Making the Most of Your Money

Your Personal Guide to Successful Financial Planning

Lawrence J. Gitman

A CBS Business Book from The Dryden Press
Chicago New York Philadelphia San Francisco Montreal Toronto
London Sydney Tokyo Mexico City Rio de Janeiro Madrid

To my mother, Edith Gitman, M.D.

Gitman, Lawrence J.
Making the most of your money.

Includes index.
1. Finance, Personal. I. Title.
HG179.G535 1985 332.024 84-25954
ISBN 0-03-003892-8

Printed in the United States of America
567-038-987654321

Address orders:
383 Madison Avenue
New York, NY 10017

Address editorial correspondence:
One Salt Creek Lane
Hinsdale, IL 60521

CBS College Publishing
The Dryden Press
Holt, Rinehart and Winston
Saunders College Publishing

Preface

For the majority of our parents, personal financial planning meant working hard, putting as much as possible away for a rainy day, and looking forward to spending their "golden years" of retirement living on income from savings, investments, and government and company pensions. Today, these are still good goals, but fluctuations in the economy have greatly affected the personal finances of most individuals. People can no longer assume that without careful planning there will be enough money to pay for the children's education, to buy that dream house in a few years, or to meet any of life's unexpected emergencies and opportunities.

In the past few years, exciting changes have heightened both the importance and complexity of personal financial planning and management. Personal computers, liberal retirement plan and tax reform legislation, new investment opportunities, expanded insurance products, and major changes in financial institutions themselves, are some of the many recent developments that have revolutionized the field of personal finance.

To maintain your lifestyle and achieve personal financial goals, you need a good understanding of the principles and concepts of personal financial management. This guide provides the broad base of knowledge necessary for making decisions that "make the most of your money." An understanding of these fundamentals will help you assess your financial situation and use available instruments and organizations to develop and implement financial plans that will meet your goals.

Topics covered in "The Guide" include the following:

☐ The importance of personal financial management and the issues that complicate personal finances today.

☐ The structure of personal financial statements and their use in personal financial management.

☐ Personal planning, budgeting, and taxation. (Relevant discussions reflect the *Tax Reform Act of 1984*.)

☐ Management of fundamental assets, such as cash and savings, housing, automobiles, and household goods.

☐ Liability management, including such areas as credit cards and consumer loans.

☐ Insurance topics, including life, health, property, and liability insurance. The concept of an insurable risk is also covered.

☐ The fundamentals of stock and bond investment. This includes a complete discussion of making transactions in the market and alternative investments.

☐ Retirement and estate planning.

Finally, this guide presents a great deal of information to assist in personal financial management. I hope that you use this important resource to make the most of your money through successful personal financial planning.

Lawrence J. Gitman
Dayton, Ohio
January 1985

Table of Contents

The Importance of Personal Financial Management 1

Throughout life, you are bombarded with opportunities and alternatives. You are required to make decisions concerning education, career, family status, lifestyle, and finances. The decisions you make greatly affect your personal financial situation. The outcome of these decisions has an impact on your personal finances. This guide should help you to understand principles and practices of contemporary personal financial management. The insight it provides will allow you to make better decisions.

Life is a process that becomes increasingly complicated with age. When you were a child, life was simple: you were the object of attention, fed and cared for. You spent most of your time playing and had few responsibilities—financial or otherwise. As you grew older, you began to care for yourself. Gradually you assumed other responsibilities involving education and work. Now, you probably find that your responsibilities are very significant.

Regardless of your current situation, you can expect that life will continue to become more complicated as you grow older. The number of your dependents may increase, your income will probably increase, you might make major purchases, and you may borrow money. You will assume many other new responsibilities. Although these responsibilities may add pleasure and satisfaction to your life, at the same time they are likely to make it a bit more complicated. One of the key factors complicating your life will be the state of your finances; as a matter of fact, most of life's problems can somehow be related to, or eliminated by, proper handling of finances.

The Goals of Personal Financial Management

Personal financial management allows individuals or families to achieve their personal financial goals more easily. Although most people do not have the same goals, similar financial principles are required in order to facilitate goal achievement. By following the procedures for effective personal financial management, individuals can get the most for their money in terms of both satisfaction and material goods. The three sections which follow contain a general discussion of personal goals as they relate to quality of life, consumption, and wealth accumulation.

Quality of Life

Your quality of life is closely tied to the level or standard of living you maintain. The presence or absence of certain material items, such as a home, cars, and jewelry, are commonly associated with *quality of life.* Large, expensive, or "fancy" items are viewed as evidence of a high *standard of living.* The ability to spend money for entertainment, health, education, variety in life, art, music, and travel also contributes to the quality of life. Although many other factors—geographical location, public facilities, local costs of living, pollution, traffic, and population density—also affect the quality of life, wealth is commonly viewed as the primary determinant of an individual's quality of life. Of course, many so-called wealthy people live quite plain lives, choosing to save or invest their money rather than spend it on luxuries and frills. However, their quality of life is not necessarily any less than that of the person who is a flamboyant consumer.

Perceptions of just what a desirable quality of life is vary among socioeconomic strata. While people in the lower socioeconomic strata might consider the ownership of a large, expensive car part of a high-quality life, those in the upper socioeconomic strata might consider membership in a country club and an annual trip abroad requisites for a high-quality life.

By planning certain future purchases and financial activities, you can set goals which are consistent with your desired quality of life, even though you may not be able to describe in precise detail the quality of life you wish to attain. In general, most people attempt to increase their wealth in order to obtain a comfortable and secure standard of living and those items commensurate with the quality of life they desire; few seriously aim at becoming millionaires. By carefully planning your finances using the principles outlined in this guide, you should be able to provide yourself with the best quality of life possible given your current financial position, your income potential, your career, and your level of motivation.

Consumption

As indicated in the preceding section, the level of consumption often has a direct effect on the quality of life. Past consumption, although no longer under your control, is important since it may have set limits on current and future consumption opportunities. Given a certain level of income, you can consume currently, or save, or invest a portion of the income for future consumption. The determination of your consumption requirements—both current and future—is an important input to your personal financial management process.

Current Your current consumption is based on the necessities of life and your average propensity to consume. A minimum level of consumption is that which obtains only the *necessities of life:* food, clothing, and shelter. Although the quantity and types of food, clothing, and shelter purchased may differ among individuals depending on their wealth, these items in some amount are essential for survival in today's society.

Average propensity to consume refers to the percentage of each dollar of income that on average is spent for consumption. People exhibiting high average propensities to consume may do so because their income is low and they must spend a large portion of it for necessities. Conversely, individuals earning large amounts quite often have low average propensities to consume, since the cost of necessities on average represents only a small proportion of their income. Still, it is not unusual to find two people with significantly different incomes and the same average propensity to consume due to differences in standards of living. The person making more money may believe it is essential to buy either better quality and/or more items and thus may on average spend the same percentage of each dollar of income during the current period as the person making far less.

Future Future consumption is based on anticipated living requirements, expected increases in the cost of living, and the desired standard of living. By considering these factors simultaneously, you can better plan your future consumption requirements, thereby allowing any residual earnings to be placed in some savings or investment media, if that is your goal.

Inflation and the CPI For 40 or so years, the United States has experienced extended periods of *inflation,* which means a general rise in the level of prices. Figure 1.1 illustrates the past inflationary behavior and its effect on consumer prices. The *consumer price index (CPI),* which is plotted in this figure, shows the relative cost of a bundle of goods and services for more than 70 years. It is an index of the price of a "market basket" containing several thousand goods and services based upon the purchasing habits of the average urban consumer. The major categories of goods and services are food, housing, clothing, transportation, health needs, and entertainment. Although the index rises during an inflationary period, it is important to recognize that the prices of some of the items in the market basket will actually decline. Figure 1.1 shows that the bundle of goods that could be purchased for \$100 in 1967 cost approximately \$218 at the end of 1979. By May 1984, the cost of this same bundle of goods had risen to \$309.70.

Since the CPI measures the general level of prices for the "average urbanite," it may not accurately reflect the effect of inflation on the *cost of living* for a given individual. For example, if the CPI increases during a given year, the cost of living for some consumers will rise, that of others will remain unchanged, and that of still others will decline. Such differences result from the differing consumption patterns of individuals whose purchases of goods and services may differ significantly from those reflected in the market basket. When assessing the impact of

Figure 1.1 Consumer Price Index (CPI), 1910–1984[a] (1967 = 100)

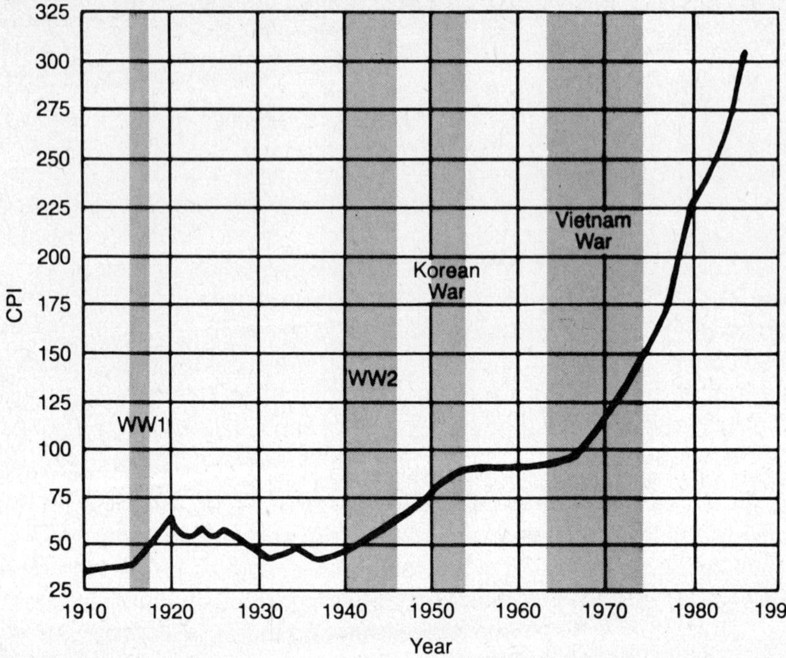

[a]1984 data supplied through May.

Source: Adapted with permission from *Changing Times* Magazine, © 1977 Kiplinger Washington Editors, Inc., "Why Inflation Is So Hard to Stop," April 1977, p. 35.

inflation as reflected in the CPI on one's cost of living, the general nature of this commonly cited index must be recognized.

Still, most consumers expect the inflationary behavior exhibited by the CPI to continue into the future. Future inflation will bring an increase in the cost of living; in other words, the cost of most goods and services will rise. Therefore, although average propensity to consume and income may remain the same in the future, inflation can cause a real decline in a person's standard of living. For this reason, you should establish future consumption goals and direct current plans and activities so as to achieve those goals. Current and future consumption goals will affect your quality of life.

Inflationary Outlook Will prices continue to rise in the future? This question is difficult to answer. Economists do not agree among themselves about the major causes of inflation. Some hold that inflation is the result of excessive government deficits; others believe it has more to do with constantly growing wage demands, particularly in sectors where labor unions are strong; and still others argue that inflation is tied directly to excessive growth in the money supply. Probably all three factors contribute to the inflation problem with varying intensities at different times, suggesting that it may take many years to reduce inflation to the one or two percent annual rates experienced in the United States during much of the 1960s.

Progress is possible, however. Persistent anti-inflation policies by the Federal Reserve System were given credit, for example, for reducing the annual inflation rate from over 10 percent in 1981 to around 4.5 percent in 1984. (The Federal Reserve is the institution responsible for controlling the money supply; it is not part of the federal government.)

Wealth Accumulation

A person's *wealth* at any point in time represents the total value of all items such as bank accounts, stocks, bonds, autos, and homes he or she owns. People accumulate wealth by saving, investing, or purchasing *tangible property,* which represents items that last for long periods of time. The accumulation of wealth quite often results from savings and investments, which represent forms of nonconsumption that act as a storehouse for future consumption. Most individuals have certain wealth accumulation goals that can be stated in terms of achieving specified levels of savings, investments, or tangible property. In general, the goal of most people is to accumulate as much wealth as possible while maintaining the level of current consumption necessary to live the desired quality of life.

Savings *Savings* represent money that has been set aside in some interest-earning form. Numerous savings institutions exist; they are described in detail in Chapter 5. Many people establish savings goals by planning to place a specified amount from each paycheck into their savings accounts. Quite often these savings goals are set in order to accumulate a specified amount needed to purchase tangible property, such as a house or a car, to pay for education, or to finance a vacation. Regardless of the motive, the establishment of savings goals as part of the overall wealth accumulation scheme is an important aspect of personal financial management.

Investments Stocks, bonds, and other types of *securities* and property when acquired to provide the purchaser with interest, dividends, or increased value are called *investments.* Although investments are viewed as more "risky" than savings, investors can expect to receive larger returns from investments than from savings. Investments, just as savings, represent a form of nonconsumption, since income that is channeled into this form cannot be used for consumption in the current period. Of course, the proceeds from selling an investment can be used for consumption. The current value of investments represents another form of accumulated wealth, which should contribute toward achieving maximum wealth accumulation. The wise investment of funds aids in the fulfillment of wealth accumulation goals.

Tangible Property Tangible property refers to long-lived physical items, for example, housing and other real estate, automobiles, and jewelry. These items, accumulated by past consumption, maintain some portion of their value over long periods of time. Some of these items, such as automobiles and boats, may depreciate in value, while other items, such as a home and jewelry, may increase in value. Some items of tangible property represent necessity items, while others may be acquired solely to enhance the quality of life. By intelligently purchasing items of tangible property, you can enhance your wealth. Because of our inflationary economy, many items of tangible property are likely to be worth more in the future than was originally paid for them; and, during the intervening years, these items provide a needed or desired service. Quite often—especially for those in the upper economic classes—tangible property is purchased solely for its expected appreciation in value. Purchases of real estate and classic automobiles fall into this category. Regardless of the motive for purchase, carefully planned tangible property purchases can make maximum contributions to your accumulated wealth.

Financial Planning

Financial planning is the key to success in achieving financial goals. Having a firm grasp on what you hope to accomplish and how you intend doing it will give you an edge over someone who does not plan and only reacts to financial events as they unfold. Purchasing a new car in two years may be important to you, for example, but evaluating and possibly arranging financing before your shopping trip—instead of accepting a financing arrangement offered by an auto dealer—might save considerable interest costs. Moreover, since some dealers advertise low-interest loans but then charge higher prices for their cars, knowing all your costs in advance helps you identify the best deal.

There are four components in financial planning: (1) setting specific *financial goals* that you expect to accomplish within certain periods of time; (2) developing *action plans* that spell out how you will achieve those goals; (3) establishing detailed *budgets* that both implement action plans and measure performance in achieving your goals; and (4) periodically *evaluating results* from an overall perspective to determine whether or not changes need to be made in your objectives or action plans.

Financial Goals

Your general aspirations in life must be made specific if they are to be financially manageable. In addition to the new car that you want in two years, you might also plan to buy a new home ten years after that; and your consumption plans might include dining out several times a week, or attending the theater once a month. Whatever your preferences are, they must be detailed and stated in monetary terms. Thus money and the utility it buys are an integral part of financial planning and goal setting.

The Role of Money Money is the common denominator by which all financial transactions are gauged. It is the medium of exchange used as a measure of value in our economy. Without the standard unit of exchange provided by the dollar, for example, it would be quite difficult to set specific personal financial goals and to measure progress with respect to those goals. Money as we know it today is, therefore, the key consideration in establishing financial goals. It is not money as such that most people want, however; it is the utility money makes possible.

Money and Utility *Utility* refers to the amount of satisfaction a person receives from purchasing certain types or quantities of goods and services. Often the utility or satisfaction provided, rather than cost, acts as the overriding factor in the choice between two items of differing price. A special feature may provide additional utility in one item, causing it to be the preferred item. This added utility may result from the actual usefulness of the special feature or may result from the status, or "snob appeal," it is expected to provide. Regardless, different people receive different levels of satisfaction from similar items, and this satisfaction is not necessarily related to the cost of the item. When alternative qualities of life, consumption patterns, and forms of wealth accumulation are evaluated, not only their cost but, even more important, their utility should be considered.

Action Plans

How will you achieve the financial goals you set for yourself? The answer to this question should come from plans that indicate how and where you will generate income and manage expenses. For example, your goals to own a new car in two years and purchase a new home ten years later may not be consistent with a high-consumption budget, given reasonable expectations of your earnings over the ten-year period. Something has to give. An *action plan* forces one to set priorities on goals and in the process it offers some assurance of success in achieving those that are really important.

An action plan should not be confused with a budget, which is far more detailed. An action plan provides the basic inputs of a budget by showing sources of revenues and broad categories of expenditures and savings. Action plans result from overall planning for your entire life. While you probably are not excited about planning far in the future—that is, for your retirement—nevertheless it may be very important to do so, particularly if different retirement plans are part of your work compensation. Life-cycle planning can be viewed in four phases: (1) career planning, (2) saving-investment planning, (3) liability and insurance planning, and (4) retirement and estate planning.

Career Planning While a person is relatively young, say, from 20 to 30, he or she will be concerned most with selecting an appealing career. You may be currently unsure about, or unhappy with, your career. Later in this chapter we look at how various factors such as education and career influence earnings, but career planning involves more than monetary compensation. Job satisfaction, working conditions, or even geographical location are examples of other important factors.

Some positions require immediate sacrifices—in lower starting salaries or less desirable working conditions, for example—but they may offer greater returns in later years. An often-cited example of such a career is public accounting. While entry-level salaries are usually competitive with comparable jobs in other fields, working conditions in early years sometimes are regarded as less attractive. A member of an audit team learning auditing procedures usually must travel extensively and spend extended periods of time away from home. Training periods, however, provide good preparation for the CPA examination. A candidate who successfully passes that test and continues in the profession can reasonably expect regular promotions and accompanying salary increases. Many accountants who start with a CPA firm directly from college are invited by their early or mid-30s to become a partner in their firm. Partners enjoy a substantial income; for example, newly-admitted partners at Arthur Andersen (one of the largest CPA firms in the world) earned compensation in excess of $125,000 in 1984. Moreover, the responsibilities of a partner are far more challenging than the routine work encountered by the trainee.

Saving-Investment Planning In the mid-life years from 30 to 50, family income is usually growing. Greater attention is devoted to accumulating wealth, either for retirement or for major expenditures such as college education for children. Wealth may be acquired through increased savings and subsequent investing of such funds in various investment media—common or preferred stocks, government or corporate bonds, real estate, and many others. Success is determined by how profitably excess funds are invested, and in a high-inflation, high-taxation economy such as the one experienced in the United States frequently, investment planning takes on added importance. If you fail

Figure 1.2 How $1,000 Invested at 10 and 12 Percent Grows Over Time

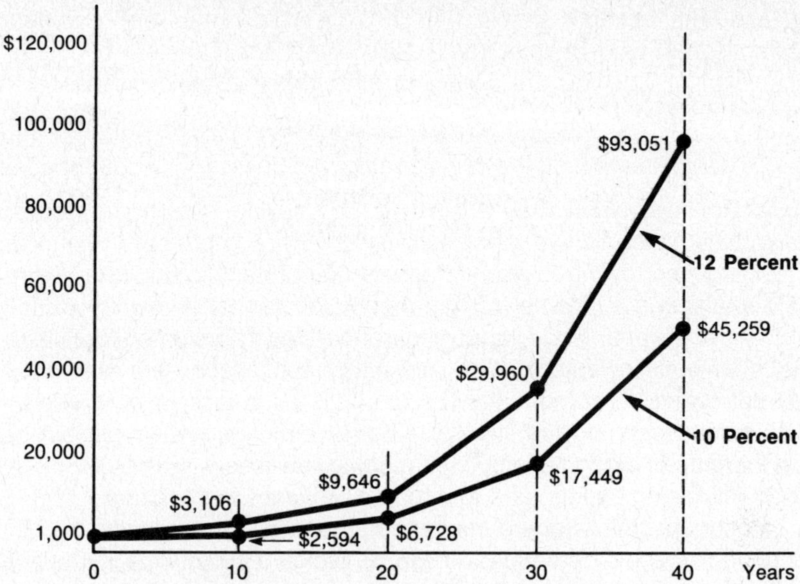

to earn a return on your investments that at least matches the CPI, the real—as opposed to nominal—value of your wealth will decline. For example, if you had held all your investment assets in passbook savings accounts, on which nominal interest is paid, over the dozen years following 1970, you would have fallen considerably behind the CPI by the early 1980s.

The impact of several rates of return on accumulated wealth is illustrated in Figure 1.2. If you had $1,000 today and could invest it at 10 percent and subsequently invest also at 10 percent all the earnings the initial investment provides, you would accumulate considerable sums of money over time; at the end of 40 years you would have $45,259 from your original $1,000. Equally important is earning higher rates of return. Some might assume that earning two percentage points more—that is, 12 rather than 10 percent—would not matter a great deal. But it certainly does. Note that if you could earn 12 percent over the 40 years, you would accumulate $93,051, or more than twice as much as you would accumulate at 10 percent.

It might be argued that if you can constantly invest at 10 or 12 percent, then inflation is probably very high also and the inflation-adjusted value of your wealth would be considerably less than the amounts shown in Figure 1.2. Of course, if the inflation rate matched your investment rate, say, both were 10 percent, then the inflation-adjusted value of $45,259 would be $1,000, which means real wealth would have remained constant. That argument is true, but it is also true that if you earned two percentage points more than the CPI, the future value of your $1,000 would have increased by $47,792 ($93,051 − $45,259), which is mathematically equivalent to a $1,056 *increase* in your real wealth. The lesson is simple: it is crucially important to maximize your potential returns over time. You must take into consideration, of course, the level of risk you are willing to undertake—a topic discussed at length in Chapter 12.

Liability and Insurance Planning The saving-investment process is closely linked to two other activities that are important in financial planning—borrowing to acquire assets and protecting both the means of sustaining our income (life and health insurance) and what we currently own (property and liability insurance). Most consumer durables—such as houses, automobiles, and major appliances—are purchased by borrowing. In some instances, credit is used also to purchase investment assets; buying stock with borrowed funds, known as "buying on margin," is a good example. Managing liabilities is no less important than managing assets, and that topic is covered in Chapters 7 and 8.

Most consumers regard insurance as absolutely essential—and for a good reason. One serious illness or accident could wipe out everything they have accumulated over years of hard work. But what kind of insurance is appropriate and how much should you have are no less important questions. Overinsuring or mis-insuring are costly too; insurance coverage is examined in Chapters 9, 10, and 11.

Retirement and Estate Planning While you are still working you will be primarily concerned with managing your finances to attain those goals you feel are important in old age. They might include extensive travel, plans for visiting children and others, dining out frequently at better restaurants, and perhaps a vacation home or boat. It is important to see that retirement planning begins long before you actually retire. For example, if a vacation condominium is one of your retirement goals, you might consider purchasing it well in advance of retirement. You might not only use it periodically during your working years, but you might also enjoy possible investment returns from rents. It could also serve as an inflation hedge if condominium prices rise.

Accumulating assets to enjoy in retirement is only part of the long-run planning process. As persons grow older they often start considering how their wealth can be passed on to heirs most effectively, an activity called estate planning. It deals with such topics as wills and trusts and how gift, estate, and inheritance taxes may have an impact upon distributions of assets to heirs. The subject is not easy to comprehend immediately because most of us are unfamiliar with its terminology, but it is extremely important. Estate planning is covered in Chapter 16, and we look at other aspects of retirement planning in Chapter 15.

Budgets

In a very practical sense, budgeting and financial planning mean the same thing. Well-executed budgets put forth in detailed form overall financial plans. The budget is where you get down to the business of spelling out all the items of income and expense you expect to incur during the budget period. As you detail each line item it will become apparent that setting goal priorities is necessary since, in most instances, the first run-through of a budget creates huge deficits that you may wish to avoid. When the budget balances, you are ready to use it as a management tool; that is, you will judge your financial performance by how well, or poorly, you stay within the budget.

Over- or under-budget amounts—that is, variances—should act as a guide to budgeting for subsequent periods. If the variance resulted because you failed to forecast prices accurately, then you must revise the next budget. On the other hand, if variances are more reflective of your unwillingness to stay within budgeted activities—you went to the movies four times last month instead of your planned one visit—then you need to re-evaluate your immediate goals. There are many aspects to budgeting, and these are covered in Chapter 3.

Periodic Evaluation

While budget variances show what is right or wrong in comparing planned and actual money flows, they do not answer the really crucial question: Are you achieving the broad quality-of-life goals that are important to you? It is easy for us to change our perspectives on life, and we should not hesitate to change our budgets if that is necessary. Moreover, your situation in life may change. For example, you may accept a job in a city, such as New York, where car ownership is both difficult and expensive. As a result, owning a new car may no longer be a high-priority budget item.

Overall evaluations are not generated easily. Often, the question is whether or not you are relatively happy in what you are doing, in your career or in your family situation. There are considerable emotional linkages to financial planning that cannot be avoided. A mid-life change in your career, for example, will have a more pervasive impact than simply changing your yearly budgets. But both finances and emotions are important in making your decision—you cannot ignore either.

The Personal Finance Environment

The environment in which personal finance goals are established, action plans are developed, and decisions are made contains three dif-

Figure 1.3 Personal Finance Environment

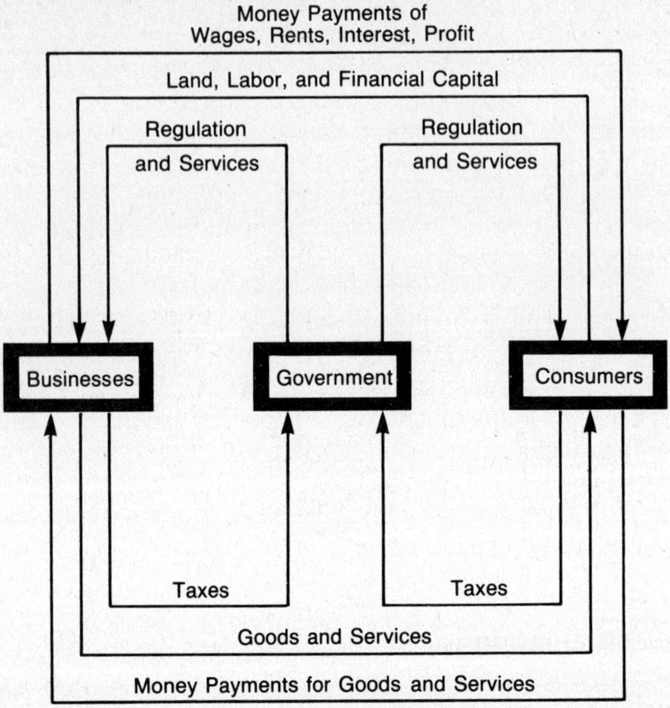

ferent groups, each attempting to fulfill certain goals. Although the goals of each of these groups are not necessarily inconsistent, they do impose certain constraints on one another. The three key groups are government, business, and consumers. Each is discussed separately in the following sections, and a final section considers the effects when these groups interact on the economy.

Government

Government—federal, state, and local—provides us with many essential services such as police and fire protection, national defense, highways, health care, and more. In making such services available, however, they also constrain businesses and consumers, as indicated in Figure 1.3.

Taxation The federal government levies taxes on income; state governments tax sales and income; and local governments levy taxes primarily on real estate and personal property. The largest tax bite for consumers results from federal income taxes, which may take as much as 50 percent of earnings. These taxes are levied on a progressive basis so that the greater the taxable income, the higher the rate at which taxes are paid. Much attention must be devoted to considering the effects of taxes on personal financial management activities. Due to the constraints of the tax structure on personal financial decisions and the potential magnitude of taxes, decisions must be evaluated on an "after-tax" basis.

Regulation Federal, state, and local governments place many regulations on consumer- and citizen-related activities. Aimed at protecting the consumer from fraudulent and undesirable actions by sellers and lenders, these government regulations require certain types of businesses to have licenses, to maintain certain hygienic standards, to adequately disclose financial charges, and to warrant their goods and services. Other laws protect sellers from adverse activities by consumers, for example, shoplifting and nonpayment for services rendered. Certainly, any decisions relating to achieving personal financial goals should take into consideration both those legal requirements that protect consumers and those that constrain their activities.

Business

As Figure 1.3 shows, businesses provide consumers with goods and services and receive money payments in return. Also, to produce these outputs they hire labor and use land and capital (what economists refer to as factors of production, or inputs) and in return they pay wages, rents, interest, and profit. Thus, businesses are a key part of the circular flow of income that sustains our free enterprise system. In general, their presence creates a competitive environment in which consumers may select from an array of goods and services. There are, of course, certain industries, such as public utilities, in which the degree of competition or choice provided the consumer is limited by the government for economic reasons. As indicated in the preceding section, all businesses are in some way directly or indirectly limited by the laws of some governmental body. Consumers need to understand the role and effects of business on their financial plans since the activities of business largely affect the cost and availability of goods and services in our economy. An understanding of various business activities should permit consumers to make better purchases and help them determine which business firms to deal with.

Consumers

The consumer is the party around which the personal finance environment centers. It is his or her choices that ultimately determine what kinds of goods and services businesses will provide. In addition, the consumer's choice to spend or save has a direct impact on the present and future circular flows of income. A cutback in spending is usually

Figure 1.4 The Economic Cycle

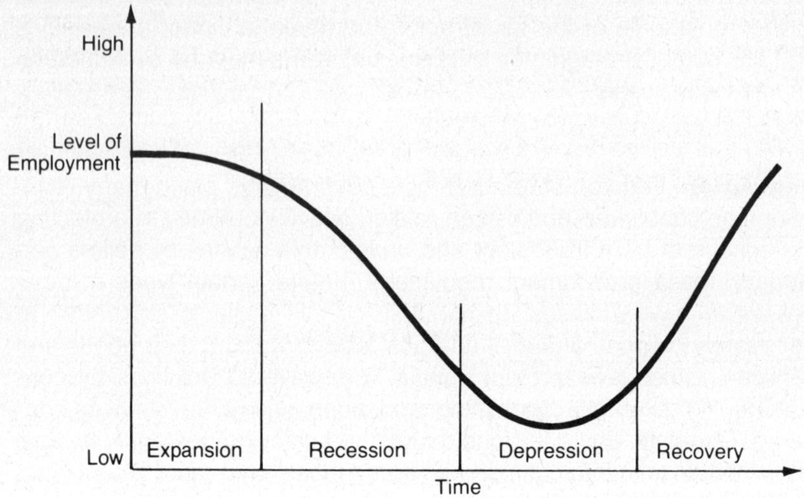

associated with a decline in economic activity while increases in spending help the economy recover. While consumers are often thought to have free choices in the marketplace, they must operate within the financial environment resulting from the actions of government and business. Of course, through their elected officials and by their purchase actions, consumers can affect government and business. But lobbies and consumer groups are necessary for any real impact; the individual consumer should not expect to change government or business independently. As a consumer, you are best off accepting the existing financial environment and planning your transactions within it.

Economic Conditions

Our economy is a result of the interaction of government, business, and consumers as well as the economic situation in other nations. Although the goal of the government is to regulate the economy and provide economic stability and high levels of employment, swings in economic activity do occur. Some political and economic factors just do not yield to governmental regulation. A typical economic cycle contains four stages: *expansion, recession, depression,* and *recovery.* Each of these stages as it relates to employment is depicted in Figure 1.4. For 40 years the government has been reasonably successful in keeping the economy out of a depression, although we have experienced periods of rapid expansion or inflation followed by periods of deep recession.

The swings in unemployment from one phase of the cycle to the next can be substantial. For example, in the great depression of the 1930s U.S. unemployment reached a level as high as 25 percent of the work force; in contrast, during the expansion in 1968, unemployment dropped slightly below 4 percent. During the most recent recession (1981–1983), unemployment rose to about 10.5 percent in late 1982, the highest level since the great depression. In mid-1984 unemployment had dropped to about 7.5 percent.

Determinants of Personal Income

The key factor ultimately controlling the quality of your life as reflected in your consumption and wealth is the amount of income you can expect to earn. In the absence of any inheritances or existing wealth, your income will depend on your age, your education, and your career. Although there are obvious exceptions, such as the shoeshine boy who develops a small business into a huge shoe polish manufacturing operation, generally, in our society, the closer you are to middle age, the more educated you are, and the more professionally or managerially oriented your job, the greater your income will be. Each of these determinants of income—age, education, career—is discussed separately in the following sections. A final section discussing your lifetime earnings is also included.

Age and Income

Although age is a variable over which you have no real control, it is interesting to look at the relationship between age and income. Typically, people with low incomes fall into the very young and very old age groups, while the period of highest earnings generally occurs between the ages of 35 and 55. (See Table 1.1 for a breakdown of annual income for various age groupings.) This distribution results because those below age 35 are often developing their trade or moving up in their jobs, while many above 55 are likely to be working only part-time or to be completely retired. When setting financial goals and making financial plans, consideration should be given to expected changes in income as they relate to your age. Of course, someone without proper education, career choice, and motivation cannot fairly anticipate the types of age-income distribution depicted in Table 1.1. As a matter of fact, for less-motivated individuals, annual income may remain relatively constant over their working life except for inflation-induced wage increases. This situation can be avoided by using the tools of personal financial management to improve the quality of your life.

Table 1.1 Distribution of Income on the Basis of Age (31 March 1981 Data)

Annual Wage or Salary Income	Age of Head-of-Household (Percent Earning Income within Ranges) 14 to 34	35 to 44	45 to 54	55 and Over	Total
$ 4,999 and below	9.0%	6.0%	6.2%	19.4%	11.7%
$ 5,000 to 9,999	14.2	8.7	9.7	23.2	15.8
$10,000 to 14,999	17.6	11.6	10.8	15.8	15.0
$15,000 to 19,999	17.6	12.6	10.9	11.0	13.3
$20,000 to 24,999	15.0	15.0	12.1	8.4	12.2
$25,000 to 29,999	10.7	12.7	10.9	6.1	9.4
$30,000 to 39,999	10.7	17.4	17.4	7.8	11.8
$40,000 to 49,999	3.2	8.4	10.8	3.8	5.5
$50,000 and above	2.0	7.6	11.2	4.5	5.3
Total	100.0%	100.0%	100.0%	100.0%	100.0%
Average Income	$17,470	$26,052	$28,169	$18,066	$21,063

Source: Adapted from data in U.S. Bureau of the Census, "Money Income of Households, Families, and Persons in the United States: 1980," *Current Population Reports,* Series P-60, No. 132 (Washington, D.C.: U.S. Government Printing Office, 1981), Table 11, p. 33.

Education and Income

Level of formal education is a controllable factor believed to affect an individual's potential income. All people with equivalent formal educations will not earn similar incomes. Formal education is a tool which properly applied can help carve out an income. The breakdown of income on the basis of formal education in Table 1.2 shows that, on the average, heads-of-households having more formal education earn higher annual incomes than those with less formal education. Although this is not a cause-and-effect relationship, it suggests that a good formal education should enhance a person's earning opportunities.

Table 1.2 Distribution of Income on the Basis of Formal Education (31 March 1981 Data)

	Years of School Completed by Head-of-Household (Percent Earning Income within Ranges)							
	Elementary		High School		College			
Annual Wage or Salary Income	Fewer than Eight Years	Eight Years	One to Three Years	Four Years	One to Three Years	Four Years	Five or More Years	Median Years School Completed
$ 4,999 and below	31.4%	23.1%	16.8%	7.7%	6.3%	3.0%	2.3%	10.10
$ 5,000 to 9,999	28.8	26.2	21.6	13.5	10.6	6.2	5.0	11.45
$10,000 to 14,999	16.4	17.4	17.3	15.3	13.7	9.1	7.1	12.35
$15,000 to 19,999	8.9	10.7	14.2	14.5	14.2	11.8	11.0	12.55
$20,000 to 24,999	5.5	8.5	10.6	14.9	14.1	13.1	11.6	12.65
$25,000 to 29,999	3.3	5.2	7.6	11.6	11.2	12.5	11.4	12.80
$30,000 to 39,999	3.8	5.9	7.6	13.5	16.3	18.6	19.0	13.02
$40,000 to 49,999	1.2	1.9	2.8	5.2	7.6	11.3	13.0	14.35
$50,000 and above	0.7	1.1	1.5	3.8	6.0	14.4	19.6	16.13
Total	100.0%	100.0%	100.0%	100.0%	100.0%	100.0%	100.0%	-----
Average Income	$10,996	$13,497	$15,846	$21,462	$24,188	$31,491	$35,416	$21,463

Source: Adapted from data in U.S. Bureau of the Census, "Money Income of Households, Families, and Persons in the United States: 1980," *Current Population Reports,* Series P-60, No. 132 (Washington, D.C.: U.S. Government Printing Office, 1981), Table 13, p. 37.

Table 1.3 Distribution of Income of Employed Heads-of-Households on the Basis of Occupation (31 March 1981 Data)

	Percent Earning Income within Range									
Annual Wage or Salary Income	Professional and Managerial Workers	Clerical and Kindred Workers	Sales Workers	Craftsmen and Kindred Workers	Operatives, Including Transportation Workers	Service Workers	Farm Laborers and Foremen	Laborers Except Farm	Farmers and Farm Managers	Total
$ 4,999 and below	0.4%	0.5%	0.6%	0.8%	0.4%	1.7%	6.7%	1.4%	19.0%	1.2%
$ 5,000 to 9,999	1.7	6.0	2.9	2.9	4.9	12.3	20.0	9.4	17.0	4.5
$10,000 to 14,999	4.6	15.7	9.0	8.6	14.0	17.4	28.8	15.0	17.0	9.9
$15,000 to 19,999	8.7	16.9	11.0	15.3	18.9	17.9	18.0	21.0	10.6	13.6
$20,000 to 24,999	13.0	17.9	12.0	19.5	20.0	16.6	10.4	20.0	11.3	16.3
$25,000 to 29,999	14.6	13.8	12.5	17.5	15.0	13.3	7.9	13.0	6.8	14.7
$30,000 to 39,999	22.9	17.9	22.0	22.7	17.3	13.7	4.8	14.0	7.5	20.0
$40,000 to 49,999	14.6	8.3	13.4	8.3	5.9	4.3	2.0	4.4	3.7	10.0
$50,000 and above	18.7	3.0	15.6	4.4	2.6	2.8	1.4	1.8	6.7	9.8
Total	100.0%	100.0%	100.0%	100.0%	100.0%	100.0%	100.0%	100.0%	100.0%	100.0%
Average Income	$36,567	$24,876	$33,752	$27,136	$24,150	$21,978	$16,175	$22,080	$18,029	$29,530

Source: Adapted from data in U.S. Bureau of the Census, "Money Income of Households, Families, and Persons in the United States: 1980," *Current Population Reports,* Series P-60, No. 132 (Washington, D.C.: U.S. Government Printing Office, 1981), Table 38, pp. 126–127.

Table 1.4 Selected Occupations and Estimated Midcareer Income

Occupation	Estimated Annual Midcareer Income
Accountant	$ 38,680
Attorney	61,579
Buyer	27,424
Chemist	46,971
Computer Operator	22,889
Computer Programmer	29,365
Dental Hygienist	20,700
Dentist	65,270
Director of Personnel	47,553
Doctor	100,980
Engineer	40,677
Engineering Technician	23,620
File Clerk	12,794
Manufacturing Inspector	23,400
Photographer	22,425
Production Worker—Durable Goods Industries	21,928
Production Worker—Nondurable Goods Industries	19,650
Secretary	18,603
Tool and Die Maker	32,760

Source: U.S. Department of Labor, Bureau of Labor Statistics, *National Survey of Professional, Administrative, Technical, and Clerical Pay,* Bulletin 2145, September 1982, Table 1, p. 10.

Career and Income

Your formal education is probably closely related to your career. Of course, formal education is not a prerequisite for many types of careers, such as sales, service, and certain types of clerical work. But generally, the more responsibilities for decision making associated with a given career, the greater the annual income that career is expected to provide. The breakdown of the average income of a head-of-household in various occupations presented in Table 1.3 demonstrates that the highest earnings occur among professional and managerial workers, whose formal education is likely to include a college degree. Table 1.4 provides a listing of the estimated annual midcareer (ten years' experience) income for various careers and clearly indicates that those requiring greater formal education or specialized skills typically earn higher annual incomes. Thus educational and career goals are closely related to personal financial goals.

Your Lifetime Earnings

During your lifetime, you will earn much income. If you establish realistic financial goals and apply the principles of personal financial man-

Figure 1.5 Lifetime Earnings and Educational Level (Head-of-Household, Thousands of 1980 Dollars)

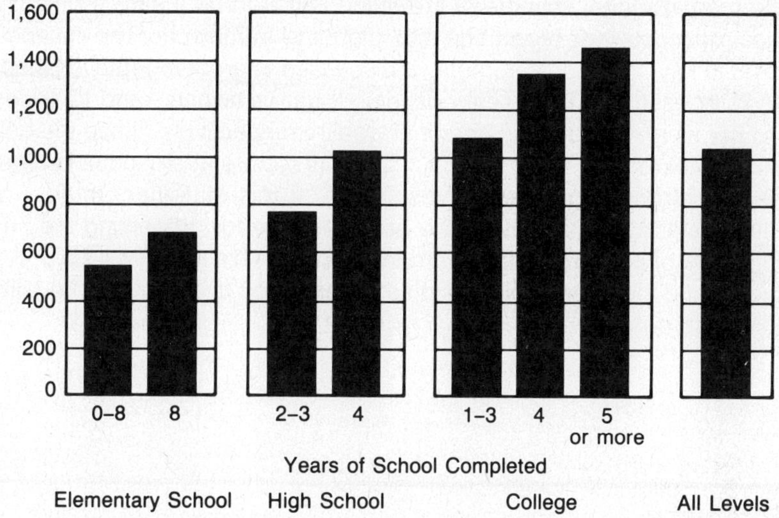

Note: The values reflected in this figure were estimated using the average annual salary figures from Table 1.2 and assuming in each case that retirements will take place at age 65. The values are measured in 1980 dollars but do not consider the timing of income received.

agement, this income can be used in a fashion that will allow you to maintain the desired quality of life. Although your current weekly income may seem small, the average head-of-household is expected to earn about $1,020,000 over his or her lifetime. Of course, estimated lifetime income increases with education. Figure 1.5 illustrates the significant relationship between educational level and estimated lifetime earnings. Individuals with college degrees can expect to earn over $1,350,000 during their lives, while those who have fewer than eight years of formal education can only hope to earn about $560,000 in their lifetimes. Comparison of the nearly $1,010,000 of lifetime earnings of persons having completed four years of high school with the $1,350,000 of those who completed four years of college suggests that the approximate lifetime value of a college degree is $340,000 (that is, $1,350,000 − $1,010,000). This tends to suggest that usually college education is financially justifiable.

Although many people tend to concern themselves with only their day-to-day financial affairs, all of the data suggest that by using a long-run time horizon, people can direct their current actions toward activities that will enhance the quality of their lives on a long-term basis.

An Overview of this Guide

The organizational scheme of the guide is based on a simple balance sheet couched in a broad financial planning framework. The *balance sheet,* a key financial statement, is discussed in greater depth in Chapter 2. In essence, it presents *assets*—what is owned—and *liabilities* and *net worth*—debts and personal wealth, respectively. Since the balance sheet reflects an individual's financial picture at any point in time, the logical breakdown and investigation of this statement in light of one's financial plans provide the best structure for presenting the key principles of personal financial management. This guide will help you understand these principles, and so prepare you to achieve the quality of life you desire.

Summary

The goals of personal financial management are related to quality of life, consumption, and wealth accumulation. To some extent, economic strata determine average propensity to consume. The enhancement of wealth, or ownership, is one of the most important goals of the personal financial management process. Inflation can have a powerful impact on consumer prices and therefore on an individual's ability to consume. The consumer price index is a commonly cited indicator of the impact of inflation on consumer prices.

Financial planning is the key to achieving financial goals. Financial goals must be framed in monetary terms, but it is important to consider the utility associated with money. Financial planning requires action plans detailing how goals will be accomplished over time and annual budgets that implement the action plans and measure performance. Action plans are drawn up over an entire lifetime and relate to four different activities: (1) career planning, (2) saving-investment planning, (3) liability and insurance planning, and (4) retirement and estate planning. Financial planning also requires periodic evaluations to assess progress from an overall perspective and to determine whether changes must be made in objectives or action plans.

The environment in which personal finance decisions are made results from the interaction of government, business, and consumers. Government affects personal finance decisions most directly through taxes and regulations. Business provides the marketplace in which these decisions must be made. As a result of the interaction of government, business, and consumers, the economy passes through various economic cycles, which include four basic stages: expansion, recession, depression, and recovery. An understanding of the economy can aid in making personal financial decisions.

Personal income is another important factor controlling the quality of life and wealth. Such factors as age, education, and career can have significant effects on income. In general, the closer to middle age, the more educated people are, and the more professional their career, the higher their personal income will be.

Your Financial Statements 2

In order to effectively manage your personal finances, procedures must be available to measure how well you are doing. Although you are accountable only to yourself, while businesses must report to the government, to lenders, and to owners, the basic financial reporting techniques of business can be adapted to the personal financial management process. An understanding of how to prepare and evaluate personal financial statements should help you in periodically assessing your progress toward achievement of whatever financial goals you have set.

Imagine you were left aboard a drifting ship. Not knowing where you were within the vast expanse of the ocean, you would first need to determine your location; and, with the assistance of certain navigational aids—the most important of which would be the compass—you would plot your course to safety. However, if you did not have a compass, you would be unable to accurately determine your location, and you could not periodically check your progress toward the desired destination. Financial statements are like compasses; people use them to gauge their financial position at various points in their lives in order to judge their progress toward their financial goals.

In order to periodically assess your financial condition, you will require some measures of both financial position and financial performance. Your *financial position* can be thought of as your wealth at a certain point in time, while your *financial performance* describes your income and expenditures over a specified period of time. An understanding of how to prepare and interpret personal financial statements is one of the cornerstones of personal financial management. Without some standards by which to measure your financial condition, establishing financial goals and evaluating your progress toward those goals would become much more difficult.

The Balance Sheet

The *balance sheet,* or *statement of financial position*, describes a family's—or individual's—wealth at a certain point in time. This statement is most commonly used as a barometer of long-run progress toward achievement of financial goals. The balance sheet derives its name from the fact that "it must balance," which means that everything must be accounted for. The statement contains three basic account classifications: *assets, liabilities*, and *net worth*.

Assets

Assets, or the items owned by the family, are normally tangible items, although in certain instances they may be intangible. An item is classified as an asset regardless of whether it has been purchased for cash or whether its purchase was financed with borrowing. In other words, even if an asset has not been fully paid for, it is considered owned by the family. An item that is leased by the family, of course, is not shown as an asset since it is actually owned by someone else. Table 2.1 lists some of the assets commonly held by a family. Assets can be grouped into two broad categories: fundamental and investment. *Fundamental assets* are those that are routinely held by a family for the service they provide as part of their day-to-day activities, while *investment assets* include assets acquired in order to earn a return rather than to provide a service. All assets should be shown on the balance sheet at their current *fair market value*, which may differ considerably from their original purchase price. Fair market value is the price that the asset can reasonably be expected to sell for at the date of the statement.

Fundamental Assets Fundamental assets, which are discussed in detail in Chapters 5 and 6 of this guide, are those that are commonly held by a family for use in their everyday lives. They include cash, savings deposits, housing, automobiles, boats, motors, trailers, recreational equipment, and personal property. Cash may be held either in the form of cash on hand or as a *demand deposit*—a checking account, in banking jargon. Savings, or *time deposits*, as they are referred to by bankers, may be held in a savings or money fund account at a bank, a savings and loan association, a credit union, or other institution. Funds held in a demand or time deposit account are *liquid* since they can be readily converted into cash. Typically, housing, representing a family's home and property, appears as a major fundamental asset on the personal balance sheet. Any automobiles, boats, motors, trailers, recreational equipment, and personal property owned for the service they provide are fundamental assets and must be shown at their fair market value.

Investment Assets Investment assets are those assets acquired in order to earn a return rather than to provide a service. These assets, which are discussed in detail in Chapters 12–14 of this guide, tend to be held for the anticipated future benefits they offer. Popular investment assets include common and preferred stocks and corporate, government, and municipal bonds. Shares in investment companies—especially mutual funds—and real estate are also popular investment assets. Business ownership, the cash value of life insurance, the cash value of pensions, and other investment vehicles, such as commodity and financial futures, options, precious minerals, and collectibles, represent some of the less popular forms of investment assets. Investment

Table 2.1 Assets Commonly Held by a Family

Fundamental Assets	Investment Assets
Cash	**Stocks and Bonds**
On Hand	Common Stock
In Checking Accounts	Preferred Stock
Savings Deposits	Corporate Bonds
At Banks	Government and Municipal Bonds
At Savings and Loans	**Investment Companies**
At Credit Unions	Closed-End
At Other Institutions	Mutual Funds
Housing	**Real Estate**
Automobiles	**Business Ownership**
Boats, Motors, Trailers	**Cash Value of Life Insurance**
Recreational Equipment	**Cash Value of Pensions**
Personal Property	**Other Investment Vehicles**
Furniture	Commodity and Financial Futures
Clothing	Options
Jewelry	Precious Minerals
Other	Collectibles

assets tend to be acquired in order to achieve long-run personal financial goals rather than to provide current benefit. They vary in liquidity from highly liquid stocks and bonds to relatively nonliquid real estate and business ownership investments.

Assets other than those included in Table 2.1 may exist and should be included in the family's balance sheet. Housing that is being leased to the family, as well as any other leased assets, should *not* be shown as an asset on the family's balance sheet. A family that is leasing the services of an asset does not own the asset and, therefore, must not represent it as such on their balance sheet.

Three points to remember are:

1. All assets should be entered on the balance sheet at their fair market value.
2. Only owned—not leased—items should be included on the family's balance sheet.
3. Even if an asset is not fully paid for, it should still be included on the balance sheet.

The best way to determine your assets is to ask the question, "What do I own?" All items eliciting positive responses should be included.

Liabilities

Liabilities represent the debts of the family. These debts could result from department store charges, bank card charges, installment loans,

Table 2.2 Liabilities Commonly Owed by a Family

Bills Outstanding	Installment Loan Balances	Other Loans
Charge Account Balances	Automobile	Bank
Bank Card Charges	Appliances and Furniture	Educational
Utility Bills	Other	Stocks and Bonds
Rent	**Mortgage Loans**	Other
Insurance Premiums	Housing	
Taxes	Real Estate Investment	
Medical Bills	Other	
Repair Service Bills		
Other Bills		

or mortgages on housing or other real estate. Regardless of the source of a given liability, it is owed by the family and must be paid for in the future. Some liabilities are due in the very near future, while others are long term and must be paid off over a period of years. Short-term liabilities are normally incurred for convenience while long-term liabilities are incurred to purchase either fundamental or investment assets, which are expected to provide service for an extended period of time. Table 2.2 presents a listing of common types of liabilities that may appear on a family's balance sheet. The level and status of an individual's liabilities are factors that potential lenders give careful consideration. Very high levels of debt and the presence of overdue debts are both viewed with a great deal of disfavor by potential lenders.

Bills outstanding include all items that must be completely paid for in the near future. These bills normally represent short-term obligations resulting from charges for the purchase of clothes, other less expensive items, consumable goods, and services. Charge account balances, bank card charges, utility bills, rent, insurance premiums, taxes, medical bills, repair service bills, and any other similar bills are classified as bills outstanding. *All outstanding charges—even if you have not received the bill—must be shown as bills outstanding*. In other words, a charge incurred prior to the balance sheet statement date that remains unpaid should be included as a liability, regardless of whether a bill for the charge has been received.

Installment loan balances include all debts (other than mortgages on housing or other real estate) for which a series of installment payments are required over a specified period of time—usually six months to five years. Installment loans are generally used to finance such purchases as automobiles, appliances, furniture, and boats. *Mortgage loans* are associated with housing and other real estate purchases and normally have lives of ten years or more. They most commonly result from the purchase of a home, although sometimes they result from real estate investments, for example, the purchase of an apartment or office building. Mortgage loans are normally paid on an installment basis, and only the outstanding loan balance should be shown on the balance sheet. Mortgage loans are described in greater detail in Chapter 6, which discusses housing purchases.

Other types of loans must be shown on the balance sheet as well. These may be bank loans requiring single payments, educational loans, loans used to purchase stocks or bonds, or other specialized loans. With these loans, as with the mortgage loans, *only the outstanding loan balance should be shown as a liability*, since at a given time it—not the initial loan balance—is the amount owed. More detailed discussions of the various types of loans and the loan negotiation process are included in Chapters 7 and 8.

Net Worth

A family's *net worth* is the amount of actual wealth, or *equity*, it has in the assets it owns, measured at a given time. Net worth can be viewed as the amount that would remain after the family sold all of its assets for their estimated value and paid all liabilities. The accounting relationship between assets, liabilities, and net worth is called the *balance sheet equation:*

$$\text{Total Assets} - \text{Total Liabilities} = \text{Net Worth.} \qquad \textbf{(2.1)}$$

Once the market value of assets and the level of liabilities have been established, net worth is easily calculated by subtracting total liabilities from total assets. If net worth is less than zero, the family is technically viewed as *insolvent.* This form of insolvency does not mean that the family will be thrown in the poorhouse, but it does reflect the absence of adequate financial planning. In the long-run financial planning process, the level of net worth is important. Once a family has established a goal of accumulating a certain level or type of wealth over a specific period of years, progress toward that goal is best analyzed by monitoring net worth. Net worth represents wealth at a given time. Increasing wealth positions are preferred to decreasing wealth positions, and high wealth or net worth positions are generally preferred to low net worth positions.

Balance Sheet Format

The balance sheet begins with the *date* at which the various asset, liability, and net worth figures recorded on it are measured. All assets are listed on the left side of the statement, and all liabilities are listed on the right. The net worth entry is shown on the right side of the statement just below the liabilities. The subheadings included in Tables 2.1 and 2.2 may be used to break the statement into various categories. Often the totals of these categories will be shown as subtotals in the

Table 2.3 General Format of the Balance Sheet

Date	
Assets	**Liabilities and Net Worth**
Total Assets	Total Liabilities
	Net Worth
Total =	Total

statement. Regardless of how the various assets and liabilities are categorized, the statement should *balance*: According to the balance sheet equation, total assets should equal the sum of total liabilities and net worth. The general format of a balance sheet is depicted in Table 2.3.

A Sample Balance Sheet—Art and Betty Johnston

The relationship between assets, liabilities, and net worth and the general format of the balance sheet are best illustrated with an example. To this end, we will examine the balance sheet of Art and Betty Johnston, a young family described briefly in the following section. Art and Betty's balance sheet for the year ended 31 December 1984 appears in Table 2.4. This statement is best evaluated by looking at Art and Betty's assets, liabilities, and net worth separately.

The Art and Betty Johnston Family

Art and Betty Johnston were married two and one-half years ago and currently have no children. Art, who is 23 years old, has just completed his second year as a sales representative for a large soap manufacturer. He is quite satisfied with his job and expects to continue his career in the sales and marketing area. Art's boss recently assured him that the company is most pleased with his performance and that they have "big plans" for him. Betty, who is 21, still has one more year of college remaining before she receives her degree in special education. She currently works part-time in the library at the university and expects to take a job in the public schools once she receives her degree. The Johnstons live in their own home, which they purchased in December 1983. Art and Betty love to travel; snow skiing is one of their favorite pastimes. They plan to have children in a few years, but wish to devote their current efforts toward developing some degree of financial stability.

Art and Betty's Assets Given their ages, Art and Betty's asset position looks quite good. The dominant asset is their home, which they

Table 2.4 Balance Sheet for Art and Betty Johnston (at 31 December 1984)

Assets		Liabilities and Net Worth	
Fundamental Assets		**Liabilities**	
Cash		Bills Outstanding	
On Hand	$ 40	Charge Account Balances	$ 90
In Checking Accounts	220	Bank Card Charges	40
Savings Deposits		Utility Bills	60
At Banks	650	Taxes	80
In Money Market Fund	800	Repair Bill	30
Housing	60,000	Installment Loan Balances	
Automobiles		Auto Loan (Credit Union)	1,500
1981 Cutlass Sedan	4,000	Furniture Loan (American	
1977 Volkswagen Rabbit	1,300	Furniture)	400
Recreational Equipment	400	Mortgage Loan	
Personal Property		(First Savings and Loan)	55,200
Furniture	2,000	Personal Loan from	
Clothing	800	Parents	3,600
Jewelry	1,000	**(2) Total Liabilities**	$61,000
Total Fundamental Assets	$71,210		
Investment Assets			
Stocks and Bonds			
Common Stock	$ 840	**Net Worth [(1) − (2)]**	$15,000
Corporate Bonds	1,000		
Government Bonds	350		
Cash Value of Life Insurance	100		
Stamp Collection	2,500		
Total Investment Assets	$ 4,790	**Total Liabilities**	
(1) Total Assets	$76,000	**and Net Worth**	$76,000

purchased one year ago. Another item that strengthens their asset position is a stamp collection, which was a wedding gift from Betty's grandparents. In addition, Art and Betty have a total of $2,290 spread among investments in common stock, corporate bonds, government bonds, and the cash value of their life insurance. The Johnstons' cash of $260 and savings deposits of $1,450 are liquid assets, which should allow them to meet their bill payments and cover many small unexpected expenditures. But the real strength of Art and Betty's financial position cannot be evaluated without examining their debts, or liabilities, since they may be highly indebted as a result of borrowing to purchase certain of their assets, especially their home.

Art and Betty's Liabilities Looking at the Johnstons' liabilities, we can see that the primary liability is the $55,200 mortgage on their home. As might be expected, since they purchased their home only one year ago, the amount of the mortgage on it is still quite large relative to its estimated market value of $60,000. The Johnstons' *equity*, or actual ownership interest in the home, is approximately $4,800 ($60,000 market value minus the $55,200 outstanding mortgage loan). The Johnstons' bills outstanding, which total $300, do not seem too great. It is likely that these bills must be paid, at least partially, within the next month, since monthly billing cycles are most common. Other debts shown on the balance sheet include a $1,500 balance on an installment loan used to purchase one of their cars, a $400 balance on an installment loan used to purchase furniture, and a $3,600 balance on a personal loan made by their parents to finance the down payment on their house. Contrasting the Johnstons' total liabilities of $61,000 to their total assets of $76,000 provides a more realistic view of their present wealth position.

Art and Betty's Net Worth The Johnstons' balance sheet in Table 2.4 shows their net worth as $15,000, the amount necessary to cause the balance sheet to balance. Considering Art and Betty's ages (23 and 21, respectively), they seem to be doing quite well. Their above average net worth can be explained by the fact that they received a $10,000 inheritance 18 months ago. The $15,000 net worth figure is the amount Art and Betty would have if they sold their assets for the $76,000 at which they are valued on the balance sheet and from these proceeds repaid their debts of $61,000. Of course, Art and Betty are not expected to take such action, but by calculating their net worth at specified points in time, they can measure the results of their financial plans and decisions on their wealth position. As might be expected, increasing wealth positions are preferred.

The Income Statement

While the balance sheet describes a family's financial position at a certain point in time, the *income statement* describes the various financial activities that have occurred over a certain period of time—normally one year—and allows the comparison of actual financial outcomes to budget goals. (This will become clearer in Chapter 3, which is devoted to financial planning and budgeting.) The statement also evaluates savings or investments made during the period, which can, of course, be positive or negative.

The income statement consists of three major parts: *income, expenditures*, and *contribution to savings or investments*. The name of the statement may be a bit misleading, for it shows not just income but also expenditures, which are deducted from income to determine the contribution to savings or investments.

Income

Items shown as income on the income statement include earnings received as wages, salaries, bonuses, and commissions; earnings on savings and investments; and proceeds from the sale of assets. Only income that has actually been received should be shown as income. This approach forces an honest representation of the way things were

Table 2.5 Sources of Income

Sources of Income
Wages and Salaries
Bonuses and Commissions
Interest Received
From Savings
From Security Investments
From Loans to Others
Dividends Received
Proceeds from Sale of Assets
Proceeds from Sale of Securities
Other Items
Rent Received
Tax Refunds
Pension or Annuity Income
Miscellaneous Income

during the year—not the way they were expected to be. A default on the payment of income earned is always possible. Common sources of income, which would be shown on the income statement, are listed in Table 2.5.

A few items in Table 2.5 require clarification. Interest can be received on savings, on certain types of securities held as an investment, and from loans made to others. Proceeds from the sale of assets, such as furniture or a car, are shown as income. Likewise, proceeds from the sale of securities are shown as income. The tax implications of these transactions are discussed in Chapter 4, which is devoted to personal taxes. Other items of income include rent received from leased assets, any tax refunds received, any pension or annuity income received, and other miscellaneous types of income for the period. Total income is determined, of course, by adding all sources of income received during the period being evaluated.

Expenditures

Items shown as expenditures on the income statement represent money used for any of numerous possible outlays. Due to the large number of possible items of expenditure, it is perhaps easiest to categorize expenditures by the types of benefits they provide, as in Table 2.6. The listing of expenditures given there is certainly not all-inclusive, but it should provide some feel for possible types and categories of personal expenditures. Other schemes for categorization are possible; for example, categories could be based on distinctions between goods and services or necessities and luxuries. The financial planning and budgeting process, which is described in detail in Chapter 3, relies quite heavily on the categorization of expenditures in order to provide meaning to personal financial forecasts.

Table 2.6 Expenditure Category Breakdown

Housing	**Taxes**
Mortgage Payment	Income
Rent	Property
Repairs and Additions	**Appliances, Furniture, or Other Assets**
Household Services	Purchases
Utilities	Installment Payments
Gas and Electric	Repairs and Maintenance
Garbage Service	Home Accessories
Telephone	**Health and Hygiene**
Water	Laundry and Dry Cleaning
Cable TV	Cosmetics
Food	Barber and Hairdresser
Groceries	**Recreation, Entertainment, and Vacation**
Dining Out	Admissions
Automobile	Alcoholic Beverages
Purchase or Loan Payment	Hobby Supplies
Gas and Oil	Film and Developing
License Fees	Cigarettes and Tobacco
Repairs	Sports Equipment
Lease	Records and Tapes
Medical	Vacation and Travel
Doctor Bills	**Other Items**
Dental Bills	Postage and Stationery
Hospital Bills	Personal Allowance
Drugs and Medicine	Books and Magazines
Clothing and Shoes	Tuition
Insurance	Legal Fees
Life	Dues and Club Memberships
Health	Gifts
Homeowner's	Church and Charity
Auto	Pets
	Child Care
	Miscellaneous Unclassified Expenditures

Just as only the amount of income received is shown as income, only the amount of expenditures actually paid out is shown on the income statement. If an item—particularly an asset—is acquired through borrowing, only the net or actual dollars of money paid out (that is, purchase price minus the amount borrowed) is included as an expenditure. Any items purchased on credit or for which a portion of the purchase was financed with borrowing are not shown as expenditures on the income statement; the financed portion of these outlays is not viewed as an expenditure until it is actually paid off. Any credit purchases of this type are instead shown as an asset and corresponding liability on the balance sheet. Payments against these loans are shown on the income statement in the year they are actually made. In other words, the income statement is presented on a *cash basis*, which means that only cash income and cash expenditures are shown. Included in the cash expenditures are actual payments against loans obtained during the period—not the amount of the loans incurred. Total expenditures for the period are determined by adding together all uses of cash, or expenditures, listed on the income statement.

Contribution to Savings or Investments

The third component of the income statement presents the net result of the period's activities. The contribution to savings or investments for the period is obtained by subtracting the period's total expenditures from its total income. Although the income statement seems to indicate that dollars for savings or investments result from "what is left over" after all expenditures are paid, the amount to be contributed to savings and/or investments must be determined by personal financial goals. The income statement is only an after-the-fact report of what actually was contributed during a particular period.

The contribution to savings or investments entry on the income statement does allow you to determine how you did during the period. Its value can be zero, positive, or negative. A zero contribution to savings or investments indicates that the period's expenditures are exactly equal to the income from the period. A positive contribution to savings or investments indicates that the period's expenditures were less than the income for the period, and therefore a *surplus* resulted, which could be used to increase savings or investments or to reduce outstanding debts (that is, liabilities). A negative value indicates that the period's expenditures have exceeded its income, thereby resulting in a *deficit* that must be covered by either reducing savings or investments or by borrowing. When businesses have expenditures in excess of income, they are said to be *operating in the red*, since red ink is used to show deficits.

When a surplus exists, a family or individual can put the surplus into savings or an investment vehicle, or use it to pay outstanding debts. The effect of repaying outstanding debts would be to reduce future expenditures. When a deficit exists, the amount of the deficit can be met by drawing down savings or investments or by borrowing. The effect of borrowing would not be felt until subsequent periods when the loan would have to be repaid.

Balance Sheet Effect of Surplus When a positive contribution to savings or investments results (and the values of all other assets and liabilities have not changed), the effect is to *increase* net worth. This increase results because an asset—savings or investments—increases without a corresponding increase in any liability. In order for the balance sheet equation (Equation 2.1) to balance, an increase in assets without any increase in liabilities must result in an increase in net worth. If the surplus is used to reduce a liability, an increase in net worth is still the result. By way of illustration, assume that Balance

Table 2.7 Impact of a Positive Contribution to Savings or Investments (a Surplus) on the Balance Sheet

Balance Sheet A
31 December 1983

Assets		Liabilities and Net Worth	
		Total Liabilities	$22,000
Total Assets	$30,000	Net Worth	8,000
Total	$30,000	Total	$30,000

Balance Sheet B
31 December 1984 ($1,500 Surplus Added to Assets)

Assets		Liabilities and Net Worth	
		Total Liabilities	$22,000
Total Assets	$31,500	Net Worth	9,500
Total	$31,500	Total	$31,500

Balance Sheet C
31 December 1984 ($1,500 Surplus Used to Repay Debts [Decrease Liabilities])

Assets		Liabilities and Net Worth	
		Total Liabilities	$20,500
Total Assets	$30,000	Net Worth	9,500
Total	$30,000	Total	$30,000

Sheet A in Table 2.7 represents a family's balance sheet at 31 December 1983. If the family's income statement for 1984 showed a contribution to savings or investments (that is, surplus) of $1,500 and these funds were used to increase an asset, Balance Sheet B would represent the family's financial position at 31 December 1984. If the $1,500 surplus were used instead to repay a debt (that is, liability), Balance Sheet C would reflect the family's financial position at 31 December 1984. Regardless of which use is made of the surplus, the family's net worth increases by the amount of the surplus ($1,500) from its level of $8,000 at the end of 1983 to $9,500 at the end of 1984.

Balance Sheet Effect of Deficit While *surpluses* add to net worth, *deficits* reduce net worth (assuming the values of all other assets and liabilities have not changed). Again, in order for the balance sheet equation (Equation 2.1) to balance, this has to be the case. If the deficit is financed by reducing an asset—savings or investments—without a corresponding change in liabilities, a reduction in net worth results. If it is financed by borrowing without changing assets, the net worth is still reduced, as the example in Table 2.8 indicates. Balance Sheet X represents a family's financial position at 31 December 1983. Assume that the family's income statement shows a negative contribution to savings or investments (deficit) of $1,500 for 1984. Balance Sheets Y

Table 2.8 Impact of a Negative Contribution to Savings or Investments (a Deficit) on the Balance Sheet

Balance Sheet X
31 December 1983

Assets		Liabilities and Net Worth	
		Total Liabilities	$22,000
Total Assets	$30,000	Net Worth	8,000
Total	$30,000	Total	$30,000

Balance Sheet Y
31 December 1984 ($1,500 Deficit Financed by a Reduction in Assets)

Assets		Liabilities and Net Worth	
		Total Liabilities	$22,000
Total Assets	$28,500	Net Worth	6,500
Total	$28,500	Total	$28,500

Balance Sheet Z
31 December 1984 ($1,500 Deficit Financed by Borrowing (Increase Liabilities))

Assets		Liabilities and Net Worth	
		Total Liabilities	$23,500
Total Assets	$30,000	Net Worth	6,500
Total	$30,000	Total	$30,000

and Z show the two alternatives for meeting the deficit. In Balance Sheet Y, the $1,500 deficit is financed by reducing assets, while in Balance Sheet Z, the deficit is financed by borrowing. Regardless of the fashion in which the deficit is financed, the family's net worth decreased by $1,500, from $8,000 at the end of 1983 to $6,500 at the end of 1984.

In summary, surpluses, regardless of how they are used, result in increases in net worth; and deficits, regardless of how they are covered, result in decreases in net worth. Since increases in net worth are associated with growing financial strength, while decreases in net worth indicate declining financial strength, surpluses are preferred.

Income Statement Format

The format of the income statement is outlined in Table 2.9. It is headed with the dates defining the period covered by the statement—typically, one year, although quarterly or even monthly statements are sometimes prepared. The first set of entries includes all income items and a total income figure. Following the income entries, the expenditures are listed and totaled. Although it is not essential, the readability of the statement is greatly enhanced by including the various expenditure category headings. These headings permit a better understanding of

Table 2.9 General Format of the Income Statement

	Dates
Income	
Item 1	
Item 2	
.	
.	
.	
(1) Total Income	
Less: Expenditures	
Item 1	
Item 2	
.	
.	
.	
(2) Total Expenditures	
Contribution to Savings or Investments	[(1) − (2)]

general areas of expenditure and simplify the budget control process, which is described in Chapter 3. The final entry representing the contribution to savings or investments is shown as the result obtained by subtracting the total expenditures from the total income. This entry constitutes the *bottom line* of the statement and is basically a summary of the results of the financial activities during the designated period.

A Sample Income Statement—Art and Betty Johnston

Art and Betty Johnston's income statement for the year ended 31 December 1984 (Table 2.10) serves to illustrate the relationship between total income, total expenditures, and the contribution to savings or investments, along with the general format of the income statement. This statement, which was prepared using the background material presented earlier, along with the Johnstons' balance sheet (Table 2.4), is best evaluated by separate analysis of their income, expenditures, and contribution to savings or investments.

Income Art's wages clearly represent the family's chief source of income, to which the $1,176 of income earned by Betty in her part-time job is a supplement. Other sources of income include $178 in interest received on their savings deposits and bond investments and $50 in dividends received on the common stock they own. Art and Betty's total income for the year ended 31 December 1984 amounts to $26,345. The amount of income becomes much more meaningful when viewed in light of the expenditures made during the year.

Expenditures Art and Betty's major expenditures, as shown in Table 2.10, can be attributed to their home mortgage loan, food, and income

Table 2.10 Income Statement for Art and Betty Johnston (Year Ended 31 December 1984)

Income	
Wages and Salaries	
Art Johnston	$24,941
Betty Johnston	1,176
Interest Received	178
Dividends Received	50
(1) Total Income	$26,345
Less: Expenditures	
Housing	
Mortgage Payment	$ 8,280
Repairs and Additions	700
Utilities	
Gas and Electric	1,400
Telephone	240
Water	200
Food	3,800
Automobile	
Loan Payments	960
Gas and Oil	1,000
Repairs	200
Licenses	200
Medical Payments and Drugs (nonreimbursed)	240
Clothing and Shoes	600
Insurance	
Life	290
Health (paid by employer)	0
Homeowner's	365
Auto (liability only)	270
Taxes	
Income (includes social security)	3,890
Property (included in mortgage payment)	0
Furniture Loan Payment	400
Health and Hygiene	340
Recreation, Entertainment, and Vacation	780
Other Items	
Tuition and Books (Betty)	890
Gifts	150
Loan Payment (parents)	300
(2) Total Expenditures	$25,495
Contribution to Savings or Investments [(1) − (2)]	$ 850

taxes. Other sizeable expenditures during the year included housing repairs and additions, gas and electricity, auto loan payments, gas and oil for the cars, clothing and shoes, insurance, furniture loan payments, health and hygiene, recreation, and tuition and books. The total of the expenditures shown on the income statement is $25,495. Note that although the expenditure categories on Art and Betty's income statement are similar to those given in Table 2.6, they are not identical. As indicated earlier, these categories should be set up in a manner most suitable to the individual's—or family's—data requirements. Keep in mind, too, that the items of expenditure shown represent actual cash outlays made by the Johnstons during the year ended 31 December 1984.

Contribution to Savings or Investments The Johnstons' contribution to savings or investments of $850 for the year is found by subtracting the total expenditures of $25,495 from the total income of $26,345. Since the $850 is greater than zero, their contribution to savings or investments is, of course, positive. This surplus of $850 could be used to increase savings; to invest in stocks, bonds, or other vehicles; or to pay outstanding debts. The correct strategy depends on Art and Betty's financial goals. (Strategies with respect to savings, investments, and debt repayment are discussed in subsequent chapters.) If the contribution to savings or investments had been negative, this would have indicated that the Johnstons had to withdraw savings, liquidate investments, or borrow an amount equal to the deficit in order to meet their financial commitments during the year ended 31 December 1984. With their *surplus* of $850 (assuming the values of all other assets and liabilities have not changed from the previous period), the Johnstons have made a positive contribution to their net worth; had this figure been negative, a decrease in net worth would have resulted.

Preparing, Interpreting, and Forecasting Financial Statements

Your financial statements—the balance sheet and income statement—should provide the information needed to examine your financial position. With a thorough understanding of your financial status, you should be able to better direct your financial plans and activities toward achievement of your personal financial goals.

Preparation of Financial Statements

Financial statements should be prepared at least once each year and are typically prepared in conjunction with the preparation of budgets. In order to simplify the financial statement preparation process, a *ledger*, or financial record book, should be set up. The ledger should contain a separate section for assets, liabilities, sources of income, and expenditure items. Separate accounts can then be established for each item within each section. Whenever a change (that is, an addition or subtraction) in any of these accounts occurs, the appropriate entry should be made in the ledger. The objective of this system is to provide up-to-date data for use in preparing financial statements as well as for financial planning. Without current data, the likelihood of omitting any of these items from the financial statements or the planning process is much greater. Of course, if your finances are not very complicated, you may be able to maintain accurate records using some other, less sophisticated arrangement. Regardless of the arrangement used, some type of records providing accurate information for use in preparing the balance sheet and the income statement must be maintained.

Interpreting Financial Statements

Each time you prepare your financial statements, you should analyze them in order to assess how well you are doing compared to past periods and in light of your financial goals. Analysis of this type is often made easier by examining certain financial ratios. These ratios can be compared over time or with those of other households to evaluate your financial performance. Moreover, if you need to apply for a loan, there is a good chance the lending agency will also look at these to judge your capacity to carry additional debt. Space limits the ability to list and explain many ratios used in credit investigation analysis, but three will be used—(1) solvency ratio, (2) liquidity ratio, and (3) savings ratio—to illustrate the approach. The first two are associated primarily with the balance sheet while the last relates solely to the income statement.

Balance Sheet When evaluating your balance sheet, you should be most concerned with the net worth figure, since it indicates your worth at a given time. As explained earlier in this chapter, you are technically insolvent when your total liabilities exceed your total assets; that is, you have negative net worth. The *solvency ratio* shows, in percentages, the degree to which this has taken place. It is calculated as follows:

$$\text{solvency ratio} = \frac{\text{total net worth}}{\text{total assets}} \tag{2.2}$$

And for the Johnstons in 1984, the

$$\text{solvency ratio} = \frac{\$15{,}000}{\$76{,}000} = 0.20\text{, or 20 percent.}$$

This tells us that Art and Betty could withstand only about a 20 percent decline in the market value of their assets before they would be insolvent. The low value for this ratio suggests they should consider improving it in the future.

While the solvency ratio gives an indication of impending financial problems, it does not deal directly with the ability to pay immediate debts. This issue is addressed more appropriately with a *liquidity ratio*. Illustrated is the ratio of liquid assets to total current debts; current means any bill or charge that must be paid within one year. We have, then,

$$\text{liquidity ratio} = \frac{\text{liquid assets}}{\text{total current debts}} \tag{2.3}$$

The Johnstons' liquid assets (from Table 2.4) are the cash on hand and in checking accounts and deposits in banks and in the money market fund; these total \$1,710 (\$40 + \$220 + \$650 + \$800). Their total current debts are the bills outstanding of \$300 (\$90 + \$40 + \$60 + \$80 + \$30) and the portions of their mortgage loan, installment loans, and personal loan that are due within one year. These total \$9,940 (\$8,280 mortgage payment + \$960 auto loan payment + \$400 furniture loan payment + \$300 parent loan payment—all found on the income statement in Table 2.10). They are detailed below, but for now let us just take the year's total, which is \$10,240. Then, the Johnstons have

$$\text{liquidity ratio} = \frac{\$1{,}710}{\$10{,}240} = 0.17, \text{ or 17 percent.}$$

This ratio indicates that Art and Betty can only cover about 17 percent of their existing one-year debt obligations with their current liquid assets; in other words, they have about two months (one month is 1/12, or 8 percent) of coverage. If an emergency took place that would stop their income, their liquid reserves would be exhausted very quickly. While there is no hard and fast rule as to what this ratio should be, it seems low for the Johnstons; they should consider strengthening it along with their effort to improve their solvency ratio. This could be done by holding any added savings in the form of liquid assets, ideally through additions to their money market fund.

Income Statement When evaluating your income statement, primary concern should be placed on the *bottom line*, which shows the amount of the contribution to savings or investments resulting from the period's activities. This figure indicates how well you have done during the period and it can be related to income by calculating a *savings ratio*. That is done most appropriately with after-tax income as shown below:

$$\text{savings ratio} = \frac{\text{contribution to savings or investments}}{\text{income after income taxes}} \tag{2.4}$$

For the Johnstons, the

$$\text{savings ratio} = \frac{\$850}{\$26{,}345 - \$3{,}890} = \frac{\$850}{\$22{,}455} = 0.04, \text{ or 4 percent.}$$

Art and Betty saved about 4 percent of their after-tax income. How much to save is your own personal choice; some families would plan very much higher levels, particularly if they were saving to achieve an important goal, such as buying a house. The Johnstons are fortunate in already owning a house, which permits them to enjoy a higher level of consumption.

Forecasting Financial Statements

Until now, we have looked at financial statements to determine historical financial performance; that is, to evaluate what has happened in the past. But they can be used also to assist in achieving future financial goals; and they serve best in that capacity when they are tied to the annual budgeting process, described in detail in the next chapter. For the moment, let us suppose Art and Betty Johnston believe that one important goal for them to achieve in 1985 is to increase their net worth by at least $3,000.

Their increase can take place in two different ways. First, the Johnstons can prepare a 1985 cash budget that will specifically provide for it by controlling their income and expenditures. Second, the Johnstons could rely upon increases in market values of some of their assets, particularly the stocks and bonds they own and, possibly, their house and stamp collection. They must be concerned, though, that some of their assets may decline in market value. This would seem to be true for their automobiles, recreational equipment, and personal property items.

Table 2.11 details how the Johnstons expect their net worth to increase in 1985. Line *a* shows a budgeted increase of $3,452, and line *b* indicates the Johnstons' estimates of increases and decreases in their assets' market values. The net increase in 1985 is expected to be $1,280. This is only an estimate, of course, and Art and Betty are not relying upon it to achieve their net worth goal. They expect that in the long run many of their assets will increase in value—that is one of the reasons they purchased them—but they are less sure of these increases on a year-to-year basis. Finally, if everything works out as planned, the Johnstons' net worth at 31 December 1985 will be $19,732 ($15,000 to start the year and the addition of $4,732).

Table 2.11 Forecasted Increase in Balance Sheet Net Worth for Art and Betty Johnston (Year to End 31 December 1985)

Increases in Net Worth Planned with the 1985 Budget:	
(1) Make $8,280 in monthly payments on home mortgage; $7,728 is interest, leaving payments to reduce the loan of	$ 552
(2) Make payments on auto loan of $960 and furniture loan of $400; combined interest on both is $260, leaving payments to reduce the loan of	1,100
(3) Reduce loan to parents	800
(4) Increase savings (and invest in money market fund)	1,000
(a) Budgeted increase in net worth	$3,452
Expected Increases (Decreases) in Market Values of Assets:	
(1) House (3% increase)	$1,800
(2) Automobiles (10% decrease)	(530)
(3) Recreational equipment (50% decrease)	(200)
(4) Personal property (jewelry will increase but furniture and clothing will decrease; assume they offset)	0
(5) Stocks and bonds (5% increase)	110
(6) Cash value of life insurance (from the policy)	50
(7) Stamp collection (2% increase)	50
(b) Expected net increase in market value of assets	$1,280
Total Expected Increase in Net Worth in 1985 = [(a) + (b)]	$4,732

Summary

Your financial statements—the balance sheet and income statement—allow you to measure your financial position and financial performance. The balance sheet, or statement of financial position, consists of three major accounts: assets, liabilities, and net worth. It describes your financial condition at a specified point in time. The balance sheet must balance, which means that the total assets must equal the sum of total liabilities and net worth. Assets include items such as cash, savings, housing, cars, and investments and are listed on the left-hand side of the statement. Liabilities, which include unpaid bills, installment and other kinds of loans, and mortgages, and net worth are shown on the right-hand side of the balance sheet. All assets are shown on the statement at their current market value, while liabilities entered on the statement represent the amounts currently owed on all outstanding debts.

The income statement describes the various financial activities that have taken place over a specified period of time, normally one year. The statement has three component parts: income, expenditures, and contribution to savings or investments. The contribution to savings or investments is found by subtracting the total expenditures from the total income of the period. The contribution may be zero, positive, or negative. A positive contribution, or surplus, can be used to increase savings or investments or to repay an outstanding loan. A negative contribution, or deficit, can be financed by reducing savings or investments or by borrowing. Since surpluses tend to increase net worth and deficits tend to decrease net worth, surpluses are preferred. Income, which includes items such as wages and salaries, interest, and dividends, is shown at the top of the statement followed by expenditures, which include items such as those related to housing, utilities, food, automobiles, and medical services. The contribution to savings or investments, which is the difference between total income and total expenditures, is shown as the bottom line of the statement.

Both the balance sheet and income statement should be prepared periodically, typically at the end of each year. These statements can be used to evaluate past performance, and ratio analysis is often used in this effort. The solvency ratio shows total net worth as a percentage of total assets; a low percentage indicates potential problems. The liquidity ratio measures liquid assets in relation to total current debts; a low percentage reveals questionable ability to meet current debts if family income falls or stops. The savings ratio shows the contribution to savings or investment in relation to after-tax income; a low percentage means the family saves very little of its earnings.

Financial statements can also be forecasted for future periods. In this regard they are often integrated with budgeting. A commonly forecasted balance sheet value is net worth since it is the most important measure of financial progress.

Financial Planning and Budgeting 3

The periodic assessment of your financial position using the balance sheet and income statement is only the first step in managing your personal finances. In order to reach your financial potential and maintain your desired quality of life, you need to initiate a positive personal financial management program. This will require you to prepare plans and budgets that can act as navigational aids in plotting the course toward achievement of both your long-run and short-run financial goals. Although conscientious planning of your finances may force you to make certain short-run sacrifices, it should allow you to achieve your long-run goals and so provide you with higher levels of overall satisfaction.

Most individuals wish to achieve certain *life goals*. Although these goals may not be entirely financial, the ability to achieve most of them depends on realizing a certain level of financial success. The absence of goals—financial and otherwise—results in a depressing and unexciting life with little direction and few prospects for the future.

Money is not necessarily the key to happiness, but its presence in amounts adequate for the fulfillment of financial goals allows people to devote more of their energy to the achievement of life goals and personal happiness. Since most people are not favored with unlimited funds throughout their lifetimes, their management of personal finances becomes a job of planning how to spend, save, and invest income in order to achieve as many lifetime goals as possible. Although it may be possible to achieve certain financial goals without financial planning, the presence of financial plans should improve goal achievement possibilities.

Establishing Financial Goals

The establishment of financial goals is the first step in the overall financial planning process. These goals, once set, provide direction for the financial planning process. In other words, you cannot prepare plans for attaining goals that are not yet formulated. Nor is it possible to enter the financial planning process without a knowledge of current financial position. Methods for evaluating the current financial position by preparing personal financial statements were described in Chapter 2. After the current financial position is evaluated, both long-run and short-run financial goals must be established. Once they have been defined, budgets consistent with them can be prepared each year. Normally, *long-run financial goals* are set first, and then a series of *short-run financial goals* are established in line with the long-run goals. Long-run goals are set for the years between the present and retirement, while short-run goals are normally set for one or two years ahead. These goals must be established with reference to the entire family unit—not on the basis of only one person's priorities.

Long-Run Financial Goals

Since it is quite difficult to be precise about future developments and desires, long-run financial goals are normally established in a somewhat general manner. They should indicate the wants and desires of the family unit over the next 30 to 40 years. Of course, it is not easy for many people to predict what they will want 30 or so years from now, but if they at least give some thought to the problem, they should be able to establish some tentative long-run financial goals.

Actually, as the size and age of the members of the family unit change, so will many of the family's long-run goals. Long-run goals must be flexible enough to allow for changes as well as strong enough to shape short-run financial decisions. For example, an individual might set a goal of retiring at age 55 with a net worth of $400,000. This same individual might later decide to purchase a condominium in Florida at age 50 and retire at age 62 with a net worth of $500,000. But, although the long-run goal is changed, the short-run goals will remain fairly consistent: either long-run goal requires substantial regular contributions to savings or investments for the accumulation of the desired net worth.

Many families have found that the best procedure for establishing a set of mutually agreeable long-run goals is a meeting of the entire family at which the suggestions of each family member can be taken into consideration. Goals are most effective when set in reference to certain *goal dates* over a period of 30 to 40 years. Goal dates are points in the future when certain financial activities are expected to be concluded; they may serve as checkpoints in the progress toward some financial goals or as deadlines for the achievement of others. For example, one goal may be the purchase of a boat in 1988 (the goal date), and another goal may be a net worth of $200,000 in 2008, with goal dates 1991 and 2001 set as checkpoints for the attainment of net worth of $75,000 and $140,000, respectively.

Goal dates are often set at intervals of 2 to 5 years for the first 10 to 12 years and at 5-year intervals thereafter. Of course, setting long-run goals and goal dates for periods extending 20 to 25 years into the future should be the prerogative of the parents, since it is likely that children will be on their own at that time and retirement will be the parents' key concern.

As time passes and long-run goals become short-run goals, adjustments in the financial plans can be made. The possibility also exists that as the actual financial outcomes are realized, the goals themselves may have to be changed. In other words, the family may recognize that goals were set either too high or too low. If the goals appear to be too high in light of the financial outcomes, they must be revised and made more realistic. If they are clearly too low, they should be reevaluated and set at a level that forces the family to make financially responsible decisions rather than squandering surplus funds.

Short-Run Financial Goals

Short-run financial goals for each year should be consistent with the achievement of the long-run goals. These short-run goals thus become the key input into the *budget*—a tool used to plan for short-run income and expenditures. The immediate goals of individual family members, the family's expected income for the year, and the family's long-run financial goals must all be taken into account when these short-run goals are defined. In addition, the family must consider both its financial position, as reflected by the current balance sheet, and its spending in the year immediately preceding, as reflected in the income statement for that period. Short-run planning should also include the establishment of an emergency fund containing three to six months of income. This special savings account serves as a safety valve that can be used in case of financial emergencies—for example, a temporary loss of income.

The family's effectiveness in reaching its short-run goals significantly affects its ability to achieve long-run goals. If many short-run goals are not attained, the likelihood of achieving long-run goals is greatly reduced. In setting short-run goals, current desires must not be allowed to override the requirements for achieving long-run goals. Given the general disposition of people to prefer current satisfactions over satisfactions in the distant future, this may be the greatest challenge involved in setting short-run goals. Short-run sacrifices may be necessary to provide for a comfortable future, and realizing this fact 10 or 20 years too late may make important financial and life goals unattainable. For example, college seniors who wish to become medical doctors may have to forgo jobs paying around $16,000 a year in order to attend medical school at a cost of $10,000 a year for three or more years. Of course, upon completion of their medical education, they can expect to earn more than $60,000 a year practicing medicine.

Examples of Goals—Art and Betty Johnston

In Chapter 2, you were introduced to Art and Betty Johnston, whose financial data were used to develop financial statements dated 31 December 1984. Throughout this chapter, the Johnstons' financial data will continue to be used to illustrate various aspects of financial planning and budgeting. The Johnstons' long- and short-run financial goals, which they set on 31 December 1984, are described in the following sections.

Table 3.1 Art and Betty Johnston's Long-Run Financial Goals (1 January 1987 to 31 December 2019)

1987
Pay off all loans other than mortgage
Save money for new home
Begin to build an investment portfolio
Start family (Betty stops teaching)
Buy new car (replace Volkswagen, trade every three years)

1991
Build investment portfolio
Have second child
Save money for new home
Buy station wagon (replace Cutlass, trade every three years)

1996
Betty resumes teaching
Buy new home
Purchase new furniture

2001
Buy sailboat
Purchase summer home
Accumulate net worth of $65,000

2006
Send children to college
Buy third car for children
Accumulate net worth of $90,000
Travel to Europe
Remodel home

2011
Children finlsh education
Buy larger sailboat
Travel to Australia
Accumulate net worth of $150,000

2019
Sell home and buy condominium
Retire from jobs
Accumulate net worth of $250,000

Long-Run Financial Goals of the Johnstons Since Art and Betty Johnston are 23 and 21 years old, respectively, they have set their most distant long-run financial goal 35 years from now—a point in time at which Art would like to retire. Table 3.1 presents a summary of Art and Betty's long-run financial goals. They arbitrarily set their goal dates at the years 1987, 1991, 1996, 2001, 2006, 2011, and 2019. With the passage of time, they will probably adjust both the goals and goal dates. Although most of their goals do not have dollar amounts attached, Art and Betty can use them to provide direction to their short-run financial plans. In the planning process, the Johnstons made rough estimates of the costs of achieving their various long-run goals and then set the short-run goals necessary to attain them. For instance, in order to have $10,000 saved by 1996 to buy a new home, they would need to save approximately $850 per year over the 1985–1996 period (that is, $10,000 saved over 12 years, or $10,000/12).

Short-Run Financial Goals of the Johnstons In the final week of December 1984, Art and Betty Johnston set their short-run financial goals for the coming year. They considered three factors: (1) their current financial condition as reflected in their balance sheet dated 31 December 1984 (Table 2.4); (2) their income statement for the year ended 31 December 1984 (Table 2.10), from which they were able to

Table 3.2 Art and Betty Johnston's Short-Run Financial Goals (Year Ended 31 December 1985)

Priority	1	Betty finish school ($500)
	2	Purchase new tires for Cutlass ($240)
	3	Purchase career clothes for Betty ($550)
	4	Buy new suits for Art ($400)
	5	Accumulate net worth of $18,000
	6	Take two-week vacation to Canada ($900)
	7	Buy workshop equipment ($500)
	8	Take ski trip to Colorado ($800)
	9	Purchase electric garage door opener ($240)

evaluate their past spending in order to estimate their spending requirements for 1985; and (3) their long-run financial goals (Table 3.1), with which the short-run goals had to be consistent. Art and Betty's short-run financial goals for the coming year along with their expected costs of achievement are given in Table 3.2.

In order to simplify the process of eliminating expenditures in the event that sufficient funds are not available, the Johnstons assigned priorities to their short-run goals. The first four items seem to be necessities, and the fifth appears to be associated with their long-run net worth goal. The remaining items are extras, or luxuries, that the Johnstons would like to acquire during the year but probably can do without. Once they have prepared their budget, the Johnstons will be able to determine which of their short-run goals they can afford to achieve during the coming year.

The Budgeting Process

Once you have established your short-run goals, you should prepare a budget for the coming year that is consistent with them. The *budget* is a short-run financial planning device designed to allow you to achieve your short-run financial goals. As such, it makes a positive contribution toward the achievement of your long-run financial goals. Your budget contains estimates of income and expenditures, including savings and investments, for the coming year. It is usually divided into monthly intervals, although in some cases other time intervals may be more convenient.

The budget preparation process has three stages: estimating income, estimating expenditures, and finalizing the budget. When estimating income and expenditures, you should take into account any anticipated changes in the cost of living and their impact on your budget components. If your income is fixed—not expected to change over the budgetary period—increases in various items of expenditure will probably cause the purchasing power of your income to deteriorate. In an inflationary economy, the effects of changing price levels on both income and expenditure must be reflected in your budget.

Estimating Income

Once the short-run financial goals have been established, the first step in the budget preparation process is that of estimating income for the coming year. Since bills are most commonly rendered and paid monthly, it is best to estimate income as well as expenditures using monthly time intervals. The forecast of income takes into consideration all income expected for the year, for example: take-home pay of husband and wife, any bonuses or commissions expected, interest income, dividend income, rental income, and annuity income. Any items expected to be received for which repayment is required are not considered income. For example, a loan is treated not as a source of income, but rather as a liability for which scheduled repayments are required.

Estimating Expenditures

The second stage of the budgeting process is the most difficult. It involves estimating (on a monthly basis) the expenditures for the coming year using the actual expenditures from previous years (as found on income statements for those past periods) along with the stated short-run financial goals. Families without past expenditure data must use a "needs approach" to develop spending forecasts. By first projecting their needs based on necessities and then attaching dollar values to these needs, estimates of expenditures can be made. Discussions of estimated expenditures with friends and relatives should help in developing realistic values for expenditures included in the budget.

Initially, achievement of all short-run goals should be built into the expenditure estimates. To do this effectively, the cost of achieving the goal as well as the timing of the expenditure should be estimated. Any current or short-run contributions toward achievement of long-run goals should also be quantified and appropriately scheduled in the budget. Scheduled additions to savings and investments are often included as expenditures, since they are required by the family's goals. If the inclusion of all of these items does not allow the budget to balance, certain of them may, in the final analysis, have to be removed from the budget. Estimates of expenditures should be based on current price levels and then increased by a percentage that reflects the anticipated rate of inflation. For example, if the monthly food bill is estimated at \$300, and 8 percent inflation is expected in food prices, the estimated monthly food expenditure would be budgeted at \$324–\$300 plus \$24 (\$300 × 8 percent). In order to avoid omitting important entries, reference to a list of common expenditure categories such as that in Table

2.6 is useful when preparing the budget. An expenditure category for *fun money* that contains an allocation for each family member should also be included. This money, which family members use as they wish without reporting how they spend it, gives each family member some degree of financial independence and thus helps provide for a healthy family budget relationship.

Finalizing the Budget

Once income and expenditure estimates have been made, the budget can be finalized. This involves comparing the projected income and the projected expenditures on both a month-to-month and an annual basis. A *balanced budget* results when the total income for the year equals or exceeds the total expenditures for the year.

Monthly Budget Deficits Yet, even though the budget for the year may balance, expenditures in certain months may exceed income, causing a monthly *budget deficit*, or income in some months may exceed expenditures, causing a monthly *budget surplus*. Two remedies exist: (1) expenditures might be transferred from months in which budget deficits occur to months in which budget surpluses exist or, conversely, income might be transferred from months with surpluses to months with deficits; or (2) savings, investments, or borrowing may be used to cover temporary deficits. Since the budget for the year is balanced, the need for funds to cover these shortages is only temporary. Once a month having a budget surplus is reached, funds used to cover deficits can be returned to savings and investments, or loans can be repaid. Either of the preceding remedies for a monthly budget deficit in a balanced annual budget is possible, but the second is probably more practical.

Unbalanced Annual Budget Situations in which the budget for the year is not in balance are more difficult to cope with. Three approaches exist. One is to *liquidate enough savings and investments*, or to *borrow enough,* to meet the total budget deficit for the year. This action is *not recommended* because it violates the objective of budgeting. The purpose of the budgeting process is to set expenditures at a level that provides for a reasonable standard of living while making positive contributions toward the achievement of long-run goals. Drawing down savings and investments or borrowing in order to make the budget balance tends to reduce net worth. People who use these approaches are not living within their means.

A second and preferred approach is to *cut lower priority expenditure items* out of the budget in order to bring the total budget into balance. This approach forces the budget to balance without using some external source of funds. Low-priority expenditures are those items associated with the short-run financial goals believed to be least important. Some people using this technique to bring their budgets into balance divide their expenditures into two groups—inflexible and flexible. *Inflexible expenditures* are those that must be made on the basis of either contracts or necessity. Items such as mortgage payments, loan payments, and utility bills are examples of inflexible expenditures. *Flexible expenditures* are for noncontractual items that are not necessities, such as recreation, entertainment, and certain clothing purchases. These flexible expenditures can be cut from the budget in order to bring it into balance.

A third approach is to *increase income* by assuming a second, part-time job or by finding an alternative job that pays more. This is probably the most difficult approach for it is likely to result in a significant change in leisure activities and lifestyle. Individuals with no savings and investments to liquidate and who are unable to meet expenditures for necessity items may find that taking a second job or changing jobs provides the only feasible course of action for balancing their budget.

Budget Summary Once all monthly deficits have been considered and the total annual budget has been balanced, the budget is finalized. The income for the year equals or exceeds the year's expenditures, and tentative plans have been made for covering expected monthly deficits. At this point, the preparation of a *budget summary*—which shows for each month the estimated income and estimated expenditures, the amount of any surplus or deficit, and the cumulative surplus or deficit at the end of each month—provides an overview of the financial situation in the year to come. By analyzing the cumulative surplus or deficit, the timing and amount of shortage or excess funds can be evaluated and the practicality of the method chosen for covering monthly deficits can be determined. The use of the budget summary statement can greatly simplify the problems in preparing and interpreting budgets. The entire budget finalization process, including the budget summary statement, is illustrated in a later section of this chapter.

The Budget Format

As shown in Table 3.3, the finalized budget is normally broken into three basic sections: income, expenditures, and the difference between them (income minus expenditures), which may be either a surplus or a deficit. Within the first two sections, the individual items of income and expenditure are shown separately. Usually, the budget shows monthly figures as well as an annual total for each income and expenditure item. In many situations, the number of budget entries dictates that it is better to break the budget into separate schedules—one for estimated income, one for estimated expenditures (including savings and investments), and a budget summary that can replace the single budget statement. The income and expenditure schedules can

Table 3.3 The Budget Format

	Jan.	Feb.	......	Dec.	Annual Total
Income					
Item 1					
Item 2					
.					
.					
.					
(1) Total Income			......		
Expenditures (Includes Scheduled Contributions to Savings and Investments)					
Item 1					
Item 2					
.					
.					
.					
(2) Total Expenditures			......		
Surplus (or Deficit) [(1) − (2)]			......		

be prepared separately, and the budget summary can be used to bring these components together to determine the amount of any surpluses or deficits.

Sample Budget—Art and Betty Johnston

Using their short-run financial goals (Table 3.2) and their past financial statements (see Tables 2.4 and 2.10), Art and Betty Johnston prepared their budget for the 1985 calendar year. The Johnstons' budget was developed using separate schedules of estimated income and expenditures along with a budget summary, as described earlier.

Schedule of Estimated Income Art and Betty Johnston's *schedule of estimated income* for the year ended 31 December 1985 shown in Table 3.4 provides an item-by-item breakdown for each month of the coming year. The Johnstons' total annual income, which is derived primarily from Art's wages, is expected to be $28,048. Using the amount of take-home pay, as the Johnstons did, rather than the entire salary to draw up this schedule eliminates the need to show taxes or social security payments in the expenditure portion of the budget. Note the lapse in Betty's income during the months of June, July, and August; she will quit her library job just before she graduates from college in June but will not take a teaching job until September.

Table 3.4 Schedule of Estimated Income for Art and Betty Johnston (Year Ended 31 December 1985)

Source	Jan.	Feb.	Mar.	Apr.	May	June	
Art's Take-Home Pay	$1,860	$1,860	$1,860	$1,860	$1,860	$1,860	
Betty's Take-Home Pay	100	100	100	100	100	0	
Art's Bonus							
Interest			45			45	
Dividends			12			12	
Total Income	$1,960	$1,960	$2,017	$1,960	$1,960	$1,917	
Source	**July**	**Aug.**	**Sept.**	**Oct.**	**Nov.**	**Dec.**	**Total**
Art's Take-Home Pay	$1,860	$1,860	$1,860	$1,860	$1,860	$1,860	$22,320
Betty's Take-Home Pay	0	0	1,000	1,000	1,000	1,000	4,500
Art's Bonus						1,000	1,000
Interest			45			45	180
Dividends			12			12	48
Total Income	$1,860	$1,860	$2,917	$2,860	$2,860	$3,917	$28,048

Schedule of Estimated Expenditures The Johnstons' initial *schedule of estimated expenditures* for the year ended 31 December 1985 is presented in Table 3.5. Most of the expenditure items the Johnstons listed were categorized and included in Table 2.6. Note that Art and Betty have built $110 into their budget as fun money. The fun money is to be divided equally between them, and they will not report to each other on the disposition of their share of it.

Another significant aspect of their schedule of estimated expenditures is the $1,000 included under savings and investments. In light of the scheduled debt repayment, Art and Betty estimate that putting that amount aside will enable them to easily exceed their net worth goal of $18,000. (Art and Betty's net worth goal was discussed at length at the end of Chapter 2.) Note also that the Johnstons built in additional costs in order to adequately reflect the effect of inflation on certain of the budgeted items. They did this by adjusting actual 1984 expenditures upward by the percentages which they believed accurately reflected the rate of price increase expected for certain budget items.

Aside from this, the schedule of estimated expenditures shown in Table 3.5 is self-explanatory. Of course, it represents only the Johnstons' first estimate of their expenditures. The first trial aims at the achievement of all of the Johnstons' short-run goals listed in Table 3.2.

Finalizing the Johnstons' Budget Reviewing Art and Betty Johnston's initial schedule of expenditures, we can see that the initial esti-

Table 3.5 Art and Betty Johnston's Initial Schedule of Estimated Expenditures (Year Ended 31 December 1985)

Item	Jan.	Feb.	Mar.	Apr.	May	June	July	Aug.	Sept.	Oct.	Nov.	Dec.	Total
Home Mortgage	$ 690	$ 690	$ 690	$ 690	$ 690	$ 690	$ 690	$ 690	$ 690	$ 690	$ 690	$ 690	$ 8,280
Electric Garage Door Opener		80	80	80									240
Gas and Electric	160	160	160	85	85	120	120	160	160	120	120	160	1,610
Water	15	15	15	15	15	25	25	25	15	15	15	15	210
Groceries	190	190	190	190	190	190	190	190	190	190	190	190	2,280
Dining Out	160	160	160	160	160	160	160	160	160	160	160	160	1,920
Workshop Equipment									250	250			500
Clothing	65	65	175	65	65	65	65	65	500	90	90	90	1,400
Betty's Tuition		500											500
Auto Loan	80	80	80	80	80	80	80	80	80	80	80	80	960
Furniture Loan	33	33	33	33	33	33	33	33	33	33	33	37	400
Parents' Loan									200	200	200	200	800
New Tires for Cutlass	80	80	80										240
Gasoline and Oil	100	100	100	100	100	100	100	100	100	100	100	100	1,200
Auto Licenses		200											200
Income Taxes (assumed equal to withholding)													0
Property Taxes (included in mortgage payment)													0
Telephone	25	25	25	25	25	25	25	25	25	25	25	25	300
Homeowner's Insurance						185						185	370
Auto Insurance (liability only)		150						150					300
Health Insurance (paid by Art's employer)													0
Life Insurance											290		290
Medical and Dental (nonreimbursed)	20	20	20	20	20	20	20	20	20	20	20	20	240
Laundry, Cosmetics, Hair Care	80	80	80	80	80	80	80	80	80	80	80	80	960
Gifts				20	40			40				200	300
Recreation and Entertainment	120	120	120	120	120	120	120	120	120	120	120	120	1,440
Vacations								900				800	1,700
Charitable Contributions	100					30			30				160
Miscellaneous	70	70	70	70	70	70	70	70	70	70	70	70	840
Fun Money	110	110	110	110	110	110	110	110	110	110	110	110	1,320
Savings and Investments (to achieve $17,000 of net worth)												1,000	1,000
Total Expenditures	$2,098	$2,928	$2,188	$1,943	$1,883	$2,103	$1,888	$3,018	$2,833	$2,353	$2,393	$4,332	$29,960

Table 3.6 Art and Betty Johnston's Adjusted Schedule of Estimated Expenditures (Year Ended 31 December 1985)

Item	Jan.	Feb.	Mar.	Apr.	May	June	July	Aug.	Sept.	Oct.	Nov.	Dec.	Total
Home Mortgage	$ 690	$ 690	$ 690	$ 690	$ 690	$ 690	$ 690	$ 690	$ 690	$ 690	$ 690	$ 690	$ 8,280
Electric Garage Door Opener													0
Gas and Electric	160	160	160	85	85	120	120	160	120	120	120	160	1,610
Water	15	15	15	15	15	25	25	25	15	15	15	15	210
Groceries	190	190	190	190	190	190	190	190	190	190	190	190	2,280
Dining Out	160	160	160	160	160	160	160	160	160	160	160	160	1,920
Workshop Equipment													0
Clothing	65	65	175	65	65	65	65	65	500	90	90	90	1,400
Betty's Tuition		500											500
Auto Loan	80	80	80	80	80	80	80	80	80	80	80	80	960
Furniture Loan	33	33	33	33	33	33	33	33	33	33	33	37	400
Parents' Loan										200	200	200	600
New Tires for Cutlass	80	80	80										240
Gasoline and Oil	100	100	100	100	100	100	100	100	100	100	100	100	1,200
Auto Licenses		200											200
Income Taxes (assumed equal to withholding)													0
Property Taxes (included in mortgage payment)													0
Telephone	25	25	25	25	25	25	25	25	25	25	25	25	300
Homeowner's Insurance						185						185	370
Auto Insurance (liability only)		150						150					300
Health Insurance (paid by Art's employer)													0
Life Insurance											290		290
Medical and Dental (nonreimbursed)	20	20	20	20	20	20	20	20	20	20	20	20	240
Laundry, Cosmetics, Hair Care	80	80	80	80	80	80	80	80	80	80	80	80	960
Gifts				20	40			40				200	300
Recreation and Entertainment	120	120	120	120	120	120	120	120	120	120	120	120	1,440
Vacations								900					900
Charitable Contributions	100					30			30				160
Miscellaneous	70	70	70	70	70	70	70	70	70	70	70	70	840
Fun Money	90	90	90	90	90	90	90	90	90	90	90	90	1,080
Savings and Investments (to achieve $17,000 of net worth)												1,000	1,000
Total Expenditures	$2,078	$2,828	$2,088	$1,843	$1,863	$2,083	$1,868	$2,998	$2,363	$2,083	$2,373	$3,512	$27,980

Table 3.7 Budget Summary for Art and Betty Johnston (Year Ended 31 December 1985)

Month	Estimated Income (1)	Estimated Expenditures (2)	Surplus (Deficit) [(1) − (2)] (3)	Cumulative Surplus (Deficit) (4)
January	$ 1,960	$ 2,078	(118)	(118)
February	1,960	2,828	(868)	(986)
March	2,017	2,088	(71)	(1,057)
April	1,960	1,843	117	(940)
May	1,960	1,863	97	(843)
June	1,917	2,083	(166)	(1,009)
July	1,860	1,868	(8)	(1,017)
August	1,860	2,998	(1,138)	(2,155)
September	2,917	2,363	554	(1,601)
October	2,860	2,083	777	(824)
November	2,860	2,373	487	(337)
December	3,917	3,512	405	68
Totals	$28,048	$27,980	$68	$68

mate results in total expenditures of $29,960. This figure is greater than that for their total estimated income of $28,048 (Table 3.4). Clearly, the budget is not balanced; a budget deficit of approximately $1,900 exists. In order to bring the budget into balance, Art and Betty cut certain low-priority goals from their budget, rescheduled some of their loan payments, and reduced their fun money allocation. The specific individual adjustments are as follows:

1. Eliminated purchase of workshop equipment costing $500.
2. Eliminated ski trip to Colorado costing $800.
3. Eliminated purchase of electric garage door opener costing $240.
4. Rescheduled $200 of loan repayment to parents.
5. Reduced allocation of fun money by $240 for the year ($20 per month).

The total expenditure reduction of $1,980 lowered the total scheduled expenditures for the year to $27,980, which falls within the total income estimate of $28,048. These changes are reflected in the adjusted schedule of estimated expenditures presented in Table 3.6. The expenditure totals after these adjustments are given in the final line of the schedule. Once these adjustments are made and estimated annual expenditures no longer exceed estimated annual income, the budget is balanced.

The Johnstons' final step in the budgeting process was to analyze monthly surpluses and deficits in order to estimate whether or not savings, investments, or borrowing should be used to meet any monthly deficits. To do this, Art and Betty prepared the *budget summary* that appears in Table 3.7. The first two columns list the estimated income and expenditure totals for each month from Tables 3.4 and 3.6, respectively. Column 3 shows the surplus or deficit for each month. The total surplus of $68 for the year should add to the Johnstons' savings and investments or allow them to repay a portion of one of their outstanding loans. Column 4 presents a cumulative total of the surpluses or deficits shown in column 3.

Note that although monthly deficits occur in January through March and June through August, the magnitude and timing of these deficits result in a cumulative deficit for the months January through November. In order to cover these deficits, Art and Betty were able to arrange an interest-free loan from their parents. Had they been required to use their savings to finance these temporary deficits, they would have had to forgo some of the interest on savings included as part of their estimated income. If the Johnstons had been completely unable to obtain funds to cover these temporary deficits, they would have had to reschedule their planned expenditures or income.

Budget Records and Control

Accurate records and control procedures must be maintained to insure that the budget has some effect on the financial planning process. A good financial plan and budget are not enough; records are needed in order to maintain control over income and spending, for preparing financial statements, and for planning future spending. The family does not need to account for every penny of income and expenditure during a given period. Since most families are not interested in devoting great amounts of time to maintaining detailed records, record-keeping and control procedures used should not be so technical as to become a burden.

A sophisticated budget record and control system includes (1) setting up the record book, (2) recording actual expenditures, (3) balancing accounts periodically, (4) controlling budget expenditures, and (5) balancing the books and preparing year-end financial statements. Personal computers are beginning to play an important part in simplifying the amount of clerical effort involved in the budget record and control process. The system described in the following sections is relatively sophisticated, but by studying it, you should be able to develop your own more practical budget record and control procedures.

Setting Up the Record Book

In order to maintain accurate records for controlling the budget and planning future expenditures, a *budget record book* should be kept. Loose-leaf binders with separate pages for each income and expenditure account serve this purpose quite well. Each account should be numbered, and an index of accounts should appear at the front of the binder. The account title and number should head each page of the record book. Grouping similar categories of accounts and tabbing these sections facilitates reference to individual accounts. Duplication and confusion can be avoided by giving only one person the responsibility for recording all income and expenditures in the record book.

Recording Actual Expenditures

At the beginning of each budget period (month, quarter), the amount budgeted for each item of expenditure should be recorded in the record book. As income is received and money is expended, entries should be made in the appropriate accounts. The amount expended for a given item should be deducted from that item's account balance in order to maintain a running balance of the amount yet available for expenditure in the current period. When the balances in each account are kept up to date in this way, the probability that accounts will be overspent is reduced. Instead of making these entries each day, many people prefer to maintain all expenditures on a *master expenditure sheet* from which the entries are posted to the record book at specified intervals of time, such as every three days. Still, these expenditures must be entered frequently enough to insure that accounts are not overspent.

Balancing Accounts Periodically

At the end of each period, all accounts should be *balanced*; that is, the end-of-period balance should be determined. Then the amount budgeted for the next period should be added to this end-of-period balance in order to determine the balance on hand at the beginning of the new period. In theory, the balance of each account should be zero at the end of each budget period, but this normally occurs only for those accounts from which a single payment equal to the budgeted amount is required—mortgages, loans, or insurance, for example. Other accounts may end up with either positive balances, indicating the budget was underspent, or negative balances, indicating the budget was overspent.

Controlling Budget Expenditures

When accounts are balanced at the end of each period, surpluses and deficits should be subjected to some analysis. The presence of a surplus need not cause concern; but a deficit, which indicates that the account is operating in the red, requires attention. An account deficit that occurs in only one period is not as problematical as a deficit that recurs in a series of periods. One way of dealing with a deficit is to cut back expenditures in future periods for the account affected. If recurring deficits indicate an account may have been underbudgeted, the budget may need to be adjusted to a level sufficient to cover the outlays. Budget adjustments of this type are usually accomplished by reducing the amount budgeted for other accounts that may be either overbudgeted or nonessential. In all cases, however, accounts must balance so that the annual budget will balance. Only in exceptional situations should budget adjustments be financed by drawing down savings and investments or by borrowing.

Envelope System Another method of monthly budget control, the *envelope system*, is often used for expenditures for which the budgeted amount is spent on a number of individual purchases, such as groceries, gas and oil, clothing, and so on. Under this system, at the start of each period an amount of money equal to the budgeted amount for each of the accounts is placed into separate envelopes labeled with the account name. All expenditures made on these accounts are paid using the money enclosed within the appropriate envelope. When the funds within the envelope are exhausted, the period's spending for that budget item is concluded. With this system, the balance of any of these accounts can be checked merely by finding out how much money remains in the envelope. The envelope system has been found to be quite effective in controlling expenditures in selected accounts.

Total Monthly Budget Control Control is important not only in individual accounts, but also in the total budget for the period. By examining end-of-period balances for the total of all accounts, it is possible to determine whether a net budget surplus or deficit exists. Based on this finding, appropriate action can be taken to insure a balanced budget for the year. The existence of total period surpluses is advantageous, since the surplus funds can be used for savings, investments, or debt repayment. Total period deficits, however, signal the need for corrective action, which normally consists of adjusting spending in subsequent months in order to end the year with a balanced budget.

Budget Records and Control—An Illustration

Two techniques are used by Art and Betty Johnston in the budget record and control process—monitoring an account and summarizing total budget activity.

Monitoring an Account Table 3.8 presents the Johnstons' grocery expenditure record for January through March of 1985. In January $190 was budgeted and only $182 was actually spent; the month ended with an $8 surplus. In February, $190 was again budgeted, but $209 was spent. Although the Johnstons' spending during February was $19 over their budget ($209 − $190), the month ended with only an $11 deficit

Table 3.8 Art and Betty Johnston's Grocery Expenditure Record (January through March 1985)

Date		Item	Amount Budgeted	Amount Expended	Account Balance
Jan.	1	**January Budget**	$190		$190
	3	Groceries		$ 78	112
	9	Milk and Eggs		5	107
	11	Girl Scout Cookies		7	100
	15	Groceries		78	22
	26	Pop and Snacks		14	8
	31	January Totals	$190	$182	$ 8
Feb.	1	**February Budget**	$190		$198
	2	Groceries		$ 91	107
	10	Snacks		19	88
	15	Groceries		69	19
	23	Dinner Party		30	−11
	28	February Totals	$190	$209	$−11
Mar.	1	**March Budget**	$190		$179
	10	Groceries		$89	90
	12	Sirloin		12	78
	16	Groceries		66	12
	26	Pop and Snacks		10	2
	30	March Totals	$190	$177	$ 2

since the $8 surplus from January was in the account. During March, $190 was budgeted and $177 was actually spent; but, since the month began with an $11 deficit, the month-end balance was $2 ($13 surplus for March minus $11 deficit carried over from February). All in all, Art and Betty appear to have made reasonable budget estimates and maintained good control over their grocery expenditures. Had there been surpluses in all months or deficits in all months, some type of budget adjustment would have been necessary.

Summarizing Total Budget Activity In addition to monitoring individual accounts, the Johnstons maintained an *actual budget summary* of accounts showing the budgeted amount, the balance at the beginning of the month, the actual expenditures made, and the end-of-month balance for each account, along with the total expenditures for all accounts. Their summary statement for January through March of 1985 appears in Table 3.9. The format of the statement makes it easy to analyze the behavior of individual accounts as well as the total budget and to make adjustments in amounts budgeted for future months, if necessary. The summary statement is also useful in preparing future budgets, since it facilitates evaluation of actual expenditures. For example, an analysis of individual items makes it quite clear that the end-of-month $111 deficit in March—which contrasts strikingly with the Jan-

Table 3.9 Art and Betty Johnston's Actual Budget Summary (January through March 1985)

Item	January			February				March			
	Beginning Balance (1)	Expenditures (2)	Ending Balance [(1) − (2)] (3)	Budget (4)	Beginning Balance [(3) + (4)] (5)	Expenditures (6)	Ending Balance [(5) − (6)] (7)	Budget (8)	Beginning Balance [(7) + (8)] (9)	Expenditures (10)	Ending Balance [(9) − (10)] (11)
Home Mortgage	$ 690	$ 690	$ 0	$ 690	$ 690	$ 690	$ 0	$ 690	$ 690	$ 690	$ 0
Gas and Electric	160	165	−5	160	155	160	−5	160	155	150	5
Water	15	15	0	15	15	14	1	15	16	14	2
Groceries (Table 3.8)	190	182	8	190	198	209	−11	190	179	177	2
Dining Out	160	135	25	160	185	175	10	160	170	205	−35
Clothing	65	115	−50	65	15	50	−35	175	140	120	20
Betty's Tuition	0	0	0	500	500	500	0	0	0	0	0
Auto Loan	80	80	0	80	80	80	0	80	80	80	0
Furniture Loan	33	33	0	33	33	33	0	33	33	33	0
Parents' Loan	0	0	0	0	0	0	0	0	0	0	0
New Tires for Cutlass	80	70	10	80	90	70	20	80	100	70	30
Gasoline and Oil	100	85	15	100	115	85	30	100	130	90	40
Auto Licenses	0	0	0	200	200	95	5	0	5	0	5
Telephone	25	35	−10	25	15	20	−5	25	20	35	−15
Homeowner's Insurance	0	0	0	0	0	0	0	0	0	0	0
Auto Insurance (liability only)	0	0	0	150	150	150	0	0	0	0	0
Life Insurance	0	0	0	0	0	0	0	0	0	0	0
Medical and Dental (nonreimbursed)	20	0	20	20	40	0	40	20	60	165	−105
Laundry, Cosmetics, Hair Care	80	65	15	80	95	90	5	80	85	95	−10
Gifts	0	0	0	0	0	0	0	0	0	0	0
Recreation and Entertainment	120	160	−40	120	80	90	−10	120	110	130	−20
Vacations	0	0	0	0	0	0	0	0	0	0	0
Charitable Contributions	100	100	0	0	0	0	0	0	0	0	0
Miscellaneous	70	55	15	70	85	85	0	70	70	100	−30
Fun Money	90	90	0	90	90	90	0	90	90	90	0
Savings and Investments	0	0	0	0	0	0	0	0	0	0	0
Totals	$2,078	$2,075	$ 3	$2,828	$2,831	$2,786	$ 45	$2,088	$2,133	$2,244	$ −111

Source Key: Columns (1), (4), and (8)—Initial Budgeted Amounts from Table 3.6 Columns (2), (6), and (10)—Actual Expenditures during Month

uary and February surpluses of $3 and $45, respectively—is attributable primarily to the high level of nonreimbursed medical and dental expenditures incurred during that month.

Balancing the Books and Preparing Year-End Financial Statements

The final steps in the budget control process are *balancing the books* for the year by calculating the end-of-year account balances and then, using this data, preparing the balance sheet and income statement (refer back to Tables 2.4 and 2.10). At the year's end, actual expenditures in each account can be determined by totalling the monthly expenditure values given in the actual budget summary for the account. Only after you have prepared your year-end financial statements can you determine whether you have achieved your stated budget goals. Your net worth as indicated on your year-end statements can then be compared to your net worth objective in order to assess the overall effectiveness of your budgeting process.

Using the Personal Computer

Unquestionably, the *personal (or micro-) computer* greatly facilitates the budgeting process. Once data are entered into storage, which is usually done on a keyboard, they can be retrieved and used in an almost endless number of applications. For example, all the budgeting procedures explained in this chapter are handled easily by even the smallest personal computer. Instead of handwritten records in a loose-leaf binder, your budget data will probably be recorded on a small flexible disk. The computer performs all arithmetic functions—without error—to save you a considerable amount of time. Equally important, though, it also gives you the flexibility of evaluating proposed or anticipated changes in income or expenditures. For instance, suppose you have an opportunity to earn an additional $1,000 of income. In an instant you could see how this change might affect certain expense items, such as automobile expenses, assuming your car will be used to produce the extra income, or income taxes. Thus you will be in a better position to evaluate whether or not you wish to pursue the additional earning opportunity. You might also wish to make certain assumptions about expenditures in relation to income and then see what would happen to savings if your income rose or fell.

In addition to budget data, the computer also can be used to store data on your tax records, insurance policies, investments, and many other bits of financial information. It is particularly helpful in updating your investment portfolio and calculating periodic rates of return. It can show you those investments that are performing well and those that are not. Finally, as part of the budget-preparing process the computer can also extend the data and prepare a balance sheet and income statement. Properly programmed, it can do this for historical budget periods that have ended and for those projected in the future. So if you would like to know at the beginning of 1985 what your year-end balance sheet will look like, it is a simple matter to add the 1985 budget to the 31 December 1984 balance sheet and project the 31 December 1985 amounts.

It is expected that throughout the remainder of the 1980s the prices of both hardware (the computer and related equipment) and software (programs that tell the computer what to do) will continue to decline, thereby increasing the availability of personal computers. As this happens, the role of budgeting will take on added importance in personal financial planning.

Summary

Personal financial planning provides a logical framework within which to make financial decisions consistent with your long-run financial goals. A good financial plan should provide funds for the achievement of both long-run and short-run goals. Long-run financial goals should be established for your productive lifetime. While they do not necessarily have to be stated in dollar amounts, they should be specified in general terms. Each year your short-run financial goals should be set in a fashion consistent with the achievement of your long-run goals. These short-run goals are stated in dollar terms so that they can be evaluated in light of your projected income.

After establishing short-run goals, the budget should be prepared in a way that is consistent with as many of these goals as possible. The first step in the budget preparation process is estimating the income to be received during each month of the coming year. Estimating monthly expenditures using past spending data along with the short-run financial goals is the next step. And finalizing the budget by bringing it into balance is the last step. In order to balance the annual budget, you may need to eliminate certain low-priority goals. Furthermore, you may have to use savings, investments, or borrowing; reduce expenditures; or increase income. A budget summary that shows monthly and cumulative surpluses and deficits can simplify the balancing procedure.

When the budget is placed into operation, appropriate records and controls must be used to insure the success of the budgeting process. A record book containing accounts for all items of income and expenditure during each budget period provides the type of information necessary for budget control. At the end of every budget period all accounts in the record book are balanced and any surplus or deficit balances are carried forward to the following month. For budget control purposes, an actual budget summary, which shows actual budget expenditures for each period, is often maintained. This facilitates any adjustments that may be necessary by making it easy to evaluate spending. At the end of each year all budget accounts are balanced and the financial statements—balance sheet and income statement—are prepared and analyzed. The personal computer facilitates the budgeting process considerably by reducing labor time and expanding capabilities. With increased availability and reduced cost, more families will begin using the personal computer to prepare and monitor their personal financial plans and budgets.

Personal Taxes 4

The payment of taxes is an important, necessary, and unpopular expenditure that can significantly affect your personal finances. Taxes are a key consideration in the financial planning and budgeting process discussed in the last three chapters. The average American family pays about a third of its income in taxes. Thus you should try to gain a thorough understanding of personal taxes. Knowledge of tax laws can help you take advantage of opportunities to reduce your taxes and thereby increase the amount of after-tax dollars available for achieving your financial goals.

In order to pay the costs of governments—federal, state, and local—a variety of taxes are levied on both consumers and business. The proceeds received as a result of taxation are used to pay the operating costs of government as well as to provide for our national defense, our highways, parks, and police, and social and educational services that are often taken for granted.

Regardless of our feelings concerning taxes and their use by government, taxes are a very real expenditure that most working people must make. Of the current taxes, the largest and most important one to the consumer is the personal income tax. Although the primary user of income taxation is the federal government, personal income taxes are also levied by state and local governments. Taxpayers are typically divided into two groups: corporations and all others. Corporations have their own tax rates, while individuals and other noncorporate taxpayers are taxed at a different set of rates. This chapter is concerned only with taxes on the individual.

Principles of Federal Income Taxation

The federal income tax law for corporations and all others was systematically outlined in the *Internal Revenue Code* of 1939. In 1954, this code was revised to further clarify and more precisely state the provisions of the 1939 law. Since 1954, a number of amendments have been added to the code that have attempted to simplify it and eliminate infrequently used provisions, as well as to repeal and modify other provisions. The sections of the code and its amendments deal with the tax effects of practically all personal and business transactions. The *Tax Reform Act of 1976* was one of the most extensive tax reform measures ever passed. It was followed by the *Tax Reduction and Simplification Act of 1977* and the *Revenue Act of 1978,* both of which further modified and simplified tax laws and procedures. Other major tax legislation includes the *Economic Recovery Tax Act (ERTA) of 1981*, the *Tax Equity and Fiscal Responsibility Act (TEFRA) of 1982,* and the *Tax Reform Act of 1984.* ERTA was designed to stimulate a sluggish economy by lessening the tax burden on savings and investments. However, prospects of huge fiscal deficits for 1983 and beyond brought forth TEFRA, which was intended to raise over $100 billion primarily by increasing excise taxes and eliminating abuses and unintended benefits (the so-called loopholes) of the existing tax code. The Tax Reform Act of 1984 was passed as part of the Deficit Reduction Act of 1984; the tax act was designed to raise approximately $50 billion in additional revenue by delaying or repealing certain provisions passed in recent years, closing various "loopholes," and enforcing compliance through additional reporting measures.

The enforcement of federal tax laws is placed in the hands of the *Internal Revenue Service (IRS),* which is part of the U.S. Treasury Department. The IRS is responsible for making sure that people pay their taxes as required by the various tax codes. Performance of this function, although greatly simplified as a result of widespread computer usage, requires the work of thousands of IRS employees.

The Economics of Taxation

Income taxes provide the major source of revenue for the federal government. Income taxation is used not only to raise revenue but also to encourage economic activity. This encouragement has been in the form of preferential tax treatment that allows investors the opportunity for tax-free returns and tax-sheltered income. Personal income taxes are scaled on progressive rates. To illustrate how this progressive rate structure works, the following data from 1984 for married taxpayers filing joint returns will be used:

Taxable Income	Tax Rate
$ 0 to $3,400	0%
$3,400 to $5,500	11%
$5,500 to $7,600	12%

Now, consider three possible incomes: (a) $3,100, (b) $4,000, and (c) $7,000. The taxes due on these incomes would be:

(a) $ 0—($3,100 − $0) × .00

(b) $ 66—($4,000 − $3,400) × .11

(c) $411—[($5,500 − $3,400) × .11] + [($7,000 − $5,500) × .12].

Notice that as taxable income goes from a lower to a higher bracket, the higher rate applies only to the additional income in that bracket and *not* to the entire income; for example, you do not pay 11 percent on the entire $4,000 or 12 percent on the entire $7,000.

An important part of the ERTA of 1981 was its attempt to mitigate the impact of inflation on the income taxes we pay—often referred to as *bracket creep.* Even when the rate of increase in your income matches the rate of inflation, you still wind up losing to inflation because your additional income is taxed at higher rates (bracket creep); thus the increase in your after-tax income falls short of the inflation rate. ERTA requires that beginning in 1985, individual tax rates as well as certain tax deductions be indexed to the Consumer Price Index and adjusted in such a way as to eliminate bracket creep.

Your Take-Home Pay

Income taxes are usually collected on a *pay-as-you-go basis:* Your employer withholds (deducts) a portion of your income every pay period and sends it to the Internal Revenue Service. After the close of your taxable year, you calculate the taxes you owe and file your income tax return. At the time of filing, you receive full credit for the amount of taxes withheld from your income over the year. Depending on whether the taxes withheld are greater than or less than the actual taxes you incurred, you will either receive a refund from or owe money to the Internal Revenue Service. Withholdings commonly include the federal withholding tax, the Federal Insurance Contributions Act tax (social security, as it is commonly called), state and local income taxes, and other items. Your *take-home pay*, or *net earnings*, can be determined by subtracting the amount withheld from the amount of your *gross earnings*.

Federal Withholding Taxes The amount of *federal withholding taxes* deducted from your gross earnings each pay period depends on both the level of your earnings and the number of withholding exemptions you have claimed on a form, called a W–4, that you must complete for your employer(s). *Exemptions* are deductions in the amount withheld from your income; they are based on the number of people your income supports. If you believe your actual taxes owed (*tax liability*) will be lower than suggested by the withholding tables, you may under certain conditions claim additional exemptions in order to allow your employer to withhold less. You can also elect to have your employer withhold amounts greater than prescribed by the withholding tables. Federal withholding taxes on earnings are levied only on the incomes of employees.

FICA The combined old age, survivor's, disability, and hospital insurance tax under the *Federal Insurance Contributions Act (FICA)* is levied on both employee and employer. This social security tax applied to the first $37,800 of an employee's wages in 1984. The employer withholds the FICA tax from the employee's gross earnings (up to $37,800) and also contributes approximately the same amount. The total FICA tax, which includes the employee's and the employer's contribution, is submitted to the Internal Revenue Service at specified times by the employer.

Both the employee and the employer thus make social security tax (FICA) contributions on the basis of the employee's wages. The past, present, and future maximum gross earnings , contribution rates, and maximum taxes are given in Table 4.1. In 1984, with a tax rate of 6.70 percent and maximum gross earnings subject to the tax of $37,800, the maximum tax an employee had to pay was $2,532.60 (6.70% × $37,800). Assume that in 1984 you earned $18,000. Your FICA contribution would be $1,206 (6.70% × $18,000). Individuals who work for more than one employer during the year and who thereby pay FICA taxes over the taxable limits can receive credit for the overpayment on their income tax returns.

State and Local Income Taxes State and local income taxes—unlike federal incomes taxes—differ from state to state. These taxes, if levied, are generally tied to the individual's level of earnings. While state and local income taxes that have been withheld (or paid) are deductible on the federal return, federal taxes may or may not be deductible on the state or local return, depending on state and local laws. Especially in large cities, local income taxes can amount to as much as 2 percent of income. And in some states, the state income tax amounts to as much as 15 percent or more of taxable income. Further discussion of state and local taxes is included in the final part of this chapter.

Other Items Employers may withhold money in addition to that already mentioned for their employees. For example, they may withhold voluntary contributions to a retirement fund or payment for life and health insurance coverage in excess of standard benefits. These additional deductions, of course, lower take-home pay.

Determining the Amount of Taxable Income

Although various sections of the Internal Revenue Code define the key components of *taxable income,* the actual amount of taxable income is often difficult to determine. The numerous conditions and exceptions surrounding the tax treatment and/or deductibility of certain items attest to the complexity of our tax system. An individual must ask many questions to determine what his or her taxable income is. Is it income? Whose income is it? Is an expenditure deductible? How much is deductible? Table 4.2 illustrates the procedure for computing taxable income. The items listed in the two right-hand columns are general classifications which are described in detail in the Internal Revenue Code.

Table 4.1 Past, Present, and Future FICA Maximum Gross Earnings, Contribution Rates, and Maximum Taxes

Year	Maximum Gross Earnings Subject to Tax	Contri-bution Rate	Maximum Tax	Year	Maximum Gross Earnings Subject to Tax	Contri-bution Rate	Maximum Tax
1978	$17,700	6.05%	$1070.85	1984	$37,800	6.70%	$2532.60
1979	22,900	6.13	1403.77	1985	*	7.05	*
1980	25,900	6.13	1587.67	1986	*	7.15	*
1981	29,700	6.65	1975.05	1987	*	7.15	*
1982	32,400	6.70	2170.80	1988	*	7.51	*
1983	35,700	6.70	2391.90	1989	*	7.51	*
				1990	*	7.65	*

*Amount uncertain—base scheduled to increase automatically to keep pace with rises in average wage levels.

Gross Income All income (before any deductions) that is subject to federal taxes is considered *gross income*. Certain types of income that are classified as *tax exempt* are excluded from gross income and are not listed on the tax return. A partial list of types of tax exempt income (income not considered income for tax purposes) is included in Table 4.3. In addition to the items included in Table 4.3, which are examples of completely excluded income, some other forms of income, such as dividend income, may be partially excluded. For example, the first $100 of dividend income ($200 on a joint return) received from domestic corporations is excluded from taxable income.

Deductions from Gross Income Table 4.2 shows that most *deductions from gross income* are various types of trade and business-related expenditures. In order for them to be allowable, they must be ordinary and necessary. *Ordinary* means that the item is common and expected in the general industry or type of activity in which the taxpayer is engaged. *Necessary* means that the item is appropriate and helpful in furthering the taxpayer's business or income-producing activity.

The acceptability of certain deductions from gross income depends upon legislative decisions. For example, ERTA in 1981 attempted to remedy the so-called *marriage penalty* that arose in the case of a married couple when each spouse earned income. Two features of the tax law, the zero bracket amount (to be explained shortly) and progressive rates, made it more attractive for two-income couples to file as two unrelated individuals, rather than as a husband and wife. A tax "penalty" arose from being married. Beginning in 1982, ERTA allowed a deduction for a married couple when both work. It is set at 10 percent of the smaller income—husband's or wife's—on the first $30,000 of earned income. It should be pointed out that while the 1981 law soft-

Table 4.2 Computation of Individual Taxable Income

Gross Income	Wages, Salaries Interest Received Dividends Received Gains on Sales or Exchanges Annuities, Pensions Net Business Profits	Farm Income Commissions, Bonuses, Tips Rents and Royalties Prizes Alimony Net Lottery and Gambling Winnings
minus		
Deductions from Gross Income	Trade or Business Expenses Travel Expenses Transportation Costs Outside Salesperson's Expenses Employee's Reimbursed Expenses Depreciation Allowable Losses from Sales or Exchanges Net Operating Loss Deduction Self-Employed Retirement Plan Payments	Individual Retirement Account Payments Moving Expenses Interest Forfeited on Premature Withdrawals from Time Savings Accounts Alimony Paid Long-Term Capital Gain Deduction Expenses Incurred from Producing Rents and Royalties Disability Income Exclusion Deduction for a Married Couple When Both Work
equals		
Adjusted Gross Income		
minus		
Excess Itemized Deductions (Itemized Nonbusiness Expenses minus Zero Bracket Amount)[a]	Charitable Contributions Taxes Paid (Nonbusiness) Interest Paid (Nonbusiness) Nonbusiness Casualty and Theft Losses	Medical and Dental Expenses Certain Investor's Expenses Certain Employee Expenses, such as Union Dues
minus		
Exemptions	Taxpayer Spouse Dependents	Blind Aged (65 or Over)
equals		
Taxable Income		

[a]*Zero bracket amount* is explained later in this chapter.

ened the marriage penalty, it did not eliminate it. When both taxpayers' incomes are about the same, a tax advantage still accrues to those filing as "separated" persons.

Adjusted Gross Income *Adjusted gross income* is gross income less the deductions from gross income. It is an important calculation in

Table 4.3 Partial Listing of Tax-Exempt Income

Accident and health insurance premiums paid by employers
Allowances received by dependents of people in the armed forces
Child support payments
Compromise settlement of will contest
Disability payments (limited in some cases)
Gifts
Inheritances
Interest on certain state and municipal bonds
Loans (principal) repaid (but interest is taxable)
Scholarships and fellowships (limited as to amount and time)
Social security and disability benefits
Veterans' disability pensions

computing an individual's federal income tax since certain itemized deductions are limited by adjusted gross income.

Itemized Nonbusiness Expenses (Deductions from Adjusted Gross Income) Deducting itemized nonbusiness expenses allows taxpayers to reduce their adjusted gross incomes by the amount of their allowable personal expenditures in excess of the zero bracket amount (explained later). The Internal Revenue Code describes the types of *itemized nonbusiness expenses*, including personal, living, and family expenses, that can be deducted from adjusted gross income. Some of the more common itemized nonbusiness expenses are listed in Table 4.2. To encourage *gifts and contributions* to charitable organizations, a deduction is allowed for the amount of such contributions up to a maximum of 50 percent of adjusted gross income. The contribution must be made to qualified recipients as outlined in a list published by the Internal Revenue Service. The Internal Revenue Code also allows the taxpayer to deduct certain taxes from adjusted gross income, including state, local, and foreign income taxes; state, local, and foreign real property taxes; state and local personal property taxes; and state and local general sales taxes (excluding gasoline taxes).

Another deduction is permitted for all interest paid or incurred on borrowing during the taxable year, although the Internal Revenue Service has not established what is a "reasonable" amount of interest. The Tax Reform Act of 1976 requires taxpayers to deduct *prepaid interest* over the period of the loan, if the interest represents the cost of using borrowed funds during each taxable year in the period. Any personal casualty losses, such as theft, are deductible (*see* Chapter 11); they are limited to the amount of each loss above $100 and only the portion in excess of an amount equal to 10 percent of adjusted gross income.

A deduction of the amount by which expenditures exceed 5 percent of adjusted gross income is allowed for medical and dental expenses paid during the taxable year. The expenses allowed are those incurred in the diagnosis, cure, mitigation, and treatment of disease and injury, and in the prevention of disease. Specifically, they include costs related to doctors, hospitals, corrective devices such as eyeglasses, transportation, medicine and drugs, education for the physically or mentally handicapped, and the cost of medical insurance. Of course, you cannot deduct any item for which you are reimbursed by medical insurance.

Zero Bracket Amount Instead of itemizing personal deductions (nonbusiness expenses), a taxpayer can use the *zero bracket amount*, which is a type of blanket deduction. The zero bracket amount is so named because a zero tax rate applies to this amount of the taxpayer's income. The amount varies depending on the filing method used. Table 4.4 summarizes the zero bracket amount for various filing alternatives. For unmarried individuals (including unmarried heads of households) the zero bracket amount is $2,300; for married taxpayers filing a joint return it is $3,400; and for married taxpayers filing a separate return it is $1,700.

Each individual taxpayer "elects" either to itemize deductions or to use the zero bracket amount (which prior to the Tax Reduction and Simplification Act of 1977 was referred to as the "standard deduction"). The decision is not irrevocable, however, and taxpayers who find they have chosen the wrong option and paid too much may recompute their tax using the other method and claim a refund for the difference. For example, suppose you computed and paid your taxes, which amounted to $2,450, using the zero bracket amount. A few months later you find that, had you itemized your deductions, your taxes would have been only $1,950. Using the appropriate forms, you can file an *amended return (Form 1040X)* showing a $500 refund ($2,450 − $1,950). In order to avoid having to file an amended return as a result of using the wrong deduction technique, you should estimate your deductions using both the itemized and zero bracket amounts and then choose the alternative that results in the lower taxes. Amended returns must also be filed in order to correct any error—mathematical or conceptual—in the original tax return, whether the correction results in a tax refund or an additional tax payment.

Exemptions Deductions from adjusted gross income based on the number of persons supported by the taxpayer's income are called *exemptions*. The ordinary exemption allowed a taxpayer, spouse, and any *dependents*—which includes children or other relatives earning less than $1,000 and for whom the taxpayer pays at least 50 percent of support—is $1,000 per person. Children who are younger than 19 or are full-time students can earn more than $1,000 during the year and still be claimed as exemptions by their parents. Students receiving more than half of their support from their parents and earning more than $1,000 (regardless of age) can be claimed as exemptions both by their parents *and* on their own tax returns (by themselves). This

Table 4.4 Zero Bracket Amount for Various Filing Alternatives (1984)

Filing Status	Zero Bracket Amount
Single Persons and Heads of Households	$2,300
Married Persons Filing Joint Returns and Surviving Spouses	3,400
Married Persons Filing Separate Returns	1,700
Dependent Children with Unearned Income[a]	Limited to earned income

[a]Where children are under 19 or full-time students and qualify as income tax dependents of their parents, they must file a return if they have taxable interest, dividends, or other unearned income of $1,000 or more. In addition, their zero bracket amount is determined only on the basis of their earned income.

double exemption is permitted for a married student as long as a joint return is not filed with the spouse. An additional exemption of $1,000 each is allowed for taxpayers and their spouses who are 65 years of age or older or who are blind. For example, a woman (age 43) filing a joint return with her blind spouse (age 45) and having three dependent children would have six exemptions—one for herself, one for her spouse, one for her spouse's blindness, and three for their children. She would therefore receive a $6,000 ($1,000 × 6) deduction in addition to those itemized or zero bracket amount deductions from her adjusted gross income.

Tax Credits Once *taxable income* has been determined, the *tax liability*, or amount of taxes owed, must be calculated. This is done either with the help of a table or by applying certain specified formulas. Because our federal income taxes are *progressive taxes*, the higher our taxable income, the higher is the rate of taxation. Taxpayers are allowed to make certain deductions known as *tax credits* from their tax liability. In reducing the tax liability, these tax credits can result in a refund. One frequently used credit introduced with the Tax Reform Act of 1976 is currently between 20 and 30 percent of child or dependent care expenses (depending on the level of adjusted gross income) paid (up to a maximum expense of $2,400 for one and $4,800 for two or more qualifying individuals) for the purpose of being gainfully employed. The maximum child or dependent care credit is therefore $1,440 (30 percent of $4,800). Another credit allows taxpayers to take one-half of their political contributions not to exceed $50 on single (or separate) returns and $100 on joint returns. Other available credits are given for the purchase of property and equipment used in a trade or business, for the installation of energy-saving components in the homes of individuals, for the federal tax on gasoline purchased for off-highway usage, for old age, and for wage earners with dependent children and little or no tax liability, to mention a few. Note that tax credits, because they are deducted directly from tax liability, directly lower taxes.

Cash Versus Accrual Basis The most common method used by taxpayers to account for income and expenditure items is the *cash basis*. In this system, all items of income and expenditure are recognized for tax purposes in the period in which the actual cash receipt or payment takes place. Under the *accrual basis*, items of income and expenditure are recognized when the obligation to receive or pay them is incurred. For example, suppose that your employer always pays you your wages two weeks after you have completed the work. If you calculate taxable income on the cash basis, the wages you earn in the last two weeks of December cannot be claimed as income for the calendar year since payment will be received during January. But if you make your calculations on an accrual basis, the wages for the last two weeks in December can be claimed as income for the calendar year, even though you do not actually receive these wages in December. The same is true for items of expenditure. The relative ease of maintaining records of cash income and expenditure during the tax year using the cash basis makes it the more popular system.

Capital Gains and Losses

Capital gains and losses are items of income or expenditure that may be eligible for special tax treatment. Because these gains and losses may be taxed differently from ordinary personal income, it is important to understand how they are taxed. Since capital gains and losses receive more favorable tax treatment than items of ordinary income, they are an important consideration in the personal tax planning process. To make the best use of capital gains and losses, it is necessary to understand the difference between capital and noncapital assets and between short-term and long-term gains, as well as how the sale of a home is taxed.

Capital and Noncapital Assets A *capital asset* is property owned and used by the taxpayer for personal purposes, pleasure, or investment—for example, a home, an automobile, household furnishings, and stocks or bonds. Items such as interest in a business and various business inventories, copyrights, and other business assets are considered *noncapital assets* for purposes of determining the taxpayer's personal income taxes. A capital gain or loss therefore can occur when the sale or exchange of a capital asset takes place. A *capital gain* results when a capital asset is sold for more than its original cost. The amount of the capital gain can be found by subtracting the cost from the sale price. If the sale price is less than the cost of the capital asset, a *capital loss* results.

Short- and Long-Term Gains A capital gain or loss can be either short- or long-term, depending on the length of time the capital asset is owned. Ordinarily, a gain from the sale or exchange of property is included in income in its entirety and taxed at ordinary income tax rates. But if the gain on the transaction is a *long-term capital gain*—that is, a gain arising from the sale or exchange of a capital asset which has been held by the taxpayer for longer than the holding period required by IRS standards—it is subject to a lower tax.

The rate at which long-term capital gains are taxed is approximately equal to 40 percent of the ordinary tax rate, since only 40 percent of the gain is shown as taxable income. A *short-term capital gain*—a gain on the sale of a capital asset that is not held for the required holding period—receives no favored income tax treatment. A short-term capital gain is treated as ordinary income and taxed at the ordinary tax rates. The holding period for long-term gains and losses currently is *greater than six months*.

The IRS allows certain capital losses—whether they are long- or short-term—to be deducted from ordinary income. These deductible losses must result from the sale of some *income-producing capital asset*, such as stocks and bonds, at less than their initial cost. A capital loss on the sale of a nonincome-producing asset such as a home or automobile does not provide any tax relief for the taxpayer except in certain situations where offsetting capital gains exist. Due to the rather technical nature of these computations, further detail is not included here.

Selling Your Home If you sell your home and purchase (or begin construction on) a new (new to you, not necessarily newly constructed) home within 24 months, any gain made on the sale of the old home will not be taxable unless the amount paid for the new home is less than that for which the old home was sold. If a new home is not purchased within 24 months of the sale of the old home, taxes must be paid on any gains from that sale. If the purchase occurs within the 24 months and the purchase price of the new home is greater than the sale price of the old home, no taxes will be levied. If the price of the new home is less than the sale price of the old home, the amount by which the price of the old residence exceeds that of the new residence is subject to capital gains tax treatment. For example, assume you sell your first home, which you purchased for $65,000 three years ago for $73,000. In this case, you would have an $8,000 ($73,000 − $65,000) long-term capital gain. Within 24 months of the sale of your old home, you purchase a new home for $70,000. In this case, you have to claim a $3,000 long-term capital gain ($73,000 − $70,000) on which taxes will be due. Had the new home instead cost $80,000, no taxes would be due in the current year since the $80,000 purchase price exceeded the $73,000 for which the old home was sold. If you decide at some point in the future to retire into a rental unit, you will have to pay a capital gain on the amount by which the proceeds on the sale of your house exceed the purchase price of the first home you bought. If you and your spouse are 55 or older when you sell your home and you meet certain other conditions, you may elect to take a one-time exclusion from gross income of up to $125,000 of the gain. Note that a married person filing separately can exclude only $62,500.

Methods of Filing

There are several methods to choose for filing your tax returns. Your choice will depend on your marital status as well as the amount of income you earn. The two basic types of returns are joint returns and individual returns.

Joint Returns A husband and wife may file a *joint return* if they are married as of the last day of the year. In the joint return, both the gross income and the deductions of the husband and wife are totaled. While there are two taxpayers on a joint return, there is only one adjusted gross income amount and only one taxable income. A couple generally benefits by filing a joint return rather than separate returns, but in some instances, separate returns can be more advantageous. For example, if one spouse has substantial medical expenditures and a moderate income while the other has no medical expenses and a low income, filing separately may provide a tax savings.

Individual Returns The taxpayer may also file an *individual return,* either as a single individual or as a head-of-household. When married persons file separately from their spouses, they file as if they are single individuals. Of course, the total exemptions claimed by married individuals filing separately cannot exceed the total exemptions they are eligible for as a married couple. A *head-of-household* is a single individual who maintains a household that is the principal residence of a dependent. One example of a head-of-household would be a single person who pays more than half the cost of keeping up his or her parents' home. Single persons, married persons filing separately, and heads-of-households all have their taxable incomes taxed under *differing tax rates*. These rates are different from the rates levied on joint returns.

Filing Requirements

The IRS filing requirements are based on achievement of specified levels of income. Individuals earning more than the specified minimums must file income tax returns. The income levels at which individuals had to file income tax returns in 1984 are given in Table 4.5 for certain of the more common situations. Persons with no tax liability but for whom income has been withheld must also file income tax returns in order to receive a tax refund of the amount withheld.

Table 4.5 Income Tax Filing Requirements (1984)

Filing Status	Minimum Income
Single Individual	$3,300
Single Individual, 65 or Older	4,300
Married Couple, Joint Return	5,400
Married Couple, Joint Return, One Spouse 65 or Older	6,400
Married Couple, Joint Return, Both 65 or Older	7,400
Surviving Spouse with Dependent Child and Under 65	4,400
Surviving Spouse with Dependent Child and 65 or Older	5,400

Estimated Taxes Because the federal withholding taxes are taken only from income earned on a regular basis and paid in the form of wages, the Internal Revenue Service requires certain people to make *estimated tax payments* on income earned from other sources. This requirement allows the principle of "pay as you go" to be applied not only to wages subject to withholding but also to other sources of income. The payment of estimated taxes is most commonly required of investors, consultants, lawyers, business owners, and various other professionals who are likely to receive income in a form that is not subject to withholding. The IRS requires taxpayers expecting to have $400 or more in 1984, and $500 or more in 1985 and subsequent years, of total estimated taxes to file a declaration of estimated taxes (Form 1040ES) in the following cases:

1. If they can reasonably expect to receive more than $500 of gross income from sources other than wages subject to withholding.
2. If they can reasonably expect that their gross income will exceed:
   (a) $20,000 in the case of a single individual (or a married individual treated as single), a head-of-household, a surviving spouse, or a married individual entitled to file a joint declaration of estimated tax, whose spouse does not receive wages;
   (b) $10,000 in the case of a married individual entitled to file a joint declaration of estimated tax, where both spouses receive wages;
   (c) $5,000 in the case of a married individual not entitled to file a joint declaration of estimated tax with his or her spouse.

The declaration of estimated taxes is normally filed with the tax return. The amount of estimated taxes must be paid in four quarterly installments (15 April, 15 June, and 15 September of the current year and 15 January of the following year). Failure to estimate and pay these taxes can result in a penalty charge levied by the IRS, although no penalties are levied unless the amount paid in is less than 80 percent of the actual tax liability *and* it is less than the preceding year's tax liability.

Year-End Tax Payments At the end of the tax year, those taxpayers required to file must determine the amount of their tax liability—the amount of taxes that they owe as a result of the past year's activities. The tax year covers the period 1 January through 31 December. Taxpayers are asked to file their returns as soon after the end of the tax year as possible. They must file their returns by 15 April of the year immediately following the tax year (or by the first business day after that date if it falls on a weekend or federal holiday). Depending on whether the taxes withheld plus any estimated tax payments are greater than or less than the taxpayer's tax liability, the taxpayer will either receive a refund or will have to pay additional taxes. For example, assume that you had $2,000 withheld and paid estimated taxes of $1,200 during the year. After filling out the appropriate tax forms, your tax liability amounts to $2,800. In this case you have overpaid your taxes by $400 ($2,000 + $1,200 − $2,800) and will therefore receive a $400 refund from the IRS. If, on the other hand, your tax liability had amounted to $4,000, you would have a balance due the IRS of $800 ($4,000 − $2,000 − $1,200).

Filing Extensions It is possible to receive an extension of time for filing your federal tax return. An automatic four-month extension, which makes the due date 15 August, can be applied for simply by submitting the appropriate form (Form 4868). In filing for an extension, however, the taxpayer must estimate the taxes due and remit that amount with the application for extension. Beyond the four-month automatic extension, other extensions can be requested, but they are not automatic; the IRS must be convinced that granting them is justified.

IRS Audits of Returns Since the taxpayers themselves provide the key information and fill out the necessary forms in paying their taxes, the IRS cannot be certain that taxes have been correctly calculated. In order to validate tax returns insofar as possible, the IRS more or less randomly selects some returns for audit. IRS audits attempt to confirm the validity of these returns by carefully analyzing the data reported in them. In the course of an audit, the IRS may deem it necessary to arrange a meeting with the taxpayer being audited. At this meeting, the taxpayer is asked to explain and document certain deductions taken. Even when documentation is provided, the IRS agent can still question the legitimacy of deductions. If the taxpayer and the IRS agent cannot settle the disputed items on an informal basis, certain formal appeal arrangements exist. IRS district personnel then hear the taxpayer's case and make a recommendation. If this recommendation is still not acceptable to the taxpayer, the case can be taken to the Appellate Division of the IRS. Finally, if satisfaction is not obtained from the hearing before the Appellate Division, the case can be brought before the U.S. Tax Court, the U.S. Court of Claims, or a U.S. District Court.

Because some day you might be audited by the IRS, satisfactory tax records should be kept. Although the IRS does not specify any type of record-keeping system, you should keep track of the source or use of all cash receipts and cash payments. Notations with respect to the purpose of expenditures are important, as well as proof that you actually made the expenditures for which you claimed deductions. Typically, audits question both the amounts and the legitimacy of deductions, as well as whether all income received is properly reported. Since the IRS can take as many as three years from the date of your filing to audit your return and, in some cases, an unlimited period of time, records and receipts used in preparing your returns are best kept on hand several years. Severe financial penalties as well as prison sentences can result from violating tax laws. In sum, at the same time, as you take advantage of all legitimate deductions in order to minimize your tax liability, you must be sure, too, that you properly report all items of income and expenditure as required by the Internal Revenue Code.

Tax Preparation Services and Advisors

Many people prepare their own tax returns each year. Typically these "do-it-yourselfers" have fairly simple returns which can be prepared without a great deal of difficulty. Of course, some taxpayers with quite complicated financial circumstances may also invest their time in preparing their own returns. The Tax Reduction and Simplification Act of 1977 was aimed at simplifying the process of filing a tax return. Each year additional simplifications are incorporated into the tax returns. The IRS estimates that 95 percent of all taxpayers can, under the simplified system, prepare their own returns. If so, nearly all taxpayers should be able to file their own returns without expert help. Further, there are numerous IRS informational publications to aid persons who do prepare their own returns. Consult your telephone directory for the IRS office closest to you, or call the IRS's toll-free number to request any form or publication. An excellent and free reference source is IRS Publication 17, *Your Federal Income Tax.*

The IRS The Internal Revenue Service, in addition to issuing various publications for use in preparing tax returns, also provides direct assistance to taxpayers. The IRS will compute taxes for those whose adjusted gross income from wages, salary and tips, interest, dividends, and pensions and annuities is $50,000 or less if they do not itemize deductions. Persons who use this IRS service are required to fill in certain data, sign the return, and send it to the IRS on or before 15 April of the year immediately following the tax year. The IRS figures your tax to "give you the smallest tax." You are then sent a refund, if your withholding exceeds your tax liability, or a bill, if your tax liability is greater than the amount of withholding. If you do not wish or qualify for this total tax preparation service, you can still obtain IRS assistance in preparing your return. The IRS provides a toll-free service through which taxpayers can have questions answered.

Private Tax Preparation Services Many taxpayers prefer to use private *tax preparation services* because (1) they are concerned about accuracy and minimizing their tax liability as much as possible, and (2) they believe the complexity of the tax forms makes preparation too difficult and/or too time consuming. Taxpayers who do not wish to prepare their returns and have relatively common types of income and expenditure might consider using a *national tax service*. Many *local tax preparation services* are also available. Caution is recommended in selecting a tax preparation service, since differing levels of competency exist.

Taxpayers with more complex finances often employ an attorney with tax training or a certified public accountant (CPA). Both types of professionals usually know the various technical points and are able to provide the taxpayer with advice on how to defer income, qualify for deductions, and generally minimize tax liability. Such advice helps the taxpayer understand how to maximize net worth over the long run. Tax attorneys generally devote most of their attention to counseling taxpayers in the area of tax planning, while CPAs tend to be more concerned with the actual preparation of returns. Since the services provided by tax attorneys and CPAs can be expensive, they are usually best used only by those taxpayers whose financial situation is relatively complicated.

When selecting a tax advisor, you should examine credentials as well as fee schedules. Friends and relatives whose financial circumstances are similar to yours may be able to recommend a tax service. The person you choose to prepare your returns typically will provide you with various guidelines and forms to be used in gathering and organizing the information needed for this task. You should follow such guidelines closely and provide all information requested in order to make sure your tax returns are completely and accurately prepared; the accuracy of the tax return can be no better than the accuracy of the information provided. If you have maintained the type of budget records described in Chapter 3, the information required should be readily available.

Before signing the completed return, you should check it closely, since you must accept primary responsibility for its accuracy. Starting in 1977, the IRS began requiring persons who prepare tax returns for pay to sign each return as preparer, enter their social security number and address, and furnish a copy of the return to each taxpayer. This requirement should encourage those who operate tax services to act responsibly in preparing tax returns.

Calculating Taxable Income

Now that we have looked at the general principles of federal income taxation we can begin to examine the key aspects of calculating taxable income: (1) tax rates applicable to the various types of personal income, (2) basic tax forms and schedules, (3) the procedures for determining one's tax liability, and (4) techniques available for reducing tax payments.

Tax Rates

Tax rates levied on personal income vary with amount of taxable income and filing status. Table 4.6 presents a portion of the 1984 Tax Table applicable to persons with a taxable income of $50,000 or less. After calculating their taxable income, taxpayers can use this table to determine their tax liability. For example, a married person filing jointly with a taxable income of $15,490 would have a $1,657 tax liability, as indicated in Table 4.6, for taxable income between $15,450 and $15,500.

Table 4.7 presents the three tax-rate schedules used when taxable income exceeds $50,000. The schedules—X, Y, and Z—are included in this table. The schedules vary according to filing status. For example, married taxpayers filing a joint return use Schedule Y. Take the case of married taxpayers who wish to file a joint return and have $68,000 of taxable income. Their tax liability is calculated from Schedule Y as follows:

$$\begin{aligned} \$15{,}168 + 0.42(\$68{,}000 - \$60{,}000) &= \$15{,}168 + \$3{,}360 \\ &= \$18{,}528 \end{aligned}$$

Note that the maximum tax rate on personal income is 50 percent, which is levied on taxable income above $81,800 for single (or separate) returns and $162,400 on joint returns.

The *average tax rate* is determined by dividing tax liability by taxable income. The married couple who filed jointly with a taxable income of $15,490 had an average tax rate of 10.7 percent ($1,657 ÷ $15,490). For the couple with the taxable income of $68,000, the average tax rate was 30.9 percent ($18,528 ÷ $68,000). A comparison of these average tax rates should further reinforce your understanding of the progressive nature of the federal tax structure: tax schedules are set up in such a way that the more you earn, the larger the percentage you pay to the government in the form of taxes. As indicated earlier, since only 40 percent of long-term capital gains is claimed as income, the tax rate on these gains is equal to only 40 percent of the taxpayer's average tax rate. For this reason, long-term capital gains are an advantageous form of income from the standpoint of taxation.

Table 4.6 Portion of 1984 Tax Table for Individuals with Taxable Incomes Less than $50,000

1984 Tax Table (*Continued*)

If line 37 (taxable income) is—		And you are—				If line 37 (taxable income) is—		And you are—				If line 37 (taxable income) is—		And you are—			
At least	But less than	Single	Married filing jointly *	Married filing separately	Head of a household	At least	But less than	Single	Married filing jointly *	Married filing separately	Head of a household	At least	But less than	Single	Married filing jointly *	Married filing separately	Head of a household
		Your tax is—						Your tax is—						Your tax is—			
5,000						**8,000**						**11,000**					
5,000	5,050	329	179	413	306	8,000	8,050	764	543	875	697	11,000	11,050	1,244	963	1,452	1,186
5,050	5,100	336	184	420	312	8,050	8,100	771	550	884	704	11,050	11,100	1,253	970	1,463	1,195
5,100	5,150	343	190	427	318	8,100	8,150	779	557	893	711	11,100	11,150	1,262	977	1,474	1,203
5,150	5,200	350	195	434	324	8,150	8,200	786	564	902	718	11,150	11,200	1,271	984	1,485	1,212
5,200	5,250	357	201	441	330	8,200	8,250	794	571	911	725	11,200	11,250	1,280	991	1,496	1,220
5,250	5,300	364	206	448	336	8,250	8,300	801	578	920	732	11,250	11,300	1,289	998	1,507	1,229
5,300	5,350	371	212	455	342	8,300	8,350	809	585	929	739	11,300	11,350	1,298	1,005	1,518	1,237
5,350	5,400	378	217	462	348	8,350	8,400	816	592	938	746	11,350	11,400	1,307	1,012	1,529	1,246
5,400	5,450	385	223	469	354	8,400	8,450	824	599	947	753	11,400	11,450	1,316	1,019	1,540	1,254
5,450	5,500	392	228	476	360	8,450	8,500	831	606	956	760	11,450	11,500	1,325	1,026	1,551	1,263
5,500	5,550	399	234	483	366	8,500	8,550	839	613	965	767	11,500	11,550	1,334	1,033	1,562	1,271
5,550	5,600	406	240	490	372	8,550	8,600	847	620	974	774	11,550	11,600	1,343	1,040	1,573	1,280
5,600	5,650	413	246	497	378	8,600	8,650	855	627	983	781	11,600	11,650	1,352	1,047	1,584	1,288
5,650	5,700	420	252	504	384	8,650	8,700	863	634	992	788	11,650	11,700	1,361	1,054	1,595	1,297
5,700	5,750	427	258	511	390	8,700	8,750	871	641	1,001	795	11,700	11,750	1,370	1,061	1,606	1,305
5,750	5,800	434	264	518	396	8,750	8,800	879	648	1,010	804	11,750	11,800	1,379	1,068	1,617	1,314
5,800	5,850	441	270	525	402	8,800	8,850	887	655	1,019	812	11,800	11,850	1,388	1,075	1,628	1,323
5,850	5,900	448	276	532	408	8,850	8,900	895	662	1,028	821	11,850	11,900	1,397	1,082	1,639	1,332
5,900	5,950	455	282	539	414	8,900	8,950	903	669	1,037	829	11,900	11,950	1,406	1,089	1,650	1,341
5,950	6,000	462	288	547	420	8,950	9,000	911	676	1,046	838	11,950	12,000	1,415	1,097	1,661	1,350
6,000						**9,000**						**12,000**					
6,000	6,050	469	294	555	426	9,000	9,050	919	683	1,055	846	12,000	12,050	1,424	1,105	1,672	1,359
6,050	6,100	476	300	563	432	9,050	9,100	927	690	1,064	855	12,050	12,100	1,433	1,113	1,683	1,368
6,100	6,150	483	306	571	438	9,100	9,150	935	697	1,073	863	12,100	12,150	1,442	1,121	1,694	1,377
6,150	6,200	490	312	579	444	9,150	9,200	943	704	1,082	872	12,150	12,200	1,451	1,129	1,705	1,386

1984 Tax Table (*Continued*)

If line 37 (taxable income) is—		And you are—				If line 37 (taxable income) is—		And you are—				If line 37 (taxable income) is—		And you are—			
At least	But less than	Single	Married filing jointly *	Married filing separately	Head of a household	At least	But less than	Single	Married filing jointly *	Married filing separately	Head of a household	At least	But less than	Single	Married filing jointly *	Married filing separately	Head of a household
		Your tax is—						Your tax is—						Your tax is—			
14,000						**17,000**						**20,000**					
14,000	14,050	1,806	1,425	2,164	1,719	17,000	17,050	2,467	1,926	2,976	2,299	20,000	20,050	3,212	2,466	3,937	2,972
14,050	14,100	1,816	1,433	2,176	1,728	17,050	17,100	2,478	1,935	2,990	2,309	20,050	20,100	3,225	2,475	3,954	2,984
14,100	14,150	1,826	1,441	2,189	1,737	17,100	17,150	2,490	1,944	3,004	2,319	20,100	20,150	3,238	2,484	3,970	2,996
14,150	14,200	1,836	1,449	2,201	1,746	17,150	17,200	2,501	1,953	3,018	2,329	20,150	20,200	3,251	2,493	3,987	3,008
14,200	14,250	1,846	1,457	2,214	1,755	17,200	17,250	2,513	1,962	3,032	2,339	20,200	20,250	3,264	2,503	4,003	3,020
14,250	14,300	1,856	1,465	2,226	1,764	17,250	17,300	2,524	1,971	3,046	2,349	20,250	20,300	3,277	2,514	4,020	3,032
14,300	14,350	1,866	1,473	2,239	1,773	17,300	17,350	2,536	1,980	3,060	2,359	20,300	20,350	3,290	2,525	4,036	3,044
14,350	14,400	1,876	1,481	2,251	1,782	17,350	17,400	2,547	1,989	3,074	2,369	20,350	20,400	3,303	2,536	4,053	3,056
14,400	14,450	1,886	1,489	2,264	1,791	17,400	17,450	2,559	1,998	3,088	2,379	20,400	20,450	3,316	2,547	4,069	3,068
14,450	14,500	1,896	1,497	2,276	1,800	17,450	17,500	2,570	2,007	3,102	2,389	20,450	20,500	3,329	2,558	4,086	3,080
14,500	14,550	1,906	1,505	2,289	1,809	17,500	17,550	2,582	2,016	3,116	2,399	20,500	20,550	3,342	2,569	4,102	3,092
14,550	14,600	1,916	1,513	2,301	1,818	17,550	17,600	2,593	2,025	3,130	2,409	20,550	20,600	3,355	2,580	4,119	3,104
14,600	14,650	1,926	1,521	2,314	1,827	17,600	17,650	2,605	2,034	3,145	2,419	20,600	20,650	3,368	2,591	4,135	3,116
14,650	14,700	1,936	1,529	2,326	1,836	17,650	17,700	2,616	2,043	3,162	2,429	20,650	20,700	3,381	2,602	4,152	3,128
14,700	14,750	1,946	1,537	2,339	1,845	17,700	17,750	2,628	2,052	3,178	2,439	20,700	20,750	3,394	2,613	4,168	3,140
14,750	14,800	1,956	1,545	2,351	1,854	17,750	17,800	2,639	2,061	3,195	2,449	20,750	20,800	3,407	2,624	4,185	3,152
14,800	14,850	1,966	1,553	2,364	1,863	17,800	17,850	2,651	2,070	3,211	2,459	20,800	20,850	3,420	2,635	4,201	3,164
14,850	14,900	1,976	1,561	2,376	1,872	17,850	17,900	2,662	2,079	3,228	2,469	20,850	20,900	3,433	2,646	4,218	3,176
14,900	14,950	1,986	1,569	2,389	1,881	17,900	17,950	2,674	2,088	3,244	2,479	20,900	20,950	3,446	2,657	4,234	3,188
14,950	15,000	1,996	1,577	2,402	1,890	17,950	18,000	2,685	2,097	3,261	2,489	20,950	21,000	3,459	2,668	4,251	3,200
15,000						**18,000**						**21,000**					
15,000	15,050	2,007	1,585	2,416	1,899	18,000	18,050	2,697	2,106	3,277	2,499	21,000	21,050	3,472	2,679	4,267	3,212
15,050	15,100	2,018	1,593	2,430	1,909	18,050	18,100	2,708	2,115	3,294	2,509	21,050	21,100	3,485	2,690	4,284	3,224
15,100	15,150	2,030	1,601	2,444	1,919	18,100	18,150	2,720	2,124	3,310	2,519	21,100	21,150	3,498	2,701	4,300	3,236
15,150	15,200	2,041	1,609	2,458	1,929	18,150	18,200	2,731	2,133	3,327	2,529	21,150	21,200	3,511	2,712	4,317	3,248

Source: U.S. Department of Treasury, Internal Revenue Service, *1984 1040 Federal Income tax Forms and Instructions* (Washington, D.C.: U.S. Government Printing Office, 1984), pages 37–38.

Table 4.7 1984 Tax-Rate Schedules for Individuals with Taxable Income Greater than $50,000

1984 Tax Rate Schedules

Your zero bracket amount has been built into these Tax Rate Schedules.

Caution: You must use the Tax Table instead of these Tax Rate Schedules if your taxable income is less than $50,000 unless you use **Schedule G,** Income Averaging, to figure your tax. In that case, even if your taxable income is less than $50,000, use the rate schedules on this page to figure your tax.

Schedule X

Single Taxpayers

Use this Schedule if you checked **Filing Status Box 1** on Form 1040—

If the amount on Form 1040, line 37 is: *Over—*	*But not over—*	Enter on Form 1040, line 38	*of the amount over—*
$0	$2,300	—0—	
2,300	3,400	.......11%	$2,300
3,400	4,400	$121 + 12%	3,400
4,400	6,500	241 + 14%	4,400
6,500	8,500	535 + 15%	6,500
8,500	10,800	835 + 16%	8,500
10,800	12,900	1,203 + 18%	10,800
12,900	15,000	1,581 + 20%	12,900
15,000	18,200	2,001 + 23%	15,000
18,200	23,500	2,737 + 26%	18,200
23,500	28,800	4,115 + 30%	23,500
28,800	34,100	5,705 + 34%	28,800
34,100	41,500	7,507 + 38%	34,100
41,500	55,300	10,319 + 42%	41,500
55,300	81,800	16,115 + 48%	55,300
81,800	....	28,835 + 50%	81,800

Schedule Z

Unmarried Heads of Household

(including certain married persons who live apart—see page 5 of the instructions)

Use this schedule if you checked **Filing Status Box 4** on Form 1040—

If the amount on Form 1040, line 37 is: *Over—*	*But not over—*	Enter on Form 1040, line 38	*of the amount over—*
$0	$2,300	—0—	
2,300	4,400	.......11%	$2,300
4,400	6,500	$231 + 12%	4,400
6,500	8,700	483 + 14%	6,500
8,700	11,800	791 + 17%	8,700
11,800	15,000	1,318 + 18%	11,800
15,000	18,200	1,894 + 20%	15,000
18,200	23,500	2,534 + 24%	18,200
23,500	28,800	3,806 + 28%	23,500
28,800	34,100	5,290 + 32%	28,800
34,100	44,700	6,986 + 35%	34,100
44,700	60,600	10,696 + 42%	44,700
60,600	81,800	17,374 + 45%	60,600
81,800	108,300	26,914 + 48%	81,800
108,300	....	39,634 + 50%	108,300

Schedule Y

Married Taxpayers and Qualifying Widows and Widowers

Married Filing Joint Returns and Qualifying Widows and Widowers

Use this schedule if you checked **Filing Status Box 2 or 5** on Form 1040—

If the amount on Form 1040, line 37 is: *Over—*	*But not over—*	Enter on Form 1040, line 38	*of the amount over—*
$0	$3,400	—0—	
3,400	5,500	.......11%	$3,400
5,500	7,600	$231 + 12%	5,500
7,600	11,900	483 + 14%	7,600
11,900	16,000	1,085 + 16%	11,900
16,000	20,200	1,741 + 18%	16,000
20,200	24,600	2,497 + 22%	20,200
24,600	29,900	3,465 + 25%	24,600
29,900	35,200	4,790 + 28%	29,900
35,200	45,800	6,274 + 33%	35,200
45,800	60,000	9,772 + 38%	45,800
60,000	85,600	15,168 + 42%	60,000
85,600	109,400	25,920 + 45%	85,600
109,400	162,400	36,630 + 49%	109,400
162,400	....	62,600 + 50%	162,400

Married Filing Separate Returns

Use this schedule if you checked **Filing Status Box 3** on Form 1040—

If the amount on Form 1040, line 37 is: *Over—*	*But not over—*	Enter on Form 1040, line 38	*of the amount over—*
$0	$1,700	—0—	
1,700	2,750	.......11%	$1,700
2,750	3,800	$115.50 + 12%	2,750
3,800	5,950	241.50 + 14%	3,800
5,950	8,000	542.50 + 16%	5,950
8,000	10,100	870.50 + 18%	8,000
10,100	12,300	1,248.50 + 22%	10,100
12,300	14,950	1,732.50 + 25%	12,300
14,950	17,600	2,395.00 + 28%	14,950
17,600	22,900	3,137.00 + 33%	17,600
22,900	30,000	4,886.00 + 38%	22,900
30,000	42,800	7,584.00 + 42%	30,000
42,800	54,700	12,960.00 + 45%	42,800
54,700	81,200	18,315.00 + 49%	54,700
81,200	....	31,300.00 + 50%	81,200

Source: U.S. Department of the Treasury, Internal Revenue Service, *1984 1040 Federal Income Tax Forms and Instructions* (Washington, D.C.: U.S. Government Printing Office, 1984), page 42.

Tax Forms and Schedules

The Internal Revenue Service requires taxpayers to file their tax returns using certain specified tax forms. These forms and a variety of instruction booklets on filling them out are made available to taxpayers free of charge. Tax forms can be obtained at the post office, at banks, at a local IRS office, or, as mentioned before, by writing or calling the IRS. All persons who filed tax returns in the previous year are automatically sent a booklet containing tax forms and instructions for preparation of returns for the current year. Inside the booklet is a form that can be used to obtain additional tax forms. Form 1040 is the main form used for filing personal taxes. Numerous others exist for filing various tax-related returns and information.

Form 1040 All individuals use *Form 1040* along with its accompanying schedules for filing their tax returns. If you do not itemize deductions, you will use *Form 1040A.* If you are single and have no dependents, you will use Form *1040EZ.* Schedules which accompany Form 1040 are named and briefly described in Table 4.8. The use of these schedules, which provide detailed guidelines for calculating certain entries on the first two pages of Form 1040, varies among taxpayers, depending on the relevance of these entries to the individual financial situation. Pages 1 and 2 of this form summarize all items of income and deduction and note the taxable income and associated tax.

Other Tax Forms Other tax forms may also be necessary: (1) to provide detailed information needed to report other sources of income, (2) to support certain deductions, and (3) to qualify for certain credits. Reference to certain of these forms can be found in the instructions for preparing Form 1040. One form that most people will at some time have to complete is Form 3903, *Moving Expense Adjustment*. Persons moving to a new residence as a result of employment at a new principal place of work are able to deduct "allowable" moving expenses, which include travel to the new location, moving household goods and personal effects, househunting trips before the actual move, temporary quarters at the new location, and disposing of an old residence and acquiring a new one. Although many other forms exist, space does not permit further description and discussion of them in this chapter.

The Richard and Evelyn Grant Family

Richard and Evelyn Grant are both age 33. They have been married for 11 years and have three children—Tom (age 9), Dick (age 7), and Jane (age 3). Richard is a staff accountant for a major oil company headquartered in the Grants' hometown of Anywhere, Ohio. Evelyn Grant, who has one and a half years of college education, works part-

Table 4.8 Description of Schedules Accompanying Form 1040

Schedule	Description
A	For itemized deductions
B	For gross dividends and interest in excess of $400 each
C	For profit (or loss) from a personally owned business
D	For income (or loss) from the sale or exchange of capital assets
E	For income from rents and royalties, partnerships, estates, trusts, etc.
F	For income from farming
G	For use in income averaging
R & RP	For credit for the elderly
SE	For reporting net earnings from self-employment
W	For a married couple to claim a deduction when both work

time as a salesclerk in a major department store. During 1984, Richard's salary totaled $30,115, while Evelyn earned $4,900. Richard's employer withheld taxes of $3,900, while Evelyn's employer withheld $443 of her income for tax purposes. During the year, the Grants earned $1,700 interest on their joint savings account, received $1,800 in dividends from stock they jointly owned, and realized $800 in capital gains on the sale of securities. Of the $800 in capital gains, $300 were short term and $500 were long term. Richard kept the books for his brother's auto sales business, from which he netted $3,600 during the year. Since no taxes were withheld from this outside income, Richard made estimated tax payments totaling $500 during the year. His detailed records indicate that he and Evelyn had a total of $8,614 of itemized nonbusiness expenses during the year. Richard also incurred $580 of nonreimbursed travel expenses attending certain accounting seminars at the suggestion of his employer. During the year, the Grants had jointly contributed $300 to the campaign fund of a close friend who was running for U.S. Representative.

Determining the Grants' Tax Liability

An examination of the 1984 tax return data for the Grant family elicits the basic calculations required in preparing Form 1040. Although the supporting Schedules A, B, D, and W are not included here, the basic calculations required by them are illustrated. Richard Grant has kept detailed records of his income and expenditures, which he uses not only for tax purposes but also as an important input to his budgeting process. Using this information, Richard hoped to prepare his 1984 tax return in a fashion that would allow him to reduce his tax liability as much as possible. He knew that filing a joint return was best in his particular case. The Grants completed Form 1040 given in Table 4.9, the details of which are described separately in the following sections.

Table 4.9 Tax Computations for the Grant Family

Form **1040** Department of the Treasury—Internal Revenue Service
U.S. Individual Income Tax Return 1984 (0)

For the year January 1-December 31, 1984, or other tax year beginning , 1984, ending , 19 . OMB No. 1545-0074

Use IRS label. Otherwise, please print or type.		
Your first name and initial (if joint return, also give spouse's name and initial) Last name	Richard and Evelyn Grant	Your social security number 000 000 0000
Present home address (Number and street, including apartment number, or rural route)	123 Main Street	Spouse's social security number 000 00 0000
City, town or post office, State, and ZIP code	Anywhere, Ohio 43215	Your occupation Accountant; Spouse's occupation Sales Clerk

Presidential Election Campaign ▶ Do you want $1 to go to this fund? ✓ Yes No
If joint return, does your spouse want $1 to go to this fund? Yes No
Note: Checking "Yes" will not change your tax or reduce your refund.

For Privacy Act and Paperwork Reduction Act Notice, see Instructions.

Filing Status (Check only one box.)

1 ☐ Single
2 ✓ Married filing joint return (even if only one had income)
3 ☐ Married filing separate return. Enter spouse's social security no. above and full name here.
4 ☐ Head of household (with qualifying person). (See page 5 of Instructions.) If the qualifying person is your unmarried child but not your dependent, write child's name here.
5 ☐ Qualifying widow(er) with dependent child (Year spouse died ▶ 19). (See page 6 of Instructions.)

Exemptions (Always check the box labeled Yourself. Check other boxes if they apply.)

6a ✓ Yourself ☐ 65 or over ☐ Blind
b ✓ Spouse ☐ 65 or over ☐ Blind
Enter number of boxes checked on 6a and b ▶ 2
c First names of your dependent children who lived with you Tom, Dick, Jane
Enter number of children listed on 6c ▶ 3

d Other dependents:

(1) Name	(2) Relationship	(3) Number of months lived in your home	(4) Did dependent have income of $1,000 or more?	(5) Did you provide more than one-half of dependent's support?

Enter number of other dependents ▶ —
Add numbers entered in boxes above ▶ 5
e Total number of exemptions claimed (also complete line 36).

Income

Please attach Copy B of your Forms W-2, W-2G, and W-2P here.

If you do not have a W-2, see page 4 of Instructions.

Please attach check or money order here.

7	Wages, salaries, tips, etc.	7	35,015 —
8	Interest income (also attach Schedule B if over $400)	8	1,700 —
9a	Dividends (also attach Schedule B if over $400) 1800 —, 9b Exclusion 200 —		
c	Subtract line 9b from line 9a and enter the result	9c	1,600 —
10	Refunds of State and local income taxes, from the worksheet on page 9 of Instructions (do not enter an amount unless you itemized deductions for those taxes in an earlier year—see page 9)	10	—
11	Alimony received	11	—
12	Business income or (loss) (attach Schedule C)	12	—
13	Capital gain or (loss) (attach Schedule D)	13	500 —
14	40% of capital gain distributions not reported on line 13 (see page 9 of Instructions)	14	—
15	Supplemental gains or (losses) (attach Form 4797)	15	—
16	Fully taxable pensions, IRA distributions, and annuities not reported on line 17	16	—
17a	Other pensions and annuities, including rollovers. Total received 17a		
b	Taxable amount, if any, from the worksheet on page 10 of Instructions	17b	—
18	Rents, royalties, partnerships, estates, trusts, etc. (attach Schedule E)	18	—
19	Farm income or (loss) (attach Schedule F)	19	—
20a	Unemployment compensation (insurance). Total received 20a		
b	Taxable amount, if any, from the worksheet on page 10 of Instructions	20b	—
21a	Social security benefits. (see page 10 of Instructions) 21a		
b	Taxable amount, if any, from the worksheet on page 11 of Instructions	21b	—
22	Other income (state nature and source—see page 11 of Instructions) Bookkeeping Services	22	3,600 —
23	Add lines 7 through 22. This is your **total income** ▶	23	42,415 —

Adjustments to Income (See Instructions on page 11.)

24	Moving expense (attach Form 3903 or 3903F)	24	—		
25	Employee business expenses (attach Form 2106)	25	580 —		
26a	IRA deduction, from the worksheet on page 12	26a	—		
b	Enter here IRA payments you made in 1985 that are included in line 26a above ▶				
27	Payments to a Keogh (H.R. 10) retirement plan	27	—		
28	Penalty on early withdrawal of savings	28	—		
29	Alimony paid	29	—		
30	Deduction for a married couple when both work (attach Schedule W)	30	490 —		
31	Add lines 24 through 30. These are your **total adjustments** ▶			31	1,070 —

Adjusted Gross Income

32	Subtract line 31 from line 23. This is your **adjusted gross income**. If this line is less than $10,000, see "Earned Income Credit" (line 59) on page 16 of Instructions. If you want IRS to figure your tax, see page 12 of Instructions. ▶	32	41,345 —

Table 4.9 (continued)

Form 1040 (1984) Page 2

Tax Computation (See Instructions on page 13.)	33	Amount from line 32 (adjusted gross income)			33	41,345 —
	34a	If you itemize, attach Schedule A (Form 1040) and enter the amount from Schedule A, line 26. **Caution:** If you have unearned income and can be claimed as a dependent on your parent's return, check here ▶ ☐ and see page 13 of the Instructions. Also see page 13 if: • You are married filing a separate return and your spouse itemizes deductions, OR • You file Form 4563, OR • You are a dual-status alien.			34a	5,214 —
	34b	If you do not itemize deductions, and you have charitable contributions, complete the worksheet on page 14. Then enter the allowable part of your contributions here			34b	—
	35	Subtract line 34a or 34b, whichever applies, from line 33			35	36,131 —
	36	Multiply $1,000 by the total number of exemptions claimed on Form 1040, line 6e			36	5,800 —
	37	Taxable Income. Subtract line 36 from line 35.			37	31,131 —
	38	Tax. Enter tax here and check if from ☑ Tax Table, ☐ Tax Rate Schedule X, Y, or Z, or ☐ Schedule G			38	5,133 —
	39	Additional Taxes. (See page 14 of Instructions.) Enter here and check if from ☐ Form 4970, ☐ Form 4972, or ☐ Form 5544			39	—
	40	Add lines 38 and 39. Enter the total ▶			40	5,133 —
Credits (See Instructions on page 14.)	41	Credit for child and dependent care expenses *(attach Form 2441)*	41	—		
	42	Credit for the elderly and the permanently and totally disabled *(attach Schedule R)*	42	—		
	43	Residential energy credit *(attach Form 5695)*	43	—		
	44	Partial credit for political contributions for which you have receipts	44	100 —		
	45	Add lines 41 through 44. These are your total personal credits			45	100 —
	46	Subtract line 45 from 40. Enter the result (but not less than zero)			46	5,033 —
	47	Foreign tax credit *(attach Form 1116)*	47	—		
	48	General business credit. Check if from ☐ Form 3800, ☐ Form 3468, ☐ Form 5884, ☐ Form 6478	48	—		
	49	Add lines 47 and 48. These are your total business and other credits			49	—
	50	Subtract line 49 from 46. Enter the result (but not less than zero). ▶			50	5,033 —
Other Taxes (Including Advance EIC Payments)	51	Self-employment tax *(attach Schedule SE)*			51	—
	52	Alternative minimum tax *(attach Form 6251)*			52	—
	53	Tax from recapture of investment credit *(attach Form 4255)*			53	—
	54	Social security tax on tip income not reported to employer *(attach Form 4137)*			54	—
	55	Tax on an IRA *(attach Form 5329)*			55	—
	56	Add lines 50 through 55. This is your **total tax** ▶			56	5,033 —
Payments Attach Forms W-2, W-2G, and W-2P to front.	57	Federal income tax withheld	57	4,343 —		
	58	1984 estimated tax payments and amount applied from 1983 return	58	500 —		
	59	Earned income credit. If line 33 is under $10,000, see page 16	59	—		
	60	Amount paid with Form 4868	60	—		
	61	Excess social security tax and RRTA tax withheld (two or more employers)	61	—		
	62	Credit for Federal tax on gasoline and special fuels *(attach Form 4136)*	62	—		
	63	Regulated Investment Company credit *(attach Form 2439)*	63	—		
	64	Add lines 57 through 63. These are your **total payments** ▶			64	4,843 —
Refund or Amount You Owe	65	If line 64 is larger than line 56, enter amount **OVERPAID** ▶			65	
	66	Amount of line 65 to be **REFUNDED TO YOU** ▶			66	
	67	Amount of line 65 to be applied to your 1985 estimated tax ▶	67			
	68	If line 56 is larger than line 64, enter **AMOUNT YOU OWE**. Attach check or money order for full amount payable to "Internal Revenue Service." Write your social security number and "1984 Form 1040" on it ▶ (Check ▶ ☐ if Form 2210 (2210F) is attached. See page 17 of Instructions.) $			68	190 —

Please Sign Here

Under penalties of perjury, I declare that I have examined this return and accompanying schedules and statements, and to the best of my knowledge and belief, they are true, correct, and complete. Declaration of preparer (other than taxpayer) is based on all information of which preparer has any knowledge.

Your signature: Richard Grant — Date: 2/18/85 — Spouse's signature (if filing jointly, BOTH must sign): Evelyn Grant

Paid Preparer's Use Only

Preparer's signature ▶	Date	Check if self-employed ☐	Preparer's social security no.
Firm's name (or yours, if self-employed) and address ▶		E.I. No.	
		ZIP code	

☆U.S.GPO:1984-0-423-073 ☆E.I.#430814328

Source: U.S. Department of the Treasury, Internal Revenue Service, *1984 1040 Federal Income Tax Forms and Instructions* (Washington, D.C.: U.S. Government Printing Office, 1984).

Gross Income The Grants' gross income during 1984 totaled $42,415. In addition to their salaries and Richard's bookkeeping income, they had income from interest, dividends, and capital gains. (Note that the dividend exclusion is $200 and that only 40 percent of the long-term capital gain is included in the $500 reported on line 13.)

Deductions from Gross Income The Grants have two deductions from gross income. The first is the $580 of expenses Richard incurred while attending accounting seminars. The deduction is taken on line 25 and, as you see, Form 2106 should also be filed. The second deduction is that allowed a married couple when both work. As mentioned earlier, this is a flat 10 percent of the smaller income of one of the two spouses. For the Grants, this is Evelyn's salary of $4,900, and 10 percent of this amount is $490. Adding this to the $580 gives the Grants a total adjustment to gross income of $1,070.

Adjusted Gross Income After subtracting the $1,070 deduction from the gross income, the Grants' adjusted gross income of $41,345 results.

Itemized or Zero Bracket Amount In order to determine whether to take the itemized or zero bracket amount, the Grants had to compare the total itemized nonbusiness expenditures of $8,614 to the zero bracket amount of $3,400. Since the itemized deductions exceeded the zero bracket amount by $5,214, this amount is then subtracted from adjusted gross income.

Exemptions For each exemption claimed, the Grants received an exemption of $1,000. Since the Grants claimed five exemptions, they received a total exemption of $5,000 (5 × $1,000). The exemption deduction is shown on line 36.

Taxes The amount of taxes owed by the Grants was calculated using their taxable income ($31,131). Since this amount was less than $50,000, they used the tax tables, a portion of which is shown in Table 4.6. The resulting tax was $5,133.

Tax Credit As a result of their $300 in political contributions, the Grants were eligible for the maximum credit of $100. After subtracting the credit on line 45, their total tax liability was $5,033. Since no other credits were earned, this value again appears on line 50.

Tax Payment or Refund Because the total amount of withheld taxes of $4,343—$3,900 from Richard's salary and $443 from Evelyn's wages—plus the total estimated tax payments of $500 amounted to only $4,843, the Grants will have a tax balance due the IRS. By subtracting the total taxes withheld from the total tax liability, the amount due the IRS is found to be $190, which is shown on line 68. Therefore, the Grants had to remit $190 along with the signed Form 1040 and supporting forms and schedules to the nearest IRS District Office by 15 April 1985. Had the total of taxes withheld and estimated tax payments exceeded the Grants' total tax liability, they would have received a refund for the difference from the IRS. Refund checks are typically received one to two months after the tax return is filed.

Reducing Tax Payments

Many taxpayers—especially those with moderate to high incomes—use various techniques to minimize their tax liability. *Tax avoidance*, or minimizing tax payments, should not be confused with tax evasion. In avoiding taxes, the taxpayer accurately reports all items of income and expenditure but attempts to use legitimate deductions and computational procedures to minimize the taxes. *Tax evasion*, which is against the law, involves a failure to report accurately income, expenditure, and tax liabilities as well as failure to pay taxes. Persons found guilty of tax evasion are subject to severe financial penalties and prison terms. A few of the more common, legitimate methods of tax reduction are described briefly in the following sections.

Income Averaging Persons whose income shows extreme fluctuations can reduce their tax liability in peak income years by *income averaging*—spreading their income evenly over a period of four years (the current year plus the three immediately preceding years). Schedule G (Form 1040) provides a step-by-step method for determining whether income should be averaged. Generally speaking, income averaging is advantageous if the balance after subtracting $3,000 from the current year's taxable income is greater than 46⅔ percent of the total taxable income for the immediately preceding three years. For example, assume your current year's taxable income is $18,000 and your taxable income in the preceding three years was $7,000, $9,000, and $14,000 (total $30,000). Subtracting $3,000 from current taxable income leaves $15,000. Since $15,000 is more than 46⅔ percent of the $30,000 of total taxable income from the preceding three years, income averaging should be considered. Because of the progressive nature of our tax structure, the averaging of increasing streams of taxable income allows the taxpayer to reduce the average tax rate applied. Taxpayers are free to average income in any year they find such action will reduce their taxes.

Income Splitting Another method of reducing income tax liability is a technique known as *income splitting*, whereby the taxpayer shifts a portion of his or her income to related individuals in lower tax brackets.

This can be done by creating a trust or custodial account or by making outright gifts of income-producing property to family members. For example, parents with $25,000 of taxable income and $18,000 of corporate bonds that pay $2,000 in annual interest might give the bonds to their two-year-old child. The $2,000 annual interest would then belong to the child, who would probably have to pay little or no tax on this income. Thus the parents' taxable income would be reduced by $2,000. Income splitting is often done in order to reduce taxes while at the same time building savings for covering future outlays such as paying for a child's college education. According to what is known as the "fruit-of-the-tree" doctrine, individuals cannot give away income (fruit) alone; they must give away or place in trust the income-producing property (fruit-bearing tree) as well. Further tax implications of gifts to dependents are discussed in Chapter 16.

Bunching Deductions Sometimes taxes can be reduced by *bunching deductions*, a technique which can be used effectively by persons with middle incomes (approximately $15,000 to $25,000 of taxable income). This involves planning to make few tax-deductible expenditures in one year and many in the following year. The zero bracket (or standard) deduction can then be used in the low-expenditure year, while deductions can be itemized in the high-expenditure year. In the low-expenditure year, the zero bracket amount will be greater than the actual expenditures made; in the high-expenditure year, the actual expenditures, which are itemized, will be considerably greater than the zero bracket amount. Taxpayers wishing to bunch deductions must, of course, take into account the fact that taxable income is computed on a cash basis. The net effect of bunching deductions is to reduce taxes by maximizing total deductions over a period of years.

Tax Shelters *Tax shelters* are forms of investment that take advantage of certain *tax write-offs*. Some forms of real estate and natural resource investments provide these desirable deductions. The favorable write-offs come from deductions from gross income that are permitted by the IRS, but do not actually involve an outlay of cash by the investor. In accounting terminology, these write-offs are called *depreciation, amortization,* or *depletion*. The presence of these noncash expenditures provides for the lowering of your tax liability. For example, an individual could invest in an apartment project that in addition to providing actual cash returns of say $5,000 also provides a depreciation deduction (from gross income) of $9,000. The net result of this investment would mean that the $5,000 of taxable income would be completely sheltered and an additional $4,000 ($9,000 − $5,000) can be deducted from other sources of gross income, such as wages, salaries, interest, dividends, capital gains, and so on. Because it ordinarily takes a sizable sum of money (that is, $10,000 or more) to acquire a tax shelter, and tax-sheltered investments often are risky, they tend to be of greatest interest to those in higher tax brackets.

Individual Retirement Accounts (IRAs) An IRA (see Chapter 15 for a detailed discussion of IRAs) can be an investment in practically anything, although the most popular investments are stocks, bonds, mutual funds, and many different types of deposits and certificates offered by financial institutions. The tax law allows you to deduct up to $2,000 of such investments each year from your taxable income. If your spouse also works, you can take another deduction up to the extent of his or her earned income, or $2,000, whichever is less; that is, your maximum total deduction can be $4,000. If your spouse does not have earned income, your deduction can be $2,250. While you are allowed the deduction in the year you make the investment, you must report as income any money taken from your IRA investment. So the tax advantage comes in the form of being allowed the deduction in years when you are probably in higher tax brackets than you will be when you withdraw from the IRA at retirement. Moreover, any distributions you take before age 59 and a half will be subject to a penalty; thus, you must be careful not to establish an IRA if there is a chance the funds will be needed before then. Finally, IRA deductions can be taken regardless of whether or not you itemize deductions.

Other Techniques Planning for capital gains instead of ordinary income, buying tax-exempt securities, and claiming business expenses are other techniques used to reduce taxes. Wealthy individuals may have an opportunity to receive future capital gains income instead of ordinary income. By receiving long-term capital gains, they can lower the taxes they must pay, since only 40 percent of these gains must be claimed for tax purposes. They therefore are effectively taxed at only 40 percent of the ordinary tax rate.

Investment in *tax-exempt securities*, which are bonds that pay interest that is not taxed as income, also provides an opportunity for reducing taxable income. Further discussion of tax-exempt securities, which are issued by state and local governments, is presented as part of the discussion of bonds in Chapter 12. Some people reduce taxes by claiming certain types of travel, meals, and entertainment as a business—rather than personal—expense. These otherwise nondeductible expenditures may be deducted from taxable income. Although the IRS takes a close look at such deductions, persons in higher tax brackets are often able to reduce their taxes with them. Still other methods of tax reduction that take advantage of certain loopholes in the tax laws do exist but will not be discussed here. Most important, however, is that before attempting to take advantage of these opportunities for tax reduction, you make certain you are operating within the law. Penalties for tax evasion can be quite severe.

Other Sources of Personal Taxation

Although federal income taxes are typically the largest taxes a person pays, there are other types of personal taxes. Additional federal taxes may be levied on income as well as on specific types of transactions. At the state and local level, sales transactions, income, property ownership, and licenses may be taxed. Because most individuals making purchase transactions, earning income, or owning property have to pay many of these other types of taxes, their implications for the individual's financial condition must be understood. For example, a person saving to purchase a new automobile costing $10,000 should realize that the state and local sales taxes as well as the cost of license plates and registration may add $800 to the total cost.

Additional Types of Federal Taxation

Social security taxes, excise taxes, and gift and estate taxes are some of the federal taxes not based solely on income. Probably the most pronounced of these are the social security taxes, which are paid by most individuals and their employers.

Social Security Taxes Most common of the social security taxes is *FICA* (Federal Insurance Contributions Act), described at the beginning of this chapter. Another social security tax is the *federal unemployment tax*, which must be paid by an employer on the basis of each employee's income. Although only employers have to pay this tax, you may benefit from it in the form of unemployment compensation should you lose your job. Unemployment benefits, although largely funded through this tax, are typically administered by state governments. Self-employed individuals must pay a *self-employment tax*, which is calculated on their income above $400. The tax is intended to pay for the same benefits that are provided to employed persons through the FICA tax.

Excise Taxes Taxes levied by the federal government on the purchase of certain luxury items and services, such as jewelry, automobiles, gasoline, telephone service, tobacco products, and liquor, are called *excise taxes*. These taxes are added on to the purchase price of these products and services. The Tax Equity and Fiscal Responsibility Act (TEFRA) of 1982, mentioned earlier, substantially increased some of these taxes.

Gift and Estate Taxes The federal government and state governments both tax gifts and estates. *Gift taxes* are levied on a gift; they must be paid by the giver and are based on the value of the gift given.

Estate taxes are levied on the value of the estate left at the death of its owners. Therefore, these taxes reduce the amount of the inheritance passed on to the heirs. A detailed discussion of these federal taxes is included in the final part of Chapter 16, which is concerned with estate planning.

Other Federal Taxes Duties on imports, entrance fees to federal facilities such as parks and museums, and taxes on special types of transactions are still other types of federal taxation. None of the federal taxes described in the preceding sections can be claimed as deductions for federal income tax purposes.

State Taxes

In order to finance their operating costs, state governments levy a variety of taxes. Probably the largest source of state revenue is taxes levied on sales transactions. Other sources are income taxes, property taxes, and licensing fees.

State Sales Tax Most consumer purchases are taxed. Although these sales taxes vary from state to state, they typically range from 3 to 6 percent. Most states exempt certain items that are viewed as necessities of life from this tax—for example, groceries, medical services, and rent. Sales taxes are levied by the merchant at the point of sale. The merchant is then responsible for remitting the taxes to the appropriate state authorities. Most states allow the merchant to retain a small portion of the taxes as payment for performing the collection function.

Taxpayers who itemize their nonbusiness expenses can deduct sales taxes from their income. The IRS provides tables for computing this deduction. Because sales taxes are tied to purchases, there is really no practical way to avoid them. When making or budgeting for large purchases, you should recognize that sales taxes will add to the cost.

State Income Taxes Most states currently have income taxes, which range as high as 15 percent or more of taxable income. Although numerous states have graduated tax rates which increase with income, some have fixed rates which apply to all levels of taxable income. Calculation of these taxes is generally similar to that for the federal income tax, which makes it relatively easy for the taxpayer to file the state tax return. Like the federal government, most states operate on a "pay-as-you-go" basis by withholding a portion of income from each paycheck. Many allow the taxpayer to deduct federal taxes from taxable income prior to calculating their state tax liability. For federal tax purposes, persons who itemize their nonbusiness expenses can deduct all state income taxes paid.

State Property Taxes, Licensing Fees, and Other Taxes Although most states obtain their revenues from sales and income taxes, some states also tax various items of property. Since *property taxes* are levied primarily by local governments, a discussion of them is included in the next section of the chapter. State governments also obtain revenue from the sale of automobile licenses and by licensing certain professions. In addition, many states have excise taxes on gasoline, tobacco, liquor, and other luxuries. Most also have gift and estate taxes similar to those levied by the federal government (see Chapter 16). Although many of the state taxes are deductible and so aid taxpayers in lowering their federal taxes, they nonetheless constitute an expenditure to be reckoned with in the financial planning process.

Local Taxes

Local governments, which include cities and counties, levy taxes in order to obtain the revenue needed to provide a variety of public services. Although the majority of local revenues come from property taxes, local governments often use income taxes, sales taxes, and licensing fees to add to their funds.

Local Property Taxes The primary source of local revenues is the taxation of real estate and other personal property, such as automobiles and boats. Since the largest source of property ownership for most people is their home, the dominant form of property taxes is the *real estate tax*. Property taxes are typically collected by the county and then distributed among other governmental units—the city and the school system, for example. The rate of taxation differs from community to community. The value of the property on which taxes are levied is determined by the governmental unit to which the tax is paid. In general, the more expensive the home, the higher the real estate taxes, and vice versa. If deductions are itemized, these taxes can be deducted in calculating federal income taxes. Further discussion of these taxes is included in Chapter 6, which is primarily concerned with housing.

Local Income Taxes Local governments—typically larger cities—sometimes levy taxes on the incomes of all those employed within their bounds. These taxes are similar to federal and state income taxes, but the rates are lower—usually about 1 percent. Most city income taxes are withheld and therefore charged on a pay-as-you-go basis with final settlement made at the end of the year. These taxes are a deductible expenditure for federal income tax purposes.

Local Sales Taxes and Licensing Fees Some cities have sales taxes, which are collected by merchants and remitted to the state government as part of the total sales tax on certain items. The state government, whose levy makes up the major portion of the tax, then returns to the cities their portion of the collections. *Licensing fees,* such as building permits, also provide local governments with added revenue. In some states, a portion of the fees collected for automobile and other licenses represents a local licensing fee or property tax.

Summary

Because taxes somehow affect all individuals, an understanding of them is essential to the intelligent management of personal finances. The dominant tax in our economy today is the federal income tax. Federal income taxes provide the federal government with money required to cover its operating costs. The Internal Revenue Service (IRS), which is a branch of the U.S. Treasury Department, is responsible for the enforcement of our federal tax laws. Because the federal government—as well as certain state and local governments—operates on a pay-as-you-go basis, employers are required to withhold a portion of their employees' taxes from each period's pay. Also withheld are FICA taxes, which are used by the federal government to pay social security benefits; state and local income taxes; and certain voluntary contributions to pension or retirement funds or for life and health insurance coverage in excess of standard benefits.

To determine your taxable income, first total your eligible income and then subtract certain deductions and exemptions from it. The IRS provides specific guidelines and tests that can be applied to determine what items can be deducted from income. Most taxpayers, when determining their tax liability, measure income and expenditures by the amount of cash received and the amount paid out, respectively, during the tax year (1 January through 31 December). When taxpayers sell personal property that has been in their possession for more than six months at a gain or loss, they can take advantage of the favorable long-term capital gains tax. The capital gains tax applies to the sale of a home, but only under certain conditions. As long as a home sold is replaced no longer than 24 months after its sale with a home of equal or greater value, this tax is not due. Taxpayers over age 55 who meet certain other conditions can receive a one-time $125,000 exclusion from the capital gains tax on the sale of a home.

Tax returns must be filed by 15 April of the year following the tax year. The IRS checks the accuracy of tax returns and levies severe penalties on taxpayers who attempt to avoid taxes by failing to report accurately income, expenditures, and tax liabilities as well as by failing to pay taxes altogether. The IRS, as well as certain private tax preparation services, provides assistance in the preparation of tax returns.

Federal tax rates on personal income vary with the manner in which the taxpayer files, the number of exemptions claimed, and, most important, the level of income. The IRS supplies taxpayers with forms and schedules for use in filing returns. Taxes are calculated using the IRS's tax tables, and if they exceed the amount withheld, plus any estimated tax payments, a check for the amount owed must be included with the return. If the amount withheld plus any estimated payments exceeds the tax liability, the taxpayer will receive a refund from the IRS. Taxpayers should attempt to minimize their taxes while fulfilling all of the legal requirements set out by the IRS. Although a number of tax-minimizing techniques are available, they are most often utilized by persons in high income brackets. Other types of personal taxes—on income, sales, and property—are levied by the federal government, state governments, and local governments.

Cash and Savings Instruments 5

Chapters 2 and 3 discussed the importance of planning for cash and savings when constructing your annual budget. Once this chore is completed, the next question will be, "In what form should these cash and savings be held?" Cash and savings balances are two of the most important fundamental assets you have. They are the primary resources available to you for meeting both planned and unexpected expenditures. The effective management and control of cash and savings will make it easier for you to attain your financial goals.

In recent years *cash management*—the management of one's liquid cash and savings resources—has taken on greater importance, and for several reasons. First, the rates of interest paid on short-term, very liquid investments have been higher than at any other time in U.S. history. Since these vehicles are capable of satisfying cash needs, investors have preferred holding a large part of their total cash reserves in them rather than in accounts that pay little, or no, interest; in other words, the opportunity cost (what you give up) of holding non-earning cash assets has been very high. Second, the Depository Institutions Deregulation and Monetary Control Act of 1980 initiated many far-reaching changes in the financial institutions industry. Prior to that act, distinctions were clear among various kinds of financial institutions. Banks, for example, were the sole issuers of checking accounts and most of their loans were to businesses. Savings and loan institutions, on the other hand, attracted the bulk of their deposits through savings accounts and limited most of their lending activity to real estate loans. All that has changed. Many savings and loans now offer checking accounts, and banks will make any type of consumer loan they deem profitable. Moreover, both offer stock brokerage services while stockbrokers, such as Merrill Lynch and E.F. Hutton, provide banking services. The trend today is toward the giant financial supermarket that provides one-stop shopping for all your financial needs.

These changes are important since you now have the opportunity to use a wide variety of checking-savings accounts and design a cash management plan that best serves your needs. This chapter discusses many of these accounts and it also describes the key kinds of financial institutions.

Cash Balances

Any form of funds that already is or can readily be converted into cash with a minimum of expense and administrative effort is a cash balance. As such, a cash balance is a *liquid balance.* There are three basic reasons why people maintain cash balances. The most common forms in which to hold them are pocket money, demand deposits, savings deposits, and combination demand-savings deposits.

Why Maintain Cash Balances?

The individual reasons for holding cash balances largely affect the form in which they are maintained. The three basic motives are (1) convenience, (2) planned expenditures, and (3) unexpected expenditures.

Convenience Cash is a readily acceptable form of payment in our country; its availability makes the purchase-sale transaction quite simple. For this reason, most people maintain some type of cash balance. In fact, since all people must make economic transactions in order to survive, convenience is probably the primary motive for maintaining some form of cash balance.

Planned Expenditures Every consumer must make certain planned expenditures. These may be large or small and may or may not be covered by 100 percent cash. Especially in the case of more expensive items, a portion of the purchase price is usually paid for with borrowed funds—a topic discussed at greater length in Part 3. Cash needed for current expenditures, for example, food and clothing, may be drawn from current income, while cash for major purchases of such items as appliances may be obtained from savings. Planning the availability of cash goes hand in hand with planning the expenditure of cash. The financial planning and budgeting process discussed in Chapter 3 presented procedures that can be used to provide the cash needed to make planned expenditures.

Unexpected Expenditures The third basic motive for maintaining cash balances is a precautionary one. Many people set aside cash in order to provide a cushion for meeting unexpected expenditures, such as automobile repairs, medical bills, and household repairs, or for taking advantage of unexpected opportunities, such as a sale or bargain price on a planned purchase. The presence of excess balances allows people to make these unexpected expenditures without lowering their standard of living. Maintenance of cash balances for this purpose thus allows individuals to achieve their financial goals without risking damaging financial setbacks.

Pocket Money

The term *pocket money* is used to refer to all currency and coin physically under the control of an individual or family. This includes cash on the person or in the home and excludes cash held by a second party (such as a commercial bank or savings and loan) on behalf of the individual or family. Although people have been known to hoard cash due to their lack of confidence in financial institutions, the only valid justification for maintaining a cash balance in the form of pocket money is its convenience in making small planned and/or unexpected expenditures. Pocket money should be kept to a minimum, since the risk of its loss, theft, or destruction always exists.

Demand Deposits

Checking accounts held at a variety of financial institutions are demand deposits. The term *demand deposit* indicates that the withdrawal of these funds must be permitted whenever demanded by the accountholder—the bank (formerly, only commercial banks provided checking accounts but that is no longer true; "bank" is now used generically and may refer to any financial institution that accepts deposits and permits issuance of checks against them), when presented with a valid check, must immediately pay the amount indicated. Money held in checking accounts is, therefore, liquid and can easily be used to pay bills and make purchases. Checking accounts are important in our economy; statistics of the *Federal Reserve System,* which is the official organization governing our nation's banking system, indicate that over 35 billion checks are written each year and that demand deposits are the largest component of the money supply.

Because checks are generally accepted in payment of bills and taxes and in the purchase of goods and services, demand deposit balances are a common and important type of cash balance. One of the primary advantages of demand deposits is that in almost all commercial banks they (and any other deposit accounts in the bank) are insured for up to a total of $100,000 per accountholder by the *Federal Deposit Insurance Corporation (FDIC)* or the *Federal Savings and Loan Insurance Corporation (FSLIC),* which insure deposits in savings and loans and similar institutions, or the *National Credit Union Administration (NCUA),* which insures deposits in credit unions. Another advantage is that the use of checks to pay bills provides a convenient type of recordkeeping system for use as proof of payment and in calculating income taxes at the end of the year. In short, the widespread use of demand deposits can be attributed to the safety and relative convenience of checks in paying bills and other obligations.

Savings Deposits

The third type of cash balance, *savings deposits,* may be kept in commercial banks, savings and loan associations, credit unions, and other institutions. Since a passbook is sometimes used to record transactions in these accounts, they are called *passbook accounts,* and the rate of interest at which they earn is referred to as the passbook rate. Savings deposits are referred to as *time deposits* since they are expected to remain untapped for a longer period of time than are demand deposits. Because interest income is received on savings deposits but not on demand deposits, savings accounts are preferable to demand deposits when the depositor's purpose is to accumulate money for a future expenditure or to hold money to cover unexpected expenditures.

While financial institutions generally retain the right to require a savings accountholder to wait a certain number of days before receiving payment of a withdrawal, most are willing to pay withdrawals immediately. The institutions that hold savings deposits insure them up to a specified maximum amount per accountholder through various insuring agencies. Of course, in addition to withdrawal policies and insurance, the rate and method of calculating interest paid on savings accounts are important considerations in choosing the financial institutions in which savings are to be placed.

Combination Demand–Savings Deposits

As a result of changes in financial institutions that took place in the late 1970s and early 1980s depositors now have far greater flexibility in choosing how to satisfy their cash balance needs. The most successful new account is the money market mutual fund (MMF); these, in turn, have been challenged by money market accounts (MMAs). Also available are negotiable order of withdrawal (NOW) accounts.

Money Market Funds Starting from zero in the mid-1970s, MMFs grew to over $230 billion in deposits by late 1982, making them the most successful mutual fund ever offered. (Mutual funds are explained in greater detail in Chapter 14.) A *money market fund (MMF)* pools the funds of many small investors and purchases short-term securities offered by the U.S. Treasury, major corporations, large commercial banks, and others. Many will never have an opportunity to buy these securities directly since a minimum purchase is at least $10,000, but the minimum deposit into a MMF can be as little as $500. The interest rate earned on a MMF depends on returns earned on the fund's investments. They fluctuate with overall credit conditions but were high in the late 1970s and early 1980s. At their peak, most MMFs were earning annual rates in excess of 15 percent, which was considerably better than the $5\frac{1}{2}$ percent then paid on typical savings deposits. Moreover, investors had instant access to their funds through checkwriting privileges, although these were usually limited by requiring a minimum amount of $500 per check. Investors learned quickly that it made good sense to keep most of their cash in the MMFs and only a bare minimum in their checking accounts, and to replenish the checking account periodically from the MMF as bills needed to be paid.

Money Market Accounts The loss of billions of deposits to MMFs created a real financial crisis for many financial institutions in the early 1980s. Partially as a result, Congress permitted them to offer their own versions of MMFs; called *money market accounts (MMAs),* they were introduced 14 December 1982. Initially, these accounts required a minimum balance of $2,500 and only three checks could be written in a month. Each financial institution was free to set its own rate on its MMA, and most set rates somewhat above those being offered on MMFs in an effort to recapture lost deposits. As expected, MMA rates later fell to a level comparable to those on MMFs. Perhaps the single most important advantage to the MMA, other than its competitive interest rate, is the insurance protection provided by the FDIC, FSLIC, or NCUA up to $100,000 per depositor; this protection has been proposed, but at this writing is not currently available on MMFs.

NOW Accounts *Negotiable order of withdrawal (NOW) accounts* were first made available on a limited basis in 1974. Initially they offered depositors unlimited check writing privileges on their savings accounts, thus effectively permitting them to earn passbook interest on demand deposit balances. Until 1983, these accounts failed to receive widespread acceptance probably because the interest they paid was substantially below that offered by MMFs. However, starting 7 January 1983, liberalized banking legislation permitted financial institutions to issue NOW accounts—called *super NOW accounts*—without any interest rate restrictions and also with unlimited checkwriting privileges. Since the minimum balance on these accounts is also only $2,500, they are expected to become very attractive. Their acceptance, of course, will depend upon the level of interest rates actually offered; if not competitive, depositors are likely to continue to use their traditional checking accounts along with MMFs or MMAs.

Checking Accounts

Most adults in the United States have at least one checking account at a commercial bank, savings and loan association, mutual savings bank, or credit union; for convenience, the following discussion concentrates on the commercial bank. Many persons open their first checking account upon graduation from high school. Checking account balances represent an important component of our money supply and streamline the purchase-sale process. The following five sections describe methods for opening a checking account, checking account procedures, monthly statements, special types of checks, and other special bank conveniences.

Opening a Checking Account

Choosing a Bank Factors that may influence your choice of the bank where you will maintain a checking account are convenience, cost, and services provided. Many people choose a bank solely on the basis of convenience factors such as business hours, location, number of drive-in windows, or number of branches. In some states (for example, California and Ohio), branches of a bank can be spread throughout a community, while in other states (for example, Illinois and Oklahoma) branch banks are prohibited. Ease of access is obviously an important consideration: most people prefer to bank near their home or place of employment.

In some areas, checking accounts are free, which means that no service charge is levied. These "free checking" arrangements typically require the depositor to maintain a specified minimum or average balance; for example, a bank may require a *minimum* daily balance of $300 or an *average* daily balance of $600 in order to receive free checking. Some banks even provide personalized checks to customers at no cost. At the other extreme are banks that charge a basic monthly fee—$2 to $5 and/or 15¢ or so per check written—in addition to their charge for check printing. The cost of checking services should be estimated based on the average number of checks to be written per month.

Services provided differ from bank to bank. Depending on their size, banks may rent safe deposit boxes, pay bills for their depositors out of their accounts, make loans, provide financial counseling, and offer various types of bank cards and check-cashing services. Although proximity to home or work is generally the basis for bank choice, consideration of all these convenience, cost, and service factors is advised.

Signature Card Once you have selected a bank, the checking account must be opened. To do this you generally fill in your name, address, phone number, and signature—and sometimes your place of employment and occupation—on a *signature card.* The signature on this card will be compared to the signature on checks drawn on your account in order to confirm their validity. A sample signature card filled out by James C. and Mary Morrison is shown in Figure 5.1.

After the signature card has been filled out, a number is assigned to your account. The signature card is filed according to this account number. The account number appears on the card and is also printed in a special ink on the checks and deposit slips you receive. (Your checks and deposit slips will have other numbers along with your account number. These routing symbols play an important part in the check-clearing process.) In order to activate your new account, a deposit must be made. The bank may require a minimum deposit—generally no more than $50—to open a new account.

Joint or Single Account Two people who wish to open a checking account may decide to have a joint account. In this case, both individ-

Figure 5.1 Signature Card for the Morrisons' Account

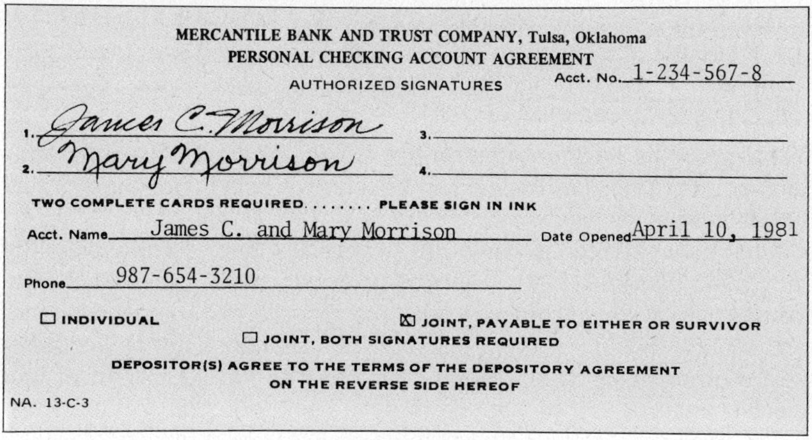

MERCANTILE BANK AND TRUST COMPANY, Tulsa, Oklahoma
PERSONAL CHECKING ACCOUNT AGREEMENT
AUTHORIZED SIGNATURES Acct. No. 1-234-567-8

1. James C. Morrison 3. ______
2. Mary Morrison 4. ______

TWO COMPLETE CARDS REQUIRED....... PLEASE SIGN IN INK

Acct. Name James C. and Mary Morrison Date Opened April 10, 1981

Phone 987-654-3210

☐ INDIVIDUAL ☒ JOINT, PAYABLE TO EITHER OR SURVIVOR
☐ JOINT, BOTH SIGNATURES REQUIRED

DEPOSITOR(S) AGREE TO THE TERMS OF THE DEPOSITORY AGREEMENT ON THE REVERSE SIDE HEREOF

NA. 13-C-3

Source: Courtesy of Bank of Oklahoma, Mercantile Center.

uals must sign the signature card. Either of them can then sign checks written on the account. The Morrisons' signature card indicates that their account is jointly held. One advantage of the joint account over two single accounts is that it lowers the cost of any service charges the bank may make. If one of the partners dies, the title to the account passes to the surviving partner. The account, then, is said to have rights of survivorship, and in the case of a married couple, this means that if one spouse dies, the surviving spouse, after fulfilling a certain legal time requirement, can draw checks on the account. If the deceased partner had a single account, the surviving partner could not take possession of it until the estate of the deceased partner had been probated, which could take years. (If, rather than having rights of survivorship, account owners are treated as tenants in common, the survivor gets only his or her share of the account. It is important when opening a joint account to specify the rights preferred.)

Accounts jointly held have disadvantages: It is difficult to keep accurate balances when each partner is writing checks against the account, and it is possible for one partner to drain the account and abscond with the money. To overcome the difficulty in keeping records of balances, partners in a joint account can share a single checkbook or use two checkbooks, dividing the account balance between them. To protect both partners, both signatures may be required on all checks drawn on the account.

Checking Account Procedures

Writing Checks When you write a *check,* you fill in on the appropriate lines the name of the person to whom it is made out, the amount, and the date. The amount of the check is both printed in numerals and written in script in order to assure accuracy; if these amounts do not agree, the written amount is considered legally correct. Sign the check the same way you signed the signature card; otherwise, it may not be accepted by your bank. It is also a good idea to write somewhere on the check the name of the item or service for which the check is payment. For example, in the personal check written by Mary Morrison shown in Figure 5.2, Mary has noted that the $65.17 made out to Gulf Oil Company is payment due on her Gulf credit card (see lower left-hand corner). This information can be used for both budgeting and tax purposes at some future date.

Whenever a check is written or a deposit made, a corresponding entry must be made in the *checkbook ledger,* which is provided with the checkbook for maintaining accurate records of all transactions in the account. By subtracting the amount of each check written and adding the amount of each deposit made to the previous balance, the account balance can be kept up to date. (See the portion of the Morrisons' checkbook ledger shown in Figure 5.2.) Good records of transactions and an accurate balance figure help avoid overdrawing the account.

Endorsing Checks When you (second party) receive a check from someone (first party), you can either cash, deposit, or make a payment to someone else (third party) with the check. Regardless of how you use the check, you will have to endorse it (in exactly the same way it has been made out on the front) on the back (generally, the left end of the check). The common forms of endorsement—*in blank, special, restrictive,* and *conditional*—are illustrated in Figure 5.3.

The Check-Clearing Process Clearing a check involves a series of bookkeeping entries on the part of the banks involved. Computer sophistication has greatly simplified and speeded up this process. One of the keys to the clearing process is the use of *Magnetic Ink Character Recognition (MICR).* Checks and deposit slips are encoded with numbers referring to the routing of the check, a bank identification number, the check number (in many cases), and the account number, all of which are read by a machine. The machine, which is linked to a computer, sorts the checks and transmits the appropriate information to the account records. The MICR encoding and routing symbols appear in the lower-left portion of a check. See them, for example, on the Morrisons' check in Figure 5.2 (1039 0106). The routing symbols are also shown on the right-hand side of both checks and deposit slips. In the case of the Morrisons' check and deposit slip in Figure 5.2, these symbols are given as (86-106)/1039. In order to further simplify the routing of checks and deposits, the account number is MICR-encoded at the bottom of each check and deposit slip. The Morrisons' account number (1 234 567 8), encoded in MICR symbols, appears on their check and deposit slip in Figure 5.2. In an effort to streamline the check reconciliation process (discussed later), most banks now include the check

Figure 5.2 Basic Checking Account Transactions

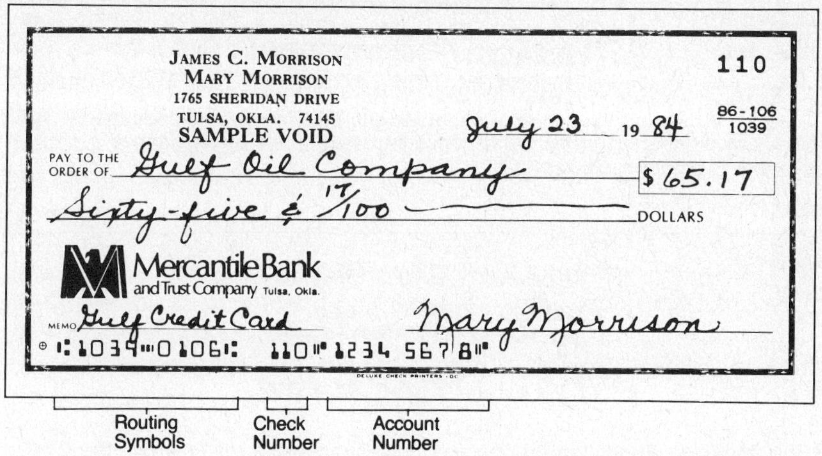

CHECK NO	DATE	CHECK ISSUED TO	AMOUNT OF CHECK		✓	DATE OF DEP	AMOUNT OF DEPOSIT		BALANCE	
									476	40
108	7/8	Safeway	53	86					422	54
109	7/11	Cash	35	00					387	54
110	7/23	Gulf Oil Company	65	17					322	37
111	7/23	First Trash Service	8	00					314	37
—	7/24	Deposit					436	15	750	52
112	7/26	First Mortgage Co.	497	60					252	92

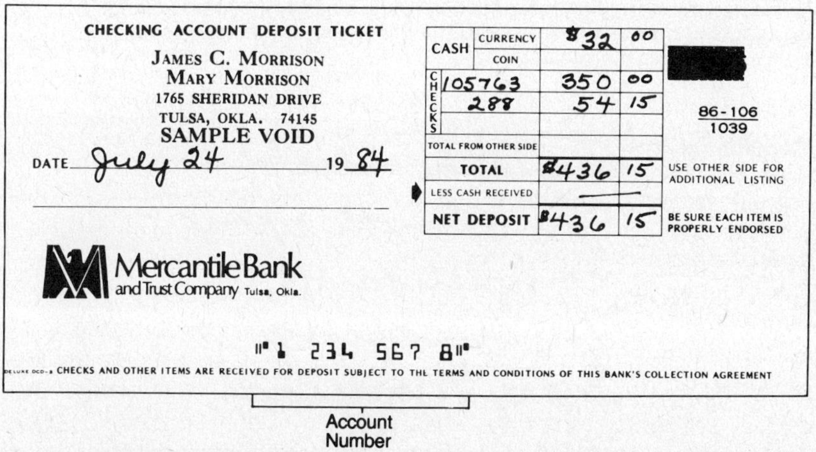

Source: Courtesy of Bank of Oklahoma, Mercantile Center.

Figure 5.3 Common Forms of Check Endorsement

In Blank

Mary Morrison

This is the most popular form of endorsement. One merely endorses the check by signing his or her name. Once endorsed, the check becomes payable to whoever possesses it.

Special

Pay to the order of
John Smith
Mary Morrison

This endorsement includes a notation indicating specifically to whom the check is to be paid. Such an endorsement does not preclude that person from endorsing the check over to yet another person (fourth party).

Restrictive

Pay to the order of
John Smith only
Mary Morrison

or

For deposit only
Mary Morrison

By adding the world *only* after the third-party's name, the check cannot be endorsed over to a fourth party. The third party in this case could be either an individual or a bank.

Conditional

Pay to the order of
John Smith upon
completion of
landscaping
Mary Morrison

This endorsement, although not legally binding, places some condition on the endorsement. Its use restricts further negotiation of the check and does make the third-party (John Smith) liable to the second party (Mary Morrison) if he or she violates the condition.

number as part of the MICR coding at the bottom of the check. Note the Morrisons' check number (110) has been encoded between the routing symbols and their account number at the bottom of their check.

Once the information has been transmitted, a series of bookkeeping entries takes place. First, the amount of the check is deducted from the balance. If there are service charges, they are accumulated and deducted at the end of the month. Second, the amount of the check is transferred to the account in which it is deposited. The check may be deposited within the same bank, or it may be deposited in a different bank. Regardless, the funds are transferred via certain bookkeeping entries to the appropriate recipient.

Even with MICR, it often takes three or four days for a check to clear. When the bank that the check is drawn on is in the same city as the bank that receives the deposit, however, the check will often clear within one day. Checks drawn on banks geographically distant from those in which the depositor's checking account is held often take as long as a week to clear. Care should therefore be taken in writing checks against recent deposits to an account, since the funds deposited may not be available. When this occurs, the check "bounces" due to an insufficient balance. On the other hand, people sometimes knowingly write checks against nonexistent balances, recognizing that the delay in the check-clearing process makes it possible for them to deposit funds to cover the check a few days later. This strategy of "playing the float" is a form of fraud and is against the law.

Making Deposits Deposit slips are normally included within your checkbook and are also readily obtained from your bank. Filling out a deposit slip on which the components of your deposit are itemized is the first step in making a deposit. Normally, separate entries for currency, coin, and checks are included. Each check to be deposited is listed separately on the slip. (See the sample deposit slip prepared by the Morrisons in Figure 5.2.) The second step is endorsing all of the checks to be deposited. To protect against possible loss of endorsed checks, it is common practice to use a special endorsement, such as "Pay to the order of XYZ Bank," or a restrictive endorsement, such as "For deposit only." If the way your name is written on the check differs from the way you signed the signature card, you should sign your correct signature below your endorsement. In order to further assure that the deposit is properly entered into your account, writing your account number below your endorsement can be helpful.

Your deposit can be submitted to your bank in several ways: at the bank during normal banking hours; at a remote banking facility, such as a drive-in window; at an *automatic teller machine (ATM),* a type of remote computer terminal at which transactions can be made 24 hours a day, 7 days a week; in the bank's *night depository,* a protected type of mail slot on the exterior of the bank, in the special envelopes banks usually provide for after-hours deposits; and by mail, in the self-addressed, sometimes prestamped deposit envelopes many banks provide for this purpose. Some employers will deposit employees' payroll checks directly into their accounts. In any case, you should obtain a receipt for your deposit and enter the amount of the deposit into your checkbook ledger.

The use of ATMs, night depositories, and banking by mail is not advised if cash is to be deposited since the opportunity for an unaccountable loss exists; the loss of checks can normally be proven. Of course, when checks are deposited, a delay in the availability of the funds may result due to the time required for the check to clear. This delay is increased when deposits are mailed, since it may take an additional two to three days for them to reach the bank. Similarly, receipts from the bank verifying the deposits will require a few more days to arrive through the mail. Time factors involved in the required availability of funds should be considered when selecting a method for making a deposit.

Overdrafts When a check is written for an amount greater than the current account balance, the result is an *overdraft.* Poor bookkeeping on the part of the accountholder or a delay in the bank's receipt of a deposit can be the cause. If the overdraft is proven to have been intentional, the bank could initiate legal proceedings against the accountholder. The action taken by a bank on an overdraft depends on the amount involved and the strength of the relationship between the bank and the accountholder. In many cases, the bank stamps the overdrawn check with the words "insufficient balance (or funds)" and returns it to the person to whom it was written. The accountholder is notified of this action, and a penalty fee of $5 to $15 is deducted from the checking account. (See, for example, the notice of insufficient balance received by the Morrisons shown in Figure 5.4.) When the bank uses this procedure, the person to whom the check was written recognizes that the check has bounced. Many vendors require an individual whose check bounces to pay a service charge of $5 to $10 in addition to the original amount for which the check was written. They also usually refuse to accept checks drawn on that account thereafter.

In instances where a strong banking relationship has been established between the accountholder and the bank, the accountholder is a major customer of the bank, or arrangements have been made for overdraft privileges, the bank will go ahead and pay a check that overdraws the account. Accountholders at most banks can arrange to receive *overdraft protection.* These arrangements are given various names, such as "checking plus," "personal line of credit," or "instant cash." They generally are either charged against a bank card (such as MasterCard or Visa) or are met by withdrawal from a companion savings account. In either case, the bank automatically initiates the transfer assuming that the customer has previously arranged to receive such an overdraft protection service. In cases where overdraft protection is not prearranged, but the bank pays the check, the accountholder is usually notified by the bank and charged a penalty fee for the incon-

Figure 5.4 A Notice of Insufficient Balance

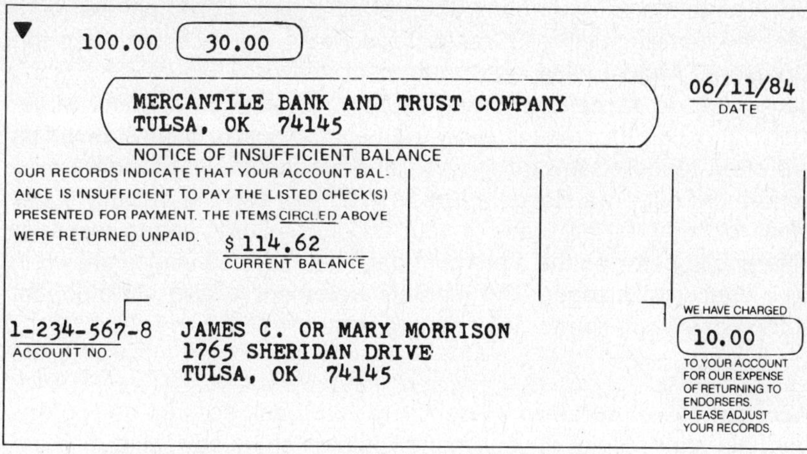

▼ 100.00 30.00

MERCANTILE BANK AND TRUST COMPANY
TULSA, OK 74145

06/11/84
DATE

NOTICE OF INSUFFICIENT BALANCE

OUR RECORDS INDICATE THAT YOUR ACCOUNT BALANCE IS INSUFFICIENT TO PAY THE LISTED CHECK(S) PRESENTED FOR PAYMENT. THE ITEMS CIRCLED ABOVE WERE RETURNED UNPAID.

$ 114.62
CURRENT BALANCE

1-234-567-8
ACCOUNT NO.

JAMES C. OR MARY MORRISON
1765 SHERIDAN DRIVE
TULSA, OK 74145

WE HAVE CHARGED
10.00
TO YOUR ACCOUNT FOR OUR EXPENSE OF RETURNING TO ENDORSERS. PLEASE ADJUST YOUR RECORDS.

Source: Courtesy of Bank of Oklahoma, Mercantile Center.

venience. The check does not bounce, and the remitter's credit-worthiness is not damaged. Making sure that all checks you write are covered by the balance in your account avoids possible embarrassment associated with overdrafts.

Stopping Payment Occasionally it is necessary to *stop payment* on a check which has been issued. This may be due to any of several possible reasons, for example: (1) checks or a checkbook are either lost or stolen, (2) a service or merchandise paid for by check is found to be faulty, or (3) a check is issued as part of a contract which is not carried out. Payment on a check is stopped by notifying the bank. Normally, the accountholder must fill out a form describing the check by number and date, amount, and the name of the person to whom it was written. Sometimes stop payment orders can be initiated over the telephone, in which case a written follow-up is normally required. Telephone-initiated stop payments generally remain in effect only 14 days while written stop payment orders can remain in effect for 6 months.

Once a stop payment order has been issued, the tellers in the bank are told not to pay on the given check. At the same time, the stop payment information is placed in the data processing system in order to reject the check if it is presented by another bank in the check-clearing process. Most banks require accountholders who wish to stop payment on a check to sign a statement relieving the bank of any liability if, by error, payment is made on the check in question. A fee ranging from $5 to $15 is also usually charged for stopping payment on a check. Note, too, that payment can be stopped only on regular checks drawn on demand or combination demand-savings deposit accounts; certified and cashier's checks (except when reported lost or stolen) cannot be stopped.

Monthly Statements

Once each month, your bank will provide a bank statement that contains an itemized listing of transactions within your account. (See the Morrisons' August 1984 bank statement shown in Figure 5.5.) Many banks include canceled checks and deposit slips with the bank statement, although the trend is away from such practice. Bank statements are often rendered toward the end of each month. Large banks may send them out on a staggered basis. You can use the monthly statement to verify the accuracy of your account records and to reconcile differences between the statement balance and the balance shown in your checkbook ledger. The monthly statement is also an important source of information for your tax records.

Account Reconciliation Reconciling your bank account as soon as possible after receipt of your monthly statement is advisable. The *account reconciliation* process can uncover errors in recording checks or deposits, in addition or subtraction, and occasionally in the bank's processing of the checks. Overdrafts can also be avoided since you are periodically forced to verify your account balance. Any differences in your account balance as reflected in your checkbook ledger and the bank statement can be attributed to four basic factors, assuming neither you nor the bank has made any errors: (1) Certain checks which you have written and deducted from your checkbook balance have not yet been received by your bank and therefore remain outstanding. (2) Certain deposits you have made and added to your checkbook balance have not been credited to your account by the bank. (3) Certain service (activity) charges levied on your account by the bank have not yet been deducted from your checkbook balance. (4) Interest earned on your account, if it is a MMA or NOW account, has not been added to your checkbook balance.

The following steps facilitate the reconciliation of your account:

1. Upon receipt of your bank statement, arrange all canceled checks in ascending order based on their sequence numbers or issuance dates. As noted in the Morrisons' statement, banks using *checks with preencoded check numbers have eliminated the need for their customers to follow this step* since check numbers are printed on the bank statement and often arranged in ascending order.
2. Compare each check (or statement entry for preencoded checks) with the entry recorded for it in your checkbook ledger to make sure no recording errors exist. Place a mark in your checkbook ledger alongside each entry compared.
3. List the checks outstanding—those deducted in your checkbook but not returned with your bank statement (those not checked off in step 2). Total their amount.
4. Compare the deposit slips returned with the statement (or statement deposit entries) to deposits shown in your checkbook. Total the amount

Figure 5.5 The Morrisons' August 1984 Statement

STATEMENT OF CHECKING ACCOUNT

POST OFFICE BOX 45448
TULSA, OKLAHOMA 74145
PHONE 918/628-1200

MAIN BANK: 42nd at SO. DARLINGTON
DRIVE-IN: 42nd at SO. FULTON
MEMBER F.D.I.C.

Mercantile Bank
and Trust Company

JAMES C. OR MARY MORRISON
1765 SHERIDAN DRIVE
TULSA, OK 74145

1
PAGE

1-234-567-8
ACCOUNT NUMBER

08/31/84
STATEMENT DATE

TRANSACTIONS POSTED SINCE LAST STATEMENT

NUMBER	DATE	AMOUNT	ID	NUMBER	DATE	AMOUNT	ID	NUMBER	DATE	AMOUNT	ID	NUMBER	DATE	AMOUNT	ID
	08/03	715.33	CR												
	08/04	200.00	CR												
	08/10	6.75	CR												
	08/31	250.00	CR												
0080	08/03	3.50													
0092	08/03	12.44													
0110	08/04	65.17													
0113	08/03	14.75													
0115	08/10	15.50													
0116	08/07	50.00													
0117	08/06	10.00													
0118	08/07	16.80													
0119	08/10	21.37													
0120	08/05	4.18													
0122	08/11	8.00													
0123	08/11	7.27													
0124	08/14	30.00													
0125	08/17	45.80													
0126	08/20	24.83													
0127	08/20	25.00													
0128	08/19	132.00													
0129	08/27	159.07													
0131	08/31	497.60													
	08/31	2.85	DR												

DATE LAST STATEMENT: 07 31 84

PLEASE EXAMINE THIS STATEMENT PROMPTLY. REPORT ANY DIFFERENCE TO THE AUDITING DEPARTMENT.

DATE THIS STATEMENT: 08 31 84

BALANCE LAST STATEMENT		NUMBER Checks-Debits	AMOUNT CHECKS-DEBITS		NUMBER Deposits-Credits	AMOUNT DEPOSITS-CREDITS		BALANCE THIS STATEMENT
65.10	LESS	20	1146.13	PLUS	4	1172.08	EQUAL	91.05

Source: Courtesy of Bank of Oklahoma, Mercantile Center.

of outstanding deposits—those shown in your checkbook ledger but not yet received by the bank as reflected by the deposit slips returned and on your statement.

5. Deduct the amount of any service charges levied by the bank from and add any interest earned to your checkbook ledger balance.
6. Subtract the total amount of checks outstanding (from step 3) from your bank statement balance, and add to this balance the amount of outstanding deposits (from step 4). The resulting amount should be the same as your adjusted checkbook balance (determined in step 5). If it is not, you should check all addition and subtraction in your checkbook ledger since you have probably made an error.

Often the reverse side of your bank statement will provide a form for reconciling your account along with a step-by-step description of how to use it. Although a number of different approaches to reconciliation exist, the one described is the most straightforward.

The reconciliation of the Morrisons' account for August 1984 appears in Table 5.1. Their checkbook ledger balance was $310.47. The bank statement showed $2.85 in service charges for the month. The Morrisons did not earn any interest during the month. The month-end balance reflected in their bank statement (Figure 5.5) was $91.05. After going through the canceled checks, the Morrisons found checks outstanding for a total of $476.59. An evaluation of the deposits received by the bank revealed that a total amount of $693.16 was still in transit at the statement date. Since the new checkbook balance after adjustment for service charges and interest earned was equal to the calculated checkbook balance, the Morrisons' checking account appeared to be in good order. If the account had not reconciled correctly, the accuracy and calculations in the checkbook ledger would have had to be checked.

Tax Records Your monthly bank statement is an important tax record. It can be reviewed along with the checkbook ledger in order to evaluate past income and expenditures. Although you may maintain accurate records of these items as part of your budgeting process, the statement can be used to provide proof of payment, which you might need if the Internal Revenue Service should decide to audit your tax return. At the time of writing, it is advisable to indicate in the checkbook ledger (as well as on the front of your checks if they will be returned with your bank statement) the name of the item(s) or service(s) they purchased. Bank statements should be retained for a period of five years since an audit can still be conducted several years after a tax return is filed.

Special Types of Checks

Because there is no way to be absolutely sure that checks are good, verification is often necessary for a seller. This is common for large purchases or when the buyer's bank or the buyer is not located in the area where the purchase is made. The most common instruments used to guarantee payment are *certified checks, cashier's checks,* and *traveler's checks.*

Certified Check To certify a check, you make it out to whomever is to be paid and take it to your commercial bank. The bank will immediately deduct the amount of the check from your account and then stamp the check to indicate its certification. There is normally a small charge for this service. In effect, the bank has guaranteed that the check is good. And since the bank has become the guarantor, it nor-

Table 5.1 Reconciliation of the Morrisons' Checking Account (August 1984)

Checkbook Balance	$310.47
Less: Service Charges	(2.85)
Plus: Interest Earned	0.00
New Checkbook Balance	$307.62
Bank Statement Balance	$ 91.05
Less: Outstanding Checks	(476.59)
Plus: Deposits in Transit	693.16
Calculated Checkbook Balance	$307.62

mally will not return the canceled check to you, but rather will keep the check for its own records.

Cashier's Check Anyone can buy a cashier's check from a bank. These checks are often used by people who do not have checking accounts. They can be purchased for about three dollars and are sometimes issued at no charge to bank customers. In exchange for an appropriate amount of money—the amount of the check plus a service charge—the bank issues a check drawn on itself.

Traveler's Check A number of the larger financial organizations—such as First National City Bank, American Express Company, VISA, and Bank of America—issue traveler's checks, which can be purchased at commercial banks and most other financial institutions in denominations ranging from $10 to $1,000. A fee of about 1½ percent is charged on their purchase. If properly endorsed, traveler's checks are accepted by most U.S. businesses and can be exchanged for local currencies in most parts of the world. Since these checks are not valid unless properly countersigned by the purchaser and since they are insured against loss or theft by the issuing agency, they provide a safe, convenient, and popular form of money for travel.

Special Bank Conveniences

Banks offer a number of other conveniences, such as safe deposit boxes, drive-in and walk-up windows, automatic teller machines, preauthorized payments, bank-by-phone accounts, and electronic funds transfer systems.

Safe Deposit Boxes A *safe deposit box* is a drawer in a bank's vault that can be rented. The annual rental fee depends on the box size; small boxes can be rented for about $10 per year, while large boxes cost hundreds of dollars per year. When you rent a box, you receive one key to it, and the bank retains another key. The box can be opened only when both keys are used. This arrangement protects items in the box from theft and makes it an excellent storage place for jewelry, contracts, stock certificates, titles, and other special documents.

Drive-In and Walk-Up Windows Both drive-in and walk-up windows handle the basic deposit-withdrawal and check-cashing transactions. Other, more complex transactions, such as the purchase of certified or traveler's checks, are not normally handled at a drive-in or walk-up facility. For the convenience of their customers, banks usually keep their drive-in and walk-up windows open before and after regular banking hours.

Automatic Teller Machines Recent advances in computer technology have resulted in the development and use of *automatic teller machines (ATMs)* by many of the nation's banks. A type of remote computer terminal at which bank customers can make deposits, withdrawals, and other types of basic transactions, the ATM is a completely mechanical device and can operate 24 hours per day, 7 days a week. Banks are beginning to locate these terminals in shopping centers, office buildings, and other places suited to enhance and protect their competitive position. Such facilities will become more numerous over the next few years.

Pre-authorized Payments Another area of growth in bank conveniences is the *pre-authorized payment.* This mechanism allows the bank to make payments from customers' accounts at their directions. This service is typically initiated over the telephone with the customer directing payments in specified amounts to various vendors. These systems are most prevalent among savings and loans and mutual savings banks. They typically require the customer to maintain a minimum deposit balance and charge a fee of about 15 cents per item paid. Not only does this mechanism allow the customer to earn interest on money held in order to pay bills, it also is a convenient payment mechanism that provides savings in postage. Continued growth in this payment mechanism is anticipated.

Bank-by-Phone Accounts Prompted by competition from other financial institutions coupled with recent advances in computer and communication technology, banks have begun offering *bank-by-phone accounts.* These accounts are similar to pre-authorized payments except that they allow the bank customer to initiate a variety of transactions using a push-button telephone. Persons with such accounts are given a secret code number that allows them access to their account over the telephone. By pushing a series of numbered codes, the customer can make a variety of transactions, such as learning the account balance, transferring money to other accounts, seeing if checks have cleared, and paying bills to participating merchants. All transactions are made directly from the customer's phone to the computer— no human intervention is involved in making the transactions. A number of checks are built into these systems in order to allow customers to confirm the accuracy of their transactions. The cost of participation in bank-by-phone varies depending upon an individual's minimum (or average) account balances. The service is generally free to those with high checking *and* savings balances, for example, a $200 checking minimum *and* a $1,500 savings minimum. At maximum, bank-by-phone will add about $2 per month to the monthly account charge and cost about 15¢ per transaction. Growth in these systems is anticipated. Their main benefits lie in the elimination of postage associated with bill payment; a reduction in the number of trips one must make to the bank and the post office; and the general convenience they provide.

Electronic Funds Transfer Systems Another recent development which uses computer technology, the *electronic funds transfer system (EFTS),* attempts to eliminate the need for cash or checks. Each person has a *debit card* which can be used to make all transactions. Stores have point-of-sale (POS) terminals similar to cash registers. By inserting the customer's card into the terminal and punching in certain data relating to a specific transaction, the amount of the transaction is transferred via computer from the customer's account to the vendor's account. Although EFTS has been used on a very limited basis, it will probably become more common in the next five to ten years. Ultimately, users will need no cash or checks; instead, they will have one debit card with which all transactions can be made. A series of computers will make the necessary bookkeeping entries at the time of the transactions, thereby allowing up-to-date information on all accounts. The bounced check will be a thing of the past.

Maintaining Savings Accounts

As indicated earlier in this chapter, savings deposits are an important method of holding cash balances, not only because they earn interest and thus provide some return on available funds, but also because they permit the accumulation of money for planned future expenditures and cover necessary but unexpected expenditures. This part of the chapter describes three important aspects of savings accounts: determining interest on savings, savings institutions, and insured savings.

Determining Interest on Savings

Interest received on savings is a form of income paid to the saver by the institution in which the savings are placed. The true or *effective rate of interest* paid on your savings differs from the stated or *nominal rate of interest.* The effective rate of interest is the annual rate of interest and reflects the actual rate at which deposits earn interest. The nominal rate of interest represents the rate that can be applied to deposits without consideration for the time period and/or methods utilized to determine the amount of interest. An understanding of the effects of the compounding period on the effective rate of interest and the methods used to calculate interest on savings provides a rational basis for selecting savings media.

Compounding Period The effective rate of interest you receive on your savings is dependent on the period over which interest is compounded. *Compounding interest* involves paying interest not only on the initial deposit but also on any interest accumulated from period to period. It is the standard method for paying interest on savings accounts. The period of time over which interest is compounded affects the effective rate of interest. For a given nominal rate, the more frequently interest is compounded, the higher the effective rate of interest. Table 5.2 presents the amount that results at the end of five years when $1,000 is compounded at a 5 percent nominal rate of interest annually, quarterly, weekly, and continuously; it clearly demonstrates that the more often interest is compounded, the higher the effective rate of interest.

Methods Used to Calculate Interest The time that a deposit is made affects the amount of interest earned on it. Some savings institutions pay interest for the entire month on all deposits received before the tenth of the month and remaining in the institution through the end of the month. Others pay interest quarterly and require deposits to remain in the account through the quarter in order to receive any interest. There are several basic techniques used by savings institutions to determine what balances are eligible to receive interest for a given compounding period. The four most commonly used are *FIFO, low balance, LIFO,* and *actual balance.*

FIFO The first-in-first-out (FIFO) technique deducts any withdrawals during the interest period from the earliest amount on deposit for the period. This approach penalizes the saver by removing the longest-lived deposits when withdrawals occur. The result is that the interest paid over the period is lower than under any of the other techniques.

Low Balance Under the low balance technique, interest is paid on the lowest balance remaining on deposit throughout the entire interest pe-

Table 5.2 Interest Earned for Various Compounding Periods Using a 5 Percent Nominal Rate of Interest ($1,000 Initial Deposit)

	Compounding Period			
Year	Annually	Quarterly	Weekly	Continuously
1	$1,050.00	$1,050.94	$1,051.25	$1,051.27
2	1,102.50	1,104.47	1,105.13	1,105.17
3	1,157.63	1,160.74	1,161.76	1,161.83
4	1,215.51	1,219.86	1,221.30	1,221.40
5	1,276.28	1,282.00	1,283.90	1,284.02
Effective Rate	5.000%	5.094%	5.125%	5.127%

riod. Interest is not paid on deposits made during the period, and withdrawals during the period tend to substantially reduce the interest earned and penalize the saver.

LIFO The last-in-first-out (LIFO) technique deducts withdrawals during the period from the most recent deposit made during the period. This provides much better interest earnings than with the FIFO technique since the interest lost through withdrawals is that on the shortest-lived deposits and is therefore minimized.

Actual Balance Interest is paid on a daily basis in the actual balance technique so that each dollar on deposit receives the appropriate amount of interest for each day. (Note: This is often called the *day-of-deposit-to-day-of-withdrawal* technique.) To be eligible to receive interest on a deposit most banks require that it be on their books at the close of the day. For example, a deposit made on the tenth of the month and withdrawn on the twentieth of the month would earn interest for the full ten days it was on deposit (that is, the close of the tenth day through the close of the nineteenth day). Deposits do not have to be made by a certain date and remain through the end of the period in order to receive interest; instead, the interest is paid on the actual balance maintained on a day-to-day basis. This technique, which many financial institutions have adopted, maximizes the interest earnings.

The differences in interest earned under each of these techniques can be demonstrated using the account transactions shown in Table 5.3 for the month of June. Assuming interest is paid on this account at a nominal annual rate of 5 percent and that a deposit must be received on or before the tenth of the month to earn interest for the month (except, of course, in the case of the actual balance technique), the total interest earned during the month under each of the four techniques would be determined as shown in Table 5.4.

Table 5.3 Account Transactions during June

Date	Transaction	Amount	Account Balance
1 (Initial Balance)	—	—	$ 0
5	Deposit	$4,000	4,000
12	Deposit	3,000	7,000
20	Withdrawal	2,000	5,000
25	Deposit	1,000	6,000
30 (Ending Balance)	—	—	$6,000

Under all but the actual balance technique, the only deposit eligible to receive interest for the month is the 5 June deposit of $4,000 since it is the only deposit made prior to the tenth of the month. Under the FIFO technique, the withdrawal of $2,000 on 20 June is deducted from the $4,000 deposit made on 5 June, therefore resulting in only $2,000 on which the monthly interest is paid. The interest amounts to $8.33. Under the low balance technique, the lowest balance remaining on deposit throughout the month, which is $4,000, earns interest for the month. The interest earned in this case amounts to $16.67. Under the LIFO technique, the $2,000 withdrawal on 20 June is deducted from the deposit of $3,000 made on 12 June. Since the initial deposit, which is the only deposit eligible to receive interest (that is, on deposit before the tenth of month), is not affected by this withdrawal, the interest is earned on the entire $4,000. The interest earned in this case totals $16.67.

Using the actual balance technique, interest is paid on a daily basis. The account balances shown in Table 5.3 are $4,000 for 7 days (5 June through 11 June), $7,000 for 8 days (12 June through 19 June), $5,000 for 5 days (20 June through 24 June), and $6,000 for 6 days (25 June through 30 June). Calculating the interest on these balances using the 5 percent nominal annual rate as shown in Table 5.4 results in interest for the period of $20.14.

Clearly, from the standpoint of the accountholder, the actual balance technique is most desirable, and finding a savings institution which pays interest on the actual balance should not present any great problem. Note, however, that this technique may be referred to as the "payment of daily interest," which should not be confused with "daily compounding of interest." *Payment of daily interest* refers to the fact that interest is paid on the actual balance, while *daily compounding of interest* indicates how the actual *rate* of interest is applied.

Savings Institutions

Several different types of savings institutions offering a variety of savings plans and services are present in our economy. Limitations of space preclude description of all aspects of these institutions, but some

Table 5.4 Interest Earned Under Alternative Computation Techniques for Account Transactions Given in Table 5.3

(Nominal Annual Rate of Interest: 5 Percent)

Technique	Balance Eligible to Receive Interest (1)	Nominal Annual Interest Rate (2)	Fraction of Year that Interest Is Earned[a] (3)	Interest Earned [(1) × (2) × (3)] (4)
FIFO	$2,000	0.05	1/12	$ 8.33
Low Balance	$4,000	0.05	1/12	$16.67
LIFO	$4,000	0.05	1/12	$16.67
Actual Balance[b]: Period				
6/5 through 6/11	$4,000	0.05	7/360	$ 3.89
6/12 through 6/19	7,000	0.05	8/360	7.78
6/20 through 6/24	5,000	0.05	5/360	3.47
6/25 through 6/30	6,000	0.05	6/360	5.00
			Total Interest Earned	$20.14

[a]Column (3) values represent the fraction of the year, which for convenience is assumed to consist of a total of 360 days (12 30-day months), that the 5 percent nominal annual rate of interest is earned on the eligible balance given in column 1.
[b]Under the actual balance technique, the period a given balance is on deposit is the number of days at the *close* of which the given balance remains on deposit.

of the important characteristics and services they provide are outlined here. The most common savings institutions are commercial banks, savings and loan associations, mutual savings banks, and credit unions.

Commercial Banks In addition to checking accounts and demand-savings accounts such as money market accounts (MMAs) and NOW accounts described earlier, *commercial banks* offer their customers several types of pure savings accounts. Most prevalent among these is the *passbook account,* which is a regular savings account on which annual interest is paid; in recent years, the rate of interest paid has averaged about 5.25 percent. Although legally commercial banks can make depositors wait 30 to 60 days to receive a requested withdrawal, they rarely, if ever, require any waiting period. The passbook account-holder may or may not be given a passbook in which all transactions are recorded. Some banks now issue separate deposit/withdrawal receipts and then at the end of the quarter send each depositor a statement on which all account transactions for the period are itemized. Passbook accounts at commercial banks offer the convenience of maintaining both checking and savings accounts at one financial institution.

Commercial banks also offer *special savings accounts.* These accounts, the names of which may vary from bank to bank, offer a slightly higher rate of interest (0.25 to 0.50 percent) than the passbook account, but in exchange they require the accountholder to maintain a specified minimum balance of $200 to $500 for a specified period of time. If the accountholder does not maintain the balance as required, the interest is paid on the account as if it were a passbook account.

A third type of savings account offered by the commercial bank is the *club account.* These accounts are established for special purposes, such as saving money for Christmas shopping. Banks set up these types of accounts in order to attract additional deposits from customers. The club account acts as a budgeting device for the customer by requiring specified weekly or monthly deposits, which are aimed at achieving some type of savings goal, for example, $500 for Christmas shopping or a vacation. To assist club members in making sure that scheduled deposits are made, the bank often issues them some type of coupon book. The book contains a series of coupons—one for each required deposit—showing the date and amount of each individual deposit. The rate of interest paid on club accounts is generally below the rate paid on passbook accounts since the bank must perform additional clerical chores to establish and maintain them.

Savings and Loan Associations *Savings and loan associations* are found in most parts of the country. The most common type is a mutual association in which the depositors actually own the institution, and the returns they receive are called dividends rather than interest. (*Note:* In finance the word *mutual* indicates a type of cooperative ownership.) Although these payments are dividends, they are classified as interest for income tax purposes. This treatment also applies to dividends received from other types of "mutual" savings institutions. The other type is owned by a group which may or may not include some depositors. Depositors in this case receive interest instead of dividends on their deposits. Regardless of their organizational structure, savings and loans are important since they channel the savings of individuals into mortgage loans for purchasing and improving homes. This role of the savings and loan is discussed in detail in Chapter 6.

The savings opportunities provided by the savings and loan association do not differ significantly from those provided by commercial banks. In addition to MMAs and NOWs, they offer a variety of passbook, special savings accounts, and club-type accounts. The dividends or interest paid on deposits are typically about 0.25 to 0.50 percent above that of comparable commercial bank savings accounts. The convenience of services available at numerous branch offices in large cities, along with the attractive rates of dividends or interest paid, contribute to the popularity of savings and loan associations.

Mutual Savings Banks *Mutual savings banks* are a special type of savings institution, similar to savings and loan associations and found primarily in the New England states. In addition to offering MMAs and NOW accounts, they accept a variety of savings deposits on which interest is paid at a rate on a par with the rates paid by savings and loans. Depositors in a mutual savings bank are actually the bank's owners. The mutual savings bank accepts deposits and, after deducting the expenses of doing business from its earnings, distributes the profits to the owners in the form of dividend payments, which are technically equivalent to interest payments. Normally, instead of distributing all profits, only enough to provide depositors with a stated return of, say, 5.5 percent is distributed. Any remaining profits are reinvested in order to provide greater protection for depositors.

Credit Unions The *credit union,* which is a type of mutual association, draws together the savings of its members. These savings are lent out to members (at favorable rates) or invested in certain types of securities. Membership in a credit union is normally limited to a group of people having some common bond, such as the same employer, the same church, or the same community. A person who qualifies for membership in a credit union may join by making a minimum deposit, which may be five dollars or less and which buys a share in the credit union. In many of the smaller credit unions, members participate on a volunteer, part-time basis in the management and operation of the institution. Larger credit unions use paid full-time employees. Because the credit union is run to benefit the members, the rate of interest paid on savings is normally 0.50 to 1.50 percent above the rates paid by other savings institutions. As a mutual association in which the savers own shares, the credit union pays dividends, not interest on savings.

Most credit unions, in addition to offering MMAs and NOW accounts, sometimes called *share draft accounts,* offer a variety of types of savings accounts to their members; the dominant one is the passbook account. The dividend rate is often not known by the savers until the end of the savings period, since the dividends paid in each period depend on the credit union's earnings for that period. The credit union does estimate expected dividends. Since credit unions permit members not only to receive a favorable return on their savings but also to borrow money at advantageous rates (no more than 1.75 percent a month on the unpaid balance in federally chartered credit unions and generally around 15 to 21 percent a year in state-chartered institutions), they are attractive to many members. Most of them also provide free life insurance up to a maximum amount for each dollar deposited at no direct cost to the member; use of a portion of their income to pay insurance fees reduces dividends accordingly.

Insured Savings

Savings deposits are almost always insured, regardless of the type of institution in which they are held. The insuring agency provides protection against failure of the institution for up to some maximum amount of a depositor's total accounts. Table 5.5 shows the insuring agencies, insurance limits, and approximate percent of institutions of each type insured by the agencies listed. In almost all cases, those institutions

Table 5.5 Insured Savings Institutions

Savings Institution	Insuring Agency	Amount of Insurance	Approximate Percent Insured[a]
Commercial Bank	Federal Deposit Insurance Corporation (FDIC)	$100,000/depositor	97
Savings and Loan Association	Federal Savings and Loan Insurance Corporation (FSLIC)	$100,000/depositor	86
Mutual Savings Bank	Federal Deposit Insurance Corporation (FDIC)	$100,000/depositor	67
Credit Union	National Credit Union Administration (NCUA)	$100,000/depositor	77

[a]These figures represent the approximate percent of all such institutions that are insured by the corresponding insuring agency listed here. The institutions not included in these percentages are, for the most part, insured by a state-chartered or independent insuring agency. Details can be learned by inquiry.
Source: The "approximate percent insured" values have been estimated using data found in the fact books or annual reports of the associations of different types of savings institutions. Data were also obtained from "The Safety of Your Savings," *U.S. News & World Report,* 12 May 1980, p. 74.

not insured by one of these federal or national plans receive insurance through a state-chartered or independent insuring agency.

The presence of insured deposits at almost all savings institutions makes it possible for consumers to feel confident that their savings deposits are protected. They must keep in mind, however, that regardless of how many accounts they have in an insured institution, the insurance limit applies to the total of their deposits in that institution and its branches. For instance, an individual with three accounts in one commercial bank totaling $125,000—a passbook savings account balance of $5,000, a money market account (MMA) with a $70,000 balance at a branch office, and a NOW account with a $50,000 balance at the home office—is covered by only $100,000 of insurance. Of course, if either the MMA or NOW deposit were transferred to another bank or savings institution, it would be insured for up to $100,000 and the total amount in all accounts would then be protected. Thus not only the existence of insurance on deposits but also the maximum amount insured *per depositor* must be taken into account in establishing checking and savings accounts.

Other Savings Instruments and Cash Management Strategies

Certificates of deposit, money market certificates, U.S. Savings Bonds, and life insurance, retirement, and pension plans are alternatives to savings accounts. But although these savings instruments may provide more attractive returns, they tend to reduce the liquidity of the savings; a penalty often exists for withdrawals prior to a specified date. These forms of savings are normally maintained for some planned expenditure or solely as investments. A cash management strategy is clearly needed to guide these liquidity-related decisions.

Certificates of Deposit (CDs)

Savings certificates or (time) *certificates of deposit (CDs)* are issued by certain savings institutions in exchange for deposits. They generally require a minimum deposit of $100 and have maturities ranging from 30 days to one or more years. The rate of interest paid on money held with a CD is higher than the rate paid on passbook accounts. Interest on a CD account may be paid periodically over its life or at maturity. CD purchasers, in effect, agree to leave their funds with the savings institution for a specified period of time in exchange for a favorable rate of interest. If they wish to get their money back prior to maturity, they normally receive only the passbook savings rate minus some penalty charge—less than the earnings from a savings account. CDs therefore should not be purchased unless they can be held to maturity. Certificates of deposit are generally available at commercial banks, savings and loan associations, and mutual savings banks; a similar instrument called a *share certificate* is offered by many credit unions. Since a wide variety of maturities and interest rates are available, the CD should be strongly considered as a savings medium for funds expected to be idle for a known period of time.

Also available are negotiable CDs, large CDs issued by commercial banks at favorable rates with 90-day or longer maturities. Negotiable CDs are normally issued in denominations of $100,000 or more. Unlike CDs of smaller denominations, these large CDs may be sold by the holder to a third party. This feature allows purchasers to get their money back prior to maturity without paying a penalty. Although these large CDs are purchased primarily by business firms, they are sometimes also obtained through commercial banks or stock brokerage firms, which break them into several parts. For large amounts of savings ($10,000 or more), this arrangement might provide the most attractive returns. Your banker or stockbroker can make you aware of such opportunities.

Money Market Certificates (MMCs)

For those savers having at least $10,000 available for deposit, the *money market certificate (MMC)* may prove to be an attractive savings vehicle. It is a special type of certificate of deposit issued by banks, savings and loan associations, mutual savings banks, and credit unions. The most common MMCs have six-month maturities (only) and pay interest at a maximum rate set equal to the rate paid on the most recently issued six-month Treasury Bills, which are securities issued weekly by the U.S. Treasury. Two and one-half year certificates with no minimum denomination and paying interest at a rate slightly below that on a government security are also available. In periods of high interest rates, such as 1979–1982, money market certificates are especially attractive because they pay higher interest than existing interest rate regulations would otherwise permit the savings institution to pay on a deposit of under $100,000.

U.S. Savings Bonds

A safe and popular savings instrument available to everyone is the *U.S. Savings Bond.* These bonds are issued in various denominations and maturities by the U.S. Treasury in order to assist in financing the federal government. Because both the payment of interest and the repayment of the principal are guaranteed by the government, U.S. Savings Bonds are a very safe investment. They can be purchased and redeemed at most banks and other financial institutions at no charge. Savings bonds are not negotiable; they are issued to a person or persons and are registered in the name(s) of the holder(s). The registration protects purchasers against their loss or destruction. They can be redeemed prior to their stated maturities without any direct penalty to the purchaser, and the interest received on them is exempt from all state and local income and personal property taxes. Two series of U.S. Savings Bonds are available currently: Series EE and Series HH.

Series EE The Series EE bonds, which were introduced on 2 January 1980, replaced the previous Series E bonds. They can be purchased for one-half of their face value in denominations ranging from $50 to $10,000. Individuals cannot purchase more than $15,000 (in issue price) each year.

Interest earned on Series EE bonds is not paid periodically; instead it takes the form of the difference between the initial purchase price and the face value at redemption. In November 1982 Congress changed the method of determining the interest paid on Series EE bonds. Prior to that time, the interest was fixed and depended only on the length of time the bond was held—the longer the period, the higher the rate up to a maximum of 9 percent. Now, however, if you hold an EE bond five years or longer, the interest you receive at redemption will be determined by the level of interest rates on Treasury securities during the years you held the bond. Suppose, for example, you buy a Series EE bond and hold it, say, six years. Every six months the Treasury will have calculated an average annual interest rate on five-year Treasury bonds and notes (explained in detail in Chapter 12). So, in this case there would be 12 interest rates; now, take the average of these and then take 85 percent of that figure and you arrive at the interest rate that would be used to determine how much you receive at redemption. Continuing the example, if you purchased a $50 face-value bond for $25 and if the average interest rate was 10 percent, you would earn an interest rate of 8.5 percent. Using semi-annual compounding, your $25 bond would be redeemed at the end of six years for $41.20.

Indexing the return on Series EE bonds was done to allow investors to earn competitive rates of return during periods of rising interest rates. But what happens if interest rates fall? In this case, bonds held longer than five years will earn a minimum rate of 7.5 percent. A bond can be redeemed any time after six months from its purchase date, but if it is not held for five years it earns less than 7.5 percent interest. These rates may change, so you should obtain current information from your bank if you are considering purchasing Series EE bonds. Also, the interest earned on a Series EE bond does not have to be reported to the IRS as taxable income until the bond is redeemed.

EE bonds can be used as a device for income splitting (a tax reduction technique described in Chapter 4). An objective might be to create a *tax-sheltered college education fund,* for example. It would work this way. When a child is young, the parents buy EE bonds in the child's name. Each year the parents file an income tax return for the child including the accumulated interest on the savings bonds as income. Owners of Series EE or E savings bonds have the option of claiming interest annually as accumulated or waiting until the bond is cashed in and claiming all accumulated interest. Unless the child's total income is in excess of $3,300 (under rules in 1982), no taxes will be due (see Chapter 4). In the case of Series EE and E bonds, the interest claimed as income is measured by the increase in the bond's redemption value over the given period of time. These values can be obtained from redemption tables available at a bank or other financial institution that sells U.S. Savings Bonds. By claiming the interest earnings on the bonds each year and avoiding taxes, the funds can be withdrawn tax free and used to pay college education expenses once the child begins college.

Series HH Series HH bonds were also introduced on 2 January 1980 to replace the previous series of H bonds. Rather than accumulating to some future value like Series EE bonds, Series HH bonds pay interest semiannually. Although Series HH bonds currently pay interest at an annual rate of 8.50 percent, they must be held for five years to do so. If the bond is redeemed earlier, the current redemption value will be less than the face amount. The reduction will represent an adjustment of the interest that has already been paid the owner at the 8.50 percent rate. Until November 1983, Series HH bonds could be obtained by either purchasing them or exchanging Series EE or Series E bonds for them. Thereafter they were no longer made available by purchase, and they could only be obtained in exchange for outstanding Series EE and Series E bonds at their current redemption value, providing they had a current redemption value of $500 or more. For income tax purposes, if an exchange is made, any deferred interest on the EE or E bonds can continue to be deferred until the HH bond is redeemed.

In sum, savings bonds provide safe and reasonably good returns—if they are held at least five years. Series EE and Series HH bonds can be redeemed after six months from their purchase without penalty. In addition, various plans exist for those who wish to set aside savings regularly; they allow Series EE bonds to be purchased on a payroll deduction basis.

Life Insurance, Retirement, and Pension Plans

In certain types of life insurance, retirement, and pension plans, a portion of each payment is allowed to accumulate as savings. Although funds are channeled into these media primarily to provide insurance and retirement income, they can coincidentally generate some savings. Since these plans require periodic payments, the funds thus accumulated are sometimes called "forced" savings. Further discussions of the savings aspects of life insurance and retirement and pension plans are presented in Chapters 9 and 15.

Cash Management Strategies

By now you are probably confused about how and where you should hold your liquid funds. Perhaps the most important question is, "How much liquidity should I have to begin with?" A rule of thumb is that you should maintain about two to three months of after-tax income in liquid reserves. Should you lose your source of income, this would act as a buffer to sustain you until it could begin again. Naturally, two or three months is not a long period of time, and if you are a conservative person you could easily double this figure.

You might recall (from Chapter 3) that Art and Betty Johnston budgeted their 1985 income at $28,048, or about $2,340 a month. Actually, in their case it probably would be better to use October or November as the representative month since that is when Betty expected to be in the work force. The figure is $2,860, and using it we arrive at a liquid balance requirement of, say, $8,580 (3 × $2,860). You might recall also that our ratio analysis of the Johnstons' situation in Chapter 2 indicated they did not have sufficient cash reserves and should, therefore, attempt to build them up over time.

Once you determine your total liquidity requirement, the next question is: How should it be maintained? How much should be kept in a checking or NOW account? How much should be held in a savings account? Should you use a money market fund, or a money market account? And finally: Should you use CDs, or MMCs, or U.S. Savings Bonds? Answers to these questions would be much simpler if we knew the future direction of interest rates. It is important to understand that interest rates fluctuate considerably over time. Money market funds became popular because they offered investors very high rates of return, as high as 16 percent in the early 1980s. But those rates did not last for long. By December 1982, most had come down to about 9 percent, and prospects were that they would decline even further. They could drop as low as passbook rates, although that is not likely. If they do continue to decline, it would be advantageous to lock in currently existing higher interest rates. One could do so by buying CDs with long maturities, such as four years. Obviously, CDs are not as liquid as a money market account, and if you guess wrong about interest rates—they might go up instead of going down—you not only have less liquidity, but you would also earn less interest. This is so because the money market account interest rate will follow current interest rates very closely. As you have probably inferred by now, there is an element of risk in cash management. This risk will be discussed in greater detail in Chapter 12.

To illustrate one plan, let us consider the Johnstons again. They could be advised that they open a money market account for about $5,000. That should give them free checking at most banks, or their credit union, and allow them to earn prevailing short-term interest rates. The additional $3,580 should be used to purchase three-year CDs, earning about 9 percent (when this was written). The $5,000 will provide a good buffer for minor emergencies and the CDs could be sold, unfortunately with a penalty, if more funds are needed. Naturally, Art and Betty hope that neither source ever has to be used.

Summary

Individuals maintain cash balances for convenience, planned expenditures, and unexpected expenditures in the form of pocket money, demand deposits, savings deposits, or combination demand-savings deposits. Checking accounts (demand deposits) may be opened by anyone willing to make the minimum deposit required. Interest is not paid on most checking accounts. Savings deposits are used to accumulate funds, while combination demand-savings deposits provide checkwriting and saving functions; each of these pays interest, which is usually tied to the money market rate of interest. Examples of the latter are money market funds (MMFs), money market accounts (MMAs), and NOW accounts.

The bank at which a checking account is maintained is normally selected on the basis of convenience, cost, and services provided. The procedures involved in opening and operating a checking account are quite simple. A variety of endorsements can be used to deposit or to make payment with a check. Maintaining accurate records of account transactions minimizes the chances of overdrafts. Each month a bank statement showing all transactions, fees, and earnings for the month is sent to the accountholder. Since the statement shows the actual account balance, it must be reconciled with the checkbook ledger. The reconciliation process should uncover any errors in either the checkbook ledger or the bank records.

Aside from the standard check written on a checking account, certified checks, cashier's checks, and traveler's checks are available to meet special checking needs. Banks also offer special conveniences, such as safe deposit boxes, drive-in and walk-up windows, automatic teller machines (ATMs), pre-authorized payments, bank-by-phone accounts, and electronic funds transfer systems (EFTSs), in order to simplify and streamline banking procedures.

Savings accounts are used to accumulate money for planned future expenditures. In the process of selecting savings institutions, special attention must be given to the effective rate of interest. The effective, or true, rate of interest is largely dependent on the length of the period over which the nominal, or stated, rate of interest is compounded. The method used to calculate interest also affects the returns received from savings. Passbook accounts, special savings accounts, and club accounts are offered by commercial banks. Other common financial institutions, including savings and loan associations, mutual savings banks, and credit unions, offer a variety of savings plans. Most are insured through federal or national agencies for up to $100,000 per depositor.

Other types of savings opportunities include certificates of deposit (CDs), money market certificates (MMCs), U.S. Savings Bonds, and savings plans connected with certain types of life insurance, retirement, and pension plans. U.S. Savings Bonds, which are available in two series—Series EE and Series HH—provide a convenient and safe savings mechanism that appeals to many people. Series EE bonds are often used as an income-splitting device (for example, to create a tax-sheltered college education fund).

Because of the wide variety of checking and savings deposits available to investors, it is often wise to develop a cash management strategy. A strategy details how funds will be allocated among the competing alternatives and is shaped by weighing the higher possible return available on deposits with long maturities against the costs of illiquidity.

Housing and Other Fundamental Assets

6

One of the largest purchases you will make during your life is a house or condominium. Americans buy four or five residences during their working years and then make at least one more housing purchase as a part of their plans for retirement. So to prepare for housing purchases, you will need to itemize carefully your housing needs and your ability to pay for them. Toward that end, you must be able to compare both the physical and legal characteristics of various properties and the financing options that are available.

Home buying is not all facts and figures. It nearly always creates an emotional undercurrent. Nevertheless, if you temper your emotions with rational analysis, you are more likely to choose the housing that will serve you best.

In addition to housing, automobiles, furniture, and appliances are other major fundamental assets. The purchase of these assets also can result in sizable expenditures over a period of time. Because acquiring such assets can have a substantial effect on your budget, you should systematically evaluate the major factors that influence their cost, maintenance, and operation.

Housing Needs, Affordability, and the Option of Renting

Everybody's housing needs differ. Some people prefer quiet privacy. Others like the hustle and bustle that accompanies life in the big city. Some like to live within walking distance of work, shops, and restaurants; others do not mind a 45-minute commute. So, because each of us has our own unique set of likes and dislikes, you should start your search for housing by listing the needs that you believe are important to you, and then classify those needs according to whether their satisfaction is essential, desirable, or perhaps merely a plus.

Such a classification is important for three reasons. First, it serves to screen out housing that does not meet your minimum requirements. Second, it helps you recognize that often you will have to make tradeoffs. Seldom will you find any single home that meets all your needs. And third, classification can help you focus on those needs you are willing and able to pay for.

Housing Needs

You may find it useful to consider your housing needs in the light of demographics and psychographics. *Demographics* relates to such factors as household size, ages, occupation, sex, and marital status. *Psychographic* needs are those that evolve from mental dispositions such as personality, lifestyle, and self-concept.

Demographic Needs Perhaps the most obvious demographic needs are the housing space requirements that derive from the number and ages of the people who will be living in your household. A family with three teenage children, for example, will need a larger home than a young couple with one small child. Similarly, a two-earner professional family in which two members need to work at home sometimes may need a larger house than a family with a single wage earner who does all work away from home. The professional couple might find in-home office work areas essential.

As another example, consider the elderly and their special housing needs. Designers are giving more attention to housing for this group. Sex can also affect housing needs. Women often place high value on security in their housing, and that can affect their choice both of neighborhood and of a specific house or apartment. A recent demographic trend is that of unrelated adults' sharing a house purchase. The large number of single persons of home-buying age coupled with the high cost of housing has brought about for many people a need to share the housing expense. Such sharing also means that floor plans suitable for a married couple may have to be modified. Generally, unmarried housing-sharers desire more private space per person than do a husband and wife. In sum, you need to consider your household's wants that stem from its demographic characteristics.

Psychographic Needs Demographics can partially explain your housing needs. But also you need to consider your personality and desired lifestyle. In shopping for housing most people want more than a roof over their heads and enough room in which to live comfortably. In addition, they are concerned with their likes and dislikes—prestige, quiet, privacy, social atmosphere, recreational opportunities, and other factors. Many now want their housing environment to enhance their social life and provide the facilities that will help them keep physically fit. If you look through the Sunday newspaper real estate section of any large or medium-size city, you will find many examples of how real estate developers and property owners are trying to satisfy their buyers' and tenants' psychographic needs. So, to select the housing best for you, list those personality and lifestyle wants that are important to you.

Housing Affordability

Generally speaking, five expense items affect housing affordability: (1) the down payment, (2) points and closing costs, (3) mortgage payment, (4) insurance and property taxes, and (5) maintenance and operating expenses.

The Down Payment The first hurdle is a *down payment.* Most buyers finance a part of their purchase price, but they also are required by lenders to invest money of their own, called equity. The actual amount of down payment or equity required varies among lenders, among types of mortgage payment plans, and among properties. To reflect the amount of down payment that will be required in specific instances, lenders use the *loan-to-value ratio*; it represents the percentage of a property's value that a lender is willing to loan. The reciprocal percentage is the down payment the buyer will have to come up with.

A property that is financed with a high loan-to-value ratio involves only a small percentage of borrower equity, and, accordingly, a property that is financed with a low loan-to-value ratio involves a relatively high percentage of equity. For example, a mortgage that equals 90 to 95 percent of a property's purchase price is a high-ratio loan. It involves only 5 to 10 percent of equity money. In contrast, a mortgage that equals, say, 50 or 60 percent of a property's purchase price is a low-ratio loan.

To illustrate, assume that you buy a property for a price of $100,000, which equals its market value. With a down payment of $5,000, and financing of $95,000, you have obtained a high loan-to-value ratio mortgage. And conversely, if the property is bought with a $40,000 down payment and a $60,000 loan, you have acquired a mortgage with a low loan-to-value ratio. Generally speaking, when buying a first home, a high loan-to-value ratio loan, i.e., one with a low down payment, is advantageous to the buyer. (Specific types of financing plans are discussed later in this chapter.)

Points and Closing Costs A second hurdle when you buy a home relates to mortgage points and closing costs. *Mortgage points* are fees charged by lenders at the time they grant a mortgage loan. In appearance compensation to lenders for loan processing and paperwork, points are like interest in that they are a charge for borrowing money. They fluctuate in correlation with the supply of loanable funds that a lender has available. One point equals one percent of the amount borrowed. If $70,000 is borrowed and loan fees equal three points, the amount due will be $2,100.

Closing costs are other expenses that borrowers ordinarily pay at the time a loan is closed and title to the purchased property is conveyed to the buyer. Included in closing costs are items such as appraisal fees, mortgage tax stamps, termite inspections, and title insurance. In many instances sellers by custom or contract will assume the responsibility to pay some portion of a buyer's mortgage points and a transaction's closing costs. Seldom, however, can a buyer escape all—or even most—of these expenses. Because mortgage points and closing costs often amount to thousands of dollars, you should make sure to include them when figuring whether you can afford a wanted property.

Mortgage Payment You next need to estimate the amount of mortgage payment you can afford. This in turn determines how much you can borrow to help finance your purchase.

In the past lenders used fairly rigid rules of thumb to judge ability to make mortgage payments. Now, though, enlightened lenders recognize that people choose widely varying lifestyles and widely different ways to spend their money. For example, a borrower is just as likely to be a debt-free $40,000-a-year-single female attorney as a $25,000-a-year construction worker who is supporting a wife and three children and paying large bills to a dentist, a pediatrician, and several clothing stores. Applying the same rule of affordability to each of these prospective borrowers makes no sense.

Many lenders start their affordability analysis with rules of thumb, but will bend those rules if you can show your budget permits you to pay more than their guidelines indicate. One such rule of thumb, for instance, states that a borrower can afford no more than 35 percent of monthly take-home pay. To illustrate how this rule works, consider an example.

35-Percent Rule of Thumb Assume that your gross annual earnings are $30,000 per year and that this leaves you with a monthly take-home pay of $1,930 per month. However, because you are single and because you choose to drive a Ford Escort rather than a BMW, the lender agrees that a 38-percent mortgage payment/take-home pay relationship could be used to qualify you for your mortgage. Thus, at 38 percent, you could afford a monthly payment of $733.40. Then, using this amount, the market mortgage interest rate, the term of the mortgage, and a mortgage payment schedule, the lender can determine how much you can borrow. Using your affordable payment and, say, an interest rate of 13 percent and a 30-year repayment period, you could borrow $66,299. (To see how the monthly payments and scheduled interest rates relate to a beginning mortgage loan balance, see Table 6.1.) To compute how much house you can buy—and assuming your budget has provided for insurance, property taxes, and maintenance expenses—all you need to do is add to the mortgage amount the cash you have for a down payment. If, say, after deducting for mortgage points and closing costs, you have $15,000 available, you could buy a house that costs approximately $81,000 ($15,000 + the $66,299 mortgage you could afford).

Table 6.1 Monthly Payments and Corresponding Beginning Mortgage Loan Balances[a]

Monthly Payment / Interest Rate	Beginning Mortgage Loan Balance					
	10%	11%	12%	13%	14%	15%
$ 500	$ 56,975	$ 52,503	$48,609	$45,200	$42,199	$39,543
600	68,370	63,004	58,331	54,240	50,638	47,452
750	85,463	78,755	72,914	67,800	63,298	59,315
900	102,556	94,506	87,496	81,360	75,958	71,178
1,000	113,951	105,006	97,218	90,400	84,397	79,086

[a]30-year fixed-rate fully amortized mortgage.

Other Rules of Thumb In addition to the rule of thumb cited above, lenders use a multiple of gross earnings rule (usually $2\frac{1}{2} \times$ annual salary equals maximum purchase price), and a percent of gross (before-tax) monthly pay rule (usually 25 to 28 percent of before-tax monthly pay equals affordable monthly mortgage payment). If you apply these rules in the above example, you will see that each of them correlates closely with the others. The important point to remember, though, is that these rules serve only as a general guide. The mortgage payment you can afford depends on your choices concerning all items in your budget.

Insurance and Property Taxes Aside from the loan costs, many mortgage payments include insurance and property tax payments. The costs of *homeowner's insurance* vary with factors such as age of house, location, materials used in construction (stone, frame, brick, and so on), and geographic area. Homeowner's insurance is only carried on the replacement value of the home, not on the land. Insurance costs usually amount to approximately 0.25 to 0.50 percent of the home's market value per year. Thus the annual cost of insurance for a $100,000 house would usually range between $250 and $500. (The various types of homeowner's insurance are discussed in detail in Chapter 11.)

Another component of the monthly mortgage payment may be *property taxes.* Since these local government taxes are levied to support schools, law enforcement, and other local services, they differ in amount from one community to another. Within a given community, individual property taxes vary with the *assessed value* of property: the more expensive the home, the higher the property taxes, and vice versa. A general rule sometimes used to estimate property taxes sets them equal to 1 percent of the market value per year. On a $100,000 home, these taxes could be estimated as $1,000 per year (.01 × $100,000). Attention should be given to property taxes in the purchase of a home for two reasons: (1) they do vary from community to community, and (2) if they are included as part of the monthly mortgage payment, differences in them can cause the mortgage payments for houses of the same price to differ.

Figure 6.1 Checklist for Houses

Outside House and Yard

- □ attractive, well-designed house
- □ suited to natural surroundings
- □ lot of the right size and shape for house and garage
- □ suitable use of building materials
- □ attractive landscaping and yard
- □ good drainage with dry, firm soil around the house
- □ mature, healthy trees—placed to give shade in summer
- □ convenient, well-kept driveway, walks, patio, porch
- □ yard for children
- □ convenient parking garage, carport or street
- □ distance between houses for privacy
- □ sheltered entry—well-lighted and large enough for several to enter the house together
- □ convenient service entrance

Outside Construction

- □ durable siding materials—in good condition
- □ solid brick and masonry—free of cracks
- □ solid foundation walls—six inches above ground level—eight inches thick
- □ weather stripped windows and doors
- □ noncorrosive gutters and downspouts, connected to storm sewer or splash block to carry water away from house
- □ copper or aluminum flashing used over doors, windows and joints on the roof
- □ screens and storm windows or Thermopane glass
- □ storm doors

Inside Construction

- □ sound, smooth walls with invisible nails and taping on dry walls; without hollows or large cracks in plaster walls
- □ well-done carpentry work with properly fitted joints and moldings
- □ properly fitted, easy-to-operate windows
- □ level wood floors with smooth finish and no high edges, wide gaps or squeaks
- □ well-fitted tile floors—no cracked or damaged tiles—no visible adhesive
- □ good possibilities for improvements, remodeling, expanding
- □ properly fitted and easy-to-work doors and drawers in built-in cabinets
- □ dry basement floor with hard smooth surface
- □ adequate basement drain
- □ sturdy stairways with railings, adequate head room—not too steep
- □ leakproof roof—in good condition
- □ adequate insulation for warmth, coolness and soundproofing

Living Space

- □ convenient floor plan and paths from room to room
- □ convenient entry with foyer and closet
- □ convenient work areas (kitchen, laundry, workshop) with adequate drawers, cabinets, lighting, work space, electric power
- □ private areas (bedrooms and bathrooms) located far enough from other parts of the house for privacy and quiet
- □ social areas (living and dining rooms, play space, yard, porch or patio) convenient, comfortable, large enough for family and guests
- □ rooms conveniently related to each other—entry to living room, dining room to kitchen, bedrooms to baths
- □ adequate storage—closets, cabinets, shelves, attic, basement, garage
- □ suitable wall space and room size for your furnishings
- □ outdoor space convenient to indoor space
- □ windows located to provide enough air, light and ventilation
- □ agreeable type, size and placement of windows
- □ usable attic and/or basement space
- □ possibilities for expansion
- □ attractive decorating and fixtures
- □ extras—fireplace, air conditioning, porches, new kitchen and baths, built-in equipment, decorating you like

Source: This material taken from the booklet, *Your Housing Dollar,* published by the Money Management Institute of Household International, Prospect Heights, Illinois. 1983, p. 10

Maintenance and Operating Expenses Aside from the monthly mortgage payments, insurance, and taxes, home buyers incur maintenance and operating expenses. Maintenance costs should be anticipated even on new homes. Painting, mechanical repairs, leaks, and lawn maintenance, for example, are inescapable facts of homeownership. These costs are generally greater in older and larger homes. Indeed, a large, old home may appear to be a good buy in view of its purchase price, but because the costs of maintaining it are high, a smaller, new home might be more economical.

Another point to consider in the selection process is the cost of operating the home: specifically, the cost of utilities, such as electricity, gas, water, and sewage. Because costs vary with geographic location, type of heating and air conditioning, size of home, amount of insulation, and other factors—and can be quite sizable—operating cost estimates should be obtained when evaluating houses for purchase. In many parts of the country the cost of one fuel, such as gas, is much less than that of another, such as electricity, therefore making homes with gas rather than electric utilities far less expensive in the long run. Also, the amount of insulation should be investigated since the better insulated the home, the lower its fuel consumption and, probably, the lower its costs. If the insulation is inadequate, it may be economical to add more.

Figure 6.1 presents a checklist that home buyers can use in uncovering and evaluating repair and remodeling problems in a house they are considering for purchase. Using estimates of these costs and those associated with homeownership mentioned earlier, a budget can be prepared to determine whether ownership of a given house will interfere with other financial goals. Since housing costs usually will be the largest single item in your budget, you should estimate them carefully prior to committing yourself to the purchase of a home. It is sometimes helpful to consult a loan officer at a savings and loan or some other mortgage lender for advice without obligation concerning how much you can afford to spend.

As a final point, note that condominium developments charge unit owners a monthly fee that covers various project maintenance and operating expenses. Often, though, such charges have been set artificially low to entice buyers into the development. After moving in, buyers have found large increases in monthly charges were necessary. Beware of unrealistically low estimates of condominium homeowner fees.

Renting

Many persons cannot afford to buy their own housing, and others choose not to buy for various reasons. For example, young adults usually rent for one or more of the following reasons: (1) they do not have funds for the required down payment; (2) they are unsettled in job and family status (single, engaged, or recently married); and (3) they do not want the additional responsibilities associated with homeownership. Those who do choose to rent should be aware of the significance of the rental contract, the various advantages and disadvantages of renting, and the procedures for comparing rental and purchase costs.

Rental Contract When you rent an apartment, house, duplex, or other type of unit, you will normally be required to sign a *rental contract,* or *lease agreement.* Although oral agreements are often binding, the written contract is a legal device intended to protect the *lessor* (person who owns the property) from nonpayment or some adverse action of the *lessee* (person who leases the property). Because the contract binds you to various actions, you should make certain you understand the rental contract prior to signing it. The contract specifies the *amount* of the monthly payment, the payment *date, penalties* for late payments, the *length* of the lease agreement, any *deposit* requirements, the distribution of *expenses, renewal* options, and any *restrictions,* for example, on children, pets, or the use of facilities.

Most leases are for either six months or one year and require regular payments at the beginning of each month and either a deposit or the last month's payment as security against damages or some infringement of the lease agreement. Most of the deposit should be refunded to the lessee at the expiration of the lease; a portion of it is sometimes retained by the lessor to cover cleaning costs and any damages, regardless of how clean and unmarred the unit is left. Because the landlord has control over the deposit, a statement in writing of any damages in evidence prior to occupancy may help the lessee avoid loss of the entire amount deposited. Renters must also be sure to ask who bears expenses such as utilities and trash collection and exactly what, if any, restrictions there are on use of the property.

Advantages and Disadvantages of Renting A number of *advantages* are often cited in favor of renting. One is that in order to rent, a down payment such as is required for buying is not needed. Renting permits greater mobility in that moving in and out of rental units is not as complex and costly as moving when homes must be sold and purchased. Renting also requires less maintenance work. Other advantages may be the presence of security systems, the appeal of community living, and access to amenities, such as swimming pools and tennis courts.

The *disadvantages* of renting are primarily financial. The renter does not get any ownership as a result of monthly rent payments, which serve only to obtain use of the property. In addition, the renter does not receive any federal tax-deductible benefit from rent payments. Renters may also find that their rental units are not quiet, repairs are not made promptly, or landlords are not cooperative. In other words, since renters have little control over other tenants, repairs, and the general management of the building in which their unit is located, they are at the mercy of their landlords. Sometimes, though, renters can form associations to effectively pressure uncooperative landlords into responding to their requests. To protect renters against large rent increases, some local governments such as New York City have imposed *rent controls,* which limit annual rent increases to a reasonable level given the recent inflation experience.

Further, protection against being evicted from one's apartment as a result of *condo conversions*—the process of converting rental units into condominiums—is also provided by some local governments. This protection is offered as a result of the problems created by displacing persons—especially retired people—from rental units when suitable replacement housing is unavailable at a comparable price. In addition to local ordinances, the federal government also has proposed legislation to restrict apartments from being converted to condominiums. Although such restrictions help people who have housing, they work against buyers who are coming into the market.

Comparing Rental and Purchase Costs During the 1970s, renting a home generally was more expensive than buying. Three factors contributed to this result.

Low Prices and Interest First of all, home buyers benefitted from relatively low housing prices and mortgage interest rates. Because of market conditions, people could buy a house, and after a 10- or 20-percent down payment, their monthly mortgage payments would just about equal the rental value of the house.

Tax Deductions Two large items of housing purchase and ownership expenses—mortgage interest and property taxes—are tax deductible. Tenants could not deduct from their taxes any amount for rental payments. As a consequence, the annual after-tax cash flows of buying actually proved to be less than a renter's costs.

The calculations for such a cost comparison are shown in Table 6.2. It assumes that a tenant could have rented a house that has a market value of $60,000 for $390 a month, or $4,680 a year. In contrast, and allowing for a $10,000 down payment and $2,000 in closing costs, the after-tax annual cost of buying was $4,389.

Appreciation Adding to the annual cost advantage, homeowners during the 1970s gained rapid appreciation in the values of their houses. As Figure 6.2 shows, between 1970 and 1980 the median price of a single family house increased from $22,840 to $62,100. Although part of this increase was accounted for by improvements (larger size, central heating, and air conditioning), the major component was appreciation.

Table 6.2 Annual Rental vs. Purchase Costs (Circa 1975)

Rental Cost	
Annual Rental Cost ($390 × 12)	$4,680
Purchase Costs (.30 Marginal Tax Bracket)	
Add:	
Mortgage Payment ($50,000 @ 8%, 30 years)	$4,402
Principal = $417	
Interest = $3,985	
Property Taxes	600
Property Insurance	180
Maintenance	400
Cost of lost interest on $12,000 @ 5% after-tax rate of return	600
Subtract:	
Principal reduction in loan balance	(417)
Tax savings due to mortgage interest deduction ($3,985 × .30)	(1,196)
Tax savings due to property tax deduction ($600 × .30)	(180)
Net annual after-tax purchase costs	$4,389
Annual Benefit of Buying	$ 291 (plus appreciation)

Figure 6.2 Housing as a Hedge Against Inflation

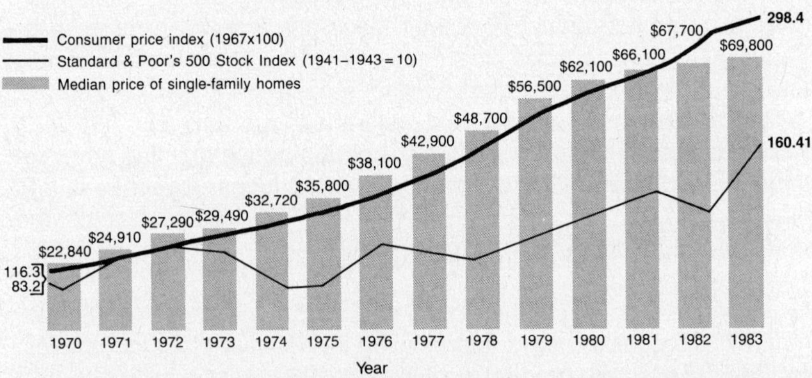

Source: Reprinted with permission from *Changing Times* Magazine, © 1976 Kiplinger Washington Editors, Inc., "How a Small Investor Can Make Money on Rental Property," May 1976, p. 16. Updated using the May 1980 and July 1984 *Federal Reserve Bulletins* (Washington, D.C.: Board of Governors of Federal Reserve System, 1980 and 1983), pp. A25, A28, A29, A42, A46, and A50.

Figure 6.3 Percentage of Families Owning Their Homes (1890–1982)

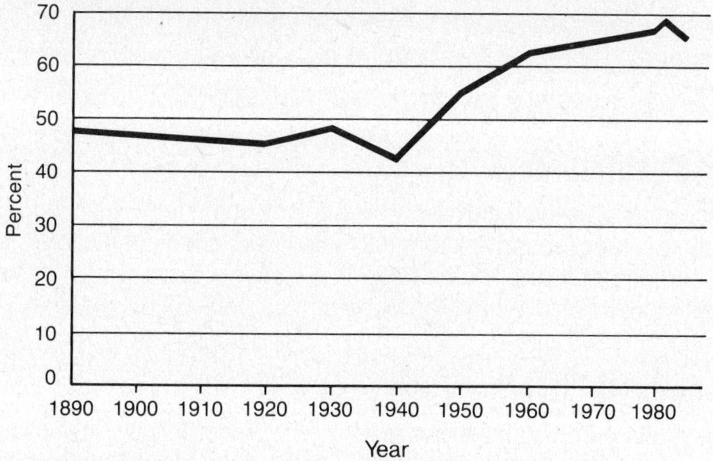

Source: U.S. Bureau of the Census. Reprinted with permission from *Savings and Loan Fact Book, 1979* (Chicago: U.S. League of Savings Associations, 1979), chart 18, p. 38. Updated data from U.S. Bureau of the Census data (1983).

Past vs. Future The financial advantages of owning over renting contributed significantly to the steady rise in home ownership that occurred in the United States up to 1980 (see Figure 6.3). In the early years of the 1980s, though, times changed dramatically. Mortgage interest rates went as high as 18 or 19 percent, mortgage payments and other ownership expenses—even after the income tax deduction—rose much faster than rent levels, and in many cities housing values leveled off or even declined. On average, between 1980 and 1984, buying a home generally proved more costly than renting, and as might be expected, the percentage of persons owning their own homes edged downward for the first time in 40 years.

Looking at population demographics, which is a prime indicator of housing demand, and the early 1983 decline in interest rates, many forecasters believe that housing will again become a good investment and that over periods of, say, from 5 to 15 years, buying a home will have economic advantage over renting. Few observers, though, are predicting the surge in housing prices that occurred between 1970 and 1980. No one really knows.

Housing Characteristics

The key to the right housing choice depends on your ability to identify explicitly and rank your wants, and then systematically compare them to the features of the homes that are available. To make this systematic comparison you should gather information about your potential housing choices in these categories: (1) legal restrictions, (2) location, (3) physical features of the property, and, (4) old, new, and custom-built.

Legal Restrictions

Restrictions on how you can use your property come from many sources. Among the most important are: zoning laws, deed restrictions, and lease and property owner association restrictions. Such restrictions can greatly improve or diminish the benefits that you will derive from your home.

Zoning Laws Zoning laws can restrict your property rights in two ways. On the one hand, they typically govern the type of property use permissible on a given site (e.g., residential, commercial, industrial). Zoning, for example, can keep a gas station operator from opening an outlet right next to your property. But zoning also might keep you from operating a beauty shop or professional office out of your home. In addition, most zoning laws divide each major classification of property use into smaller categories. For residential use, categories such as single-family, duplex-fourplex, and multiple-family are common. As a result, if your home is in an area zoned single-family, you could be prohibited by law from, say, converting your basement to an apartment and renting it.

Besides regulating use, zoning laws may also regulate the size of building that can be built on a site, the placement of buildings on a site, and, in some cases, even the appearance of the building. For instance, a zoning law might specify both the minimum and maximum number of square feet that a house must have. If your house were already at the maximum size permitted, this type of zoning law could prohibit you from building an additional room. Also, zoning usually specifies setback and sideyard requirements, i.e., how far a house must be set back from the street or sidewalk, and how much space between neighbors' houses must be preserved. Further, in many communities zoning laws are being extended to apply to the types of exterior colors and materials that property owners may use.

Deed Restrictions Deed restrictions are controls placed by a seller of a property upon a buyer. Since typically deed restrictions run with the title to a property, they are often used by subdivision developers to insure that subsequent builders and property owners will preserve the intended nature of the development. Although deed restrictions are private rather than governmental, courts can still be used to enforce them just as any other valid contractual agreement between individuals.

Figure 6.4 Example of Residential Subdivision Deed Restrictions

1. No structure shall exceed 4000 sq.ft.
2. No structure shall exceed two stories or an equivalent height.
3. No detached garages, storage buildings, or other structures shall be permitted.
4. All exterior color schemes are subject to approval of the aesthetics committee.
5. All exterior design changes or modifications are subject to approval of the architectural committee.
6. All roofs shall have a tile exterior.
7. No fence shall exceed three feet, except for those protecting a swimming pool.
8. All driveways and walks shall be constructed of concrete.
9. No structure shall be less than 2400 sq.ft.
10. All foundation exteriors shall be brick or other approved material.
11. No clothes lines, poles, or other apparatus shall be permitted.
12. No laundry shall be hung outside in any manner.
13. All decks, patios, or other structures must meet association guidelines.
14. No parking of recreational vehicles on the street.
15. Yard landscaping must meet minimum association standards.
16. Homeowners' association retains right of first refusal in all sales transactions.

As can be seen in Figure 6.4, deed restrictions can be extensive. Therefore, you should make sure that while they are satisfactory to protect you from undesirable acts of nearby property owners, they also do not prevent you from satisfying your own needs.

Lease and Property Owner Association Restrictions Some of the most specific real estate controls on tenants and homeowners stem from lease and property owner association agreements. Leases are the contracts that tenants sign (or orally agree to) when they rent a property. In consideration of the needs of other tenants and the wishes of a particluar landlord, most leases itemize a number of do's and don'ts. For example, a lease might prohibit dogs and cats, or even children. It also might limit tenants' rights to paint, wallpaper, or otherwise redecorate their units, and it might restrict the volume level of stereos and televisions.

In essence, *property owner association agreements* have the same purpose as lease restrictions. They are intended to make living in a specific complex or subdivision more enjoyable for the majority of its residents. Often these types of restrictions are drawn up and approved by owners of condominiums and other developments where owners share the use of property or facilities. Typical property owner association restrictions might: (1) prohibit owners from altering the exterior appearance of their homes or units; (2) prevent owners from doing anything that would create noxious odors, noise, or smoke for other owners; (3) detail rules and regulations that apply to day-to-day resident activities and use of the premises (e.g., hours of pool operation, procedures for tennis court sign-up, procedures for settling disputes among neighbors, and penalties for rule violators along with methods of enforcement).

Figure 6.5 Example of Condominium Rules and Regulations

I. Parking
   A. Each owner shall have two designated parking spaces. Parking elsewhere on the premises is prohibited.
   B. All boats, campers, and other recreational vehicles must be parked in the RV parking area.
   C. Owners' guests and visitors shall only park in the designated visitors' parking area.
   D. No parking of immobile vehicles permitted anywhere.

II. Swimming Pool
   A. No glass containers permitted.
   B. Swimming permitted during posted hours only.
   C. No unattended children permitted.
   D. No more than two guests per owner at any one time.
   E. All guests shall be accompanied by owner.
   F. Owners and guests must abide by all posted swimming pool rules.

III. Appearance
   A. No modification of the exterior appearance of any unit.
   B. No posting of "For Sale" signs on any unit.
   C. Drapes and curtains visible from the outside must meet association standards.
   D. No toys, yard equipment, or other items shall be left outdoors overnight.
   E. No window air conditioning units.

IV. Pets
   A. No pet more than 20 pounds nor 18" in height.
   B. No unattended or unleashed pets.
   C. Pets shall be walked only in the pet-run area.
   D. Troublesome pets may be banned from the premises.

V. Quiet
   A. No more than 4 guests permitted in a unit at any one time.
   B. No playing of stereos, televisions, radios, or other devices at volumes that create a nuisance for other unit owners.
   C. No loud talking, running, or shouting in hallways.

VI. Miscellaneous
   A. All refuse shall be placed in metal containers with lids fastened.
   B. No charcoal grills may be lit on unit patios.
   C. Bicycles shall not be left in hallways or lobbies.
   D. All waterbeds must meet standards of safety.
   E. No cooking of foods that create noxious odors on the premises.

If you are considering the purchase of a condominium or a home in a community-type development, make sure you look closely at the property owner association bylaws, rules, and regulations that you and your neighbors will have to live by. They may or may not be to your liking. As one surveyed condominium resident complained, "I don't appreciate the restrictions of the association. It's just too socialistic for me." For a sample of one condominium complex's rules and regulations, see Figure 6.5.

Location

A second major housing characteristic is its location. In this sense, location refers to a property's interrelationships with its neighborhood and city. For an analysis of location, these interrelationships are usually divided into convenience and environment.

Convenience Convenience refers to how accessible a home is to the places that you frequently need to go. In judging the relative accessibility of a residential location, most tenants and homebuyers try to see how close are schools and colleges; recreational facilities such as parks, swimming pools, and tennis courts; sources of employment; cultural facilities such as churches, libraries, and museums; and retail stores, household services, restaurants, and places of entertainment.

Another element of convenience might be the availability of bus, taxi, subway, or commuter train services. In Evanston, Illinois, a suburb of Chicago, for example, homes close to commuter train stations are generally preferred to similar homes farther away.

Environment In the analysis of real estate, "environment" has broad meaning. When you choose a home to rent or buy, you should consider the following environments: aesthetic, socio-economic, legal, and fiscal.

Neighborhoods with aesthetic appeal are those where houses and landscaped yards are well-maintained. There is little or no intrusion of noise, sight, or air pollution, and encroaching nonharmonious land uses are not evident. The socio-economic environment refers to the demographics and lifestyles of the people who live in nearby properties; and the legal environment relates to the restrictions on use that apply to neighborhood properties. Remember, in absence of zoning or deed restrictions, properties near the home you buy might be developed in a way that would lower your property's value. Further, you need to consider your potential home's fiscal environment—the amount of property taxes and municipal assessments that you will be required to pay—and, correspondingly, the government services that you will be entitled to receive (e.g., police, fire, schools, parks, water, sewers, trash collection, and libraries). Recognize that property taxes are a two-sided coin: on the one side they pose a cost; on the other, they give the property owner the right to specified services that may be of substantial benefit.

Physical Features

The next step in matching a potential home to your needs consists of an analysis of its physical features—site size, quality, and extras; housing size and floor plan; and housing amenities, style, and construction quality.

Site Analysis One of the most important features of a site is its size. Some people want a large yard for children or a garden. Others may prefer virtually no yard at all. Also, with respect to site size, if you are planning a later addition of space, make sure the site is large enough to accommodate it—both physically and legally. Site quality refers to such things as soil fertility, topography, elevation, and drainage capacity. These features are important, for example, because grass may be difficult to grow in certain types of soil, and sites with relatively low elevation may be subject to flooding. Nobody likes a basement full of water after a hard rain. In examining a site you should also note extras such as fencing, storage sheds, paved driveway, and landscaping. Each of these items can add to a property's package of benefits.

Housing Size and Floor Plan Typically housing size is measured in square footage. By American standards a small house is one of fewer than, say, 1400 square feet, medium-size houses range between 1400 square feet and 2200 square feet, and to most people a house of more than 2200 square feet would be thought of as large. Because square footage is so important in housing comparison, you should get accurate square footage measures on the homes that you are considering.

Another measure of house size is room count and floor plan. A well-designed, 1800-square-foot house might in fact be more livable than one that contains 1900 square feet. You should determine whether the sizes of individual rooms are in proportion to their intended uses. One way to check for this feature is to take measurements of your furniture (now owned or planned) and see if rooms are too small, adequate, or too large. Also, you should make sure floor plans are logical, that traffic flows throughout the house will pose no inconveniences, that closet, cabinet, and other storage space is sufficient, and that the right mix of rooms exists. For example, you should not have to cross through a bedroom to get to a home's only bathroom, or as an exclusive access to any other room; and if a house has, say, four bedrooms, it probably should also have at least two, and perhaps three, bathrooms.

Amenities, Style, and Construction Quality You should determine what amenities and personal property might be included with your potential housing choices. Houses, condominiums, and apartments are now commonly furnished with items such as draperies, carpeting, disposal, refrigerator, dishwasher, and compactor. In addition, when buying an existing property, amenities such as window air conditioners, chandeliers, fireplace equipment, and even some furniture might be included in the purchase price. Also, going through houses and reading architectural books and magazines can help you develop some preference for style and some knowledge of construction materials and quality workmanship.

Old, New, and Custom-Built

Many people develop a strong preference for either older housing, new housing, or custom-built housing. Each has certain advantages and disadvantages.

Older Home Homes ranging in age from 1 to 10 years are likely to be fully landscaped and otherwise adequately equipped, thereby providing cost savings over the new home. Homes 10 to 20 years old may appeal to some because they are in mature neighborhoods which have developed a charm of their own and have established residents. And for any of these reasons, homes that are even older may also seem attractive. Regardless of its exact age, an older home is expected to have higher maintenance costs than would a similar size and type of new home. On the other hand, the quality of construction and insulation is often better in older homes than in new homes, and they are generally conveniently located relatively close to town and near established shopping and churches. The plumbing and wiring, as well as certain structural and mechanical aspects, of an older home may not be adequate by modern standards, however; and qualified experts should be hired to evaluate these features before any purchase is made.

New Home If you buy a new home, you can be confident that it has not been abused and that all mechanical and electrical systems are probably in good working order. In most localities, builders construct homes on speculation that a buyer will be found. These *spec homes* vary in price, size, and other features and can be found in various stages of construction. If you can find and purchase a spec home in the final stages of construction, you will then have an opportunity to select the colors and types of carpeting, fixtures, and window treatments you wish. Like the houses themselves, the reputations of builders vary and should be checked as an indication of the quality of the home and the degree of cooperation to be expected in righting any defects after a purchase is made. In most states, the builder will warrant the new home against any mechanical defects for one year. Opportunities also exist to purchase insurance against mechanical failures and material defects for up to ten years.

Custom Homes You may, if you wish, employ an established builder or architect to design and build a custom home meeting your budget and layout requirements. Though this might seem the best approach, it is actually preferable to buy an old home or new spec home rather than to build your first house. It is difficult to know what types of houses and what design features best suit your lifestyle until you have had the practical experience of living in one or more houses. And although the custom home does seem to be the ideal solution to the problem of selecting a house, only certain types of people find custom building a worthwhile experience given the headaches that almost always arise from disagreements with the builder, the numerous decisions involved, and the uncertainty as to costs incurred in the construction and decorating process. There is also a limit to the creativity that can be exercised in the construction of a custom home; a home is not a good investment if it is so unique that it will not be easily resalable.

Alternative Forms of Housing

Thus far we have briefly referred to several forms of housing that you might consider. Houses, condominiums, and apartments have been mentioned. Now we will look at these and other forms of housing in a little more depth.

Single-Family House

The single-family house remains the American people's first choice in housing. It generally offers buyers privacy, adequate space, prestige, pride of ownership, and maximum property control. In recent years, however, the cost of single-family residences—and especially residential lots—has increased dramatically. In addition, as of 1982, more than 25 million Americans lived by themselves. Between 1960 and 1980 the average size U.S. household decreased from 4.2 persons to 2.7 persons. In the face of increased costs and since there are many small households, many more people are now actively considering other types of housing for long-term residency.

Mobile Homes

Factory-produced living units, such as mobile homes, can be transported on the highways to a desired location, where they can then be connected to utilities and used as residences. They generally provide between 400 and 1400 square feet of living space and range in cost from $10,000 to $40,000, depending upon size and features; the average price ranged from $15,000 to $20,000 in the early 1980s. Although occasionally used as temporary housing, mobile homes provide permanent residences for many. Their prices are low, and 7- to 15-year loans with low down payments are available. Low maintenance costs are another attractive feature. Still, because in most parts of the country the market price of mobile homes is likely to decline over time, they are not considered good investments. In many mobile home parks, however, residents are now buying the site on which their home rests. In these instances homeowners have seen appreciation because of this land component.

Cooperative Apartments

Apartment buildings in which each tenant owns a share of the corporation that owns the apartment building are *cooperative apartments.* Residents lease the units they occupy from the corporation and are assessed monthly in proportion to their ownership shares, which are based on the amount of space they occupy. The assessments cover

Table 6.3 Questions to Consider Before Buying a Cooperative Unit or Condominium

1. Who manages the building or project?
2. What control do owners have over management decisions?
3. What common grounds, facilities, and services are available to occupants?
4. How large is the monthly maintenance charge? What does it cover? When and under what circumstances can it be increased?
5. What financial responsibilities must occupants assume beyond their monthly payments?
6. How does the appraised value of the property compare with its selling price?
7. How does the investment plus the monthly assessment compare with the cost of other types of housing?
8. What rules govern the occupant's right to occupy, decorate, remodel, rent, or sell his or her individual unit?
9. What types of individuals and families live in the building?

Source: Your Housing Dollar (1984, p. 13), published by the Money Management Institute of Household International: Prospect Heights, Illinois.

the cost of services, maintenance, taxes, and the mortgage on the entire building. These can change, depending on the actual costs of operating the building and the actions of the board of directors, which determines policies of the corporation. Members of cooperatives may find that the value of their ownership interest increases over time as a result of increased market values and the reduction in the outstanding loan balance. Because profit is not the purpose of cooperative apartments, monthly assessments are likely to be less than the rent on similar accommodations in the more common type of apartment. Also, the cooperative owner receives the tax benefits resulting from interest and property taxes attributable to his or her proportionate ownership interest. As a result, coop ownership tends to be less expensive than renting a similar unit.

Condominiums

The purchaser of a *condominium* receives a title to an individual unit in a group of units and a joint ownership to any areas and facilities provided for residents of all units, such as lobbies, swimming pools, lakes, and tennis courts. Since purchasers of a condominium own their own units, they arrange their own mortgages, pay their own taxes, and pay for maintenance and building services. They are typically assessed on a monthly basis an amount deemed sufficient to cover their proportionate share of the cost of maintaining common facilities. The owners of condominium units elect a board of managers to supervise their buildings and grounds. The cost of condominiums is generally less than that of homeownership since they tend to be built in a fashion that results in better use of land and lower construction costs. Due to the phenomenal growth in the cost of new homes over the past few years, many existing apartment projects have been "condominiumized" in order to provide affordable homes. Although condominiums have traditionally appealed primarily to retired persons who do not want the responsibilities of maintaining and caring for their property, many younger people have now begun to buy them for similar reasons. This trend is expected to continue in future years. Table 6.3 lists some of the key questions to answer before buying a cooperative unit or condominium.

Rental Apartments and Houses

A variety of apartments, of various sizes and with various features, are available. Garden apartments, which are built in groups of four to six units that may be either one or two stories, are separated by landscaped green areas. Efficiency apartments are generally one-room apartments for single people. Townhouses are "up and down," or two-story apartments, usually with the bedrooms upstairs. High-rise apartments, in buildings several stories high, often have views of the city or surrounding countryside. Frequently entire houses can be rented from their owners either because they will be temporarily empty or because they are owned for rental purposes. In many parts of the country, various combinations of houses with common walls are available. The most popular among these is the duplex, which is a two-unit building resembling two separate houses joined together by a common wall.

The cost and availability of rental units vary from one geographic area to another. Unfurnished units, of course, rent for less than furnished ones. The Department of Housing and Urban Development (HUD) administers various programs which provide low-rent housing opportunities for people in lower income brackets. Because such a wide variety of rental units are available, those people who wish to rent can usually find units that conform to their location, physical, and financial requirements.

Second or Summer Homes

Second or summer homes may be regular houses, beach houses, mobile homes, cooperative apartments, or condominiums. The characteristic that differentiates summer homes from other housing is that they are used as secondary or recreational residences. Sometimes they are leased during periods when they might otherwise be idle. Tax laws permit these homes to be categorized as investments only when the owner spends less than two weeks a year in them (or less than 10 percent of the number of days during the tax year it is rented, whichever is greater). For this reason, ownership of a second or summer home is, in most instances, a luxury that only the wealthy can afford.

Time-Sharing

A relatively recent concept in real estate is *time-sharing.* Under this concept, which is also called interval ownership, buyers purchase the rights to a resort condominium or hotel unit, but only for a specified time each year, usually in one-week periods. Time-sharing has been popular, for example, in vacation spots such as Aspen, Colorado; Sarasota, Florida; and Myrtle Beach, South Carolina. Often time-share developers join national and international networks. Networks permit their buyers to swap their weeks with buyers in other resorts throughout the country and the world. Usually the time-share units are priced to approximate the long-term rental costs that a vacationer would have to pay. At present the primary drawback to buying into a time-share is resale. Appreciation can occur, but it is speculative as an investment. A prudent buyer probably should consider a time-share unit principally a consumption item.

Buying and Selling a Home

The process of buying a home often consumes time, money, and effort. Getting to know what properties are available and at what prices requires systematic search and property analysis. The buyer should also have some knowledge of real estate sales contracts.

Shopping the Market

Most people who shop the housing market rely on real estate agents for information and advice. In addition, numerous other sources of information can be used, and some buyers (renters) of properties have found it useful to advertise their needs and then let sellers initiate contact with them.

Using an Agent Most home buyers rely on real estate agents because agents are in touch on a day-to-day basis with the housing market. When you tell an agent your needs, he or she can keep a look out for properties that might be good for you. Agent service can save you a lot of time. Also, most agents will help you negotiate with the seller; assist you in finding satisfactory financing; and, although agents cannot explicitly give legal advice, they can help you fill out a real estate sales contract.

On the negative side, however, recognize that, typically, agents are employed by sellers. Unless you have agreed to pay a fee to the sales agent you are working with, by law that agent's primary responsibility is to get the seller's house sold at the highest possible price. Further, because as a rule agents get paid only if they make a sale, some might pressure you to "sign now" or miss the "chance of a lifetime." You should avoid that type of agent. Instead, you need someone who will listen to your wants, and then set about to match you with a seller in a way that will benefit both of you. Ethical and responsible agents recognize that their best interests are served when all parties to a transaction walk away happy.

Other Sources of Information Real estate agents are a good source of information about properties that are for sale (or rent). But you can also benefit by looking through the real estate advertising section in local newspapers; keeping an eye on bulletin boards where you work and in public places; and, in coming years, utilizing real estate data banks that can be accessed by personal computer. Also, in some cities experiments with real estate cable television channels are in progress.

One of the most useful ways to get information about homes that are for sale (or rent) is to drive through neighborhoods that appeal to you and look for signs on properties. This drive-around can turn up properties that are available through real estate firms as well as houses that are offered "for sale by owner." Since by-owner sellers do not have to pay a real estate sales commission, they may be willing to discount their selling price. But if you do choose to deal directly with an owner, make sure you condition your purchase agreement on the approval of both a real estate attorney and a qualified real estate appraiser.

Advertise Your Wants One way to save time in looking for housing is to make your needs known. Most newspapers publish a "real estate wanted" classified advertising section. Bulletin boards at work or in public places also can prove helpful. And informal talks with acquaintances, friends, and relatives often produce good results. The more ways you use to get the word out about what you are looking for, the better chance you have to find it.

What Price to Pay?

After you have found a property that you think will meet your needs, you must then decide what price to pay. In most cases, there is some room between the price that sellers are asking and the price that they are willing to accept. As a limit, though, you want to make sure that you do not pay more for a property than its market value. To help you decide the maximum price to pay for housing, several methods are available to you: the cost approach, the comparative-sales method, and the advice of an expert.

The Cost Approach The *cost approach* is based on the notion that a person should not pay more for a property than it would cost to rebuild it at today's prices for land, labor, and construction materials. This approach to estimating value works well for new or relatively new homes. Since older houses often suffer from wear and tear, and out-dated materials or design, the cost approach is more difficult to apply to them. To value older properties, you would have to subtract some amount for physical and functional depreciation from the replacement cost estimates. Generally, the cost approach is a good method to use as a check against a price estimate, but rarely should it be used in isolation.

Comparative-Sales Method The *comparative-sales method* uses the sales prices of properties that are similar to a subject property as the basic input variable. It is based on the principle that the value of a given property is about the same as the prices for which other similar properties have recently sold. The catch here is that all houses are unique in some respect. Therefore, the price that a subject property could be expected to bring must be adjusted upward or downward to reflect its superiority or inferiority to its comparables. Nevertheless, because the comparable-sales method is based on *selling* prices, not asking prices, it can give you a good idea about the market. In addition, if you—or your agent—can find at least one sold house slightly better than the house under consideration, and one slightly worse, their recent sales prices can serve to establish an upper and lower limit to the value of the property you are considering.

Using an Expert Real estate appraisal is a complex and technical procedure that requires good information about specific properties, their selling prices, and applicable terms of financing. Rather than rely exclusively on their own judgment, many buyers hire a real estate agent or a professional real estate appraiser to advise them about the market value of a property. As a form of insurance against paying too much, the use of an expert can be well worth the cost.

Real Estate Sales Contract

Generally, state laws specify that to be enforceable in court, real estate buy-sell agreements must be in writing and conform to certain requirements. They include: (1) names of buyers and sellers, (2) a description of the property sufficient to permit positive identification, (3) specific price and terms, and (4) usually signatures of all sellers and buyers. Real estate sales transactions often take weeks and even months to complete. Contract requirements help keep the facts straight and reduce the chance for misunderstanding, misrepresentation, or fraud.

Although these requirements fulfill the minimum necessary for court enforcement, in practice, real estate sales contracts usually treat many other contract terms. Among them are provisions that relate to earnest money deposits, contingencies, personal property, and payment of closing costs. An *earnest money deposit* is the money you are asked to pledge to show good faith. If, after you sign a sales contract, you withdraw from the transaction without a valid reason, you forfeit this deposit. For example, a valid reason for withdrawal would be one stated in the contract as a contingency clause. With a *contingency clause* you can condition your agreement to buy on such things as the availability of financing, a termite or other physical inspection of the property, or the advice of a lawyer or real estate expert. Generally speaking, your lawyer should approve all agreements *before* you sign them.

One of the most common areas for misunderstanding between buyers and sellers pertains to *personal property.* As mentioned earlier in this chapter, housing purchase agreements often include not only real estate, but also appliances, rugs and carpeting, special lighting fixtures, or portable heating or air conditioning units. When these items are included in a sale, each one should be specifically described in the contract. Also, contracts of sale often allocate closing costs between buyers and sellers. Since these amounts can be substantial, it is to the buyer's advantage to try to get the seller to pay as much as possible, and then make sure it is all written into the contract of sale.

Selling Your House

In trying to sell a house you should consider three items: preparing the home for sale, to list or not to list, and the cost of selling.

Preparing the Home for Sale Real estate agents agree that the houses that are most attractively presented to the market sell faster and at higher prices. In addition, homes should be in good repair. Although some buyers shop the market especially for "fixer-uppers" or "re-do's," these buyers expect sellers to discount their prices substantially. To help you prepare your house for sale, you can use the checklist in Figure 6.1. Since this—or a comparable checklist—is like the one buyers will use to inspect your house, you can also let it guide you to the shortcomings of your home that you should remedy.

To List or Not to List Selling your home on your own by advertising in the newspaper, by posting a "For Sale by Owner" sign in your yard, or by word of mouth can often be advantageous. The price at which you offer the house should be based upon a thorough analysis of the recent sale and asking prices of comparable properties in your general area. Often you can get the needed price data from a realtor; many of them will be most cooperative since they expect to get the listing in the event you are unable to sell the home by owner. If you try to sell by owner, you can expect to be bothered by realtors who "want to list your home" or "have a buyer lined up." If after a few weeks the house is unsold, listing it with a real estate company is probably advisable. This may be done by signing an exclusive contract giving the realtor the right to act as your agent in the sale of your home over a specified period of months. In its role as your agent, the real estate company will ordinarily advise you on the appropriate asking price for your home, advertise it, show and publicize it through multiple-listing services, and qualify prospective buyers—screen out so-called buyers who do not have the requisite funds or who merely entertain themselves by looking at houses. A listing contract with a short life, 90 days or so, will give your realtor greater incentive to sell your house quickly.

Cost of Selling If you sell your home on your own, your selling costs are usually limited to expenditures for advertising, for having a sales contract drawn up, and for updating the title. Occasionally a seller will agree to pay a fee in order to assist the buyer in obtaining the financing needed to allow the purchase of the home. If you list your house, in addition to legal and title costs, you will have to pay your realtor a commission. The 6 to 7 percent commission may seem high, but a realtor can often help you sell your house quickly at an advantageous price. Also, a commission payment may be at least partially tax deductible.

Financing and Closing the Transaction

After you and a seller negotiate the contract of sale, finalize a written agreement, and sign it, your next step toward homeownership is to obtain a *mortgage loan.* For this task you should be familiar with the kinds of lenders who grant mortgage loans, the types of mortgage contracts available, and the loan underwriting standards you will have to meet. Then, when your financing is approved, the closing date is scheduled and final legal and financial preparations are made.

Sources of Mortgage Loans

Most mortgage loans are made by savings and loan associations, which use customers' savings deposits for this purpose. The second largest source of such loans is commercial banks, which often make mortgage loans to their better customers. The third largest source is mutual savings banks (90 percent of which are located in the New England states); these banks use the money they receive in the form of customer deposits to make the loans. Another source of mortgage loans is *mortgage companies*; these companies do not accept deposits but instead use the money of large investors such as life insurance companies and pension funds to buy real estate mortgages. Although not a major source of mortgage loans, some credit unions do make mortgages available to their members. One other source for a mortgage loan is the seller of the property. Although such loans have long been in use, they have become increasingly popular in recent years. For example, during 1980–1981, more than 50 percent of the homes sold in California involved some type of seller financing.

Types of Mortgages

Technically, a real estate *mortgage* (in some states called a deed of trust) conveys a legal interest in real property to a lender as security for the payment of a debt. In addition, most mortgages on homes also include a promissory note. The lender's legal interest in a mortgaged property gives it the right to have the property sold to pay off a debt if a borrower defaults. And with the promissory note, the lender, as an additional remedy against a defaulting borrower, can take legal action to seize that borrower's savings account, automobiles, or any other assets that can be used to generate funds to pay off the mortgage.

There is no single way to classify mortgages. But for purposes here, we can look at them in two ways: (1) terms of payment and (2) whether it is conventional, insured, or guaranteed.

Terms of Payment Several different terms of payment plans are offered by most mortgage lenders. The *fixed-rate-and-payment mortgage* is the traditional type of mortgage in which both the rate of interest and the monthly payment are fixed over the life of the loan. The *graduated-payment mortgage* is a special type of fixed-rate mortgage in which the monthly payments are lower in the early years of the loan than they are in its later years. The payments are scheduled in this way in order to make it easier for a young person or family to buy housing in anticipation of future income. The *adjustable-rate mortgage* is becoming more widely used. Unlike the fixed and graduated mortgages, the rate of interest, and therefore the monthly payments, are adjusted up and down based upon the movement of a specified mortgage index at intervals ranging from six months to five years over the life of the loan. When money is in short supply, the adjustable-interest rate will increase, and when money is plentiful, it will drop. An expanded discussion of fixed-rate-and-payment, graduated-payment, and adjustable-rate mortgages along with a description of a few other types of mortgage payment plans is given in Table 6.4. An understanding of the available mortgage payment plans should assist the prospective home buyer in choosing the most suitable mortgage.

Table 6.4 Mortgage Payment Plans

Type of Payment Plan	Pros and Cons	Who Benefits
Fixed-rate-and-payment mortgage (FRPM). Both the interest rate and the monthly payment are fixed over the life of the mortgage. This is the traditional form of mortgage loan.	The size of the payments being fixed over the life of the loan allow you to know with certainty your payment obligation. On the other hand it does not offer any of the special purpose benefits that one might get from other payment plans described below.	No special group benefits from this traditional or most basic form of payment plan.
Graduated-payment mortgage (GPM). Monthly payments are arranged to start out low but get bigger later, perhaps in a series of steps at specified intervals. The term of the loan and the interest rate remain unchanged.	The main object is to make buying easier in the beginning. Initial payments have to be balanced by larger payments later. One disadvantage: Possible "negative amortization" in the early years, which means that for a time your debt grows instead of diminishing.	Mainly first-time home buyers, who have a hard time becoming homeowners, but can reasonably look forward to higher earnings that will enable them to afford the bigger payments coming later.
Adjustable-rate mortgage (ARM). Instead of a fixed interest rate, this loan carries an interest rate that may change within limits—up or down—from time to time during the life of the loan, reflecting changes in market rates for money.	Because the size of the payments you'll have to make in the future is uncertain, this loan is a bit of a gamble. If money rates go down in the future, your payments will go down. But if rates go up, so will your payments.	Helps lenders keep their flow of funds in step with changing conditions, and this in turn could make home loans easier to come by when money is tight. You may get fractionally lower interest at first or other inducements to make future uncertainties more palatable.
Rollover mortgage (ROM). The rate of interest is fixed, but the whole loan—including principal, rate of interest, and term—is renegotiated, or rolled over, at stated intervals, usually every five years.	If interest rates go up, you can expect to be charged more when you renegotiate. But you'll also have the opportunity to adjust other aspects of the loan, such as term and principal. Or you can pay off the outstanding balance without penalty. Renegotiation is guaranteed.	Lenders benefit for the same reason adjustable-rate loans are good for them. Benefits to borrowers are as shown for adjustable-rate loans, with this plus: Periodic renegotiation gives you a chance to rejigger the loan to suit your changing needs without all the expense of refinancing.
Growing-equity mortgage (GEM). The interest rate remains fixed, but the payments are scheduled to rise by 4 to $7\frac{1}{2}$ percent a year, causing the loan to be paid off within about 15 years.	Because of the accelerated payback, most lenders are willing to give borrowers a break on the interest rate. Provides an accelerated payoff of the loan, but forces the consumer to make larger mortgage payments each year.	Both lenders and borrowers benefit since the lender gets its money back sooner and the borrower who wishes to repay a mortgage quickly can do so at a lower and fixed interest rate.
Shared-appreciation mortgage (SAM). The rate of interest is lower—a mortgage banker might knock 4 percent off a 12 percent rate of return—in exchange for a partial—about one-third—interest in any gain in the property's value.	The main object is to make it easier to afford today's high-priced homes. The major drawback is that the lender usually wants to claim its share after 10 years. If the borrower cannot raise the cash, the home has to be sold.	Homeowners who could not otherwise afford to buy the home they desire. Benefits to borrowers come in the ability to share in any anticipated appreciation in the value of the home.

Source: Adapted, revised, and updated from *Changing Times*. Reprinted with permission from *Changing Times* Magazine, © 1978 Kiplinger Washington Editors, Inc., "New Ideas for Home Loans," May 1978, p. 22.

Conventional, Insured, and Guaranteed A *conventional mortgage* is a mortgage offered by a lender who assumes all the risk of loss. Typically, to protect themselves on this type of mortgage, lenders require a down payment of at least 20 or 25 percent of the value of the mortgaged property. Experience has shown that high borrower equity greatly lessens the chance of a mortgage default and a subsequent loss to a lender. However, such a high down payment requirement makes home buying unaffordable for many families and individuals.

To expand homeownership the federal government through its Federal Housing Administration (FHA) offers lenders mortgage insurance on high loan-to-value ratio loans. The *FHA mortgage insurance* program helps people buy homes even when they may have only a few thousand dollars for a down payment and for closing costs. In exchange for an annual mortgage insurance premium of one-half percent of the outstanding loan balance (which is paid by the borrower), the FHA agrees in the event of buyer default to reimburse lenders for their losses up to a specified amount. In the past, the maximum mortgage amount that the FHA could insure has just about kept pace with the national median sales price of homes. As a result, the FHA program does not offer much potential for people buying expensive homes; but for those who plan to buy homes equal to or less than a median price range, the FHA program can serve well.

In addition to the FHA, a number of private companies also insure low-down-payment mortgage loans for lenders. These plans work in a way similar to the FHA program, but the credit standards, insurable loan amounts, and insurance premiums charged by the private plans do differ somewhat. If you would like to buy a house, cooperative, or condominium, but only have a small amount for a down payment, you should ask your real estate agent or a mortgage lender whether you might qualify for either the FHA or a *private mortgage insurance (PMI) program.* These insurance plans have helped millions of home buyers.

Guaranteed loans are like insured loans, only better—if you qualify. Guarantees of mortgage loans are given by the U.S. Veterans Administration to lenders who make qualified mortgage loans to eligible veterans. This program, however, does not require lenders or veterans to pay a premium for the guarantee, and in many instances, an eligible veteran need only pay closing costs. The mortgage loan—subject to a maximum amount—can go up to 100 percent of a purchased property's appraised value. The *VA loan guarantee* is a great "fringe benefit" for those who have served in the armed forces.

Mortgage Loan Underwriting Standards

All lenders screen their mortgage loan applications on the basis of underwriting standards. Generally, these standards take into account the four C's: (1) character, (2) credit history, (3) capacity, and (4) collateral. Only if an application meets at least some minimum requirement in each of these areas will the lender grant a mortgage loan.

In the context of mortgage loan applications, character refers to a person's moral behavior, economic stability, and general attitude and appearance. Although lenders cannot deny people mortgage loans because of their race, creed, religion, national origin, or sex, they can turn down a person's application because of a tarnished image, lifestyle, or occupation. As the term implies, credit history refers to how well a mortgage applicant has met his or her past financial obligations; and capacity refers to whether potential borrowers have the earning power to meet their mortgage payments as well as their other bills and living expenses. And last, collateral refers to the relationship between the requested loan amount and the market value of the pledged property. A sure way for a lender to invite default is to loan more than a property is worth.

Because of the importance of collateral, lenders will not accept a mortgage loan application until a prospective borrower has a signed purchase contract on a house. This means that when shopping for a house, you cannot get a lender to approve a mortgage loan based simply on the amount you can afford. The property comes first.

The Closing

After your loan application has been approved, the closing process begins. It can be discussed in three steps: (1) the RESPA statement, (2) the title check, and (3) the closing statement.

RESPA Since 1974, closings on owner-occupied houses, condominiums, and apartment buildings of four units or less have been governed by the *Real Estate Settlement Procedures Act (RESPA).* This act (and its succeeding 1975 amended version) intended to spur closing cost reductions primarily by prohibiting kickbacks made in conjunction with closing services and by requiring advance notice of costs to buyers.

The idea was that real estate closing costs were higher than necessary because in many areas real estate agents, attorneys, and others received kickbacks from lenders or title insurance companies for steering business to them. Furthermore, because buyers often learned the total amount of closing costs late in the closing process, they did not have time to shop for competing providers of services (e.g., legal, financial, inspections, title insurance, property insurance). With steering and delayed notice of costs, price competition could not work.

The specific requirements of RESPA are given in a U.S. Department of Housing and Urban Development booklet *Settlement Costs and You: A HUD Guide for Homebuyers.* The law requires that lenders give a copy of this guide to potential borrowers. If read, the guide can take much of the mystery out of the closing process. And although closing expenses still may climb into the thousands of dollars, home buyers often can save significant amounts if they do shop for financing, insurance coverages, and other closing items, rather than merely accept the costs given to them by any one lender or other provider of closing services.

The Title Check Numerous legal interests can exist in real estate simultaneously. For example, there can be the rights of the owner(s), the rights of the lender(s), the rights of lienholders (such as those held by an unpaid roofing contractor), and rights of easement holders. Before you take title to a property, therefore, you want to make sure that the title is free of all liens and encumbrances (except those that are specifically referred to in your purchase agreement) and that the owners who are conveying title to you actually have the legal interest they claim.

Although it is up to you to question the quality of the title to the property you are buying, in most cases an attorney or title insurance company performs the necessary research of legal documents and courthouse records. The customary practices and procedures used to verify title, and the costs involved in doing so, vary widely throughout the country. But regardless of the specific custom in your area, some title check should be an essential part of your closing process.

The Closing Statement A closing statement, provided to both buyer and seller at closing, accounts for the monies that change hands at closing. Many agents use the form recommended for use under RESPA and written by the U.S. Department of Housing and Urban Development. Because a closing statement sets forth who gets how much, and who pays how much, understanding the logic of its entries is crucial to determining whether the contracted values-in-exchange have been realized.

Other Fundamental Assets

The automobile is probably the first major expenditure most persons make. Typically, an individual purchases an automobile every one to four years and pays anywhere from $1,000 to $20,000 for it, depending on its make, model, and age. Because you will probably make an automobile purchase decision ten or more times during your life, a systematic approach to selection and financing can help you achieve significant savings.

Furniture and appliances are other important fundamental assets. Although they are probably not purchased as often as automobiles, they nonetheless represent major budget items that require careful analysis. This part of the chapter briefly considers the purchase of automobiles, followed by furniture and appliances and several other fundamental assets.

Automobiles

The automobile plays a major role in our society. It is an important factor in the economy, since the automobile industry provides hundreds of thousands of jobs and is a major consumer of raw materials produced by other vital industries, such as steel. Although the primary motive for automobile ownership is to provide transportation, automobiles are sometimes viewed as a status symbol or purchased as part of a hobby or investment. There is a wide variety of types, styles, sizes, and colors. In addition to domestically (U.S.) produced automobiles, imported cars have been gaining a large share of the American automobile market.

Affordability Before you shop for a car, you should determine how much you can afford to spend. This estimate should be stated on a monthly basis in order to be consistent with your budget. The amount available should result from a careful analysis of your available resources in view of other necessary expenses (including housing) and your transportation requirements. Once the monthly amount available has been estimated, you should evaluate the costs of owning various types of automobiles in order to select the most suitable one for you.

Ownership Costs The monthly cost of automobile ownership consists not only of payment for the car but also includes the cost of insurance, licenses, fuel, oil, tires, and other operating and maintenance outlays. Certain of these costs—*fixed costs*—are the same regardless of how much you drive, while others—*variable costs*—depend directly on the number of miles you drive. The biggest fixed cost is likely to be the monthly *installment payments* associated with the repayment of a loan you use to finance the car; the biggest variable cost will be for fuel (that is, gas, diesel fuels, or gasahol). Table 6.5 gives an illustration of an itemized listing of the monthly costs associated with a proposed purchase. The total ownership cost per month in this illustration is $351—that is, $260 in fixed costs and $91 in variable costs. Based on an expected 12,000 miles of driving each year, the cost per mile will be 35.1 cents. In order to afford the car under consideration, you would need $351 a month to meet the total ownership costs. By comparing this amount to that amount available for meeting this expenditure, you could decide whether the car is affordable for your budget.

Other Purchase Considerations A variety of other items should be addressed when considering an auto purchase.

Table 6.5 Estimating Total Monthly Auto Ownership Costs

Ownership Cost	Monthly Amount	Cost per Mile[a]
(1) Fixed Cost		
Installment Loan Payment	$185	$.185
Auto Insurance	30	.030
License Plates and Property Taxes	15	.015
Parking Cost	30	.030
Total Fixed Cost	$260	$.260
(2) Variable Cost		
Fuel	$ 60	$.060
Oil	3	.003
Tires	6	.006
Repairs and Maintenance	22	.022
Total Variable Cost	$ 91	$.091
Total Ownership Cost [(1) + (2)]	$351	$.351

[a]The number of miles driven per month is assumed to be 1,000.

Depreciation *Depreciation cost* can be viewed as the difference between the price at which you purchase a car and the price at which you can sell it at some future date. Although it does not represent a cash outlay affecting the monthly ownership costs, depreciation does merit attention since some cars depreciate more rapidly than others in the same price range.

New or Used? The advantages of buying a used car are (1) it is less expensive than a comparable new car; (2) it will not depreciate in value as quickly as a new car; and (3) because it is less expensive, the purchaser does not have to put down as much money as is required on a new car. On the other hand, the main disadvantage of buying a used car is the uncertainty of its mechanical condition. The *federal odometer disclosure law* offers some protection by requiring the seller to give the buyer a signed statement attesting to the accuracy of the mileage shown on the odometer of a used (or a new) car; you still have to figure whether the additional repair costs on the used car will be less than the depreciation amount a new car will incur.

To compare the retail or wholesale prices of various autos, you can consult automobile price guides that are published periodically. These booklets are available at bookstores and newsstands and probably from automobile loan officers.

American or Imported? Many imported cars are smaller and lighter in weight and therefore offer better fuel economy than American cars, although the differences have tended to narrow. When considering the purchase of an imported car, you should determine the availability of local service (and parts) at a reasonable price.

Size, Body Style, and Features The size, body style, and features selected on a given automobile are largely dependent upon your motive for purchasing it. When considering these items, you should give some thought to their cost and effects, not only on performance, handling, and appearance, but also on fuel economy, reliability, repair problems, and the resale value of the car.

Reliability and Warranties The *reliability* of a car can be assessed by talking with friends owning similar cars and through objective assessments published in various consumer magazines and buying guides, such as *Consumer Reports.* The *warranty* offered by the manufacturer of new cars should also be studied and compared to that offered by other competing manufacturers. Significant differences may exist. In addition, at extra cost some auto manufacturers and dealers offer extended warranty contracts. Whether such a contract is a good buy for you partially depends on how hard you are on your car, as well as your budget's capacity for unexpected repair expenses.

Old Car: Trade-In or Sell? When buying a new or used car from a dealer in order to replace an old car, the question of a trade-in arises. Although trading-in is convenient, you are generally better off financially to sell your old car outright. If you are willing to take the time, you can usually sell your car above the wholesale price typically offered by a dealer on a trade-in.

Other Purchase Considerations You should carefully consider fuel economy. When considering a new car, the *EPA (Environmental Protection Agency) mileage ratings* are especially useful. Manufacturers are required to post on new vehicles a sticker indicating the number of miles per gallon each model is expected to get (as determined through EPA tests) for both city and highway driving. The number of *safety features* built into the car should also be considered. These features are likely to be similar in new cars as a result of government regulations, but many features may not be present in used cars. *Auto insurance costs,* which vary depending upon make, model, and other factors (and are discussed in detail in Chapter 11), also should be assessed when considering automobile purchase alternatives.

The Purchase Transaction Once you have selected two or three cars that meet your requirements, you will begin the purchase process by making an offer. If a dealer is involved in the transaction, the offer will form a written *sales contract.* To show good faith, you may be required to include a deposit of $100 or more with your offer. Since such a contract becomes binding when accepted by the dealer, you should make certain that your offer is not too high. Always offer less than the asking or sticker price (on a new car); all the seller can do is say no. The seller will likely counter with a price somewhere between your offer and the asking price. New cars can typically be purchased for around 15 percent below the sticker price for American cars and at about 10 percent below the sticker price for imported cars. Once your offer has been accepted by the seller, you will have to pay him/her and take possession of the car. At the time you pay, you should also receive the title to the car. If you are not paying cash for the car, you will need to arrange financing through the dealer or some other financial institution. (The key aspects of an automobile loan, which is an installment loan that can be quickly negotiated with good credit, are included in Chapter 8.)

Maintaining Your Automobile Like any tangible asset, the automobile must be properly maintained and repaired in order to preserve its function as well as to enhance its resale value. Maintenance and repairs should be performed by a dealership or independent garage that will stand behind its work and not do unneeded repairs. Performing *preventive maintenance,* which typically involves regularly scheduled changes and checks of various fluids, filters, and other key components, should reduce the frequency and seriousness of repairs.

Leasing an Automobile An alternative to purchasing a car is *leasing,* which typically involves receiving the use of a car in exchange for contractually agreeing to make monthly lease payments over a specified period of time, typically two to three years. The size of the lease payments depends upon the car's cost, the term of the lease, the number of miles the car is expected to be driven, and other financial factors. Because lease payments are tax deductible if the car is used in a business, leasing is most often done for business reasons. The convenience and general predictability of costs (since maintenance costs are usually borne by the lessor) also make this arrangement attractive to many individuals. Leasing sometimes allows people to obtain the use of a car they could not have otherwise acquired because they do not need to pay a sizable down payment. In most cases, however, leasing for nonbusiness purposes is more costly than buying.

Furniture and Appliances

Another group of fundamental assets that you will purchase during your lifetime consists of furniture and appliances. Although these assets can be leased, most people purchase them. Since the cost of furniture and appliances can be great, a few comments about purchase and financing should be helpful to you when acquiring them.

Purchase Considerations When buying furniture or an appliance, attention should be given to the purchase cost, function, operating and repair expenses, and appearance. By shopping around you should be able to find pieces that perform the desired function at the best price. Often by paying an extra $50 to $100 you can purchase an asset that will provide significantly greater satisfaction. In order to get an indication of the quality and general reliability of a given item of furniture or an appliance, it is helpful to consult some type of consumer *buying guide,* such as the monthly magazines *Consumer Reports* (which publishes its *Annual Buying Guide* in December), *Changing Times,* and *Consumers Digest.* These are valuable sources of ratings and comparative statistics on furniture, appliances, and many other consumer goods. The operating, including energy, costs and repair costs of items requiring power and/or having moving parts or fabric components should also be considered. In spite of a low purchase price an item of furniture or an appliance often will have a high total ownership cost if its operating and repair costs are above average or if its energy costs are excessive. Information on operating, maintenance, and repair costs can be obtained from consumer publications and from friends who have purchased similar items. Many appliances come with an "Energy Guide" rating that is attached to the appliance. A final consideration that might enter into your purchase decision is appearance, which may offer a desired degree of personal satisfaction. Clearly, when shopping for furniture and appliances, you should give the quality with which they function, purchase costs, and expected operating and repair costs primary attention.

The Purchase Transaction You can benefit greatly by shopping around for furniture and appliances. Once you have selected the basic brands and models you are interested in, you should check several stores for the best deal. Many furniture and appliance dealers will negotiate prices. You may be able to pay less than the amount shown on the price tag if you simply ask. You may be able to learn from friends and business associates which dealers have the best prices. Considering the purchase of a floor model or a second-hand item is sometimes worthwhile. Because furniture and appliances have fairly long lives, you may find that the savings resulting from the purchase of used items more than compensates for the slight wear they show. However, you should know what model you are buying—the preceding year's model or the floor model. And before finalizing your purchase, you should also look into who pays for delivery, whether taxes are included in the price quoted, and whether there are any installation costs. If you are able to plan the timing of your purchases, you can often take advantage of sales on furniture in January and August and on appliances in October and November.

Financing the Purchase Because of the magnitude of the purchase of many items of furniture or appliances, borrowing money may be necessary to make the purchase. Of course, before you begin to shop, you should have some idea about whether or not you need financing. Some furniture and appliance dealers offer "90 days same as cash" or "30-60-90 day" financing arrangements, which allow you to pay for the merchandise in three monthly installments without interest. A number of the installment payment plans used to purchase these types of assets are discussed in detail in Chapter 8. If you will need financing on a purchase, you will want to analyze and compare the cost of financing plans offered by various dealers. Differences in the total amount expended can be significant.

Some Other Fundamental Assets

Attention thus far in the chapter has been devoted to the more expensive fundamental assets that most Americans would agree are necessities. Two other groups of relatively expensive fundamental assets are personal and household goods and recreational items.

Personal and Household Goods Many assets, such as clothing, dishes, silverware, and small appliances, are necessary to allow you to function in today's society. Items that are faddish should be avoided since their use is limited. Once in a while, though, it may give you an emotional boost to buy some article that is much in vogue. Try not to buy on pure emotion or impulse; ask yourself whether you really need the item and whether the same money might be better spent elsewhere or put into savings and investments. Since personal and household goods normally decline in value quickly and cannot be easily sold, they are not good investments. Plan purchases of all items to coincide with sale months.

Recreational Items Leisure time is often devoted to some type of recreational activity that necessitates the purchase of certain assets. Before buying recreational items, you should make sure their purchase does not upset your budget or delay your progress toward your personal financial goals. Many of these assets—boats, campers, motorcycles—may depreciate rapidly in the first year or so of their lives. With this in mind, you might want to consider buying used items.

If you are convinced that some type of major recreational expense is justified on the basis of both expected use and your ability to afford it, then you should carefully shop for the item that best fulfills your needs. Ask someone who is an expert in the activity about best choices for your type of usage. You do not want to buy a high-powered ski boat if your primary objective in purchasing a boat is to fish. As for all major outlays, research the quality, safety, warranties, operating costs, and repair costs of alternative items. Try to get the best value per dollar. Be sure, too, that you consider insurance costs in your analysis. Separate insurance policies are required on major recreational assets. If you do not intend to make a cash purchase, study the various financing plans available. Once you acquire a major recreational asset, be sure to properly maintain it. If you find that you are not really using the asset, sell it quickly so that you can recover as much of your investment as possible.

Summary

The first step toward fulfilling your housing needs is to define those needs, usually in light of demographic and psychographic considerations. Next, you should decide how much you can afford to spend. Although rules of thumb can give you a general idea, the exact amount depends on the lifestyle and personal spending habits you choose. To estimate the costs of buying and ownership you should consider five cost items: (1) down payment, (2) points and closing costs, (3) monthly mortgage payment, (4) insurance and property taxes, and (5) maintenance and operating expenses. Many families and individuals decide to rent. Over longer periods, however, most experts believe that renting is less desirable than owning—both from economic and non-economic viewpoints.

Shopping for housing requires that you identify those housing characteristics that will affect how much you will enjoy your home. Among them are legal restrictions, location, physical features, and age. These characteristics apply to the many forms of housing available, such as single-family homes, mobile homes, cooperatives, condominiums, apartments, second or summer homes, and time-sharing. After deciding the characteristics and form of housing you want, you should systematically shop the market. Often, real estate agents can help you in buying (and also when it is time to sell). Obtaining the right financing and attending to the details of closing also are essential steps in buying a home.

Other fundamental assets, such as automobiles and furniture and appliances, are important since they are relatively expensive items that people are likely to purchase a number of times during their lives. When evaluating potential automobile purchases, you must estimate ownership costs, considering them in light of the amount of money available for buying a car. Other factors to consider include the anticipated depreciation; new versus used cars; American versus imported cars; differing sizes, body styles, and features; reliability and warranties; the disposition of one's old car; and other factors relative to fuel economy, safety, and insurance. Once purchased and financed, if needed, a car should be properly maintained and repaired. As an alternative to buying a car, some people find leasing attractive.

Furniture and appliances should be purchased only after carefully considering alternative costs, function, operating and repair expenses, and appearance. A number of consumer publications providing such information is available. Other major fundamental assets include personal and household goods and various types of recreational items. Careful selection and conscious avoidance of impulsive buying are important in the purchase of these types of assets.

Borrowing on Open Account: Credit Cards and Bank Cards

7

The ability to plan, select, and acquire fundamental assets is not enough to insure your financial success. You must also become familiar with the opportunities and techniques available for using liabilities to finance the acquisition of assets. One important aspect of liability management is concerned with borrowing on open account, which involves using some type of store charge account or credit card in order to make transactions.

Because the availability, costs, and conditions normally included as part of open account credit are likely to vary, you must learn when, in what amounts, how, and where to obtain and use this form of borrowing. A knowledge of these fundamental aspects of open account credit should enhance your ability to achieve your personal financial goals.

The economy we live in today is often called a "credit economy" because of the ready availability as well as liberal use of credit to make various types of purchases. This chapter discusses borrowing on an open account, an informal method of borrowing commonly used to finance less expensive goods and services.

Fundamentals of Borrowing

Consumers, businesses, and governments all rely heavily on the use of borrowing to make transactions. Without credit, businesses could not supply the goods and services needed to satisfy consumer demand. The availability of credit to business also provides for higher levels of employment and helps raise our overall standard of living. Local, state, and federal governments use borrowing to implement various projects and programs that result not only in an increased standard of living but in additional employment opportunities as well. Borrowing, therefore, helps fuel our economy and enhance the overall quality of our lives. Of course, consumers in a credit economy need to know how to establish credit. They must also be aware of the dangers of improperly using credit.

Why Borrow?

People typically borrow money for use in paying for goods and services. Many reasons exist for borrowing. Most commonly, borrowing is used because the total outlay is too large to be paid out of current resources. This is particularly true for people age 25 to 44, since in many cases they have not had time to accumulate the liquid assets required to pay cash outright for major purchases and expenditures. As people begin to approach their mid-forties, their investment assets begin to increase and their debt obligations tend to be reduced.

Most people do not pay cash for *large outlays*, such as purchases of houses and cars, but rather borrow a portion of the purchase price. They then repay their loan on some scheduled basis. In this way, borrowing allows people to obtain the immediate use of an expensive asset even though this loan may not be fully repaid for many years. Another reason people sometimes borrow is to meet a *financial emergency*—for example, to cover living expenses and make payments on other loans during a period of unemployment or to purchase plane tickets in order to visit an ill relative. As was indicated in Chapter 5, however, savings should be maintained to meet such financial emergencies, and the necessity of borrowing should be avoided if at all possible.

An increasingly common motive for borrowing is *convenience.* Merchants as well as banks have made available a variety of charge accounts and cards that readily allow consumers to charge the purchase of many goods and services. Although in many cases no interest is levied, these credit card purchases represent a form of borrowing since payment is not made at the time of the transaction, and they should be shown as liabilities on the personal balance sheet. Borrowing is also done for *investment* purposes. As will be discussed in Chapters 13 and 14, investors can arrange to finance partially the purchase of certain securities with borrowed funds. Real estate investments, too, commonly involve borrowed funds.

Benefits of Borrowing

The ability to borrow, regardless of the underlying motive, provides certain benefits to borrowers, savers, merchants, and society in general.

Borrowers The *borrower* benefits by being able to obtain expensive goods or services while spreading the payments for them over the future. Borrowers may also benefit from two other factors—taxes and inflation.

Taxes Because those persons who itemize their tax deductions can deduct all interest paid during the year (see Chapter 4), our tax structure provides favorable treatment for borrowers. Of course, the tax deductibility of interest does not fully eliminate the cost of borrowing. For example, assume that you paid interest of $1,000 in the current year, that you are in the 25 percent tax bracket, and your itemized

Table 7.1 Impact of Interest Deduction on Taxes

	Without Interest Deduction	With Interest Deduction
Income After All Deductions and Credits Other Than Interest	$18,000	$18,000
Less: Interest	0	1,000
Taxable Income	$18,000	$17,000
Taxes (25 Percent)	4,500	4,250
Income After Taxes	$13,500	$12,750

deductions exceed the zero bracket amount. Table 7.1 illustrates the impact of this interest deduction on taxes if your income after all deductions and credits other than interest is $18,000. The tax deductibility of the $1,000 in interest causes the taxes to be reduced by $250 ($4,500 − $4,250) and therefore results in only a $750 ($13,500 − $12,750) drop in income after taxes. The $1,000 interest payment reduced income by $750 due to the favorable tax treatment of interest. Thus, although interest must be paid, our tax structure provides some relief by treating it as a tax-deductible expenditure.

Inflation Because inflation reduces the purchasing power of money, the consumer who borrows money and repays it during a period of increased inflation may benefit. The benefit results because the borrower in this situation can repay the debt in dollars "cheaper" than those initially borrowed. For example, assume that you borrowed $2,000 exactly one year ago and you must repay this amount today. Also assume that the purchasing power of a dollar, as reflected in the consumer price index, is such that what cost $1.00 a year ago costs $1.09 today. In other words, the dollar today can purchase only about 92 percent ($1.00 ÷ $1.09) of what it would buy one year ago. Therefore, the $2,000 being repaid today would be worth only $1,840 (92% of $2,000) in terms of the money originally borrowed. Lenders attempt to adjust the interest rates they charge to reflect the impact of expected inflation on the purchasing power of the dollar.

Savers As was pointed out in Chapter 5, certain financial institutions accept savings deposits from which they obtain funds to loan out. A major portion of the interest paid to the savings institutions on these loans is returned to the depositors. This process of *financial intermediation* benefits savers by giving them a return on their unused funds, while at the same time satisfying the needs of borrowers. Clearly, without the interest paid by borrowers, financial institutions would not be able to pay their depositors interest on savings accounts.

Merchants By offering credit to their customers, merchants can often attract and retain business that might otherwise go elsewhere. The use of credit enables them to sell expensive items, such as automobiles, appliances, and boats, that purchasers would not be able to afford were they required to pay in full at the time of purchase. Borrowing arrangements are vital to merchants in two other ways as well: they generally receive credit from their suppliers and borrow the funds needed to extend credit to their customers.

Society In the formative years of our country, borrowing from abroad enabled settlers to buy machinery and equipment needed to build production facilities. As the nation matured, institutions and mechanisms were created to gather and make available funds for borrowing by consumers, business, and government. The borrowing mechanism still remains of key importance to the growth and development of our society. Not only must consumers be able to purchase expensive goods, but business and government too must be able to obtain the financing needed to increase productive capacity, economic growth, and employment and to fulfill growing consumer demand. The ability to borrow is one of the cornerstones of a capitalistic economy.

Establishing Credit

The willingness of lenders to extend credit to you depends upon their assessment of your credit worthiness—your ability to repay the debt, along with interest, on a timely basis. They will look at many factors in making this decision, such as your present earnings and net worth. Equally important, they will look at your credit history. Thus it is worth your while to build a good credit rating; if you are a woman, you may have to take extra steps to do this.

Things To Do First, open checking and savings accounts. These signal stability to lenders and also indicate that you handle your financial affairs in a businesslike fashion. If you pay cash for everything and use the mattress to store savings, only you will know you are a good credit risk. Second, use credit. Open charge accounts and use them periodically even if you prefer paying cash; for example, get a credit card from a major oil company and charge your gas and oil. You might pay higher prices for these products but you will partially offset them by having the use of your money for a longer period of time. In the process, you become identified as a reliable credit customer.

Third, obtain a small loan whether you need it or not. If you do not actually use the money, put it in a liquid investment such as a money market account or certificate of deposit. The interest you earn should offset much of the interest expense on the loan, and the difference can be viewed as a cost of building good credit. (It goes without saying that you repay the loan promptly, perhaps even ahead of schedule to minimize the difference in interest rates.) Your ability to obtain a large loan in the future to purchase a car, or other major item, will depend upon the availability of information on how you managed smaller loans in the past.

Credit Problems for Women Limitations on credit for women are changing rapidly. If you are a woman and credit is important to you, then make sure the following steps are taken. First, use your own name when filing a credit application. If you are single, you will use your given name—Joan Brown, for example. If you are married—suppose Joan Brown marries Thomas Watkins—*do not* use a social title, such as Mrs. Thomas Watkins. This is not your legal name and it could belong to many other women. In marriage, a woman can select several legal names; for example, if she takes her husband's name, she could choose Joan Watkins or Joan Brown Watkins. By selecting a legal name and using it consistently, you build your own credit history. Second, make sure information reported to the credit bureau is in your name as well as your husband's. This has been done automatically since June 1977, but account activity prior to then may be in your husband's name only. Third, when you marry you may wish to retain a credit file separate from your husband's, particularly if you have already established a good credit rating. You should then notify creditors of your name change and of your intention to maintain your own file.

Dangers of Borrowing

Although borrowing provides a mechanism whereby borrowers, savers, merchants, and society in general can benefit, certain dangers are associated with its use.

Inflationary Effects on the Economy One problem believed to result from the excessive use of consumer credit is inflation. If consumers have too little difficulty in borrowing to purchase goods and services, the demand for these items may rapidly increase, thereby causing prices to rise. This type of *demand-pull inflation* results from too many dollars chasing too few goods and services. Although various types of governmental controls exist for regulating consumer credit, the danger of inflationary pressures from liberal use of credit is real. A common argument denies that credit has an inflationary effect. It has been held that if credit or charge account use increases the volume of sales significantly, the fixed costs per unit of producing the item are reduced, thereby resulting in no increase in cost and possibly even a decrease—a portion of which may be passed on to the consumer.

Effects of Borrowing Costs Another aspect of borrowing that causes the prices of goods and services to rise is the borrowing costs themselves. Sellers must be compensated for extending credit to consumers; if consumers borrow or use credit to purchase a good or service, they pay interest either directly at a specified rate or indirectly in the form of an increase in the purchase price. Given the fact that consumers pay more when they use credit than when they do not, the use of credit reduces the amount they can purchase. On the other hand, some would argue, again, that the increased cost of goods and services may be offset by the fact that with credit available more goods and services are demanded, thereby possibly lowering their unit costs of production.

Overspending Probably the biggest danger in consumer credit is that it makes it easy for people to *overspend,* or incur more obligations for future payments than they have income available from which to pay. People who overspend eventually arrive at a point where they must choose either to be delinquent on their payments or sacrifice necessities such as food and clothing. If payment obligations are not met, the consequences are likely to be lawsuits, a damaged credit rating, or personal bankruptcy. The use of a budget as described in Chapter 3 provides a means of assessing your borrowing potential and planning for and using consumer credit while not subjecting yourself to the dangers of overspending.

Bankruptcy

In recent years, around 500,000 people annually file for *personal bankruptcy* in the United States. For those people, personal bankruptcy is the end of the line for deteriorating financial affairs. Filing a petition in bankruptcy is a serious act and should be taken only as a last resort to solving credit problems. Insolvency is not something that happens overnight; it usually reflects continually increasing use of credit until the total monthly payments simply cannot be met. The family may be pursuing a lifestyle beyond its means, or an unfortunate event, such as an illness or loss of a job, may have taken place. If one cannot resolve the insolvency situation on one's own, then protection from the courts is needed. Two remedies are available: (1) a Wage Earner Plan, and (2) straight bankruptcy.

Wage Earner Plan A *Wage Earner Plan* is a plan for scheduled debt repayment over future years. It may be a viable alternative to straight bankruptcy when a person has a steady source of income and there is a reasonable chance he or she can repay the debts in three to five years. The majority of creditors must agree to the plan, and interest charges along with late payment penalties are waived for the repayment period. Usually, creditors will go along with this plan because they stand to lose more in a straight bankruptcy. After the plan is approved, the individual will make periodic payments to the court, which in turn pays off the creditors. Meanwhile, he or she retains the use of, and keeps title to, all of his or her assets.

Straight Bankruptcy *Straight bankruptcy* can be viewed as a legal procedure that results in "wiping the slate clean and starting anew." However, it should be noted that bankruptcy does not eliminate all the debtor's obligations, nor do they necessarily lose all their assets. For example, alimony and child support payments continue, but the debtor does not lose certain payments from Social Security, retirement, veterans', and disability benefits. In addition, one may retain equity in a home (up to $7,500), a car (up to $1,200), and other personal assets, such as clothing, books, and tools of one's trade.

The bankruptcy laws have undergone important changes in recent years. Professional legal advice is obviously needed if a formal petition is filed. Agencies that can assist—usually without charge—in credit counseling include the National Foundation for Consumer Credit, which provides counseling services in over 200 locations throughout the country. Another good place to start looking for help is the local Better Business Bureau or Chamber of Commerce. Such organizations are very concerned that consumer credit be widely available and used properly. In most instances, a debtor can work with a *credit counselor* who will help prepare a budget and may even negotiate with creditors to establish workable schedules for repaying outstanding debts. The counseling service will often go so far as to collect money from the debtor and distribute it to the creditors.

There are also profitmaking organizations that specialize in acting as intermediates between borrowers and creditors and provide counseling services. Their counselors generally attempt to reduce the size of payments, the size of the debt outstanding, or both. Because of their high fees, profitmaking credit counseling services are not recommended.

Open Account Credit

Open account credit, often referred to as *charge accounts*, is a form of credit extended to a consumer in advance of any transactions. Typically a store or bank agrees to allow the consumer to buy or borrow up to a specified limit on open account. Credit is extended as long as the consumer does not exceed the established *credit limit* and payments are made in accordance with the terms specified. When a store issues open account credit, it is usually applicable in that store or its branches. A Penney's charge card, for example, is useful only in Penney's stores; open account credit issued by banks, such as *MasterCard* and *VISA* accounts, however, can be used to make purchases at a wide variety of businesses. In the remainder of this chapter, attention is devoted to various characteristics and types of open account credit.

Open Account Credit Illustrated

Consumers who use open account credit can generally avoid paying interest charges if they pay the full amount of the unpaid account balance each time they are billed. For example, assume that in a given month an individual has charged $15.58 worth of purchases on an open account at a department store. Sometime within the next month, that individual will receive a statement from the store. The statement will show any past unpaid balances, any new charges during the past month, any finance charges (interest) on the unpaid balance, the preceding period's payment, any other credits, such as those for returns, and the new balance. A minimum payment is also generally specified. One such statement is shown in Figure 7.1. By evaluating this statement, you should be able to gain an understanding of how open account credit works.

Transactions The statement includes the itemized transactions that have occurred between the last billing date (10 October 1984) and the current billing date (10 November 1984). The first of these items is a $25 payment on the account received on 22 October. The other four items are two purchases and the state taxes on them that were charged on 5 November. The total cost of these four items is $15.58, as indicated. Had any merchandise been returned for credit, these items would also be shown on the statement as "credits," and the amounts charged for them would be deducted from the account balance.

New Balance Calculation The $182 previous balance shown at the bottom of the statement represents the account balance at the end of the previous billing period. The charges during the current month are added to the previous month's balance; thus $15.58 in charges during the current period is added to the $182 previous account balance. Also added to the previous balance are any interest charges applicable to the account—in this case, a finance charge of $2.49. (A detailed discussion of how finance charges are determined is given in a later section of this chapter.) Finally, any payments received and other credits are subtracted from the unpaid balance to arrive at the new account balance. The $25 payment is the only deduction shown in Figure 7.1; apparently no other credits were received during the month. The resulting new balance on the account is $175.07.

Figure 7.1 Sample Statement: Open Account

DEPARTMENT NUMBER	DATES MONTH	DATES DAY	TRANSACTION DESCRIPTION	CHARGES	CREDITS
99	10	22	PAYMENT		25.00
65	11	05	GLOVES	4.98	
	11	05	STATE TAX	.20	
64	11	05	SKIRTLINER PT	10.00	
	11	05	STATE TAX	.40	

TO YOUR PREVIOUS BALANCE	WE ADDED YOUR CHARGES	*WE ADDED YOUR FINANCE CHARGES	WE DEDUCTED PAYMENTS	WE DEDUCTED OTHER CREDITS	THIS IS YOUR NEW BALANCE
$ 182.00	$ 15.58	$ 2.49	$ 25.00	$	$ 175.07

Account Number	Billing Dates This Month	Billing Dates Next Month	Finance Charge 1½ %(Annual Percentage Rate 18%) Computed On Avg. Daily Balance Of		Minimum Amount To Send
	11-10-84	12-10-84		$ 165.87	$ 20.00

*To Avoid Additional Finance Charges, Pay "New Balance" Before "Billing Date" Next Month

EXPLANATION OF FINANCE CHARGES

If the "NEW BALANCE" is received by Renberg's, Inc., by the "BILLING DATE NEXT MONTH", no additional FINANCE CHARGE is imposed.

If a FINANCE CHARGE is shown on the front hereof, it is computed as follows:

> 1½% of the AVERAGE DAILY BALANCE as shown on the front hereof; this being an ANNUAL PERCENTAGE RATE of 18%. When the AVERAGE DAILY BALANCE for a monthly billing period is $33.33, or less, the FINANCE CHARGE for that monthly billing period, at Renberg's option, will be 50c.
>
> The AVERAGE DAILY BALANCE is determined by dividing the sum of the balances outstanding for each day of the monthly billing period by the number of days in the monthly billing period. The balance outstanding each day of the monthly billing period is determined by subtracting all payments and credits (excepting credits for merchandise purchased and returned within the same monthly billing period) from the previous day's balance, excluding any purchases added to the account during the monthly billing period and excluding any unpaid finance charges.

MINIMUM PAYMENT

A minimum payment of one-tenth (1/10) of the unpaid balance (adjusted to the next highest increment of $5.00) appearing on each monthly billing statement (but not less than $10.00 monthly) PLUS any amount which is past due from previous months must be received by Renberg's, Inc., by the "BILLING DATE NEXT MONTH" as shown on the front hereof.

Source: Courtesy of Renberg's Department Store, Tulsa, Oklahoma. Receivable statement invoice was designed by Herman J. Stokes, credit manager, Renberg's. Revised for third edition.

Minimum Payment Most open accounts do not require payment of the entire new balance, but they do require some *minimum payment* amount, usually a specified percentage of the new balance. For example, the statement in Figure 7.1 indicates that a minimum payment of $20.00 is required. At the bottom of the reverse side of the statement (included in the bottom half of Figure 7.1), the method of calculating this minimum is explained. It is figured as 10 percent of the new balance (in this case, $17.51) adjusted to the next highest increment of $5.00 (in this case, $20.00). Of course, any past due charges are added to this amount. Sometimes the open account statement will have a schedule of minimum payments that will specify the minimum payment for various ranges of account balances. In our example, as long as the $20.00 minimum payment is made before the next month's billing date (10 December 1984), the customer's credit privileges will not be jeopardized.

Types of Charge Accounts

Charge accounts are available in a wide variety and differ primarily with respect to the type of institution issuing the credit. A brief description of each of the key types of charge accounts follows.

30 Day, or Regular, Charge Accounts Commonly offered by certain types of businesses for the general convenience of their customers, the *30 day,* or *regular, charge account* requires the customer to pay the full amount billed within 10 to 20 days after the billing date. If payment is made within the specified period, no interest is charged. Only when payments are received after the due date is an interest penalty levied. These accounts generally do not require the use of a charge card and are typically offered by gas and electric companies, telephone companies, doctors and dentists, and repair services.

Revolving Charge Accounts One very popular form of credit is the *revolving charge account,* which allows customers to continue to purchase goods as long as they do not exceed the credit limit established or let their account become delinquent through failure to make specified minimum payments. The *line of credit*, or total amount of credit customers can have at any point in time, varies with their net worth and past credit record. These types of accounts generally require charge cards and are most common in department and clothing stores where it is likely that customers will make several purchases each month. Sometimes revolving charge accounts are referred to as *budget* or *option charge accounts*. The example discussed earlier and the statement in Figure 7.1 illustrate the technical aspects of a revolving charge account. The finance charge levied on the unpaid balance of this kind of account is usually 1.5 percent per month. In addition to department and clothing stores, most large oil companies offer revolving charge accounts through their gasoline credit cards. Some of these companies, however, exclude gasoline from the revolving charge, thereby allowing only items such as tires, batteries, and accessories to be charged on a revolving basis.

Bank Credit Card Accounts An increasingly popular type of charge account is the *bank credit card account,* which is issued by a commercial bank and allows consumers to charge purchases at any stores accepting the appropriate credit card. This kind of account is similar to the revolving charge account except that it is not issued by a specific store. Cardholders are given credit limits beyond which they are prohibited from charging. At the end of each month the cardholder will receive a statement itemizing all charges, payments, and interest. Stores that accept these types of cards must pay a fee in the form of a specified percentage of the sales made to people using the card. In addition to being able to make purchases on credit, holders of bank credit cards can also obtain *cash advances*—loans on which interest begins to accrue immediately—from designated commercial banks without having to make any formal application. The two dominant bank credit cards are MasterCard and VISA. These cards are accepted by various retail stores and banks worldwide and in the United States by state governments, universities, medical groups, and record clubs, for example. A detailed discussion of bank credit cards is included in a later section of this chapter.

Travel and Entertainment Credit Card Accounts *Travel and entertainment credit card accounts* are similar to bank credit card accounts in that a credit card enabling the holder to charge purchases at a variety of locations is issued to qualified applicants. Typically, the businesses willing to accept these cards are travel and entertainment related—hotels, motels, airlines, and restaurants. In order to obtain one of these cards, the applicant must agree not only to pay interest on any outstanding balances but also to pay an annual fee of about $30 for the privilege of using the card. Because holders are expected to remain current, a delinquency charge is levied against unpaid balances. Issuers are private businesses, such as *American Express, Diners Club,* and *Carte Blanche.* These travel and entertainment cards are most popular among business executives because of the convenience of charging travel and entertainment related to business. Not only the charges for such business expenses but also the fee paid to purchase the card is deductible for tax purposes. Because of the business orientation of these cards, the credit standards that must be met in order to hold them are higher than those required for bank credit cards, and the credit limit is also higher than that received on bank credit cards.

Opening a Charge Account

For the sake of convenience, people often maintain a variety of charge accounts. The ranking of items purchased using credit cards shown in

Table 7.2 Ranking of Items Purchased with Credit Cards

Rank[a]	Item
1	Clothing for Adults
2	Gasoline
3	Major Appliances
4	Children's Clothing
5	Christmas Presents
6	Gifts
7	Household Goods
8	Vacations
9	Drugs and Medicines
10	Eating Out in Restaurants for Pleasure
11	Food and Groceries
12	Toys

[a]Rankings are from the most common to the least common items purchased using credit cards.
Source: Reprinted with permission from *The General Mills American Family Report, 1974–1975: A Study of the American Family and Money* (Minneapolis: General Mills, 1975), p. 89.

Table 7.2 tends to confirm their popularity as a device for making relatively routine purchases. Although open account charges do increase the accountholders' risk of overextending their budget, at the same time they serve as a useful way to keep track of expenditures. Generally, formal credit application procedures are not required for 30 day charges. Revolving charge accounts, bank credit card accounts, and travel and entertainment credit card accounts, however, all require formal application procedures.

Credit Application To obtain open account credit, an application must be filled out. Applications are usually available at the store or bank with which the account is to be held. Sometimes you can have them mailed to you. Applications for bank credit cards and travel and entertainment credit cards can be found at businesses accepting these cards or obtained by request from the companies that issue the cards. The information normally requested on these applications is concerned with family, housing, employment and income, assets and liabilities, existing charge accounts, and credit references. When applying for credit, you should provide this information as accurately and thoroughly as possible since it will be verified in the process of the credit investigation.

Credit Investigation Once the credit application has been completed and returned to the store or bank, the applicant is subjected to a *credit investigation.* In the case of local department store charge accounts requested by people who have lived in the community for a few years, the entire investigation may take only a matter of minutes since the store can get a credit report from the local credit bureau over the telephone. But in situations where the local credit bureau does not have sufficient data on the applicant, the store may ask the credit bureau to investigate the applicant's credit. This may involve contacting the credit references listed on the credit application or, in the case of someone who is new to the community, corresponding with the credit bureau in the town in which the applicant previously lived. Because most local credit bureaus are connected to one another by computer, they sometimes can get credit information from other cities in a matter of minutes. Stores themselves will sometimes check with the references the applicant has provided in order to avoid having to pay a credit bureau to do so.

The local *credit bureau* is typically established and mutually owned by local merchants and banks. It collects and stores credit information from its members on people living within the community and makes this information available for a specified fee to members who request it. If the information requested can be transmitted over the phone, the cost of an inquiry is typically only about five dollars. In situations where the credit bureau must obtain, either through its own investigations or from another credit bureau, additional information in order to update the applicant's file, the cost of the report may run as high as ten dollars. Local credit bureaus are linked together nationally through the Associated Credit Bureaus, Inc., and TRW Credit Data, Inc.—each of which provides guidelines and mechanisms for obtaining credit information from almost any area of the United States. Note that credit bureaus merely provide credit information; they do not analyze the information and make the credit decision. That is the responsibility of the store or bank involved.

Credit Decision Using the data provided by the credit applicant along with any credit information obtained from the credit bureau, the store or bank must decide whether or not to grant credit. Often some type of *credit scoring scheme* is used to make the credit decision. By assigning values to factors such as income, existing debts, and credit references, an applicant's overall credit score can be developed. If it compares favorably with the established acceptable range of scores, the applicant will be given credit; if not, credit will not be extended. Sometimes borderline cases are granted credit only on a limited basis. For example, a large department store that normally limits the outstanding balance of its revolving charge accounts to $500 might give a customer who scores poorly in the credit analysis a revolving charge account with a $100 credit limit. Even when a formal credit scoring scheme is used, the credit analyst is normally empowered to offer nonstandard credit terms if such action seems appropriate. Applicants who are granted credit are notified and sent a charge card along with materials describing the credit terms and procedures to be used.

Important Consumer Credit Legislation

When you apply for consumer credit of any kind, you should be aware of the legal obligations of the store or bank from which you are requesting credit. There is always a possibility that your rights may be violated. Over the last decade, several important pieces of consumer legislation affecting the extension of credit have been passed. The major concerns of this legislation have been credit discrimination; disclosure of credit information; mailing, error complaints, and cash discounts on bills; disclosure of finance charges; loss of credit card; recourse on unsatisfactory purchases; and protection against collector harassment.

Credit Discrimination As of October 1975, the *Equal Credit Opportunity Act* made it illegal for a creditor to discriminate on the basis of sex or marital status when considering a credit application. The act was passed in order to extend to women the credit rights already held by men; it does not say that credit *must* be extended to women but that everyone has a right to apply and be treated equally. Specifically, the act prohibits prospective creditors from asking about an applicant's sex, marital status, and childbearing plans. Lenders are required to view the income of women in exactly the same fashion as they do the income of men. In addition, they must consider alimony and child support as part of women's income. Severe penalties exist for the violation of this law.

On 23 March 1977, the Equal Credit Opportunity Act was expanded to prohibit credit discrimination based on race, national origin, religion, age, or the receipt of public assistance. A subsequent extension of the act—effective 1 June 1977—requires that if a husband and wife open a joint account or cosign a loan, the credit grantor must report the information to the credit bureau in the name of both parties. This change was intended to allow a wife to establish a credit history which would make it easier for her to obtain credit if death (of her husband) or divorce occurs. Prior to this modification of the Equal Credit Opportunity Act, the credit files were maintained only in the name of the husband.

Disclosure of Credit Information On 25 April 1971, the *Fair Credit Reporting Act* went into effect. It includes numerous provisions, among which are the following. First, credit reports must contain accurate, relevant, and recent information about the personal and financial situation of credit applicants. Second, only bona fide users of financial information may review credit files. Third, consumers who are refused credit or who find their borrowing costs increased as the result of a credit investigation must be informed of the reasons for such actions as well as the name and address of the reporting credit agency. And perhaps most important, the credit reporting agencies must let individuals review their credit files personally and correct any inaccurate information. For example, if you find erroneous or unverifiable data in your file, you may have it deleted and force the credit bureau to notify all creditors of the past six months and employers of the past two years of such changes. If you and the credit bureau disagree on the validity of certain data in your file, you are allowed to include your refutation in your file. Furthermore, you cannot be charged for any of these actions.

Mailing, Error Complaints, and Cash Discounts on Bills As a result of errors and abuses in credit billing and the poor handling of credit complaints that resulted primarily from the use of computer-generated bills, the *Fair Credit Billing Act* became effective in October 1975. One provision of the act requires creditors to mail bills at least 14 days prior to the payment due date and to include all credits and refunds on the bill for the period in which they occur. Another provision requires customers to notify (in writing) the creditor, within 60 days of the date they receive the statement, relative to any billing errors. The creditor is required to respond within 30 days to customer inquiries concerning a billing error complaint and to resolve the complaint within 90 days from receiving the customer's complaint. During the period the complaint is being resolved, the creditor is prohibited from collecting the bill or issuing an unfavorable credit report as a result of the disputed charge. A third provision of the act allows merchants to give cash discounts of any size to customers who pay cash instead of using credit. Since the merchants have to pay credit card companies, such as MasterCard, VISA, and American Express, for the privilege of accepting customers' cards, this act allows them to pass the savings on to those who choose not to use credit cards. The Fair Credit Billing Act also includes a provision concerned with the credit purchaser's recourse to the creditor; this provision is discussed in greater detail in a later section of this chapter.

Disclosure of Finance Charges Another major piece of consumer legislation is the *Consumer Credit Protection Act*. Commonly referred to as the *Truth in Lending Act*, it initially went into effect 1 July 1969 and has been amended several times since then. The directives for complying with the act are outlined in *Regulation Z*, which was issued by the Federal Reserve Board. Its most significant provision is the requirement that, prior to extending credit, all lenders disclose both the dollar amount of finance charges and the annual percentage rate (accurate to the nearest 0.25 percent) charged. This enables credit applicants to make valid comparisons of alternate sources of credit. Such a disclosure is included on the reverse side of the statement shown earlier in the bottom half of Figure 7.1.

The *dollar amount* of finance charges includes all interest and fees that must be paid in order to receive the loan. The *annual percentage rate (APR)* is the true rate of interest paid over the life of the loan and must be calculated in the manner outlined by the law. Note that on open account credit, creditors cannot specify in advance the dollar amount of interest since they do not know how much will be purchased on the account. The annual percentage rate on these accounts can be stated, however, since there are no fees charged other than interest. Remember, it is your right as a consumer to be told the dollar amount of charges and APR on any financing you consider.

Loss of Credit Card The Consumer Credit Protection Act requires each credit card to contain some form of user identification on it—generally a picture or user signature—and limits the liability of the credit card owner in the instance the card is lost or stolen to a maximum of $50 per card. Credit card issuers are also required to send to their accountholders a self-addressed form (used to notify the issuer if the card is lost or stolen) and an explanation of the card holder's rights at the time of issue. Some issuers also have toll-free numbers that can be used to report lost or stolen credit cards. If the issuer fails to do this, the card holder cannot be held liable for even the first $50 of loss. In addition, companies are prohibited from sending unrequested credit cards to potential users. Credit cards can be sent only in response to a request or application for them.

Recourse on Unsatisfactory Purchases One of the provisions in the Fair Credit Billing Act concerned the right of credit card holders to recourse on unsatisfactory goods or services charged on their account. This provision applies for the most part to situations in which the credit used to make a purchase is provided by someone other than the seller—through the use of a bank credit card or a travel and entertainment credit card, for example. This feature allows people who have used credit to purchase goods or services that do not peform satisfactorily to stop paying the creditor if they, after good faith attempts, cannot satisfactorily work out their disagreement with the seller.

By placing some of the burden of guaranteeing the value of what is purchased on the creditor, the provision has caused creditors to be more concerned with the reputation of the providers of the goods or services being financed. This provision applies only to situations where the transaction has been made within 100 miles of the card holder's current mailing address or within the card holder's state of residence and the amount contested exceeds $50. It allows you to protect yourself when you have used your credit card to purchase goods or services that prove to be unsatisfactory.

Protection Against Collector Harassment Beginning 20 March 1978, the *Fair Debt Collection Practices Act* gave consumers protection against unreasonable collection practices. To begin with, the credit customer has five days after being first contacted by a debt collector to be informed *in writing* as to: (1) how much money is owed, (2) to whom, and (3) steps that can be taken if the debt is disputed. If the customer disagrees with the claim, he or she has 30 days to send the collector written notification of the dispute. Then the collector cannot continue collection efforts until the customer is provided with written verification of the debt. Furthermore, the customer can prevent a collector from communicating with him or her by notifying the collector in writing. Finally, if the collector presses suit for payment, it must be filed in the judicial district where the customer lives or where the contract was signed.

You may have heard stories of unsavory credit collectors gaining access to people's homes by posing as ministers, or policemen—and once inside, grabbing a television set or other item on which credit payments are supposedly unpaid and overdue. Frequently, violence was threatened, and sometimes used, to collect unpaid bills. All these tactics are illegal. The act specifically makes it a federal offense for collectors to: (1) use abusive language, or threaten the customer, or call at inconvenient times or at the place of work; (2) misrepresent themselves; (3) use unfair tactics in an effort to collect the debt; (4) contact anyone else about the customer's debt unless they are trying to locate him or her; and (5) collect an amount greater than the debt, or apply payments to another disputed debt.

Credit Card Insurance

Before the passage of the Consumer Credit Protection Act, the liability of credit card holders for charges made on lost or stolen cards was virtually unlimited. The card holder was held liable for all charges made prior to the time when the issuer received written notice that the card was lost or stolen. In order to protect themselves against the consequences of the possible loss or theft of their credit cards, many people would purchase *credit card insurance.* This is no longer necessary since the credit card holder's liability in the instance of loss or theft of the card is limited to $50. In fact, under the Consumer Credit Protection Act, your liability is the lesser of two amounts: that charged on your card prior to notification of the issuer or $50. Clearly, quick notification of the issuer when a card is lost or stolen is important. In order to afford yourself maximum protection, it is a good idea to keep a list of credit card numbers along with the addresses and phone numbers provided by the issuers for use if cards are lost or stolen. Destroy credit cards that you do not plan to use.

Store Charges

Open account credit offered by various types of retail merchants is referred to as *store charges*. Because it is quite likely that you will use these types of charge accounts, you should understand the methods of computing finance charges, advantages and disadvantages of using store charges, and precautions that should be taken in using them.

Methods of Computing Finance Charges

Since merchants do not know how much you will charge on your account, they cannot specify the dollar amount of interest you will be charged. But they can and must, according to the Truth in Lending Act, disclose the percent interest they charge and the method they use to compute finance charges. (See the example of such a disclosure on the reverse of the statement presented earlier in the bottom half of Figure 7.1.) The four basic techniques for computing finance charges are the previous balance method, the average daily balance method, the adjusted balance method, and the past due balance method.

In the examples that follow, the transactions noted are taken from the statement presented in Figure 7.1. The monthly interest rate used is 1.5 percent, which represents an annual rate of 18 percent. (Although 1.5 percent is the most common rate, in some states *usury laws* governing interest rates may establish a lower interest rate ceiling on balances above a specified amount, such as $1,000. In other states, rates in excess of 1.5 percent per month may be levied on these accounts.) As is customary, any credit purchases made during the current month are not subject to a finance charge if paid before the billing date specified. Finance charges are computed only on unpaid balances from previous months' purchases. In other words, if the full amount of the monthly bill is paid before the billing date of the following month, no further finance charges will result.

Previous Balance Method A commonly used method for computing finance charges, the *previous balance method* is the most expensive for the consumer since interest is charged on the outstanding balance at the beginning of the billing period. In Figure 7.1, $182 is the balance at the beginning of the period—the previous balance on which interest would be calculated. The resulting finance charge for the period using this method would be 1.5 percent of $182, or $2.73.

Average Daily Balance Method In the *average daily balance method,* the interest is applied to the average daily balance of the account over the billing period. In this illustration, the calculations used to compute this balance do not reflect purchases or returns of purchases made

Table 7.3 Calculation of Average Daily Balance

	Number of Days (1)	Balance (2)		Weighted Balance [(1) × (2)] (3)
	11	$182		$2,002
	20	157		3,140
Total	31		Total	$5,142

$$\text{Average Daily Balance} = \frac{\$5,142}{31 \text{ days}} = \$165.87$$

during the billing period; one should realize that some companies include as a standard practice any new purchase as part of the average daily balance. The interest charges and the methods of computing interest using the average daily balance are shown in Figure 7.1.

The billing period, which extended from 10 October 1984 through 10 November 1984, included 31 days. The outstanding balance for the first 11 days of the period (11 October through 21 October) was $182, while the outstanding balance for the remaining 20 days of the period (22 October through 10 November) was $157.00 ($182.00 − $25.00 payment). The average daily balance of $165.87 can, therefore, be calculated as shown in Table 7.3 by weighting the various balances according to the number of days they were in existence and then averaging them. By multiplying the average daily balance of $165.87 by the 1.5 percent interest rate, the $2.49 finance charge shown on the statement in Figure 7.1 results. When the average daily balance method is used, $2.49 is the finance charge, while the previous balance method yielded a $2.73 finance charge. Thus the average daily balance method is clearly less expensive than the previous balance method and therefore preferable for the consumer. It is commonly used by stores that offer revolving charge accounts.

Adjusted Balance Method In the *adjusted balance method* of calculating interest, the interest charge is applied to the balance remaining at the end of the billing period (ignoring purchases or returns made during the billing period), which results in lower finance charges than under either of the other methods described. In the example, the account balance at the end of the billing period would have been $157.00 ($182.00 − $25.00 payment). When the 1.5 percent interest charge is applied to this balance, the resulting finance charge is $2.36, as compared to $2.73 and $2.49 in the other two cases.

Past Due Balance Method Occasionally a merchant will use the *past due balance method* in order to stimulate customers to fully repay their

Table 7.4 Summary of Finance Charges in Example

Method of Determining Balance	Balance (1)	Monthly Interest Rate (2)	Finance Charge [(1) × (2)] (3)
Previous Balance	$182.00	1.5%	$2.73
Average Daily Balance	165.87	1.5	2.49
Adjusted Balance	157.00	1.5	2.36
Past Due Balance	______[a]	1.5	0.0

[a]The finance charge, which does *not* have to be paid if full payment is remitted by a specified date, would be calculated using one of the other three methods.

accounts. Under this method, customers who pay their account *in full* within a specified period of time, such as 30 days from the billing date, *are relieved* of the finance charge, which would otherwise be determined by one of the three preceding methods. If this method were applicable in the statement presented in Figure 7.1, the customer would have had the $2.49 finance charge waived if payment of the full amount of $172.58 ($175.07 − $2.49) was made prior to a specified date, say 10 December 1984. By paying the full amount by the specified date the finance charge is effectively reduced to $0.0; otherwise it would have been equal to one of the values calculated using one of the preceding three methods. A comparison of the results of using these methods is given in Table 7.4. Because the finance charge varies with the method used to determine the account balance, the wise consumer determines which method is used prior to buying on credit.

Advantages of Using Store Charges

The most significant advantage of store charges is that by charging purchases, customers can delay payment until the end of the billing period. Note, however, that because of the high cost of the finance charges levied on balances carried from period to period, there is no real advantage to delaying payment beyond the end of the billing period. The advantages to be obtained from proper use of store charges are briefly described as follows.

Interest-Free Loans Carrying charge accounts costs merchants money. Since this is one of their business expenses, it is reflected in the price you pay for their goods or services. Therefore, you might as well maximize the benefits you receive from them. By delaying payment to the end of the billing period during which your purchases were made, you can (in most cases) receive an interest-free loan for up to 30 days. You can thus, without penalty, keep your money in some interest-earning form until the payment is due. Money market accounts and NOW accounts, discussed in Chapter 5, provide good opportunities to do this.

Recordkeeping, Unsatisfactory Purchases, and Credits Store charges provide detailed records of transactions in the form of monthly statements. Because there may be errors in these statements, receipts should be saved and checked against the statement entries before paying. It is also easier to resolve any disagreements you might have with businesses over goods or services purchased if you have not yet paid for them. If you charge your purchases, you will have approximately 30 days to make sure that they are satisfactory. If they are not, you can refuse to pay off your account. In addition, when you purchase an item on credit and later wish to return it, you need only have the store credit your account. Some stores credit your account for returns whether the purchase was charged using the store charge or a bank charge. In this way the purchase price can be written off the books and no cash need change hands. Some stores use due bills to compensate customers who return items purchased for cash. Due bills can be used only to make purchases within the store and thus are less advantageous than the system of crediting the account, since they make another purchase necessary.

Preferred Customer Status Customers who have charge accounts normally receive preferred customer status, which provides benefits such as notification of forthcoming sales, invitations to special shopping events limited to credit card holders, and check cashing privileges. Although these benefits may be rather limited, many people find them appealing.

Convenience Some people find the use of store charges convenient since they eliminate the need to write a check each time a purchase is made. By charging all transactions during the month, the customer has only to write one check to pay each monthly bill. This convenience is a particularly important consideration for people who make a large number of transactions at a given store during the month.

Use in Emergencies A final advantage of store charges is that they provide a means for purchasing needed items when sufficient cash is unavailable. With proper planning and budgeting, the consumer should be able to avoid running short of cash, but charging a needed item because of a shortage of cash may be justifiable in some situations. A tendency to run short of cash on a regular basis, however, signals the need to reevaluate one's budget.

Disadvantages of Using Store Charges

The use of store charges has two major disadvantages: (1) there is a tendency to overspend and (2) high interest costs add to the price of purchases.

Tendency to Overspend People who do not use budgets tend to forget that what they charge must eventually be paid for. The credit card gives them a sense of buying power that may not be supported by actual income. One of the consequences of this type of overspending is a tendency not to pay the full amount of the bill. And since consumers who overspend end up without sufficient funds to cover their bill, they make only the minimum payment and thus incur finance charges. If their overspending is not curtailed, the size of their unpaid balance carried from period to period may become so large it cannot be paid without curtailing the purchase of some necessity items. A realistic budget as well as good budget control should help avoid this type of overspending.

High Interest Costs on Unpaid Balances The rate of interest charged on unpaid balances carried from month to month is usually quite high. The 1.5 percent per month commonly charged represents an 18 percent annual rate. Since most consumer loans can be obtained at annual rates between 10 percent and 15 percent, people who need to borrow money should not do so through the use of store charges. Clearly, store charges should be paid off in full each period and not used as a type of loan to finance the purchase of goods and services.

The Effective Use of Store Charges: Some Precautions

If you use charges without close coordination with your budget, you may overspend and have to carry an unpaid account balance to the following period. In order to avoid doing this, enter all charges (as if you had paid cash) on your budget expense record as soon as they are made (see Chapter 3). If you wait to record expenditures until you are billed for them, you will probably overspend your budget. You should charge only as much as your budget indicates you can afford.

When charging a purchase of goods or services, be sure to read the charge slip before you sign it. Make sure that the items and amounts as well as the total amount shown are correct. Once you sign the charge slip, you have in effect indicated that you have purchased and agreed to pay for whatever is shown on the slip. Most merchants will correct errors if you later discover them, but this process usually provides unneeded headaches. Also, always keep your receipts and check them against the amounts shown on your monthly statement. Make sure that the amounts charged have been correctly recorded on your statement. By checking both charge slips and monthly statements for accuracy, you may save yourself many dollars. Merchants can make mistakes in recording transactions, and, unless you check for errors, they may go unnoticed at your expense.

Figure 7.2 Number of Card Holders Worldwide for Major Bank and Travel and Entertainment Credit Cards (1982)

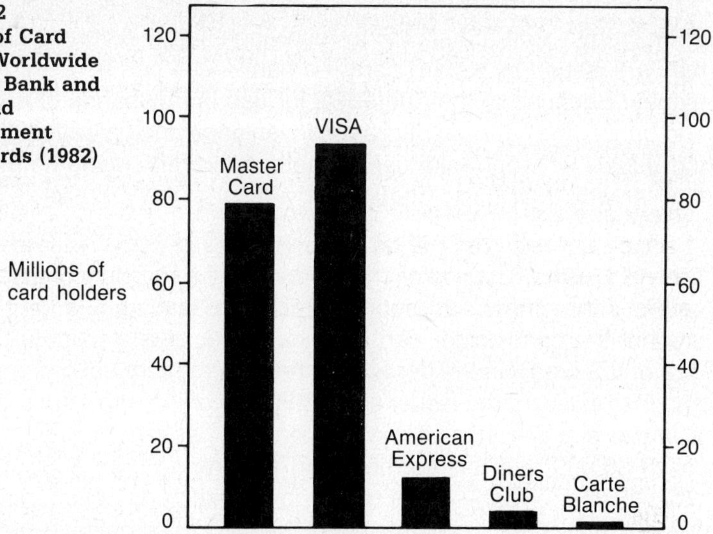

Source: Data from "Are Credit Cards a Good Deal?", *Consumers Digest,* May/June 1982, pp. 42–46.

Bank Credit Cards

As indicated earlier, bank credit cards are becoming an increasingly popular form of open account credit. The two dominant bank credit cards, MasterCard and VISA, should not be confused with travel and entertainment credit cards, such as American Express, Diners Club, and Carte Blanche. As illustrated in Figure 7.2 in the comparison of the approximate number of card holders in 1982, the bank credit cards are far more prevalent than travel and entertainment cards.

Although bank credit cards used to be free to those who qualified financially, in 1980 many issuers began to charge an annual or monthly fee and/or levy a service charge on each transaction. Applications for bank cards can be obtained from sponsoring banks and participating merchants. Many people have both MasterCard and VISA cards. These cards can be used not only to charge goods and services but also to obtain cash advances at any of the many banks that sponsor them. Merchants who accept bank credit cards must pay a fee ranging as high as 5 percent of the dollar amount of bank credit card transactions accepted. Although this may seem costly, the opportunity to make purchases on credit is expected to appeal to consumers and add significantly to the volume of business. The remainder of the chapter briefly considers the features, use, and future prospects of bank credit cards.

Features of Bank Credit Cards

Bank credit cards are similar to revolving charge accounts except that they are issued by a third party—a bank—and can be used to borrow money. Because of their potential for use in thousands of businesses and banks, they can be of great convenience and value to consumers. Individuals who do make use of them, however, should be thoroughly familiar with their basic features.

Line of Credit The line of credit provided the recipient of a bank credit card is set by the card issuer for each card issued. It is the maximum amount the card holder can owe the issuer at any point in time. The size of the credit line is dependent on both the request of the applicant and the results of the issuer's investigation of the applicant's credit and financial status. Lines of credit offered by issuers of bank cards can reach $5,000, but for the most part they range from $300 to $1,000. Most issuers of bank credit cards do not take any action against card holders until they have extended their account balance beyond the stated maximum by 20 percent or more. For example, if your credit limit were $500, you would probably not be notified you had exceeded your credit limit until your outstanding balance had exceeded $600, which is 20 percent above the $500 line of credit. Because in most cases account balances are only checked prior to transactions greater than $50, exceeding the credit limit established is not difficult. Of course, as new and more sophisticated computer-based systems are used to monitor bank credit card accounts, credit limits will be more strictly controlled.

Merchandise Purchases Merchants who participate in a given bank credit card program can generally be recognized by the bank credit card insignia they affix to the door of their business and display in their advertisements. When you purchase goods or services with bank credit cards, the key information—account number, name, and expiration date—is imprinted from the card onto the sales slip, the amount of the purchase is filled in on the sales slip, and you are asked to sign. Be sure to check the accuracy of the purchase prices recorded before you sign the sales slip. You will be given a copy of the slip for your records. Merchants can determine whether you are the legitimate user of the card by comparing your signature with that on the card, by checking the card's number with a printed list of numbers of invalid cards, by requiring additional identification (such as a driver's license), or by verifying over the telephone that you are an accountholder in good standing and that the card you present has not been reported lost or stolen. (They must also verify by telephone purchases in excess of a specified amount—typically, $50.) Merchants make these checks because bank credit card issuers hold them responsible for losses experienced as the result of accepting a lost or stolen bank credit card charge.

Cash Advances A bank credit card holder can obtain a *cash advance,* or loan, from any bank participating in the given credit card program. Cash advances are transacted in the same fashion as merchandise purchases except that they take place at a commercial bank. Of course, the bank, like the merchants who participate in these programs, checks to be sure the card user is legitimate and the line of credit will not be exceeded as a result of the advance. Some banks will not make cash advances for amounts less than $50.

Interest Rates on Bank Card Charges The rate of interest applied to bank card charges is usually between 1.5 and 1.75 percent per month or an annual percentage rate of 18 to 21 percent, whether transactions involve purchases or cash advances. In some states these rates may be limited by *usury laws*, and in some areas the rate of interest on merchandise purchases may differ from that on cash advances. Generally speaking, the rate of interest on bank credit cards is comparable to rates on store charges. The legal requirements with respect to disclosure of interest costs and related information are no different for bank credit cards than for other forms of consumer credit. In the case of purchases of merchandise and services, the specified interest rate is comparable to rates on store charges, and as with store charges, it is normally applied only to unpaid balances carried from previous periods. Interest on cash advances is charged on a daily basis for the actual number of days the cash advance remains unpaid. In addition, some banks charge a cash advance fee equal to as much as 2 percent of the cash advance.

The Statement If you use a bank credit card, you will receive monthly statements showing all transactions, payments, account balances, finance charges, credit available, and the minimum payment. A sample bank card statement is given in Figure 7.3. Although merchandise and cash advance transactions are separated on this statement, the finance charge in each case is calculated at the rate of 1.75 percent per month (21 percent per year); in some areas different interest rates might apply to merchandise and cash advance transactions. The average daily balance method is used to compute the finance charge in the statement shown. The minimum payment required for the statement in Figure 7.3 was $22; it was noted on the portion of the statement that was returned with the payment to the issuing bank.

Payments Users of bank credit cards can avoid *future* finance charges by paying the total new balance shown on their statement each month. For example, if the $534.81 total new balance shown in Figure 7.3 is paid by the due date of 21 September 1984, no additional finance charges will be incurred. If card holders cannot pay the total new balance, they can pay any amount as long as it is greater than the mini-

Figure 7.3 **Sample Bank Credit Card Statement**

Please detach the above portion and return it with your payment to insure proper credit.

Bank Card Statement

Retain this statement for your records

MasterCard VISA UNITED CALIFORNIA BANK

Account Number	Name(s)	Statement Date	Payment Due Date
		8-26-80	09-23-80

Account Activity

Previous Balance	203.64
Payments −	119.89
Credits −	.00
Subtotal	83.75
New Transaction +	445.93
Finance Charge +	5.13
Late Charge +	.00
NEW BALANCE	534.81

Credit Status	
Your Credit Limit is:	2000.00
Your Available Credit is:	1465.19

Finance Charge Calculation

Amounts Subject to Finance Charge		This Month's Charge	ENTIRE BAL.
A *Average Daily Balance	293.25	5.13	1.75% Monthly Periodic Rate; 21.00% Nominal Annual Rate
B *Cash Advance	.00	.00	
C *Loan Advance	.00	.00	
		5.13 Finance Charge	21.00% Annual Percentage Rate

* Finance Charges explained on reverse side.

Mail Billing Inquiries to: Post Office Box 7760, Van Nuys, California, 91409, or call 800/000-0000

For inquiries on Past Due Accounts, Overlimits or Credit Line Increases, call 800/000-0000

Posted Mo./Day	Transaction Description or Merchant Name and Location		Purchase Mo./Day	Bank Reference Number	Purchases/ Advances/ Debits	Payments/ Credits
8-08	AIR WEST	LOS ANGELES	07-25	850000008823395192	42.00	
8-13	HACIENDA MOTOR	COSTA MESA	08-05	015400018537022316	166.86	
8-15	RICOS RESTAURANT	PALM SPRG	08-10	114500018856161722	132.47	
8-12	PAYMENT - THANK YOU		08-11	4501000182MD02139		119.89
8-26	RENEES RESTAURAN T	NEWPORT	08-13	114500068201632483	104.60	
	Notice: See reverse side for important information.				Total Debits 445.93	Total Credits 119.89

Source: Courtesy of United California Bank.

mum payment specified on the statement. They do, however, incur additional finance charges in the following month. The minimum payment of $22 for the statement in Figure 7.3 represents 4 percent of the total new balance, rounded to the next dollar. Had the new balance been less than $250, the bank and card issuer would have required a $10 payment or the total new balance if it were less than $10. If card holders fail to make the minimum payment, they are in default of the bank credit card agreement they signed when they received the card, and the bank issuing the card can take whatever action is deemed necessary.

Returning Merchandise When you return merchandise purchased with your bank credit card, the merchant to whom you return it will issue a credit on your bank credit card. The credit is transacted in the same fashion as a purchase and will appear on your statement as a deduction from the statement balance. If you purchase a good or service and have problems with it, you may not have to pay the bank credit card company for the purchase if you have attempted in good faith and failed to resolve the problem with the merchant. This protection is provided by the Fair Credit Billing Act. Of course, if the problem is resolved in the merchant's favor, you will ultimately have to pay.

Effective Use of Bank Credit Cards

Bank credit cards, like store charges, can be helpful tools if used properly. They have the same basic advantages and disadvantages as do store charges.

Interest-Free Loans Like store charges, many bank credit cards provide short-term, interest-free loans on the purchase of goods or services as long as each monthly statement is paid in full by the due date. Recent high interest rates have caused a growing number of bank credit card issuers to include purchases made during the current period when computing the period's average daily balance. The high rate of interest—1.5 percent per month or 18 percent per year—on balances carried from period to period makes it inadvisable to make purchases on bank credit cards that cannot be paid off in full at the end of the current period. The use of the bank credit card to obtain cash advances is also inadvisable due to the high rate of interest charged on such loans. Bank credit cards should be used only to charge merchandise and services, and monthly statements should always be paid in full to avoid any finance charges. If the card issuer includes current purchases in the average daily balance, the card should only be used in financial emergencies, since interest would be charged beginning at the time of the transaction. Use of the card in any other fashion signals poor personal financial management.

Consolidated Statement of Expenses Probably the most valid reason for using a bank credit card is to consolidate your records of purchases. No matter how many and varied the stores at which bank credit card transactions occur, the consumer receives only one statement that records them all. This greatly simplifies the recordkeeping process. Another benefit of a consolidated statement of purchases is that only one check need be used to make the payment for the many purchases transacted. Thus not only time but also the service charges on checks can be saved.

A Word of Caution One of the real dangers of bank credit cards results from the fact that they are so easy to use. Many people have a tendency to forget they must eventually pay for the merchandise charged with their bank card. But each time they make a transaction using their bank credit card, they are incurring a liability to the issuer of the card. Bank card charges should be limited to those items budgeted. Only in financial emergencies should bank credit card holders use their credit to make nonbudgeted transactions, leave a portion of the bank card balance unpaid, or receive cash advances on account. If used properly, the convenience and widespread acceptance of bank credit cards makes them worthwhile devices for the efficient management of personal finances.

The Future of Bank Credit Cards

Due to their widespread acceptance and the rapid advances in computer technology, bank credit (or debit) cards are expected to replace cash in transactions of all types. As was discussed in Chapter 5, the development and linking together of electronic funds transfer systems (EFTSs) and point-of-sale (POS) terminals will virtually eliminate the use of currency, coin, and checks in our society. In the not too distant future, each person will have a card that can be used to make all transactions. Paychecks will be deposited directly into people's bank accounts, and the banks will be authorized to make certain fixed payments from these deposits. All other transactions will be made using the bank credit (or debit) card. They will be electronically transmitted to the appropriate bank account and result in a series of bookkeeping entries. For example, if you buy a $50 radio at Store X, your bank card will be inserted in a terminal at the store, and the account number and information regarding the purchase will be transmitted to your bank. Upon receipt of this information, the bank will deduct $50 from your account or loan you $50 and deposit it in Store X's account. If the store's account is not at the same bank as the customer's, the bank will electronically transfer the $50 to the appropriate bank.

Loans, loan payments, and payment of bills will all be transacted using the bank card. Regular statements will continue to be issued, but the system will make it virtually impossible to overdraw an account or credit line. Merchants will be certain to receive immediate and full payment for their goods and services. Although the need for pocket money to pay for inexpensive convenience items may continue for some time into the future, eventually bank cards will be used exclusively in all transactions.

Summary

People who use open account credit, whether in the form of store charges or bank credit cards, do so for several basic reasons: to finance large outlays, to cover financial emergencies, for the sake of convenience, or to finance investments. The ready availability of credit provides benefits: consumers can obtain a good or service now and pay for it later; interest payments receive favorable tax treatment; and inflation makes delayed payments advantageous. Savers, merchants, and society in general benefit from the opportunity to buy on credit. Consumers who have never used credit can do several things to establish a good credit rating; these would include opening and using checking and savings accounts, obtaining credit cards and using them, and obtaining a small loan. Women often have extra problems in establishing credit since previous credit activity may have been in a husband's name only; thus it is important that women use their legal names in credit activities.

There are disadvantages to the use of open account credit, such as possible inflationary effects on the economy, the high cost of finance charges, the consumer's tendency to overspend, and the possibility of bankruptcy. Bankruptcy should be used only as a last resort to solving credit problems. A Wage Earner Plan is a court-directed settlement plan that allows debtors to continue owning and using their assets while paying off their past bills; straight bankruptcy disposes of assets and uses the proceeds to settle creditors' claims.

The key types of open account charges include 30 day, or regular, charge accounts; revolving charge accounts; bank credit card accounts; and travel and entertainment credit card accounts.

Certain important pieces of credit legislation, including the Equal Credit Opportunity Act, the Fair Credit Reporting Act, the Fair Credit Billing Act, the Consumer Credit Protection Act, or Truth in Lending Act, and the Fair Debt Collection Practices Act, have provided the consumer with numerous protections related to credit discrimination; the disclosure of credit information; mailing, error complaints, and cash discounts; disclosure of finance charges; loss of credit card; recourse on unsatisfactory items purchased on credit; and protection against collector harassment.

Store charges are open accounts offered primarily by retail merchants who currently charge interest only on the unpaid account balance. The account balance on which interest is charged may be determined using the previous balance method, the average daily balance method, the adjusted balance method, or the past due balance method. The use of store charges is appealing. They provide short-term, interest-free loans; the cost of issuing them is included in the price of the merchandise; they simplify recordkeeping; unsatisfactory purchases and credits can be more easily handled; the accountholder receives preferred customer status; they are convenient; and they can be generally helpful in financial emergencies. Still, these charges facilitate overspending, and the interest charges levied on unpaid balances are high.

Bank credit cards can be used to make purchases or to obtain cash. Although they used to be available free to those who met certain financial requirements, in 1980 many issuers began to charge an annual or monthly fee and/or levy a service charge on each transaction. The amount of the line of credit extended depends on the credit worthiness of the individual. If used correctly, bank credit cards can provide short-term, interest-free loans and also allow accountholders to consolidate the records of numerous purchases in one statement. The cost of carrying unpaid balances and/or cash advances is usually 18 percent per year, which is normally too expensive to justify their use in this fashion.

In the future, the use of bank credit (or debit) cards in conjunction with the computer will replace the use of both cash and checks for making most transactions.

Consumer Loans: Single Payment and Installment 8

In addition to borrowing on open account, liability management must also consider the equally important problem of determining appropriate methods for financing major purchases other than housing. (Note: Mortgage loans were discussed in Chapter 6.) In the course of a lifetime, almost every individual must find answers to questions such as: "How do I obtain temporary financing?" "Where can I borrow money?" "How can I finance the purchase of a new automobile?" Knowledge of the sources, types, characteristics, costs, and methods for obtaining single payment and installment loans should provide you with the ability to resolve these and other problems related to asset financing.

The preceding chapter illustrated that although the use of open account credit is not essential to the achievement of financial goals, it does help people plan and live within their personal financial budget. More important to the long-run achievement of financial goals are single payment loans and installment loans. These long-term liabilities are most commonly used to finance the acquisition of durable assets, such as automobiles, furniture, and appliances, that are likely to be too expensive to purchase out of current funds. Sometimes, too, they may serve to finance nondurable items, for example, education and vacations. Of course, the extent to which these types of borrowing are used must be dictated by personal financial plans and budgets. And since they provide financing to cover the cost of necessity items that cannot be purchased with current resources, proper management of these long-term liabilities is quite important.

Types and Sources of Consumer Loans

The major difference between open account credit, which was discussed in the preceding chapter, and consumer loans is the formality of the lending arrangement. While open account credit results from a rather informal arrangement, consumer loans are negotiated formal contracts that specify terms for borrowing and repaying relatively large amounts. The formality of the consumer loan is necessary since, compared to open account charges, it is long-lived and involves significant amounts of money.

Types of Consumer Loans

Consumer loans can be broken into two main categories based on type of repayment arrangement: single payment and installment.

Single Payment Loans *Single payment loans* are made for a specified period of time at the end of which full payment is due. They are generally used to finance purchases that are expected to be repaid within a year and usually have maturities ranging from 30 days to one year. Sometimes single payment loans are made to finance purchases or pay bills when the cash to be used for repayment is known to be forthcoming in the near future. Thus they serve as a form of *interim financing.* In other situations single payment loans are negotiated on short notice in order to meet some unexpected need.

Installment Loans *Installment loans* are repaid in a series of fixed, scheduled payments rather than a lump sum. These loans are typically made to finance the purchase of a good or service for which current resources are inadequate. Mortgage loans, which are used to finance housing (and were described in detail in Chapter 6), are a form of installment loan. The repayment period on most installment loans is six months or more. Table 8.1 shows the monthly payments, finance charges, and total costs of a $1,000 installment loan for a variety of annual percentage rates and maturities. Installment loans have become a way of life for most consumers; they are popular because they provide an organized mechanism that permits people to "buy now and pay later" in fixed monthly amounts that can readily be incorporated into the budget. The process of using installment loans to finance purchases is often referred to as "buying on time."

Sources of Consumer Loans

Loans can be obtained from any of a number of possible sources, including commercial banks, consumer finance companies, credit unions, life insurance companies, savings and loan associations, sales finance companies, pawnshops, remedial loan societies, and friends and relatives. The selection of a lender often depends on both the rate of interest charged and the ease with which the loan can be negotiated. Table 8.2 provides a summary of the characteristics of the major sources of nonhousing consumer loans.

Commercial Banks Because they offer various types of consumer loans at good rates of interest, commercial banks are a popular source of consumer loans. Their rates of interest on single payment and installment loans are generally in the range of 11% to 21%. They are lower than those charged by many other lenders because they take only the best credit risks and are able to obtain relatively inexpensive

Table 8.1 Cost and Payment Data for a $1,000 Installment Loan

Annual Percentage Rate	Maturity of Loan (Months)	Monthly Payment	Finance Charge	Total Cost
9	6	$171.07	$ 26.42	$1,026.42
	12	87.45	49.40	1,049.40
	24	45.68	96.32	1,096.32
	36	31.80	144.80	1,144.80
	48	24.89	194.48	1,194.48
10	6	171.56	29.36	1,029.36
	12	87.92	55.04	1,055.04
	24	46.14	107.36	1,107.36
	36	32.27	161.62	1,161.62
	48	25.36	217.40	1,217.40
11	6	172.05	32.33	1,032.33
	12	88.38	60.58	1,060.58
	24	46.61	118.59	1,118.59
	36	32.74	178.64	1,178.64
	48	25.85	240.59	1,240.59
12	6	172.55	35.30	1,035.30
	12	88.85	66.20	1,066.20
	24	47.07	129.68	1,129.68
	36	33.21	195.56	1,195.56
	48	26.33	264.02	1,264.02
15	6	174.03	44.18	1,044.18
	12	90.26	83.12	1,083.12
	24	48.49	163.76	1,163.76
	36	34.67	248.12	1,248.12
	48	27.83	335.88	1,335.88
18	6	175.53	53.18	1,053.18
	12	91.68	100.16	1,100.16
	24	49.92	198.08	1,198.08
	36	36.15	301.40	1,301.40
	48	29.37	410.00	1,410.00

funds from their depositors. The demand for their loans is generally high, and they can be selective in making consumer loans. Typically, banks lend only to customers with good credit ratings who can easily demonstrate an ability to make repayment in accordance with the specified terms. They also give preference to loan applicants who are accountholders. The fact that an applicant is a good customer of the bank greatly enhances his or her chances of receiving requested financing. Although banks prefer to make loans secured by some type of collateral, they also make unsecured single payment loans to their better customers. Often they will lend against a passbook savings account balance or certificates of deposit. People obtain such loans in order to avoid losing interest by withdrawing deposits or cashing in

Table 8.2 Major Sources of Nonhousing Consumer Loans

Credit Source	Commercial Banks	Consumer Finance Companies
Type of Loan	• single payment loans • personal installment loans • passbook loans • check-credit plans • credit card loans • second mortgages	• personal installment loans • second mortgages
Lending Policies	• seek customers with established credit history • often require collateral or security • prefer to deal in large loans such as auto, home improvement and modernization, with the exception of credit card and check-credit plans • determine repayment schedules according to the purpose of the loan • vary credit rates according to the type of credit, time period, customer's credit history and the security offered • may require several days to process a new credit application	• often lend to consumers without established credit history • often make unsecured loans • often vary rates according to the size of the loan balance • offer a variety of repayment schedules • make a higher percentage of small loans than other lenders • maximum loan size limited by law • process applications quickly, frequently the same day as the application is made
Cost	lower than some lenders because they: • take fewer credit risks • lend depositors' money, a relatively inexpensive source of funds • deal primarily in large loans which yield larger dollar income without raising administrative costs	higher than some lenders because they: • take greater risks • must borrow and pay interest on money to lend • deal frequently in small loans which are costly to make and yield a small income
Services	• offer several different types of consumer credit plans • may offer financial counseling • handle credit transactions confidentially	• provide credit promptly • make loans to pay off accumulated debts willingly • design repayment schedules to fit the borrower's income • usually offer financial counseling • handle credit transactions confidentially

Source: This material taken from *Managing Your Credit,* published by the Money Management Institute of Household International, Prospect Heights, Illinois, 1983, pp. 18–19.

certificates of deposit before the end of some specified period. The interest rate on a bank loan may be affected by the loan's size, terms, and whether it is secured by some type of collateral.

Consumer Finance Companies Sometimes called *small loan companies, consumer finance companies* make secured and unsecured, or signature, loans to qualified individuals. These companies do not accept deposits but rather obtain funds from their stockholders and through borrowing. Because they do not have the inexpensive sources of funds that banks and other deposit-type institutions have, their interest rates are generally quite high, not infrequently ranging from 15

Table 8.2 (*continued*)

Credit Unions	Life Insurance Companies	Savings and Loan Associations
• personal installment loans • share draft credit plans • credit card loans • second mortgages	• single or partial payment loans	• personal installment loans (generally permitted by state-chartered savings associations) • home improvement loans • education loans • savings account loans • second mortgages
• lend to members only • make unsecured loans • may require collateral or cosigner for loans over a specified amount • may require payroll deductions to pay off loan • may submit large loan applications to a committee of members for approval • offer a variety of repayment schedules	• lend on cash value of life insurance policy • no date or penalty on repayment • deduct amount owed from the value of policy benefit if death or other maturity occurs before repayment	• will lend to all credit-worthy individuals • often require collateral • loan rates vary, depending on size of loan, length of payment and security involved
lower than some lenders because they: • take fewer credit risks • lend money deposited by members, less expensive than borrowed money • often receive free office space and supplies from the sponsoring organization • are managed by members whose services, in most cases, are donated • enjoy federal income tax exemptions	lower than some lenders because they: • take no risk • pay no collection costs • secure loans by cash value of policy	lower than some lenders because they: • lend depositors' money, a relatively inexpensive source of funds • secure most loans by savings accounts or real estate
• design repayment schedules to fit the borrower's income • generally provide credit life insurance without extra charge • may offer financial counseling • handle credit transactions confidentially	• permit repayment at any time • handle credit transactions confidentially	• often offer financial counseling • specialize in mortgages and other housing-related loans • handle credit transactions confidentially

to 36 percent per year. The actual rates charged by consumer finance companies are regulated by interest rate ceilings set by the states in which they operate. The maximum allowable interest rate may vary with the size of the loan. State regulatory authorities also limit the maximum size and repayment period of these loans. Typically, loans made by consumer finance companies are for $5,000 or less and are secured by some type of asset. Repayment is required on an installment basis over a period of five years or less. Consumer finance companies generally make small loans to high-risk borrowers. Of course, these loans are quite costly, but they may be the only alternative for people who have poor credit ratings. Some people are attracted to consumer finance companies due to the ease with which loans may be obtained from them. Because of the high rates of interest charged, the individual should consider this source only after exhausting others.

Credit Unions Only members can obtain installment loans and, in some cases, single payment loans from credit unions, which are described in Chapter 5. Because they are nonprofit organizations with minimal operating costs, credit unions charge relatively low rates on their loans. The maximum rate of interest that federally chartered credit unions can charge their customers is 1.75 percent a month, or 21 percent per year; state-chartered credit unions typically can charge no more than 21 percent annual interest. Most credit unions currently make loans at annual percentage rates ranging from 9 to 15 percent. They make both unsecured and secured loans depending on the size and type of loan being requested. The maximum size of loan made by credit unions to their members is often set by certain regulatory agencies. In addition, the directors of the credit union frequently set their own in-house loan limits. Generally speaking, membership in a credit union provides the most attractive borrowing opportunities available since their interest rates and borrowing requirements are commonly more favorable than other sources of nonhousing consumer loans. An added convenience of credit union loans is that loan payments can often be deducted from payroll checks.

Life Insurance Companies Life insurance policyholders can often obtain loans from their insurance companies. Certain types of policies not only provide a death benefit but also have a savings function, and these can be used as collateral for loans. (A detailed discussion of life insurance is presented in Chapter 9.) Life insurance companies are required by law to make loans against the *cash value*—the amount of savings accumulated—of their customers' policies. The rate of interest on these loans is stated in the policy, and the trend in state regulation today is to allow market rates set at the time the loan is taken out, and revised as often as every few months, although in the past the legal limit was 8 percent. Such loans typically have no repayment date, and interest is charged on the actual amount for the period of time the loan is outstanding. A loan on a life insurance policy may never be repaid, in which case the amount of the loan outstanding plus any accrued interest is deducted from the proceeds of the policyholder or beneficiaries when the policy is retired.

When you take out a loan against the cash value of your life insurance policy, you are really borrowing your own money, and the procedure is simple. Forms can be obtained from your agent or by writing the company. Once completed, they are returned to the insurance company, which (normally) promptly issues you a check for the specified amount. Interest on the loan is then included as part of your premium payment. Generally these loans are attractive. The chief danger of life insurance loans is that they do not have a firm maturity date. Therefore, borrowers may lack motivation to repay them. Delay in repaying these loans increases their cost to the borrower, who must pay interest until the loan is retired. As indicated earlier, all borrowing must be budgeted—both in amount and with respect to repayment.

Savings and Loan Associations Savings and loan associations and mutual savings banks, both of which are discussed in detail in Chapter 5, primarily make mortgage loans as described in Chapter 6. They are also permitted to make loans on consumer durables such as televisions, refrigerators, and ranges; in addition, they make certain types of home improvement and mobile home loans that are secured by assets, as well as some personal and educational loans using passbook savings as collateral.

The rate of interest on nonmortgage loans ranges from $7\frac{1}{4}$ to 21 percent. In each case the rate depends on several factors, including the type and purpose of the loan, the duration and type of repayment (single payment or installment), and the overall credit worthiness of the borrower. Although savings and loan associations and mutual savings banks primarily offer mortgage loans, in some parts of the country you can get the type of loan you require from them at rates competitive with those of other lenders.

Sales Finance Companies Businesses who sell more expensive items, such as automobiles, furniture, and appliances, often provide installment financing to purchasers of their products. Because dealers cannot afford to tie up their funds in installment contracts, they sell them to a *sales finance company* for cash. This procedure is often referred to as "selling paper" since merchants in effect sell their loans to a third party. When the sales finance company purchases these notes, the customer is normally notified to make payments directly to it. Should the customer fail to make payments to the finance company, the merchant may be held liable if the paper was sold *with recourse;* if it was sold *without recourse,* the merchant can no longer be held liable. The customer has an obvious concern in the sale of his or her loan. For example, suppose the merchandise proves defective: can the customer withhold payments from the finance company in an effort to pressure the merchant to correct the defects? Under the *holder in due course doctrine,* the answer would have been, no. However, the Fair Credit Billing Act of October 1975, a Federal Trade Commission regulation put into effect in May 1976, and other state regulations have more or less eliminated this clause from loan agreements. In cases in which the seller and the financing agency cooperate to arrange the financing, the holder in due course doctrine is no longer valid. (But when a purchaser independently arranges financing in order to make a purchase, it is likely to remain in effect, since the lender can be considered an independent third party.) Future legislation will probably cause any holder of a consumer credit contract to be subject to all claims and defenses made by the purchaser (debtor). Such action will provide the consumer with the best protection possible on installment purchases.

The largest sales finance companies are the *captive finance companies* owned by manufacturers of big-ticket items—automobiles and appliances. General Motors Acceptance Corporation (GMAC) and General Electric Credit (GEC) are examples of captive (sales) finance companies that purchase the installment loans made by dealers in their products. Some large commercial banks act as sales finance companies by buying paper from certain types of businesses. The cost of financing through sales finance companies is generally in the range of 12 to 24 percent per year. Rates tend to be higher than those charged on similar loans by commercial banks and credit unions. Often when consumers let a dealer arrange financing for a purchase, they end up owing a sales finance company for a loan with an unnecessarily high interest rate. The reverse sometimes occurs, such as in the case when low-cost credit is used as a marketing tactic. This was done by automobile manufacturers in late 1982 and early 1983 when interest rates began falling from their previous historic highs. You should be sure, of course, that you also are getting the best price for the product you want. If cheap credit is substituted for lower prices, it might be better to buy the product elsewhere and arrange your own, and perhaps more favorable, financing.

Pawnshops Loans can be obtained in exchange for some kind of collateral, or *pawn,* as it is often called, at *pawnshops.* The pawnshop accepts certain types of goods such as jewelry, guns, and stereos against which it lends 25 to 75 percent of their estimated market value. An individual who needs money and is unable to obtain it from other sources may turn to the pawnshop as a last resort. To pawn an item, a person need only take it to a pawnshop and have the pawnbroker appraise it and specify the amount that he or she will lend using it as collateral. The pawnbroker is required by the Truth in Lending Act to disclose both the dollar amount and annual percentage rate of interest that will be charged on a proposed loan. If both parties agree, the pawnbroker gives the customer the specified amount of money along with a pawn ticket to be used in reclaiming the pawned merchandise and receives possession of the merchandise in return. The loan might be for anywhere from one to twelve months. It is a single payment loan that is, in effect, secured by the pawned item. If the borrower does not repay the loan as well as the interest according to the terms of the agreement, the pawnbroker will sell the pawned item and use the proceeds to satisfy the outstanding loan. If the pawnbroker nets more from this sale than is owed on the loan, this excess is supposed to be returned to the borrower. The rate of interest, which typically ranges from 20 to 40 percent per year, and many other aspects of pawnshop operations are regulated by various local and state governments. In states that do not regulate their interest rates, such as Florida, the rate of interest charged by pawnbrokers can go as high as 10 percent per month, which is equivalent to an annual percentage rate of 120 percent.

Borrowers who use pawnshops are usually from low-income groups and often do not repay the loans they receive on pawned merchandise. Because pawnshops end up with a great deal of merchandise to sell, they operate as retail stores in which jewelry, stereos, and other items are offered for sale at attractive prices. In fact, many sell not only the used merchandise they have claimed as the result of unpaid loans but also new items they have purchased solely for resale purposes. Due to the high costs involved, the use of pawnshops as a source of loans is not advised. But as a consumer looking for a bargain on merchandise, you might find that the pawnshop offers interesting purchase opportunites.

Remedial Loan Societies In some metropolitan areas, nonprofit organizations have been set up to provide a mechanism through which the poor can get a fair deal. These *remedial loan societies* operate in a manner similar to a pawnshop in that they lend against personal assets, which are held as collateral. The borrower is expected to repay the amount lent along with the interest at maturity of the loan. The annual percentage rate of interest on these loans, most of which are made for a period of one year or less, is relatively low given the risks involved—15 to 21 percent per year. Like pawnbrokers, these societies sell the collateral to satisfy an unpaid loan. And similarly, if excess proceeds are obtained through the sale, the borrower will be entitled to receive these funds. Probably only about 20 of these societies exist today.

Friends and Relatives Often a close friend or relative who has excess funds will be willing to lend you money. In many cases such loans are attractive because little or no interest is charged. The terms will, of course, vary depending on the financial needs of the borrower, but they should be specified in a loan agreement that states the costs, conditions, and maturity date of the loan as well as the obligations of both borrower and lender. Not only does a written loan agreement reduce opportunities for disagreement and unhappiness, but it also legally protects both borrower and lender should either of them die or other unexpected events occur. Still, given the potential for disagreement and conflict among friends and relatives inherent in this type of arrangement, borrowing from friends or relatives is advisable only when the terms are considerably better than those available from one of the more traditional sources or when there are no other alternatives.

Single Payment Loans

The single payment loan differs from other loans in that it is to be repaid in full on a given date. It is useful when funds for a necessary purchase are currently inadequate but expected to be available in the future. Thus it can aid in meeting emergency cash requirements, serving as a form of interim financing until more permanent financing can be arranged. This part of the chapter examines two aspects of single payment loans: finance charges and annual percentage rate computations and the important features of loan agreements.

Finance Charges and Annual Percentage Rate (APR) Computations

As indicated in the preceding chapter, the Consumer Credit Protection Act, or Truth in Lending Act, requires all lenders to disclose both the dollar amount of finance charges and the annual percentage rate (APR) of interest. A sample disclosure statement applicable for either a single payment or an installment loan is given in Figure 8.1. Although disclosures such as this allow you to compare the cost of various borrowing alternatives, you still need to understand the methods used to compute finance charges, since similar loans with the same *stated* interest rates may have different finance charges and APRs. The two basic methods used to calculate the finance charges on single payment loans are the simple interest method and the discount method.

Simple Interest Method Interest is charged only on the *actual loan balance outstanding* in the *simple interest method*. This method is commonly used on revolving open account charges, by commercial banks, and by credit unions. To see how it is applied to a single payment loan, assume that you borrow $1,000 for two years, at a 12 percent stated annual rate of interest. On a single payment loan, the actual loan balance outstanding for the two years would be $1,000 since no payments are made until the two years have elapsed. The finance charge calculated using the simple interest method, F_s, is obtained by multiplying the actual *principal amount* outstanding by the stated annual rate of interest and then multiplying this product by the term of the loan (Equation 8.1).

$$F_s = Prt \tag{8.1}$$

where:

F_s = finance charge calculated using the simple interest method

P = the principal amount of the loan

r = stated annual rate of interest

t = term of the loan stated in years

Substituting $1,000 for P, .12 for r, and 2 for t in Equation 8.1, F_s becomes $240 ($1,000 × .12 per year × 2 years).

Figure 8.1 Disclosure Statement from a Loan Agreement

DISCLOSURE STATEMENT OF LOAN

BORROWERS (NAMES AND ADDRESSES): ______ LOAN NO.______ DATE______

LENDER: MERCANTILE BANK & TRUST COMPANY

4115 So. Darlington
(Mailing Address)
Tulsa, Oklahoma 74135
(City) (State) (Zip)

DISCLOSURES REQUIRED BY FEDERAL LAW:
(Supplementing Those Above Given and Those Given in Note and Security Agreement)

PAYMENT TERMS: Payable:______ after date; or Payable in______equal monthly payments of $______, commencing on ______, 19____, and on the same day of the month thereafter, plus an irregular payment of $______, due on______, 19____; (Delete payment terms inapplicable.); together with a delinquency or late charge not exceeding the lesser of $5.00 or 5% of each installment in default for 10 or more days. Further, if suit is instituted, upon borrowers' Default, to collect outstanding balance or otherwise to enforce Note and Security Agreement, borrowers are liable for lender's legal expenses not exceeding 15% of the unpaid balance at the time of suit.

BALLOON PAYMENT, if any, and conditions (if any) for refinancing same, if not paid when due: $______, ______

BASIC TERMS OF LOAN CONTRACT:

1. LOAN PROCEEDS: ...... $______
2. OTHER CHARGES: (TOTAL) ...... $______
   a. Premium, Credit Life: ...... $______
   b. Premium, Disability Ins.: ...... $______
   c. Premium, Physical Dam. Ins.: ...... $______
   d. Title & Notary Fees: ...... $______
   e. Filing & Related Fees: ...... $______
   f. Other:______ ...... $______
3. LESS: Prepaid FINANCE CHARGE: ...... $______
   Required Deposit Balance: ...... $______
   TOTAL PREPAID FINANCE CHARGE & REQUIRED DEPOSIT BALANCE: ...... $______
4. AMOUNT FINANCED (No. 1 + No. 2 minus No. 3): $______
5. FINANCE CHARGE: ...... $______
6. TOTAL OF PAYMENTS: ...... $______
7. ANNUAL PERCENTAGE RATE: ...... ______%

Source: Courtesy of Mercantile Bank and Trust Company, Tulsa, Oklahoma.

To calculate the true, or annual, percentage rate (APR) of interest on this loan, the average annual finance charge is divided by the average loan balance outstanding, as specified in Equation 8.2.

$$\text{APR} = \frac{\text{average annual finance charge}}{\text{average loan balance outstanding}} \qquad \textbf{(8.2)}$$

The average annual finance charge is found by dividing the finance charge by the life of the loan (in years). In our example, the result is \$120 (\$240 ÷ 2). Because the loan balance outstanding remains at \$1,000 over the life of the loan, the average loan balance outstanding is \$1,000. When the \$120 average annual finance charge is divided by the \$1,000 average loan balance outstanding, an APR of 12 percent results. Thus the APR and the stated rate of interest (also 12 percent) are equivalent. This is *always* the case when the simple interest method is used to calculate finance charges, whether loans are single payment or installment.

Discount Method The finance charges are calculated and then subtracted from the amount of the loan in the *discount method*. The difference between the amount of the loan and the finance charges is then lent to the borrower. In other words, finance charges are paid in

Table 8.3 Finance Charges and APRs for a $1,000 Single Payment Loan with a Stated Interest[a]

Method	Finance Charges	Approximate APR
Simple Interest	$240	12.0%
Discount	240	15.8

[a]At a stated annual rate of interest of 12 percent to be repaid at the end of two years.

advance and represent a discount from the principal amount of the loan. The finance charge on a single payment loan using the discount method, F_d, is calculated in the same way as for the simple interest loan:

$$F_d = F_s = Prt \tag{8.3}$$

Using the above method, the finance charge, F_d, is $240.

To find the annual percentage rate (APR) on this discount loan, substitute the appropriate values into Equation 8.2. For this two-year loan, the average annual finance charge is $120 ($240 ÷ 2). But since on a discount loan the finance charges for the life of the loan are deducted from the stated amount of the loan, the borrower receives only $760 ($1,000 principal amount of loan − $240 in finance charges). Because this is a single payment loan, the amount of the average loan balance is thus $760. When Equation 8.2 is applied to these figures, the APR for the discount loan is found to be 15.8 percent ($120 ÷ $760). Clearly, the discount method yields a higher APR on single payment loans than does the simple interest method. Table 8.3 depicts these results for the single payment loan example discussed here. Two important points should be noted: (1) the computations shown pertain only to single payment loans and (2) interest is assumed to represent the only component of the finance charge. The calculation of finance charges and APRs for installment loans is discussed later in this chapter.

Important Features of Loan Agreements

Although the finance charges on a single payment loan are an important consideration, other features of the loan agreement also deserve attention. The Truth in Lending Act made mandatory the explicit disclosure of all conditions and features of loans.

Loan Collateral Most single payment loans are secured by certain specified assets. Lenders will only grant unsecured loans to the highest quality borrowers with proven credit histories. For *collateral*, lenders accept only items that are readily marketable at a price sufficiently high to cover the principal amount of the loan—for example, an automobile, jewelry, or stocks and bonds. If a loan is obtained to purchase some personal asset, that asset may be used to secure the loan. In most cases lenders do not take physical possession of the collateral, but rather file a *lien*, a legal claim that permits them to liquidate the items that serve as collateral to satisfy their claim in the event of default. The lien is filed in the county courthouse and is a matter of public record. If borrowers maintain possession or title to *movable* property used as loan collateral, the instrument that gives the lenders title to the property in the event of default is called a *chattel mortgage.* Chattels are movable assets such as cars, TVs, and jewelry. If lenders actually take possession of loan collateral or the title to collateral, as in the case of stocks and bonds, the agreement giving them the right to sell these items in the instance of default is a *collateral note*.

Sometimes single payment loans are secured using second mortgages on homes. A *second mortgage* is a secondary claim on the proceeds from liquidating a home in order to satisfy unpaid claims. Because the market value of a home is likely to be greater than the amount owed on it, second mortgages can provide an excellent source of loan collateral. For example, if you owe $50,000 on a home that currently has a net market value (that is, after all expected sales costs) of $75,000, you have $25,000 ($75,000 − $50,000) of unused collateral value. You may be able to use some of this amount to secure a loan with a second mortgage.

Sometimes, too, borrowers can secure loans by having a creditworthy friend or relative *cosign* for them. Of course, if they default, their cosigner is required to repay the loan, since by cosigning he or she has guaranteed it.

Maturity, or Term, of the Loan As indicated earlier, the maturity, or term, of a single payment loan is typically one year or less. When you request such a loan, you should be sure its term is long enough to allow you to receive the money needed for repayment but no longer than necessary since the dollar amount of finance charges paid increases with time. Because the loan is to be paid in a single payment, the lender must be assured that you can repay it at the specified future date even if certain unexpected events occur in the meantime. The term of your single payment loan must therefore be reconciled with your budget as well as your ability to pay. If the money you plan to use for repayment will be received periodically over the term of the loan, an installment type of loan would probably be more suitable.

Repayment: Early or Late? The repayment of a single payment loan is expected to take place on its maturity date. Occasionally, the funds needed to repay this type of loan will be received prior to maturity. Depending on the lender, the borrower might then be able to repay the loan prior to its maturity and thereby reduce the finance charges on it. Credit unions often permit early repayment of these loans with reduced finance charges, but commercial banks and other single payment lenders either do not accept early repayments or charge a *prepayment penalty* on them. This penalty normally amounts to a set percentage of the interest that would have been paid over the remaining life of the loan. The Truth in Lending Act requires lenders to disclose in the loan agreement whether or not and in what amount prepayment penalties are charged on a single payment loan. This information should be understood prior to signing a loan agreement.

Paying back a loan late should be avoided at all costs. For if you are unable to repay a single payment loan at maturity, you will be in default, and the lender could force you into bankruptcy. If you cannot pay on time, inform the lender in advance so that a partial payment, a loan extension, or some other arrangement can be made. If you wait until payment is already past due before talking with the lender, your credit rating as well as the possibility of working out an agreement with the lender will probably be reduced. Whatever you do, do not try to trick or avoid the lender; such action can severely damage your credit rating. Maintaining a favorable credit rating is vital since it can significantly affect both your cost and availability of credit.

Installment Loans

Installment loans, which are made to purchase certain goods and services, require the borrower to make scheduled payments over the life of the agreement. They typically require equal monthly payments over a period of six or more months. This part of the chapter discusses finance charges and APR computations on installment loans, the installment purchase agreement, special features of the agreement, and early repayment considerations related to installment loans.

Finance Charges and APR Computations

In the preceding part of this chapter, the finance charges and annual percentage rates (APRs) of interest on single payment loans were discussed. The simple interest and discount methods of determining finance charges on single payment loans were described and illustrated. In this section, the simple interest and add-on methods of computing finance charges on installment loans are the subject. For illustrative purposes, a $1,000 installment loan with a stated interest rate of 12 percent and 12 monthly installment payments will be used. As in the earlier illustration for single payment loans, interest is assumed to rep-

Table 8.4 Payment Analysis for a $1,000 Loan at a 12 Percent Annual Interest Rate to Be Repaid in 12 Monthly Installments

Month	Outstanding Loan Balance (1)	Monthly Payment (2)	Interest [(1) × 0.01] (3)	Principal [(2) − (3)] (4)
1	$1,000.00	$ 88.85	$10.00	$ 78.85
2	921.15	88.85	9.21	79.64
3	841.51	88.85	8.42	80.43
4	761.08	88.85	7.61	81.24
5	679.84	88.85	6.80	82.05
6	597.79	88.85	5.98	82.87
7	514.92	88.85	5.15	83.70
8	431.22	88.85	4.31	84.54
9	346.68	88.85	3.47	85.38
10	261.30	88.85	2.61	86.24
11	175.06	88.85	1.75	87.10
12	87.96	88.85	0.89	87.96
Totals		$1,066.20	$66.20	$1,000.00

Notes: Column (1) values for months 2 through 12 are obtained by subtracting the principal payment shown in column (4) for the preceding month from the outstanding loan balance shown in column (1) for the preceding month. In column (3) the 0.01 value represents the monthly interest charge of 1 percent, since the stated rate of interest is 12 percent per year.

resent the only component of the finance charge; the presence of any other loan charges, such as credit life insurance or title and notary fees, is ignored.

Simple Interest Method In the case of installment loans, simple interest is charged only on the outstanding balance. The required payments can be determined from financial tables, which, due to their complexity, are not discussed here. As shown in Table 8.4, the monthly payment on a $1,000, 12-percent installment loan to be repaid in 12 monthly installments is $88.85. Since the stated interest rate is 12 percent per year, monthly interest of 1 percent (12 percent ÷ 12 months) is applied to the outstanding loan balance each month. Table 8.4 illustrates how loan payments are divided into interest and principal components in calculating simple interest on an installment loan. Of the payment total of $1,066.20, $66.20 represents interest and the remaining $1,000 represents repayment of the principal. Since no finance charges other than interest have been assumed, the total finance charges are $66.20. And because interest is charged only on the outstanding balance of the loan, the annual percentage rate of interest on an installment loan calculated by the simple interest method equals the stated rate, in this case 12 percent.

Add-On Method Finance charges and monthly payments on installment loans are commonly computed on the basis of the *add-on method.*

Equation 8.1, which was presented in the section on single payment loans, can be used for this purpose. Given the \$1,000, 12-month loan with a stated rate of interest at the 12-percent annual rate, $P = \$1{,}000$, $r = .12$, and $t = 1$; thus the computations prescribed in Equation 8.1 yield a finance charge of \$120 (\$1,000 × .12 × 1). The finance charge is added to the principal amount, and the total is divided by the number of payments to be made; this results in the amount of the monthly payment, in this case \$93.33 ([\$1,000 + \$120] ÷ 12).

The formula given in Equation 8.4 can be applied to calculate the approximate APR on an add-on loan. It represents the *N-ratio method,* the most accurate method currently available for estimating the annual percentage rate.

$$\text{Approximate APR} = \frac{M(95N + 9)F}{12N(N + 1)(4P + F)} \tag{8.4}$$

where:

APR = annual percentage rate of interest

M = number of payments in a year

N = number of loan payments scheduled over life of loan

F = total finance charges

P = the principal amount of the loan

If $M = 12$, $N = 12$, $F = \$120$, and $P = \$1{,}000$, the approximate APR is 21.5 percent:

$$\begin{aligned}\text{Approximate APR} &= \frac{(12)[(95)(12) + 9](\$120)}{(12)(12)(12 + 1)[(4)(\$1{,}000) + \$120]} \\ &= \frac{\$1{,}654{,}560}{\$7{,}712{,}640} = \underline{\underline{21.5\%}}\end{aligned}$$

A less accurate, but also less detailed, estimate of APR can be made using the *constant ratio method*. Using the symbols above, this equation is

$$\text{APR} = \frac{2MF}{P(N + 1)}. \tag{8.5}$$

Substituting the numbers above,

$$\text{Approximate APR} = \frac{2(12)(\$120)}{\$1{,}000(12 + 1)} = \frac{\$2{,}880}{\$13{,}000} = \underline{\underline{22.2\%}}$$

Table 8.5 Finance Charges and APRs for a $1,000 Installment Loan[a]

Method	Finance Charges	Approximate APR
Simple Interest	$ 66.20	12.0%
Add-On	120.00	21.5

[a]At a stated annual rate of interest of 12 percent to be repaid in 12 equal monthly installments.

There is somewhat of a difference between the two answers. The constant ratio method can be used when a quick calculation is needed, but for greater accuracy, the N-ratio method is preferred.

Whichever of these methods is used, the approximate APR using the add-on method is considerably higher than the APR of 12 percent found when the simple interest method was used. When add-on interest is applied to an installment loan, the interest included in each payment is charged on the initial principal even though the outstanding loan balance is reduced as installment payments are made. Like the approximate APR, the exact APR calculated with the add-on method is higher than the APR calculated with the simple interest method. A summary of the finance charges and approximate APRs for this example is presented in Table 8.5.

Under the Truth in Lending Act, the exact APR (accurate to the nearest 0.25 percent) must be disclosed to borrowers. Sophisticated formulas or financial tables derived from such formulas are necessary to find the exact value of the APR. You will probably never have to calculate it yourself, but as a well-informed consumer, you should understand the differences in the simple interest and add-on methods of computing finance charges. Note, too, that not only interest but also any other fees required to obtain a loan are considered part of the finance charges used in the computation of the APR. In the illustrations presented in this chapter, interest was assumed to represent the only finance charge on the loan.

The Installment Purchase Agreement

All of the information relevant to the transaction being financed on an installment basis is included in an *installment purchase agreement*. This agreement specifies the obligations of both the purchaser (or borrower) and the lender. Although its form is likely to vary with the lender, it will probably contain four basic components: a sales contract, a security agreement, a note, and an insurance agreement. A sample purchase agreement used for installment sales of autos or trucks by General Motors dealers in the state of Michigan and containing all four of the components mentioned is presented in Figure 8.2. The back side of the agreement (not shown) has all of the detailed provisions printed on it.

Sales Contract An important part of the purchase agreement, the *sales contract* is drawn up to provide adequate protection for the lender in the event that the purchaser defaults on the installment loan. The actual content and form are regulated by the state in which the contract is drawn. Sales contracts specify all key information with respect to identification of borrower, lender, and the merchandise being purchased as well as any down payment, the amount of payments, all other fees, and the finance charges and APR. The upper portion (through item 5) of Figure 8.2 represents the sales contract for the sample installment purchase agreement.

Security Agreement The *security agreement* (or *security interest*), which may be part of the sales contract, gives the installment lender control over the item being purchased. Although state laws determine whether or not the borrower retains legal title to the collateral, the lender files a lien on the collateral in order to make his or her "security interest" public. In either case, the lender retains legal control over the collateral. If default does occur, the lender can sell the collateral and use the proceeds to satisfy the unpaid loan balance and cover any costs incurred in this process. The lender must pay the borrower any excess funds obtained from the liquidation of the collateral. If the proceeds from liquidation are not sufficient to satisfy the loan, the borrower remains liable for the unsatisfied portion of the debt. The security agreement appears near the bottom of the installment purchase contract illustrated in Figure 8.2.

Note The formal promise on the part of the borrower to repay the lender as specified in the sales contract is contained in the *note.* It states the legal obligations of both the borrower and lender and outlines all details about repayment, default, and disposition of collateral. The note is normally secured by the sales contract or security agreement, which provides the lender with a security interest in the assets being acquired. It is the document which, when signed by both borrower and lender, legally binds them to the terms and conditions stated therein. Although many of the detailed provisions of the note in Figure 8.2 are on the reverse side of the contract (not shown), the entire document, when signed, is considered to be the note.

Insurance Agreement Sometimes, as a condition of receiving an installment loan, the borrower is required to buy *credit life insurance* and possibly credit disability insurance. These policies insure the borrower for an amount sufficient to repay the outstanding loan balance.

Figure 8.2 Sample Installment Purchase Agreement

GMAC FINANCING **General Motors Acceptance Corporation**

RETAIL INSTALMENT SALE CONTRACT Dealer Number Contract Number

Buyer (and Co-Buyer)—Name and Address (Include County and Zip Code)	Creditor (Seller Name and Address)

You, the Buyer (and Co-Buyer, if any), may buy the vehicle described below for cash or on credit. The cash price is shown below as "Cash Price." The credit price is shown below as "Total Sale Price." By signing this contract, you choose to buy the vehicle on credit under the agreements on the front and back of this contract.

Descrip:ion of Vehicle. You agree to buy and the Creditor agrees to sell the following vehicle:

New or Used	Year	Make and Model	Body Type	Vehicle Identification No.	Use for Which Purchased
					☐ personal ☐ agricultural ☐ business ☐ ______

If truck—Give GVW and describe body and major items of equipment sold:

FEDERAL TRUTH-IN-LENDING DISCLOSURES

ANNUAL PERCENTAGE RATE The cost of your credit as a yearly rate.	**FINANCE CHARGE** The dollar amount the credit will cost you.	**Amount Financed** The amount of credit provided to you or on your behalf.	**Total of Payments** The amount you will have paid after you have made all payments as scheduled.	**Total Sale Price** The total cost of your purchase on credit, including your downpayment of $ ______ is
______%	$______	$______	$______	$______

Your Payment Schedule Will Be:

Number of Payments	Amount of Payments	When Payments Are Due	Or as Follows
		Monthly beginning	

Late Charge. If a payment is not paid in full within 10 days after it is due, you will pay a late charge of 2% of the late payment per month, computed on the basis of a full calendar month for any fractional month period in excess of 10 days.

Prepayment. If you pay off all your debt early, you may be entitled to a refund of part of the finance charge.

Security Interest. You are giving a security interest in the vehicle being purchased.

Additional Information: See the other side of this contract for more information including information about nonpayment, default, any required repayment in full before the scheduled date, prepayment refunds and security interest.

ITEMIZATION OF AMOUNT FINANCED

1 Cash Price (including any accessories, services, and taxes) $ ______ (1)

2 Total Downpayment = Net Trade-in $ ______ + Cash Downpayment $ ______
Your Trade-in is a ______ Year ______ Make ______ Model $ ______ (2)

3 Unpaid Balance of Cash Price (1 minus 2) $ ______ (3)

4 Other Charges Including Amounts Paid to Others on Your Behalf:

A Cost of Required Physical Damage Insurance Paid to the Insurance Company Named Below—Covering Damage to the Vehicle $ ______

B Cost of Optional Credit Insurance for the Term of this Contract Paid to the Insurance Company or Companies Named Below. Life $ ______ Disability, Accident and Health $ ______ $ ______

C Official Fees Paid to Government Agencies $ ______

D Taxes Not Included in Cash Price $ ______

E Government License and/or Registration Fees (Itemize) $ ______

F Government Certificate of Title Fees $ ______

G Other Charges (Seller must identify who will receive payment and describe purpose)
to ______ for ______ $ ______
to ______ for ______ $ ______

Total Other Charges and Amounts Paid to Others on Your Behalf $ ______ (4)

5 Amount Financed—Unpaid Balance (3 + 4) $ ______ (5)

Insurance. If any insurance is checked below, the policies or certificates issued by the Companies named will describe the terms and conditions.

Required Physical Damage Insurance. Physical damage insurance is required, but you may obtain it from anyone you want who is acceptable to the Creditor. The cost of this insurance is shown in 4A of the Itemization above.

Insurance Company ______ Term: ______ months

☐ Regular $ ______ Deductible Collision; or
☐ Broadened $ ______ Deductible Collision; or
☐ Limited Collision (private passenger car); or
☐ Limited $ ______ Deductible Collision (commercial vehicle)

and either:

☐ Comprehensive Coverage
☐ $ ______ Deductible Comprehensive Coverage
☐ Fire-Theft and Combined Additional Coverage

Optional, if desired—☐ Towing and Labor costs ☐ Rental Reimbursement ☐ CB Radio Equipment

Optional Credit Insurance. Credit life insurance and credit disability insurance are not required to obtain credit and will not be provided unless you sign for them and agree to pay the additional cost. If you want this insurance, check the insurance desired and sign below. If you have chosen this insurance, the cost is shown in 4B of the itemization above.

Check the insurance desired: ☐ Life (Buyer ☐ Co-Buyer ☐ Both ☐)
☐ Disability, Accident and Health (Buyer Only)

Name of Insurer ______

Home Office Address ______

APPROVAL: I DESIRE TO OBTAIN THE CREDIT INSURANCE CHECKED ABOVE FOR THE PERSON PROPOSED FOR INSURANCE.

Buyer Signature ______ Date ______ Co-Buyer Signature ______ Date ______

You signed this contract on (Do not date on Sunday) ______, 19 ______ at ______ (City) (County) (State)

Warning: The Insurance afforded hereunder does not cover liability for injury to persons or damage to property of others.

NOTICE TO BUYER: 1. Do not sign this contract in blank. 2. You are entitled to a true copy of the contract you sign without charge. 3. Keep it to protect your legal rights.

Buyer Signs ______ Co-Buyer Signs ______

Co-Buyers and Other Owners—A co-buyer is a person who is responsible for paying the entire debt. An other owner is a person whose name is on the title to the vehicle but does not have to pay the debt. The co-buyer or other owner knows that the Creditor has a security interest in the vehicle and consents to the security interest.

Other owner signs here ______ Address ______

Creditor Signs ______ By ______ Title ______

Each undersigned acknowledges receipt from seller of a true, correct and complete copy of this contract at time of execution.

Buyer Signs ______ Co-Buyer Signs ______

This contract is assigned with recourse under the terms of the "Seller's Assignment" on the reverse side.	This contract is assigned without recourse or with limited recourse under the terms of the "Seller's Assignment" on the reverse side.
Seller By (If Corp. or Partnership) (Title)	Seller By (If Corp. or Partnership) (Title)

Z111 MI. 10-84 (For use in the State of Michigan) (1 of 4) **Notice: See Other Side** **ORIGINAL**

Source: Courtesy General Motors Acceptance Corporation.

By requiring this coverage, the seller and lender are assured that if the borrower dies or is disabled, the loan will be repaid. The seller's or lender's ability to dictate the terms of these insurance requirements is restricted by law in some states. The statement with respect to credit life insurance and credit disability insurance in the sample installment purchase agreement given in Figure 8.2 is contained in item 4B. If insurance is required as a condition of purchase, its cost must be included in the finance charges and APR disclosed by the lender. State laws specify the maximum premiums that can be charged on credit life and disability insurance. Buyers should always make sure that the cost of such insurance is reasonable since sellers or lenders often receive commissions on the sale of credit life and disability insurance. Purchasing the required insurance at a lower cost from another source is often possible.

Special Features of Installment Purchase Agreements

The general content of installment purchase agreements was described in the preceding section. Some of the more important features of these agreements, which are normally included as clauses in the sales contract and/or note, are further highlighted in the following sections.

Add-On Clause An *add-on clause* allows the lender to hold as security a number of items that are purchased over a period of time. The lender does not release the security interest in any of these items until the entire loan has been paid off. In the past, this would have allowed lenders to repossess items of merchandise already purchased and paid for if the borrower defaulted on other items purchased under the agreement. The Consumer Credit Protection Act disallowed such practices; it is still advisable, however, to use separate purchase agreements for each item purchased rather than one agreement with an add-on clause.

Acceleration Clause The *acceleration clause* allows the lender to demand immediate repayment of the entire amount of the unpaid debt if the purchaser misses a payment. Although this clause is always included in installment loans, the lender is likely to allow a late payment or levy a fixed penalty instead of accelerating the loan by exercising the acceleration clause.

Wage Assignment and Garnishment Some purchase agreements allow the lender to collect a portion of the purchaser's (borrower's) wages if the purchaser defaults on payments. By signing a purchase agreement with such a clause, the purchaser agrees to these terms and enables the lender to collect part of his or her wages without obtaining a court order. Even if an *assignment clause* is not enforceable (as often is the case) or not included in the agreement, a lender can still *garnish* a borrower's wages, which is a legal method of getting an employer to pay a portion of a borrower's wages to the lender. The borrower must, of course, be in default, and a court order must be issued to the employer in order for such action to be taken.

The *Federal Garnishment Law,* which was included as part of the Truth in Lending Act and became effective 1 July 1970, places limitations on the portion of an employee's wages that can be garnished. It specifically limits the amount of an employee's weekly wage that can be garnished to no more than the smaller of the following: (1) 25 percent of take-home pay, or (2) the amount by which take-home pay exceeds 30 times the federal minimum hourly wage ($3.35/hour in 1983, and likely to increase in subsequent years). The law also prohibits firms from firing employees as a result of their wages being garnished to repay a single debt. Many state laws have completely prohibited garnishing or have placed more severe restrictions than the federal law on the portion of a person's wages that can be garnished.

Repossession The act of seizing collateral when the borrower defaults on an installment loan is termed *repossession*. In many states the ability of the lender to repossess collateral in the case of default is limited. But in some states collateral can be repossessed without notice and even "in effect" stolen from the borrower. Still other states require a court order to repossess loan collateral. Quite a few states have detailed procedures that must be followed by the lender when selling repossessed items in order to satisfy unpaid debts. Because there have been many abuses in the repossession of collateral—especially in automobile financing—you should avoid the possibility of its occurrence. Repossession is a poor way to settle a debt. The repossessed item is usually sold—perhaps not very enthusiastically—by the merchant and the amount due him or her, along with legal and other expenses in connection with the repossession, is taken from the sale proceeds. If this is not enough to cover the loan, the customer can still be held liable for the remaining portion. In the event the sale proceeds are greater than the loan, the difference is returned to the borrower.

Balloon Clause Sometimes installment purchase agreements are set up in such a fashion that the final payment is considerably larger than all other payments. The Truth in Lending Act requires that any *balloon payment,* which is defined as a payment more than twice the normal installment payment, included in a loan agreement must be clearly identified as such. For example, a loan requiring monthly payments of $200 per month for 23 months, followed by a final payment of $1,000 in the 24th month, would have to clearly disclose the $1,000 balloon payment. A statement to this effect appears in the disclosure statement in Figure 8.1 and on the reverse side of the installment purchase agreement in Figure 8.2. Because balloon clauses have been abused by some lenders and can place borrowers in an undesirable position, some states prohibit their inclusion in a loan agreement. It is best not to enter into an agreement that includes such a clause, since it is difficult to know if you will be able to afford the balloon payment when it falls due. Only when the borrower is expecting a known sum of money at some exact future date can the use of a balloon payment be justified.

Early Repayment: The Rule of 78 (Sum of the Digits)

In most loan agreements (and according to some state laws), the borrower is permitted to repay a loan prior to its maturity. If interest has been prepaid, the loan agreement may provide for a refund of interest when an early repayment is made. In most cases, the *Rule of 78* (sometimes called *Sum of the Digits*) is used to determine the portion of the total finance charges the lender receives upon paying off a loan prior to its maturity. The rule is best illustrated using a simple example. Suppose you borrowed $1,000 to be repaid in 12 monthly installments of $90. Assume that the total finance charge over the life of the loan is $80. To determine the amount the lender will receive if you repay the loan after 3 months, you must first add all whole numbers between 1 and 12 (1 + 2 + 3 + . . . + 10 + 11 + 12). The total is 78. If the loan is repaid after 1 month, the lender receives 12/78 of the total interest. If it is repaid after 2 months, the amount of interest paid is 23/78 of the total interest ([12 + 11] ÷ 78), and so on. In the example, since the loan is repaid after 3 months, the lender receives 33/78 of the total interest ([12 + 11 + 10] ÷ 78). This amounts to $33.85 ([33/78] × $80).

Since the lender will receive $33.85, this means the borrower will be refunded $46.15 ($80.00 − $33.85) of the add-on interest. The "payoff" on the loan—that is, the amount required to eliminate the loan—is $763.85, calculated as follows:

Amount borrowed, including add-on interest	$1,080.00
Less interest refunded the borrower	46.15
Amount due the lender	$1,033.85
Less payments to date, 3 × $90.00	270.00
Payoff on the loan	$ 763.85

The purpose of the Rule of 78 is to allow the lender to get a fair return on loans that are repaid prior to maturity. Note that in spite of the name of this rule, the denominator in the fraction used may not always be 78. The denominator depends on the number of months in the total repayment period, while the numerator is determined by the principle illustrated earlier. For example, if you repay a 10 month loan after 2 months, the lender receives 19/55 ([10 + 9] ÷ [1 + 2 + ... + 9 + 10]) of the total finance charges. Although the use of the Rule of 78 to determine interest charges on prepayments of installment loans is most common, other rules do exist. On the reverse side (not shown) of the sample installment purchase agreement given in Figure 8.2, a statement indicates that the Rule of 78 is used on prepayments under that contract.

Summary

There are two basic types of consumer loans that are not open account forms of credit. Single payment loans are made for a specified period of time at the end of which full payment is due. They are used as interim financing and to meet emergency needs. Installment loans are repaid through a series of payments scheduled over a period of months. They are used to finance purchases of more expensive goods and services such as automobiles and appliances. Mortgage loans are a special type of installment loan; they are used to finance the purchase of housing. Consumer loans can be obtained from a variety of sources including commercial banks, consumer finance companies, credit unions, life insurance companies, savings and loan associations, sales finance companies, pawnshops, remedial loan societies, and friends and relatives.

Either the simple interest method or the discount method is normally used to compute the finance charges on single payment loans. While the stated rate of interest and the annual percentage rate (APR) of interest are equal using the simple interest method, the APR that results from the discount method is higher than the stated rate of interest. Most single payment loans are secured by loan collateral on which the lender obtains a security interest by filing a lien against the property. To have this legal claim on movable property, the lender must obtain either a chattel mortgage or a collateral note. Sometimes a single payment loan can be secured by a second mortgage on one's home. Another method is to have a second party cosign the note. Although lenders may allow early repayment of a single payment loan, they are likely to charge a fee for such action. Late payment of these loans can result in a damaged credit rating and possibly even personal bankruptcy.

Financial tables and formulas are required to calculate finance charges and APRs for installment loans because of the periodic nature of the payments. When the simple interest method is used on these loans, the APR and stated rate of interest are equal. However, the use of the add-on method to calculate finance charges results in an APR that is considerably higher than the stated interest rate. The installment purchase agreement, which may include a sales contract, a security agreement, a note, and an insurance agreement, contains all the relevant information pertaining to the purchase and installment repayment plan. Various aspects of purchase agreements that consumers should be aware of and understand include the following: add-on clauses, acceleration clauses, wage assignment or garnishment, repossession, and balloon clauses. Often installment lenders use the Rule of 78 to determine what portion of the total prepaid interest is refunded to the borrower when a loan is repaid before its maturity.

Life Insurance 9

Over a period of years, the difference between buying life insurance wisely and unwisely can easily amount to thousands of dollars in extra premiums and tens of thousands of dollars in lost protection. Wide differences exist among the types of life insurance policies that are available, the costs of those policies, and the quality of the companies and agents that sell them.

This chapter begins with a discussion of some fundamental concepts of risk and insurance that provide a base for your life insurance purchase decisions. In addition, you can apply these fundamental risk and insurance concepts to help you choose the right health, homeowner's, and automobile insurance coverages (treated in Chapters 10 and 11). Next, this chapter shows how you can logically figure out how much life insurance protection you and your family need. Following is an explanation of the types of life insurance policies that are widely available. Although the uninformed may come to feel overwhelmed by the diversity of market offerings, this explanation will show you that in essence many policies with different names are simply variations of several basic types of policies. Similarly, even with a number of different life insurance policies available, many share standard provisions. So, in the next major topic, this chapter explains the contract terms that are subject to analysis in nearly all types of policies. Analysis often means learning the right questions to ask. After reading these sections, you should be able to talk intelligently with a life insurance agent about your needs and the products he or she offers.

In the last sections of this chapter, we briefly look at how life insurance as a financial product compares with other types of financial assets such as savings accounts and U.S. bonds. The last discussion guides you through the life insurance buying process. By the chapter's end, you should know how to go about buying life insurance wisely.

Insurance Fundamentals

All insurance contracts are based on several fundamental concepts. These concepts center on risk, insurable exposures, and underwriting. If you learn these three concepts, you will better understand the role insurance can play in society, and the role it can play in your financial planning.

Concept of Risk

In insurance, *risk* is defined as uncertainty with respect to economic loss. Whenever you and your family have a financial interest in something—whether your life, health, home, car, boat, or your job—you face risk. You face the chance that your budget will be upset and that, perhaps, your net worth will be drastically reduced. Therefore, because of the great effect that losses can have on your financial well-being, you must plan ways to deal with risk. They include risk avoidance, risk assumption, loss prevention, and insurance.

Risk Avoidance Perhaps the simplest way to deal with risk is to avoid the act that creates the risk. For example, people who are afraid they might lose all they own because of a successful lawsuit against them resulting from an automobile accident could avoid driving. Many people seeking a job avoid the risk of unstable or low earnings by refusing to accept employment that pays on a commission-only basis.

Although avoidance can be an effective way to handle some risks, such action is not costless. For instance, the people who avoid driving suffer considerable inconvenience, and the person seeking a job may forfeit an opportunity for commission earnings in excess of guaranteed salary. Risk avoidance is an attractive way to deal with risk when the estimated cost of avoidance is less than the estimated cost of handling it in some other way.

Risk Assumption With *risk assumption* you choose to accept and bear the risk of loss. Risk assumption can be an effective way to handle many types of potentially small exposures to loss when insurance would be too expensive (for example, the risk of having this Guide stolen). It is also a reasonable approach in the face of very large exposures that the individual cannot ordinarily avoid or prevent or cannot secure insurance against (nuclear holocaust, for instance). Unfortunately, people often assume risks because they are unaware of various exposures to loss or because they think that their insurance offers adequate protection when in fact it does not. Therefore, an objective of these three chapters on insurance is to help you recognize exposures to loss that you will face and provide you with an understanding of when risk assumption is the preferred manner for handling given risks.

Loss Prevention In a broad sense, *loss prevention* can be defined as any activity that reduces the probability a loss will occur (for example, driving within the speed limit) or lessens the severity of the loss should it occur (for example, wearing a safety belt and shoulder strap). Loss prevention should be an important part of the risk management program of every individual and family. In fact, insurance provides a reasonable means for handling risk only when people use effective loss prevention measures. For example, if everybody drove fast and recklessly, risk avoidance might be the way to deal with the risk of an automobile accident because automobile insurance would be too expensive to buy.

Insurance *Insurance* permits society to reduce financial risks and share losses. Risk or uncertainty can be reduced because insurers are able to combine the loss experiences of large numbers of people, and with the resulting data they can estimate the chance of loss faced by the insured population. This prediction then allows each person to contribute a specified relatively small amount (the insurance premium) to an insurer in exchange for a promise that he or she will be reimbursed for covered losses. Individual insureds gain because they are able to transfer their risk to the insurer. The insurance company may benefit because, if the amount of insured losses has been accurately estimated, the company can realize a gain.

Characteristics of an Insurable Exposure

Even though insurance can be an ideal method for handling the risk of economic loss, not all risks are insurable. In order for the insurance mechanism to work well, certain criteria must be met. Several of the more important of these criteria are (1) there must be a large number of similar exposures to loss, (2) the potential loss must be fortuitous, (3) the cost of the insurance must be relatively low, and (4) losses must be noncatastrophic.

Large Number of Exposures Insurers need a large group of similar exposures because they base rate calculations on what may loosely be called "the law of averages." Unless the number is large enough to permit a good estimate of average expected losses, premiums cannot be computed accurately. If rates are set too low, the insurer may not have enough funds to pay claims, and if set too high, people will pay more than is necessary or desirable.

Fortuitous Loss A *fortuitous loss* is one that happens by chance or accident—its timing and/or occurrence is for the most part unintentional and unexpected from the standpoint of the insured. If individual losses that were intentional or certain could be insured, insurance companies would be plagued by *adverse selection,* that is, the tendency for those who anticipate a loss in the near future to seek insurance more often than the norm.

Low Cost The cost of an insurance premium should be relatively low with respect to the potential loss that is covered by the insurance. Thus insurance should only be used for protection against large losses that are suffered by a very small percentage of those who buy a given coverage. A company cannot economically insure against small losses because the expenses of selling and administering such policies when coupled with the claims that would be made could total nearly as much or more than the potential loss covered. Similarly, insurance cannot be offered economically for losses that occur too frequently because the premiums would exceed the amount that most people are willing to pay.

An excellent example of the application of the low cost criterion is life insurance for persons over age 70. Few insurance companies will issue a new policy to people in this age category because the relatively high frequency of loss makes the premiums larger than most people believe they can afford. However, life insurance is certainly not the only type of insurance for which increased frequency of loss can make the premium too high. This phenomenon has in recent years contributed to increased health, homeowner's, automobile, and professional malpractice insurance premiums.

Insurance works best when in any given year only a relatively few people file claims. The total amount paid in premiums (plus interest earnings) should exceed the total amount paid out for losses and administrative expenses.

Noncatastrophic This last criterion—*noncatastrophic loss*—means that insurers should not accept risks that have the potential for widespread catastrophe. Foremost for insurance companies is the need to protect their solvency. A company that goes bankrupt is no good to anyone. Thus, such catastrophic occurrences as war, nuclear explosion, and large-scale flooding generally cannot be safely insured by private insurance companies.

Underwriting

In all types of insurance, the company must decide who it can insure and determine the applicable rates. This function is called *underwriting*. Through underwriting insurers try to guard against adverse selection. In addition, underwriters design rate classification schemes so that people who buy insurance will pay a premium commensurate with their chance of loss. The success of any insurance company is highly dependent on the quality of the work performed in its underwriting department. If the underwriting standards and/or rates are set too high, people are unjustly denied coverage. On the other hand, if standards are set too loose and/or the rates too low, many insureds pay less than their fair share and the insurer could become insolvent.

A basic problem facing underwriters is the choice of appropriate criteria to apply when they select and classify insureds. Since a perfect relationship does not exist between available criteria and loss experience, invariably some insureds believe that they are charged more than they should be for their insurance. This situation is probably quite apparent in underwriting automobile insurance. Many young male motorists who have never had an auto accident must pay two or three times the premium that a person age 35 would pay. Similarly, a car owner who has never had a claim but who lives in Manhattan is likely to pay a considerably higher amount than a small town driver with a poor driving record.

In recognition of the difficulties experienced in selecting and classifying insureds, some vocal consumer advocates have urged the removal of rate classifications and the application of the same rate to everyone. This idea, however, is not the solution to the problem. In fact, it would probably increase the number of complaints made about insurance because, even though a few hazard-prone people would receive large decreases in premiums, many more would get rate increases. Similarly, several states have moved toward eliminating age and sex as legal criteria for automobile underwriting decisions. Insurers have often opposed such action because they do not know what other criteria to use that would be as practical or accurate.

You can see from this discussion that underwriting is a difficult task. It is an art, perhaps, as much as it is a science. Insurers are trying to improve their underwriting capabilities to set rates that are adequate to protect against insolvency and yet are reasonable for most policyholders. From your standpoint, though, recognize that various insurers often use dissimilar underwriting standards and rate classification systems. Therefore, you can often save money by shopping around for a company that has underwriting practices most favorable to your specific characteristics and needs. For instance, some life insurers offer discounts to nonsmokers, and several automobile insurers offer reduced rates to car poolers.

With the basic risk and insurance concepts in mind, we begin our discussion of specific types of insurance. The remainder of this chapter is devoted to life insurance. The following two chapters are concerned with health insurance plans and with property and liability coverages.

Determining the Need for Life Insurance

"Life insurance is sold—not bought" is an axiom in the life insurance business. As a rule people seldom get a strong urge to buy life insurance as they might a house, car, or a new television set. The majority normally wait until an agent contacts them, and then in reluctance they accept "being sold." Perhaps a partial explanation for this tendency to wait is that life insurance is intangible; upon its purchase, you cannot see, smell, touch, or taste its benefits. In addition, although most people (especially family breadwinners) recognize they should buy life insurance, many believe it can be delayed another month or two or three, and so on. The need is felt—but it is neither obvious nor pressing. Still, even with people's tendency to postpone the purchase of life insurance, sales have grown substantially since 1960. (See Figure 9.1.)

Figure 9.1 Relative Growth in Life Insurance in Force, Purchases of Life Insurance, and Benefit Payments in the United States, 1960–1980

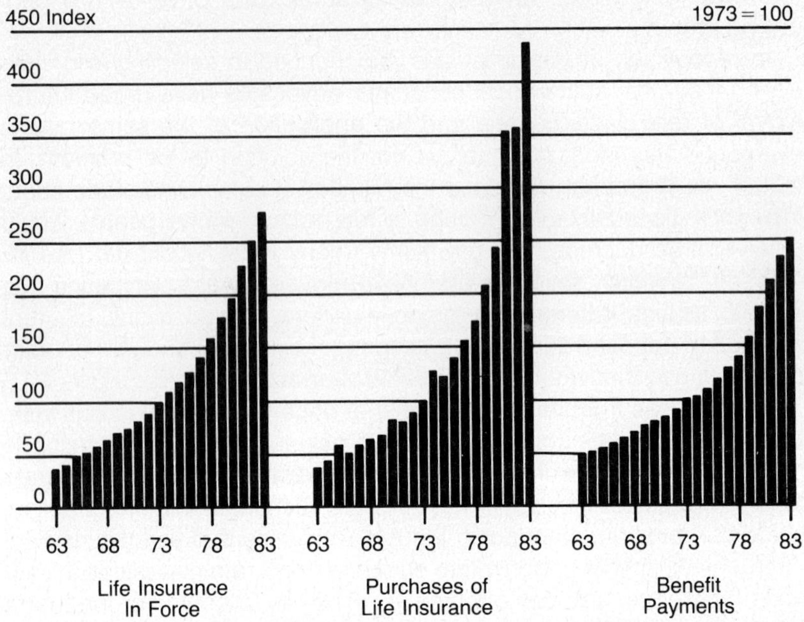

Source: Life Insurance Fact Book 1984 (Washington, D.C.: American Council of Life Insurance, 1984), p. 9.

The reason for these increased sales is that eventually most people realize that the benefits of life insurance are tangible. The benefits consist of all the things that a family will still be able to buy after a loss occurs, benefits that they would not have been able to enjoy otherwise. And with respect to the need being "pressing"—such as when a car quits running or a television goes on the blink—then it is usually too late to act. The head of family who just learns she has terminal cancer will not be able to buy the coverages she needs.

The point here, however, is not to push you to stock up immediately on as much life insurance as you can get. Rather, it is to give you a sound basis for discovering whether you do need life insurance. If you do, then you should give its purchase a high priority. If you do not, then you should recognize it and resist any sales pressure that you might be subject to.

In practice, three methods can be used to compute an individual's need for life insurance: the human life value approach, the multiple earnings approach, and the needs approach. By far, financial planners prefer the needs approach. Because the other two approaches are so widely used, though, they are discussed to help you learn their shortcomings. Choosing the correct approach also means avoiding those that are incorrect. (Some key life insurance statistics are shown in Table 9.1.)

Table 9.1 Key Life Insurance Statistics (1980)

Life Insurance in Force in the U.S. (in Millions)	
Ordinary (Individual Policies)	$1,760,474
Group	1,579,355
Industrial	35,994
Credit	165,215
Total	$3,541,038
Average Amounts of Life Insurance in Force in the U.S.	
Per Family	$41,500
Per Insured Family	$48,300
Life Insurance Purchases in the U.S. (in Millions)	
Ordinary	$371,114
Group	170,184
Industrial	3,275
Total	$544,573
Benefit Payments in the U.S. (in Millions)	
Payments to Beneficiaries	$12,884
Payments to Policyholders and Annuitants	25,158
Total	$38,042
Premium Receipts of U.S. Life Insurance Companies (in Millions)	
Life Insurance	$40,829
Annuity Considerations	24,030
Health Insurance	29,366
Total	$94,225
Net Rate of Investment Income of U.S. Life Insurance Companies, Including Separate Accounts (Before Federal Income Taxes)	8.02%

Source: Adapted with permission from *Life Insurance Fact Book 1981* (Washington, D.C.: American Council of Life Insurance, 1981), p. 7.

Human Life Value Approach

One of the oldest—and perhaps the most misused—techniques for determining the amount of life insurance a person should have is the *human life value approach.* This approach attempts to convert the future earnings of an individual into a present value. This sum is then defined as the human life value of that person. Specifically, this computation considers two factors: (1) the total amount of income that you will earn from the present to retirement minus related income taxes and personal maintenance expenses and (2) an appropriate interest rate at which these anticipated future net earnings can be discounted into a present value amount. For example, assume that a person age 25 expected to net $17,000 per year after taxes and personal maintenance expenses during the next 40 years and that an appropriate interest rate is 8 percent. The human life value of that person would equal $202,718. (This amount was determined by using special financial computations that are too rigorous for coverage in this text.)

The human life value concept may be useful in certain legal proceedings or by economists concerned with studying the human capital of a nation. It should not be used in computing the amount of life insurance you should buy because it fails to consider both the financial obligations and any resources external to life insurance that are available to you.

Multiple Earnings Approach

The *multiple earnings approach* gained its popularity on the basis of simplicity rather than soundness. To calculate the amount of life insurance to purchase using this technique, you simply multiply gross annual earnings by some arbitrarily selected number. Frequently, 3, 5, or, in some cases, 10 is used. For example, if the multiplier is 5, a person who has a gross annual income of $20,000 should have $100,000 of life insurance coverage. The major shortcomings of the multiple earnings approach are that it considers neither the financial obligations nor the resources of the individual—the same shortcomings cited for the human life value approach.

Needs Approach

Most professional life insurance agents have abandoned the human life value and/or multiple earnings approach and use the *needs approach.* This method considers the specific financial obligations that a person may have and the financial resources available in addition to life insurance. Essentially, the needs approach involves three steps: (1) estimating the total economic resources needed; (2) determining all financial resources that would be available; and (3) subtracting the amount of resources from the amount needed in order to determine the amount of funds required to provide for an individual's financial program.

Economic Needs Although life insurance often is used in retirement planning, it primarily protects families from financial loss resulting from death. (Insurance in retirement planning is discussed in Chapter 15.) In this role life insurance can provide money for six important financial needs: (1) family income, (2) additional expenses, (3) debt liquidation, (4) surviving spouse's income, (5) money for special requirements, and (6) liquidity.

Family Income For most people with dependents, their most important financial need is to protect their families' income. If they die they want to make sure that their families' ability to live comfortably is not seriously impaired. Perhaps the best way to estimate the amount of monthly income necessary to sustain a family is to develop a budget for all expenses that will be incurred. As is discussed in Chapter 3, major items in the budget are housing costs; utilities; food; automobile; medical and dental needs; clothing; life, health, property, and liability insurance; property taxes; recreation and travel; and savings.

One important question that you have to face in developing a post-death family budget is, "What standard of living do I want my family to have?" Some feel a reduced level of consumption is in order; some

Figure 9.2 Distribution of Amount of Ordinary Life Policies Purchased by Sex of Insured (in the United States)

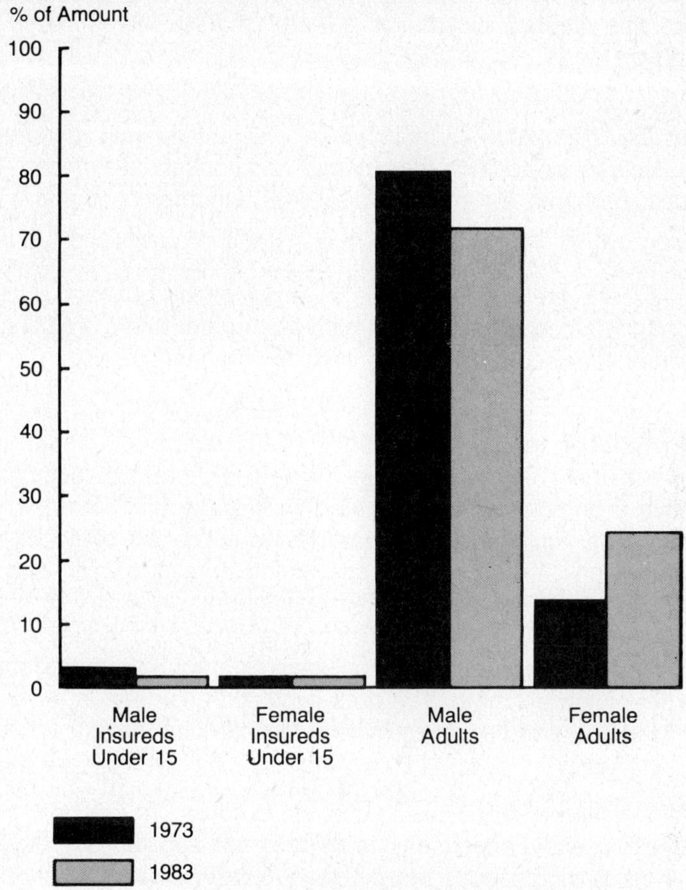

Note: Figures exclude credit life insurance.
Source: Life Insurance Marketing and Research Association.

Source: Life Insurance Fact Book 1984 (Washington, D.C.: American Council of Life Insurance, 1984), p. 15.

want their family to maintain its present standard of living; and others would like to leave their family with the level of consumption that would have been achieved had the provider continued to live and work.

One other matter to remember concerning family income is that today many families depend on two incomes. Traditionally, emphasis has been placed on insuring the family against the income loss of the father. But working mothers also can die unexpectedly. So, to the extent a family (either a one- or two-earner) depends on a woman's income, that income should be counted as a part of the family income need. In keeping with this need and the increasing importance of women in the work force, life insurance sales on the lives of women have increased dramatically in recent years. (See Figure 9.2.)

Still, even with this increase, only 64 percent of female heads of household are currently insured; the comparable number for male heads of household is 85 percent. Life insurance on working females to help protect the family's income is a need that deserves much more attention.

Additional Expenses In most households, adult family members are responsible for performing many family and household services. These services, perhaps, are most evident with a homemaker and mother. She cooks, cleans, shops, looks after the children, and does whatever is necessary to keep the family happy and cared for. If she dies many of these services will have to be paid out of the husband's income. Such additional expenses can stretch the budget to the breaking point and should be recognized as an important economic need.

Pay Off Debts In the event of their death most breadwinners prefer to leave their families relatively debt free. Therefore, to accomplish this objective a person must determine the average amount due for outstanding bills. Included in this amount would be the balances on installment loans, credit cards, department store accounts, and other similar obligations, as well as estimated funeral expenses. In addition, some heads of households will want to leave enough money to pay off their home mortgages and will include this amount in their debt liquidation expense estimate. The debt liquidation component of financial needs can be viewed as an estimate of the individual's average liabilities.

Surviving Spouse's Income After the children are independent, the monthly household expenses should decrease substantially. Nevertheless, the surviving spouse will still need monthly income for support for the remainder of his or her life. Therefore, the amount of income needed as well as the duration of the survivor's life needs to be estimated.

Special Financial Needs In addition to these economic needs, some families also would like to have the resources available to meet certain special financial requirements, such as a college education fund for the children and/or surviving spouse, an emergency fund for unexpected financial burdens, or, as previously mentioned, a fund to pay off the mortgage.

Liquidity Often we may have assets but not cash. Real estate investors, for example, are notorious for owning several million dollars worth of properties but bouncing checks for $100. Similarly, many farmers are land rich and cash poor. People who keep a very high percentage of their wealth in illiquid assets often need life insurance to provide enough cash to avoid estate shrinkage. The life insurance proceeds keep the mortgages paid and assets maintained until they can be sold at their fair market value.

Available Resources After estimating the amounts of financial needs that a family must try to satisfy upon the death of a family member, a list of all available resources for meeting those needs must be prepared. For most families, money from savings and social security benefits make up the largest non-life insurance financial resources. In addition, another important source is income that can be earned by the surviving spouse or children. If the surviving spouse is skilled and readily employable, those earnings could be a family's largest available resource. Also, a majority of large employers offer some cash benefits that are payable upon the death of an employee. Many families have real estate (not including the home), jewelry, stocks, bonds, and other assets that can be liquidated in order to obtain funds to meet financial needs. After developing a complete list of available resources, some reasonable estimate of their value should be made. Although this step can be difficult because the values of some assets are not constant, coming up with a reasonable minimum value should be possible.

Needs Less Resources The last step in determining the amount of life insurance required is to subtract the amount of available resources from the total needed to satisfy all of the financial objectives of the family. If the amount of available resources exceeds the needs, then no life insurance for death protection should be purchased. (Of course, it still might be useful for retirement, savings, or to guarantee insurability, but these uses are considered elsewhere in this text.) If, as in most families with children, the resources are less than the needs, that difference is the amount of life insurance necessary to provide the family with its desired standard of living.

By now you can see that financial planning based upon the needs concept can become quite complex. When a family uses a competent life insurance agent who knows the process, however, the planning stage can proceed quite smoothly. Many major life insurance companies have computer programs set up to determine the life insurance requirements of families using the needs approach.

Remember, though, that your life insurance needs are not static. The amount and type of life insurance you need today probably will differ from the amount and type suitable for you five years from now. Life insurance programs should be reviewed and adjusted at least every five years or after major changes in the family have occurred (for example, the birth of a child or purchase of a home).

Programming Example: Using the Needs Approach

To illustrate how the needs approach can be used in life insurance programming, the hypothetical case of Bill and Joan Black will be used

Figure 9.3 Programming Life Insurance Needs for Bill and Joan Black

Name: The Blacks (Bill and Joan)

Date: 31 January 1985

Program Objectives: The Blacks wish to protect against the economic loss resulting from the premature death of Bill or Joan. Their objectives are to fund debt liquidation, final expenses, family income, spouse reeducation, and a children's opportunity fund. With respect to Joan, their objective is to fund for a period of eight years the household services that she now provides.

Program Review Date: 31 January 1990, or upon the occurrence of a major change in family needs or resources, whichever comes first.

Needs (Bill's Death)		
Debt Liquidation	$ 70,000	
Final Expenses	5,000	
Family Income (Present Value)	200,000	
Reeducation (Joan)	25,000	
Children Opportunity Fund	50,000	
Total Needs		$350,000
Available Resources		
Savings	$100,000	
Group Life Insurance	30,000	
Total Available Resources		$130,000
Needs Less Resources (Bill's Death)		$220,000
Needs (Joan's Death)		
Replaced Services (Present Value)		$ 85,000
Available Resources		
None to be Allocated		0
Needs Less Resources (Joan's Death)		$ 85,000

(see Figure 9.3). At this time Bill and Joan Black primarily want to provide for Joan and their two children (ages 6 and 8) should Bill die. Their priorities are (1) leave the family debt free; (2) assure an income for Joan and their children until the youngest child is age 18; (3) provide funds for Joan to make the transition from homemaker to employment; and (4) establish a fund that will permit the children to have a college education or begin a career. In addition, the Blacks recognize the substantial time and effort that Joan contributes to caring for the family and running the household. Thus, in the event of Joan's death, the Blacks would like to have cash available—without straining the family budget—to replace many of the functions that Joan now performs. Because the Blacks know that insurance needs change, they believe a five-year planning horizon is appropriate. At the end of that period, the family's needs and resources will be reevaluated to see if its life insurance program warrants modification.

Economic Needs Since Bill and Joan use credit sparsely, their average outstanding balance for debts is limited to a mortgage ($65,000), an automobile loan ($4,000), and miscellaneous charge accounts ($500). These debts now total $69,500. The mortgage is in its early years and will not be reduced significantly during the five-year planning period. Although the existing auto loan will be amortized, a new loan for a replacement vehicle will probably be necessary. Bill therefore believes that $70,000 will be adequate to meet their need for paying off debts. In addition, the Blacks would like to have $5,000 available to pay estate administration expenses, taxes, and funeral charges.

Bill's current take-home pay is $1,800 per month. However, because of inflation, Bill and Joan believe that a larger income will be necessary to support the family at their present standard of living until their youngest child reaches age 18 (that is, 12 years). Therefore, the Blacks set their goal for the family income during the period at $2,200 per month. Using financial interest tables (available in various financial texts), Joan computes that the immediate amount necessary to provide $2,200 per month for 12 years is approximately $200,000 (at an assumed 8 percent interest rate).

Although Joan is trained as a stockbroker, Bill and Joan both believe that Joan should not go to work until both children are raised. By that time, her previous education may be somewhat out of date. So, they would like to have enough money to allow Joan to return to college for several years. For this purpose they believe $25,000 would be sufficient. If Bill dies prior to his next life insurance program review date (that is, in five years), the $25,000 could be invested and would also provide a cushion against any major unforeseen economic setbacks for the family.

Bill and Joan want to guarantee that their children will have the money necessary to take advantage of education or other opportunities that may be available to them when the children reach age 18. To do this they want to establish an opportunity fund of $50,000. This fund would also grow substantially before it was needed should Bill die during the five year time horizon. Based upon the needs of the Blacks, the total amount necessary to meet their financial goals should Bill die within the next five years would be $350,000.

With respect to Joan, the Blacks feel her services to the family (those that could be replaced) would cost $15,000 per year. They want to fund these services for the next eight years, at which time the children should be old enough to take care of themselves and the house. At 8 percent the present value of $15,000 per year for eight years equals about $85,000.

Available Resources Bill is employed as an accountant at a government agency. Although the agency has a retirement program, no preretirement survivor's benefits are available. Furthermore, Bill's employer does not participate in the federal social security program. However, due to a recent inheritance of $80,000 coupled with accumulated savings of $25,000, the Blacks have approximately $100,000 in total liquid savings. Also, Bill is covered by an employer-sponsored group life insurance policy in the amount of one year's gross salary ($30,000).

Other potential resources, such as a promised gift of $20,000 from Joan's Aunt Sarah, a travel accident life insurance policy with a $10,000 face value, and assorted personal property, are ignored in the programming process because of uncertainty as to either their amount or their availability. For example, Aunt Sarah may decide to donate the money to charity, or Bill may die from a cause unrelated to his travel insurance. Overall then, the resources that can be counted upon to help achieve the Blacks' economic objectives if Bill dies total $130,000. On the other hand, if Joan dies, the family would like to keep its present budget and savings intact. So no resources are available to pay for her services that will need to be replaced.

Needs Less Resources The difference between the monies available and those that will be required is $220,000; this sum thus equals the amount of life insurance the Blacks would need to buy to insure Bill's life and the family's desired standard of living. Since the Blacks have not allocated any of their resources to replace Joan's services, the amount of life insurance necessary to cover this need equals $85,000, the present value of $15,000 per year discounted at 8 percent for the eight-year period.

Often the amount of life insurance needed to meet all of a family's desired expenditures will exceed the family's willingness or ability to pay for it. Even after a careful search for the right type of policy at the best price, a family might decide they just cannot afford all of the insurance they would like. In these cases, a priority ranking of needs coupled with a reassessment of available resources is necessary. For example, in the preliminary plans a college education fund might have been included while consideration was not given to income from employment of the surviving spouse or children. The family could decide, however, to let the children work their way through college and have the surviving spouse seek employment. In this manner, capacity and willingness to pay for life insurance can be adjusted to meet economic needs.

As a final comment, here, note that to reduce its complexity this programming example has been limited in scope. Other questions that could be treated pertain to the benefits provided by social security, disability income insurance for Bill or Joan or both, and retirement income objectives. In fact, one of the most often overlooked items in family insurance programs is long-term disability insurance for breadwinners and homemakers. Disability income coverage is important because a severe disablement can cause economic loss the same as would death. The purchase of replacement services for a disabled homemaker, for example, could severely strain a family's budget. These topics are discussed in later chapters.

Types of Life Insurance Contracts

After you determine the amount of life insurance necessary to meet the financial requirements of your family, you must decide on the types of insurance contracts best suited to your needs. In general, families can most efficiently satisfy their economic requirements through the use of either term or whole life insurance. However, numerous other types of policies (which are primarily modifications of these types) are available.

Term Insurance

Under the provisions of a *term life insurance* policy, the insurance company agrees to pay a stipulated sum if the insured dies during the policy period. The period of coverage is often five years with premiums payable annually or semiannually. Many other periods of coverage and payment plans are also available. Term insurance can be an economical way to purchase life insurance on a temporary basis for protection against financial loss resulting from death, especially in the early years of family formation. A premium schedule from a company with average rates for five-year renewable term insurance is shown in Table 9.2.

Nearly all life insurance agents sell some form of term life insurance. In addition, employer-sponsored group life insurance plans and companies that sell directly to the public through the mail or newspaper and magazine advertisements often offer term insurance at low rates. Unfortunately, many families in the past, because of either lack of knowledge or poor advice, did not properly incorporate term life insurance into their insurance programs. But as consumers have become more knowledgeable, term life insurance sales have increased dramatically.

Types of Term Insurance The most common types of term insurance are straight term, renewable term, convertible term, and decreasing term. Term insurance features are not necessarily unique; for instance, a policy may be a straight term with both guaranteed renewable and convertible features.

Straight Term Policies written for a given number of years—for example, 1, 5, 10, or 20—are called *straight-term policies.* The annual premium on a straight-term policy may increase each year or each five

Table 9.2 Level Premium Term Insurance Premium Schedule
(Premiums per $1,000 of Insurance; Minimum Policy Issued, $20,000—Disability Waiver of Premium Included)

Age Nearest Birthday		Five-Year Renewable Term		
Male	Female	Annual	Semi-Annual	Quarterly
20	25	$ 2.37	$ 1.23	$ .64
21	26	2.40	1.25	.65
22	27	2.44	1.27	.66
23	28	2.50	1.30	.68
24	29	2.55	1.33	.69
25	30	2.58	1.34	.70
26	31	2.62	1.36	.71
27	32	2.67	1.39	.72
28	33	2.73	1.42	.74
29	34	2.78	1.45	.75
30	35	2.88	1.50	.78
31	36	2.97	1.54	.80
32	37	3.11	1.62	.84
33	38	3.27	1.70	.88
34	39	3.49	1.81	.94
35	40	3.73	1.94	1.01
36	41	3.99	2.07	1.08
37	42	4.28	2.23	1.16
38	43	4.59	2.39	1.24
39	44	4.93	2.56	1.33
40	45	5.30	2.76	1.43
41	46	5.69	2.96	1.54
42	47	6.12	3.18	1.65
43	48	6.59	3.43	1.78
44	49	7.08	3.68	1.91
45	50	7.74	4.02	2.09
46	51	8.47	4.40	2.29
47	52	9.25	4.81	2.50
48	53	10.13	5.27	2.74
49	54	11.10	5.77	3.00
50	55	12.16	6.32	3.28
51	56	13.34	6.94	3.60
52	57	14.69	7.64	3.97
53	58	16.14	8.39	4.36
54	59	17.76	9.24	4.80
55	60	19.55	10.17	5.28
56		18.76	9.76	5.07
57		20.56	10.69	5.55
58		22.52	11.71	6.08
59		24.66	12.82	6.66
60		27.03	14.06	7.30

Note: All policies shown are participating. This means that the company will pay policyholders a dividend at the end of each year. Of course, the amount of the dividend cannot be determined beforehand.

years. Or in many cases, it will remain level throughout the policy period. Of course, a policy with a premium that increases each year will start off below the level premium amount, subsequently equal it, and then exceed it. The face amount, or coverage, of a straight-term policy remains unchanged throughout the period of the policy.

Renewable Term A *renewable-term policy* is one that may be renewed at its expiration for another term of equal length. Renewal is at the option of the insured, but the premium will increase to offset the greater chance of death at older ages. Generally, term policies may be renewed each period until the insured attains age 65 or 70. If you buy term insurance, you would be wise to obtain a *guaranteed renewable provision* in your policy. Otherwise, if you become uninsurable due to accident or illness during the policy period, you will lose your option to renew protection at the end of the period. This valuable feature usually is available at a modest cost.

Convertible Term A term insurance policy that allows the insured to convert coverage into a whole life or endowment life insurance policy (discussed in a later section) is a *convertible term.* The convertibility feature serves as a guarantee to insureds that (1) they do not have to lose their insurance protection at the end of the period and (2) upon conversion they will have lifelong protection—as long as they pay their premiums, of course. The convertible term can be useful to persons who need a large amount of death protection for a relatively low cost but who also want to continue their insurance coverage throughout their entire life. Thus, a convertible term policy can be purchased to provide immediately for a large amount of needed death protection, and then later when the insured has more income, the policy can be converted to whole life when saving for retirement and permanent liquidity for estate taxes becomes a dominant influence. The convertibility option is available with most term insurance contracts at an attractive price. You should note that many convertible-term policies place some limitation upon when the conversion can take place. For example, a ten-year term policy may stipulate that the conversion must be made before the end of the eighth year, or a term policy to age 65 may require conversion prior to age 61.

Decreasing Term Because the death rate increases for each year of life, the premium for straight-term policies for each successive period of coverage must increase. Table 9.3 presents mortality rates per 1,000 persons and life expectancies for various ages. Many companies offer a term policy that maintains a level premium throughout all periods of coverage, while the amount of protection decreases. These policies are called *decreasing term* since the protection decreases over the life of the policy. Decreasing term can be conveniently used when the amount of coverage needed declines over time. For example, a de-

Table 9.3 Mortality Rates and Life Expectancies
(United States Total Population, 1969–1971)

Age	Deaths per 1,000	Expectation of Life (Years)	Age	Deaths per 1,000	Expectation of Life (Years)	Age	Deaths per 1,000	Expectation of Life (Years)
0	20.02	70.75	37	2.44	37.23	74	50.75	9.82
1	1.25	71.19	38	2.66	36.32	75	55.52	9.32
2	.86	70.28	39	2.90	35.42	76	60.60	8.84
3	.69	69.34	40	3.14	34.52	77	65.96	8.38
4	.57	68.39	41	3.41	33.63	78	71.53	7.93
5	.51	67.43	42	3.70	32.74	79	77.41	7.51
6	.46	66.46	43	4.04	31.86	80	83.94	7.10
7	.43	65.49	44	4.43	30.99	81	91.22	6.70
8	.39	64.52	45	4.84	30.12	82	98.92	6.32
9	.34	63.54	46	5.28	29.27	83	106.95	5.96
10	.31	62.57	47	5.74	28.42	84	115.48	5.62
11	.30	61.58	48	6.24	27.58	85	125.61	5.28
12	.35	60.60	49	6.78	26.75	86	137.48	4.97
13	.46	59.62	50	7.38	25.93	87	149.79	4.68
14	.63	58.65	51	8.04	25.12	88	161.58	4.42
15	.82	57.69	52	8.76	24.32	89	172.92	4.18
16	1.01	56.73	53	9.57	23.53	90	185.02	3.94
17	1.17	55.79	54	10.43	22.75	91	198.88	3.73
18	1.28	54.86	55	11.36	21.99	92	213.63	3.53
19	1.34	53.93	56	12.36	21.23	93	228.70	3.35
20	1.40	53.00	57	13.41	20.49	94	243.36	3.19
21	1.47	52.07	58	14.52	19.76	95	257.45	3.06
22	1.52	51.15	59	15.70	19.05	96	269.59	2.95
23	1.53	50.22	60	16.95	18.34	97	280.24	2.85
24	1.51	49.30	61	18.29	17.65	98	289.77	2.76
25	1.47	48.37	62	19.74	16.97	99	298.69	2.69
26	1.43	47.44	63	21.33	16.30	100	306.96	2.62
27	1.42	46.51	64	23.06	15.65	101	314.61	2.56
28	1.44	45.58	65	24.95	15.00	102	321.67	2.51
29	1.49	44.64	66	26.99	14.38	103	328.17	2.46
30	1.55	43.71	67	29.18	13.76	104	334.14	2.41
31	1.63	42.77	68	31.52	13.16	105	339.60	2.37
32	1.72	41.84	69	34.00	12.57	106	344.60	2.34
33	1.83	40.92	70	36.61	12.00	107	349.17	2.30
34	1.95	39.99	71	39.43	11.43	108	353.33	2.27
35	2.09	39.07	72	42.66	10.88	109	357.12	2.24
36	2.25	38.15	73	46.44	10.34			

Source: Reprinted with permission from *Life Insurance Fact Book 1983–1984* (Washington, D.C.: American Council of Life Insurance, 1983), pp. 108–9.

creasing-term policy can be purchased when children are young in order to provide sufficient family income until they reach maturity. As they grow older, the amount of coverage needed decreases until the last child becomes independent and the need expires. For example, in our programming case, the Blacks may have found decreasing term the least expensive way to meet their life insurance needs. Also, some families find it desirable to purchase a decreasing-term policy which declines in coverage at the same rate as the balance on their home mortgage or other installment loans.

Advantages and Disadvantages of Term The primary strength of term insurance is that it can offer an economical way to purchase a large amount of protection against financial loss resulting from death. Such protection is especially useful during the child-rearing years. With the guaranteed renewable and convertible options, coverage can be continued throughout the life of the insured. Of course, the costs of continued term coverage will grow due to the increased chance of death. In this characteristic, then, lies the most commonly cited weakness of term insurance: the rates increase as the insured ages. And not infrequently, many people discontinue needed coverage because of the increasing cost.

Criticizing term insurance on the basis of increasing cost is similar to finding fault with homeowner's insurance for not paying for a loss caused by an automobile accident. Clearly, the purpose of homeowner's insurance is not to provide automobile coverage just as the purpose of term insurance is not to provide lifelong coverage. The objective of term insurance is to provide a large amount of protection for a limited period of time—something it accomplishes very well.

Whole Life Insurance

Few people ever outlive the need for some type of life insurance. Accordingly, as the name implies, *whole life insurance* is designed to offer financial protection for the whole life of an individual. In addition to death protection, whole life insurance has a savings element called *cash value,* which results from the manner in which premiums are paid. In fact, whole life is normally available through several different payment plans, including continuous premium, limited payment, and single premium payment. All of these payment plans provide for accumulation of cash values.

Life insurance companies set aside assets to pay the claims expected from the policies they issue. As time goes by, the cash value of a policy—the amount of assets allocated for each person insured—increases to reflect the greater chance of death that comes with age. If policyholders decide to cancel their contracts prior to the death of the insured, that portion of assets set aside to provide payment for the death claim which did not take place is available to them. This right to a cash value is termed the *nonforfeiture right* of the policyholder. If the insured does not wish to take this nonforfeitable right as cash, he or she may elect one of several other options. This right arises because the company collects premiums in order to pay death claims. Policyholders, by terminating their insurance contract, forfeit their right to a death benefit. Correspondingly, the company must forfeit its right to

Table 9.4 Whole Life Premium Schedule
(Premiums per $1,000 of Insurance; Minimum Policy Issued, $5,000—Disability Waiver of Premium Included)

Age Nearest Birthday		Ordinary Life			20-Pay Life			30-Pay Life		
Male	Female	Annual	Semi-Annual	Quarterly	Annual	Semi-Annual	Quarterly	Annual	Semi-Annual	Quarterly
20	25	$10.13	$ 5.27	$ 2.74	$16.44	$ 8.55	$ 4.44	$12.85	$ 6.68	$ 3.47
21	26	10.50	5.46	2.84	16.91	8.79	4.57	13.23	6.88	3.57
22	27	10.86	5.65	2.93	17.40	9.05	4.70	13.61	7.08	3.67
23	28	11.26	5.86	3.04	17.89	9.30	4.83	14.02	7.29	3.79
24	29	11.68	6.07	3.15	18.41	9.57	4.97	14.43	7.50	3.90
25	30	12.07	6.28	3.26	18.87	9.81	5.09	14.82	7.71	4.00
26	31	12.47	6.48	3.37	19.34	10.06	5.22	15.21	7.91	4.11
27	32	12.90	6.71	3.48	19.83	10.31	5.35	15.62	8.12	4.22
28	33	13.34	6.94	3.60	20.34	10.58	5.49	16.05	8.35	4.33
29	34	13.81	7.18	3.73	20.87	10.85	5.63	16.50	8.58	4.46
30	35	14.30	7.44	3.86	21.42	11.14	5.78	16.98	8.83	4.58
31	36	14.82	7.71	4.00	21.99	11.43	5.94	17.46	9.08	4.71
32	37	15.37	7.99	4.15	22.57	11.74	6.09	17.98	9.35	4.85
33	38	15.94	8.29	4.30	23.18	12.05	6.26	18.52	9.63	5.00
34	39	16.54	8.60	4.47	23.83	12.39	6.43	19.09	9.93	5.15
35	40	17.18	8.93	4.64	24.50	12.74	6.62	19.68	10.23	5.31
36	41	17.86	9.29	4.82	25.19	13.10	6.80	20.31	10.56	5.48
37	42	18.58	9.66	5.02	25.90	13.47	6.99	20.96	10.90	5.66
38	43	19.32	10.05	5.22	26.66	13.86	7.20	21.64	11.25	5.84
39	44	20.11	10.46	5.43	27.45	14.27	7.41	22.37	11.63	6.04
40	45	20.94	10.89	5.65	28.27	14.70	7.63	23.13	12.03	6.25
41	46	21.80	11.34	5.89	29.13	15.15	7.87	23.93	12.44	6.46
42	47	22.72	11.81	6.13	30.02	15.61	8.11	24.74	12.86	6.68
43	48	23.69	12.32	6.40	30.95	16.09	8.36	25.63	13.33	6.92
44	49	24.71	12.85	6.67	31.91	16.59	8.62	26.55	13.81	7.17
45	50	25.91	13.47	7.00	33.07	17.20	8.93	27.66	14.38	7.47
46	51	27.17	14.13	7.34	34.30	17.84	9.26	28.84	15.00	7.79
47	52	28.52	14.83	7.70	35.56	18.49	9.60	30.08	15.64	8.12
48	53	29.95	15.57	8.09	36.90	19.19	9.96	31.43	16.34	8.49
49	54	31.47	16.36	8.50	38.34	19.94	10.35	32.84	17.08	8.87
50	55	33.10	17.21	8.94	39.84	20.72	10.76	34.35	17.86	9.27
51	56	34.82	18.11	9.40	41.42	21.54	11.18	35.97	18.70	9.71
52	57	36.65	19.06	9.90	43.10	22.41	11.64	37.71	19.61	10.18
53	58	38.61	20.08	10.42	44.89	23.34	12.12	39.56	20.57	10.68
54	59	40.70	21.16	10.99	46.80	24.34	12.64	41.56	21.61	11.22
55	60	42.95	22.33	11.60	48.83	25.39	13.18	43.69	22.72	11.80
56	61	42.79	22.25	11.55	48.34	25.14	13.05	43.43	22.58	11.73
57	62	45.01	23.41	12.15	50.32	26.17	13.59	45.55	23.69	12.30
58	63	47.36	24.63	12.79	52.40	27.25	14.15	47.82	24.87	12.91
59	64	49.85	25.92	13.46	54.62	28.40	14.75	50.24	26.12	13.56
60	65	52.50	27.30	14.18	56.97	29.62	15.38	52.81	27.46	14.26

Note: All policies shown are participating.

keep all of the monies paid by these policyholders for the future death benefit it will no longer be required to pay. This logic cannot be applied to term life insurance or various types of property and liability insurance because, upon issuing these policies, insurance companies assume that they will have to pay a claim on only a tiny fraction of the contracts sold, and consequently they collect premiums on that basis.

Types of Whole Life Policies Although a wide variety of types of whole life policies exist, only the major ones—continuous premium, limited payment, and single premium—are described here. A sample premium schedule for several types of participating whole life policies is shown in Table 9.4.

Continuous Premium Under a *continuous premium whole life* policy, individuals pay a level premium amount each year until they die or exercise a nonforfeiture right. The earlier in life the coverage is purchased, the lower the amount of the annual premium. This concept is a selling point used by some life insurance agents to convince younger persons to buy now. Their argument is that the sooner you buy, the less you pay. What they mean by this is what you pay *annually,* not the total payments over the life of the policy. Of course, the sooner people purchase whole life, the longer they have coverage in force, but (all other things being equal) the *more* they pay in total. While good reasons (such as securing needed protection, savings, and insurability) do exist for many young persons to buy whole life, it should seldom be purchased by anyone simply because the annual premium will be less than if it is purchased at a later date. Of the variety of whole life policies available, continuous premium whole life offers the greatest death protection and the least savings per dollar of premium paid. Since the emphasis of whole life insurance for most families is death protection rather than savings, the continuous premium policy is usually the wisest choice when filling a permanent life insurance need.

Limited Payment A *limited payment whole life* policy is one that offers coverage for the entire life of the insured but schedules the payments to end after a limited period. For example, 20-pay life, 30-pay life, paid-up age 55, and paid-up age 65 are types of limited pay whole life policies which are frequently sold. Under the 20-pay and 30-pay life contracts, the policyholder is most often required to make 20 or 30 annual level premium payments, respectively. Under the premium schedule of paid-up at age 55, 65, or other stipulated age policies, the policyholder makes premium payments until the insured attains the stated age. Of course, for any individual, the shorter the period of time over which premiums are payable, the larger the amount of the annual premium. Upon completion of the scheduled payments, the insurance remains in force at its face value for the remainder of the life of the insured.

Some insurance companies emphasize the sale of limited pay policies to the detriment of those who purchase them. In the sales presentation, considerable attention is focused on the "large" savings element that will develop and the fact that the policyholder is relieved of having to pay premiums for the entire life of the insured. However, this logic is often misguided on two counts. One is that for most people the primary purpose of whole life insurance is permanent protection against financial loss resulting from death—not the accumulation of savings. Second, even though people buy a continuous premium whole life policy, they need pay the premium only as long as they wish to keep the policy in force for its full face value. Policyholders may stop payment of premiums at any time after some nonforfeiture value has been accumulated. Rather than take this benefit in cash, they can convert the policy to one that is paid up for some amount less than the original face value of the policy. (This is discussed in subsequent sections.)

The preceding discussion is not intended to imply that limited pay policies are not desirable. Rather, it stresses that, if lifelong death protection is the primary aim of the life insurance policy, continuous premium whole life should be purchased instead of a limited payment policy. Since more continuous premium whole life insurance can be purchased with the same number of dollars than limited payment whole life, people who need whole life insurance are probably best off using continuous premium life insurance when insurance needs are greatest. Once their insurance needs are reduced, they can convert the policy into a smaller amount of paid-up life insurance. On the other hand, if people have sufficient life insurance already in force to protect against income loss, then they can use limited payment policies as part of a savings or retirement plan.

Single Premium Continuous premium and limited payment whole life policies represent methods of acquiring life insurance on an installment basis. In contrast, a *single premium whole life* policy is one that is purchased on a cash basis. One premium payment at the inception of the contract buys life insurance coverage for the insured for the rest of his or her life. The single premium policy has little use in the life insurance programs of most families. However, because of its investment attributes, the single premium life insurance contract does appeal to some as a medium for accumulating savings, and in some instances, the single premium policy can be an effective tool in planning for estate liquidity (see Chapter 16).

Advantages and Disadvantages of Whole Life The most noteworthy feature of whole life insurance is that premium payments contribute toward building an estate, regardless of whether the insured lives or dies. This feature results because the face value of the policy is paid upon death, or the cash value may be withdrawn when the need for insurance protection has expired. A corresponding benefit of whole life (except single premium) is that it permits individuals who need insurance for an entire lifetime to budget their premium payments over a relatively long period, thus eliminating the problems of unaffordability and uninsurability often encountered with term insurance in later years. Also, some people like whole life insurance because the periodic payments force them to save regularly.

The most frequently cited disadvantages of whole life insurance are that (1) more death protection can be purchased with term insurance and (2) higher yields can be obtained on other savings plans. Like the negative aspects of term insurance, the shortcomings of whole life arise only when the policy is used in a manner inconsistent with its purpose. In other words, if maximum return on investment is the sole objective, funds should not be put toward buying a whole life policy. However, if a person wishes to combine the acquisition of a given amount of death protection for the entire life of the insured (or until the policy is terminated) with a savings plan that provides a good return with high liquidity and minimum risk, then whole life insurance can be a wise purchase.

Programming Example: Conclusion

The choice of life insurance contract can be illustrated by returning to our family, the Blacks. The primary objective of this family's insurance program was to help it attain certain economic goals in the event of Bill's or Joan's death. Thus, death protection was their primary objective. Furthermore, the amount of life insurance needed was quite high compared to Bill's present income, and the bulk of these needs would expire as the children reached majority. Therefore, in this case straight term or decreasing term insurance could serve well. However, savings for retirement and estate liquidity will become more important to the Blacks as the need for family income support diminishes. Also, the premiums for term insurance will begin to become more costly as Bill and Joan age. Consequently, after the children are grown, their life insurance needs will likely switch from an emphasis on term to an emphasis on whole life.

Remember, also, that this example excludes social security survivors' benefits. Bill's employer did not participate in this government plan. In a majority of instances, though, potential family resources from this source amounts into the tens of thousands of dollars. Therefore, in view of its extreme importance, survivors' benefits from social security are discussed in Chapter 15 in detail.

Other Types of Life Insurance

Endowment life insurance, credit life insurance, mortgage life insurance, industrial life insurance, special purpose policies, group life insurance, variable life insurance, universal life insurance, and deferred premium life insurance are other types of life insurance that are readily available. With the exception of group life insurance, these types of contracts generally should be avoided.

Endowment Life Insurance *Endowment insurance* offers life insurance protection for a stated period of time, such as 20 years or until age 65. If the insured has not died by the end of the period, the policy may be redeemed for its face value. In other words, an endowment policy provides for the payment of the policy's face value upon the death of the insured or at the end of the policy period, whichever comes

Table 9.5 Comparison of Selected Life Insurance Contracts of Two Companies for a Male Age 25 at Date of Issue
($1,000 Annual Premium for Each Contract)

Type of Policy	Company	Face Value	Cash Value at Age 35	Cash Value at Age 45	Cash Value at Age 65	Paid-Up Amount at Age 45	Paid-Up Amount at Age 65
Continuous Premium Whole Life	Co. 1	$71,377	$6,424	$16,987	$41,113	$37,687	$58,529
	Co. 2	$59,490	6,961	18,502	37,717	31,273	48,153
Paid-Up Whole Life Age 65	Co. 1	63,870	7,026	18,650	45,092	38,332	63,870
	Co. 2	53,280	7,353	19,181	41,772	32,421	53,280
20-Pay Whole Life	Co. 1	44,117	8,816	20,823	31,147	44,117	44,117
	Co. 2	35,402	8,285	20,958	27,400	35,402	35,402
Endowment at Age 45	Co. 1	18,077	7,148	18,077	Matured at Face Value at Age 45		
	Co. 2	22,170	8,891	22,170			
Endowment at Age 65	Co. 1	53,500	7,661	19,771	53,500	28,195	Matured at Face Value
	Co. 2	45,872	5,148	16,452	45,872	26,000	

Note: All contracts shown are for participating policies.

first. The endowment policy is similar to the whole life policy in that it combines savings with insurance protection. It differs, however, because the endowment contract does not provide coverage for the entire life of the insured. It does provide for savings accumulation at a faster rate than in a whole life policy. For example, a $10,000 20-year endowment policy issued to a male age 25 would have a cash value of $10,000 when the insured became age 45. In contrast, the cash value of a $10,000 whole life policy does not equal its face amount until the insured reaches age 100. Of course, the annual premium per $1,000 of coverage under an endowment policy is usually substantially more than the rate per $1,000 of coverage under a comparable whole life policy.

Because of its high cost, persons interested in life insurance for protection against premature death should never buy an endowment policy. Endowment policies are best for those who desire a systematic and semicompulsory form of savings. Table 9.5 compares several types of whole life and endowment policies on the bases of face value, accumulated cash values, and paid-up amounts. The data in this table illustrate the trade-offs that exist among these policies in terms of the variables shown.

Credit Life Insurance Banks, finance companies, and other lenders generally sell *credit life insurance* in conjunction with installment loans. Usually credit life is a term policy with a face value that decreases at the same rate as the outstanding balance on the loan. Although liquidating debts upon death of a family breadwinner is often desirable, the funds for this need should be fulfilled through an individual's term or whole life insurance program. Buying credit life insurance per se is one of the most expensive ways to buy life insurance. Furthermore, contrary to popular belief, a lender *cannot* legally reject a loan because the potential borrower chooses not to buy life insurance.

Mortgage Life Insurance *Mortgage life insurance* is a form of credit life insurance designed to pay off the mortgage balance upon the death of the borrower. As in the case of credit life insurance, this need can usually be met less expensively by shopping the open market for a suitable decreasing term policy. Credit life and mortgage life are relatively expensive because lenders are often influenced by the amount of sales commission they receive in selecting the insurers with whom they place the coverage. And as might be expected, an insurer who pays high commissions is frequently one who charges a high premium.

Industrial Life Insurance *Industrial life insurance,* now called *home service life,* is whole life or endowment life insurance that is issued in policies with small face amounts, often $1,000 or less. It is sold by agents who call on policyholders weekly or monthly to collect the premiums. The term *industrial* arose because, when these policies first became popular, the primary sales market was low-paid industrial wage earners. Because of its high marketing costs, industrial life insurance costs more per $1,000 of coverage than whole life and endowment policies that are issued with larger policy limits requiring annual or semiannual premium payments. Nevertheless, some insurance authorities believe that industrial life insurance offers the only practical way to deliver coverage to low-income families. Presently, industrial/home service life represents less than 5 percent of the life insurance in force in the United States.

Special Purpose Policies Certain types of policies frequently combine some form of term and whole life insurance for coverage on one or more members of a family. These joint-life policies have often been developed by life insurers because of the highly competitive nature of the life insurance business. You should try to determine if such a policy truly meets your needs, or whether it is primarily a marketing gimmick. Although many of the special purpose policies are sold under various company trade names, several general designations for these policies are family income policies, family maintenance policies, multiple protection plans (especially joint husband-wife policies), and jumping juveniles. One appealing feature of certain family-type policies is that they may offer the guaranteed insurability of children. The policy may specify that when children reach a certain age (say, 21 or 25), they may buy a specified type of life insurance at a predetermined price, regardless of their physical condition. While you may find that a certain special purpose policy will meet the needs of your family, more than likely these needs can be satisfied at less cost if you simply buy convertible term and continuous premium whole life as separate policies.

Group Life Insurance Under *group life insurance,* one master policy is issued and each eligible member of the group receives a certificate of insurance. Group insurance is nearly always term insurance, and the premium is based on the characteristics of the group as a whole rather than related to any specific individual. Often group life insurance is obtained by employers as a fringe benefit for their employees. However, nearly any group can secure a group life insurance policy as long as the insurance is only incidental to the reason for the group.

Accounting for about 50 percent of all life insurance in force in the United States, group life insurance is one of the fastest growing areas of insurance. The amount of group protection in force has increased over threefold just since 1968. Many group life policies now offer coverage not only for the group members but also for their dependents. In addition, group life policies generally provide that if individual members leave the group, they may continue the coverage by converting their protection into an individually issued whole life policy. Of course, after exercising the option to convert, these individuals assume all responsibility for the payment of premiums.

The availability of group life insurance definitely should be considered when a family develops its life insurance program. However, because of its potentially temporary nature and relatively low face amount (often equal to one year's salary or more), it should fulfill only low priority insurance needs. Only in rare cases should a family rely on group life insurance to fulfill its primary income protection requirements.

Variable Life Insurance In *variable life insurance* policies the benefits payable are related to the value of the company's assets that support its payment obligation. The basic concept behind variable life insurance is that policyholders should be able to reap the benefits the insurer receives from investment returns in excess of the minimum return upon which premium computations are based. Furthermore, some persons believe that in periods of inflation a variable policy is essential for keeping an insurance coverage in line with the cost of living. However, while variable life may be a convenient way to guard against inflation, families can currently accomplish this just as well by simply buying additional policies as needed or by purchasing contracts which give the policyholder the right to increase the face amount of the policy at stipulated intervals. Moreover, experience has shown that a rising consumer price index is not necessarily accompanied by increases in the returns on security investments. Consequently, variable life insurance cannot be relied on to replace fixed-dollar (nonvariable) life insurance to any significant extent, since there is no guarantee that the investment returns of the insuring company will increase with inflation.

Universal Life Insurance Recent years have witnessed the merger of different types of financial service companies. For example, Prudential Life Insurance has acquired the investment brokerage firm Bache and Company; and E. F. Hutton, an investment brokerage firm, now owns a subsidiary life insurance company. With the expected growth in the financial services market, firms want to be able to offer a full range of products.

One such blended product is *universal life insurance*. It combines the features of an investment that earns current money market interest rates with a term life insurance policy. The essence of the idea behind the universal life contract is to offer policyholders a product that blends the favorable features of a whole life policy with the higher yields that money market and bond market funds pay. Because of different tax and cost considerations, universal life and whole life policies differ in several important respects. Still, market acceptance of universal life has been great. High interest rates during 1982 helped universal life capture 10 percent of the business for individual life insurance policies during that year. As an added feature, universal life policies allow policyholders to vary both their premium payments and the face amount of protection.

Deferred Premium Life Insurance Several life insurance companies actively market their products to college students. These companies recognize, though, that most college students have little money to spend on life insurance. So their answer is to sign you up for *deferred premium life insurance.* Apart from the fact that many college students do not have enough significant financial responsibilities to need life insurance, these deferred-payment plans are generally undesirable because they place you in (greater) debt. Generally, students who accept this type of payment plan are required to sign a legally binding installment loan contract. Although deferred-payment plans have some legitimate business and tax-planning uses, in the majority of instances their purchase by college students is unwise.

Contract Provisions and Competitive Features

All life insurance contracts have various provisions which establish the rights and obligations of the policyholder and the insurance company. Standard or uniform life insurance policies do not exist, and the wording of policy provisions and features varies among companies and according to the state in which the policy is sold. Nevertheless, even though the wording of the provisions may differ, many elements are common to most life insurance contracts. They can be broken into two groups: (1) life insurance contract features and (2) other policy features. An understanding of the competitive features of life insurance is also important.

Life Insurance Contract Features

The key features found in most life insurance contracts are (1) the beneficiary clause, (2) settlement options, (3) policy loans, (4) payment of premiums, (5) nonforfeiture options, (6) policy reinstatement, and (7) change of policy.

Beneficiary Clause All life insurance policies should have one or more *beneficiaries.* This is the person or persons who receive the death benefits of the policy if the insured dies. Otherwise the money is paid to the estate of the deceased and is often subject to lengthy legal and other proceedings associated with estate settlement (see Chapter 16). In addition, if a beneficiary is not named, the policy benefits may not go to the person the insured wants them to. When naming the beneficiary, the policyholder should make certain the identification of the beneficiary is clear. For example, a man could buy a policy and simply designate the beneficiary as "my wife." Later, if a divorce and marriage to another woman took place, a controversy could arise as to which "wife" was entitled to the benefits. Similarly, if children are the intended beneficiaries, problems can arise when other children become a part of the insured's family. For instance, if a man named "my children" as beneficiaries, would proceeds be payable only to his natural and legitimate children? Or would his adopted, illegitimate, or stepchildren also share in the proceeds? Since no definite answer to these questions exists, the need to precisely identify policy beneficiaries should be quite clear. As a precaution, a secondary beneficiary should also be named to reduce the possibility that the insurance proceeds would go to unintended persons via the estate. This could occur if the primary beneficiary were to die before or at the same time as the insured and a new primary beneficiary had not been designated.

In sum, make sure you have named both a primary and a secondary beneficiary in any life insurance policies you buy and that no mistake can be made in determining who the beneficiaries are. Note, too, that the person you name as a beneficiary can be changed at any time. Therefore, if your wishes change, all you need do is to notify the insurance company—easy to do but also easy to forget. So, each year when you write the premium check, verify that your policy's named beneficiary is also your desired beneficiary. (Similarly, you should also keep any prescribed settlement options—discussed below—up to date with desired changes.)

Settlement Options Insurance companies generally offer several ways in which death proceeds of a life insurance policy may be paid. The decision as to how the funds will be allocated may be permanently established prior to the death of the insured, or the beneficiary may be allowed to select the desired *settlement option* when the policy matures. The most common settlement options besides lump-sum cash payment are (1) interest only, (2) payments for a stated period, (3) payments of a stated amount, and (4) income for life.

Interest Only Under the interest only settlement option, the policy proceeds are left on deposit with the insurance company for a period of time. In exchange, the insurer guarantees to make interest payments to the beneficiary during the time it holds the funds. In some cases the beneficiary is not permitted to withdraw the proceeds, and upon his or her death the funds are paid to a secondary beneficiary. In other cases, the beneficiary may have the right to fully withdraw policy proceeds at any time. The interest only option can be useful when there is no current need for the principal amount, or when the principal sum is large enough to provide a satisfactory annual income (in the form of interest) to the beneficiary. Typically, however, the rate of interest paid by insurers will be less than that paid by other types of savings media.

Payments for Stated Period With the payments for a stated period option, the face amount of the policy is systematically liquidated along with interest earned over a selected number of years. For example, a beneficiary at age 55 may not be eligible for social security benefits until age 65 but may be in need of a monthly income for that 10-year period. Consequently, the option of receiving a monthly income for that duration may be more attractive than taking a lump sum. The amount of the periodic payment is determined by the face amount of the policy and the length of time over which the funds are to be distributed. For any given amount, the shorter the period, the larger the monthly benefit; and conversely, the longer the period of time over which the payments are made, the smaller the payment.

Payments of Stated Amount The payments of a stated amount option is similar to the preceding alternative in that it provides for a systematic liquidation of the policy proceeds. However, it provides for the selection of the amount of periodic benefit desired rather than the number of years over which income is to be received. The payment of a stated amount option offers more flexibility than the payments for a stated period, because beneficiaries usually retain the right to change the amount of income as their needs dictate. Under the stated period option, the term cannot be modified except that in some cases total withdrawal is permitted. In essence, the payment for a stated amount option can be used to accomplish the same objective as the stated period option. All beneficiaries need to do is estimate the period of time over which they will want to receive payments and determine the amount that will be payable. Then they can select the stated amount option to provide that amount of income. Should their needs change during the period, they can modify the terms of the settlement agreement.

Life Income Under the life income option, the insurer guarantees a certain payment amount to the beneficiary for the remainder of his or her life. In contrast to the preceding options, payments under the life income alternative are related to the age of the beneficiary at the inception of the periodic benefits. The amounts are essentially a function of the face value of the policy, interest rate assumptions, and the life expectancy of the beneficiary. (Technically, mortality rates rather than life expectancy are used in these computations. A *mortality rate* designates the number of deaths per 1,000 that will occur at specified ages each year, whereas *life expectancy* is the mean number of years of life remaining at a given age. Table 9.3 gives both types of statistics for a variety of ages.)

The life income option can be attractive to people who want to be certain that they will not outlive the income from the policy proceeds and subsequently have to depend on others for support. Usually a company will agree under the life income option to guarantee payments for five or ten years to a secondary beneficiary should the original recipient die prior to the passage of that period of time. This arrangement is sometimes referred to as a *guaranteed payment life income option.* Of course, if the guaranteed payment life income option is selected, the monthly benefit is less than if the option providing income only for the life of the primary beneficiary is chosen. The younger the primary beneficiary when payments begin, the smaller the difference in the amount of monthly payments between the life income option and the guaranteed payment life income option.

Policy Loans An advance made by a life insurance company to a policyholder is a *policy loan.* These loans are secured by the cash value of the life insurance policy. A provision in nearly all whole life and endowment policies grants this right. Typically, the maximum amount that may be withdrawn is 95 percent of the policy's cash value. Although no specific repayment terms are necessary, any balance plus interest on the loan remaining at the death of the insured is subtracted from the proceeds of the policy. The rate of interest charged on policy loans is customarily 5 to 8 percent per annum and is stated in the policy. In some new policies, though, the interest rate charged is initially set at the market rate and revised as often as every few months.

Policy loans should not be obtained except in unusual circumstances because of the reduction of death proceeds that can result. One longtime advocate of whole life insurance has decried policy loans as "stealing from your widow." Although not all would agree with this emotional appeal, life insurance does provide basic financial protection for most families, and spending those proceeds prematurely is an unwise practice. On the other hand, because these loans are less expensive than borrowing from other financial institutions, they may appeal to certain persons who wish to keep their borrowing costs low and are not bothered by the accompanying loss of death proceeds if the loan is not repaid.

Payment of Premiums All life insurance contracts have a provision that specifies when premiums are due. With most insurers, the policyholder may elect the option of paying premiums on an annual, semiannual, or monthly basis. Some premium checks are mailed directly to the company, and in other instances a sales agent collects premiums from the policyholder. Another method of payment allows policyholders to pay premiums through an automatic deduction from their bank accounts. In the case of death of a policyholder who has paid premiums more than one month in advance, many companies refund those premiums along with the policy death proceeds.

Nonforfeiture Options As discussed earlier, a nonforfeiture option provides policyholders with some benefits when a policy is terminated prior to its maturity. State laws provide that all whole life and endowment policies (and term contracts which extend coverage over a long period) contain a nonforfeiture provision. In addition to a cash withdrawal, companies ordinarily offer the following options to the policyholder: (1) a paid-up policy for a reduced amount or (2) a term policy for an extended period. Table 9.6 shows a variety of these options per $1,000 of coverage for a whole life policy issued to a male age 21.

Paid-Up for Reduced Amount Under the reduced amount option, the policyholder receives a policy exactly like the one that was terminated except that it has a lower face value. In effect, the policyholder has purchased a new policy with his or her cash value at the single-premium rate. For example, you can see in Table 9.6 that if this insured cancelled the policy after ten years, it would have a cash value of $90.84 per $1,000 of face amount. The $90.84 would buy $236 of paid-up whole life insurance. Under that option, the $90.84 cash value would continue to grow because of future interest earnings, even though the policyholder is relieved of any further premium payments. This option is useful when a person's income and need for death protection decline while at the same time some coverage is still desired. Many elect this option on whole life policies when the insured attains age 60 or 65.

Extended Term The extended term option provides that upon the relinquishment of the cash value by the policyholder the company issues a term life insurance policy for the same face value as the policy that has lapsed. The period of coverage is determined by the amount of term protection a single premium payment equal to the total cash value would have purchased at the present age of the insured. If the insured in Table 9.6 chose the extended term option instead of the paid-up insurance, he or she would receive $1,000 in coverage for a period of 22 years and 29 days. The extended term option is usually the option that automatically goes into effect if the policyholder quits paying premiums and gives no instructions to the company.

Table 9.6 Nonforfeiture Options for a Male, Age 21
(Dollar Amount for Each $1,000 of Face Amount of Insurance)

End of Policy Year	Cash or Loan Value	Paid-up Insurance	Extended Term Insurance	
			Years	Days
1	$ 0.00	$ 0	0	0
2	0.00	0	0	0
3	4.79	15	1	315
4	16.21	48	6	161
5	27.91	81	11	15
6	39.91	113	14	275
7	52.20	145	17	158
8	64.78	176	19	157
9	77.66	206	20	342
10	90.84	236	22	29
11	104.33	265	22	351
12	118.13	294	23	231
13	132.25	322	24	54
14	146.69	350	24	191
15	161.43	377	24	290
16	176.47	403	24	356
17	191.79	429	25	28
18	207.38	454	25	42
19	223.22	478	25	36
20	239.29	502	25	13
Age 60	563.42	806	17	26
Age 65	608.49	833	15	272

Source: George E. Rejda, *Principles of Insurance* (Glenview, Ill.: Scott, Foresman and Company, 1982), p. 359.

Policy Reinstatement While a policy is under the reduced paid-up option or the extended term option, the policyholder may reinstate the policy by paying all back premiums plus interest at a stated rate and providing evidence that he or she can pass a physical examination and meet any other insurability requirements of the company. *Reinstatement* means that the original contractual relationship between the company and the policyholder is revived. Most often the policyholder must reinstate the policy within a specified period (three or five years) after the policy lapsed. However, before you exercise a reinstatement option, you should make some effort to determine if buying a new policy (from the same or a different company) might be less costly.

Change of Policy Many life insurance contracts contain a provision which permits the insured to switch from one policy form to another. For example, policyholders may decide that they would rather have a paid-up age 65 policy as opposed to their current continuous premium whole life policy. A change of policy provision would allow this change without penalty. When policyholders change from a high premium policy to one with lower premiums, the insured may need to prove insurability. This requirement reduces the possibility of adverse selection against the company.

Other Policy Features

In addition to the key contractual features described in the preceding section, a number of other life insurance policy features include (1) a grace period, (2) a multiple indemnity clause, (3) a disability clause, (4) insurability options, (5) a suicide clause, (6) an incontestability clause, (7) a misstatement of age or sex clause, (8) exclusions, and (9) participation. A basic understanding of these features should provide you with better knowledge of the coverages provided.

Grace Period The grace period permits the policyholder to retain protection for a short while (usually 31 days) after failing to remit a premium when due. If the insured dies during the grace period, the face amount of the policy less the scheduled premium is paid to the beneficiary.

Multiple Indemnity Clause *Multiple* (most often double or triple) *indemnity* clauses double or triple the face amount of the policy if the insured dies as a result of an accident. This benefit is usually offered to the policyholder at a small additional cost. Many insurance authorities dismiss the use of a multiple indemnity benefit as irrational. This coverage should be ignored as a source of funds when programming insurance needs, since it provides no protection in the event of death due to illness.

Disability Clause A *disability clause* in a life insurance contract may contain either a waiver of premium benefit or a waiver of premium coupled with disability income. A *waiver of premium* benefit excuses the payment of premiums on the life insurance policy if the insured becomes totally and permanently disabled prior to age 60 (or sometimes age 65). Under the *disability income portion,* the insured is entitled to a monthly income equal to $5 or $10 per $1,000 of policy face value. Some insurers will continue these payments for the life of the insured, and others will terminate them at age 65. Disability riders providing waiver of premium and disability income protection are relatively inexpensive and can be added to most whole life and endowment policies. They are generally not available with term policies.

Insurability Options The policyholder who has an *insurability option* may purchase additional coverage at stipulated intervals even if the insured becomes uninsurable. This option is frequently offered with the purchase of a whole life or endowment policy to buyers under age 40. The increases in coverage usually can be purchased every three, four, or five years in amounts equal to the amount of the original policy, or $10,000, whichever is the lower. This option should be quite attractive to individuals whose life insurance needs and ability to pay are expected to increase over a 5- to 15-year period.

Suicide Clause Nearly all life insurance policies have a *suicide clause* which voids the contract if an insured commits suicide within two years (sometimes one) after its inception. In these cases the company simply returns the premiums that have been paid. If an insured takes his or her own life after this initial period has elapsed, the policy proceeds are paid without question.

Incontestability Clause All life insurance policies have an *incontestability clause* which gives the insurance company one to two years to investigate all information provided by the insured in the application. If during that period a material false statement is discovered, the company can seek a recision of the contract. After the elapsed period, the insurer is prohibited from challenging the validity of the policy regardless of whether the insured has died or is still living.

Misstatement of Age or Sex Clause Notwithstanding incontestability, the insurance company can adjust the payment made under a policy at any time if the insured misstated his or her age or sex in the application. For example, assume that a male age 35 applied for a life insurance policy by mail and stated that he was a female age 35. The incentive for making this misstatement is that for a given amount of coverage, females of the same age as males are required to pay a lower premium because of lower mortality rates. If upon death 10 years later the company discovered the error, it would award a sum equal to the amount of insurance that the premiums paid would have purchased had the insurer known the applicant was a male. Note that this is not technically a violation of the incontestability provision because the policy has not been voided but simply modified to conform to the facts. However, some observers say that the misstatement of age and sex clause is in conflict with the spirit of the incontestability rule and places an undesirable burden upon the beneficiaries.

Exclusions Although all private insurance policies have some types of losses that are excluded from coverage, life policies offer very broad protection. In addition to the suicide clause, only aviation and war exclusions are used more than infrequently. In aviation exclusions, the primary types of losses not covered are when the insured is a relatively inexperienced private pilot or is flying in military aircraft. No restrictions apply to fare-paying passengers of commercial airlines. (Most life insurers accept without premium surcharge the pilots and crews of scheduled airliners.) War exclusions often are inserted in policies in anticipation of or during periods of combat. Typically, they provide that should the insured die as a result of war, a return of premiums with interest will be made. War exclusions are intended to guard against adverse selection which could materially disrupt the mortality experience of the company and, correspondingly, its solvency. When the potential insured has a hazardous occupation or hobby, the company will either exclude coverage for that activity or charge an additional premium to cover the added risk exposure. Seldom, if ever, would a company be able to modify the premium charged or coverage offered should the insured, say, take up motorcycle racing or hang gliding after a policy has been issued.

Participation Many life insurance companies offer participating policies. A policy is defined as *participating* when the policyholder is entitled to receive policy dividends which reflect the difference between the premiums that are charged and the amount of premium necessary to fund the actual mortality experience of the company. When the base premium schedule for participating policies is established, a company will estimate what it believes its mortality and investment experience will be and then add a more than adequate margin of safety to these figures. The premiums charged the policyholder are based on these somewhat overly cautious estimates. When company experience is more favorable than that estimated, a return of the overcharge is made to policyholders in the form of *policy dividends.* These policy dividends may be accepted by the policyholders as a cash payment (which, since they are viewed as a return of premium, are not subject to taxation), left with the company to earn interest (which is subject to income taxation), used to buy additional paid-up coverage, or applied toward the next premium payment. The dividend option selected is simply a matter of preference based upon the wishes of the individual policyholder. Note that it is advantageous to use the dividends to buy paid-up options when more insurance coverage is desired since these additions are available at their "net" rates. This means that the rates contain no load for sales expenses and consequently provide an economical way to increase coverage.

Competitive Features of Life Insurance

In addition to the elements that make up the insurance contract and the other policy features, the following competitive features of life insurance require discussion: (1) protection from creditors, (2) medium for savings, and (3) tax benefits.

Protection from Creditors When an insured dies, all assets and liabilities are totaled and the heirs receive what is left after all legitimate claims against the estate are satisfied. However, the purchase of life insurance can be structured so that death benefits are paid to a named beneficiary, rather than the deceased's estate, and the cash proceeds, therefore, do not become a part of the estate. Even if the insured had more liabilities than assets, the proceeds would not be used to liquidate them. Similarly, creditors who are successful in securing judgments against persons with substantial accumulations of life insurance cash values often cannot levy any claim on those cash values. State laws differ with respect to the rights of creditors to the death benefits or cash values of life insurance policies, but in nearly all cases, both can be better protected than assets such as stocks, bonds, mutual funds, and investment real estate.

Medium for Savings In addition to protection from creditors, life insurance can be an attractive medium for savings for the reasons of safety of principal, competitive return, liquidity, and forced savings. Many life insurance companies are more than 100 years old and have assets totaling into the billions of dollars. Even the banking industry encounters insolvencies more frequently than the life insurance industry. No major life insurance company has failed to meet its financial obligations in at least the last 45 years. No other industry can match that record. Some wish to contrast adversely the financial return on the savings element in life insurance to investments in stocks, bonds, mutual funds, and real estate. However, that is an inaccurate comparison. These other media differ not only with respect to safety of principal but also in stability of earnings (risk), liquidity, and the contractual nature of deposits (premium payments). Unfortunately, the life insurance industry has spawned this erroneous exercise because of the overemphasis of "investment" in the sales presentation. More accurately, returns on life insurance cash value should be compared to those of savings accounts and U.S. bonds. In this area, they compare favorably in providing *after-tax* returns ranging from 5 to 8 percent for recently issued policies.

Tax Benefits Life insurance proceeds, as a rule, are not subject to state or federal income taxes. Further, if certain requirements are met, policy proceeds can pass to named beneficiaries free of any estate taxes. Generally, though, to qualify for this estate tax exemption, insureds must relinquish various "incidents of ownership" in the policy. Such incidents of ownership, for example, include the right to change the beneficiary, the right to take the policy's cash surrender value, and the right to choose a settlement option. When the named beneficiary is a spouse, the sacrifice of these rights is unnecessary. Typically, in these cases the life insurance proceeds can be excluded from estate taxes as a part of the marital deduction.

Another tax advantage of life insurance is that when cash values are withdrawn from an insurer, income taxes are payable only on the amount by which the cash value exceeds the total premiums that have been paid. In practice, this excess seldom results because part of the premium that is paid is allocated to the death benefit cost incurred by the company during the time the policy is in force. Consequently it does not become a part of the cash value of the policy.

Guide to Buying Life Insurance

Before buying life insurance, you should (1) estimate the amount of life insurance necessary to cover you and your family's financial requirements, (2) consider the types of policies available to meet your needs, and (3) familiarize yourself with the various provisions that life insurance contracts typically include. With this understanding of life insurance in mind, you can then shop the market for the insurance protection best for you.

To help you in shopping, the following discussion reviews the needs concept and the types of policies you probably should seriously consider; shows you how to compare policy costs; and explains several criteria you can use to select life insurance companies and agents that can offer good service.

Review Needs and Coverages

As discussed earlier, life insurance is used in a person's financial program to fill the gap between the resources that will be available after death and those that will be needed. In addition, some life insurance policies can be effectively used as a savings medium. For most young families on limited budgets, though, the need for a large amount of death protection greatly exceeds the need for a savings plan. If you fall into this category, guaranteed renewable and convertible term insurance should account for the largest portion of your insurance protection. Most families also have the need for some amount of permanent insurance and savings, which a continuous premium whole life policy can satisfy. Limited payment whole life and endowment policies should be purchased only when the primary need is savings instead of protection against financial loss resulting from death. Overall, then, parents of young children should give highest priority to term life insurance, some attention to continuous premium whole (or universal) life, and little or no attention to limited payment and endowment policies.

Comparing Costs—Term Insurance

When you shop for term insurance you should find out the annual premium rate per $1,000 of coverage as it applies to your present age as well as later ages over the time period you plan to keep the policy.

Table 9.7 Illustration of the Net Cost Method

Total premiums for 20 years ($132.10 × 20)	$2642
Subtract dividends for 20 years	599
Net premiums for 20 years	$2043
Subtract the cash value at the end of 20 years	2294
Insurance cost for 20 years	−$ 251
Net cost per year (−$251 ÷ 20)	−$12.55
Net cost per $1,000 per year (−$12.55 ÷ 10)	−$ 1.26

Source: George E. Rejda, *Principles of Insurance* (Glenview, Ill.: Scott, Foresman and Company, 1982), p. 382.

Some policies will steeply graduate their premiums, whereas others will go up more gradually—at least during the period important to you. In addition, if there is a good chance you will later convert your term coverage to a whole life policy, make sure you check the policies you are comparing to see how their conversion terms compare. (Cash value cost comparisons are discussed next.) Because term policies typically cover short periods of time, and because policyholder dividends play a less important role than they do in cash value policies, cost comparisons among term policies are relatively straightforward. For a female age 20, a one-year renewable and convertible term policy annual premium might range—depending on the company—between $1.50 and $3 per $1,000 of face value: a difference of 100 percent.

Comparing Costs—Cash Value Insurance

Enormous cost differences separate cash value life insurance policies just as they do term life insurance coverages. Cash value policy cost differences, though, are complex to calculate. As a result, many life insurance companies, state and federal government offices, consumer magazines, and insurance industry groups have prepared various cost analyses. A reference librarian can probably help you find several cost comparison publications in your college or public library.

Cost comparisons frequently use one of two methods: the net cost method or the interest adjusted method.

Net Cost Method The traditional manner in which life insurance companies have computed policy costs for purposes of comparison is known as the *net cost method.* Under this approach, the amount of premiums paid over a period of time (usually 10 or 20 years) is totaled. From this total, both the estimated dividends of the policyholder for the period and the cash value at the end of the period are subtracted. The remainder is divided by the number of years in the period. Assume that you are offered a $10,000 participating whole life policy that requires

Table 9.8 Illustration of the Surrender Cost Index

Total premiums for 20 years, each accumulated at 5%	$4,586
Subtract dividends for 20 years, each accumulated at 5%	824
Net premiums for 20 years	$3,762
Subtract the cash value at the end of 20 years	2,294
Insurance cost for 20 years	$1,468
Amount to which $1 deposited annually will accumulate in 20 years at 5%	34.719
For the interest-adjusted cost per year, divide $1,468 by 34.719	$42.28
For the cost per $1,000 per year, divide $42.28 by 10	$ 4.23

Source: George E. Rejda, *Principles of Insurance* (Glenview, Ill.: Scott, Foresman and Company, 1982), p. 383.

an annual premium of $132.10 and that over a 20-year ownership period policyholder dividends are expected to total $599. Furthermore, at that time, the guaranteed cash value of this policy will equal $2,294. As you can see in Table 9.7, the net cost method shows that this policy has a cost of −$12.55 per year. In other words, according to this cost figure you can have your cake and eat it too. Of course, in reality no business is going to pay you to take its product.

Regardless of its wide use, the net cost method has several technical flaws. The first and most important is that it does not consider the time value of money. A second problem is that the dividend amounts are only estimates. Actual experience may be more or less favorable than these assumptions. Third, the cost is computed only at a certain time. The rankings of the net cost of three policies at 10-, 20-, and 30-year periods could be different. And fourth, it considers only the cash involved in the contractual arrangement. Although the cash value of one policy may be larger, other nonforfeiture and dividend options as well as contractual and competitive policy features may be more favorable in policies offered by competitors.

Interest Adjusted Method More recently, considerable attention has focused on the *interest adjusted method* of calculating the cost of life insurance. The primary difference between the net cost and the interest adjusted methods is that the latter method adjusts the premium and dividend payment amounts for unearned interest. In other words, if the policyholder had not purchased life insurance he or she would have had use of his or her funds to earn interest. Thus, these lost interest earnings represent an opportunity cost that should be considered as a part of the cost of the life insurance. To incorporate these opportunity costs involves the use of financial interest functions which is beyond the scope of this book. The interest adjusted method uses two different indexes to display its cost comparisons: the surrender cost index and the net payment cost index.

Table 9.9 Illustration of the Net Payment Cost Index

Total premiums for 20 years, each accumulated at 5%	$4,586
Subtract dividends for 20 years, each accumulated at 5%	824
Insurance cost for 20 years	$3,762
Amount to which $1 deposited annually will accumulate in 20 years at 5%	34.719
For the interest-adjusted cost per year, divide $3,762 by 34.719	$108.36
For the cost per $1,000 per year, divide $108.36 by 10	$ 10.84

Source: George E. Rejda, *Principles of Insurance* (Glenview, Ill.: Scott, Foresman and Company, 1982), p. 384.

Surrender Cost Index Like the net cost method, the *surrender cost index* tells the price you have paid for life insurance if you terminate the policy at the end of some specified period. As you can see in Table 9.8, which shows the surrender cost (assuming termination at the end of 20 years) for the same policy as that in Table 9.7, adjusting premiums and dividends for interest earnings increases the annual policy cost from −$12.55 to $42.28.

Net Payment Cost Index The cost of a policy upon its surrender is relevant only to the extent that you are likely to cancel your coverage. If, instead, you plan to keep your policy in force, the *net payment cost index* represents the more useful cost measure. It calculates your policy cost exclusive of its cash value (and, of course, exclusive of its payment of the face value at death). To illustrate this costing method, Table 9.9 shows that if you died at the end of 20 years, your premium payments less dividends—interest adjusted—would amount to $3,762, or a cost of $108.36 per year.

Summary of Cost Comparisons Although cost is an important dimension in your buying process, keep in mind that the quality of the company and agent should be given due consideration. (These topics are discussed next.) Also, make sure that your cost analyses compare the same types of policies; that you consider the various value differences among all nonforfeiture and settlement options; that you realize all cost estimates on participating policies are projections—not guarantees; and that changing the year of policy surrender or maturity can affect your policy cost rankings significantly. In other words, cost comparisons offer you good information, but they cannot reduce your buying decision to a simple formula. Judgment is still required.

Selecting a Company

Selecting a life insurance company is a step that may precede to a certain degree the choosing of an agent. This approach is necessary since in the life insurance business many agents represent only one company. Consequently, before looking for an agent, you might want to develop useful criteria with which to screen out companies. Usually companies can be evaluated on the basis of their financial stability, reputation in the community and nation, liberality of policy provisions, and whether they offer participating policies (if this feature is important to you). In addition, some attention should be given to the relative costs of similar policies from the competing companies. For a view of how costs vary among 45 large life insurance companies, see Table 9.10. Notice that the annual premium of the lowest 20-year-surrender-cost-index company (Teachers Ins. & Annuity Assoc. Ordinary Life) is greater than the annual premium for some companies with higher indexes [see Massachusetts SBLI Straight Life or Connecticut Mutual LIC Econolife (Whole Life) for example]. Table 9.10 compares policies via the surrender cost index method; similarly wide differences also would show up with the net payment cost index method.

In shopping around, you might find that one company is preferable for your term protection while another company is more desirable for meeting your whole life needs. Age and size of company are useful indicators of the financial stability of life insurance companies. Unless good reason exists to do otherwise, you are probably best off limiting your choice of companies to those that have been doing business for more than 25 years and have annual premium volume in excess of $50 million. Although these criteria screen out many smaller companies, they still leave more than 75 companies from which to choose. Information on financial stability can be obtained from *Best's Reports,* and premium rates can be obtained from *Best's Flitcraft Compend.* Both are available in most university and public libraries.

Selecting an Agent

Your selection of a life insurance agent is important because you will be relying on your agent for advice and guidance with respect to some very important financial decisions. Do not assume that just because agents are licensed by the state they are competent and will necessarily serve your best interests. What you need to look for when evaluating agents is their formal and professional levels of educational attainment. Does the agent have a college degree with a major in business or insurance? Does the agent have a *CLU (Chartered Life Underwriter)* designation? The CLU is awarded only to agents who meet certain experience requirements and pass college-level examinations in such fields as life and health insurance, estate and pension planning, economics, and federal income tax law. In addition, observe how an agent reacts to your questions. Does the agent use fancy buzz words and stock answers? Or does he or she listen attentively and then after a period of thought logically answer your questions? These and other personal characteristics can provide you with information

Table 9.10 Ranking of Cash Value Life Insurance Policies: $25,000 Participating Policy Issued to a Male, Age 25

Company[a] and Policy	Annual Premium	20-Year Surrender Cost Index
The 40 Lowest-Cost Policies		
Teachers Ins. & Annuity Assoc. Ordinary Life	$302	$ 10
State Mutual LAC of Amer. Non-Smoker Whole Life	331	13
Massachusetts SBLI Straight Life	236	27
New York SBLI Straight Life	280	48
New England Mutual LIC Ordinary Life	296	48
Massachusetts Mutual LIC Convertible Life	302	55
Standard Ins. Co. Whole Life	306	55
New England Mutual LIC Ordinary Life	305	57
Northwestern Mutual LIC Whole Life	364	60
Home LIC Whole Life NSR	277	31
Phoenix Mutual LIC Ordinary Life, NSB	384	35
Home LIC Whole Life	289	43
Central LAC Special Whole Life	340	52
Phoenix Mutual LIC Ordinary Life	388	39
Union Mutual LIC Whole Life	391	49
Guardian LIC of Amer. Pension Trust Whole Life	376	51
Guardian LIC of Amer. Modified 3 Whole Life	385	53
Guardian LIC of Amer. Whole Life	376	55
Guardian LIC of Amer. Pension Trust Whole Life	382	57
Union Mutual LIC Whole Life	399	58
Guardian LIC of Amer. Modified 3 Whole Life	391	59
Mutual LAC of New York Whole Life	417	49
Continental Assurance Co. Whole Life	335	56
Mutual LAC of New York Whole Life	427	59
USAA LIC Modified-One Whole Life	282	65
Manufacturers LIC Permanent Economic Protection	306	64
Standard Ins. Co. Whole Life	316	66
Connecticut Mutual LIC Econolife (Whole Life)	281	74
Guardian LIC of Amer. Whole Life	382	61
Union Mutual LIC Exec. Life (Non-NY)	400	68
Indianapolis LIC Ordinary Life	345	69
New York LIC Modified 2 Whole Life	374	69
Columbus Mutual LIC Life—100	288	71
Farm Bureau (Iowa) Exec. Pfd. Par	349	72
USAA LIC Ordinary Life	345	68
Indianapolis LIC Exec. Protector	386	68
John Hancock Mutual LIC Pfd. 25	397	70
State Mutual LAC of Amer. Non-Smoker Exec. Protector Endowment	391	71
Minnesota Mutual LIC Econo-Life	310	72
Bankers Life Co. Special Whole Life	303	73
The 5 Highest-Cost Policies		
All Amer. Life & Casualty Co. Life Paid up at 85	452	136
Aetna LIC Whole Life	453	141
Imperial LAC of Canada Exec. Protector	475	148
Security Life & Acc. Co. Whole Life	438	153
Fidelity Life Assoc. Ordinary Life	468	181

[a]The following abbreviations are used: LIC—Life Insurance Company; LAC—Life Assurance Company; and SBLI—Savings Bank Life Insurance.

Source: George E. Rejda, *Principles of Insurance* (Glenview, Ill.: Scott, Foresman and Company, 1982), pp. 385–86.

upon which to base your decisions. In most instances, you should talk with several agents before deciding from whom to buy. Also, do not make your decision while under the influence of a specific agent. Wait until you (and your spouse, if you have one) have a chance to evaluate the pros and cons of each agent. Then, when you have decided, call and ask that agent to return for another visit.

When seeking a good life insurance agent, try to obtain recommendations from other professionals who work with agents. For example, bankers in trust departments, professional financial planners, and attorneys and accountants who are specialists in estate planning are typically good sources. In contrast, be a bit wary of selecting an agent simply because of a recommendation by a friend or relative or the aggressiveness of the agent in soliciting your patronage.

Summary

This chapter has introduced you to the concept of risk and has explored various ways that risk can be handled by families. Among these methods are risk avoidance, risk assumption, loss prevention, and insurance. Risks that can be effectively handled by insurance must meet the following criteria: (1) the group insured must have a large number of exposures, (2) the loss involved must be fortuitous, (3) the cost to the insurer of assuming financial responsibility must be relatively low—the losses covered must occur relatively infrequently but still have a high potential of severity, and (4) the loss potential should not be catastrophic to the insurer. To determine the exposure to loss it can insure and the rates to charge, the insurance company performs the underwriting function.

The most widely accepted method for assessing the amount of life insurance a family should have is the needs approach. With this technique, the family estimates how much insurance it will need after a loss to provide cash for the following: (1) family income, (2) additional expenses, (3) debt liquidation, (4) surviving spouse's income, (5) money for special requirements, and (6) liquidity. Once the amount of available resources is determined, it is compared to the total resources needed in order to find the amount of life insurance necessary to meet the financial requirements of the family. Other approaches sometimes used to determine life insurance needs are the human life value approach and the multiple earnings approach.

The two most accepted types of life insurance available to meet the needs of a family are term and whole life. Term insurance is written for a stated number of years and terminates at the end of that period. Term insurance builds cash values only rarely and when the period of coverage is relatively long (20 years or more); it offers a large amount of death protection at an economical rate for persons age 40 or younger. Whole life insurance is coverage that is necessary to fulfill a need for death protection that will exist throughout the life of the insured. It also builds cash value and can provide a good way to accumulate savings.

Another form of life insurance, endowment insurance, is like term insurance in that it provides protection for a stated period of time. In contrast to term, endowment insurance matures to its face value, which is payable upon the death of the insured or at the end of the policy period, whichever comes first. Other types of life insurance include credit life, mortgage life, industrial or home service life, special purpose policies, group life, variable life, and deferred premium life. These policies have very limited usefulness in most insurance programs. In addition, a new type of insurance—universal life—has been growing in popularity.

A number of significant features of life insurance policies are (1) the beneficiary clause, (2) settlement options, (3) policy loans, (4) payment of premiums, (5) nonforfeiture options, (6) policy reinstatement, and (7) policy changes. In addition, other important policy features such as disability clauses, insurability options, and participation are included in most life insurance policies. Other competitive features of life insurance external to the policy include the protection of cash values and death proceeds from creditors, its use as a competitive medium for savings, and the lower taxation of life insurance benefits.

Comparison of life insurance costs can be made using either the net cost method or the interest adjusted method—using either the surrender cost index or the net payment cost index. Before purchasing life insurance, careful selection of both the company and the agent is important since differences exist in the quality as well as the cost of various types of life insurance.

Health Care Plans and Insurance

10

Perhaps the next best thing to good health is a good health insurance plan. When we suffer serious illness or accident—as most of us will sometime during our lives—the road to recovery can hurt in more ways than one. We are all aware of the physical pain that disablement can bring, but there is also economic pain. The price of medical care today can often run into the tens of thousands of dollars. Without adequate health insurance to pay those expenses, a person's economic health can suffer long after he or she has recovered physically.

Health care costs have been increasing at a rate that substantially exceeds the rise in the consumer price index (CPI). As Table 10.1 shows, the costs of medical care have risen more than any other component of the CPI. Of the various costs that make up the medical care portion of the CPI, hospital charges lead the list of price increases. Hospital charges have more than tripled since 1967, and hospital room charges of $200 per day are not uncommon. Physicians' fees, nurses' salaries, and other products and services essential to health care also have increased in cost faster than the increases in price reflected by the overall consumer price index. Although the rate of increase in these fees and prices does not match the increase experienced in hospital rates, it is nonetheless significant.

Several major factors account for the inflation that has occurred in the health care field. The chief cause probably stems from the increased demand for health care services stimulated by the government's medicare and medicaid programs, as well as the rapid growth in the broad base of private health plans. More than 95 out of every 100 noninstitutionalized Americans are now eligible for at least some cost reimbursement for losses resulting from accident or illness. In addition, large acquisitions of expensive new health care equipment and facilities by hospitals and clinics have pushed costs upward. A poor distribution of demand for and the supply of health care facilities and services may also contribute to today's high costs of health care. Unfortunately, no immediate relief is foreseen. In light of these spiraling costs, the need for health financing plans and insurance is greater now than it has ever been, and continued growth is expected. Without insurance few families can afford to pay the high financial costs that would arise if any family member required substantial medical attention.

As a case in point consider the likely costs incurred by a man who while painting his house fell off his ladder. An ambulance was called, and the man was taken to the hospital. There he was admitted, examined, x-rayed, and assigned to a semiprivate room. The results of the examination showed a broken leg and a sprained back. Treatment

Table 10.1 Consumer Price Index in the United States (1967 = 100.0)

Calendar Year	All Items	Food	Apparel	Housing	Transportation	Medical Care	Entertainment	Other Goods and Services
				Urban Wage and Clerical Workers				
1935	41.1	36.5	40.8	49.3	42.6	36.1	41.8	44.6
1940	42.0	35.2	42.8	52.4	42.7	36.8	46.1	48.3
1945	53.9	50.7	61.5	59.1	47.8	42.1	62.4	56.9
1950	72.1	74.5	79.0	72.8	68.2	53.7	74.4	60.9
1955	80.2	81.6	84.1	82.3	77.4	64.8	76.7	79.8
1960	88.7	88.0	89.6	90.2	89.6	79.1	87.3	87.8
1965	94.5	94.4	93.7	94.9	95.9	89.5	95.9	94.2
1966	97.2	99.1	96.1	97.2	97.2	93.4	97.5	97.2
1967	100.0	100.0	100.0	100.0	100.0	100.0	100.0	100.0
1968	104.2	103.6	105.4	104.2	103.2	106.1	104.7	104.6
1969	109.8	108.9	111.5	110.8	107.2	113.4	108.7	109.1
1970	116.3	114.9	116.1	118.9	112.7	120.6	113.4	116.0
1971	121.3	118.4	119.8	124.3	118.6	128.4	119.3	120.9
1972	125.3	123.5	122.3	129.2	119.9	132.5	122.8	125.5
1973	133.1	141.4	126.8	135.0	123.8	137.7	125.9	129.0
1974	147.7	161.7	136.2	150.6	137.7	150.5	133.8	137.2
1975	161.2	175.4	142.3	166.8	150.6	168.6	144.4	147.4
1976	170.5	180.8	147.6	177.2	165.5	184.7	151.2	153.3
1977	181.5	192.2	154.2	189.6	177.2	202.4	157.9	159.2
1978	195.3	206.2	159.5	202.6	185.8	219.4	176.2	183.2
				All Urban Consumers[a]				
1978	195.4	211.4	159.6	202.8	185.5	219.4	176.6	183.3
1979	217.4	234.5	166.6	227.6	212.0	239.7	188.5	196.7
1980	246.8	254.6	178.4	263.3	249.7	265.9	205.3	214.5
1981	272.4	274.6	186.9	293.5	280.0	294.5	221.4	235.7

[a]Beginning January 1978, the Bureau of Labor Statistics introduced a new index for all urban consumers.
Source: Source Book of Health Insurance Data, 1981–1982 (New York: Health Insurance Institute, 1982), p. 62.

included setting the fracture, four days of traction for the back sprain, and four weeks of recuperation before returning to work. As shown in Table 10.2, total expenses and lost income for this disablement amount to $4,250. Certainly charges of this size could devastate the family budget.

To show you how to reduce your health care exposures, this chapter first explains why preparing for health care protection can be complex. Next, the popular types of health care coverages, typical health insurance policy provisions, and the various sources of health care expense protection are discussed. Last, this chapter brings the previous discussions together to guide you through the process of buying health care insurance coverages wisely.

Table 10.2 Disablement Costs of a Hypothetical Accident

Ambulance	$ 65
Hospitalization (5 Days)	1,000
X-Rays	100
Emergency Room Service	95
Physician	700
Traction Equipment Rental	110
Prescription Drugs	55
Anesthetist	125
Lost Wages (4 Weeks)	2,000
Total	$4,250

The Complexity of Health Care Insurance

If we ranked consumer insurance programs on a complexity scale, life insurance would be at the "simple" end of the scale, health insurance at the opposite extreme. In all but rare instances, life insurance pays regardless of the cause of loss, the loss itself is seldom arguable, and the amount of the loss is the face amount of the policy (or some multiple thereof). In addition, with life insurance each policy you own will pay regardless of any other policies you have; there are no deductibles, waiting periods, participation clauses, or chances of cancellation; and differences in policy provisions among leading insurers are relatively slight.

In contrast, each of the above issues is pertinent to health insurance coverages. Specifically, here we look at two major problem areas: the large number of health care financing coverages and the numerous types of sources of these coverages.

Large Number of Coverages

Around 1850, when health insurance policies were first sold, they were most commonly accident policies that paid a small amount when an insured was injured in a specific type of accident. As more health insurers began writing health coverages, the number of accident perils insured against increased. By the turn of the 20th century, individual accident policies were being written for nearly all types of accidents. At about this same time, health insurers began issuing "sickness insurance policies," which offered protection for a small amount of income loss if the insured contracted any of several named diseases. In other words, comprehensive coverage was impossible to obtain, and "extensive" coverage could only be achieved through buying a basketful of policies—each one representing different types of accidents and illnesses.

Not until the 1930s was the modern concept of broadly based health care insurance born. At that time Blue Cross began selling policies that provided families with the costs of hospital and surgical care. Although from the 1930s to the present, great strides have been made in health care plan coverages offered, amounts of reimbursement provided, and number of persons protected, no standardized all-risk policy has yet been adopted. Needed coverage is often obtained only through a collection of types of health insurance policies. The heritage of the 1800s and early 1900s is still with us. Unfortunately, this piecemeal approach often causes double coverage in certain areas, while other areas of need lack any coverage at all.

Multiple Sources

Compounding the complexity wrought by the large number of health insurance coverages is the fact that many people are covered by at least three or four different health care financing plans. Employer sponsored group plans, social security, worker's compensation, automobile medical payments, veterans' benefits, and individually purchased coverages represent several of the most popular. Unfortunately, these financing plans seldom force a coherent and comprehensive health care program that adequately and efficiently meets the needs of any one person or family. Instead, the multiple sources contribute to the problem of coverage duplication for some risks and gaps in coverages for others.

Making Sense of It All

Because of these complicating factors, designing the best way to meet your health care needs truly requires a systematic approach. You need to learn what coverages are available, their various policy provisions, and from whom they can be obtained. Next, you need to inventory your needs and existing coverages. With that task completed, you then can shop the market for the right protection at the best price. It is toward this goal that the remainder of this chapter is devoted.

Types of Coverages

Even though many of today's health insurance policies provide much broader coverages than policies offered in the predepression era, the wide variety and quality of policies available today make it imperative that one be cautious when shopping for health insurance. The individual can best guard against purchasing the wrong kinds of coverage by understanding the basic differences and uses of the various types of

Table 10.3 Disability Income Insurance Premiums
(Male Age 35, Class #1: Desk-Type Job)

Waiting Period	Term of Disability Benefits			
	1 Year	3 Years	5 Years	Age 65
7 Days	$30.88	$34.40	$37.30	$53.80
14 Days	24.40	29.10	32.00	47.90
30 Days	14.16	17.60	19.90	31.80
60 Days	9.70	12.75	15.00	26.20
90 Days	—	10.20	12.50	23.50
1 Year	—	—	10.90	19.50

Note: Premiums shown are *annual* charges per $100 per *month* of coverage.

policies. Thus the most popular types of health insurance coverages are discussed in the following sections: (1) disability income, (2) hospital, (3) surgical expense, (4) physicians expense, (5) major medical, (6) comprehensive major medical (7) dental, and (8) other special coverages.

Disability Income Insurance

Disability income insurance is designed to provide families with weekly or monthly payments to replace income when an insured person is unable to work as a result of a covered illness, injury, or disease. Some companies also offer disability income protection for an unemployed spouse; in that case, the coverage helps pay for the services that the spouse would normally provide. Disability income policies frequently include *waiting period* provisions, which require that the insured wait a specified length of time after the inception of the disability before payment begins. A waiting period provision is similar to the deductibles that are found in property insurance contracts. The purpose of both is to omit coverage for the frequent small loss, which is very expensive to administer. A family can save a substantial amount in premiums by purchasing a policy that has a relatively long waiting period.

The maximum period for which disability payments are made normally ranges from 13 weeks to age 65. In some cases, a disability policy will state that payments will continue for a specified period if the disability occurred because of sickness (for example, 5 years) and another period if the disability resulted from accident (for example, age 65). With most companies, the insured can trade off, say, an increase in the waiting period from 7 days to 90 days for an increase in the duration of benefits from 5 years to age 65. In fact, as can be seen in Table 10.3, the premium for a policy with a one-year term and a seven-day waiting period for the company shown is about the same as the premium charged for benefits payable to age 65 with a 30-day waiting period. Since the purpose of all insurance is to protect against a catastrophic loss rather than smaller losses that could be better handled through budgeting or savings, accepting this type of trade-off usually makes sense. Because the prolonged disability of the breadwinner of a family can have a severe adverse impact on its finances (often more than in the case of death), disability income insurance should be an integral part of the insurance program of most families. The lack of adequate long-term disability income insurance is the most common weakness in the health insurance program of most families.

Normally, in rating most types of health insurance, underwriters consider an applicant's occupation, age, sex, and medical history. In addition, to avoid "encouraging" a disability, most insurers will limit the monthly payment amount to 60–70 percent of an insured's wages. Also, disability income policies often specify a shorter maximum period for illness-created disabilities as opposed to those caused by accident. The reasons are that determining sickness is more subjective and poses a larger chance for the insured to pretend to be ill. As mentioned in Chapter 9, many life insurance companies offer disability income riders to their life insurance policies.

Hospital Insurance

Hospital insurance policies offer reimbursement plans covering the costs of hospital room and board and other expenses incidental to hospitalization. More people in the United States are covered by some type of hospitalization insurance than any other kind of private health insurance. Basically, hospital insurance pays for a portion of (1) the per day hospital room and board charges, which typically include floor nursing and other routine services, and (2) ancillary expenses, such as use of the operating room, laboratory tests, x-ray examinations, and medicine taken by the patient while hospitalized. Although a few hospital insurance policies will pay for an in-hospital private duty nurse, most do not. In some cases, the hospital plan will simply pay a flat daily amount for each day the insured remains in the hospital, regardless of the actual amount of charges levied. Numerous hospital plans now also offer reimbursement for some outpatient and out-of-hospital services, among which might be in-home rehabilitation or ambulatory center care, diagnostic and preventive treatment, and preadmission testing.

In most policies, hospital insurance is written to provide the daily benefit room and board charges up to a specified number of days, such as say 90, 120, or 360. The maximum reimbursement for ancillary expenses, in contrast, may be a stated dollar amount, or sometimes a multiple of the daily room rate. In the first instance, frequently found maximums are $1,000, $2,000, and $5,000; whereas in the second instance the multiple might be, say, 15 or 20. So, if the room and board rate were $150 per day, applying this multiple would result in an ancillary expense limit of either $2,250 or $3,000. The average hospital cost per day, the average length of hospital stay, and the average cost per stay are shown in Table 10.4 for each state.

Table 10.4 Community Hospital Statistics, 1980

State	Average Cost to Hospital Per Day	Average Length of Hospital Stay in Days	Average Cost to Hospital Per Stay
Alabama	$210.10	7.0	$1,470.70
Alaska	409.00	5.6	2,290.40
Arizona	290.60	7.0	2,034.20
Arkansas	185.60	6.3	1,169.30
California	362.60	6.6	2,393.20
Colorado	247.50	7.1	1,757.30
Connecticut	271.70	7.5	2,037.80
Delaware	238.20	8.2	1,953.20
District of Columbia	358.30	8.9	3,188.90
Florida	247.30	7.3	1,805.30
Georgia	217.60	6.3	1,370.90
Hawaii	245.80	7.5	1,843.50
Idaho	208.80	6.0	1,252.80
Illinois	277.60	7.9	2,193.00
Indiana	214.30	7.6	1,628.70
Iowa	199.30	7.4	1,474.80
Kansas	207.30	7.7	1,596.20
Kentucky	189.40	6.7	1,269.00
Louisiana	233.10	6.4	1,491.80
Maine	217.10	7.9	1,715.10
Maryland	251.20	8.5	2,135.20
Massachusetts	294.40	8.8	2,590.70
Michigan	267.00	7.8	2,082.60
Minnesota	203.10	9.0	1,827.90
Mississippi	174.80	6.7	1,171.20
Missouri	230.40	8.0	1,843.20
Montana	160.20	8.3	1,329.70
Nebraska	194.70	7.9	1,538.10
Nevada	343.90	6.4	2,201.00
New Hampshire	203.20	7.1	1,442.70
New Jersey	212.60	8.7	1,849.60
New Mexico	263.70	5.9	1,555.80
New York	257.40	9.6	2,471.00
North Carolina	186.90	7.5	1,401.80
North Dakota	177.10	8.7	1,540.80
Ohio	241.40	7.9	1,907.10
Oklahoma	239.80	6.4	1,534.70
Oregon	277.40	6.0	1,664.40
Pennsylvania	234.90	8.3	1,949.70
Rhode Island	260.50	8.3	2,162.20
South Carolina	186.60	7.3	1,362.20
South Dakota	189.60	6.7	1,270.30
Tennessee	204.10	7.0	1,428.70
Texas	227.00	6.6	1,498.20
Utah	271.70	5.4	1,467.20
Vermont	183.40	8.0	1,467.20
Virginia	209.50	7.8	1,634.10
Washington	262.50	5.8	1,522.50
West Virginia	195.20	7.2	1,405.40
Wisconsin	218.20	8.1	1,767.40
Wyoming	242.80	4.9	1,189.70
Total United States	$245.60	7.6	$1,866.60

Source: Source Book of Health Insurance Data, 1981–1982 (New York: Health Insurance Institute, 1982), p. 65.

Table 10.5 Examples of Surgical Payments, Hospital-Surgical Policy

	Maximum Payment		
	$1,200 Schedule	$2,000 Schedule	$2,800 Schedule
Appendectomy	$ 240.00	$ 300.00	$ 560.00
Brain tumor, suboccipital craniectomy	900.00	1,500.00	2,100.00
Breast tumor, removal (one breast involved)	90.00	150.00	210.00
Gall bladder, removal	360.00	600.00	840.00
Heart, replacement of aortic valve (open)	1,200.00	2,000.00	2,800.00
Hernia, repair of inguinal, femoral, or epigastric	210.00	350.00	490.00
Hip or knee dislocation, closed reduction	120.00	200.00	280.00
Hysterectomy			
Subtotal or supracervical	330.00	550.00	770.00
Total (uterus and cervix)	360.00	600.00	840.00
Kidney, removal	480.00	800.00	1,120.00
Knee joint, excision of cartilage	300.00	500.00	700.00
Lung, removal	600.00	1,000.00	1,400.00
Spinal fusion, with removal of disc	720.00	1,200.00	1,680.00
Suturing wound(s), not as a hospital inpatient, up to a total of 2½ inches	12.00	20.00	28.00
Tonsils, or tonsils and adenoids, removal			
Under age 18	90.00	150.00	210.00
18 or over	120.00	200.00	280.00

Note: A more complete list of procedures and the related maximum payments is usually contained within the policy itself.
Source: A major life and health insurance company.

Surgical Expense Insurance

Surgical expense insurance provides coverage for the cost of surgery. Typically, a schedule of benefits will be available that prescribes the amount the insurer is obligated to pay for listed surgical procedures (for instance, $300 for an appendectomy, $800 for removal of a kidney, or $200 for a tonsillectomy). Sample surgical benefit payment schedules for selected procedures are shown in Table 10.5. The three schedules ($1,200, $2,000, and $2,800) differ on the basis of the premiums charged for the policy. By paying a little more, the insured can receive benefits under a schedule providing higher maximum payments. Usually surgical expense coverage is quite extensive and will pay for almost any type of surgery that is required to maintain the health of the insured. In the event a necessary surgical procedure is not named in the policy, the company will pay the amount listed for a comparable operation. The amounts shown in the schedule usually approximate the average fees charged in a specific geographic area. Reimbursement for the cost of anesthetics and their administration is provided in some surgical expense policies. However, more frequently these are paid under the additional benefit provision of a hospital insurance policy. Surgical expense policies may also allow payment for the treatment of tumors and other afflictions using x-rays or radium. Surgical expense coverage is typically sold in conjunction with a hospital insurance policy either as an integral part of that policy or as a rider. In some cases, a surgical schedule is also available as a rider to certain accident policies.

Physicians Expense Insurance

Physicians expense insurance, previously called regular medical expense, can provide coverage for the cost of such services as physician fees for nonsurgical care in a hospital, at home, in a clinic, or in the doctor's office. Also covered are x-rays and laboratory tests performed outside of a hospital. These plans usually provide maximum amounts payable for services as listed in a schedule of allowances. Often the first few visits with the physician for any single cause will be excluded. This exclusion serves the same purpose as the deductible and waiting period features found in other types of insurance.

Major Medical Insurance

Major medical plans are those that provide benefits for nearly all types of medical expenses resulting from either accidents or illnesses. As the name implies, the amounts that can be collected under this coverage are relatively large. Limits of $25,000 or $100,000 or higher are common, with some policies providing unlimited protection. The trend in recent years has been toward the higher benefit levels. For example, in a recent survey, 94 percent of the persons covered under group major medical had benefits of $100,000 or more available. In contrast, in 1966 only 14 percent of this class of insureds had policies with limits greater than $20,000.

Major medical coverage was first offered in the early 1950s to supplement the basic coverages of hospital, surgical, and physicians expenses discussed earlier. This basic concept still applies today since the other three hospital and physicians expense coverages are available to meet the smaller health care costs while major medical is used to finance medical costs of a more catastrophic nature. Approximately three out of every four Americans are covered by some type of major medical health plan. The popularity of this insurance has grown more since its inception than that of any other kind of health insurance in history. To give insureds an incentive to avoid unncessary medical costs major medical plans typically are written with provisions for deductibles, participation or coinsurance, and internal limits.

Deductibles Because major medical plans are designed to supplement the basic hospital, surgical, and physicians expense policies, they frequently have a relatively large *deductible* of $500 or $1,000. In many plans, the deductible is on a per accident or per illness basis. This means that if you were covered by a policy with a $1,000 deductible and suffered three separate accidents in the course of a year, each requiring $1,000 of medical expenses, you would not be eligible to collect any benefits from the major medical plan.

Participation or Coinsurance Another feature of major medical insurance is that most policies contain some type of *participation, or coinsurance, clause.* This provision stipulates that the company will pay some portion—say, 80 or 90 percent—of the amount of the covered loss in excess of the deductible, rather than the entire amount. The purpose of requiring the insured to participate as "coinsurers" is to reduce the possibility that they will pretend to be ill, and to discourage them from incurring unnecessary medical expenses.

Because major medical limits now go up to $1,000,000 or more, many plans place a cap on the amount of participation required. If this were not the case, a $1,000,000 medical bill could still leave the insured with, say, $200,000 of costs. Often such caps limit the insured's payment to less than $10,000, and sometimes as little as $2,000.

Internal Limits Most major medical plans in recent years also have been written with *internal limits.* Internal limits place constraints on the amounts that will be paid for certain specified expenses, even if the overall policy limits are not exceeded by the claim. Charges which are commonly subject to internal limits are hospital room and board, surgical fees, and nursing services. Providing internal or inside limits is similar in purpose to participation and coinsurance clauses. The insurer wants to give the insured an incentive not to incur unreasonably high medical expenses. Therefore, if an insured elects a highly expensive physician or medical facility, that insured is responsible for paying the portion of the charges that are above a "reasonable and customary" level, or beyond a specified maximum amount. The example in the following section illustrates how deductibles, coinsurance, and internal limits constrain the amount a company is obligated to pay under a major medical plan.

Major Medical Policy: An Example Assume that an insured person has coverage under a major medical insurance policy that specified a $25,000 overall limit of protection, a $1,000 deductible, an 80 percent coinsurance clause, internal limits of $140 per day on hospital room and board, and $1,000 as the maximum payable surgical fee. Assume further that the insured was hospitalized for 14 days at $185 a day and required an operation that cost $900. Other covered medical expenses that were incurred with this illness totaled $1,800. Therefore, the medical expenses incurred by the insured amount to $5,290, the total of $2,590 for hospital room and board plus $900 for the surgeon plus $1,800 for the other medical expenses.

Because of the coinsurance clause in the policy, however, the maximum the company has to pay is 80 percent of the covered loss in excess of the deductible. In the absence of internal limits the company would pay $3,432 (.80 × [$5,290 − $1,000]). The internal limits further restrict the payment. Even though 80 percent of the $185 per diem hospital charge is $148, the most the company would have to pay is $140 per diem. Therefore, the insured becomes liable for $112 ($8 per day × 14 days). The internal limit on the surgery is not exceeded, since, after considering coinsurance, the insurer will have to pay $720 (.80 × $900), which is below the $1,000 internal limit. The company's obligation is reduced to $3,320 ($3,432 − $112), while the insured must pay a total of $1,970 ($1,000 deductible + .20 [$5,290 − $1,000] coinsurance + $112 excess hospital charges). The lesson here is that even though major medical insurance can offer very large amounts of reimbursement, you may also remain responsible for substantial payments.

Comprehensive Major Medical Insurance

A *comprehensive major medical insurance* plan combines the basic hospital, surgical, and physicians expense coverages with major medical protection to form a single policy. In contrast to an ordinary major medical plan, the deductible under a comprehensive major medical plan is relatively small, often $100 or less. Some of these plans also have a more favorable participation feature than major medical policies since they may require no coinsurance on basic hospital and surgical expense claims. Frequently, comprehensive major medical insurance is written under a group contract. However, some efforts have been made to make this type of coverage available on an individual basis.

Dental Insurance

Dental insurance covers necessary dental health care as well as dental injuries sustained through accidents. The coverage may provide for oral examinations including x-rays, cleanings, fillings, extractions, inlays, bridgework, dentures, oral surgery, root canal therapy, and orthodontics. Of course, dental policies vary with respect to the number of these items included within the coverage. Some dental plans contain deductible and coinsurance provisions, and others have "first dollar protection"—they pay for all claims. Most present dental coverage is written through group insurance plans, although some companies do offer individual and family policies. However, since many types of dental insurance function more as budgeting techniques than as true insurance, premiums are often relatively large in light of the dollar amount of coverage obtained.

Other Special Insurance Coverages

An examination of every type of health insurance coverage available would fill a book twice the size of this one. However, the types of health insurance plans previously discussed are sufficient to meet the protection needs of most families and individuals. Other popularly available contracts often are simply frills and gimmicks. These plans may be classified as accident policies, sickness policies, and hospital income policies. Sound insurance programming seldom dictates the purchase of these types of policies. Nevertheless, large-scale marketing efforts by some insurers coupled with public misunderstanding has brought about their proliferation. The following discussion will help you guard against a potentially unwise purchase.

Accident policies are those that pay a specified sum to an insured who is injured in a certain type of accident. The most common types of accident policies are those relating to travel accidents. These first became widespread with the growing passenger traffic of the railroads during the 1800s and today include private and for-hire automobiles and commercial and private aviation. Often these policies are sold in conjunction with oil company and travel and entertainment credit cards. A primary shortcoming of these policies is that the amount of the payment is not directly related to the amount of a loss. Also, as noted earlier, since only certain types of accidents are covered, it becomes impossible to structure a systematic insurance program using these coverages that does not have serious gaps in some places and duplicate coverage in others.

Sickness policies are similar in design and shortcomings to accident policies except that a named disease, as opposed to an accident, conditions the payment. Sickness policies may be written separately or in conjunction with an accident policy. *Dread disease policies* are a popular version of sickness insurance. Today's renditions limit health care coverage to a specific type of disease or illness. Cancer policies appear to be the most common, with some organ transplant policies also being offered.

Hospital income policies typically guarantee the insured a specified daily, weekly, or monthly amount as long as the insured remains hospitalized. However, the policies generally exclude illness that could result in extended hospitalization (for example, mental illness or those resulting from health conditions that existed at the time the policy was purchased). Several of these plans have been accused of returning in benefits only 10¢ to 20¢ of each $1 of premiums collected.

The basic problem with buying policies that cover only a certain type of accident, illness, or financial need is that major gaps in coverage will occur. However, the financial loss can be just as great regardless of whether the insured falls down a flight of stairs or contracts cancer, lung disease, or heart disease. Most limited peril policies should be used only to supplement a comprehensive insurance program if the coverage is not overlapping. Both dread disease and hospital income policies are frequently offered directly through television and newspaper advertisements.

Evaluating Policy Provisions

To compare the health insurance coverages offered by different insurers, you need to evaluate whether they contain liberal or restrictive provisions. Generally, these provisions can be divided into two classes: terms of payment and terms of coverage.

Terms of Payment

Five provisions govern how much your health care plan will pay: (1) deductibles and waiting periods, (2) duration of benefits, (3) policy limits, (4) coordination of benefits, and (5) method of payment.

Deductibles and Waiting Periods In order to reduce administrative costs and frequent small claims, nearly all types of health insurance policies include deductible and/or waiting period clauses. On individual and family policies, the policyholder usually has a broad range of deductibles and waiting periods from which to choose. Of course, with all other things equal, the higher the deductible and the longer the waiting period, the lower the annual premium.

Duration of Benefits Another item that you should look for in health insurance policies concerns the length of the benefit period. For disability coverage, this time period typically ranges from six months to life. The benefit period under health care expense policies is often limited to three years after the first charge is incurred on a given claim.

Policy Limits Almost all private health insurance contracts place some limit on the benefit amounts they will pay. Often specific dollar amounts are stipulated. In their absence, the payments are limited to an amount considered *reasonable and necessary.* Reasonable usually means the prevailing charges are in line with those given for similar services in the same geographic area. Remember that, in a fashion similar to major medical coverage, many health policies not only have maximum total amounts payable, but they also specify internal limits for certain types of expenses and services.

Coordination of Benefits In contrast to most property and liability insurance coverages, which are discussed in Chapter 11, health insurance policies are not contracts of *indemnity.* This means that insureds can collect multiple payments for the same accident or illness unless a *coordination of benefits provision* is included in their health insurance contracts. For example, many private health insurance policies have coordination of benefits provisions with medical benefits paid under worker's compensation. In contrast, some companies widely advertise that their policies will pay claims regardless of how much other coverage the policyholder has. Of course, these latter types of insurance contracts are often more expensive per dollar of protection than those policies that provide for coordination of benefits. From the standpoint of insurance planning, use of policies with coordination of benefit clauses can help you prevent coverage overlaps and, ideally, reduce your premiums.

Method of Payment The type of financing method used to pay your covered medical expenses will be specified as: (1) the indemnity approach, (2) the valued approach, or (3) the service approach.

Under the *indemnity approach,* insurers reimburse insureds for their actual amount of covered losses up to the stated policy maximums. Sometimes, this stated maximum is specified as the amount that is reasonable and customary. In other policies it is a specified dollar amount such as shown in Table 10.5 for surgical expense payments. Under the *valued approach,* the amounts to be paid are specified in the policy and do not necessarily bear a direct relationship to costs incurred. And under the *service approach,* typically no monies pass to the insured. He or she is simply entitled to some level of medical and hospital care. As is pointed out later, Blue Cross/Blue Shield plans and HMOs are typically service-providing organizations. Among these methods of payment, your best protection comes from service plans, since you are guaranteed care—not partial reimbursement. These plans, though, can cost higher premiums.

Terms of Coverage

Some of the major terms of health insurance coverage derive from the following: (1) persons and places covered, (2) definition of accident, (3) change of occupation, (4) definition of disability, (5) house confinement, (6) cancellation, (7) renewal, (8) rehabilitation, (9) pre-existing conditions, (10) pregnancy and abortions, and (11) mental illness.

Persons and Places Covered Some health insurance policies cover only the named insured, while others offer protection to all family members. Of those that offer family coverage, some terminate benefits payable on behalf of children at age 18 and others continue them to age

22 as long as the child remains in school or is single. If your policy does not include this coverage, sometimes it can be added by paying an additional premium. Also, some policies protect you only while you are in the U.S. or Canada; others offer worldwide coverage, but exclude certain named countries.

Definition of Accident Health policies that pay for losses caused by accident define an *accident* in one of two ways. The majority have a liberal definition indicating that as long as the result of a given action is accidental, coverage will apply. This is called an *accidental injury clause.* Other health insurance policies contain an *accidental means clause.* Under this provision, both the act and the injury must have been accidental. Consider the following example: After cleaning leaves out of the gutters on his house, Steve Urse purposely jumped to the ground from the roof and accidentally broke his leg in the process. Payment would be made under the policy with an accidental injury clause, but no payment would be available if an accidental means provision applied, since the cause of the injury (jumping from the roof) was not accidental.

Change of Occupation In underwriting disability income policies, insurance companies consider the hazards related to the insured's job. Consequently, people who work in dangerous occupations must pay a higher premium than those in less accident-prone positions. In order to protect the insurance company, most disability income contracts explicitly state that a lower level of benefits will be paid if an insured person switches to a more hazardous occupation during the policy period.

Definition of Disability In some disability income policies, people are defined as disabled if they no longer have the capacity to undertake gainful employment. In fact, this is the definition used by the Social Security Administration to qualify a covered worker for disability payments. The practical enforcement of this provision, however, is often more liberal than might be expected from reading the policy. In contrast, more liberal policies classify insureds as disabled if they simply cannot pursue an occupation for which they have been trained. Under some coverages, an insured person may be eligible for disability benefits if he or she loses sight, both arms or both legs or, in other cases, one of each. In these instances no employment test would be applied in order to determine the benefit eligibility of the insured.

House Confinement Another requirement imposed by some disability income policies is that insureds must be confined to their home in order to become eligible for benefits. Obviously, policies with this provision should be avoided.

Cancellation Many health insurance policies are written to permit *cancellation* at any time at the option of the insurer. Some policies explicitly state this; others do not. To protect yourself against premature cancellation, you should buy policies that contain a provision which specifically states that the insurer will not cancel coverage as long as premiums are paid.

Renewal Whereas cancellation pertains to termination of the contract during the policy period, *renewal* refers to the right of the insured to continue coverage upon expiration of the policy period. For maximum protection, you should find health coverage contracts that either provide for guaranteed renewal or are noncancellable to at least age 65.

Rehabilitation Coverage In the past health insurance plans focused almost exclusively on reasonable and necessary medical expenses. If an illness or accident left an insured partially or totally disabled, no funds normally would be available to help the person retrain for employment and a more productive life. Now, though, many policies include expense reimbursement for counseling, occupational therapists, and even some educational or job training programs. With this *rehabilitation coverage* the goal is not to medicate but to rehabilitate. This is a good feature to look for in disability income and major medical policies.

Pre-Existing Conditions Most health insurance policies that are sold to individuals (as opposed to group-employer sponsored plans) contain a *pre-existing condition clause.* This means that the policy might exclude coverage for any physical or mental problems that you might have at the time you buy the policy. In some policies the exclusion is permanent, in others the exclusion only lasts for the first year or two that the coverage is in force. Group insurance plans may also have a pre-existing condition clause, but these tend to be less restrictive than those found in individually written coverages.

Pregnancy and Abortions Many individual and group health insurance plans include special clauses that pertain to medical expenses incurred through pregnancy or abortion. The most liberal of these policies pay for all related expenses, including sick-leave pay during the final months of pregnancy. Other middle-of-the-road policies will pay for medical expenses that result from pregnancy or abortion complications, but not for routine procedure expenses. And, in the most restrictive cases, no coverage for any costs of pregnancy or abortion is granted.

In recent years, the federal government and many states have passed laws that require certain employer-sponsored group health insurance programs to provide more liberal pregnancy and abortion reimbursement plans. Even in absence of law, though, many employers are expanding their coverage for employees in this area. Because of adverse self-selection problems, individual health insurance will continue to restrict this policy feature.

Mental Illness Mental illness and emotional disorders are perhaps America's most prevalent, but least talked about, health problems. The high pressure "get ahead" lives that many people lead often give rise to drug and alcohol abuse, stress-related physical disability, and various forms of psychosis or neurosis. In addition, family problems, economic setbacks, and chemical imbalances within the body all can contribute to poor mental health. Yet, even though mental illness or emotional disorder at some time strikes one out of three families, many of those affected will not admit they need help.

Compounding this problem of denial is the fact that many health insurance coverages omit or offer reduced benefits for treatment of mental disorders. Both hospital insurance and major medical insurance often restrict the duration over which they will reimburse victims. For example, one widely marketed health insurance policy offers hospital benefits that continue to pay as long as you remain hospitalized—except for mental illness. Under this policy payment for mental illness is restricted to one-half the normally provided payment amounts and for a period not to exceed 30 days. Unfortunately, mental illness is the number one sickness that requires long-term hospital care.

As you can see from this discussion, coverage for mental illness is an important type of insurance protection. So make sure you check your policies to learn how liberal—or how restrictive—they are with respect to this feature.

Sources of Health Care Coverage

Five traditional sources of financial aid for losses arising from accident or illness are available on a large scale. These are (1) social security, (2) worker's compensation insurance, (3) group health insurance, (4) Blue Cross/Blue Shield, and (5) individual health coverages from insurance companies. In certain parts of the country, health maintenance organizations also help families and individuals meet their health care needs. In addition, several other sources of health care coverage are available. And although not presently enacted, national health insurance legislation has been suggested as a means to fund health care costs.

Social Security

Many people think of social security as only a retirement system. It can, however, provide a considerable amount of coverage for losses arising from disability. In fact, the official name for what is commonly referred to as social security is *Old-Age, Survivor's, Disability, and Health Insurance (OASDHI).* Health benefits are provided under two separate programs: (1) disability income and (2) medicare. Although the *medicaid* program also provides medical benefits under social security, it is not discussed here since it is a public assistance program designed to provide benefit for those persons who are unable to pay for health care.

Disability Income The disability income benefits under social security can be important to families during child-rearing years as well as thereafter. Nearly all families in the United States are covered by social security. The only major exceptions are certain groups of state and local employees and most employees of the federal government (legislation was proposed in 1983 to include federal employees), who are enrolled in a special system. In order to be eligible for disability income benefits, a covered employee needs 20 quarters (5 years) of coverage out of the 40 quarters (10 years) immediately preceding the date of disability and must have suffered a total disability that has been in effect for at least 5 months and is expected to prevent employment for a minimum of 12 months. After becoming eligible for disability benefits, the worker and his or her family can receive benefits for the duration of the disability, even if it lasts for life. The amount of the monthly family benefit paid on behalf of the disabled worker, say, under age 35, often would range between 40 and 80 percent of his or her predisability monthly earnings. The exact percentage used decreases as a covered worker's average earnings increase.

Eligibility requirements for workers who become disabled before age 31 are more liberal. Benefits may be paid on behalf of young workers if they have coverage in one-half of the quarters elapsing in the period after they attained age 21, up to and including the quarter in which the disability occurred. A minimum of 6 quarters of coverage is required. Unmarried children 18 or under whose disabled, retired, or deceased parent is covered under social security can draw benefits under that parent's account without ever having worked.

A very desirable feature of disability income, as well as the other cash benefit programs of social security, is that all payments are automatically adjusted periodically to reflect increases in the cost of living. No private insurance plan can make such a guarantee. Of course, the reason that social security can make this promise is that the financing mechanism is based on the assumption that taxes can always be raised, if needed, to fund the social security benefits. (The financial soundness of social security is discussed in Chapter 15.) Disability income can also be paid during periods of rehabilitation even though the recipient may have some type of gainful employment.

Medicare *Medicare* is a health care plan that has two primary components: (1) basic hospital insurance and (2) supplementary medical insurance. Although medicare was primarily designed to help persons over age 65 meet their health care costs, it now also covers many persons under age 65 who are current recipients of monthly social security disability benefits.

Basic Hospital Insurance Under the basic hospital insurance coverage of medicare, inpatient hospital services are included for 90 days per benefit period. A *benefit period* begins when an insured enters a hospital or skilled nursing facility and ends 60 days after the hospital or nursing home stay is terminated. In addition, a person has a lifetime "safety cushion" of 60 days of care which may be used at any time to extend coverage for a prolonged hospital stay beyond the standard 90 days per benefit period. Along with the coverage of hospital room and board, medicare hospital insurance contributes toward the payment of all services normally provided to inpatients as well as covering stays for limited periods in post-hospital extended care facilities. Moreover, some post-hospital health services, such as intermittent nursing care, therapy, rehabilitation, and home health aid, are provided. Benefits offered under the basic hospital plan of medicare are subject to deductibles, coinsurance provisions, and time limits. These amounts are revised each year to reflect changes in medical costs. The funds for medicare benefits come from the social security taxes paid by covered workers and their employers.

Supplementary Medical Insurance (SMI) The supplementary medical insurance program under medicare provides payment for the following items: (1) physicians' and surgeons' services that are provided either at home or in a health care facility; (2) home health service (visitations by a registered nurse); and (3) medical and health services such as x-rays, diagnostics, laboratory tests, rental of necessary durable medical equipment, prosthetic devices, and ambulance trips. Limited psychiatric care is also covered under this part of medicare. In contrast to the basic hospital plan, this supplementary protection is a voluntary program. Financing is provided by charging premiums to those who participate. These premiums are then matched by funds from general tax revenues of the United States. Unlike private health insurance, SMI assesses no premium differential because of differences in enrollees' ages, health status, or sex. The coverage under SMI is open to nearly anyone age 65 or over, as long as he or she is properly enrolled in the program and pays the required monthly premiums. (As a budgeting device, the SMI premium may be subtracted from the social security check the covered worker is receiving.) SMI is similar to many other types of health insurance in that payments are subjected to deductibles and the insured participates at the rate of 20 percent of costs incurred in excess of the deductible. However, SMI pays only 80 percent of the *allowable* amount of the bill—not 80 percent of whatever amount is charged by the physician for the service. As a result, an insured may receive substantially less than 80 percent of his or her total bill.

Worker's Compensation Insurance

Worker's compensation statutes have been enacted in every state in the union. These laws generally provide for compensation to workers for job-related injuries or illness. Although the worker's compensation legislation differs in each state, benefits often include disability income, medical expenses, rehabilitation, and scheduled lump sum amounts for certain injuries, such as dismemberment. Wide variations are found among the individual states in benefit amounts and payment periods.

In most instances, covered employees become eligible for worker's compensation benefits when they show that an injury or illness has occurred in the course of their employment. Payments are made without question of fault—employee or employer—except in certain cases where the worker was intoxicated or acted outside the scope of his or her authority. The primary purpose of these laws is to lighten the burden of job-related injury or illness to the worker. The cost of worker's compensation plans in all states is borne directly by employers. However, the amount of premium charged is computed on a merit basis; employers with the highest claims experience pay at the highest rates. Consequently, employers try to reduce accidents and injuries to help keep their premiums low. Employees are not required to make any direct premium payments for this coverage. Self-employed persons who are covered under the law have to make contributions for themselves and their employees. The four basic areas of coverage provided by worker's compensation insurance are discussed below.

Disability Income Disability income benefits are most often paid to covered workers suffering loss due to injury or disease. The amount paid represents a set percentage of their predisability earned wages up to some maximum amount. The duration of disability payments is as short as 50 weeks in some states and as long as a lifetime in others. The maximum weekly benefit payable is seldom more than one and one-half times the average weekly wage of workers within the state in which the worker is employed, and often much less.

Medical and Rehabilitation Expenses A basic objective of worker's compensation legislation is to help the recovery of employees and to assist them in reentering the work force as productive members of society. Thus the laws provide for the payment of hospital, surgical, and other related expenses, including such prosthetic devices as artificial limbs, which may be required to aid in the worker's recovery. In addition, a number of jurisdictions provide compensation for retraining seriously injured victims for new employment.

Lump Sum Payments Worker's compensation legislation also provides for the payment of lump sum amounts to employees who suffer dismemberment in a work-related accident or to their beneficiaries in the case of death. The lump sum amounts payable for any specific type of loss are usually listed in a schedule of benefits that applies to all covered workers. These scheduled amounts vary considerably from state to state. In some states, payment for the loss of an arm exceeds the payment for death allowed by other states.

Second Injury Funds *Second injury funds* are established by the states to operate in conjunction with worker's compensation statutes. Their purpose is to relieve employers of the additional worker's compensation premium burden they might incur if a worker already handicapped sustained further injury on the job. For example, an employer might be reluctant to hire a worker with one eye, because if that individual's other eye were lost, the injury would constitute total disablement under the law. And rather than being charged with an accident which resulted in the loss of one eye, the employer would be charged with a total disability. In light of the merit-rating system used in worker's compensation, this would adversely affect the employer's claims experience and premiums. Established to relieve employer's of this burden, second injury funds are financed in some jurisdictions from state tax revenues and in others from an assessment levied against worker's compensation insurers.

Group Health Insurance

Group health insurance consists of health care contracts that are written between a group (usually an employer, union, credit union, college or university, or other organization) and an insuring organization. The coverages of each specific plan are subject to negotiation between the group and the insurer. All of the health care coverages that have been discussed, except disability income, are widely provided by group plans. Group insurance accounts for a large majority of all private health insurance benefits paid in the United States. As can be seen in Table 10.6, of the $37 billion in health insurance *benefits paid* in 1980, more than $33 billion were accounted for by group insurance. In addition to private insurance companies, Blue Cross/Blue Shield plans—prepaid medical expense plans discussed in the following section—also provide health care coverage for groups. In fact, total benefits paid in 1980 by Blue Cross/Blue Shield and a few other minor hospital-medical plans also nearly equaled $33 billion.

Table 10.7 clearly indicates how the *premium volume* for both private health insurers and Blue Cross/Blue Shield grew between 1970 and 1980 in relation to disposable personal income. In 1940 (not shown) only .42 percent of disposable personal income went for health care premiums, while by 1970 this figure had reached 2.87 percent. As of

Table 10.6 Health Insurance Benefits of Insurance Companies by Type of Policy and Type of Protection (in Millions of Dollars)

		Group				Individual and Family Policies		
Year	Total Benefits	Total	Medical Expense	Dental Expense	Loss of Income	Total	Medical Expense	Loss of Income
1970	$ 9,089	$ 7,476	$ 6,043	$ 140	$1,293	$1,613	$1,090	$ 523
1971	9,497	8,018	6,541	175	1,301	1,480	1,006	474
1972	10,622	8,943	7,315	201	1,427	1,679	1,148	531
1973	11,863	9,764	7,924	262	1,578	2,099	1,462	637
1974	13,636	11,439	9,260	332	1,847	2,197	1,517	680
1975	16,470	14,191	11,607	599	1,985	2,279	1,557	722
1976	20,217	17,795	14,425	1,187	2,183	2,422	1,691	731
1977	22,113	19,479	15,683	1,452	2,344	2,634	1,869	765
1978	26,352	22,868	18,696	1,771	2,401	3,484	2,480	1,004
1979	31,692	27,934	22,159	2,185	3,590	3,758	2,644	1,114
1980	37,002	33,002	25,895	2,795	4,312	4,000	2,970	1,030

Source: Adapted from *Source Book of Health Insurance Data, 1981–1982* (New York: Health Insurance Institute, 1982), p. 24.

1980, the figure had risen to 4.27 percent. The proportion of personal disposable income spent on health insurance is expected to continue to increase.

The chances are that if you go to work for an organization of more than just a few employees, you will be covered by some type of group health care plan. In many group plans, the employer pays the total premium for basic coverage on employees and their dependents. In others, employees must pay the portion of their premium that provides protection for their family. Much of the rapid expansion of both benefits and persons covered under group plans has been a direct result of the collective bargaining process of unions and employers. In recent years many employee-benefit plans have included, in addition to the coverages previously discussed, medical expenses for maternity (in or out of wedlock), abortion, alcoholism, mental and nervous disorders, and drug addiction.

Blue Cross/Blue Shield

In a technical sense, *Blue Cross/Blue Shield* plans are *not* insurance policies. Blue Cross contracts can be viewed as nonprofit prepaid hospital expense plans. They include hospitals that have joined together and, in exchange for a prepaid fee, agreed to provide certain hospital services to members of groups protected by Blue Cross. Similarly, Blue Shield plans are nonprofit contracts providing for prepaid surgical and medical services. These plans serve as intermediaries between groups that want these services and physicians who contractually agree to provide them. Although technically Blue Cross/Blue Shield organizations are nonprofit, they compete for business with private insurance companies (many of which are nonprofit mutual insurance companies) and attempt to retain a portion of their income to finance growth. However, if premium income is substantially larger than necessary to meet

Table 10.7 Health Insurance Premiums and Ratio to Disposable Personal Income (in Millions of Dollars)

Year	Private Health Insurance Companies	Blue Cross/ Blue Shield and Other Hospital-Medical Plans	Total Premiums (1)	Disposable Personal Income (2)	Ratio (Percent) [(1) ÷ (2)] (3)
1970	$11,546	$ 8,439	$19,985	$ 695,288	2.87%
1971	12,777	10,058	22,835	751,751	3.04
1972	14,771	11,465	26,236	810,322	3.24
1973	16,104	12,908	29,012	914,495	3.17
1974	17,915	14,533	32,448	998,345	3.25
1975	20,795	16,943	37,738	1,096,068	3.44
1976	24,502	19,955	44,457	1,194,359	3.72
1977	28,676	23,187	51,863	1,311,537	3.95
1978	32,713	27,362	60,075	1,462,939	4.11
1979	37,941	30,300	68,241	1,641,729	4.16
1980	43,666	34,058	77,724	1,821,700	4.27

Source: Adapted from *Source Book of Health Insurance Data, 1981–1982* (New York: Health Insurance Institute, 1982), p. 28.

all expenses and surplus requirements, dividends are paid to subscribers in the form of either lower premiums or expanded coverage.

Currently, approximately 40 percent of the U.S. population is covered by some type of Blue Cross/Blue Shield protection. Blue Cross/Blue Shield organizations have been formed on a geographical basis and now total 111 separate plans. Because they are producer cooperatives, benefit payments are seldom made to the enrollee. Instead, direct payments to the participating hospitals and physicians are the norm. When Blue Cross/Blue Shield first began, premiums were based upon a communitywide rating structure. No experience rating and rate adjustment were utilized. However, because of resulting adverse selection, the original rating system was dropped, and premiums are now calculated in much the same way as those for policies from insurance companies. From the standpoint of individuals, both Blue Cross/Blue Shield and group private insurers can provide good protection against medical expenses. Since Blue Cross/Blue Shield are prepaid health service plans, they do not offer disability income programs.

Individual Health Coverages

Individual health insurance policies provide protection directly to policyholders and/or their families. Consequently, individuals can tailor the coverage to their needs. In contrast, an individual under a group plan is entitled only to the benefits that are available in the master group plan. All of the coverages discussed previously (including disability income) can be purchased in the open market. Existing group plan coverage can also be converted to an individual plan when an individual leaves the group. Even though the protection afforded under many group plans is excellent, most families still need to supplement this coverage with an individual health plan. This situation is especially true with respect to disability income insurance for upper middle income wage earners. In contrast to group life insurance (which is not recommended as a basis for a life insurance plan in Chapter 9), *group health insurance* can serve as the foundation upon which a family builds its individual health insurance program because of the comprehensive nature of many employer-sponsored health care coverages.

Health Maintenance Organizations (HMOs)

A *health maintenance organization (HMO)* consists of a group of hospitals, physicians, and other health care personnel who have joined together to provide necessary health maintenance and corrective services to its members. HMOs are also called *group practice plans.* Members are charged a monthly fee based upon the number of persons in the family. The fee entitles them to receive the various preventive and corrective health care services. Health maintenance organizations may be started by physicians and hospitals themselves, a community, a university, an employer, an insurance company, or another organization. HMOs attempt to reduce the costs of health care to families and individuals by employing health care resources more efficiently. The presumption is that by providing opportunities for preventive (as well as corrective) medicine, the long-run costs of health care can be reduced while simultaneously improving the health of the general population.

The formation of HMOs has been encouraged by legislation of the federal government. Grants, contracts, and loan guarantees for the planning, development, and initial costs of HMOs are authorized under federal law. Between 1971 and 1981, the number of people who subscribed to HMO plans increased from 3.6 million to 10.3 million.

Other Sources of Health Care Coverage

Supplementing the traditional health payment plans are several other sources of funds or services. As is discussed in Chapter 11, both homeowner's and automobile insurance policies contain limited amounts of medical expense protection. The homeowner's covers accidents that happen around the home to people who are visiting you (although not to members of the insured household). And the automobile protection covers you if you are involved in an automobile accident regardless of whether you are in a car, walking, or riding a bicycle. Further, if someone negligently injures you, you have legal grounds to collect from them or their liability insurer.

In addition to social security, various other government programs help pay for medical expenses. Among these are included medical care for people who have served in the armed services and were honorably discharged, care for military personnel and their dependents, and public health programs to treat communicable diseases, handicapped children, and mental health disorders. In total, federal, state, and local governments now spend more than $100 billion a year on health care expenses. When people—especially the elderly and low-income—suffer accident or illness, a government program is often available to help out.

National Health Insurance

In recent years attention has been given to our health care delivery system by the news media, government officials, and others. As a result, several *national health insurance* plans have been proposed, although none has been enacted. The programs that have been suggested range from a complete replacement of private health insurance with a government scheme that would cover the entire population to plans that would preserve the private system while at the same time providing greater availability of health services to the aged and poor. Regardless of the approach that is taken, a national program must be more than simply a financing plan that increases the demand for health care. Such a plan must improve the efficiency and effectiveness of the manner in which health care is delivered to the public. Certainly, the mistakes that have been made with the medicare and medicaid programs should not be repeated in a national health insurance plan.

Guide to Buying Health Insurance

We bring together here this chapter's earlier discussions to show you how to plan your health insurance purchases systematically. In many ways the approach here is similar to the approach proposed for life insurance programming in Chapter 9. The primary difference is that with health insurance you generally must consider both a variety of coverages and a variety of sources for your coverages.

You should list your potential areas of loss; you should determine what types of coverages and other resources are available to you; and, to spot gaps in your present protection, you should subtract your coverages and resources from the amount of your potential losses. Then, with gaps in protection identified, you should structure a health care plan that is best for you.

Table 10.8 Checklist of Sources and Types of Coverages

1. **Social Security**
   a. disability income
   b. medicare (medical expenses)
   c. medicaid (medical expenses)
2. **Worker's Compensation**
   a. disability income
   b. medical expenses
   c. rehabilitation
   d. lump sum
3. **Group Health Plans**
   a. hospital expenses
   b. surgical expenses
   c. physicians expenses
   d. major medical
   e. comprehensive major medical
   f. pharmaceuticals
   g. chiropractic, optometry, etc.
   h. dental
   i. mental illness
   j. rehabilitation
4. **Blue Cross/Blue Shield**
   a. hospital expenses
   b. surgical expenses
   c. physicians expenses
   d. other expenses
5. **Existing Individual Resources**
   a. present individual coverages
   b. family dependency
   c. savings
6. **Wage Continuation Plan (Employer)**
   a. sick-leave
   b. short-term disability
   c. long-term disability
7. **Other Plans**
   a. homeowner's medical expenses
   b. auto medical expenses
   c. negligence claim
   d. veterans' medical benefits
   e. Indian health services
   f. public health clinics (e.g., communicable diseases, maternal and child health, migrant health expense)

Needs

Most people need protection against two types of losses that can result from accident or injury: (1) loss of income because of time spent away from work and (2) additional expenses to pay for medical bills, rehabilitation counseling, training, and education, and in some cases—such as loss of a homemaker—replacement services. The income need is relatively easy to calculate. It is usually stated as a percentage of your (or your spouse's) current monthly earnings. For planning purposes, most people believe that a 60–75 percent replacement of lost income is sufficient. In contrast, the amount needed to pay additional expenses cannot be estimated so easily. In cases of long-term serious illnesses, medical bills and related expenses can run into the hundreds of thousands of dollars. So, as a minimum, we might note that each of us faces potential hospital, surgical, pharmaceutical, and other charges of at least $250,000, and with a protracted disability, charges can go upward to $1,000,000.

Matching Needs and Resources

In the next step of your health insurance purchase planning, you should match your present resources against your needs. Table 10.8 should help you perform this task. It sets forth a checklist for sources of re-

Table 10.9 Checklist of Policy Features

Type of Coverage	
A. Terms of Payment	3. Definition of accident
1. Deductibles and waiting periods	a. accidental injury
a. per occurrence	b. accidental means
b. per period	4. Change of occupation
2. Duration of benefits	5. Definition of disability
3. Policy limits	a. gainful employment
a. internal limits	b. reasonably trained
b. maximum payable	c. blindness or loss of limbs
4. Coordination of benefits	6. House confinement
5. Method of payment	7. Insurer rights of cancellation
a. indemnity	8. Insured renewal rights
b. valued approach	9. Rehabilitation
c. service approach	10. Exclusions
6. Participation/Coinsurance	a. pre-existing conditions
a. percentage	b. pregnancy
b. amount of cap	c. abortion
B. Terms of Coverage	d. named activities or illnesses (e.g., student pilot, drug abuse, or mental disorders)
1. Persons covered	
2. Places covered	e. cosmetic surgery

covery and the types of coverages that you might already have. Among these resources you should rely most on social security, present group coverages, Blue Cross/Blue Shield, individual coverages, savings, and employer wage continuation plans. The remaining sources of recovery typically restrict payments to specified types of accidents or illness. Thus, for planning purposes their use is limited because you need protection against all types of potential losses, not just those that occur in specific instances.

After you identify your present coverages, you then should examine them to learn what terms of payment and coverage apply. Table 10.9 can aid you in this analysis. It summarizes earlier discussions of policy features. By checking these listed features against your health care plan, you can evaluate the quality of your existing protection. In those places where you find gaps that are not provided for by your coverages, savings, or family dependency, you need to prepare ways to meet potential losses.

Preparing a Health Care Plan

Throughout this chapter we have emphasized the need for good health insurance protection to cover the costs of accident or illness. But a good health care plan encompasses much more than a means to finance lost income, medical expenses, and replacement services. It also should incorporate other means of risk reduction. Accordingly, recall from Chapter 9 that you can deal with risk in four ways: risk avoidance, loss prevention and control, risk assumption, and insurance. Although these four methods apply to all types of risks, each is especially useful in developing health care plans.

Risk Avoidance Risk avoidance means avoiding the exposure that creates potential for loss. For example, people who do not stand on the backs of chairs to reach into high places never fall off chairs; people who do not take illegal drugs never have to worry about disability from overdose; people who refuse to ride on motorcycles avoid the risk of injury from this relatively dangerous means of transportation; and people who do not smoke in bed will never doze off and start a fire on themselves, their families, or their houses. Looking for ways to avoid exposure to loss is a good starting point for a health care plan.

Loss Prevention and Control Although you can handle many health risks through risk avoidance, in many other instances this means is not feasible. In these instances you can turn to loss prevention and control. This method of handling risk works well to reduce potential losses that can result from either accident or illness.

Accidents The National Safety Council reports that more than one-half of all automobile accidents could be prevented if motorists followed highway safety laws. Topping the list of violations is driving under the influence of alcohol and drugs (DUI). This unnecessary exposure to loss accounts for nearly 50 percent of automobile fatalities; and specifically, alcohol abuse is a leading cause of injury and death among college students and other young persons. (This toll on youth has prompted, since 1976, 17 states to raise the minimum legal drinking age.)

Furthermore, accident data overwhelmingly document the loss-preventing and control effectiveness of safety belts, shoulder straps, and child passenger seats. In addition, smoke alarms, bathtub safety mats, and proper storage of chemicals, pesticides, cleaning fluids, and prescription drugs pose easy and effective measures to reduce loss frequency and severity. So, regardless of whether you are at home, school, work or play—or traveling in between—you should integrate accident prevention and control measures into your health care plans.

Illness Steven Tiger, the Senior Editor of *Hospital Physician,* has written (as cited in *The Wall Street Journal,* 2 February 1983, p. 25), "The majority of [poor health] conditions treated by medical doctors are totally—and easily—preventable. The answer [to high health care costs] is to encourage a wellness-oriented lifestyle, with individuals recognizing and accepting responsibility for their own well-being." Mr. Tiger believes that instead of self-reliance, "We slavishly worship high tech medical marvels that cost more and more. . . ." Without a doubt, Mr.

Tiger's assertions are backed up by fact. Life and health insurance company as well as public health statistics show that smoking, alcohol and drug dependency, improper diet, inadequate sleep, and lack of regular, vigorous exercise contribute to more than 60 percent of all diagnosed illnesses. Heart disease, cancer, tuberculosis, and mental disorders all have been positively linked to these forms of self-abuse. In contrast, the odds are overwhelming that if you maintain a basic program for fitness, you will miss fewer days of work, you will spend less on medical bills, and you will live a healthier and happier life.

Risk Assumption The next step necessary to prepare a health care plan requires you to consider the risks you are willing to retain. Some risks pose relatively small loss potential and therefore you can budget for them. Of course, this is a primary reason to choose insurance coverages that include deductibles and waiting periods. Rather than insure them, it is economical to pay small losses from savings. Similarly, although you are wise to buy policies with high limits, few people are willing to pay the premium for 100 percent reimbursement of all losses above the deductible. To increase insurance affordability, most assume part of the risk for large losses through participation or coinsurance, internal limits, and maximum aggregate limits. It is impossible to live in a world in which all of your risks are either avoided, prevented, or insured. Thus, before you buy health care coverages—or for that matter any type of insurance coverage—you should explicitly identify the types and amounts of risk that you are willing and able to bear.

Shopping for Health Insurance

Now we return to the focus of this discussion. It is very important for you to recognize that a health care plan should incorporate methods of risk avoidance, loss prevention and control, and risk assumption. But our goal throughout this chapter has been to give you a systematic way to decide what health insurance (or other health care financing plan—e.g., Blue Cross/Blue Shield, HMO) you should buy. To proceed, then, through this step of shopping for health insurance, you need to consider two items: (1) costs of coverage and (2) quality of agent and company.

Costs of Coverage In some ways shopping for health insurance is like shopping for a car. You would not simply compare, say, a major medical coverage from Blue Cross/Blue Shield to that of Prudential, any more than you would simply choose between a Chevrolet and a Ford. In each instance you need to size up competitive offerings on a feature-for-feature basis. What size engines do the cars have; does either have air conditioning, AM-FM stereo, radial tires, higher gas mileage, a longer warranty, or better styling? Similarly, with the available health insurance policies, what provisions do they contain? What is the definition of an accident; what exclusions apply; what persons and places are covered; what are the applicable deductibles, methods of payment, duration of benefits, and participation percentages? Big cost differences exist among health insurance coverages just as they do among different models of Chevrolets and Fords; but you can judge which is the best buy only after you compare the costs of the coverages in relation to the desired features they offer.

Quality of Agent and Company As with all types of insurance, you should buy your health care coverages from an agent who listens to your needs and answers your questions with well thought out responses—not sales jargon and pressure—and from a company that is rated A or A+ for financial soundness by *Best's Reports.* Also, your health care insurer should settle claims fairly and promptly. You should avoid companies with narrow and unusual legalistic claims practices. Friends with claims settlement experience and the consumer division of your state's department of insurance regulation can help you learn about an insurer's record for service after a loss.

Summary

Because both the frequency and potential severity of economic loss resulting from accidents and illness are high, health insurance is essential. The costs of delivering health care continue to soar, making adequate coverage even more important. In addition, the large number of coverages available and the many sources offering them make health protection planning a complex process.

A variety of types of health coverage are available. Disability income insurance is primarily used to replace wages lost due to the disablement of a breadwinner. Because the largest gap in the health insurance program of most people is inadequate long-term disability income protection, this type of insurance merits close examination. Hospital insurance policies offer reimbursement for the costs of hospital room and board and other necessary expenses incidental to hospitalization. Surgical expense coverage pays for the cost of nearly all types of operations and surgical procedures. Physicians expense insurance provides for the cost of such services as physician fees for nonsurgical care, x-rays, and laboratory tests. To protect against catastrophic medical expenses resulting from accident or sickness, major medical policies are available. Some health insurers offer a comprehensive major medical policy that combines basic hospital, surgical, and physicians expense coverage with major medical to provide a package health care protection policy. Other less important coverages offered by some health insurers include dental policies, specified accident policies (for example, airplane), specified sickness policies (for example, cancer), and hospital income policies.

Some of the most important health insurance policy features that you should be familiar with are those that pertain to terms of payment and terms of coverage. The five provisions governing how much your health care plan will pay are deductibles and waiting periods, duration of benefits, policy limits, coordination of benefits, and method of payment. Some of the terms of coverage derive from persons and places covered, definition of accident, change of occupation, definition of disability, house confinement, cancellation, renewal, rehabilitation, preexisting conditions, pregnancy and abortions, and mental illness.

Several important sources of health care coverage exist. An often overlooked provision of social security provides both long-term disability and hospital and medical insurance coverage. A source of financial recovery for job-related injuries or illness is worker's compensation, which often pays disability income, medical and rehabilitation expenses, and a lump sum in the case of dismemberment or death. Within the nongovernment insurance market, group insurance is by far the most prevalent source of recovery. Group insurance consists of health care contracts that are written between a group (usually an employer) and an insurance company or Blue Cross/Blue Shield. A variety of individual health insurance policies are available from a large number of insurers. In recent years increasing attention has been focused on health maintenance organizations (HMOs), which emphasize preventive medicine in addition to corrective care as a means for delivering health care to the public. Other sources of health care coverage are available to various groups. In the future, some form of national health insurance may replace many of the existing health insurance coverages.

In evaluating present health protection, you must first list potential losses and estimate the amount of protection needed to cover them. Next in your health insurance planning, you should match your present resources against your needs. After identifying your present coverages, you should examine them to learn what terms of payment and coverage apply. Where gaps are found you need to prepare ways to meet potential losses. The resulting plan should reflect a reasonable program of risk avoidance, loss prevention and control, and risk assumption. In shopping for the needed coverages, you should carefully consider the cost of coverage and the quality of both the agent and the insurer.

Property and Liability Insurance 11

Because you own assets, you are exposed to a variety of losses that could result in financial disaster. Suppose a severe storm destroyed your house. Could you afford to replace it? Most people could not. So, to protect yourself from this and similar types of property loss, you need property insurance. Also, every day you face the risk of negligence. For example, you might be distraught over a personal problem and unintentionally run a red light and kill a pedestrian. Because the consequences of this and other potentially negligent acts can cause financial ruin, appropriate liability insurance is essential. Once you know how to assess your property and liability exposures, you will be able to select the coverages needed to assure the achievement of your personal financial goals.

American families and businesses are now spending more than $100 billion annually on premiums for property and liability insurance. Property insurance helps people guard against catastrophic losses to their real and personal property caused by perils such as fire, theft, vandalism, wind storms, and many other calamities. Liability insurance offers protection against the financial ruin that stems from certain types of legal actions. Although insurance outlays are large, few people know what they are receiving for their premium dollars. Few people are aware of the gaps, overinsurance, and underinsurance that exist in their property and liability insurance programs. Since such inadequate insurance programs are completely at odds with the objectives of personal financial management, you should become familiar with the basics of property and liability insurance. This chapter discusses the property and liability risks that most families face and explains the coverages available to deal with them. However, before discussing property and liability insurance needs and available protection, attention is given to several principles that underlie property and liability insurance.

Some Basic Principles

The basic principles of property and liability insurance pertain to types of exposures, criteria for an insurable exposure, the principle of indemnity, and coinsurance. Each of these is discussed on page 300.

Types of Exposures

Most individuals face two basic types of exposures: physical loss of property and loss through liability.

Exposure to Property Loss Most property insurance contracts define the property that is covered in the policy and name the perils (causes of loss) for which insurance proceeds will be available. Some property contracts do offer protection on a comprehensive basis, however, and limit coverage by excluding certain types of property and perils. The nature of these contracts imposes two obligations on the property owner: (1) developing a complete inventory of the property in need of insurance coverage and (2) identifying the perils against which protection is desired.

Property Inventory Most people neither fully appreciate the value of all the property they own nor attempt to itemize their property for insurance purposes. Nevertheless, a *property inventory* should be prepared not only to help you select coverages but also to help you settle a claim if a loss occurs. All property insurance companies require you to show proof of loss when making a claim. Consequently, a prepared schedule of property with corresponding values can serve as evidence to satisfy the company.

Ordinarily, families have a home, household furnishings, clothing and personal accessories, lawn and garden equipment, and motor vehicles intended for road use, all of which need to be insured. Fortunately, the majority of homeowner's and automobile package insurance policies provide coverage for these types of belongings. Many families also own items such as motorboats and trailers, motor vehicles intended for off-road use, business property and inventories, jewelry, stamp or coin collections, furs, cash, gold or silver bullion, manuscripts, important papers and documents, antiques, paintings, bonds and other securities, and items of special value, such as expensive cameras, golf clubs, electronic recording and playing equipment, or citizen-band radios. Often coverage for these types of properties must be specially arranged with the insurer. In order to help policyholders prepare an inventory, many property insurance companies have easy-to-complete personal property inventory forms available. A sample of a portion of such a form is shown in Figure 11.1. In addition, you can supplement the inventory form with photographs of your belongings. For insurance purposes, a picture may, indeed, be worth a thousand words.

Identifying Perils A *peril* is a cause of loss. Since certain perils cannot be reasonably insured against, very few property insurance contracts offer protection against every conceivable loss. Therefore, when obtaining property insurance protection, you should be certain to evaluate the various types of losses that are and are not covered by a policy. (Many persons feel a false sense of security after buying insur-

Figure 11.1 Personal Property Inventory Form

Living Room				**Dining and/or Family Room**			
Items	Model & Serial No.[a]	Original Cost	Year Purchased	Items	Model & Serial No.[a]	Original Cost	Year Purchased
Books (see page 12)				Buffet			
Bric-a-brac (Total estimate)				Cabinets			
Cabinet, contents				China Closet			
Chairs				China (see page 11)			
Clocks				Chairs			
Curtains, Drapes				Curtains, Drapes			
Desk, Desk Sets				Glassware (see page 11)			
Fireplace Accessories				Lamps			
Lamps				Linens			
Mirrors				Mirrors			
Musical Instruments				Pictures, Paintings (see page 12)			
Pictures, Paintings (see page 12)				Rugs, Carpeting			
Stereo, Hi-Fi				Silver (see page 11)			
Phonograph				Tables			
Radio				Electrical Appliances			
Records							
Rugs, Carpeting							
Sofas				Other Articles			
Tables							
Television							
Other Articles							
Total:				Total:			

[a]Law enforcement officers will often not release recovered items unless the owner can identify them by a serial number.

Source: Insurance Record and Household Inventory, Farmers Insurance Group, pp. 2–3. Reprinted by permission of Fire Insurance Exchange, a member company of the Farmers Insurance Group, Los Angeles.

ance because they believe that they are safeguarded for all contingencies.) For example, several perils that are uninsurable or demand special attention under many homeowner's or automobile insurance policies include flood, earthquake, earth movement such as mud slides, theft, mysterious disappearance, war, nuclear radiation, and wear and tear. In addition to limiting coverage resulting from certain perils, property insurance contracts also routinely limit coverage on the basis of location of the property, time of loss, persons involved, and the types of hazards to which the property is exposed. These limitations are explained further in subsequent sections of this chapter.

Liability Exposures Every day you face the risk that you might negligently cause property damage or bodily injury to someone else. For example, when golfing you might become impatient and tee off before the people in front of you are clearly out of range. If your ball struck one of them, and you were found legally liable for that injury, a judgment ranging into the thousands, or in some cases millions, of dollars could be levied against you. Of course, a debt of that size could force many families into financial ruin and bankruptcy. Many different liability exposures are encountered every day. Driving a car, entertaining guests in a home, and being careless during the performance of professional duties are some other common liability risks. However, even if you were never negligent and always prudent, you still would run the risk that someone might think that you were the cause of a loss and therefore bring a lawsuit. High legal fees required to defend against suits that may or may not have merit are another exposure sometimes encountered. Fortunately, various types of *liability insurance* are available for protecting families from losses resulting from each of these risks. Before discussing the methods available for insuring against liability exposures, the ways in which legal liability arises, as well as the defenses available for defeating claims, are briefly described.

Liability Based upon Negligence Legal definitions of negligence and liability have evolved over hundreds of years of court decisions and enactments of statutes, and these definitions are expected to continue to be modified as society's values change. In addition, specific rules of law not only vary over time, but their interpretations vary depending on judges, juries, and locations throughout the country. Consequently, only a general overview of these concepts can be presented here.

A person is said to have been *negligent* when his or her behavior has been inconsistent with the *reasonable man doctrine.* This doctrine holds that if a person fails to act in a reasonable manner—as would one with normal intelligence, perceptions, and experiences common to the community—that person is negligent. However, evidence that someone was negligent is only the first step in establishing liability. In addition, the defendant (the person accused of negligence) must be proven to have had a duty toward the plaintiff (the accuser) and that a breach of duty caused the plaintiff a compensable loss. If any of these elements is missing, the defendant is relieved from legal liability. The defendant can also escape payment if one of several defenses available against a charge of negligence can be successfully used.

Defenses to a Negligence Action The two most common defenses to a charge of negligence are assumption of risk and contributory negligence. Under the *assumption of risk defense,* the allegation is that some action of the plaintiff relieved the defendant of his or her duty to protect the plaintiff. For example, assume that Bill Putnam voiced his intent to try to cover a 12-mile stretch of highway in less than ten minutes on his motorcycle. If Janice Morris asked to go with him on this daredevil ride, she would forgo any right to later collect from Bill should an accident develop because of his reckless behavior.

With a *contributory negligence defense,* the defendant maintains that the plaintiff contributed to his or her own loss by also acting in a negligent manner. This defense might be successful, for example, in a case in which motorist A fails to yield the right-of-way (a negligent act) and is struck by motorist B, who has the right-of-way but is speeding. If it could be shown that the accident would not have occurred had motorist B been in reasonable control of his or her vehicle, motorist B's claim against motorist A might be defeated. However, because of the potential harshness of the doctrine of contributory negligence, some states have enacted *comparative negligence statutes.* Under this legislation an attempt is made to allocate the loss to each party in proportion to the degree to which each contributed to the accident.

Note that the preceding discussion relates to the legal elements necessary for the successful defense against damages based upon a negligence action. In practice, though, juries often make awards which derive from their sympathy for the plaintiff rather than from the facts pertaining to the case. This is especially apparent when the defendant has substantial ability to pay—or as plaintiffs' lawyers say, look for defendants with deep pockets.

Criteria for an Insurable Exposure

As noted in Chapter 9, insurance can be an effective way to deal with risk only when the following conditions are met: (1) there are a large number of similar exposure units, (2) the loss covered is fortuitous, or accidental, (3) the cost is relatively low, and (4) losses are non-catastrophic. For certain types of property and liability exposures, such as medical malpractice, product liability, and automobile collision and liability, insurance is becoming less and less able to provide the necessary protection. This undesirable situation is developing because losses in these areas are increasing in both frequency and severity, thereby pushing premiums beyond the levels that many insured persons are willing or able to pay. In fact, over the last several years property and liability insurers have lost billions of dollars through their underwriting activities. Therefore, unless these losses are reduced to tolerable levels, fewer and fewer types of risks will meet the criteria of an insurable exposure. While some people believe that letting the state or federal government establish insurance operations will solve the problem, such optimism is unjustified. Unless losses are reduced, premiums are going to increase regardless of whether private companies or the government administers the program.

Principle of Indemnity

The *principle of indemnity* states that the insured may not be compensated by their insurance company in an amount exceeding their economic loss. Most property and liability insurance contracts are based upon this principle. You might recall from Chapters 9 and 10 that, in contrast, life and health insurance contracts are not specifically contracts of indemnity. Four important concepts that are related to the principle of indemnity are implemented in property and liability insurance: (1) insurable interest, (2) actual cash value, (3) subrogation, and (4) other insurance.

Insurable Interest The concept of *insurable interest* means that the individuals who insure property must stand to lose something if that property is subject to loss, and they cannot receive more in payment than their financial interest in the property. For example, assume that John and Mary own equal shares in an apartment house that has a market value of $200,000 (excluding the value of the land, which is uninsurable). If the building is destroyed, the maximum the insurer would pay to each partner is $100,000 since that is the extent of either's economic interest in the property. If these partners sell the property but forget to cancel their insurance policy and the property is destroyed by fire, the insurance company will pay them nothing.

Ownership, however, is not the only way someone can develop an insurable interest in a property. For instance, an owner of a dry cleaning operation has a legal obligation to return the clothing received in the course of business. If a fire damages the clothing, the proprietor may be liable to the customers for the value of the damaged clothing. Thus the proprietor—though not the owner of the clothing—does have a legal obligation to maintain the clothing in good condition and may insure it in order to be protected against loss.

Actual Cash Value The principle of indemnity also limits the amount an insured may collect to the actual cash value of the property. *Actual cash value* is defined as replacement cost less depreciation, although some insurers do guarantee replacement cost without taking depreciation into account. Since depreciation is usually deducted in order to obtain the actual cash value, only that is considered here. If an insured property is damaged, the insurer is obligated to pay no more than what the property would cost new today (its replacement cost) less accrued depreciation. For example, assume that fire destroys two rooms of furniture that have a replacement cost of $5,000. The average age of the furnishings was six years, and they were estimated to have a useful life of ten years. Therefore, at the time of loss the items were subject to total depreciation of 60 percent (6 years ÷ 10 years)—in this case, $3,000. Since the actual cash value is estimated at $2,000 ($5,000 replacement cost minus $3,000 depreciation), the maximum the insurer would have to pay is $2,000.

Subrogation After the insurance company pays a claim, its *right of subrogation* allows it to request reimbursement from the person who caused the loss or that person's insurance company. For example, assume that you are in an automobile accident in which the other party damages your car. You may collect from your insurer or the at-fault party's insurer, but not from both (at least not for the same loss). If you receive payment from your insurance company, you must subrogate (transfer) to it your right to sue the other person. To collect the full amount from both parties would leave you better off after the loss than before it. Such an action would represent a violation of the principle of indemnity.

Other Insurance Nearly all property insurance contracts have an *other insurance clause,* which also supports the concept of indemnity. This provision prohibits insured persons from insuring their property with two or more insurance companies and then collecting in full for a loss from all companies. The "other insurance" clause normally states that if a person has more than one insurance policy on a property, each company is liable only for a pro rata amount of the loss based upon its proportion of the total insurance covering the property. For example, assume that John and Mary in the earlier example purchased two policies of $200,000 each on their $200,000 building. If a total loss occurred, each company would pay 50 percent, because the ratio of the coverage purchased from each company to the total coverage on the property is one-half ($200,000/$400,000). Similarly, if each of three companies had issued a $200,000 policy, their individual shares would be one third ($200,000/$600,000). Without this provision, insured persons could use duplicate property insurance policies to profit from their losses.

Coinsurance

Coinsurance, a provision commonly found in property insurance contracts, requires policyholders to buy insurance in an amount equal to a specified percentage of the value of their property. If the insureds comply with this requirement, they will be reimbursed for covered losses dollar-for-dollar up to the amount of the policy limits. Otherwise, payment is based upon a specified percentage of loss. For example, assume that John and Mary's fire policy on their apartment building, which had a value of $200,000 excluding the land value, contained an 80 percent coinsurance clause. This means that the policy limits must equal or exceed 80 percent of the value of their building. Further assume that they had run short of money and decided to save by buying a single $120,000 policy instead of a minimum of $160,000 (80% × $200,000) as required by the coinsurance clause. If a loss of any amount occurred, the company would be obligated to pay only 75 percent

Table 11.1 Guide to Homeowner's Policies

Coverage	HO-1 (Basic Form)	HO-2 (Broad Form)	HO-3 (Special Form)
		Section I Coverages	
A. Dwelling	$15,000 min.	$15,000 min.	$20,000 min.
B. Accompanying Structures	10% of A	10% of A	10% of A
C. Personal Property	50% of A	50% of A	50% of A
D. Loss of Use	10% of A	20% of A	20% of A
	Fire or lightning	Fire or lightning	All-risk coverage on buildings
	Windstorm or hail	Windstorm or hail	Same perils as HO-2 on personal property except for glass breakage
	Explosion	Explosion	
	Riot or civil commotion	Riot or civil commotion	
	Aircraft	Aircraft	
	Vehicles	Vehicles	
	Smoke	Smoke	
	Vandalism or malicious mischief	Vandalism or malicious mischief	
	Theft	Theft	
	Breakage of glass or safety glazing material	Breakage of glass or safety glazing material	
		Falling objects	
		Weight of ice, snow, or sleet	
		Collapse	
		Accidental discharge or overflow of water or steam	
		Explosion of steam or hot water system	
		Freezing	
		Damage from artificially generated electricity	
		Section II Coverages	
E. Personal Liability	$25,000	$25,000	$25,000
F. Medical Payments to Others	$500 per person	$500 per person	$500 per person

Note: Coverage E and Coverage F limits can be increased to higher limits.

($120,000 ÷ $160,000) of it up to the amount of the policy limit. Thus, on damages of $40,000, the insurer would pay only $30,000 (75% × $40,000). Clearly, you should closely evaluate the coinsurance clause of any property insurance policy you may buy in order to make sure that you will not have an unexpected additional burden in the event a loss does take place.

Homeowner's Insurance

Although homeowner's insurance is often thought of as a single type of insurance policy, five different forms (HO-1, HO-2, HO-3, HO-5, and HO-8) are actually available to homeowners, and two other forms (HO-4 and HO-6) are designed to meet the needs of renters and owners of condominiums (see Table 11.1). An HO-4 policy offers essen-

HO-4 (Contents-Broad Form)	HO-5 (Comprehensive Form)	HO-6 (Condominium Unit-Owners Broad Form)	HO-8 (Modified Coverage Form)
		Section I Coverages	
Not Applicable	$30,000 min.	Not Applicable	Same as HO-1 except losses are paid on an actual cash value basis
Not Applicable	10% of A	Not Applicable	
$6,000 min.	50% of A	$6,000 min.	
20% of C	20% of A	40% of C	
Same perils as HO-2 on personal property except for glass breakage	All-risk coverage on both the buildings and personal property	Same perils as HO-2 except for glass breakage	Same perils as HO-1 except for reduced coverage for theft, off-premises coverage for personal property, and other items
		Section II Coverages	
$25,000	$25,000	$25,000	$25,000
$500 per person	$500 per person	$500 per person	$500 per person

Source: George E. Rejda, *Principles of Insurance* (Glenview, Ill.: Scott, Foresman and Company, 1982), pp. 122–123.

tially the same protection as an HO-3 policy, except that the coverage does not apply to the rented dwelling unit because tenants usually do not have a financial interest in the real property. All HO forms are alike in that each is divided into two sections. Section I applies to the dwellings, its contents, and accompanying structures and Section II is comprehensive coverage for personal liability and for medical payments to others. They differ in that the scope of coverage under Section I is least with an HO-1 policy and greatest with an HO-5 policy. HO-8 is a modified coverage policy for older homes. It is used by homeowners to insure houses that have market values well below their costs to rebuild. The coverage in Section II is the same for all forms. In the following paragraphs, the important features of homeowner's forms HO-2 and HO-3 are emphasized because these policies are sold most frequently. The coverage offered under these forms is basically the same; the differences lie only in the number of perils against which protection applies.

Perils Covered

As mentioned previously, a peril is defined as a cause of loss. Some property and liability insurance agreements called comprehensive policies cover all perils except those that are specifically excluded in the policy, while others name the perils covered individually. The latter type is the more common variety and is called a *named peril policy.*

Section I Perils The perils against which the home and its contents are insured are shown in Table 11.1. The coverage on household belongings is the same for the HO-2 and HO-3 forms, but coverage on the house is comprehensive under HO-3 and named peril in HO-2. Thus, an HO-3 offers the same coverage as an HO-2 for contents, but the same as an HO-5 for the house and other buildings. Whether homeowners should buy an HO-2 or an HO-3 form depends primarily on the amount they are willing to spend to secure additional protection. In some states, the premium differential is small, and consequently an HO-3 policy is the better buy. In other states, though, the HO-2 form has a substantially lower premium. Also, the size of the premiums for the HO-2 and HO-3 policies can differ substantially among insurance companies. Because of its more limited coverage, the purchase of an HO-1 is not recommended; and, because the relative cost of an HO-5 is usually more than most people are willing to pay, its popularity is rather limited. (A special note on the HO-8 is presented later.)

Section II Perils The peril insured against under Section II of the homeowner's contract is the negligence (alleged negligence) of an insured. As discussed earlier in this chapter, negligence is defined as failure to act in a reasonable manner. The coverage is called comprehensive personal liability coverage because it offers protection against nearly any source of liability (major exclusions are noted later) resulting from negligence. It does not insure against other losses for which one may become liable, such as libel, slander, defamation of character, and contractual or intentional wrongdoings. For example, coverage would apply if you carelessly, but unintentionally, pushed someone down your stairs. If you purposely struck and injured another person, however, or harmed someone's reputation either orally or in writing, the homeowner's liability coverage would not protect you. As an additional feature of Section II, the insurer offers a limited amount of medical payment coverage to persons other than the homeowner's family in certain types of accidents involving insureds or their premises. The basic purpose of this coverage is to help homeowners meet their moral obligations and perhaps also to deter possible lawsuits. The limited medical payment coverage pays without proof of negligence or fault.

Property Covered

The homeowner's policy offers property protection under Section I for the dwelling unit, accompanying structures, and the personal property of the homeowners and their families. In addition, coverage for certain types of losses also applies to the lawn, trees, plants, and shrubs. However, structures on the premises used for business purposes (except incidentally) are excluded from coverage, as are animals (pets or otherwise) and motorized vehicles not used in the maintenance of the premises. This latter exclusion means there is no coverage for motorcycles, autos, golf carts, or snowmobiles (an exception is small boats). Furthermore, business inventory (goods held by an insured who is a traveling salesperson or cosmetics and other goods held for sale) is not covered. Even though business inventory is excluded, business property (books, typewriters, working materials) is covered while it is on the insured premises.

Also, the homeowner's policy offers less protection than is desirable for many expensive items of personal property. To meet this need, insurers have developed the *personal articles floater policy* to provide either blanket or scheduled coverage of such items. These coverages, which are described in more detail later in the chapter, extend protection to items otherwise slighted by the homeowner's contract form.

Types of Losses Covered

A person can suffer three different types of property-related losses when misfortune occurs: (1) the direct loss of property, (2) an indirect loss through the loss of use of damaged property, and (3) extra expenses that result from direct and indirect losses. The homeowner's insurance contract offers compensation for each of these types of losses.

Section I Coverage When a house is damaged by an insured peril, the company will pay living expenses that a family might incur while the home is being repaired. Also, in many instances, the insurer will pay for damages caused by perils other than those mentioned in the policy if a named peril is determined to have been the underlying cause of the loss. Assume, for instance, that lightning (a covered peril) strikes a house while a family is away and knocks out all the power, which causes $400 of food in the freezer and refrigerator to spoil. The company will pay for the loss even though temperature change (the direct cause) is not mentioned in the policy.

Section II Coverage In addition to paying successfully pursued liability claims against an insured, the homeowner's policy includes coverage for (1) the cost of defending the insured, (2) any reasonable expenses incurred by an insured in helping the company's defense, and (3) the payment of court costs. Since these three types of costs apply even in cases in which the liability suit is without merit, coverage in these areas is an added benefit that can save you thousands of dollars in attorney fees.

Persons Covered

The homeowner's policy covers the persons named in the policy and the members of their family who are residents of the household. A person can be a resident of the household even while temporarily living away from home. For example, college students who live at school part of the year and at home during vacations are normally regarded as household residents. The homeowner's contract also extends limited coverage to guests of the insured for property losses that occur at the insured house, if the insured wants such coverage to apply. If the insured does not choose to file a claim for the guest's property loss, the guest will be reimbursed only if he or she can prove negligence on the part of the homeowner. If the home is financed, coverage for loss to the house will also apply to the mortgage lender, provided that the lender is named in the insurance policy.

Locations Covered

Although some insurance contracts (for example, automobile insurance contracts) have territorial exclusions, the homeowner's policy offers coverage worldwide. Consequently, an insured's personal property is covered regardless of whether it is loaned to the next-door neighbor or is kept in a hotel room in Outer Mongolia. Coverage of property away from the insured premises is normally limited to 10 percent of the total amount of personal property coverage applicable. Coverage of property left at a second home, such as a beach house or resort condominium, is in effect only while the insured is actually residing there. Homeowners and their families have liability protection for their negligent acts wherever they occur. This liability protection does not include negligent acts involving motorized vehicles or arising in the course of employment or professional practice. It does, however, include golf carts when used for golfing purposes and recreational vehicles such as snowmobiles and minibikes when they are used *on* the insured premises.

Periods of Coverage

Most homeowner's policies are written for either a one-year or a three-year period. The advantage of the three-year contract is that the annual premium is not increased during the policy period. Homeowner's contracts begin coverage at 12:00 noon, standard time, on the date of the policy and terminate at noon on the expiration date. Some states, though, have changed the inception of homeowner's policies to 12:01 A.M. of the date of issue.

Limitations on Payment

The insurable interest, actual cash value, subrogation, and other insurance features that restrict the amount paid under a property and

Table 11.2 Illustration of Replacement Cost Calculation

Replacement Cost Calculation	**Date: February 15, 1984.**	
Dwelling 1800 Sq. Ft. @ 50 $ p.s.f.	=	$ 90,000
Extra Features Built-in appliances, mahogany bookcases, three ceiling fans with lighting	=	7,700
Porches, Patios Back screened and trellised patio	=	2,700
Garage 400 Sq. Ft. @ 20 $ p.s.f.	=	8,000
Other Site Improvements Driveway, storage building, landscaping	=	4,250
Total Replacement Cost (Today's Prices)	=	$112,650

liability insurance contract and thus enforce the indemnity principle have already been described. In addition to these items, replacement cost, policy limits, and deductibles can influence the amount an insurance company will pay for a loss.

Replacement Cost The amount necessary to repair, rebuild, or replace an asset at today's prices is the *replacement cost.* The homeowner's coverage on a house and the accompanying structures is based upon replacement cost coverage. (An illustration of the replacement cost calculation is given in Table 11.2.) This means that the insurer will repair or replace damaged items without taking any deduction for depreciation. In order for homeowners to be eligible for reimbursement on a replacement cost basis, they must keep their home insured for at least 80 percent of the amount it would cost to build it today exclusive of the value of the land.

In periods of inflation, homeowners must either increase their coverage limits on the dwelling unit every few years or take a chance of falling below the 80 percent requirement. If the 80 percent condition is not met, the maximum compensation allowable for total or partial losses will be determined on an actual cash value basis. In some cases when the amount of insurance on the house is much less than the required 80 percent, the insuring company will pay even less than the actual cash value of the loss. This can happen because an insurer is not required to pay a higher percentage of the replacement cost amount than the total insurance on the building bears to 80 percent of its replacement cost. For example, if a person has only 50 percent of the replacement cost insured, the insurer can limit the payment to 5/8 (50% ÷ 80%) of the replacement cost even if the actual cash value of the loss is greater than this amount.

Neither actual cash value nor replacement cost has any necessary relationship to the market value of a home. Because replacement cost and actual cash value relate only to the physical structure and do not consider the influence of location, as does market value, a home's market value can be in excess of its replacement cost or below its actual cash value. Also, even though a home is in an excellent state of repair, its market value may be lessened because of functional obsolescence within the structure. In fact, the HO-8 homeowner's form was adopted in partial response to this problem. In many older neighborhoods, a 3,000-square-foot home might have a market value, excluding land, of, say, $60,000; the replacement cost, though, might total $160,000. Thus, to get good protection a homeowner would have to buy a policy with limits of $128,000 (.80 × $160,000). This was expensive to the homeowner and created a moral hazard to the insurer. Now, with the HO-8, generally homeowners can get their property repaired in full up to the amount of their loss or up to its market value, whichever is less. This reduced limit saves the insureds premiums, and reduces the risk that people will burn their house down to make money on the insurance proceeds.

Although coverage on a house is often on a replacement cost basis, standard coverage on the contents may be on an actual cash value basis. Therefore, depreciation is taken into account in calculating the amount of any payments made for losses to furniture, clothing, and other belongings. The depreciation amount is subtracted from the *current replacement cost* of the items—not from what may have been paid for the property several years ago. And thus it is possible to collect more in insurance than the property's original price if the rate of inflation has exceeded the rate of depreciation.

Recently, many insurers began offering, for a slight increase in premium, replacement cost coverage on contents. It seems likely that in the future, the standard coverage on contents will become replacement cost—rather than actual cash value. Because the additional premium required to buy replacement cost coverage is generally small, when buying homeowner's insurance, you should strongly consider this option.

Policy Limits In Section I of the homeowner's policy, the amount of coverage on the dwelling unit (coverage A) establishes the amounts applicable to the accompanying structures (coverage B), the unscheduled personal property (coverage C), and the temporary living expenses (coverage D). Generally, the limits under coverages B, C, and D are 10, 50, and 20 percent, respectively, of the amount of coverage under A. (See Table 11.1.) For example, if the house were insured for $50,000, the respective limits for coverages B, C, and D would be $5,000, $25,000, and $10,000 (10% × $50,000; 50% × $50,000; 20% × $50,000, respectively). Each of these limits can be increased if it is insufficient to cover the exposure. Also, for a small reduction in premium, some companies will permit a homeowner to reduce coverage on unscheduled personal property to 40 percent of the amount on the dwelling unit.

Remember that homeowner's policies also specify internal limits for certain types of properties. For example, a $100 limit applies to money, bank notes, bullion, silver, and coins and metals; a $500 limit applies to securities, manuscripts, evidences of debt, passports, tickets, and stamps; a $500 limit applies to loss by theft of jewelry, watches, furs, and precious and semi-precious stones; and a $1,000 limit applies to the loss of firearms by theft. Internal limits give rise to the need for either a homeowner policy schedule of personal property for additional protection, or the purchase of a personal articles floater policy.

In Section II, the standard liability limit (coverage E) is $25,000, and the medical payments portion (coverage F) normally has a limit of $500 per person and $25,000 per accident. These split limits under medical payments mean that no individual who suffers injury will be paid more than $500 but that as many as 50 people could be paid this maximum amount for the same accident. Additional coverages often included in Section II include claim expenses such as court costs and attorney fees, first aid expenses such as ambulance costs, and damage to the property of others of up to $250 per occurrence.

Although these limits are the ones most commonly sold, most homeowners need additional protection, especially liability coverage. In these days of high damage awards by juries, no less than a $100,000 liability limit seems adequate, and a greater amount is advisable for persons with higher incomes and net worths. The liability limit with most companies can be increased for only a nominal cost. For example, in Dallas, Texas, the annual premium difference between a $50,000 personal liability limit and a $300,000 limit is only $17.

Deductibles Each of the preceding limits on recovery constrains the maximum amount payable under the policy. In contrast, *deductibles* place constraints on what a company must pay for small losses. Deductibles help reduce insurance premiums, because they do away with the frequent small loss claims that are proportionately more expensive to administer. The standard deductible in most states is $50 or $100 on the physical damage protection in Section I. However, deductible amounts of $250, $500, and $1,000 are available on an optional basis. The premium savings on policies with larger deductibles are often significant. For example, in some states an increase in the deductible from $50 to $250 results in an annual premium savings of $40 to $75 depending on the amount of coverage purchased. Homeowners should check with their insurance agents to see whether it is attractive to increase the deductible. Deductibles do not apply to the liability and medical payments coverage since insuring companies want to be notified of all claims, no matter how trivial. If companies did not set this procedure, the insurer in some cases might be notified too late to properly investigate and prepare an adequate defense for a resulting lawsuit.

Homeowner Premiums

Perhaps it might be useful to bring together here previous comments concerning the premiums on homeowner's insurance policies. Generally speaking, a homeowner's contract form is selected by an insured. Usually the policy is written with physical damage coverage on the dwelling up to at least 80 percent of the dwelling's cost to rebuild at today's prices. With the amount of coverage on the dwelling set, basic amounts of coverage then apply to the other structures on the site, personal property, and loss of use. As you will recall, these other coverages are stated as a percentage of the amount of protection placed on the dwelling unit. As a standard provision, each of these property damage coverages is subject to a $50 or $100 deductible. Also included in the homeowner's policy are basic amounts of protection for liability losses ($25,000), medical payments to others ($500), and additional coverages such as damage to property of others ($250). For this basic package of protection, an insurer will quote a premium.

As we have discussed, most people need to modify this basic package of coverages. Some will want to increase coverage on their house to 100 percent of its replacement cost; also, changing the contents protection from actual cash value to replacement cost and scheduling some items of expensive personal property may be desirable. Most insurance professionals further advise homeowners to increase their liability and medical payments limits. Each of these changes will result in an additional premium charge.

As another issue to consider, you can reduce your total premium by increasing the amount of your deductible. Since it is better to budget small losses, rather than insure them, larger deductibles are becoming more popular. In sum, recognize that although the homeowner's policy is good protection for some people, most homeowners (and tenants) will need to modify the basic coverages offered. Thus, when you compare premiums among insurers, make sure the premiums quoted reflect the same additions to and subtractions from the standard coverages, limits, and deductible.

Automobile Insurance

Another asset that provides major exposure to loss for most families is the automobile. Damage to this asset as well as negligence in its use can result in significant loss. As can be seen from Figure 11.2, U.S. motor vehicle accidents accounted for 50,800 deaths, 1.9 million disabling injuries, and economic loss of $40.6 billion in 1981. In addition, indirect monetary losses to society result from police and legal

Figure 11.2 U.S. Motor Vehicle Accident Data, 1981

Deaths	50,800
Disabling Injuries	1.9 million
Costs	$40.6 billion
Motor Vehicle Mileage	1,544 billion
Death Rate per 100,000,000 Vehicle Miles	3.29
Registered Vehicles in the U.S.	165.7 million
Licensed Drivers in the U.S.	148.0 million

Accident Totals (Rounded)	Number of Accidents	Drivers (Vehicles) Involved
Fatal	45,300	65,000
Disabling Injury	1,300,000	2,200,000
Property Damage and Nondisabling Injury	16,700,000	27,700,000
Total	18,045,300	29,965,000

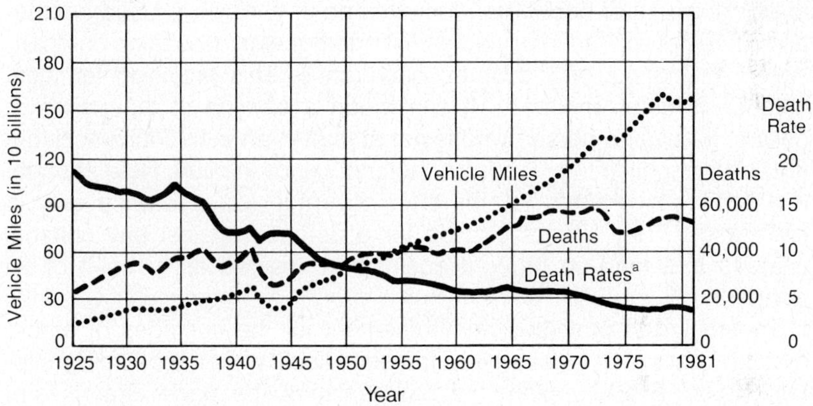

[a]Deaths per 100,000,000 vehicle miles.

Source: Accident Facts, 1982 (Chicago: National Safety Council, 1982), p. 40.

costs, as well as from the lost productive capacity of capital and human resources. Fortunately, from the standpoint of the individual, the major portion of these costs can be protected against through insurance. The major features of automobile insurance are discussed in the next several sections of this chapter. In the first of these sections, the coverages of a typical private passenger automobile policy is discussed. However, now approximately 25 states have legislatively provided for the modification of automobile insurance coverages through automobile no-fault insurance. Therefore, following the section on the automobile policy is an explanation of how no-fault laws typically affect reimbursement for losses caused by automobile accidents. Next, auto insurance premiums and financial responsibility laws are discussed.

Insurance Coverages

The major coverages available under the automobile policy include liability, uninsured motorists, medical payments, collision, and comprehensive. Although two different forms of automobile insurance—the family auto policy (FAP) and the personal auto policy (PAP)—are used widely throughout the United States, both forms offer similar coverages. Some variations between these two forms will be pointed out in the following discussions. Nearly all policies issued contain provisions for liability, uninsured motorists, and medical payments protection. Many insureds, however, choose not to purchase collision or comprehensive insurance.

Liability Policy Provisions Under the provisions of a typical automobile liability insurance policy, the insurer agrees (1) to pay on the insured's behalf all sums which the insured becomes legally obligated to pay because of accidental damages he or she has caused another and (2) to defend the insured against another who is seeking compensation arising out of a covered occurrence. This provision for legal defense is quite important. It can mean a savings of thousands of dollars, for even a person who is not at fault in an automobile accident may be compelled to prove his or her innocence in court. Note, though, that liability insurance policies offer coverage for a defense only in civil cases. They do not provide for a defense against any criminal charges that may be brought against the insured as a result of an accident.

In addition to providing reimbursement for the damages of others and the costs of defense, the automobile liability insurance policy stipulates that certain supplemental payments may be made. Examples of supplemental payments include expenses incurred by the company in settling the claim, expenses incurred by an insured party at the time of the accident to render medical help to others, and all reasonable expenses other than loss of earnings incurred by the insured at the request of the insurance company (for instance, food and travel expenses).

Supplemental payments can also take the form of reimbursement for premiums up to $250 expended for appeal bond, bonds to release attachments of the insured's property, and bail bonds required of an insured as a result of an accident involving an insured automobile. (The family auto policy, but not the personal auto policy, also provides bail bond premiums for traffic violations and for supplemental immediate medical payments to those injured in an auto accident.) The amount of these supplemental payments is *not* restricted by the applicable policy limits. In other words, the insurance company does not reduce your policy limits by the amount it costs to protect you in these ways.

Policy Limits Typically, the family automobile liability insurance policy provides for different policy limits depending on whether the damage is bodily injury or property damage. Policy limits to protect individuals against claims made for *bodily injury liability losses* are most frequently available in the following combinations: $5,000/$10,000; $10,000/$20,000; $25,000/$50,000; $30,000/$85,000; $50,000/ $100,000; $100,000/$300,000; and $500,000/$1,000,000. (Note that some companies do not make available all of these various policy limits.) The first amount in each combination is a limit per individual, and the second amount is a limit per accident. For example, if you purchased the $50,000/$100,000 policy limits, the maximum amount any person negligently injured in an accident could receive from the insurance company would be $50,000. And the total amount that the insurer would pay to all injured victims in one accident normally would not exceed $100,000. Thus, if a jury awarded a claimant $80,000, the defendant whose insurance policy limits were $50,000/$100,000 could be required to pay $30,000 out of pocket ($80,000 award − $50,000 paid by insurance). For the defendant, this could mean loss of home, cars, bank accounts, and other assets. In many states, if the value of these assets is too little to satisfy a claim, the defendant's wages may be garnished (taken by the court and used to satisfy the outstanding debt).

The policy limits available to cover *property damage liability losses* are typically $5,000, $10,000, $25,000, and $50,000. In contrast to bodily injury liability insurance limits, property damage policy limits are stated as a per accident limit, without specifying any limits applicable on a per item or person basis. Often the combination bodily injury and property damage liability insurance policy limits are designated, for example, $10,000/$20,000/$5,000, where the first two amounts pertain to the available bodily injury coverage and the latter figure to the amount of property damage protection.

Single limit automobile liability insurance policies are available from some insurance companies. These policies specify a single maximum amount, for example, $300,000, per accident that can be paid to cover all losses incurred (bodily injury and property damage). The single limit liability insurance policy appears to make more sense than the so-called split limit coverages. Attempting to determine the total amount of damage one might cause appears to be a simpler task than determining internal per person limits, bodily injury limits, and property damage limits. Single limit automobile liability insurance policies are the norm under the personal auto policy.

Persons Insured The automobile liability insurance policy extends protection to the named insured and residents of his or her household with respect to an owned automobile. In a majority of cases, an unmarried college student away from home would remain a resident of the household for automobile insurance purposes. Also protected are any other persons who use the automobile with the permission of the named insured as long as they stay within the scope of such permission. Children of named insureds may not lend a parent's automobile or allow others to operate it unless the parent has authorized it. If such a loan were made without permission, liability insurance protection would not exist for the operator. Coverage is also afforded under automobile liability insurance to persons or organizations on whose behalf the automobile of the named insured is being driven. For example, if Marilyn Zorr was involved in an automobile accident while running an errand for her employer, her liability insurance would extend protection to the firm.

In addition to offering liability protection to those operating the automobile of the named insured, automobile liability insurance extends coverage to the named insured while operating any other nonowned automobile and to his or her household relatives while they are operating any nonowned private passenger automobile or trailer. The important distinction here is between "any automobile" and "any private passenger automobile." The former has a much broader definition. Thus, for instance, a named insured is protected under his or her own policy while operating a rental truck, whereas other members of the household would not have similar coverage because the rental truck is not a private passenger automobile. As a desirable feature of the personal auto policy, insureds are now covered under their own policy for losses that they negligently cause to a borrowed car. The family auto policy does not include this coverage.

When a motorist who is involved in an automobile accident is covered under two or more liability insurance contracts, the coverage *on the automobile* is primary, and the other coverages are secondary. For example, if Bob Burnkrant, a named insured in his own right, is involved in an accident while driving George Clark's automobile (with permission), a claim settlement in excess of the limits of George's liability policy would be necessary before Bob's liability insurance would apply. If George's insurance had lapsed, Bob's policy would then offer primary protection.

Uninsured Motorists Coverage *Uninsured motorists coverage* is available to meet the needs of "innocent" accident victims negligently injured by uninsured, underinsured, or hit-and-run motorists. Legislation requiring that uninsured motorists insurance be included in each liability insurance policy issued has been enacted in nearly all states. The insured is allowed, however, to reject this coverage in most of these states. In many states, a person may also collect if the negligent motorist's insurance company is insolvent. Under uninsured motorists insurance, an insured is legally entitled to collect an amount equal to the sum that could have been collected from the negligent motorist's liability insurance, if such coverage had been available.

Three points must be proven in order to receive payment through uninsured motorists insurance: (1) another motorist was at fault; (2) this motorist has no available insurance; and (3) damages were incurred. Property damage is not included in this coverage in most states. Therefore, under uninsured motorists coverage, you generally can collect only for losses arising from bodily injury. If the motorist and insurer cannot agree on the terms of the settlement of a claim under uninsured motorists coverage, the motorist can seek an attorney to negotiate the claim. If a mutually agreeable settlement still cannot be worked out, the insured has the right to have the case arbitrated by a neutral third party. In most cases, the accident victim and the company are then bound to accept the decision of the arbitrator.

Policy Limits Uninsured motorists insurance is available at minimum cost (usually less than $10 per year). It often is sold with basic limits of $10,000/$20,000, with additional amounts available for a small increase in the premium. At the least, uninsured motorists insurance should be purchased with the minimum limits available. The cost of this coverage is small relative to the amount of protection it provides.

Persons Insured In contrast to liability insurance coverage, distinction is not made between the uninsured motorists coverage applicable to named insureds and that applicable to resident relatives. The unnamed members of the household are protected if injured in the named insured's automobile, as pedestrians, or as passengers in the automobile of someone else.

Automobile Medical Payments Insurance *Automobile medical payments insurance* provides for payment to an eligible insured of an amount no greater than the policy limits for all reasonable and necessary medical expenses incurred within one year (three years under the personal auto policy) after an automobile accident. It provides for reimbursement even if other sources of recovery, such as health or accident insurance, also make payment. In addition, in most states the insurer reimburses the insured for medical payments even if the insured proves that another was negligent in an accident and receives compensation from that party's liability insurer.

As with liability and uninsured motorists insurance, a person does not have to be occupying an automobile when the accidental injury occurs in order to be eligible for benefits. For example, the eligible insured is covered for injuries sustained in traffic accidents, as a pedestrian, or on a bicycle. (Motorcycle accidents normally are not covered.) This insurance also pays on an excess basis. For instance, assume that you are a passenger in an automobile of a friend and suffer $8,000 in medical expenses as a result of an accident. You can collect under your friend's medical payments insurance up to his or her policy limits. And you can then collect (up to the amount of your policy limits) from your insurer the amount in excess of what the other medical payments provide. Of course, you may also collect from the liability insurance of another person involved in the accident if that person can be shown to have been at fault; in addition, you may be able to collect from your own health insurance protection.

Policy Limits Medical payments insurance usually is available with per person limits of $1,000, $2,000, $3,000, $5,000, and $10,000. Thus an insurer conceivably could pay $60,000 or more in medical payments benefits for one accident involving a named insured and five passengers. Most families are advised to buy the $5,000 or $10,000 limit because even if they have other adequate health insurance coverages available, they cannot be certain that their passengers are equally well protected. Having automobile medical payments insurance also reduces the probability that a passenger in your auto will sue you (in those states that permit it) and attempt to collect under your liability insurance coverage.

Persons Insured Coverage under an automobile medical payments insurance policy applies to a named insured and household relatives while occupying either an owned or an unowned automobile (with permission) or if struck by an automobile or trailer of any type. Also, auto insurance contracts sometimes cover any other person occupying an unowned private passenger automobile that is being operated by a named insured or a covered relative.

Automobile Collision Insurance *Collision insurance* is a first-party property damage coverage that pays for collision damage to an insured automobile regardless of fault. The amount of insurance payable is the actual cash value of the loss in excess of a stated deductible. Remember that actual cash value is defined as replacement cost less depreciation. Therefore, if a car is demolished, an insured will be paid an amount equal to the car's depreciated value minus any deductible. In contrast to automobile insurance for bodily injuries, an insured cannot receive duplicate payments from automobile property damage insurance.

Lenders often require the purchase of collision insurance on cars they finance. In some cases—especially when the auto dealer is handling the financing—the lender will attempt to sell this insurance. Generally, the purchase of automobile insurance from car dealers or finance companies should be avoided. These firms have been known to sell policies covering only collision and excluding other coverages at premiums that are nearly large enough to insure the entire Hertz fleet. This is not to imply that all insurance purchases through automobile dealers or finance companies are bad. Still, a full-time insurance agent is better trained to properly assess and meet a motorist's insurance needs.

Individuals who purchase collision insurance may select from one of several *deductibles* available—$50, $100, or $250 in most cases, and for the most expensive automobiles, $500 or more. Significant premium savings often can be obtained by increasing the amount of the deductible. For example, one large automobile insurance company reports that a $50 deductible on a relatively new car can be purchased for an annual premium of $177 whereas the $100 deductible costs $150. Thus, a motorist who buys the $50 deductible is paying $27 for this additional $50 worth of protection. Note, though, that regardless of the amount of the collision deductible chosen, under the family auto policy (but not the personal auto policy) full reimbursement is provided if an insured has an accident involving another motorist who has insurance with the same company.

Automobile Comprehensive Insurance *Comprehensive insurance* protects against loss to an insured automobile caused by any peril (with few exceptions) other than collision. As one might imagine, this coverage offers broad protection and includes, but is not limited to, damage caused by fire, theft, glass breakage, falling objects, malicious mischief, vandalism, riot, and earthquake. Contrary to popular belief, theft of personal property kept or left in the insured automobile is normally *not* covered under the automobile insurance policy. (It may, however, be covered under the off-premises coverage of the homeowner's policy if the auto was locked at the time the theft occurred.) The maximum compensation provided under the comprehensive coverage is the actual cash value of the automobile. In recent years this coverage ordinarily has been written with a $50 or $100 deductible.

Under the personal auto policy comprehensive protection is offered, but there is no separate insuring agreement. Therefore, the deductible for noncollision damage would be the same as the deductible for collision coverage. Both coverages are written in the personal auto policy under the heading "Coverage for Damage to Your Auto."

Automobile No-Fault Insurance

The purchase of automobile insurance has been widespread. Nevertheless, over the years, many accident victims have not received adequate compensation for their losses. Critics of this undercompensation have complained that the existing first-party medical payments portion of the family policy is too low. Furthermore, to collect from the automobile policy liability coverage, an injured victim needs to prove that another motorist was at fault (that is, negligent) in the accident. In addition, even in those cases in which fault is proved, the liability limits of, say, $10,000 or $20,000, or even greater, may still be too small to provide full reimbursement for a seriously injured victim. Medical costs, lost wages, and funds spent for replacement services have accounted for the bulk of the economic losses that remain undercompensated. In contrast, these critics have maintained that the liability system pays too much for pain and suffering (called *general damages*), especially for minor injuries.

An early critic of the auto liability insurance system has alleged that automobile insurance companies have been selling the wrong product (auto liability insurance) because today the public is more concerned with the compensation of all accident victims, not just those who can prove another was at fault for the accident. As a consequence, a major reform movement began during the mid-1960s to push adoption of no-fault automobile insurance.

The No-Fault Concept The concept of *no-fault auto insurance* is based on the belief that the liability system should be replaced by a system that reimburses without regard to negligence. The principle is that "my insurance policy should pay the cost of my injuries, and your insurance policy should pay the cost of yours"—regardless of who is at fault in an accident. Under pure no-fault insurance, the driver, passengers, and injured pedestrians are reimbursed by the insurer of the car for economic losses stemming from bodily injury. The insurer thus does not have to provide coverage for claims made for losses caused to other motorists. Each insured party is compensated by his or her own company, regardless of which party caused the accident. Legal remedies and payments for pain and suffering are abolished.

Unfortunately, the advocates of no-fault forgot that liability insurance was never intended to serve as the primary system for the compensation of the injured. Its sole purpose is to protect the assets of the insured, not to pay losses per se. This same concept applies to all liability insurance. The coverages of medical payments, collision, and comprehensive insurance, which were discussed earlier, do serve this compensation purpose to a certain extent. In addition, families can and should purchase widely available life, health, and disability income protection, which will protect them not only for losses resulting from automobile accidents but also for nearly all other types of economic losses resulting from accident or illness. In fact, the numerous cries that no-fault auto insurance is needed so that people can be compensated for their losses incurred in automobile accidents have probably had a harmful effect since they detract from public understanding of the need for full life and health insurance programming. Although there is no reason to be more concerned about the person who is injured in an automobile accident than for the homeowner who sustains injury while repairing his or her house, the widespread publicity given to the no-fault issue suggests that such concern may exist. Nevertheless, because some valid arguments have been put forth by proponents of no-fault insurance, about one-half of the states in the United States have legislatively required a modification of the coverages offered by the family automobile policy. However, as of yet no state has adopted a pure no-fault insurance plan.

Laws in Effect A listing of the states currently having no-fault (also called first-party) statutes is given in Table 11.3. The 24 states, the District of Columbia and Puerto Rico are presented in five groups, differentiated by whether or not (1) no-fault and liability insurance is compulsory and/or (2) any restrictions on lawsuits exist. The laws of

Table 11.3 States with No-Fault (First-Party) Insurance Statutes

Compulsory first-party and liability insurance; some restrictions on lawsuits		
Colorado, 1 April 1974	Kansas, 1 January 1974	New York, 1 February 1974
Connecticut, 1 January 1973	Kentucky, 1 July 1975	North Dakota, 1 January 1976
District of Columbia, 1 October 1983	Massachusetts, 1 January 1971	Pennsylvania, 19 July 1975
Georgia, 1 March 1975	Michigan, 1 October 1973	Utah, 1 January 1974
Hawaii, 1 September 1974	Minnesota, 1 January 1975	
	New Jersey, 1 January 1973	
Compulsory first-party, optional liability insurance; some restrictions on lawsuits		
Florida, 1 January 1972	Puerto Rico, 1970	
Compulsory first-party and liability insurance; no restrictions on lawsuits		
Delaware, 1 January 1972	Maryland, 1 January 1973	Oregon, 1 January 1972
Compulsory liability, optional first-party insurance; no restrictions on lawsuits		
South Carolina, 1 October 1974	Texas, 17 June 1981	
Insurance not compulsory; first-party benefits optional, no restrictions on lawsuits		
Arkansas, 1 July 1974	South Dakota, 1 January 1972	Virginia, 1 January 1972
New Hampshire, 1 October 1971		

Source: Insurance Facts, 1983–1984 edition (New York: Insurance Information Institute, 1984), p. 96.

the separate states vary substantially as to both the amount of no-fault benefits provided and the degree to which the restrictions for legal actions apply. For example, the Virginia statute places no limit on the right to damages for pain and suffering and only requires that automobile insurers make available (that is, the purchase is optional) modest amounts of medical expense, funeral expense, and wage replacement coverage. At the other extreme is the Michigan law, which eliminates legal action for bodily injury claims for pain and suffering except when the accident victim is killed or incurs serious bodily dysfunction or disfigurement. Michigan is also the only state that restricts the right of a victim to legal recovery for property damage caused by someone else's negligence. For its no-fault benefits, Michigan requires the insured to buy coverage that provides reimbursement for unlimited medical and hospital expenses. In addition, it covers rehabilitation, lost wages, replacement services, and funeral expenses. Most states, in contrast to Michigan, provide from $2,000 to $10,000 in first-party benefits (often called personal injury protection) and restrict legal recovery for pain and suffering to cases in which medical or economic losses exceed some threshold level such as $500 or $1,000. In all states, recovery based upon negligence is permitted for economic loss in excess of the amount payable by no-fault insurance.

Overall, most of the no-fault laws that have been passed accomplish neither objective desired—that is, elimination of liability as a basis for recovery and provision of adequate compensation for all accident victims. Furthermore, the no-fault concept gained its largest public support because its advocates promised that it would contribute to lower insurance premiums. As might be expected, based upon the laws that are now on the books, that has not always been achieved. In those states with substantive laws, though, some efficiencies have been gained. Still, because only a few states have required first-party benefits of substantial size, most seriously injured accident victims will continue to turn to the liability system or their life and health insurance coverages for large amounts of compensation.

Automobile Insurance Premiums

The starting point for determining the automobile insurance premium in nearly all states is the rating territory. Since more accidents occur in some geographic areas than others, higher rates are applied where claims are greatest. Even an insured who is the pillar of the community and has a sterling driving record will be charged the rates in effect for the territory in which he or she resides regardless of how high the rates might be. Usually the location where an automobile is principally garaged determines the applicable rating territory. Herbert Dennenburg, former insurance commissioner of Pennsylvania, stated that he had found a magic formula for reducing auto insurance premiums: "I moved from Philadelphia [a high-rate area] to Harrisburg [a low-rate area]." The effect of geographic location on the automobile insurance premiums charged by one insurer is shown for several selected areas in Texas in Table 11.4.

Among the other factors which influence automobile insurance rates and premiums are (1) the amount of use the automobile receives, (2) the personal characteristics of the drivers, (3) the type of automobile, (4) the driving record of the insured, and (5) applicable discounts. Note

Table 11.4 Annual Automobile Insurance Premiums for Selected Areas in Texas (February 1983)

Coverage	Dallas	Houston	Coke County
Collision			
$200 Deductible	$210	$288	$176
Comprehensive			
$50 Deductible	102	146	82
Personal Injury Protection, No-Fault			
$10,000	39	41	38
Medical Payments			
$5,000	19	20	18
Uninsured Motorist			
$15,000/$30,000	11	11	11
Bodily Injury			
$100,000/$300,000	72	108	45
Property Damage			
$50,000	96	108	62
Total	$549	$722	$432

Note: All premium quotations shown are for a married male, age 35, who has a clean driving record, drives to work fewer than 10 miles one way in a six-cylinder, automatic 1982 Ford Granada, and accumulates annual mileage of less than 15,000 miles. The rates are quoted for the same insurer in each of the cities shown.

Source: Premiums provided courtesy of Allstate Insurance, Dallas, Texas.

that while these have been and are presently the determining factors for rates in all but a few states, several jurisdictions have outlawed the use of rating territories, age, and/or sex factors. The belief has been that these factors unfairly discriminate against the urban, the young, and the male. The debate over the proper rating classification scheme will continue to be a major issue in many states throughout the 1980s.

Use of the Automobile If an insured has a nonbusiness automobile that is not customarily driven to work—or if an automobile is driven fewer than three miles one way to work—it probably will be classified as a pleasure car. This is a favorable rating for the use classification. A motorist who drives more than 3 but fewer than 15 miles to work will pay a slightly higher premium. And if an auto is driven more than 15 miles each way to work, an even higher premium is charged. Generally, higher premiums are charged for automobiles driven for business purposes than for those that qualify for other classifications, and a farm use designation qualifies for the lower rates.

Personal Characteristics of Drivers Such items as the age, sex, and marital status of the insured affect the premium that is assessed for automobile insurance. As many young people and their parents realize, the rates applicable to youthful motorists can be relatively high. Figure 11.3 shows how the rate structure for certain young persons

Figure 11.3 Auto Insurance Rate Comparisons for Youthful Motorists

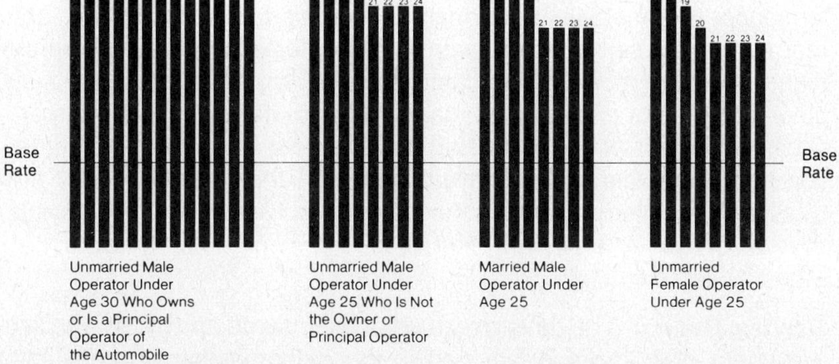

Note: The *base rate* includes no surcharges or discounts. It represents the auto insurance premium charged persons over 30 years old or married who drive a non-high-performance automobile for ordinary (nonbusiness) use and have clean driving records.

Source: Reprinted by permission from *A Family Guide to Property and Liability Insurance* (New York: Insurance Information Institute, 1978), p. 10.

Table 11.5 Accidents by Age of Driver, 1981

Age Group	Number of Drivers	Percent of Total	Drivers in All Accidents	Percent of Total	Drivers in Fatal Accidents	Percent of Total
Under 20	14,500,000	9.8	4,800,000	16.0	9,500	14.6
20–24	17,600,000	11.9	6,000,000	20.0	13,700	21.1
25–29	17,800,000	12.0	4,400,000	14.7	9,500	14.6
30–34	17,000,000	11.5	3,600,000	12.0	8,200	12.6
35–39	14,100,000	9.5	2,200,000	7.3	4,600	7.1
40–44	11,800,000	8.0	2,000,000	6.7	4,600	7.1
45–49	11,600,000	7.8	1,600,000	5.3	3,400	5.2
50–54	11,800,000	8.0	1,200,000	4.0	2,700	4.2
55–59	10,200,000	6.9	1,300,000	4.4	2,500	3.8
60–64	7,700,000	5.2	1,000,000	3.3	2,200	3.4
65–69	6,500,000	4.4	1,000,000	3.3	1,500	2.3
70–74	4,400,000	3.0	300,000	1.0	1,100	1.7
75 and over	3,000,000	2.0	600,000	2.0	1,500	2.3
Total	148,000,000	100.0%	30,000,000	100.0%	65,000	100.0%

Source: Accident Facts, 1982 (Chicago: National Safety Council, 1982), p. 54.

compares to the base auto rate. Generally, unmarried females age 24 or under and unmarried males age 29 or under are placed in higher-rate categories than individuals who are older. Married males under age 25 also fall into a relatively high-rate category. Females over age 24 and married females of any age are exempt from the youthful operator classification and correspondingly need not pay the higher premiums. Insurance companies believe that such premium differentials based upon age are justified because of the great number of accidents that involve youthful operators. For example, as can be seen in Table 11.5, drivers in the age group 20–24 made up 11.9 percent of the driving population but were involved in 20.0 percent of all automobile accidents and 21.1 percent of those accidents in which a fatality occurred.

Type of Automobile Automobiles may be classified as standard performance, intermediate performance, high performance, sports, and rear engine. In some states even four-door cars are rated differently than a two-door model of the same make. As might be expected, if an automobile is not classified as standard performance, higher rates are usually charged. Automobiles that have high horsepower-to-weight ratios and more than three forward gears on the floor frequently are classified in higher-rate categories. So, if you are thinking of buying, say, a Corvette or a Firebird, first check the insurance premiums.

Driving Record The driving records of the insured and those who live with them play an important part in the determination of premiums. Both traffic violation convictions and traffic accidents are normally considered in assessing driving records. The more severe types of traffic convictions are for driving under the influence of alcohol or drugs (DUI), leaving the scene of an accident without properly reporting it, homicide or assault arising out of the operation of a motor vehicle, and driving while having a revoked or suspended driver's license. In addition, but on a less severe basis, any conviction for a traffic violation that results in the accumulation of points under a state point system may result in higher insurance premiums. Included in this category are such violations as speeding, running a red light, failure to yield the right-of-way, and illegal passing. Typically, points under a state system are assigned only for moving traffic violations. Therefore, convictions for offenses such as parking violations, improper registration, lack of an operator's license, and lack of a valid safety sticker usually do not result in increased insurance premiums. In several states, a *premium surcharge* is made for traffic offenses. A surcharge schedule is shown in Table 11.6. Under this plan, designated points are charged against the household of the insured. The first point earned eliminates the safe driving discount for the household. Subsequent points each result in a $20 additional liability premium and a $20 additional collision premium. For example, a motorist convicted of driving under the influence would experience a $560 premium increase ([15 − 1 points] × [$20 + $20]) over the base rate. Under this plan, points are also assessed for nonmoving violations. The idea behind surcharge plans is that motorists will exercise safer driving practices to avoid the expense of a surcharge.

Sometimes traffic violations do not directly enter into the premium computations but influence instead whether a motorist will be offered a regular policy or placed in an *automobile insurance plan* (formerly called an assigned risk plan). These plans have been organized in many states to provide automobile insurance to drivers who are refused coverage when they have sought it in a normal manner. Motorists who are placed in an automobile insurance plan generally pay higher premiums. Still, even with the high premiums, in a recent five-year period insurers lost $2.3 billion on this type of business.

Discounts Many automobile insurers give *discounts,* for one of several possible reasons, to individuals who purchase automobile insurance. Some give overall safe-driving discounts, and others give youthful operators lower rates if they have had driver's training. Youthful drivers may also receive discounts for maintaining at least an equivalent of a B grade average or by being on the dean's list at their school. These discounts apply to both high school students and college students. Nearly all insurance companies provide discounts to families with two or more automobiles if each of them is insured by the same company. Some also offer discounts to owners of compact automobiles. Nonsmoker and nondrinker discounts are offered by a growing number of insurers. Several companies specialize in insuring certain portions of the general population. For example, certain insurers accept only persons who are educators or executives, and others accept only

Table 11.6 Point-Surcharge Schedule for Traffic Offenses (South Carolina)

Offense	Points
Speeding Convictions	
First conviction, less than 10 mph over limit	0
Second conviction, less than 10 mph over limit	1
Third and all after, less than 10 mph over limit	2
First conviction, over 10 mph over limit	1
Second conviction, over 10 mph over limit	2
Third and all after, over 10 mph over limit	3
Each speeding with any bodily injury or property damage over $200	4
Each racing on public highways	10
Reckless driving, but no accident resulting	4
Chargeable Accidents	
First accident with no bodily injury but property damage under $200	0
Each additional accident with no bodily injury but property damage under $200	1
Each accident involving bodily injury or death	2
First accident with no bodily injury, but property damage over $200	1
Each additional accident with no bodily injury, but property damage over $200	2
First and each additional accident while driving under the influence which results in any bodily injury or property damage over $200	20
First and each additional accident involving reckless driving which results in any bodily injury or property damage over $200	15
Hit and run convictions which result in property damage only	10
Hit and run convictions which result in bodily injury	20
Moving Violations (Other than Accidents and Speeding)	
First moving violation, if not listed here	1
Each additional moving violation, if not listed here	2
If moving violation conviction for offense not listed here occurs in connection with accident, assign points for accident only	
Driving under the influence, no accident resulting	15
Homicide or assault with auto	15
Failure to stop when signaled by law enforcement	10
Failure to stop for school bus	10
Transporting illegal whiskey	15
First, brakes and lights defective	1
Second and each additional, brakes and lights defective	2
Other Violations	
Principal operator not licensed for one year	1
Knowingly permitting an unlicensed person to drive	4
Knowingly permitting operation of an uninsured vehicle	8
Lending operators license	8
Operating without valid license	8
Operating while under suspension	8
Making false statements in application for license registration	8
Impersonating an applicant for license or registration	8
Procuring any license or registration through impersonation	8
Operating a motor vehicle without a reasonable belief that use is authorized by owner	8

Note: The first point earned eliminates the safe driving discount for the household while each subsequent point results in a $20 increase in the liability premium and a $20 increase in the collision premium.

Source: "South Carolina Auto Insurance Guide" (Columbia, South Carolina: South Carolina Department of Insurance, 1982).

Table 11.7 U.S. Automobile Financial Responsibility Requirements

State	Liability Limits[a]	State	Liability Limits[a]
Alabama	10/20/5	Montana	25/50/5
Alaska	25/50/10	Nebraska	25/50/25
Arizona	15/30/10	Nevada	15/30/10
Arkansas	25/50/15	New Hampshire	25/50/25
California	15/30/5	New Jersey	15/30/5
Colorado	15/30/5	New Mexico	15/30/5
Connecticut	20/40/5	New York	10/20/5[b]
Delaware	10/20/5	North Carolina	25/50/10
District of Columbia	10/20/5	North Dakota	25/50/10
Florida	10/20/5	Ohio	12.5/25/7.5
Georgia	10/20/10	Oklahoma	10/20/10
Hawaii	25/unlimited/10	Oregon	15/30/5[c]
Idaho	25/50/15	Pennsylvania	15/30/5
Illinois	15/30/10	Rhode Island	25/50/10
Indiana	25/50/10	South Carolina	15/30/5
Iowa	15/30/10	South Dakota	15/30/10
Kansas	25/50/10	Tennessee	10/20/5
Kentucky	10/20/5	Texas	10/20/5[d]
Louisiana	5/10/5	Utah	20/40/10
Maine	20/40/10	Vermont	20/40/10
Maryland	20/40/10	Virginia	25/50/10
Massachusetts	10/20/5	Washington	25/50/10
Michigan	20/40/10	West Virginia	20/40/10
Minnesota	25/50/10	Wisconsin	25/50/10
Mississippi	25/50/10	Wyoming	10/20/5
Missouri	25/50/10		

[a]The first two figures refer to bodily injury liability limits and the third to property damage liability. For example, 10/20/5 means coverage up to $20,000 for all persons injured in an accident, subject to a limit of $10,000 for one individual and $5,000 coverage for property damage.
[b]50/100 in cases of wrongful death.
[c]25/50/10 on January 1, 1984.
[d]15/30/15 on January 1, 1984.

Source: Insurance Facts, 1983–1984 edition (New York: Insurance Information Institute, 1984), p. 95.

government employees. While not offering discounts in a normal sense, these companies frequently do have lower premiums because, through more selective underwriting, they are able to reduce losses and operating expenses. Lower premiums can sometimes be secured by purchasing automobile insurance from insurers that mass market through groups such as labor unions, credit unions, and employers.

Financial Responsibility Laws

The annual losses from automobile accidents in the United States run into billions of dollars. Because of the increasing losses, most state governments have taken steps to encourage (and in many cases require) motorists to buy automobile liability insurance. These actions have primarily been in the form of financial responsibility laws and automobile insurance plans (discussed earlier). A summary of the financial responsibility requirements in each of the 50 states and the District of Columbia is given in Table 11.7. As pointed out earlier, many states are now forcing insurance companies to develop policies that conform with no-fault insurance statutes. And, indeed, federal legislation with respect to financial responsibility as well as no-fault insurance may soon be forthcoming.

As their name implies, *financial responsibility laws* attempt to force motorists to be financially responsible for the damages they become legally obligated to pay as a result of automobile accidents. Two basic types of laws compel motorists to assume financial responsibility. The first variety is one in which all automobile owners in a given state are required to show evidence that they have liability insurance coverage prior to obtaining registration for their motor vehicles. Until 1971, only three states had these compulsory liability insurance requirements. Approximately 50 percent of the states now require you to show evidence of insurance coverage before they will sell you your license plates.

In the second type of financial responsibility legislation, motorists do not have to show evidence of their insurance coverage until after they are involved in an accident. If they then fail to demonstrate compliance with the law, their registration and/or driver's license is suspended. This latter type of law has been criticized on the basis that it allows negligent motorists to have one "free" accident. Even though the motorists who are not financially responsible lose their driving privileges, the losses to their victims may remain uncompensated.

Other Property and Liability Coverages

While the homeowner's and automobile insurance policies represent the basic property and liability protection needed by most families, other insurance contracts of this type may be appropriate for some persons. Among those discussed here are the personal articles floater policy, umbrella personal liability policy, mobile home insurance, boat insurance, recreational vehicle insurance, automobile repair insurance, earthquake insurance, flood insurance, professional liability insurance, group plans, and executive job loss insurance.

Personal Articles Floater (PAF) Policy

This policy provides comprehensive coverage on a blanket basis for virtually all personal property of the insured. It is designed for persons who desire the maximum protection available. In fact, this insurance on personal property is the same as the personal property coverage applicable on the HO-5 form contract. Because floater coverage is on an all-risk basis, the only property or perils not covered are those listed in the exclusions. Most notably these exclusions are for wear and tear, damage from insects or vermin, nuclear energy, and gradual deterioration.

As stated earlier, the personal articles floater policy offers protection on a blanket basis supplemental to coverage under a homeowner's policy. In addition, many types of scheduled personal property floaters are available to supplement coverage under a homeowner's contract. These coverages are especially useful for the types of property that may not receive adequate protection under the homeowner's policy because of limits on amount payable and perils insured. Coverage under a scheduled personal articles floater is extensive and is a good way to guard against serious economic loss for expensive belongings. Some of the more popular policies apply to furs, jewelry, photographic equipment, silverware, fine art and antiques, musical instruments, and stamp and coin collections.

Umbrella Personal Liability Policy

Persons with relatively high levels of income and assets may find the *umbrella personal liability policy* useful. It provides excess liability coverage for both the homeowner's and automobile insurance, as well as coverage in some areas not provided for in either of these policies. These policies are often sold with limits of $1 million or more. In addition, some also include excess coverage for a family's major medical insurance.

Because upper-income individuals are often viewed as good targets for liability claims, umbrella personal liability protection can be a desirable coverage. In addition, the premiums are usually quite reasonable (under $200 a year for as much as $1 million coverage) considering the broad coverage afforded. While the protection is written on a comprehensive basis, it does contain a number of exclusions that purchasers should be aware of.

Mobile Home Insurance

Several hundred thousand mobile homes are sold each year, and several million now serve as homes for young couples, transients, and retirees. Because of this widespread use, insurers offer special package insurance policies for mobile home owners in the same manner as they do for owners of single-family residences. Coverage on mobile homes may be written to offer protection on a blanket basis against the same perils that are covered on an HO-2 form. In addition, personal property and personal liability coverage is included. Even though the coverage offered for mobile home owners is similar to that available for more permanent structures, rates per $100 of protection are typically higher for mobile homes since mobile homes present a greater chance of wind and fire loss. Total losses on mobile homes occur much more frequently than they do for either wood or brick houses.

Boat Insurance

Most people underinsure their boats. This situation exists partly because homeowner's policies do offer some limited protection for boat owners. This misleads many into a false sense of security. Insurance protection for boats should most often consist of liability, physical damage, theft, and medical payments coverage. However, only boats less than 23 feet (or some other stipulated maximum) in length or those that have motors under 25 horsepower are typically afforded liability coverage under a homeowner's policy. The physical damage coverage is limited to only a few perils, and in most cases reimbursement cannot exceed $500. In addition, medical payment is not provided to persons injured in boat accidents off the insured premises. Consequently, for all but small fishing or sailboats, the coverage of the homeowner's policy is insufficient. Fortunately, this problem is easily remedied either through a boat and motor endorsement of the homeowner's policy or through a specially designed package boat owner's policy. These endorsements or policies typically contain liability, physical damage and theft, and medical payments coverage. The liability and medical payments protection is similar to that offered in an automobile policy.

The physical damage and theft coverage under boat policies can be either limited or comprehensive, excluding only a few perils such as nuclear explosion, warfare, and government action. Perils commonly insured against are fire and lightning, collision, overturning of a transporting land conveyance, windstorm, and theft. Other contingencies that can also be covered include damage resulting from submersion, vandalism, motor falling overboard, and burglary from a closed and locked garage or boathouse. Because the physical damage and theft provisions of boat policies are not highly standardized, you should not assume that coverage exists for any given type of loss. Make certain your insurance agent explains what coverage applies and what losses are not covered.

Recreational Vehicle Insurance

Although a consistent definition of the term recreational vehicle does not exist, the following vehicles generally fall within this classification: all-terrain vehicles, antique automobiles, dune buggies, go-carts, minibikes, trail and motor cross motorcycles, camping vehicles (both motorized and trailer type), snowmobiles, and customized vans. Generally, complete coverage is available for these vehicles, including bodily injury and property damage liability, medical payments, physical damage, and theft. You may have to shop around for the policy that best fits your needs since not all insurance companies write coverage for recreational vehicles. In addition, the specific types of losses for which payment will be made are also likely to be more restrictive than for, say, a family automobile policy. Rates will also vary substantially depending on the age of the driver, how the vehicle is used, and the location of the policy owner. In insuring a recreational vehicle, as well as a boat, you need to discuss with a property insurance agent how your recreational vehicle can best be insured giving particular attention to who, where, and what are covered.

Many types of recreational vehicles—including motorcycles and mopeds—can be insured under the personal auto policy through a Miscellaneous Type Vehicle Endorsement. With this endorsement insureds get the same protection for their recreational vehicles as they do for their private passenger automobiles.

Automobile Repair Insurance

Some automobile dealers are offering plans under which a person buying an automobile can pay an additional fee to warrant the repairs resulting from certain mechanical problems. These plans, however, do not represent insurance but rather an arrangement whereby a fee is paid in exchange for contracted services.

Earthquake Insurance

Although most people think of California when earthquakes are mentioned, areas in every other state are also subject to this type of loss. At the present time, very few homeowners buy this coverage even though the premiums are relatively inexpensive. Surprisingly, perhaps, the vast majority of Californians were without earthquake coverage when the major San Fernando Valley quake occurred in 1971.

Flood Insurance

Before 1969, flood was regarded by most private insurers as an uninsurable peril because the risk could not be spread among enough people who were not located in flood-prone areas. But in 1969, the federal government established a subsidized flood insurance program through the U.S. Department of Housing and Urban Development in cooperation with private insurance agents, who can now sell this coverage. In addition, the flood insurance program is encouraging communities to initiate land-use controls in order to reduce future flood losses.

Professional Liability Insurance

Lawsuits against medical doctors for malpractice have increased substantially in recent years. And in fact, liability claims against nearly all types of professionals, including lawyers, architects, professors, and engineers, are also rising rapidly. *Professional liability insurance* is available to these individuals, but because of the increasing claims, rates are becoming much higher, and stricter underwriting standards are being imposed by insurers.

Group Plans

As a benefit to members of some groups (labor unions, credit unions, fraternal organizations, and various other organizations), *group property and liability plans* are being introduced. These plans are not true group plans as are life and health insurance agreements because they do not issue a single master policy to the group. Instead, they are arrangements for mass marketing homeowner's and automobile policies, and the policies are individually sold and issued. The primary benefit of group plans is that the lower marketing expense of the insurance company is passed along to the group members in lower premiums. Some groups also have *group legal insurance.* These plans are fee-for-services agreements that the group enters into with a given law firm on behalf of its members. The plans typically cover only basic legal matters such as divorce, writing of wills, small claims settlement, and landlord-tenant problems. In some cases, the group member is entitled to lower charges on other legal services provided by the participating firm.

Executive Job Loss Insurance

Executive job loss insurance is a new coverage being offered in Canada—and on an experimental basis in the United States. Although technically this type of policy is not property and liability insurance, several property and liability insurers have shown an interest in writing it. With one form of this coverage, executives pay 1.6 percent of salary as a premium, and in return they receive the right to compensation should they be involuntarily removed from their jobs. Such coverage includes amounts to replace after-tax earnings, fringe benefits, and normal bonus pay. Insurers are optimistic that the market will accept "Career Guard" policies because many executives live with job insecurity, and depending on the particular state, government unemployment insurance typically pays no more than $150–$250 per week.

Buying Property and Liability Insurance and Settling Claims

When preparing to buy property and liability insurance, you should first develop an inventory of exposures to loss and arrange them from highest priority to lowest priority. Losses that lend themselves to insurance protection are those that seldom occur but have a potential for high severity—for example, damage to a home and its contents or liability arising out of a negligence claim. Of less importance, but nevertheless desirable, is insurance to cover losses that could be disruptive to the financial plans of a family but would not result in insolvency. Such risks include physical damage to automobiles, boats, and other personal property of moderate value. Lowest priority should be given to insuring exposures that can easily be covered by savings or from current income. Low-dollar deductibles, for instance, usually serve only to increase premiums. And personal property of minor value, such as an old auto, normally does not merit coverage. In addition to inventorying exposures and deciding on appropriate coverages, you should exercise care in selecting both the property insurance agent and insurer. Knowledge of the procedures involved in settling property and liability claims is helpful in obtaining maximum benefits from policies when claims arise.

Property and Liability Insurance Agents

Most property insurance agents can be classified as either captive or independent. A *captive agent* is one who represents only one insurance company and is more or less an employee of that company. Allstate, Nationwide, and State Farm are major insurance companies that market through captive agents. *Independent agents* typically represent between 2 and 20 different property insurance companies. These agents may place your coverage with any of the companies with which they have an agency relationship as long as you meet the underwriting standards of that company. Names of companies which may be familiar to you that operate through independent agents include Aetna, Hartford, and Travelers. It is difficult to generalize with respect to the superiority of agents. In some cases, an independent agent will provide the best combination of low-cost insurance and good service, while in others, the captive agent might be the better choice. Because of wide differences in premiums charged and services rendered, however, it can pay to shop around.

Property insurance agents should be willing to take the time to go over your total property and liability insurance exposures with you. As you now should know, there is much more to the purchase of property insurance than simply signing a homeowner's and an automobile insurance application. Decisions must be made about types of property and uses, perils to be covered, limits, deductibles, and floater policies, as well as other items that have been discussed throughout this chapter. Only an agent willing to talk with clients about these items can adequately serve their needs. In property insurance, agents who meet various experience and education requirements and pass a series of written examinations qualify for the *CPCU* designation. This abbreviation stands for *Certified Property and Casualty Underwriter.* Agents who have been awarded the CPCU have above-average knowledge and experience in their field.

Property and Liability Insurance Companies

Although the selection of the agent is probably the most important step in the purchase of property and liability insurance, some questions should also be asked about the company. Included among these are its financial soundness, claims settlement practices, and the geographical extent of its operations (this could be important if you are involved in an accident 1,000 miles from home). The agent should be a good source of information about the technical aspects of a company's operations, whereas friends and acquaintances often can provide insight into its claims settlement policy.

Settling Property and Liability Claims

Generally speaking, insurance companies settle claims promptly and fairly, especially for life and health insurance coverages. In settling property and liability claims, though, some chance for claimant-insurer disagreement does exist. So, to help you settle any claims you might file, the following discussion reviews the claims settlement process. In addition, we look at the persons who participate in claims adjustment. But before we look at these topics, you should learn what to do immediately following an accident.

Following an Accident After an accident, the names and addresses of all witnesses, drivers, occupants, and injured parties, along with the license numbers of the automobiles involved, should be recorded. Law enforcement officers as well as your insurance company representative should be immediately notified of the accident. You should never admit liability at the scene of an accident or discuss it with anyone other than the police and your insurer. Remember, prior to determining who, if anyone, is legally liable for an accident, the requisites of liability must be established. Also, the duties of the police are to assess the probability of a law violation and maintain order at the scene of an accident—not to make judgments with respect to liability.

Steps in Claim Settlement The typical insurance claim involves four steps. First, you must give notice to the company that a loss (or potential for loss) has occurred. Timely notice is extremely important because it leads into the second step, which is the investigation of the claim. To properly investigate a claim, insurance company personnel may have to talk to witnesses or law enforcement officers, gather physical evidence to tell whether the claimed loss is covered by the policy, and check to make sure the date of the loss fell within the policy period. If you delay filing your claim, you hinder the insurer's ability to check the facts. Thus, all policies specify the time period within which you must give notice. Failure to report can result in your loss of the right to collect.

Third, you must prove your loss. This step usually requires you to give a sworn statement. But also, as they are applicable, you must show: medical bills, an inventory and certified value of lost property (e.g., a written inventory, photographs, and purchase receipts), an employer statement of lost wages, and, if possible, physical evidence of damage (e.g., x-rays if you claim a back injury; a broken window or pried door if you claim a break-in and theft at your house). Then, after submitting proof of loss, the insurer either pays you the amount you asked for; offers you a lesser amount; or denies that the company has legal responsibility under the terms of your policy. In the case of a disputed amount—when you are a named insured or covered family member—most policies provide for claim arbitration. You are entitled to hire a third party, the company hires a third party, and these two arbitrators together select one more person. When any two of the three arbitrators reach agreement, their decision binds you and the company to their solution.

When a company denies responsibility, you do not get the right of arbitration because that is a right contained in the policy. In such an instance, the company is saying the loss does not fall under the policy coverage. You must then either forget the claim or bring in an attorney or, perhaps, a public adjustor (discussed below).

Claims Adjustment Usually the first person to call when you need to file a claim is your insurance agent. If your loss is relatively minor, the agent can quickly process it. If it is more complex, your company will usually assign a claims adjustor to the case.

Adjustors The *claims adjustor* will either work for the insurance company, work as an independent adjustor, or work for an adjustment bureau. In any case, the adjustor is primarily looking out for the interests of the company—which might very well be to keep you, its customer, satisfied. But many claimants think insurance companies have more money than they know what to do with. So they are out to collect all that is possible. Thus, the adjustor walks a fine line. He or she must diligently question and investigate, while at the same time offer service to minimize settlement delays and financial hardship. To help your own interest you should cooperate with the adjustor and answer inquiries honestly; yet, you should not forget the company writes the adjustor's paycheck.

Public Adjustors and Attorneys To this point we are primarily referring to the claims that you collect from your own insurance company. In accidents in which a question of fault arises, you may have to file a claim against a negligent party's insurer. In these instances, the insurer will still use an adjustor, but this adjustor will be looking out for the insurer's (and its policyholders') economic interests without the problem of keeping you satisfied. Therefore, if you are not happy with the offered settlement, you might have to hire a public adjustor or an attorney to negotiate the claim for you. They generally will know better than you the law, the policy provisions, and the chances for collecting a larger amount. For such service, they will often charge 25 to 50 percent of any amount they get you. The exact amount of the fee is negotiable, but many times even with the fee their services are worthwhile if you are not being treated fairly by the insurance company's adjustor.

Summary

Property and liability contracts protect insureds against loss of their real and personal property from numerous types of perils. They also protect against loss from lawsuits based upon negligence. A loss exposure is insurable when (1) it involves a risk with a large number of exposures, (2) the potential loss is fortuitous, (3) the cost of insurance is relatively low, and (4) the loss is noncatastrophic. The principle of indemnity holds that insurance should not be used to make people better off after a loss than before it. This principle is supported by the concepts of (1) insurable interest, (2) actual cash value, (3) subrogation, and (4) other insurance. Coinsurance is the provision found in many property insurance contracts that requires an insured to buy policy limits equal to at least a certain percentage of the property value.

Homeowner's insurance contracts for owners of residences are divided into two major sections. Section I covers the dwelling unit, accompanying structures, and personal property of the insured. Section II pertains primarily to comprehensive coverage for personal liability and medical payments. The tenant owner's insurance form also contains these two sections except that the rental dwelling itself is not covered. The major difference among the various forms of homeowner's insurance contracts is in the number of perils insured against. Because specific limitations apply to certain types of property covered under a homeowner's policy, special attention should be given to the following items of property: expensive cameras, jewelry, furs, and coin and stamp collections; business inventories; cash and bullion; important papers, such as deeds and manuscripts; antiques; and some boats and recreational vehicles. Homeowner's insurance normally provides for the payment of all losses except the house and garage on an actual cash value basis subject to applicable deductibles and policy limits. Losses to the house and garage are reimbursed on a replacement cost basis if the required coverage has been purchased. Because of consumers' needs, many insurers now offer replacement cost coverage on personal belongings—but, of course, this protection requires an additional premium.

The automobile insurance policy ordinarily contains the following coverages: liability, uninsured motorists, medical payments, collision, and comprehensive. Liability insurance is used by motorists to protect their assets if they should be found liable for damages in an automobile accident. Uninsured motorists coverage pays for medical expenses and general damages when insureds show that someone else was at fault in an accident and that the person has no applicable liability insurance. Medical payments coverage normally reimburses insureds for medical expenses incurred in an automobile accident. Collision coverage pays for physical damage losses resulting from collision accidents, whereas comprehensive covers nearly any other type of noncollision damage your car might suffer. In many states modified no-fault automobile insurance plans have been enacted. These plans typically increase the amount of first-party benefits available for economic losses. They also reduce the right to receive awards for pain and suffering under a liability claim. Other important considerations include automobile insurance premiums and financial responsibility laws.

In addition to the major forms of homeowner's and automobile insurance, a variety of other types of property and liability coverages are available, including personal articles floater policies, umbrella personal liability policies, mobile home insurance, boat insurance, recreational vehicle insurance, automobile repair insurance, earthquake insurance, flood insurance, professional liability insurance, group plans, and executive job loss insurance. Before buying property and liability coverages, you should first evaluate your exposures to loss and determine the coverages needed. Both the insurance agent(s) and the insurance company should be carefully selected in order to assure that good coverage is obtained at a reasonable price and—just as important—to assure that your agent and company have a reputation for fair claims settlement practices. An understanding of the claims settlement process, which includes knowing what to do after an accident, understanding the steps in the process, and knowing how to deal with claims adjustors and attorneys, is helpful in obtaining maximum benefits from policies when claims arise.

Fundamentals of Stock and Bond Investments 12

Investment planning is an important part of financial planning that must be given attention—*only after* acquiring fundamental assets of savings and housing (discussed in Chapters 5 and 6) and adequately insuring life, health, and property (discussed in Chapters 9, 10, and 11). This point needs to be emphasized because it is often thought that imaginative and successful investing can overcome poor financial planning elsewhere. The temptation to get rich quick in the stock market or in real estate, or through some other scheme, is strong, and it is continually encouraged by promoters claiming to have done it and eager to show you how to do it too—for a fee, naturally. There are, indeed, investment opportunities offering returns above those usually available on low-risk savings instruments, but these always involve higher risks.

Although there are different kinds and degrees of risk associated with various investment media, there is a risk theme common to all of them—the shorter the period of time you are willing to hold an investment, the greater the potential risk. Most investment vehicles are subject to abrupt and sharp price changes, and if investment funds must be returned on short notice, there is a good possibility they can be recovered only at a loss. Most investment advisors recommend against undertaking risky investments with funds that may be needed for other purposes. This and the following two chapters explain the basics of many kinds of investments, and also profile their risk-return behaviors.

Investment Prerequisites, Risks, and Returns

Successful investment can serve a dual purpose: it can provide a source of income supplemental to job earnings and it can increase net worth through appreciation in the market value of investments. Depending upon your age and other personal goals, you may select investments emphasizing one of these functions. Before any investment is undertaken, though, it is a good idea to specify the objectives you hope the investment will achieve, and to understand the risk-return behaviors of the alternative investment vehicles available.

Investment Objectives

What you hope to accomplish by investing will very often determine the specific kinds of investments you make. The most frequent *invest-*

ment objectives are: (1) enhancing current consumption, (2) saving for a major expenditure, (3) accumulating retirement funds, and (4) sheltering current income from taxes. Each of these is discussed below.

Enhancing Current Consumption The ability of an investment to accomplish this objective depends upon the amount of income, usually dividends or interest, it offers the investor. Retired people frequently choose investments offering a high current income since their other sources of income are below the levels they earned during their working years. The picture of an elderly person clipping coupons from high-yielding bonds is a fair description of what most older persons should do during their later years in life. One would hardly recommend to them purchase of common stock of a highly speculative oil-drilling venture that might not pay off for ten or more years—if ever.

Saving for a Major Expenditure Most families save for many years to make major outlays such as a down payment on a house, or sending children to college. Whatever the reason, if you know the final amount you need and the length of time your investment funds can be at work, you have far greater flexibility in choosing investment vehicles to help achieve your savings goal. As an example, suppose you need $10,000 in ten years and plan to accumulate this sum by investing now, or over the period. By planning the purchase of certain kinds of bonds you can design a plan to achieve your goal. Similar to Series EE bonds, discussed in Chapter 5, you buy these bonds (called zero-coupon bonds) at a discount and receive back their full face value at maturity. Most major brokerage houses offer them under a variety of names, such as "money multiplier notes." As an example of how they might fit into a savings plan, certain bonds purchased for about $3,200 in mid-1984 were guaranteed to return $10,000 about 10 years later. Income taxes would have to be considered, of course, as would the possible effects of inflation on the cost of the outlay you are saving for. This example illustrates only one of many approaches for accumulating funds over a specific period of time. Whether it would be the correct approach for you depends upon your attitude toward risk and your expectations about future investment opportunities during the investing period. If you thought investment returns would improve over the period, and were willing to take the chance that they would, then you would probably avoid these bonds and invest in some other vehicle.

Accumulating Retirement Funds Accumulating funds for retirement is perhaps the single most important reason for investing. In many cases, however, it occupies a small amount of our time since retirement plans are often provided by employers as well as through social security. (Detailed discussion of retirement plans is in Chapter 15.) You need to review the amounts you can realistically expect to receive from these sources and decide, based upon your retirement goals, whether or not they will be adequate to meet your needs. If they are not, you must supplement them through personal investing. The earlier in life you make this assessment of retirement needs, the greater your chance of success in accumulating funds. Again, this occurs because of the longer period of time over which your investment funds can grow. For example, if you could invest $1,000 today and earn 10 percent each year and continually reinvest each year's earnings also at 10 percent, after 30 years you would accumulate $17,449—a rather nice sum. But, if you let the investment grow for just seven more years, you would have $34,004—over double the total accumulation!

Sheltering Current Income from Taxes As Chapter 4 explains, the federal income tax law does not treat all sources of income equally. For example, certain forms of investment income are either not taxed at all or taxed at lower effective rates. If you own real estate—either directly or through some pooling arrangement—you may be able to take depreciation deductions against your other sources of income, thereby reducing your final taxable income. This tax write-off characteristic of real estate can make it a very attractive investment even though its pre-tax rate of return may not be very high.

Often the goal of sheltering current income from taxes goes hand in hand with the goals of saving for a major outlay and retirement. Obviously, if you can avoid paying taxes on the income from an investment, all other things considered, you will have more funds available for reinvestment during the period. An ideal vehicle, for example, to accomplish both the tax sheltering goal and the retirement goal is the Individual Retirement Account (IRA)—mentioned in Chapter 4 and more fully explained in Chapter 15. The current tax law allows individuals to invest $2,000 ($2,250 for an individual and an unemployed spouse) each year in an IRA account and then deduct this amount from taxable income. Moreover, you can invest in practically any investment vehicle you choose, such as those described in this chapter and the two following, or the variety of savings instruments described in Chapter 5. All you need to do is find a financial institution—a stockbroker, bank, insurance company, credit union, or other—to help set up the IRA. For many IRAs, once they are established, there is virtually nothing else to do until you withdraw funds at retirement.

Investment Alternatives

After you have established your investment objectives, you can choose from a variety of investment vehicles to satisfy them. For the most part, they are *securities,* which are obligations of issuers that provide purchasers with a stated or expected return. In this chapter and the two following, the investment vehicles briefly defined here are examined.

Common and Preferred Stock These represent ownership interests in a corporation; return comes from dividends and possible price appreciation of the shares. *Preferred stock* differs from *common stock* in several respects, the most important being that preferred pays a fixed dividend each year, while dividends on common are variable—they can increase or decrease over time.

Bonds In contrast to stocks, bonds are liabilities of the issuer; the bondholder actually loans money to the issuer. Governments and corporations issue bonds and, like preferred stock, bonds pay a stated return, called interest, each year. Also like preferred and common stocks, bond prices fluctuate daily in the marketplace.

Investment Companies These are pooling arrangements that provide for the diversification of investment funds. Risk and return behaviors result from the specific investment vehicles the investment company acquires; they usually include stocks and bonds of other corporations or governments.

Real Estate This investment can take on many forms ranging from raw land speculation to limited partnership shares in a commercial property. Estimating both risk and return in a real estate venture can be difficult and usually requires some expert advice, particularly relative to income-tax implications.

Commodity and Financial Futures These are contracts to buy or sell commodities or financial instruments at a future time. They do not pay interest or dividends, so their return depends solely upon the change in the price of the underlying commodity or financial instrument. These are very risky securities because losses can be far greater than the amount invested.

Options Similar to futures, options give the holder the right to buy or sell common stocks (and some bonds and futures contracts) at a set price sometime in the future. Again, to earn a positive return one must correctly anticipate future price movements in the underlying stock. In contrast to futures contracts, the price paid for an option is the maximum amount that can be lost; however, options have very short maturities and consistent losses can quickly eliminate one's investment capital.

Precious Minerals and Collectibles These are specialized investments that are sometimes associated with a hobby. While price appreciation for many precious minerals and collectibles has been rather good in the past, there is no assurance it will continue in the future.

Before investing in them, consideration should be given to the ability to sell them in the future. Very often, resale markets are hard to find and/or sales agents receive large commissions.

Investment Risks

In selecting investments, the possible risks or uncertainties associated with them should be considered. The basic types of risk are business risk, financial risk, market risk, purchasing power risk, and interest rate risk.

Business Risk If you invest in a business firm by purchasing its stocks or bonds, you face the possibility that the firm issuing the securities will fail. Failure of a firm may be due to economic or industry conditions and/or management actions. It is not unusual for stockholders to receive nothing when a business fails. Bondholders, on the other hand, are likely to receive some—but not necessarily all—of the amount owed them due to their preferential situation. Although failure of the firm is the most severe outcome, in general *business risk* is the degree of uncertainty associated with the firm's earnings and consequent ability to pay interest and dividends.

Financial Risk *Financial risk* is also associated with stock or bond investments, and it is related to the mix of debt and equity financing used by the firm. The greater the proportion of debt to equity the firm has, the larger its financial risk. High proportions of debt indicate that the firm must meet large interest payments; if the firm is unable to meet contractual interest payments, it could be forced into bankruptcy.

Market Risk *Market risk* results from the behavior of investors in the securities markets. Changes in their behavior as reflected in the market price of any one security may or may not be related to fundamental changes in the issuing firm's performance. Changes in political, economic, and social conditions or changes in investor tastes and preferences may cause the market price of a security to rise or fall. Although it is difficult to estimate this type of risk, the potential investor can evaluate past price movements in order to get a feel for the degree of market risk for a given security.

Purchasing Power Risk Possible changes in price levels within the economy also result in risk. In periods of rising prices, the purchasing power of the dollar declines. This means that a smaller quantity of some commodity can be purchased with a given number of dollars than could have been purchased in the past. In periods of declining price levels, the purchasing power of the dollar increases. An awareness of *pur-*

chasing power risk and changes in purchasing power allows investors to select investments that are best for the given price levels and thus protect themselves against changes in purchasing power. In general, investments whose values move with price levels are most profitable during periods of price rise and those that provide fixed returns are preferable for periods of price decline.

Interest Rate Risk *Fixed income securities*—securities including preferred stocks and bonds that offer purchasers a fixed periodic return—are most often affected by *interest rate risk.* As interest rates change, the prices of these securities fluctuate, decreasing with increasing interest rates and increasing with decreasing interest rates. The prices of fixed income securities drop when interest rates increase in order to provide purchasers of the security with the same rate of return as would be available on similar securities. Increases in price due to declining interest rates result from the fact that the return on a fixed income security is adjusted downward to a competitive level by upward adjustments in its market price. The changes in the interest rates that cause these adjustments are a result of fluctuations in the supply of and/or demand for money. These fluctuations are caused by various economic actions of the government or the interactions of business firms, consumers, and financial institutions.

Investment Returns

As mentioned previously, the returns from investments are available as income or growth (that is, appreciation in value). While some investment vehicles provide either income or growth, most offer both types of return. Of course, the mix of the two types of return differs among investments.

Income Income, such as dividends on stock and interest from bonds, is often the primary motive for investment. People who invest to obtain income look for investment vehicles that provide regular and predictable patterns of income distribution. Preferred stocks and bonds, which are expected to pay known amounts at specified times (quarterly or semiannually, for example), are usually good income investments.

Growth The other type of return available from investments is growth, which is reflected in an increase in the market value of the investment. Generally, investments that provide greater growth potential through capital appreciation have lower levels of income, since the firm achieves its growth by reinvesting its earnings instead of paying dividends to the owners. For example, many common stocks are usually acquired for their growth potential. And, as indicated earlier, many investment vehicles provide returns only in the form of growth; but the risk of a decline in value is also present in such vehicles.

Figure 12.1 Risk-Return Relationship

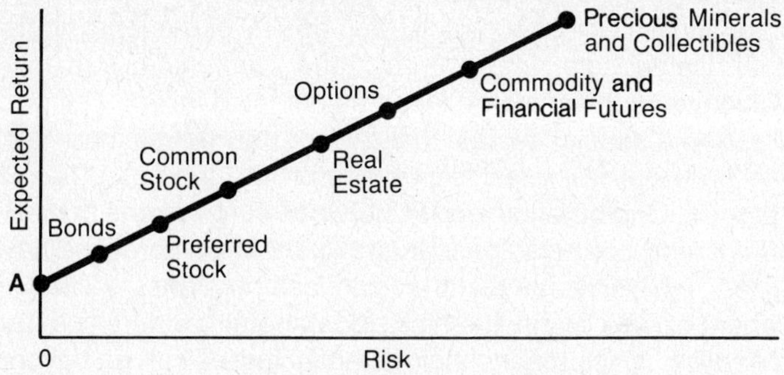

Risk-Return Trade-Off

The risk associated with a given investment vehicle is inversely related to its expected return. This means that the higher the risk, the greater the expected return from the investment. Investors are compensated for taking higher levels of risk by the expectation of higher returns. Since most people are believed to be risk averse—they dislike taking risks—some incentive to take risks must be given. If the same return a high risk investment offered could be received from one with lower risk, investors would naturally opt for the latter. Or, looking at it in another way, investors would choose the highest return available for a given level of risk. The inverse relationship between risk and return is shown in Figure 12.1, which generalizes the risk-return trade-off for some popular investment vehicles. Note in Figure 12.1 (point A) that it is possible to receive a positive return for zero risk; this is sometimes referred to as the risk-free rate of return, which is often measured by the return on a short-term government security. Also, the relationship between risk and expected returns from the various investments is generalized. For example, it is possible to find many common stocks that are less risky than some bonds; but, *on balance,* common stocks are the riskier of the two.

Characteristics of Stock and Bond Investments

Having considered the overall role of investing, you are now in a position to evaluate specific investment vehicles. The most popular are stocks and bonds. *Stocks* are shares of ownership in a corporate form of business, while *bonds* are certificates indicating that a corporation has borrowed a certain amount of money which it has agreed to repay in the future.

Stocks and bonds have several key characteristics. Both are issued by *corporations,* which are business firms that have been chartered by the state and given legal status. The corporation can sue and be sued, can make and enter into contracts, and has all of the legal rights of an individual. Unlike *sole proprietorship* and *partnership* forms of business, which have their income taxed as personal income, corporations are subject to a special tax rate that may or may not be more favorable than the personal tax rates, depending on the amount of taxable income earned. One other difference between corporations and sole proprietorships and partnerships is that owners of corporations have *limited liability,* which means that they can lose no more than they invest. The owners of sole proprietorships and general partnerships have *unlimited liability,* which means their potential losses can go beyond their investment in the firm. This feature has contributed greatly to the dominance of the corporate form of business in the United States.

Common Stock

Common stock, the most basic form of corporate ownership, is a form of *equity capital,* which means that each share purchased represents an investment in equity, or ownership, of the firm. The purchaser of common stock normally receives the right to one vote in all corporate elections for each share that is owned. Common stockholders do not receive any type of guarantee or assurance that they will receive favorable returns on their investments. They are last in line to recover any portion of their investment should the firm fail; in most cases, they do not receive much of their investment if a business is liquidated (that is, all assets are sold and proceeds are used to satisfy debts). The amount paid in *dividends,* or earnings distributed to the stockholders, is normally determined quarterly by the board of directors of the corporation, who are elected by the stockholders. Dividend income is one of two possible motives for purchasing shares of common stock. The other is price appreciation. Many people buy stock in the expectation that its price will increase, thereby allowing them to sell it at a profit.

As indicated in Chapter 4, income received in the form of dividends is taxed as ordinary income, while income earned as the result of selling a security for more than its original purchase price may be taxed as a *long-term capital gain.* A security must be held for more than six months before the profit on its sale can be taxed at the favorable long-term capital gains rates.

If this time requirement is met, capital gains are taxed at a rate equal to 40 percent of the ordinary tax rate but no more than 20 percent of the amount of the gain. If the security is not held for at least six months, a *short-term capital gain,* which is taxed at ordinary rates, results. Assume, for example, that you just sold 100 shares of the RZX Company common stock for $30 per share. Also assume that the stock was originally purchased two years ago for $20 per share, and that during the current year you received $1.25 per share in cash dividends from the stock. For tax purposes, you would have a long-term capital gain of $1,000 ([$30/share − $20/share] × 100 shares) and $125 ($1.25/share × 100 shares) of dividend income. Ignoring the dividend exclusion (see Chapter 4), your taxable income from this transaction would be $525 ($400 from long-term capital gain + $125 from cash dividends) since only 40 percent of the long-term capital gain is taxed, while all of the dividend income is subject to taxes.

Preferred Stock

Preferred stock is a special type of ownership, or equity, capital. Purchasers of preferred stock expect to receive a stated dividend periodically. The amount of this dividend is *stated* when the stock is first issued. The board of directors of the issuing corporation can elect not to pay this dividend in any period. However, such action is not viewed favorably by the common stockholders since the claims of the preferred stockholders must be satisfied before dividends can be paid to the common stockholders.

Most preferred stock is *cumulative,* which means that all dividends *passed* (not paid in a period) accumulate and must be paid prior to giving the common stockholders any dividends. Preferred stockholders not only receive preference with respect to dividends, but they also have preference over the common stockholders in the case of liquidation of the firm. Because they have these privileges, however, preferred stockholders normally do *not* receive any voting rights. Although preferred stock is traded in the marketplace, most purchasers buy it for the fixed dividend return rather than for any anticipated appreciation in its market price. Since its dividend return is fixed, preferred stock is not nearly as popular an investment as is common stock. In addition, because it takes precedence over common stock in these cases, many corporations avoid using preferred stock financing on the ground that it is not in the best interest of the true owners of the firm, the common stockholders.

Bonds

Bonds represent a form of *debt capital,* which means that funds raised through the sale of bonds are borrowed funds. Bond purchasers do not normally receive any voice in the management of the firm. They expect to receive interest payments at specified times and to be paid back the face value or bond *principal* at maturity. Corporate and government bonds normally have face values of $1,000 and maturities of 5 to 30 years. Interest on corporate or government bonds is usually paid semiannually and is expected to be higher than that paid on savings instruments. Failure to pay interest by the corporation or government will

Table 12.1 Generalized Risk-Return Ratings for Better-Quality Securities

Security	Risk	Return: Income	Return: Growth
Common Stock	Most	Variable	Most
Preferred Stock	Average	Steady	Variable
Corporate Bonds	Least	Very Steady	Usually None

result in *default,* which may then force the corporation or government into bankruptcy. A corporation must pay all interest due bondholders prior to distributing dividends to preferred and common stockholders.

Risk-Return for Stocks and Bonds

As Table 12.1 illustrates, although common stocks are generally more risky than preferred stocks or bonds, they do provide opportunities to earn very large returns through appreciation in value. The return potential on preferred stocks and bonds is much more limited. Another aspect of the appeal of common stock investments over bond investments is that common stock prices can range anywhere from less than one dollar per share up to hundreds of dollars per share. Bonds, however, normally sell at $500 or more per bond. The lower prices of common (and preferred) stocks thus make them quite attractive to the small investor.

Common Stock Investments

If you own common stock, you are an owner of the underlying business. If the firm prospers, your ownership shares will increase in value; if it fails, you may lose your entire investment. There are many aspects of common stocks that you need to understand before you begin investing in them.

Issuers of Common Stock

Common stock can be issued by any corporation in any line of business whose charter authorizes the issuance of shares. A certificate for stock in NCR Corporation is shown in Figure 12.2. Although all corporations have stockholders, not all have publicly traded shares. Corporations whose shares are not publicly traded are often referred to as *closed corporations,* while corporations whose shares are traded publicly are

Figure 12.2 Sample Stock Certificate for NCR Corporation

Source: Courtesy of NCR Corporation, Dayton, Ohio.

called *open corporations.* Of course, the stock of some public corporations is not traded on the major security exchanges and is therefore difficult for investors to obtain. Aside from the initial sale of common stock when a corporation is formed, subsequent sales of additional common stock may be made through public offerings, rights offerings, or with warrants. Rights offerings and warrants have some special characteristics that should be understood.

Rights Offerings When a firm makes a new issue of common stock, it is required (in many states) to allow the current stockholders to purchase new shares in proportion to their existing share ownership. This right of the existing stockholders to be given an opportunity to maintain their proportional ownership is known as a *preemptive right.* For instance, if a stockholder currently owns 10 percent of the firm's stock and the firm plans to issue 5,000 additional shares, that stockholder will be given an opportunity to purchase 500 shares, or 10 percent of the new shares issued. In order to efficiently carry out the *rights offering,* the firm issues rights—negotiable instruments allowing the holder to purchase a certain number of shares of the new issue at a specified price—to each shareholder. These rights normally must be exercised within a few months. Because the *exercise price* at which the new shares can be purchased is usually below the prevailing market price, rights have value and may be sold in the marketplace.

Warrants Another technique used to sell shares of common stock, a *warrant*, provides for the purchase of shares at a certain price over some specified period of time. The purchase price of shares specified by warrants is usually higher than the market price at the time of issue. This means that it is not desirable to exercise warrants when issued; they become valuable only after the market price of the stock rises above the exercise price. For instance, a warrant may allow the holder to purchase three shares of common stock at $30 per share. If the current market price of the stock is $25 per share, the holder will not want to exercise the warrant. But when the market price of the shares exceeds $30, rising to $40 per share, for example, the exercise of the warrant becomes very profitable. Warrants, therefore, do have value and are traded in the security markets. They are commonly issued by corporations in order to make preferred stocks and bonds more attractive investments or as part of a merger or acquisition. When warrants are exercised, a corporation issues new shares of common stock.

Voting Rights

The holders of common stock normally receive *voting rights,* which means that for each share of stock held, they receive one vote. In certain instances common stock may be designated as nonvoting stock at the time of its issue, but this is the exception, not the rule. Although two basic voting systems exist, the small stockholders need not concern themselves with them, since regardless of the system, the chance that they will be able to affect the corporate control with their votes is quite slim. Corporations have annual stockholders' meetings at which new directors are elected and any special issues are voted on. Since most small stockholders are unable to attend these meetings, they are asked to assign their votes by proxy to another person in order to vote their stock. A *proxy* is merely a written statement assigning voting rights to another person. In Figure 12.3, a proxy for NCR Corporation common stock is shown. Normally the existing directors are able to gain proxy voting rights for the majority of shares and thus perpetuate their terms in office. Occasionally, if a large group of dissident stockholders exists, a proxy battle may occur between the directors and the dissident group of stockholders.

Types of Dividends

Corporations can pay dividends to the common stockholders in cash and/or additional stock. *Cash dividends* are most common. Since firms can pay dividends from earnings accumulated from previous periods, stockholders may receive dividends even in periods during which the firm shows a loss. Cash dividends are normally distributed on a quarterly basis in an amount determined by the firm's directors.

Figure 12.3 A Proxy for NCR Corporation Common Stock

P R O X Y

NCR CORPORATION | **Annual Meeting April 21, 1982** | Reinvestment Shares | Proxy No. 98765 | Shares In Your Name 500

Solicited by the Board of Directors of NCR CORPORATION

The undersigned hereby appoints W.S. Anderson, C.E. Exley, Jr., J.E. Rambo and L.P. Scriggins, and each of them, proxies, with full power of substitution, to act for the undersigned and to vote all stock of the undersigned in NCR Corporation at the Annual Meeting of its stockholders to be held on April 21, 1982 and at any adjournment thereof, upon the matters set forth in the Notice of Annual Meeting and Proxy Statement, dated March 5, 1982, copies of which have been received by the undersigned, and upon all other matters properly coming before said meeting or any adjournment thereof. Without otherwise limiting the generality hereof, said proxies are directed to vote as indicated on the other side hereof.

NCR

A. Small Stockholder
1234 Any Street
Any Town, U.S.A. 54321

(Continued and to be signed on the other side)

DDX-22815-OF

P R O X Y

NCR CORPORATION | Annual Meeting April 21, 1982

UNLESS DIRECTED TO THE CONTRARY, THIS PROXY WILL BE VOTED "FOR" THE ELECTION OF DIRECTORS AND "FOR" PROPOSALS (2) AND (3).

A MAJORITY OF SAID PROXIES OR SUBSTITUTES AS SHALL BE PRESENT AND ACTING AT SAID MEETING SHALL EXERCISE ALL POWERS HEREUNDER.

(1) Election of 13 directors — nominees are:
C.A. Anderson, W.S. Anderson, W.G. Bowen, N.F. Brady, G.A. Constanzo, C.E. Exley, Jr., C.H. Hardesty, Jr., H. Holiday, Jr., J.J. Horan, C.S. Morawetz, J.E. Rambo, E.J. Schlegel, and R.L. Terrell

☒ For all nominees
☐ Vote withheld from all nominees
☐ Vote withheld from nominees listed below:

(2) Approval of 1982 Employee Stock Purchase Plan
☐ For ☒ Against ☐ Vote withheld

(3) Appointment of Price Waterhouse & Co. as independent auditors
☒ For ☐ Against ☐ Vote withheld

Dated the 12 day of April, 1982

A Small Stockholder
Signature of Stockholder(s) as shown on this proxy.

PLEASE MARK, SIGN, DATE AND RETURN THE PROXY CARD PROMPTLY USING THE ENCLOSED ENVELOPE.

DDX-22817-OB

Source: Courtesy of NCR Corporation, Dayton, Ohio.

Occasionally, the directors may declare a *stock dividend* as a supplement to or in place of cash dividends. Stock dividends are new shares of stock issued to existing stockholders. Although they often satisfy the needs of investors, stock dividends have no value, since in an accounting sense, they represent the receipt of something already owned by the stockholder. Usually after a stock dividend has been paid, the per share stock price drops by just enough to cause the value of the old share plus the stock dividend to just equal the original share price. When a firm declares a 10 percent stock dividend, each shareholder receives one-tenth of a share of stock for each share owned. In other words, a stockholder with 100 shares of stock in a firm which declared a 10 percent stock dividend would receive 10 new shares of stock. Since all stockholders receive 10 percent increases in their ownership, their proportion of ownership in the firm remains unchanged by stock dividends.

The shareholder who has received a stock dividend may sell the new shares in order to get a cash dividend. (Stock dividends are not taxed until they are sold, whereas cash dividends—excluding the dividend exemption—are taxed in the year they are received.) But the value of that shareholder's holdings in the firm is reduced by the amount of the proceeds from such a sale. Stock dividends, therefore, do not represent real dollar income but rather a type of "psychic income," which may satisfy the stockholder's need to receive something from the firm.

Stock Splits

Stock splits are often initiated by a firm's directors in order to affect the trading activity of the stock in the marketplace. *Stock splits* are a type of trade—old shares for a given number of new shares. In the normal stock split, the stockholder receives more than one share of the new stock for each old share. For instance, in a 2 for 1 stock split, a person owning 200 old shares would receive 400 new shares of stock. Of course, the market price of the new shares is expected to decline in proportion to the increase in the number of shares; in a 2 for 1 split, for example, the market price per share would be reduced by half. If the before-split market price was $50 per share, the after-split market price would be $25 per share. The person owning 200 shares at $50 per share prior to the 2 for 1 split would hold 400 shares at $25 per share after the split.

Occasionally, in order to stimulate trading activity in a stock selling at a low price, firms announce *reverse stock splits,* which means that each existing share is exchanged for less than one new share. A 1 for 2 stock split, for instance, means that one new share is issued in exchange for two old shares of stock. The effect of reverse stock splits is to increase the market price of the stock in proportion to the stock split. For instance, if a stock currently selling for $5 was split 1 for 2, the new price would be $10 per share. Regardless of how stocks are split, stock splits have no value in and of themselves; they are merely intended to enhance the trading activity of the stock. If this effect is obtained, it may then tend to drive up the stock price. Generally speaking, investors prefer regular stock splits and look unfavorably on reverse splits.

Common Stock Measurements

A number of terms are commonly used to describe certain attributes of common stock—par value, book value, earnings per share, price/earnings ratio, and beta. Some pertain to the value of stock, while others refer to its return and risk.

Par Value A stated value that used to be placed on stock certificates, *par value* was not intended to represent the value of a stock, but rather the minimum price at which the stock could sell without causing the shareholder to assume any liability for the firm's actions. Par value is no longer important; it does not reflect value. Many stocks issued today are, in fact, no-par stocks, which should attest to the virtual insignificance of par value. Occasionally, stocks do sell for less than their par value, although in most instances they sell above par.

Book Value The value of a firm, as determined by accounting, represents the *book value* of common stock. The firm's liabilities and preferred stock value are subtracted from the value of its assets. Thus, if a firm's assets were sold for amounts just equal to its book (accounting) value and all debts (and preferred stock) were paid off, what would remain would be the book value of common stock. For example, assume the RZX Company has total assets of $12 million, liabilities of $9 million, and preferred stock valued at $1 million. The book value of the firm's common stock is $2 million ($12 million − $9 million − $1 million). If book value is divided by the number of shares outstanding, the result is the book value per share. If the RZX Company has 100,000 shares of common stock outstanding, its book value per share is $20 ($2,000,000 ÷ 100,000 shares). Some stocks that have market prices below their book values are not necessarily poor investments; they may be excellent investments.

Earnings per Share The claim on earnings for each share owned during the current period is what is known as *earnings per share (EPS).* EPS is calculated by dividing all earnings that remain after the claims of preferred stockholders (if any) are satisfied by the number of shares of common stock outstanding. For example, assume RZX Company had earnings of $250,000 available for its common stockholders as a result of the current year's operations. Since the firm has 100,000 shares of common stock outstanding, its annual earnings per share would be $2.50 ($250,000 ÷ 100,000 shares). The magnitude of earnings per share is considered important by most stockholders because it represents the amount that the firm has earned on behalf of each outstanding share of common stock. Note, however, that the firm's directors may choose not to pay dividends in this amount, or in any amount.

Price/Earnings Ratio When the prevailing market price per share is divided by the annual earnings per share, the result is the *price/earnings ratio (P/E),* which is viewed as an indicator of investor confidence and expectations with respect to a given security. The higher the P/E, the more confidence investors are presumed to have in a given security, and vice versa. In the case of the RZX Company, whose shares are currently selling for \$30, its price/earnings ratio is 12 (\$30/share ÷ \$2.50/share). This means that the RZX Company stock is selling for 12 times earnings. P/E ratios are important to many investors since they provide a feel for the general expectations or growth of the firm.

Beta Over recent years, the use of betas to measure the risk of common stock has become widely accepted. *Beta,* an index of the inescapable risk in a share of common stock, indicates the amount of risk possessed by the stock if it is held as part of a diversified portfolio of securities. The beta for a given stock is determined through the application of various statistical techniques to the historic returns on the stock as compared to the market, which is defined as a portfolio representing all securities. The beta for a risk-free security is set equal to zero, while the beta for the market is set equal to one. The majority of common stock betas fall in the range of .5 to 2.0. A stock's beta can be either positive or negative; however, almost all are positive, which means that they move in the same direction as the market (that is, if the return in the market is generally rising so will the return on the given stock). Low beta stocks, which move less sharply than the market, are often called defensive stocks (a topic discussed in the next section).

The larger a stock's beta, the more risky it is considered to be. For example, assume the beta for RZX Company is currently 0.8 while the beta for the KLM Company is currently 1.8. The 0.8 beta for RZX means that the company's returns are 80 percent as responsive as the market; KLM's 1.8 beta indicates that its returns are 1.8 times as responsive as the market. For example, if the return in the market were to increase by 10 percent, RZX's return would only increase by 8 percent (0.8 × 10%) while KLM's return would increase by 18 percent (1.8 × 10%). It should be clear that beta is an index of the variability, or overall risk, of a stock relative to the market. The higher the stock's beta, the greater is its risk; in the example, KLM Company is clearly more risky than RZX Company. Because betas are easily obtainable from many stockbrokerage firms and investment services, their use in assessing the risk of common stock is commonplace today.

Classifications of Common Stock

Common stock is often classified on the basis of its performance under various conditions as blue-chip, growth, income, speculative, cyclical, or defensive stock.

Blue-Chip Stocks Those stocks known to provide a stable and safe return are *blue-chip stocks.* They are issued by the most stable and strongest companies, such as IBM and General Electric, and provide uninterrupted streams of dividends and good long-term growth prospects. Their proven records of earnings and dividends make them attractive investments when stable and reasonably predictable returns are desired. Due to the high levels of investor confidence and the higher than average predictability associated with blue-chips, they normally sell at high P/E ratios and have betas near 1.0.

Growth Stocks Stocks whose earnings have increased at an above average level over the recent past are *growth stocks.* These stocks normally do not pay out more than about 25 percent of earnings since the firm's rapid growth potential requires that its earnings be retained and reinvested. The very high growth expectations for these stocks usually cause them to sell at relatively high P/E ratios; they typically have betas in excess of 1.0. Because these stocks are expected to achieve high levels of price appreciation, they appeal to investors desirous of capital gains income rather than dividend income. Growth stocks in the early 1980s included companies such as Apple Computer, American Hospital Supply, and Coleco Industries.

Income versus Speculative Stocks Stocks which have appeal primarily on the basis of the dividends they pay out are known as *income stocks.* They have fairly stable streams of earnings, a large portion of which are distributed in the form of dividends. Investors buy these stocks for the income they provide and do not concern themselves with their P/E ratios or their potential for price appreciation. Because of their low risk, these stocks commonly have betas of less than 1.0.

Speculative stocks, on the other hand, are purchased in the hope that their price per share will increase. Rather than basing their investment decisions on a proven record of earnings, those who purchase speculative stocks gamble that some new information, discovery, or production technique will favorably affect the growth of the firm and inflate the price of the stock. For example, a company whose stock is considered speculative may have recently discovered a new drug or located a valuable resource such as oil. The value of speculative stocks and their P/E ratios tend to fluctuate a great deal as additional information with respect to the firm's future is received. The betas for speculative stocks are nearly always in excess of 1.0. Investors in speculative stocks should be prepared to experience losses as well as gains.

Cyclical versus Defensive Stocks Stocks whose price movements tend to follow the business cycle are called *cyclical stocks.* This means that when the economy is in an expansionary stage (recovery or inflation), the prices of cyclical stocks increase; and when the economy is in a contractionary stage (recession or depression), they decline. Most cyclical stocks are found in basic industries—automobiles, steel, and lumber, for example—which are sensitive to changes in economic activity. Investors who purchase cyclical stocks try to do so just prior to their expansionary phase and to sell the stocks before the contraction occurs. Since they tend to move with the market, these stocks always have positive betas.

The prices and returns from *defensive stocks,* unlike those of cyclical stocks, are expected to remain stable during periods of contraction in business activity. For this reason, they are often called countercyclical. The stocks of certain public utilities and gold mining companies are examples of defensive stocks. Basically income stocks, their earnings and dividends in effect hold up the market price during periods of economic decline. This characteristic makes them popular investments for those desiring a safe but certain return. Betas on these stocks are quite low, and occasionally even negative.

Common Stock Value

The value of common stock as viewed by current and potential investors may be based on several considerations. Probably most important of these is the level of expected future earnings and its relationship to the supply and demand for the stock. The greater the expected earnings, the more shares sought for purchase (demand) relative to the number of shares offered for sale (supply) and, therefore, the higher the price and vice versa. There are three basic theories of stock value—fundamental, technical, and random walk and efficient markets.

Fundamental Theory The *fundamental theory* is based on the belief that the true value of a security such as common stock is determined by its expected stream of future earnings. The higher the expected future earnings, the higher the value of the stock; and the lower the level of expected future earnings, the lower the value of the stock. The fundamental value of a security can be estimated by an analysis of the potential sales and earnings of a company using economic and industry based factors. One of the most common fundamental approaches involves estimating the average annual earnings per share expected in the future and then multiplying this value by the expected P/E. For example, assume that a stock that normally sells for nine times earnings is expected to earn (annually) $3.50 per share in the future. Using this method, the fundamental value of the stock would be $31.50 per share (9 × $3.50). Once the fundamental, or true, value of the stock has been determined, purchase or sale decisions can be made. If the true value is above the current market price, the stock is a good buy, since it is underpriced, but if the fundamental value is below the current market price, the stock is overpriced and should be sold.

Technical Theory The belief that security prices are solely the result of the forces of supply and demand characterizes the *technical theory* of stock value. Technical analysis does not rely on earnings data but rather is concerned with forecasting changes in supply and demand and the resulting stock price movements. The basic premise underlying the technical theory is that past patterns of market movement will occur again in the future and can therefore be used to make predictions. The advocates of technical analysis are often called *chartists,* since they normally keep charts plotting daily stock price and market index movements in order to find patterns and trends. Numerous terms such as "ascending triangle" and "head and shoulders" have been developed to describe patterns that are believed to signal certain price movements. Investors who believe in the technical theory base their purchase and sale decisions on the signals generated by their charts. Although the technical analysts rely strictly on predictions of supply and demand and ignore true value, they have been able to perform reasonably well over the recent past.

Random Walk and Efficient Markets Theory Some would suggest that stock price movements are strictly random events, that there are really no patterns in stock price movements. Known as the *random walk theory,* this hypothesis actually rejects both fundamental and technical theories on the basis that price changes are really random. The findings of numerous researchers who have investigated this theory suggest that stock prices have indeed tended to move randomly. To explain these findings researchers developed the concept of an *efficient market,* which is a market in which the price of stock accurately reflects all available information. This theory, which has been statistically validated, suggests that the market price of stock accurately reflects its value. Those who accept the efficient markets theory argue that since stocks are properly valued, the use of fundamental or technical analysis is a waste of time; there are no under- or over-valued stocks. In spite of the growing support for the efficient markets theory, the use of fundamental analysis and technical analysis by the small investor is expected to continue. Many investors strongly believe that use of fundamental and/or technical analysis greatly improves their investment returns . . . and they may be right!

Common Stock Investment Considerations

Common stock has both advantages and disadvantages. Its advantages are twofold: First, its potential returns in the form of both dividend income and price appreciation may be quite good. The record of the average share of common stock over the recent past as well as extended periods of years has been favorable. The returns on some common stocks are considered virtually unlimited since there are no constraints on dividend payments or stock price. Second, at least part of the income from stock investments—that due to its appreciation in price—may be taxed as long-term capital gains at 40 percent of the ordinary tax rate.

Risk, the problem of timing purchases and sales, and the uncertainty of dividends are disadvantages associated with common stock. Although potential common stock returns may be high, the risk or uncertainty associated with the actual receipt of an expected return may also be great. In general, the higher the expected return, the greater the risk involved in actually receiving the return. Even though careful selection of stocks may somewhat reduce risk, the risk-return trade-off cannot be completely eliminated. In other words, high returns on common stock are not guaranteed; they may or may not occur depending on numerous economic, industry, and company factors—all of which are beyond the investor's control.

The timing of purchases and sales is closely related to risk. Many investors purchase a stock, hold it for a period of time during which the price drops, and then sell it below the original purchase price, at a loss. The proper strategy, of course, is to buy stocks low and sell high, but the problem of predicting price movements makes it difficult to implement. The investor must always be abreast of the stock market and stock price movements. In general, because of the risk associated with common stock price movements and because common stock dividends do not have to be paid, common stock is probably not the best investment if a steady income is desired. However, many stocks do provide generous, dependable incomes plus moderate growth.

Preferred Stock Investments

Preferred stock is an income-oriented security commonly purchased by large institutional investors and often issued by public utilities. It is sometimes issued as part of a merger transaction between firms. Preferred stock is a form of ownership, but its fixed return characteristic often causes it to be viewed as a type of debt. Although preferred stocks are traded in the securities markets, their investment appeal can be attributed to the income they provide to their holders in the form of dividends.

Types of Preferred Stock

Several types of preferred stock are available for investment consideration. While the most popular types are not widely divergent, certain key features of preferred stock do affect investment planning.

Cumulative or Noncumulative Most preferred stock is *cumulative,* which means that any dividends passed by the directors in past periods must be paid prior to distributing any dividends to common stockholders. For example, assume a firm has outstanding a $4 preferred stock, which means that $4 per year or $1 per quarter is the stated dividend, on which the last two quarterly dividends have been passed. Before any dividends can be paid to the common stockholder, the preferred stockholder must be paid the $2 of past dividends plus the current quarterly dividend of $1. Had the preferred stock been *noncumulative,* only the current $1 dividend would have had to be paid prior to distributing any earnings to the common stockholders.

Participating or Nonparticipating Most preferred stocks are *nonparticipating,* which means that the preferred stockholder receives only the stated amount of dividends. Occasionally a *participating* preferred stock issue is made. These issues allow the preferred stockholder to share in the distribution of dividends once the common stockholder has received a specified dividend. An example might be a preferred stock in which the preferred stockholders participate equally with the common stockholders on a per-share dividend basis once the common stockholders have received a specified per-share dividend. Participating preferred stock is issued only when a firm is unable to obtain needed financing using more conventional types of securities.

Conversion Feature Preferred stocks are often *convertible,* which means that the holder has the opportunity to exchange the preferred stock for shares of common stock. Convertible preferred stock can be exchanged for a specified number of shares of common stock during a specified period of time. For example, a share of preferred stock may be convertible into two shares of common stock anytime after 1 April 1991. The holder of a share of convertible preferred stock may elect to convert the stock or may continue to hold the convertible preferred instead.

The decision whether or not to convert depends on many factors, including the market price of the common stock and the length of time remaining until the conversion option expires. Convertible preferred stock has appeal since it provides fixed dividend income while offering price appreciation opportunities similar to those obtained with the common stock into which it is convertible. By including this conversion feature in new preferred stock issues, many firms have been able to make preferred stock an attractive investment.

Call Feature Preferred stock may be *callable,* which means that the issuing company can repurchase the stock at a specified price during a certain period of time. All convertible preferred stock has this feature, and quite often nonconvertible issues will be callable. The *call price* is normally stated in advance or is somehow tied to the prevailing market price of the preferred stock. The call feature allows the issuer to retire the preferred stock. In the case of convertible preferred stock, the issuer can force the preferred stockholders into converting the preferred by calling it when the call price is lower than the prevailing market price.

Preferred Stock Investment Considerations

Preferred stock may be an attractive investment for those interested in receiving a fixed income while still being an owner of the firm. Although the fixed income of preferred stock along with its possible appreciation in value does have appeal, preferred stock is not especially popular among small investors. Because of its fixed dividend return, fluctuations in the market price of preferred stocks are primarily attributable to changes in interest rates and/or dividend rates of other fixed income securities.

As pointed out earlier, preferred stock is commonly held by certain financial institutions in order to "round out" their investment portfolios. When investments in preferred stock are being considered, those that are convertible should be given high priority, for they provide not only a guaranteed return but also some of the benefits of common stock price movements. Of course, the purchase of any security depends largely on the needs of the investor. For example, a retired person who wishes to receive regular income but does not have enough money to buy a $1,000 bond may find preferred stock the perfect investment. Preferred stock investments lack popularity probably because other more attractive investment vehicles exist.

Bond Investments

Bonds, which are the negotiable debt instruments of corporations or governments, are far more popular investments than preferred stocks for establishing a fixed income. The purchaser of a bond receives periodic interest over the life of the bond and the face value of the bond—the amount that was originally lent to the issuer—at maturity. Bond interest is generally paid semiannually, and bond maturities range from 5 to 30 years. Because the denominations of bonds are commonly in the $1,000 range, generally only large institutions and wealthy individuals actively deal in bond investments.

A certificate for a bond issued by NCR Corporation is shown in Figure 12.4. Notice that this bond is referred to as a 9% note. A note and a bond mean virtually the same thing—the only distinction is that notes are issued for shorter periods of time (usually less than 10 years) than bonds. The 9% tells you the note will pay $90 a year in interest (per $1000 of principal); the interest is almost always paid semiannually. NCR's note pays interest on May 15 and November 15. Al-

Figure 12.4 Sample Bond Certificate for NCR Corporation

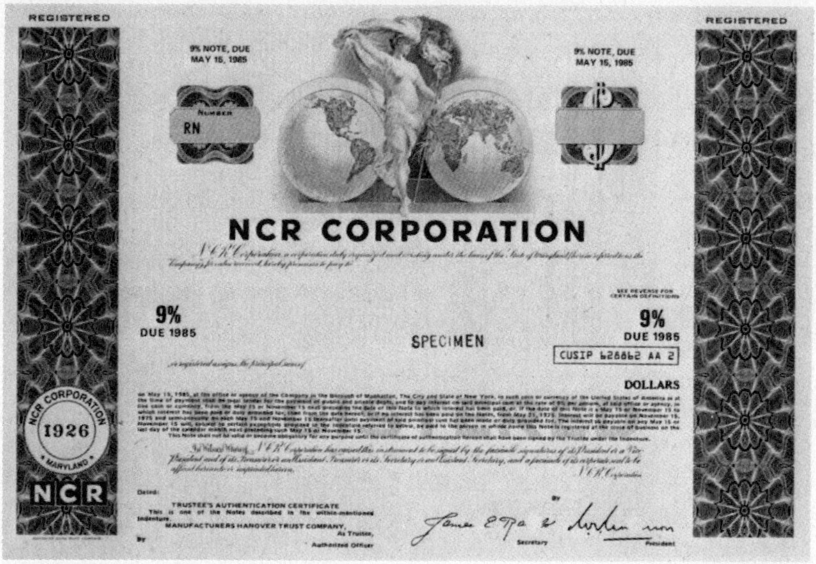

Source: Courtesy of NCR Corporation, Dayton, Ohio.

though certain risks relating to both purchasing power and interest rates are associated with bond investments, a wide variety of bonds are available; investors willing to devote sufficient time can find bonds that conform to their investment needs.

Issuers of Bonds

The issuers of bonds available for investment consideration include corporations, municipalities, and the federal government. Their special roles and the characteristics of the bonds they issue are described separately.

Corporate Bonds Corporations, including industrial firms and utilities, sell bonds in order to raise funds needed for expansion and growth. Most corporate bonds have maturities of 20 to 30 years and are listed and traded on an organized security exchange or in the over-the-counter market. Although the most common denomination of these bonds is \$1,000, their prices in the marketplace are quoted as a percentage of the \$1,000 face value. For example, a \$1,000 bond selling at 87⅛ has a market value of \$871.25 (0.87125 × \$1,000). The stated interest return on corporate bonds at time of issue varies depending on the quality of the bond, which is determined by the financial condition of the issuer.

Table 12.2 Converting Tax-Exempt Yields to Taxable Equivalent Yields for Persons in High Tax Brackets[a]

	Individual Income Brackets (Thousands of Dollars)								
Single Return		\$23.5 to \$28.8		\$28.8 to \$34.1	\$34.1 to \$41.5		\$41.5 to \$55.3		Over \$55.3
Joint Return	\$29.9 to \$35.2		\$35.2 to \$45.8		\$45.8 to \$60.0	\$60.0 to \$85.6		\$85.6 to \$109.4	Over \$109.4
Tax Bracket[b]	30%	32%	35%	36%	40%	44%	45%	48%	50%
Tax-Exempt Yields	Taxable Equivalent Yields								
5.0%	7.1%	7.4%	7.7%	7.8%	8.3%	8.9%	9.1%	9.6%	10.0%
6.0	8.6	8.8	9.2	9.4	10.0	10.7	10.9	11.5	12.0
7.0	10.0	10.3	10.8	10.9	11.7	12.5	12.7	13.5	14.0
7.5	10.7	11.0	11.5	11.7	12.5	13.4	13.6	14.4	15.0
8.0	11.4	11.8	12.3	12.5	13.3	14.3	14.5	15.4	16.0
8.5	12.1	12.5	13.1	13.3	14.2	15.2	15.5	16.3	17.0
9.0	12.9	13.2	13.8	14.1	15.0	16.1	16.4	17.3	18.0
9.5	13.6	14.0	14.6	14.8	15.8	17.0	17.3	18.3	19.0
10.0	14.3	14.7	15.4	15.6	16.7	17.9	18.2	19.2	20.0
10.5	15.0	15.4	16.2	16.4	17.5	18.8	19.1	20.2	21.0
11.0	15.7	16.2	16.9	17.2	18.3	19.6	20.0	21.2	22.0
11.5	16.4	16.9	17.7	18.0	19.2	20.5	20.9	22.1	23.0
12.0	17.1	17.6	18.5	18.8	20.0	21.4	21.8	23.1	24.0
12.5	17.9	18.4	19.2	19.5	20.8	22.3	22.7	24.0	25.0
13.0	18.6	19.1	20.0	20.3	21.7	23.2	23.6	25.0	26.0
13.5	19.3	19.9	20.8	21.1	22.5	24.1	24.5	26.0	27.0
14.0	20.0	20.6	21.5	21.9	23.3	25.0	25.5	26.9	28.0
14.5	20.7	21.3	22.3	22.7	24.2	25.9	26.4	27.9	29.0
15.0	21.4	22.1	23.1	23.4	25.0	26.8	27.3	28.8	30.0

[a]To see what a taxable security would have to yield to equal the tax-exempt yield on a tax-exempt bond, find your taxable income and read down.

[b]Based on tax tables effective beginning 1 January 1983.

Source: An Investor's Guide: Tax Exempt Securities (New York: Public Securities Association, 1983), pp. 14–15.

Municipal Bonds State and local governments often issue bonds to finance certain projects. These *municipal bonds* are quite popular among persons in high tax brackets, even at lower interest rates than those on corporate bonds, since the interest received on them is exempt from federal and in many cases state taxes. Table 12.2 indicates the difference in yields between taxable interest bonds and tax-exempt municipal bonds for taxpayers in high tax brackets. According to the table, for instance, a tax-exempt municipal bond that pays interest at a rate of 8 percent is equivalent to a bond that receives no exemption and pays interest at a rate of 13.3 percent for an individual paying taxes at a 40 percent rate. One can calculate the taxable equivalent yield of a tax-exempt bond for a given tax bracket using Equation 12.1.

$$\text{Taxable equivalent yield} = \frac{\text{Tax-exempt yield}}{(1 - \text{tax bracket stated in decimal form})} \quad (12.1)$$

For example, in the preceding case, the taxable equivalent yield on the 8 percent municipal (tax exempt) bond for a person in a 40 percent tax bracket would be 13.3 percent (8% ÷ [1 − .40]). In general, the higher the tax bracket, the more attractive municipal bonds become; they are especially attractive to wealthy individuals desiring fixed income from their investments.

Because there is such a diversity of municipal bonds available, investors must be careful to assess the quality of the bond in order to make sure that the issuer will not default and the bond can be sold prior to maturity, if necessary. Although it may not seem that the issuer of municipals would default on either interest or principal payments, it does occasionally occur, especially on issues of small communities.

Federal Government Bonds The federal government also sells bonds in order to finance its activities. These bonds make up part of the so-called *national debt.* Ranging in maturity from 3 months to 28 or more years, they come in many forms, including treasury bills, treasury notes and treasury bonds, and savings bonds, which are discussed in Chapter 5. The interest returns on these government issues are lower than returns on corporate issues since the risk of default is viewed as nonexistent. Because of their risk-free nature and fixed returns, investment in government bonds appeals to more conservative investors who wish to receive a reasonable, but certain, return.

Treasury bills are issued in 91- to 360-day maturities with interest returns that reflect the existing financial conditions. They are readily marketable and can be purchased in denominations of $10,000 or more through a broker or bank or directly from the Federal Reserve. They are sold below their face value (at a discount) and can be redeemed for face value at maturity. The size of the discount from face value and the time required to attain maturity determine the interest return received.

Treasury notes normally have one- to five-year maturities and generally sell with interest rates slightly above that on treasury bills. They are also quite marketable and may be purchased in denominations of $1,000 or more. They have a stated rate of interest that is paid semiannually to all holders.

Treasury bonds are issued with initial maturities of 5 to 28 years and generally have interest rates above treasury bills and notes due to their higher purchasing power and interest rate risks. Treasury bonds are also very marketable and can be purchased in $1,000 denominations. As in the case of treasury notes, the stated rate of interest on treasury bonds is paid semiannually.

Characteristics of Bonds

Bonds differ according to specifications and conditions under which they are issued. The following discussion considers some of the characteristics of bonds, particularly of corporate bonds, since they are probably most appealing due to the diversity of risk-return possibilities they offer.

Legal Aspects When corporations issue bonds, an *indenture,* which is a legal contract clearly stating all obligations of the issuer, is drawn up. Within the indenture, the dates and amounts of interest and principal payments are stated along with other provisions designed to protect the quality of the bond. In order to make sure that the indenture is not violated by the issuer, a *trustee,* which is generally a large commercial bank, is appointed to enforce the indenture. Although hired by the issuer, the trustee protects the interests of the bondholders. In order to aid in the bond preparation and sale process, the issuer may use an *investment banking firm,* which is paid for its advisory and selling assistance.

Unsecured or Secured Bonds can be issued on the credit worthiness of the company or with specific assets pledged as collateral. Unsecured bonds are called *debentures,* while secured bonds are referred to as *mortgage bonds, collateral trust bonds,* or *equipment trust obligations.* Mortgage bonds, which are the most common type of secured bond, have tangible property (land, buildings, equipment) pledged against them; collateral trust bonds have stocks and bonds owned by the issuer pledged against them; and equipment trust obligations are secured by certain types of equipment.

In the instance of default, the holders of debentures have a general claim on the firm's assets. When a firm defaults on secured bonds, the specific assets held as collateral are liquidated and the proceeds are used to satisfy the bondholders' claims. If, after liquidating the collateral, the claims of secured bondholders have not been satisfied, they become general creditors for the remainder of their claims. In order to protect debenture holders from having assets pledged against subsequent bond issues, a clause can be included in the indenture requiring that the debenture holders share equally in the liquidation of any pledged assets. Secured bonds are generally viewed as a safer investment than debentures since specific assets stand behind them and can be used to satisfy the bondholders' claims. Since only firms having strong financial positions can sell debentures, they are still generally considered safe investments.

Senior or Subordinated The claims of certain bondholders are sometimes subordinated to the claims of other bondholders or lenders. The claims of *subordinated debentures* are not especially strong; normally they are viewed as nearly equivalent to those of a stockholder. The bonds to which the debentures are subordinated are often referred to as *senior debt* since the claims of these lenders are superior to those holding subordinated bonds. Purchasers of subordinated debentures are normally given higher interest returns and an opportunity to convert their bonds into common stock as compensation for the higher degree of risk they assume.

Conversion Feature Like preferred stocks, some corporate bonds are convertible into a specified number of shares of common stock. The *conversion feature* is outlined in the indenture at the time of issuance. The price per share at which conversion can be made is set above the market price at the time of issuance, but the expectation is that when the stock price exceeds the conversion price, bondholders will convert to common stock. Sometimes conversion is limited to only a certain period of years while the bond is outstanding. Most convertibles are debentures, and most subordinated debentures are convertibles. The conversion feature enhances the marketability of these issues since it provides purchasers with an opportunity for investment appreciation; they share in the growth of the firm in a fashion similar to that of the common stockholder. Because they offer this advantage, convertible bonds typically have a lower interest rate than do similar nonconvertible bonds.

For a better understanding of the alternatives a convertible bond offers its purchaser, consider a $1,000 bond that is convertible into 25 shares of common stock. This means that the conversion price is $40 per share of common stock ($1,000 ÷ 25). If, at the time of issue, the common stock had a market price of $30, conversion would not be attractive since the bond would be worth only $750 (25 × $30) once converted. If the stock price rises above the $40 conversion price, the price of the bond will probably rise also. For instance, if the market price of the stock rises to $50, conversion will be attractive; but, since the bond price will rise to $1,250 (25 × $50), many people may not convert the bond. They still have the benefit of the fixed interest payment of the bond along with the price movement of the stock. Convertible bonds, because they offer fixed income as well as prospects for price appreciation similar to common stocks, are attractive to people who are not necessarily interested in receiving maximum current income from their investments.

Call Feature The *call feature,* which allows the issuer to repurchase the bond at a prespecified price, is often included as part of a bond issue. Call features do not normally come into effect until the bond has been outstanding for five or more years. The call feature is always included as part of a convertible bond because it allows the issuer to force bondholders to convert the bonds into common stock once the common stock price exceeds the conversion price. In other cases, the use of the call feature permits a firm that no longer needs debt financing to retire debts prior to their maturity.

Table 12.3 **Moody's and Standard & Poor's Bond Ratings**

Moody's	Interpretation	Standard & Poor's	Interpretation
Aaa	Prime Quality	AAA	Extremely strong
Aa	High Grade	AA	Very strong
A	Upper Medium Grade	A	Strong
Baa	Medium Grade	BBB	Adequate
		BB	Speculative
Ba	Lower Medium Grade or Speculative	B	
		CCC	
B	Speculative	CC	
		C	Income Bond
Caa	From Very Speculative		
Ca	to Near or in Default		
		DDD	In Default (Rating Indicates
C	Lowest Grade	DD	the Relative Salvage
		D	Value)

Source: Reprinted by permission of Moody's Investors Service, Inc., and Standard & Poor's Corporation.

Bond Ratings

Potential bond investors can obtain unbiased evaluations of the quality of various bonds through bond ratings. The two chief bond ratings are provided by Moody's Investors Service, Inc., and Standard & Poor's Corporation. These companies assign ratings to bonds on the basis of quality and degree of risk. As Table 12.3 illustrates, Moody's and Standard & Poor's ratings are quite similar. As one moves down the classification schemes, the bonds become lower quality investments. Investors should consult either of these bond ratings in order to make sure that the bonds they purchase are consistent with the level of risk they are willing to take. These ratings can be obtained at banks, brokerage firms, or libraries. Although they are not infallible, bond ratings do provide free and useful insights for investors.

Bond Prices

The price of a bond depends on many factors, including its interest rate, the number of years to maturity, and the prevailing returns on similar bonds. The most common type of corporate bond is the *registered bond,* on which interest checks are automatically mailed to the bondholder. The other type of bond is the *coupon bond,* which provides interest coupons that are detached and redeemed at specified dates. Registered bonds are popular because there is too much risk involved in handling coupon, or "bearer," bonds; coupons can be easily lost or

Table 12.4 Bond Prices for Varying Market Rates of Interest (9 Percent Coupon Interest Rate, 20-Year Maturity, $1,000 Bond)

Market Rate of Interest	Bond Price	Premium, Discount, or Face Value
6%	$1,347	Premium
7	1,214	Premium
8	1,099	Premium
9 (Coupon Rate)	1,000	Face Value
10	914	Discount
11	840	Discount
12	774	Discount

stolen. In order to understand why the market price of these bonds may differ from their face values, you must understand discounts and premiums, yields, and interest rate effects.

Discounts and Premiums Once a bond is issued, it is not unusual for its market price to deviate from its face value. When a bond is selling below its face value, it is said to be selling at a *discount;* when it is selling above its face value, it is selling at a *premium.* Bond discounts and premiums result when other bonds of similar risk (with similar ratings) are selling for higher or lower rates of interest, respectively, than the *coupon* (or stated) rate on the bond. Changes in the interest returns on similar-risk bonds are brought about by changes in the supply and demand for money. Supply and demand changes normally result from changes in economic activity. In order for the bond to be attractive to investors, it must provide a return that is competitive with similar-risk bonds; since the rate of interest paid to bondholders is fixed, the price must be adjusted in order to allow investors to receive a competitive return on the bond.

For example, a bond with a face value of $1,000 and a 9 percent coupon rate would be expected to sell for $1,000 as long as similar-risk bonds are selling at 9 percent returns. If the *market rate of interest* on the similar-risk securities increases, the price of the bond will drop in order to allow the investor to receive a competitive return. The amount of the discount will depend on the prevailing interest rates and the time to maturity of the bond. The closer the market rate to the coupon rate and the closer to maturity the bond, the smaller the amount of the discount.

In effect, the discount allows the coupon rate of the bond to become competitive, since, as the price drops, the coupon rate represents a higher percentage return. Of course, when the market interest rates fall below the coupon rate on the bond, the reverse process will result, and the price of the bond will rise above its face value. Table 12.4 presents the bond prices associated with varying market rates of interest for the bond with a 9 percent coupon interest rate. The bond is assumed to have just been issued with a 20-year maturity.

Yields: Current and to Maturity The *yield* on a bond investment is the rate of return that would be earned on the bond if held for a stated period of time. The two most commonly cited bond yields are the current yield and the yield-to-maturity. The *current yield* reflects the amount of current income the bond provides relative to its current market price. The formula for current yield is given in Equation 12.2.

$$\text{Current yield} = \frac{I}{N} \qquad \textbf{(12.2)}$$

where:

I = annual interest payment in dollars

N = the current market price of the bond

Assume, for example, that a 9 percent coupon bond with \$1,000 face value is currently selling for \$910. Since I would equal \$90 (.09 × \$1,000) and N equals \$910, its current yield would be 9.89 percent (\$90 ÷ \$910). This yield, which is commonly quoted in the financial press, would be of interest to investors seeking current income.

The annual rate of return that a bondholder purchasing the bond today and holding it until it matures would receive is the bond's *yield-to-maturity.* The yield-to-maturity reflects two types of return: the actual interest income and the payment of face value at maturity. If a bond is purchased at its face value, its yield-to-maturity equals the stated rate of interest. But if it is purchased at a discount, its yield-to-maturity is greater than the stated rate because in addition to receiving the stated rate, the face value, which is greater than the initial investment, is received at maturity. Of course, if a premium is paid for the bond, the opposite is true; the yield-to-maturity is less than the coupon rate.

Equation 12.3 provides the formula for calculating an approximate yield-to-maturity for a \$1,000 bond where I and N are defined as earlier and n equals the number of years remaining to maturity of the bond.

$$\text{Approximate yield-to-maturity} = \frac{I + \dfrac{\$1{,}000 - N}{n}}{\dfrac{N + \$1{,}000}{2}} \qquad \textbf{(12.3)}$$

Assume, for example, that you are contemplating the purchase of the \$1,000, 9 percent coupon bond, with 15 years remaining to maturity, at a discount for \$910. If I = \$90, N = \$910, and n = 15 years, the approximate yield-to-maturity for this bond will be 10.5 percent:

$$\text{Approximate yield-to-maturity} = \frac{\$90 + \dfrac{\$1{,}000 - \$910}{15}}{\dfrac{\$910 + \$1{,}000}{2}} = \frac{\$96}{\$955} = 10.05\%$$

This is above both the 9 percent stated rate and the 9.89 percent current yield since the bond is purchased at a discount from its face value. Equations 12.2 and 12.3 are valid for any \$1,000 bond whether it sells at a discount or a premium. Had the bond been selling at \$1,090, it would have had a current yield of 8.26 percent and an approximate yield-to-maturity of 8.04 percent—both below the 9 percent coupon rate since the bond was selling at a premium.

Interest Rate Effects Interest rate fluctuations in the marketplace directly affect the prices at which bonds sell. If market rates of interest increase, the prices of bonds are discounted in order to provide competitive yields; if market rates of interest decline, bond prices are increased in order to adjust the yield to a level that is competitive with the prevailing rate of interest. If you purchase a bond with the intention of holding it to maturity, changes in the market rates of interest will not affect the actual return you receive; in other words, you will get the yield expected as long as you hold the bond to maturity. If you must sell a bond prior to maturity, however, the effects of changing interest rates upon the price at which you sell may be significant.

Bond Investment Considerations

Bonds are attractive investments for those who wish to receive periodic and predictable patterns of income from their investments. High-grade (bank investment quality) bond investments provide nearly certain income along with the return of the principal at maturity. Although investment in high-grade bonds is viewed as quite conservative, its appeal is that it provides a safe return exceeding that available from various savings instruments.

The primary danger of corporate bond investments lies in the potential effects of interest rate movements on the bond price. Over the past ten years, the general trend in interest rates has been upward, which has tended to lower prices on outstanding bonds having lower-than-market interest rates. Bonds, therefore, do not protect investors from the inflationary pressures of our economy. The bond investor should assess the potential effects of interest rate movements and inflation on bond prices when evaluating various investment alternatives.

Summary

Investment planning is an important part of financial planning that must be given attention after acquiring necessary fundamental assets and providing for adequate insurance coverage. Before specific investment alternatives are considered, investment objectives should be formulated. These generally include enhancing current consumption, saving for a major expenditure, accumulating retirement funds, and sheltering current income from taxes. Investment alternatives considered in this chapter and Chapters 13 and 14 are common and preferred stocks, bonds, investment companies, real estate, commodity and financial futures, options, and precious minerals and collectibles.

The basic risks that must be considered when selecting security investments include business risk, financial risk, market risk, purchasing power risk, and interest rate risk. An inverse relationship exists between these risks and the expected security returns, which may be received in the form of periodic income or growth in the market price of the securities.

Common stock is a popular investment due to the diversity of risk-return combinations available. Common stock may be purchased in the marketplace, through public offerings or rights offerings, or by exercising warrants. Common stockholders vote in corporate elections and may pass their votes to others by signing a proxy statement. Dividends on common stock may be paid in either cash or stock. Sometimes stock splits are initiated in order to stimulate trading activity in the firm's shares. Par value and book value are measures of stock value. The earnings per share and the price/earnings ratio are often used to assess the returns on common stock. Beta is an index used to measure the risk of a common stock relative to the market risk. On the basis of performance, common stock is often classified as blue-chip, growth, income or speculative, and cyclical or defensive. The three basic theories of common stock value are (1) the fundamental theory, (2) the technical, or chartist, theory, and (3) the random walk and efficient markets theory. Common stock investment offers opportunities for both income and profit through price appreciation. Disadvantages are related to the risk associated with its returns, the difficulty of timing purchases and sales, and the uncertainty of dividends.

Preferred stock, which is a form of ownership that is given preference over common stock in the distribution of dividends and—in case the firm is liquidated—assets, is occasionally issued by corporations. Preferred stockholders do not normally receive voting privileges. Most preferred stock pays dividends on a cumulative and nonparticipating basis. Preferred stock can be convertible and/or callable. Its appeal lies in the fixed income it provides, while its chief disadvantage is that many other more attractive investments are available today.

Bonds may be issued by corporations, municipalities (in which case they are tax-exempt), and the federal government. Since corporate issues—both industrials and utilities—have the broadest appeal, they are given primary attention. An indenture is the legal document describing a corporate bond issue; it is enforced by the trustee. Bonds may be unsecured debentures or they may be secured by a variety of corporate assets. Bonds may also be senior to the claim of another security or subordinated to another security's claim. Like preferred stocks, bonds may be convertible or callable. Bond ratings are published by a number of companies. The market price of a bond depends on the relationship between its coupon, or stated, rate of interest, the number of years to maturity, and the market rate of interest. Depending on the relationship of these factors, a bond may sell at a discount (below), at a premium (above), or at its face value. A bond investor can measure return using either the current yield or the yield-to-maturity. Bond investments provide fixed and relatively safe returns, but upward interest rate movements and inflation do affect them adversely.

Making Transactions in Securities Markets 13

An individual may have an excellent understanding of the physical characteristics of boats but still be unable to operate them and navigate across a body of water. In the same sense, a thorough knowledge of alternative investment vehicles is not enough to permit you to carry out your investment goals. In order to operate an investment program, you need to understand the institutions, mechanisms, and procedures involved in making security transactions. To navigate through the vast array of securities and tangible investment assets, you must know how to gather and interpret relevant information and be familiar with the strategies available for making purchase and sale decisions.

The preceding chapter presented investment fundamentals, placing primary emphasis on stock and bond investing, including the basic characteristics of the most common types of those securities and the differences in their risk-return behaviors. In this chapter, the nature of the various markets and the process of making stock and bond transactions are discussed.

Securities Markets

The phrase *securities markets* describes the marketplace in which stocks, bonds, and other financial instruments are traded. The *capital market* is the marketplace in which long-term securities (those with lives or maturities greater than one year) are traded, while the *money market* is the marketplace for short-term securities. Both types of markets provide a vital mechanism for bringing together the purchasers and sellers of securities for the purpose of making transactions. This chapter considers only the capital market in which stock and bond transactions take place. Without the development of securities markets, it would have been difficult for business firms to grow into the large corporations of today.

Types of Markets

The securities markets can be divided into two basic parts—the primary market and the secondary market. The *primary market* is the market in which new securities are sold to the public. The *secondary market*

Figure 13.1 Organization of a New Security Selling Process

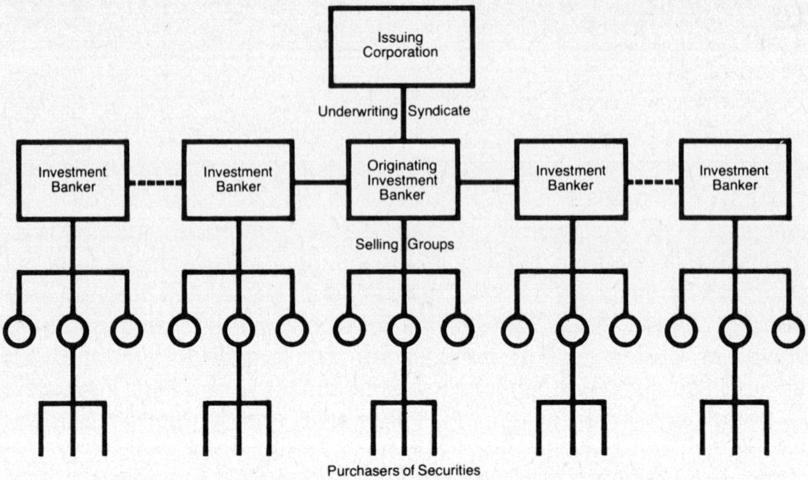

is the market in which old securities are sold. A security is traded in the primary market only when it has just been issued by a corporation. Subsequent transactions in which it is sold by one investor to another take place in the secondary market. Trading in the secondary market, where various types of "stock exchanges" exist, is more prevalent, especially among small investors who may not be able to conveniently make purchases in the primary securities market.

Primary Markets When a corporation sells a new security issue, several financial institutions participate in the transaction. The corporation will probably usc an *investment banking firm,* which specializes in *underwriting* (selling) new security issues. The investment banker will give the corporation advice on pricing and other aspects of the issue and will sell the new securities or arrange for a *selling group* to do so. The selling group is normally made up of a large number of stock-brokerage firms, each of which accepts the responsibility for selling a certain portion of the new issue. Occasionally on very large issues of securities, the originating investment banker will bring in other underwriting firms as partners and form an *underwriting syndicate* in an attempt to spread the risk associated with selling the new securities. In such cases, each underwriter forms a selling group responsible for selling its portion of the new issue. Figure 13.1 depicts this selling process for a new security issue.

In the course of selling a new security, both the underwriting firm and the selling firms are compensated by receiving discounts from the anticipated sales price. In other words, the underwriting and selling firms buy the securities at a price below that at which they will sell them. The discount is the difference between the price they pay and the sale price.

A potential purchaser of a new issue must be provided a *prospectus,* which is a document describing the firm and the issue. Certain agencies of the federal government have the responsibility of making sure that all information included within a prospectus is an accurate representation of the facts. Sometimes investors have trouble purchasing new security issues because all shares allocated to the stockbrokers have been sold—often prior to the official sale date. Of course, if new shares are sold using *rights* or *warrants,* which are discussed in Chapter 12, the ability to purchase new shares may be considerably more limited, since only the holders of these instruments can purchase the shares.

Secondary Markets The secondary markets for securities exist in order to permit the buyers and sellers of securities to make transactions. Included among the secondary markets are the various *securities exchanges,* in which the buyers and sellers of securities are brought together. Both organized and over-the-counter securities exchanges exist. The organized exchanges typically handle transactions in the securities of larger, better-known companies, and the over-the-counter exchange handles transactions in the securities of smaller, less well-known firms. The *organized securities exchanges* are well-structured institutions where the market forces of supply and demand are brought together, while the *over-the-counter (OTC) market* is basically a mass telecommunications network linking buyers and sellers. Since most transactions of small investors are made in the secondary market, primary emphasis will be given to it throughout this chapter.

Organized Securities Exchanges

The forces of supply and demand for various securities are brought together in the organized securities exchanges. Approximately 66 percent of all shares traded are traded on an organized securities exchange. In these exchanges, the floor is laid out according to the different types of securities, and *members* of the exchange can trade only *listed securities* on the floor of the exchange. Members of an exchange are said to own a seat on the exchange. This privilege is obtained by meeting certain financial specifications and requirements. Only the securities of companies that have met certain listing requirements are traded on the exchange, and those companies must comply with regulations established to assure that they do not make financial or legal misrepresentations to their stockholders. Not only must the firms comply with the rules of the specific exchange, but they must also fulfill certain requirements established by the Securities and Exchange Commission.

Table 13.1 Ten NYSE Companies[a] Having the Largest Number of Common Stockholders, Early 1983

Company	Number of Stockholders
American Telephone & Telegraph[b]	3,148,000
General Motors	1,035,000
Exxon Corporation	865,000
International Business Machines	726,000
General Electric	481,000
GTE Corporation	467,000
Sears Roebuck	434,000
Texaco Inc.	373,000
Southern Company	347,000
American Electric Power	346,000

[a]Foreign companies not included in survey.

[b]AT&T became eight separate companies on January 1, 1984.

Source: The New York Stock Exchange 1983 Fact Book (New York: New York Stock Exchange, 1983), p. 37.

New York Stock Exchange The *New York Stock Exchange (NYSE)* is the largest and most prestigious organized securities exchange. It handles the major portion of the dollar volume of securities transactions and accounts for approximately 81 percent of the total annual share volume on organized security exchanges. Membership on the NYSE is limited to 1,366 seats. During this century, the cost of a seat has ranged from $17,000 (in 1942) to $515,000 (in 1968 and 1969); most recently seats have sold for $250,000 to $300,000 or more. Most are owned by stock brokerage firms, the largest of which—Merrill Lynch Pierce Fenner & Smith, Inc.—owns over 20 seats.

The NYSE has the most stringent requirements of all organized exchanges. In order to be listed on the NYSE, a firm must have at least 2,000 stockholders, each owning 100 shares or more. It must also have a minimum of 1 million shares of publicly held stock outstanding; it must have demonstrated earning power of $2.5 million before taxes at the time of listing and $2 million pre-tax for each of the preceding two years; it must have $16 million in market value of publicly held shares; and, finally, it must pay a listing fee. The ten companies listed on the NYSE with the largest number of common stockholders in 1982 are shown in Table 13.1. Firms failing to continue to meet listing requirements can be *delisted.* More than 1,500 firms accounting for over 2,200 different stocks and over 3,100 different bonds are currently listed on the NYSE.

American Stock Exchange The *American Stock Exchange (AMEX)* is the second largest organized exchange. Its organization and procedures are similar to those of the NYSE. Membership costs and listing requirements on AMEX are not quite as stringent as the NYSE's. There are approximately 660 seats on AMEX, and over 950 listed stocks and 240 listed corporate bonds. AMEX is believed to handle approximately 9 percent of the total annual share volume on organized security exchanges. The NYSE and the AMEX are the dominant organized securities exchanges; in combination, they handle about 90 percent of all shares traded.

Regional Stock Exchanges A total of 14 *regional stock exchanges* also exist, including the Midwest Stock Exchange, the Pacific Stock Exchange, and the Boston Stock Exchange. These exchanges deal primarily in the trading of securities with local and regional appeal. Most regional exchanges are modeled after the NYSE, but their membership and listing requirements are considerably more lenient. Regional exchanges will often list securities also listed on the NYSE or AMEX in order to enhance their trading activity. The total activity on the regional stock exchanges accounts for only about 10 percent of the annual share volume on organized exchanges.

Over-the-Counter Market

The over-the-counter (OTC) market is not a specific institution like the organized securities exchanges but rather an intangible relationship between the buyers and sellers of securities. It is the fastest growing market, with a volume of 7.82 billion shares traded in 1981, compared to only 2.76 billion in 1978. The market is linked together by a mass telecommunications network. Unlike the organized securities exchanges, many of the trades in the OTC market are negotiated directly between buyer and seller. Approximately 34 percent of all share trades take place in the over-the-counter market. Most government and corporate bonds as well as a numerical majority of stocks are traded in the OTC market, which has no listing requirements: all nonlisted securities are traded there. Traders known as *broker-dealers* make markets in certain securities by offering to either buy or sell them at stated prices.

The *bid* and the *ask* price represent, respectively, the highest price offered to purchase a given security and the lowest price at which the security is offered for sale. The OTC market is linked through the National Association of Securities Dealers Automated Quotation System (NASDAQ), which provides up-to-date bid and ask prices on thousands of securities and allows buyers and sellers to locate each other in order to consummate transactions. Buyers and sellers of the less active OTC securities, which are not traded on the NASDAQ system, must find each other through references or through known *market makers,* who specialize in making markets in certain securities.

Regulation of Securities Markets

The *Securities and Exchange Commission (SEC),* an agency of the federal government, was established to enforce the Securities Exchange Acts of 1933 and 1934. These acts were aimed at regulating not only the operation of securities exchanges and the securities markets, but also the disclosure of information on both new and outstanding listed securities. In addition to the regulations of the SEC, most states have laws on the sale of securities within their borders. These blue sky laws protect investors by preventing firms from attempting to sell nothing but "blue sky." The exchanges themselves also perform a self-regulatory function through their governing bodies.

The OTC market is regulated by the *National Association of Securities Dealers (NASD),* which is made up of all brokers and dealers in OTC securities. The NASD is a self-regulatory organization that polices the activities of brokers and dealers in order to make sure the association's standards are upheld. The SEC supervises the activities of NASD, thus providing investors further protection from fraudulent activities.

General Market Conditions: Bull or Bear

The market is said to be bullish or bearish depending on whether the prices of stocks are generally rising or falling, respectively. Changing market conditions generally stem from changing investor attitudes, changes in economic activity, and certain governmental actions generally aimed at stimulating or slowing down the economy. *Bull markets* are favorable markets normally associated with investor optimism, economic recovery, and governmental stimulus, while *bear markets* are unfavorable markets normally associated with investor pessimism, economic slowdowns, and government control. It is not unusual to find individual securities that are bullish in a bear market or bearish in a bull market. Market conditions—bull or bear—are difficult to predict and usually can only be identified once they exist.

Making Securities Transactions

To take advantage of the full spectrum of market opportunities, you must not only be aware of the mechanism available for accessing the securities markets, but you must also understand the various types of orders that may be placed and the services available to help you make transactions.

Stockbrokers

Stockbrokers, or account executives, purchase and sell securities for their customers. They must be licensed by the exchanges on which they place orders and abide by the strict ethical guidelines of the exchanges and the SEC. Stockbrokers work for brokerage firms, which own seats on the organized security exchanges. Thus the members of the security exchange actually execute orders transmitted to them by the brokers in the various sales offices. For example, the largest stockbrokerage firm, Merrill Lynch Pierce Fenner & Smith, Inc., has brokerage offices in most major cities in the U.S. Orders from these offices are transmitted to the main office of Merrill Lynch and then to the floor of the stock exchange (NYSE, AMEX, or other), where they are executed. Confirmation that the orders have been executed is transmitted back to the broker placing each order and then to the customer. This process, which can be carried out in a matter of minutes with the use of sophisticated telecommunications networks, is illustrated in Figure 13.2.

Orders for the over-the-counter (OTC) securities must be executed through market makers in the given security. The NASDAQ system, along with available information on who makes markets in certain securities, allows the broker to execute orders in OTC securities. Normally, OTC transactions can be executed rapidly since most market makers maintain inventories of the securities in which they deal in order to provide a continuous market. Although the procedure for executing orders on organized exchanges differs from that in the OTC market, you as an investor place orders with your broker, regardless of the market in which the security is traded.

Selecting a Stockbroker You should select a stockbroker who understands your investment objectives and can effectively assist you in pursuing them. If you choose a broker whose own disposition toward investing is similar to yours, you should be able to avoid conflict and establish a solid working relationship. It is probably best to ask friends or business associates to recommend stockbrokers. It is not important—and often not even advisable—to know your stockbroker personally. A strict business relationship eliminates the possibility that social concerns will interfere with achievement of your investment objectives. This does not mean, of course, that your broker's sole interest should be commissions. Responsible brokers make a concerted effort to establish a long-term broker-client relationship with their clients; they do not "churn accounts"—that is, attempt to cause their clients to make many transactions in order to get numerous commissions.

Brokerage Services In addition to facilitating purchase and sale transactions for a commission, stockbrokers offer their clients a variety of other services. The stockbrokerage firm, or house, normally provides

Figure 13.2 How Stocks Are Bought and Sold on the New York Stock Exchange

Source: Courtesy of the New York Stock Exchange and Loewi Financial Companies, Ltd.

a wide variety of free information ranging from stock and bond guides that summarize the activity of securities to research reports on specific securities or industries. Quite often the house will have a research staff that will periodically issue analyses of economic, market, industry, or company behavior and events and relate them to recommendations it makes to buy or sell certain securities. Your stockbroker should provide you with the type of information that is most relevant to your investment goals. As a client of a large brokerage firm, you can expect to receive periodically monthly bulletins discussing market activity and possibly including a recommended investment list. Also, you will receive a statement describing all of your transactions for the month, commission charges, interest charges, dividends and interest received, and your account balance.

Most brokerage offices have electronic equipment of some sort that provides up-to-the-minute stock price quotations and world news. Stock price information can be obtained from either the quotation board (a large screen that electronically displays all NYSE and AMEX security transactions within a few minutes after they take place) or by keying into the telequote system, which relies on a computer terminal to provide a capsule description of almost all securities and their prices. World news, which can significantly affect the stock market, is obtained from a news wire service subscribed to by the brokerage office. Most offices also have a reference library for use by the firm's clients.

Brokerage firms will also hold your certificates in their safe for you in order to protect against their loss. The stocks kept thus by the firm are said to be held in "street name" since the broker can liquidate them for you without having to obtain your signature. You are protected against the loss of the securities that are held by your broker by the *Securities Investor Protection Corporation (SIPC),* an agency of the federal government that insures each customer's account against the financial failure of the brokerage firm. SIPC insurance covers each customer's account for up to $500,000, of which up to $100,000 may be in cash balances held by the firm. Note, however, that the SIPC insurance does not guarantee that the dollar value of the securities will be recovered; it only guarantees that the securities themselves will be returned. Certainly, in light of the diversity and quality of services available among stockbrokerage houses, careful consideration should be given not only to your selection of a stockbroker but also to your choice of a firm.

Odd- or Round-Lot Transactions Security transactions can be made in either odd or round lots. An *odd lot* consists of fewer than 100 shares of a security, while a *round lot* represents a 100-share unit or multiple thereof. Since all transactions made on the floor of the major stock exchanges (New York and American) are made in round lots, the purchase or sale of odd lots requires the assistance of the *specialist* who is an exchange member dealing in the given security. The additional fee charged by the specialist for making these types of transactions

Table 13.2 Suggested Brokerage Fee Schedule (March 1983)

Value of Transaction	Fees for an Odd Lot or 100 Shares	
Up to $800	$8.43 + 2.7% of the value of the transaction	
$800 to $2,500	$16.85 + 1.7% of the value of the transaction	+3.15¢/share
$2,500 to $5,000	$29.50 + 1.3% of the value of the transaction	+3.15¢/share

Source: A major stockbrokerage firm.

encourages round-lot transactions. Small investors, who are generally in the early stages of their investing programs and do not account for the majority of security transactions, are primarily responsible for odd-lot transactions.

Brokerage Fees For executing purchase and sale transactions on behalf of their clients, brokerage firms receive commissions. Brokerage commissions are currently said to be negotiated, which means that the fees are not fixed. But, in practice, brokerage firms establish fee schedules that are applied to small transactions; these fees are not really negotiated. The small investor may nonetheless find that the fee schedule differs from brokerage firm to brokerage firm. On the larger, institutional trades, the negotiation of commissions actually does take place.

The suggested fee schedule currently used by one large brokerage firm is given in Table 13.2. Although this schedule does not specifically levy a premium on odd-lot transactions, the fixed-cost fee component does tend to raise the per-share cost of odd-lot transactions. (In addition to the fees shown in the schedule, *some* brokerage firms will charge an odd-lot differential of 12½¢ per share on odd-lot transactions.) Using the fee schedule in Table 13.2 to calculate brokerage fees on a purchase of 80 shares of stock XYZ at $30 per share, the total value of the transaction would be $2,400 (80 shares × $30/share) and the brokerage fee would therefore be $16.85 + 1.7%($2,400) + $.0315(80 shares) = $16.85 + $40.80 + $2.52 = $60.17. A common rule of thumb is that brokerage fees on a round lot are approximately 2 percent of the transaction value.

Aside from the brokerage fees, certain transfer taxes are charged by the state in which the transaction takes place, which is usually New York, since both the NYSE and AMEX are there. Transfer taxes are levied only on the seller. In addition, a relatively insignificant federal registration fee of approximately 1¢ per $500 is levied by the SEC on the seller in the transfer of listed securities.

The brokerage commissions on bond transactions differ from those on stock transactions. Brokerage firms typically charge a *minimum* fee of $25 to $30 on a bond transaction regardless of the number of bonds involved. For multiple bond transactions, the brokerage cost per $1,000 corporate bond typically ranges around $10 and is thus decidedly lower than the commissions on stock transactions. The magnitude of brokerage commissions is an important consideration in making security transactions since they tend to raise the overall cost of purchasing securities and lower the overall proceeds from the sale of securities.

Discount Brokers

A growing number of discount brokers—many of which are now affiliated with major financial institutions such as banks and savings and loan associations—are also available for making securities transactions. The use of discount brokers is especially attractive to investors who do not care about obtaining the full array of brokerage services and wish to make transactions at a minimum cost. *Discount brokers* tend to have low overhead operations and to offer no or very limited customer services, such as research reports, advisory services, and so on. Transactions through discount brokers are commonly initiated by calling a toll-free 800 number and placing the desired buy or sell order; the discounter confirms the order by return mail. In order to discourage small orders, most discounters charge a minimum transaction fee ranging between $18 and $35. Depending upon the size of the transaction, discount brokers can save investors between 30 and 80 percent of the commission charged by full-service brokers. Figure 13.3 is an advertisement run in *The Wall Street Journal* by one large discounter; it is interesting to note the absence of any mention of support services offered by the discounter. The small investor who does not need the research and advisory help available from full-service brokers may find the use of discount brokers especially attractive.

Types of Orders

Investors can place several different kinds of orders to make security purchase or sale transactions. The type of order chosen normally depends on the investor's goals and expectations with respect to the given transaction. The three basic types of orders are the market order, the limit order, and the stop-loss order.

Market Order An order to buy or sell stock at the best price available at the time the order is placed is a *market order.* The process by which these orders are transacted is depicted in Figure 13.2. These orders are executed through an auction process which attempts to allow *buy orders* to be filled at the lowest price and *sell orders* to be filled at the

Figure 13.3 An Advertisement for a Discount Broker

Source: Reprinted by permission of Charles Schwab & Co., Inc., San Francisco, California.

highest price, thereby providing the best possible deal to both purchasers and sellers of a security. Because of the speed with which market orders are transacted, the purchaser or seller of a security can be sure that the price at which the order is transacted will be very close to the market price at the time the order is placed.

Limit Order An order to either buy at a specified price or lower or sell at or above a specified price is a *limit order.* When a limit order is placed, the broker transmits the order to a specialist dealing in the given security on the floor of the exchange. The specialist makes a notation in his or her "book" indicating the limit order and limit price. The order is executed as soon as the specified market price or better exists and all other such orders with precedence have been satisfied. The order can be placed to remain in effect until a certain date or until canceled. Also, specialists may periodically clear their books, thereby eliminating all unexecuted limit orders.

Assume, by way of example, that you place a limit order to buy 100 shares of a stock currently selling at $20\frac{1}{2}$ (stock market terminology for $20.50) at a limit price of $20. Once the specialist has cleared all similar orders received before yours and once the market price of the stock has fallen to $20 or less, the order is executed. Of course, your order might expire before the stock drops to $20. Although a limit order can be quite effective, it can also keep you from making a transaction. If, for instance, you wish to buy at $20 or less and the stock price moves from its current $20.50 price to $32 while you are waiting, your limit order has caused you to forgo an opportunity to make a profit of $11.50 ($32 − $20.50) per share, or $1,150. Had you placed a market order, this profit would have been yours. Limit orders for the sale of a stock are similarly disadvantageous when the stock price closely approaches but does not attain the minimum sale limit before dropping substantially. Generally speaking, limit orders are most effective when the price of a stock is known to fluctuate greatly, since there is then a better chance the order will be executed.

Stop-Loss Order An order to sell a stock when the market price reaches or drops below a specified level is a *stop-loss* or *stop order.* Used to protect the investor against rapid declines in stock prices and limit loss, the stop order is placed on the specialist's book and activated when the stop price is reached. At that point in time, the stop order becomes a market order to sell. This means that the stock is offered for sale at the prevailing market price, which is likely to drop below the price at which the order was initiated by the stop. For example, imagine that you own 100 shares of OEF, which is currently selling for $25. Because of the high uncertainty associated with the price movements of the stock, you decide to place a stop order at $21. If the stock price drops to $21, the specialist will sell all your OEF stock at the best price then available. If the market price increases, nothing will be lost by placing the order. It may be advisable to raise the level of the stop and thus lock in a higher level of profit when the price does increase.

Short Sale Transactions

Most security transactions are "long transactions" made in anticipation of increasing security prices in order to profit by buying low and selling high. The *short sale* transaction is made in anticipation of a decline in the security price. Although not as common as long transactions, the short sale is often used by the more sophisticated investor to profit during a period of declining prices.

When investors sell a security short, their broker borrows the security and then sells it on their behalf. The borrowed shares must, of course, be replaced in the future. If the investors can repurchase the shares at a lower price and then return them to the owner, their profit is the difference between the proceeds of the initial sale and the repurchase price. If they repurchase the shares at a price higher than the price at which the security was sold, they sustain a loss. Because the shares sold are borrowed shares, numerous rules and regulations govern the short sale process. One, for example, permits stocks to be sold short only when the last change in the market price of the stock has been upward.

The short sale process can be illustrated using a simple example, which ignores brokerage fees. Assume that Pat Jackson wishes to sell short 100 shares of ABC at $52.50 per share. After Pat meets the necessary requirements, her broker borrows the shares and sells them, obtaining proceeds of $5,250 (100 shares × $52.50/share). If the stock price goes down, as Pat expects, she will repurchase the shares at the lower price. Say the price drops to $40 per share and Pat repurchases the 100 shares. Pat will make a profit since she has been able to replace the shares for $4,000 (100 shares × $40/share), which is below the $5,250 in proceeds obtained from the sale of them. Pat's profit will be $1,250 ($5,250 − $4,000). If on the other hand the stock price rises to, say, $60 per share, Pat will sustain a loss of $750 ([$60.00/share × 100 shares] − [$52.50/share × 100 shares]). Pat, or anyone who sells short, is betting on a price decline. In the preceding example, Pat, of course, would have to pay brokerage fees, which would result in decreased profits or increased losses. Because of the high risk involved in short sales, you should ask your broker to familiarize you with all their possibilities and pitfalls before committing yourself to them.

Borrowing to Purchase Securities

It is possible to borrow a portion of the amount necessary to purchase securities. *Buying on margin,* as this is called, is a common practice that allows investors to use other people's money (borrowed money) in an attempt to heighten their overall return.

Making Margin Purchases The *margin requirements,* which specify the proportion of each dollar used to purchase a security that the investor must provide, are set by the Federal Reserve System (Fed). Most recently, the margin requirement has been around 50 percent, which means that at least 50 percent of each dollar invested must be the investor's; the remaining 50 percent or less may be borrowed. For example, you could purchase $5,000 worth of stock by putting up only $2,500 of your own money and borrowing the remaining $2,500 if the margin requirement is 50 percent. It is believed that the Fed can depress or stimulate, respectively, stock market activity by raising or lowering the margin requirement.

In order to make *margin purchases,* approval of your broker is required. You must also have minimum equity of $2,000 in cash or securities on deposit with your broker and agree to let the shares you purchase be loaned out to short sellers. Once the necessary requirements are met, the brokerage firm will loan you the needed funds and retain the securities you purchase as collateral. Brokerage houses usually charge interest on those funds at a rate .5 to 2 percent above the prime rate of interest (that is, the rate of interest charged on loans to the highest quality business borrower). Brokerage houses often establish their own in-house margin requirements, which are more restrictive than those of the Federal Reserve System. Loans for purchasing securities can also be obtained from your commercial bank, but the Fed's margin requirements still apply, even though they may be a bit more difficult to enforce. In addition, stock exchanges and brokerage houses insist that margin purchasers put up additional money as collateral when the stock price falls to a level at which their equity represents less than 25 percent or so of the current market value. This is called a *maintenance margin* requirement and is illustrated as follows.

Assume that the margin requirement is currently 50 percent but your brokerage firm has an in-house margin requirement of 60 percent. In addition, the maintenance margin requirement is 25 percent and your brokerage firm charges 14 percent interest on margin loans. If you wish to purchase a round lot (100 shares) of LMN, which is currently selling for $50 per share, you can either make the purchase entirely with your own money or you can borrow a portion of the purchase price. The cost of the transaction is $5,000 ($50/share × 100 shares). If you borrow, you will have to put up only $3,000 of your own money (60 percent × $5,000); you can borrow the $2,000 balance ($5,000 purchase price − $3,000 of your money). Table 13.3 compares the rates of return you will receive when margin is not used and when it is in two cases: (1) a $10 per share increase in the stock price to $60 per share and (2) a $10 per share decrease in the stock price to $40 per share. It is assumed the stock was held for one year, and all brokerage commissions are ignored.

As indicated in Table 13.3, the use of margin allows you to increase the return on your investment when the stock price increases. The return on your investment when the stock price increases from $50/share to $60/share is 20 percent without margin and 24 percent with the use of margin. But when the stock price declines from $50 to $40/share, the return on your investment is negative 20 percent without margin and negative 43 percent with margin; the use of margin magnifies the loss on your investment. If the stock price drops below $26.67/share, the total market value of your stock will be less than $2,667 ($26.67 × 100 shares). If you have used margin to borrow $2,000, your investment or equity will be less than $667 ($2,667 market value − $2,000 borrowing). Your investment will thus be less than 25 percent ($667 ÷ $2,667) of the current market value of your stock. Since you will be in violation of the maintenance margin requirement, your broker will probably require you to increase your investment. Clearly, the risks inherent in buying on margin make it vital for you to acquaint yourself thoroughly with the risk-return trade-offs involved before using margin

Table 13.3 The Impact of Margin on Investment Returns

Transaction	Without Margin			With Margin		
Dollars invested						
Your investment	$5,000			$3,000		
Borrowing	0			2,000		
Total purchase (100 shares @ $50)	$5,000			$5,000		
Sell stock for $60/share one year later						
Gross proceeds (100 shares @ $60)	$6,000			$6,000		
Less: Interest @ 14% of borrowing	0			280		
Net proceeds	$6,000			$5,720		
Less: Total investment	5,000			5,000		
Net profit (loss)	$1,000			$ 720		
Return on your investment	$1,000 / $5,000	=	20%	$720 / $3,000	=	24%
Sell stock for $40/share one year later						
Gross proceeds (100 shares @ $40)	$4,000			$4,000		
Less: Interest @ 14% of borrowing	0			280		
Net proceeds	$4,000			$3,720		
Less: Total investment	5,000			5,000		
Net profit (loss)	($1,000)			($1,280)		
Return on your investment	($1,000) / $5,000	=	(20%)	($1,280) / $3,000	=	(43%)

purchases in your investment program. But, on the other hand, the broker's loan may be the least expensive loan available to you; and in this sense, it can be looked upon as another source of consumer credit.

Sources of Investment Information

Information about companies of interest, specific industries, securities markets, and the economy in general can be important for investment decisions. There are thousands of sources of investment information, including raw data on performance, various indexes of market and economic activity, and advisory information about security purchase and sale decisions. Naturally, individuals have personal preferences for certain types of analyses, but as a beginning investor, you should probably concentrate on the more common sources of information such as stockholders' reports, financial news, brokerage firms, subscription services, and investment advisors.

Figure 13.4 A Page from a Stockholder's Report (NCR Corporation, 1981)

The Company

Cover

This year's Annual Report cover depicts video screen images used in designing NCR's new 4,000-bit Non-volatile Random Access Memory. The highest-density non-volatile RAM commercially available, it is one of a number of NCR-developed semiconductor components the Company began marketing during 1981.

NCR Corporation develops, manufactures, markets, installs and services business information processing systems for selected worldwide markets. These markets are primarily in the retail, financial, commercial, industrial, healthcare, education, and government sectors.

The Company offers one of the broadest hardware and software product lines in the industry. NCR computers range from small business systems to powerful general-purpose processors, and are supported by a broad spectrum of terminals, office automation products, peripherals, data communications networks and an extensive library of software products. Supplemental services and products include field engineering, data centers, systems engineering, educational centers, semiconductor components and a comprehensive line of media.

Contents

Source: Courtesy of NCR Corporation, Dayton, Ohio.

Stockholders' Reports

Operating data on individual business firms can be obtained from their stockholders', or annual, reports. *Stockholders' reports* provide a wealth of information, including balance sheets and income statements for the most recent period of operation, as well as summarized statements for several prior years. The balance sheets and income statements for business firms are similar in form to the personal financial statements examined and illustrated in Chapter 2. Many stockholders' reports describe the firm's business activities, development, and plans for future operation and discuss the firm's future outlook. Financial ratios describing past and future performance may also be included among other relevant statistics. The first page of NCR Corporation's 1981 Stockholders' Report is shown in Figure 13.4. A review of the table of contents should make it obvious that a great deal of insight into the company's past, current, and future operations can be obtained by studying the information in the stockholders' report. These reports are sent to all stockholders and can be obtained by anyone directly from the company, through a brokerage firm, or at a large library. They are a free and useful source of investment information.

Financial News

The most common source of financial news, which describes the behavior of the economy, the market, an industry, or a particular company, is the local newspaper. In most cities with a population of 200,000 or more, newspapers devote at least two pages to the presentation of financial items, and, of course, big city newspapers, such as the *New York Times* and the *Los Angeles Times,* provide investors with an abundance of financial information.

Other, more specific sources of financial news include *The Wall Street Journal* and *Barron's.* These financial newspapers, sold by subscription and at newsstands, are devoted in their entirety to articles on the behavior of the economy, markets, industries, and specific companies. The most comprehensive and up-to-date coverage of financial news is provided daily by *The Wall Street Journal. Barron's* concentrates on the week's activities as they relate to the financial markets and individual security prices. Other sources of investment information are business publications such as *Forbes, Fortune,* the *Commercial and Financial Chronicle, Business Week, U.S. News & World Report,* and *Financial World.* In addition, the government publishes magazines containing financially related items that can be found in most libraries or may be subscribed to, sometimes free of charge. The *Federal Reserve Bulletin* and the newsletters of the Federal Reserve Banks are such free sources of information.

Economic Data Summaries and analyses of economic events can be found in all the sources of financial information mentioned previously. Economic data include news items related to the actions of government and their effects on the economy, political and international events as they pertain to the economy, and statistics related to price levels, interest rates, the federal budget, and taxes.

Market Data Most commonly presented in the form of averages, or indexes, *market data* describe the general behavior of the securities markets. The averages and indexes are based on the price movements of a select group of securities over a long period of time. Most frequently cited are those calculated by Dow Jones, Standard & Poor's, the New York Stock Exchange, and the American Stock Exchange.

Figure 13.5 The Dow Jones Industrial Average (DJIA) (Thursday, 24 February 1983)

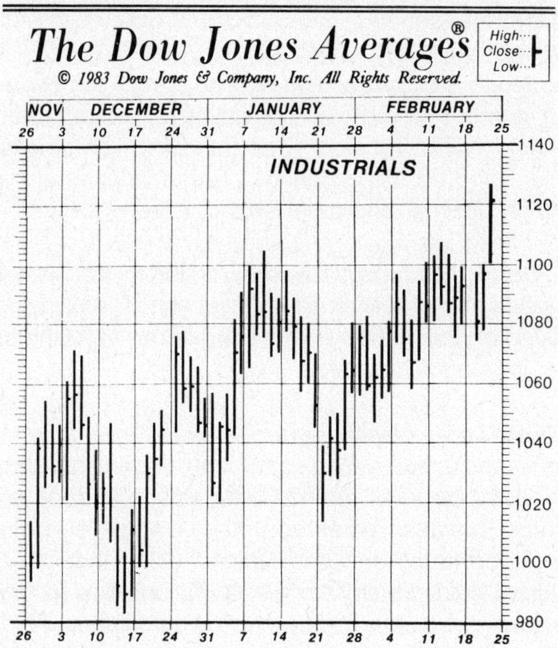

Stocks in the DJIA

Allied Corp	DuPont	Inco	Proctor&Gamble	Westinghouse Electric
Aluminum Co	EastKodak	Int'lBusMach	SearsRoebuck	Woolworth
Amer Brands	Exxon	Int'lHarvest	StdOilCal	
Amer Can	GenElectric	Int'lPaper	Texaco	
Amer Express	GenFoods	Merck	UnionCarbide	
AT&T	GenMotors	MinnesotaM&M	UtdTechnologies	
Beth Steel	Goodyear	Owens-Illinois	USSteel	

Source: The Wall Street Journal, 24 February 1983, p. 41. Reprinted by permission of *The Wall Street Journal.* © Dow Jones & Company, Inc., 1983. All rights reserved.

Dow Jones Averages The Dow consists of four basic averages: (1) an industrial average based on 30 stocks; (2) a transportation average based on 20 stocks; (3) a utility average based on 15 stocks; and (4) a composite average based on 65 industrial, transportation, and utility stocks. Most often cited is the industrial average, which is shown in Figure 13.5 along with a list of the 30 stocks included in it.

Standard & Poor's Indexes Standard & Poor's indexes are similar to the Dow Jones averages except that they consist of a larger number of stocks. There are five basic indexes: (1) an industrial index based on 400 stocks; (2) a transportation index of 20 stocks; (3) a public utility index of 40 stocks; (4) a financial index of 40 stocks; and (5) a composite index for all 500 stocks used to determine the first four indexes. The Standard & Poor's indexes, like the Dow Jones averages, are quoted in *The Wall Street Journal* as well as many other sources of investment information.

New York Stock Exchange Index The New York Stock Exchange publishes a number of indexes consisting of all common stocks, all industrial stocks, all utility stocks, all transportation stocks, and all finance stocks listed on the exchange. These indexes are also cited in *The Wall Street Journal* and other financial news sources.

American Stock Exchange Index Similar to the New York Stock Exchange Index, the American Stock Exchange Index includes indexes of stocks listed on the AMEX and is cited in basically the same places as the other indexes discussed.

Industry Data Local newspapers, *The Wall Street Journal, Barron's,* and various financial news magazines contain industry data. Standard & Poor's *Industry Surveys* provide descriptions and statistics for various industries. *Business Week* and other magazines include indexes of industry performance and price levels. Other industry-related data can be obtained from industry trade associations, one example of which is the American Petroleum Institute for oil companies.

Company Data Articles about the performance and new developments of companies are included in local newspapers, *The Wall Street Journal, Barron's,* and most news magazines. The prices of the securities of all listed companies and the most active over-the-counter stocks are quoted daily in *The Wall Street Journal* and weekly in *Barron's.* Many daily newspapers contain stock price quotations, though in the smaller ones the listing may be selective; in some cases, only stocks of local interest might be included.

The quotations in *The Wall Street Journal* give not only the most recent price of each stock but a great deal of additional information. Figure 13.6 contains a portion of the 24 February 1983 NYSE stock price quotations from *The Wall Street Journal.* The NCR Corporation (NCR) quotation is highlighted in the listing and will be used for illustrative purposes. A glance at the quotation shows that the stock prices are quoted in eighths of a dollar, with the fractions reduced to their lowest common denominator ($\frac{2}{8}$, $\frac{4}{8}$, and $\frac{6}{8}$ are expressed as $\frac{1}{4}$, $\frac{1}{2}$, and $\frac{3}{4}$, respectively). Since the quotation presented was published in the 25 February 1983 *The Wall Street Journal,* the actual transactions reported are those of 24 February 1983. There is a one-day lag in reporting. A closer look at the quotation reveals that the first two columns, labeled High and Low, contain the highest and lowest price at which the stock sold during the past 52 weeks; note that NCR traded between $40\frac{3}{8}$ and $107\frac{1}{4}$ during this period. The figure immediately following the abbrevi-

Figure 13.6 NYSE Stock Quotations (24 February 1983)

52 Weeks High	52 Weeks Low	Stock	Div.	Yld %	P-E Ratio	Sales 100s	High	low	Close	Net Chg.
18 7/8	10	MorseS	.20	1.1	18	158	18 7/8	18 1/4	18 3/8	– 1/8
59 3/4	27 3/4	Morton	1.60	2.7	6	299	58 1/2	57 1/4	58 1/4	+ 1 1/4
115	49 1/4	Motrola	1.60	1.4	24	3106	114	111 1/4	113 1/2	+ 2
39 5/8	24 3/4	MtFuel	2.60	7.0	6	61	37	36	37	+ 1 1/4
19 3/8	9 7/8	Munfrd	.50a	2.6	7	125	u19 1/2	18 3/4	19 1/2	+ 3/4
11 1/4	6 3/8	Mnfd pf	.40	3.5	..	1	u11 1/2	11 1/2	11 1/2	+ 1/4
16	9 1/2	Munsng		..	..	31	12 5/8	12 1/2	12 5/8	+ 3/8
21 7/8	9 5/8	MurphC	1.28	5.9	20	91	21 3/4	21 1/4	21 3/4	+ 1/2
27 3/4	15 1/2	MurpO	1	4.2	6	1668	24 1/2	23 1/2	23 7/8	+ 1/4
23 1/8	13	MurryO	1.20	5.3	14	100	22 3/4	22 1/2	22 1/2	.....
13 7/8	10 1/2	MutOm	1.44e	11.	..	53	13 3/8	13 1/8	13 1/8	– 1/4
14 1/2	6 1/2	MyersL		..	..	182	u14 3/4	14 3/8	14 5/8	+ 3/8
		– N–N–N –								
33 1/4	19 3/4	NBD	2.08	6.8	5	354	30 1/2	29 3/4	30 3/8	.....
50	19 3/8	NBI		..	37	446	50	48	49 3/4	+ 1 3/4
19 3/8	12 1/8	NCH	.72	3.9	16	29	18 1/2	18 1/4	18 1/2	+ 1/4
23 3/8	11 3/4	NCNB	1	4.5	7	1449	22 1/2	21 7/8	22 1/8	– 1/4
107 1/4	40 3/8	NCR	2.60	2.4	12	1334	107 1/4	105 1/2	106 7/8	+ 3/4
30 3/4	14 1/4	NL Ind	1	5.8	6	1630	17 1/4	16 1/4	17 1/4	+ 1
2 7/8	1 1/4	NVF	.08r	3.8	..	1507	2 1/8	1 7/8	2 1/8	+ 1/8
42 3/4	30 1/4	NabscB	2.28	6.7	7	2232	34 1/2	34	34 1/4	+ 1/8
41	29	NbscB pf	3.50	9.7	..	z70	36	35	36	+ 2
34	18	Nalco s	1.12	3.6	22	1138	31 5/8	30 3/4	31 1/2	+ 3/4
15 7/8	7 5/8	Napco	.24	2.4	500	214	10 1/4	9 7/8	10	.....
29 1/2	10 3/4	NaplFd	.80b	2.8	23	105	28 7/8	27 5/8	28 7/8	+ 1 1/2
19 1/8	8 1/2	Nashua		..	..	90	11	10 7/8	11	+ 1/8
24 7/8	15 5/8	NatCan	1	4.1	7	55	24 1/2	24 1/4	24 1/2	+ 1/8
47	28	NCan pf	1.50	3.3	..	1	45 1/2	45 1/2	45 1/2	– 1 1/2
19 3/4	10 1/8	NtCnv s	.54	3.1	13	120	17 3/4	17	17 5/8	+ 1/2
26 7/8	18 7/8	NatDist	2.20	8.9	12	270	25	24 5/8	24 3/4	+ 1/8
18 5/8	13 5/8	NDist pr	1.85	10.	..	2	18 1/8	18 1/8	18 1/8	.....
40 1/8	10	NatEdu		..	18	123	39	38 1/4	38 3/8	– 1/8
33 5/8	25 1/2	NatFG	3.16	9.7	6	9	32 1/2	32 1/4	32 1/2	+ 1/8
29 7/8	16 1/4	NatGyp	1.48	5.7	29	430	26 1/4	25 1/2	26	– 1/8
7 5/8	1 7/8	NtHom		..	..	536	7 1/2	7 1/4	7 1/2	+ 1/4
15 1/4	5 3/8	NMdCre	.46	3.1	16	2767	14 7/8	13 3/4	14 5/8	+ 1/2
30 1/2	12 1/4	NMdEn	.50	1.7	18	1533	29 7/8	28 7/8	29 7/8	+ 1 1/8

Source: The Wall Street Journal, 25 February 1983, p. 40. Reprinted by permission of *The Wall Street Journal,*

ated company name (the ticker symbol used for quotations) is the cash dividend expected to be paid on each share during the year. It is followed by the dividend yield, the ratio of the dividend to the prevailing market price. (*Note:* Since NCR is expected to pay a cash dividend of \$2.60, its dividend yield is 2.4%, which is \$2.60 ÷ \$106.875.) The next entry is the P/E ratio, the current market price divided by the per share earnings for the most recent one year period. Since it is believed to reflect investor expectations concerning the firm's future activities, the P/E ratio is commonly considered by investors in the process of evaluating potential investments. NCR's P/E ratio was 12.

The daily volume follows the P/E ratio; 133,400 shares of NCR were traded 24 February 1983. The next entries, in the High, Low, and Close columns, contain the highest, lowest, and last (closing) price, respectively, at which the stock sold on 24 February. The final column shows the net change between the current day's closing price and the closing price on the preceding day. NCR closed up $\frac{3}{4}$ on 24 February 1983, which means that it must have closed at $106\frac{1}{8}$ on 23 February 1983. Not all price quotations are as easy to read as this one, since often a number of other notations and footnotes are included. In *The Wall Street Journal,* a key explaining notations follows the stock price quotations.

Figure 13.7 Cover of a Prospectus for a Common Stock Issue (Hechinger Company)

PROSPECTUS

1,400,000 Shares

HECHINGER

COMPANY

Common Stock

Of the shares offered hereby, 600,000 will be sold by the Company and 800,000 will be sold by shareholders of the Company. See "Selling Shareholders." The Company will not receive any proceeds from the sale of shares by the Selling Shareholders.

The Common Stock is traded in the over-the-counter market. The highest closing bid price and lowest closing asked price on February 14, 1983, as reported by the National Association of Securities Dealers Automated Quotations System, were $23.25 and $23.75, respectively. See "Price Range of Common Stock."

THESE SECURITIES HAVE NOT BEEN APPROVED OR DISAPPROVED BY THE SECURITIES AND EXCHANGE COMMISSION NOR HAS THE COMMISSION PASSED UPON THE ACCURACY OR ADEQUACY OF THIS PROSPECTUS. ANY REPRESENTATION TO THE CONTRARY IS A CRIMINAL OFFENSE.

	Price to Public	Underwriting Discount	Proceeds to the Company(1)	Proceeds to the Selling Shareholders(1)
Per Share	$23.50	$.92	$22.58	$22.58
Total(2)	$32,900,000	$1,288,000	$13,548,000	$18,064,000

(1) Before deducting expenses estimated at $140,000, of which the Selling Shareholders will pay $35,000.

(2) The Selling Shareholders have granted the Underwriter an option to purchase up to an additional 140,000 shares at $22.58 per share to cover over-allotments. If all of such shares are purchased the total Price to Public, Underwriting Discount and Proceeds to the Selling Shareholders will be increased by $3,290,000, $128,800 and $3,161,200 respectively.

The shares of Common Stock are offered by the Underwriter when, as and if delivered to and accepted by the Underwriter, and subject to certain other conditions. It is expected that delivery of certificates will be made in New York, New York, on or about February 22, 1983.

Merrill Lynch White Weld Capital Markets Group
Merrill Lynch, Pierce, Fenner & Smith Incorporated

February 15, 1983

Source: Hechinger Company, Landover, Maryland.

Brokerage Firms

Brokerage firms provide their clients with investment information prepared by their own research staffs or, in the case of new issues, with prospectuses. The cover of the 28-page prospectus describing a 1983 common stock issue of Hechinger Company is shown in Figure 13.7.

Reports on certain industries or securities prepared by the house's *back-office research* staff may be issued on a scheduled basis and often contain lists of securities within certain industries classified as to the type of investment return they provide and the type of market behavior they are expected to exhibit. Often the brokerage house will issue lists of securities classified as either "buy" or "sell," depending on the research staff's analysis of their anticipated market behavior.

Occasionally brokerage houses issue extensive analyses of specific securities along with recommendations as to the type of investment returns expected and whether or not to buy or sell. Recognizing that brokerage houses receive their income from commissions generated through the purchases and sales, you should be certain that you—not your broker or the house research staff—are making the final decision on how your money is to be invested.

Subscription Services

Several subscription services provide information and recommendations on various industries and specific securities. The services normally cost from 50 to several hundred dollars a year; the cost is tax deductible. They should be subscribed to only by the more active investor. You will normally be able to review such materials at the office of your brokerage firm, and your broker may provide you with relevant portions of these reports. Many university as well as public libraries have these services available for reference use. Probably the best-known financial services are those provided by Standard & Poor's Corporation, Moody's Investors Service, and the Value Line Investment Survey. Each of these companies offers an array of subscription services. Both Standard & Poor's and Moody's publish manuals that contain historical facts and financial data on thousands of corporations. The manuals are broken down into industry groups. On a monthly basis, Standard & Poor's publishes a *Stock Guide* and a *Bond Guide,* each of which summarizes the financial condition of a few thousand issues.

Separate reports on specific companies are another valuable type of subscription service. An example of one such stock report is given for NCR Corporation, in Figure 13.8. This report presents a concise summary of the firm's financial history, its current finances, and its future prospects. Recommended lists of securities broken down into groups on the basis of investment objectives constitute still another type of service. In addition to these common subscription services, numerous *investment letters,* which periodically advise subscribers on the purchase and sale of securities, are available. Through subscription chart books, investors may also obtain graphs showing stock prices and volume over a period of time.

Investment Advisors

Successful investors often establish themselves as professional investors and investment advisors. As advisors, they attempt to develop investment plans consistent with the financial objectives of their clients. Professional investment advisors may operate their own individual business, or they may be associated with large firms that employ research staffs and often publish various subscription materials. Many of

Figure 13.8 A Standard and Poor's Stock Report (NCR Corporation, 28 December 1982)

NCR Corp. 1570T

NYSE Symbol NCR Options on CBOE (Mar-Jun-Sep-Dec)

Price	Range	P-E Ratio	Dividend	Yield	S&P Ranking
Dec. 20'82	1982				
82	97⅞-38¾	10	2.40	2.9%	A–

Summary

This company is one of the largest manufacturers of business information processing systems, with products ranging from large, general-purpose computers and peripherals through electronic cash registers. Earnings for 1983 should rise moderately, benefiting from new products, improving economies in the U.S. and Europe, and possibly more favorable effects from foreign currency exchange rate changes.

Current Outlook

Earnings for 1983 are projected at $9.75 a share, up from $8.75 estimated for 1982.

Dividends at $0.60 quarterly are the minimum expectation.

Revenues for 1983 should increase at a healthy pace, aided by numerous new products and the anticipated improvement in economic conditions in the U.S. and Europe. Margins should widen on the higher volume and cost control measures. A move to breakeven from a loss in the microelectronics business, and a smaller loss in the office systems division, should aid earnings comparisons. More favorable effects from foreign currency exchange rate changes could also benefit earnings. A continued commitment to new product development enhances longer-term prospects.

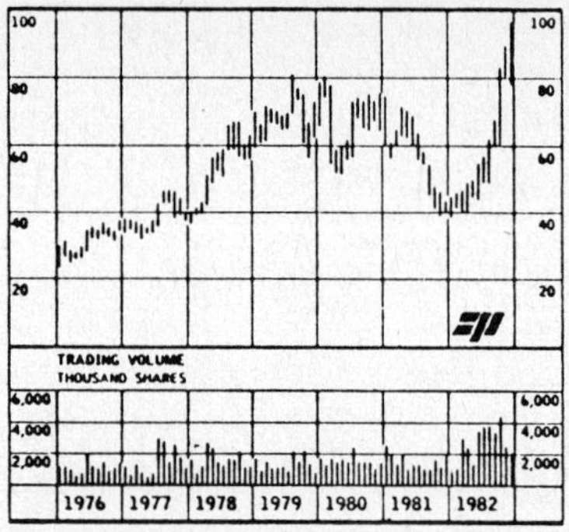

Revenue (Million $)

Quarter:	1982	1981	1980	1979
Mar.	755	733	658	590
Jun.	[4]869	854	788	718
Sep.	840	801	792	707
Dec.		1,045	1,084	988
		3,433	3,322	3,003

Revenues for the nine months ended September 30 1982 rose 3.2%, year to year, as a 3.0% rise in sales and a 5.5% increase in services offset a 2.7% decline in rentals. Profitability was aided by a gain from the repurchase of debentures, benefits from a change in the actuarial assumptions, and much lower interest expense. Pretax income advanced 23%. After taxes at 43.6%, against 41.8%, net income was up 19%, to $5.26 a share from $4.37. Adoption of FAS 52 for foreign currency translations increased earnings for the 1982 period by $0.63 a share.

Common Share Earnings ($)

Quarter:	1982	1981	1980	1979
Mar.	1.14	1.02	0.96	1.13
Jun.	[4]2.25	1.94	2.12	2.23
Sep.	1.87	1.41	2.03	1.74
Dec.		3.35	4.38	3.68
		7.72	9.51	8.78

Important Developments

Sep. '82—NCR developed a set of 32-bit microprocessor chips that computer makers can use to build the "next generation" of small and medium-sized mainframe computer systems.

Apr. '82—NCR said that virtually every major product line would be replaced by new generation products over the next 30 months.

Next earnings report due in late January.

Per Share Data ($)

Yr. End Dec. 31	1982	1981	[1]1980	[1]1979	1978	1977	1976	1975	1974	1973
Book Value	NA	64.68	58.86	51.92	49.39	38.74	34.14	33.15	31.24	28.26
Earnings[2]	NA	7.72	[3]9.51	8.78	[3]7.22	[3]5.35	[3]3.53	[3]2.72	[3]3.67	[3]3.10
Dividends	2.40	2.20	2.00	1.60	1.00	0.80	0.72	0.72	0.72	0.48
Payout Ratio	NA	28%	21%	18%	14%	15%	21%	26%	19%	15%
Prices—High	97⅞	75½	81	81½	67¾	47¼	38	39⅞	40½	46¼
Low	38¾	39¼	51¾	56¾	36¾	32	23⅝	14½	13⅝	26⅞
P/E Ratio—	NA	10-5	9-5	9-6	9-5	9-6	11-7	14-5	11-4	15-9

Data as orig. reptd. 1. Reflects merger or acquisition. 2. Bef. results of discont. opers. of +4.63 in 1978 & spec. item(s) of +0.22 in 1976, +0.27 in 1975. 3. Ful dil.: 9.50 in 1980, 6.90 in 1978, 5.09 in 1977, 3.40 in 1976, 2.65 in 1975, 3.53 in 1974, 3.00 in 1973. 4. Reflects 9 mos. reclassification for 6 mos. NA-Not Available. d-Deficit.

Standard NYSE Stock Reports
Vol. 49/No. 248/Sec. 11

December 28, 1982

Standard & Poor's Corp.
25 Broadway, NY, NY 10004

the better-known investment advisors limit their business to a select group of wealthy individuals who have similar investment objectives, while others accept clients with diverse objectives. Generally, professional advisors do not accept clients with investment assets of less

1570T

NCR Corporation

Income Data (Million $)

Year Ended Dec. 31	Revs.	Oper. Inc.	% Oper. Inc. of Revs.	Cap. Exp.	Depr.	Int. Exp.	Net Bef. Taxes	Eff. Tax Rate	Net Inc.	% Net Inc. of Revs.
1981	3,433	586	17.1%	362	244	72.5	[2]363	41.3%	208	6.1%
[1]1980	3,322	683	20.6%	371	227	55.9	[2]469	43.0%	255	7.7%
[1]1979	3,003	626	20.8%	322	210	39.7	[2]449	47.0%	235	7.8%
[5]1978	2,611	561	21.5%	220	186	47.8	[2]365	43.6%	194	7.4%
1977	2,522	496	19.7%	196	205	58.6	[2]269	43.9%	144	5.7%
1976	2,313	361	15.6%	219	179	59.6	[2]174	45.5%	[4] 90	3.9%
1975	2,166	316	14.6%	271	161	63.8	[2]124	43.5%	[4] 66	3.0%
1974	1,979	353	17.8%	240	145	55.5	[2]173	46.9%	87	4.4%
1973	1,816	312	17.2%	186	146	48.2	[2]142	44.0%	72	4.0%
1972	1,558	197	12.7%	153	142	46.1	[2] d98	NM	d60	NM

Balance Sheet Data (Million $)

Dec. 31	Cash	Current Assets	Current Liab.	Ratio	Total Assets	Ret. on Assets	Long Term Debt	Common Equity	Total Cap.	% LT Debt of Cap.	Ret. on Equity
1981	182	2,172	1,099	2.0	3,387	6.2%	300	1,853	2,221	13.5%	11.7%
1980	119	2,237	1,200	1.9	3,366	8.0%	322	1,704	2,091	15.4%	15.9%
1979	148	1,947	965	2.0	2,918	8.5%	345	1,476	1,877	18.4%	16.9%
1978	248	1,781	815	2.2	2,596	7.9%	348	1,298	1,700	20.5%	16.7%
1977	307	1,563	698	2.2	2,341	6.1%	514	1,022	1,582	32.5%	14.9%
1976	310	1,480	704	2.1	2,312	3.8%	626	887	1,554	40.3%	10.3%
1975	189	1,358	650	2.1	2,195	3.0%	664	797	1,498	44.3%	8.5%
1974	56	1,358	759	1.8	2,110	4.4%	541	731	1,307	41.4%	12.5%
1973	121	1,133	577	2.0	1,834	4.1%	539	643	1,216	44.4%	11.7%
1972	107	995	512	1.9	1,689	NM	538	579	1,146	47.0%	NM

Data as orig. reptd. 1. Reflects merger or acquisition. 2. Incl. equity in earns. of nonconsol. subs. 3. Bef. results of disc. oper. in 1978 & spec. item(s) in 1976, 1975. 4. Reflects accounting change. 5. Excl. disc. opers. NM-Not Meaningful. d-Deficit.

Business Summary

NCR manufactures business information processing systems primarily for retail, financial, commercial, industrial, healthcare, education and government markets. Revenues in recent years were divided as follows:

	1981	1980
Equipment sales	50%	51%
Equipment rentals	10%	10%
Services	30%	29%
Forms, supplies & other	10%	11%

Equipment revenues (sales and rentals) principally derived from computer systems (50%), retail terminals and systems (22%), financial terminals and systems (20%) and general purpose terminals and systems (8%).

Operations are conducted worldwide. Business outside the U.S. provided 52% of revenues and 37% of operating income in 1981.

NCR makes computers ranging from small business systems to large general purpose processors. A broad spectrum of terminals, office automations products, peripherals, data communications networks and software products is also available. Other services and products include field engineering, data centers, systems engineering, educational centers, semiconductor components and a line of media, such as business forms and microfiche products.

Dividend Data

Dividends have been paid since 1934. A dividend reinvestment plan is available.

Amt. of Divd. $	Date Decl.	Ex-divd. Date	Stock of Record	Payment Date
0.60	Jan. 20	Mar. 15	Mar. 19	Apr. 30'82
0.60	May 19	Jun. 14	Jun. 18	Jul. 30'82
0.60	Jul. 21	Sep. 13	Sep. 17	Oct. 29'82
0.60	Nov. 17	Dec. 13	Dec. 17	Jan. 28'83

Next dividend meeting: mid-Jan. '83.

Capitalization

Long Term Debt: $334,580,000.

Minority Interest: $58,200,000.

$1.25 Conv. Preferred Stock: 12,486 shs. ($5 par); conv. into one com.

Common Stock: 26,560,176 shs. ($5 par). Institutions hold about 66%. Shareholders: 37,251.

Office—1700 South Patterson Blvd., Dayton, Ohio 45479. Tel—(513) 445-5000. Pres—C. E. Exley, Jr. Secy—J. E. Rambo. Treas—N. A. Cocke. Investor Contact—G. R. Stechmesser. Dirs—W. S. Anderson (Chrmn), C. A. Anderson, W. G. Bowen, G. A. Costanzo, C. E. Exley, Jr., C. H. Hardesty, Jr., H. Holiday, Jr., J. J. Horan, D. L. McIntosh, C. S. Morawetz, J. E. Rambo, E. J. Schlegel, R. L. Terrell. Transfer Agent & Registrar—AmeriTrust [illegible], Cleveland, Ohio. Incorporated in Md. in 1926.

Information has been obtained from sources believed to be reliable, but its accuracy and completeness are not guaranteed. Sheila Peck

Source: Standard and Poor's Corporation, *Standard NYSE Stock Reports,* 28 December 1982, p. 1570T. Reprinted by permission.

than $50,000, and the more elite advisors are likely to require considerably larger holdings. Annual fees for advisory services, which may involve the complete management of the client's money, are likely to range from 0.25 percent to 2 percent of the money managed.

A recent trend is for the large commercial banks, such as First National City Bank of New York, and other independent advisory services to provide investment advice to those with investment assets of $5,000 to $10,000 for fees in the 1 to 2 percent range. In any case, there is no guarantee that investment advisors will perform better than their clients could independently. Care should be taken in the selection of advisors to assure that their investment planning is based on their clients' financial objectives and not the advisors'.

Investment Strategies

Without a plan for attaining your broad investment objectives, your investment activities may be more of a hobby than an integral part of your overall financial plans. It is, therefore, of utmost importance that you carefully formulate strategies for selecting securities that fit your investment objectives. Your investment activities must be timed properly in order to take advantage of changes in the securities markets. This portion of the chapter describes some of the key aspects of investment strategy.

Investment Targets

The investment objectives detailed in Chapter 12 are achieved more easily when investment targets are specified; one such target was stated as: "To accumulate $10,000 over a 10-year period by investing in bonds." Another specific target might be: "To earn an 8-percent after-tax return by investing in a portfolio evenly split between blue-chip and speculative stocks." It is generally advisable not only to specify the level of return and type of securities, but also to specify the *form* in which the *total return* is expected to be received. This makes it easier to select securities that are consistent with established objectives. The two basic forms of investment return are dividend (or interest) yield and capital gains.

Dividend Yield The *dividend yield* on a common stock represents the percent return provided by the dividends paid. It is calculated by dividing the per share dividend by the prevailing market price. Dividends provide a form of current income, which often appeals to investors whose goal is to receive retirement or supplementary income from their investments. Take, for example, the stock of the RST Company, which is currently selling for $60 a share and paid cash dividends of $2.40 per share during the past year. Its dividend yield would be 4 percent ($2.40 ÷ $60). Similarly, as discussed in Chapter 12, bond yields—current yield and yield-to-maturity—can be used to assess bond returns. Yields are published in a variety of outlets, including *The Wall Street Journal* (which presents current yields). The important point to remember is that if periodic income is one of your investment goals, you should select securities that offer high dividend or interest yields.

Capital Gains As was indicated in Chapter 4, capital gains result from selling a security for a profit. Many people purchase securities, especially common stock, for this kind of long-run profit rather than to provide income in the form of dividends or interest. For an example of a capital gain, assume that the RST Company stock was purchased for $56.60 and held for one year, at the end of which it was sold for $60.00. Excluding brokerage costs and personal taxes, this would produce a $3.40 capital gain ($60.00 − $56.60). Expressed as a percentage of the original purchase price, this gain would represent a 6 percent ($3.40 ÷ $56.60) return, which, when combined with the 4 percent dividend yield calculated earlier, would result in a 10 percent total return on the investment. Some *speculative traders* purchase stocks with the intention of gaining on the day-to-day fluctuations in price. *Day traders* are gamblers, and their strategies are risky in the extreme.

The total return on a security should be evaluated in light of your investment objectives. Since it is often difficult to select securities that provide only dividends or only capital gains, you will be wise to recognize and measure the contribution each security might make to your overall investment return. Careful selection of securities on this basis should result in a mix of dividend (or interest) yield and capital gains appropriate to your objectives.

Security Analysis

Various kinds of analyses—of the economy, of the securities markets, of the industry of concern, and of the firm on which the security is issued—can help in the evaluation of the quality and general desirability of a security investment. Most such analyses are done by the research departments of large brokerage firms.

Economic Analysis The first step in security analysis is assessing the present and future behavior of the economy. By studying certain economic indicators, expectations can be formulated. Actions of the government in regard to spending, taxes, and interest rates are important factors that must be considered. Although actual economic outcomes cannot be predicted, the study of various statistics and economic forecasts can aid in the judicious selection of securities. For instance, during a recessionary period, bonds may be more attractive; while in an expansionary period, stocks generally have greater appeal. In fact, specific bonds or stocks chosen for investment will depend on anticipated economic activity.

Market Analysis The second step in analyzing a security is an examination of the securities markets—both their current state and movements anticipated in them. If a recession is predicted, a bear, or downward, market would be expected; if inflation is anticipated, a bull, or upward, market would be anticipated. The analysis of market behavior is vital to those who are interested in capital gains and do not necessarily wish to hold securities for a long period of time. Forecasts of security market behaviors based on the relevant stock averages, such as the Dow Jones Industrial Average, can be obtained either from a broker or through various subscription services. Expectations about the behavior of the securities markets can significantly affect an investor's choice of stock or bond investments.

Industry Analysis The goal of industry analysis, which is the third stage in security analysis, is to determine the general behavior of a particular industry under various economic and market conditions. This is accomplished by studying the past behavior of the industry and drawing some conclusions about its future behavior, as well as by examining whether the demand for its products and services enhances its potential success. These findings should be related to the results of the economic analysis in order to determine whether or not the performance of the given industry over the near future will be favorable. Also, the market behavior of the securities of companies within the industry during periods of economic activity similar to that which is forecast should be examined to determine the future attractiveness of the industry's securities. Often security analysts will analyze a number of industries in order to determine the best industry to invest in under the economic circumstances they expect will evolve. These industry analyses are generally available from your stockbroker.

Company Analysis Once an industry has been determined to have investment potential, the analyst will look at the securities of companies within the industry to determine the "best" investments. Two of the variables investors and security analysts concern themselves with are earnings per share and the price/earnings ratio.

Earnings per Share As indicated in Chapter 12, the amount earned by the firm for each share of common stock outstanding is the *earnings per share (EPS).* Investors concern themselves with both the reported and the projected EPS value. Historic, current, and sometimes projected values for EPS for stocks of major interest are periodically reported in *The Wall Street Journal* and other financial publications. Individuals interested in investing in the common stock of a certain company should evaluate the level and expected trend of its EPS; in general, the higher the EPS, the more attractive the securities are as investment opportunities.

Price/Earnings Ratio Another popular tool in security analysis, the *price/earnings ratio (P/E)* is calculated by dividing the current market price per share by the most recent annual earnings per share (see Chapter 12). The P/E ratio is also cited in numerous places. It is generally believed that the higher the P/E, the more confidence investors have in the future of the firm, and vice versa. This relationship stems from the fact that the higher the P/E ratio, the more investors are paying for expected future benefits and the less they are paying for current earnings. P/E ratios in recent times have been in the range from 5 to 20, although during periods of economic expansion, the stocks of growth firms such as Apple Computer have been known to sell for more than 30 times earnings.

The analysis of P/E ratios as part of the stock selection process is more or less standard, since a true reading of a firm's stock cannot really be obtained by looking at its price or earnings separately. The P/E ratio offers some insight into stock price behavior because it considers both price and earnings movements simultaneously. For example, when the stock price increases from $40 to $60 per share, while annual earnings per share increase from $2.50 to $4.00, the P/E ratio decreases from 16 ($40 ÷ $2.50) to 15 ($60 ÷ $4). In this case, although the earnings per share have increased from $2.50 to $4.00, the per share price has not increased correspondingly, and so the P/E ratio has declined. Basically, the P/E ratio of a stock reflects the general sentiment of those in the marketplace toward it as an investment.

In short, the formal process of security analysis attempts to link expected economic behavior to market activity and then to the behavior of individual industries and the securities of the firms within them. The type of analysis performed by the small investor is limited primarily to company analysis. This normally involves a study of price, earnings, and the relationship between them as reflected in the price/earnings ratio. A basic investments text or materials available from your stockbroker will provide you with a more detailed discussion of the various aspects of security analysis.

Security Selection

Although numerous techniques of analysis exist for selecting security investments, small investors normally make their investment decisions without resorting to very sophisticated analytical procedures. Stockbrokers' reports, prospectuses for new issues, research studies provided by brokers, and other information can help you become familiar with proposed security investments and analyze the basic financial data on earnings, dividends, and price behavior. Once you feel comfortable with a proposed investment and find other sources (broker, research studies, friends) who agree with your selection, you should make the investment. Of course, no matter how much formal analysis you use in the selection process, there is no guarantee that you will pick a winner.

Security Portfolios

Sophisticated investors often devote their attention to constructing diversified *portfolios* of securities. Such portfolios consist of stocks and bonds selected not only for the returns expected but also for their combined risk-return behaviors. According to the *theory of diversification,* combining securities with dissimilar risk-return characteristics can build a portfolio of securities with an acceptable and relatively certain return. This type of portfolio selection, however, can become quite complex and is generally practiced only by the large financial institutions. Nonetheless, small investors can and should combine securities with different earnings behaviors to reduce the risk in their investments. For example, investing in the stock of a meat packer and the stock of a flour mill may provide a relatively stable level of earnings if certain industry patterns persist—when meat sales increase flour sales ordinarily decrease and vice versa.

In recent years, investments researchers have shown that by naively diversifying one's investments through random selection of securities to be included in a portfolio, some amount of risk reduction can be achieved. For the small investor with a moderate amount of money to invest, this means that the investment in a number of securities—rather than a single security—should be beneficial. The payoff from diversification comes in the form of reduced risk without significant impact on return. For example, Sarah James, who has $2,000 invested in Stock A, might find that by selling two thirds of her holdings and using the proceeds to buy equal amounts of Stocks B and C, she will continue to earn the same level of return—say, 10 percent—while greatly decreasing the associated risk. Investors are advised by many counselors not to put all their eggs in one basket and to hold portfolios diversified across a broad segment of business—manufacturing, services, retail and wholesale trade, and others—rather than a single security. In short, diversify!

Timing Investment Decisions

Several basic techniques can be used for timing investment decisions. Three of the more common ones are dollar cost averaging, formula timing, and the chartist approach.

Dollar Cost Averaging To use the *dollar cost averaging* approach, investors purchase a fixed dollar amount of a security at specified times. This tends to keep the cost of the security at an average level over its broad price cycle. For example, suppose you operated on a strategy of investing $300 per quarter (every three months) in the stock of BCE Company, as indicated in Table 13.4. Although the price per share of your stock ranged from $10 to $25, the average cost per share at the end of the year was $15.58 ($1,200 ÷ 77 shares). Your strategy allowed you to purchase more shares when the price was low and thus

Table 13.4 Dollar Cost Averaging Example

Quarter	Amount Invested (1)	Price per Share (2)	Number of Shares [(1) ÷ (2)] (3)
1	$ 300	$25	12
2	300	15	20
3	300	10	30
4	300	20	15
Total	$1,200		77

average out the purchase of the smaller number of shares when the price was high. Had you invested the total $1,200 in quarter 1, you would have been able to purchase only 48, instead of 77, shares. Dollar cost averaging is best used as part of a long-run investment strategy by individuals who are willing to make a fixed-dollar investment at specified times.

Formula Timing By establishing certain indicators for buying or selling, *formula timing* plans attempt to force an investor to buy low and sell high. They often rely on price/earnings ratios as signals. When the P/E of a given security drops to a certain point, that is a signal to buy; while when it rises to a predetermined level, that is a signal to sell. For example, the rule might be to buy BCE when its P/E ratio is less than 8 and to sell it if its P/E ratio is greater than 18. The use of formula plans is intended to introduce some degree of rationality into investment activities. The basic principle is to substitute these decision rules for human judgment, since people have a tendency to wait too long, thereby losing some of the potential profit, when it comes to purchasing or selling a security. Formula plans may also be based on variables other than the price/earnings ratio, such as price, earnings, economic indicators, or proportions of securities held. Care should be taken in making formula plans to be sure that the formulas established are consistent with the investor's objectives.

Chartist Approach Discussed in the preceding chapter, the *chartist approach* is a type of formula plan founded on charting trends in security prices and stock market averages. Chartists prespecify, on the basis of given chart formations, when purchase or sale actions are to be taken. The chartist theories and formations are well developed, and there are numerous books on charting available to the interested investor. There also is a great deal of disagreement among investment analysts about the effectiveness of charts. Evidence is growing that buy-and-hold strategies do just as well as chart-directed purchases and sales, particularly when brokerage commissions are considered.

Special Security Purchase Arrangements

A number of special arrangements exist whereby investors can purchase stocks. The more common of these include stock purchase options and plans, dividend reinvestment plans, monthly investment plans (MIP), and investment clubs.

Stock Purchase Options and Plans As part of their compensation, key employees of a corporation are often given an opportunity to purchase a specified number of shares of the corporation's stock at a price set above the prevailing market price when the option is granted. At issue, *stock purchase options* therefore have no value. The firm's purpose in issuing them is to motivate employees to work hard and move the firm forward so that the market price of the stock will rise above the option price and, therefore, the option will have value. A few years after the issue, the employees may be able to exercise their options and purchase the stock at a price below its market value. They can then either sell it for an immediate profit or hold it to achieve further gains from the future price appreciation. The gain on the sale, if the stock is held the required length of time, would be a long-term capital gain, which would be taxed at a lower rate than ordinary income. (See Chapter 4 for discussion of this tax treatment.) These options, if offered to you, may provide a very attractive source of income.

Stock purchase plans allow all employees to buy into the firm. These plans often include some kind of arrangement for the employer to make matching contributions toward the purchase of shares by the employees. The price at which shares are purchased is normally based on some type of average. Employees are often required to hold the stock purchased for a specified period of time before selling it. Like stock purchase options, purchase plans serve as a form of employee compensation, as well as to stimulate employee interest in the firm's success.

Dividend Reinvestment Plans A growing number of firms offer *dividend reinvestment plans,* an approach long used by mutual funds (discussed in Chapter 14), which enable stockholders to acquire shares—even fractional shares—at little or no transaction cost. Sometimes discounts are even offered, especially among the utilities. Starting in 1982, shareholders of public utilities such as electric companies, telephone companies, and natural gas distributors gained a new tax break if they participated in the utility's dividend reinvestment program. This is because up to $750 in reinvested dividends ($1,500 for married taxpayers filing joint returns) may be excluded from current income taxes. Normally cash dividends are taxed as ordinary income, except for the $100 or $200 dividend exclusion (see Chapter 4). When the acquired utility shares are sold, a capital gains tax may have to be paid if the proceeds are in excess of the original purchase price. However, the much lower capital gains tax rate results in a smaller tax bite than would have been incurred if the utility dividends were taxed as ordinary income. The existence of dividend reinvestment plans—especially in the case of public utility stocks—may enhance those securities' appeal for inclusion in one's portfolio.

Monthly Investment Plans A form of dollar cost averaging and a type of forced savings, the *monthly investment plan (MIP)* is an arrangement that benefits long-term investors. For each plan, a monthly or quarterly investment, typically in the range of $50 to $1,000, is made in the same NYSE security on a regular basis. Since a fixed dollar amount is invested periodically, fractional shares are issued as needed. For example, if you invest $100 per month in BCE and during a given month pay $16 per share, you would receive 6.25 shares of BCE ($100 ÷ $16/share) for that month. Certain rules and regulations for participating in these plans are established by the various brokerage firms. Since brokerage commissions are charged on transactions, the broker has the option of discontinuing the plan if the participant skips a payment. If your investment goal is long-run price appreciation, you may wish to look into the MIPs and other similar arrangements available at brokerage firms and large commercial banks.

Investment Clubs *Investment clubs* are often formed by a group of people in order to pool their knowledge in the hope of making better investment decisions and to further educate members on how to make investments. Club members are required to make scheduled contributions into the club's treasury. The resultant pool of funds is then invested in securities that are mutually agreed on by the club's members. A legal partnership agreement binds and protects club members. The clubs generally attempt to make investments of good quality aimed at providing favorable returns over the long run; they normally do not speculate in high-risk securities. Generally, various members of the club are responsible for analyzing certain possible stock or bond investments and presenting their findings to the membership. Through this process, the club selects what it believes to be the best investments given the overall investment goals of its membership. These clubs provide an excellent opportunity for the inexperienced investor to learn more about the investment world and how to make intelligent investment decisions. The National Association of Investment Clubs (NAIC) offers various publications and regional and national meetings through which club members can learn new investment techniques and strategies. Your broker can assist you in forming or becoming a member of an investment club. For the beginning investor, club membership is an excellent idea.

Some Investment Guidelines

The small investor often can do as well as professionals if simple—but very sound—procedures are followed. They do not guarantee success, but neither can the professional guarantee that he or she will continuously earn superior returns despite the general behavior of the economy and securities markets. In the long run, adherence to these guides should earn you a reasonable return relative to the risk you are willing to take. Six guidelines are:

1. You must have adequate diversification, which means an equal investment in no fewer than 10 different securities representing a cross-section of business. If you lack adequate funds to achieve this diversification, then stick to mutual funds (to be discussed in the next chapter) until you have enough. While the absolute amount of funds needed will vary depending upon what securities you buy, a broad rule would be that at least $10,000 is required. This leads to a $1,000 investment in each security, which means you are probably buying odd lots and incurring the slightly higher commissions. If you do not trade frequently, that will not be a severe penalty.
2. Buy securities only after your research indicates they have good investment quality. Your research may consist of nothing more than reading investment advice in financial publications, such as *Barron's* or Standard and Poor's. If the advisory service has a good reputation, it will forewarn you of both the risks and potential returns in a security, making your selection easier.
3. Be extremely cautious of "hot tips"; more often than not, they are cold news items. By the time they reach you, they are often useless.
4. Stick to a disciplined plan for purchasing securities and try to reinvest dividends or interest as they are earned. Do not try to forecast the market to buy at lows and sell at highs—you will probably end up doing just the reverse.
5. Beware the philosophy, "If I don't sell a security that is below what I paid for it, then I don't have a loss." Nothing is farther from the truth: you have a loss the moment the market price of your security dips below the purchase price. The only relevant question is whether or not the security is worth holding; if your research indicates the contrary, then sell it and take the loss, which is better than holding it for even greater losses. Studies have shown that many first-time investors are eager to take profits but reluctant to take losses. As you might suspect, after a while their trading activity shows a large number of small realized gains and one or two huge unrealized losses that far outweigh all the gains; these investors still think they are doing "pretty good" in the market, since they have not *taken* any losses.
6. Do not hesitate to take losses for tax purposes. (This is closely related to point 5 above.) Suppose you bought Gulf Oil because you thought the petroleum industry would increase in profitability in the

future. Five months later the situation has changed and, while you are still optimistic about the long-run future for the industry, your investment is down $2,000. Suppose you now think that Exxon is just as likely as Gulf to benefit in future industry growth and it does not matter to you whether you own Gulf or Exxon. Should you switch? By all means! The proceeds from selling Gulf can be reinvested in Exxon to maintain your position in the industry. In the process of taking the loss on Gulf you will also reduce your income taxes (by $600, if you are in a 30% tax bracket). It would be a mistake to sell a security *only* for tax purposes, but in instances such as the one given here, it would be a mistake not to.

Like most rules in life, the six guidelines are easier to give than to follow. When you start investing, you will notice that emotions often get in the way of good common sense. Your primary objective is to keep that from happening.

Summary

Investment transactions take place in securities markets. They include the capital market, where long-term securities are bought and sold, and the money market, where short-term securities are traded. New issues of securities are traded in the primary market, while the resale of securities takes place in the secondary market. Investment banking firms often underwrite new security issues. A prospectus is normally prepared and distributed to interested parties when a new security issue is made. Securities are listed and traded on an organized exchange or are traded in the over-the-counter market. The securities markets are regulated by the Securities and Exchange Commission, as well as various state securities commissions. The conditions of the securities markets are described as "bull" or "bear" depending on whether the security prices in general are rising or falling.

Stock and bond transactions can be made through stockbrokers, who are paid a commission to purchase and sell securities for their customers. Aside from executing purchase and sell orders, stockbrokers perform numerous other services for their clients. For persons not desiring other brokerage services, the use of a discount broker to execute purchase and/or sales transactions can provide considerable brokerage fee savings. Although the standard unit in which securities are traded is 100 shares, security transactions can be made in smaller quantities. The basic types of security orders include the market order, the limit order, and the stop-loss order. Some investors sell short in the hope of gaining from an expected decrease in the security's price. Customers who meet certain legal and brokerage firm requirements can establish margin accounts enabling them to borrow money in order to finance a portion of their security purchases.

Information for use in making investment decisions can be obtained from a wide range of sources, including stockholders' reports, the financial news, and business publications. Additional investment information can be obtained from stock averages and indexes, from brokerage firms, through any of a number of subscription services, or from an investment advisor. Before formulating an investment strategy, investment targets, which are an integral part of an individual's overall personal financial plan, should be established. The dividend yield and capital gains from a security are used to compute its total return. The formal security analysis process includes an analysis of the economy, the market, the industry, and the company. Sophisticated security analyses are normally performed by the back-office research staffs of large brokerage firms. Earnings per share and price/earnings ratios are the variables most commonly considered when analyzing securities.

Selection of securities should be based on inputs from the various sources of investment information, the findings of security analyses, and the individual's investment goals. Investors attempt to create portfolios of securities thereby gaining the advantages of diversification. The common techniques for timing investment decisions include dollar cost averaging, formula timing, and the chartist approach. A number of special security purchase arrangements, such as stock purchase options, stock purchase plans, dividend reinvestment plans, monthly investment plans, and investment clubs, are available to those who qualify and are interested. Useful guidelines for the small investor are to diversify, research potential securities, avoid so-called hot tips, stick to a disciplined purchase plan, take losses when a rebound seems unlikely, and consider the timing of losses for tax purposes.

Investment Companies, Real Estate, and Other Investment Vehicles 14

Investment planning is concerned with finding investment vehicles possessing risk-return characteristics consistent with your financial objectives. In order to fully understand the investment opportunities available to you, you need to complement your understanding of the basics of stock and bond investments with a knowledge of the functions, characteristics, and risk-return behavior of investment companies, real estate, and other investment vehicles, such as commodity futures, financial futures, options, gold, and so on. Each of these media offers risk-return opportunities that you may not be able to obtain from stock and bond investments.

The investor who is interested in receiving the benefit of professional portfolio management but does not have sufficient funds to purchase a diversified portfolio of securities may find the purchase of investment company shares attractive. An *investment company* is a company that owns a diversified portfolio of securities professionally chosen on the basis of certain specified criteria. The best-known type of investment company is the *mutual fund.* Sometimes real estate is purchased as an investment. Although there may be some similarities between housing and investment purchases of real estate, persons interested in real estate investments must justify them not on the basis of need but rather on strict economic grounds. Investors willing to take higher risks in expectation of higher returns may find commodity futures, financial futures, or options attractive. Other attractive forms of investment include precious minerals, such as gold, silver, and diamonds, and collectibles, such as stamps, coins, antiques, art, books, autographs, and so on. The costs, risk-return characteristics, institutional structure, and methods for making transactions in investment company shares, real estate, commodity futures, financial futures, options, precious minerals, and collectibles are the subject of this chapter.

Investment Company Fundamentals

An *investment company* can be viewed as a financial institution that gathers funds from numerous investors. It uses these funds to purchase securities issued by a variety of corporations. The investors actually receive shares of stock in the company in exchange for their money. Since the sole function of the investment company is to invest

Figure 14.1 Basic Investment Company Structure

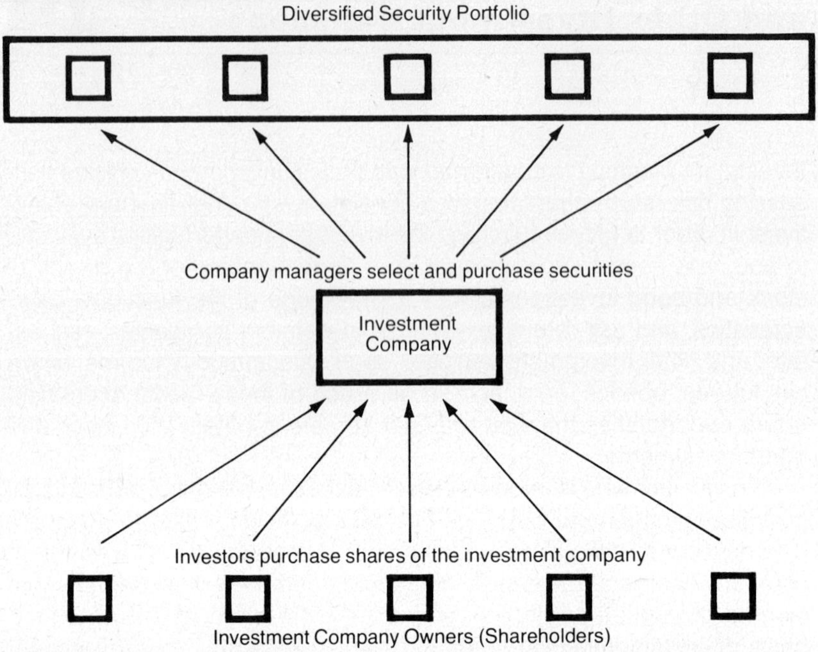

in the securities of other companies, the company shareholder is in effect indirectly investing in a wide variety of securities. The main appeal of the investment company for the investor is based on the fact that one share of its stock gives the holder a claim on a diversified portfolio of securities, while in the market, the amount of money paid for that share might not permit the purchase of more than one share of a single stock. The professional portfolio managers employed by the company to lend their expertise to the selection of good security investments can be another advantage of the investment company. The basic investment company structure is depicted in Figure 14.1.

Types of Investment Companies

There are two basic types of investment companies: in *closed-end companies* the number of ownership shares is limited, while in *open-end companies* it is not. In both, the managers of the company exercise the voting rights of shares held, and investment activities are regulated either directly or indirectly by various governmental agencies, such as the Securities and Exchange Commission.

Closed-End Companies Only a small portion of investment company activity is accounted for by closed-end companies. They issue a fixed number of shares, which may be listed and traded on an organized security exchange, and therefore have only a fixed amount of funds to invest in various securities. Once issued, their shares can be purchased or sold only in the securities markets. Shares are traded in the same fashion as for any corporate stock; brokerage commissions must be paid on purchase and sale transactions. Note that closed-end investment company share prices are affected not only by the value of the securities that underlie them but also by the general behavior of the securities markets. Some of the better-known closed-end investment companies are Lehman Corporation and Madison Fund.

Open-End Companies (Mutual Funds) The dominant type of investment company is the open-end or *mutual fund.* These funds issue as many shares as are demanded and thus, unlike the closed-end companies, do not have a fixed amount to invest. A few of the better-known mutual funds are those of the Dreyfus Group, Oppenheimer Funds, and Putnam Funds. The *open-end investment company* will sell or buy back its own shares at a price that is based on the current value of the securities the fund owns. The price at which it buys back its own shares is referred to as the *net asset value (NAV) per share.* This value is calculated at least once a day and represents the worth of a share in the fund; it is calculated as shown in Equation 14.1.

$$\text{NAV} = \frac{\begin{pmatrix}\text{market value of all} \\ \text{securities in fund}\end{pmatrix} - \begin{pmatrix}\text{liabilities of} \\ \text{the fund}\end{pmatrix}}{\text{number of fund shares outstanding}} \tag{14.1}$$

Application of Equation 14.1 can be illustrated with a simple example. Assume at the end of the day, the value of all assets held by the OPQ Fund was \$10,500,000, the fund's liabilities resulting primarily from management and operating costs were \$500,000, and there are 400,000 shares in the fund outstanding. Substituting into Equation 14.1, the net asset value (NAV) per share is:

$$\text{NAV} = \frac{\$10{,}500{,}000 - \$500{,}000}{400{,}000} = \frac{\$10{,}000{,}000}{400{,}000} = \$25$$

Therefore, the current worth of a share in the OPQ Fund is \$25.

Figure 14.2 is an excerpt of the mutual fund quotations reported for Thursday, 24 February 1983, in *The Wall Street Journal* on Friday, 25 February 1983. An explanation of the values reported is given at the top of the figure. The quotation for the Dreyfus Fund, which is highlighted, indicates that a share of this fund will cost \$14.89 (with the maximum commission included), while it can be sold for its NAV of \$13.62, which is 15 cents higher than the NAV for the previous day.

Figure 14.2 Mutual Fund Quotations (24 February 1983)

Mutual Funds

Thursday, February 24, 1983

Price ranges for investment companies, as quoted by the National Association of Securities Dealers. NAV stands for net asset value per share; the offering includes net asset value plus maximum sales charge, if any.

	NAV	Offer Price	NAV Chg.
Delaware Group.			
Decatr	14.73	16.10	+ .16
Delchs F	7.99	8.73	+ .03
TxFr Pa	6.82	7.14	+ .02
Delw Fd	21.30	23.28	+ .19
Delta Td	13.82	15.10	+ .21
Destiny Fd	12.80	(z)	+ .27
Direct Cap	.97	N.L.	+ .01
DodgC Bal	25.85	N.L.	+ .30
DodgC Stk	23.06	N.L.	+ .42
Drx Burnh	16.87	N.L.	+ .22
Dreyfus Group:			
A Bonds	13.80	N.L.	+ .02
→ Dreyf Fd ←	13.62	14.89	+ .15
Dreyf Lv	18.24	19.93	+ .19
Numbr 9	10.71	N.L.	+ .17
Spl Incm	7.24	N.L.	+ .05
Tax ExB	11.13	N.L.	− .01
Third Cn	7.11	N.L.	+ .08
Eagle Gth	9.74	10.64	+ .15
Eaton & Howard:			
Balncd F	8.33	8.98	+ .10
Equites	22.70	24.47	+ .40
Foursq	10.93	N.L.	+ .15
Income	4.82	5.27	...
Inc Bost	8.88	9.70	+ .02
Stock Fd	12.84	13.84	+ .18
Eberstadt Group:			
Chem Fd	11.30	12.35	+ .20
Enrgy R	9.53	10.42	+ .28
Surveyr	17.07	18.66	+ .15
Energy Utl	20.71	N.L.	+ .09
Evrgrn Fd	38.30	N.L.	+ .40
Evrgrn TR	14.33	N.L.	+ .08
Farm B Gr	14.92	N.L.	+ .21
FedrlSt Fd	49.92	N.L.	+ .93
Federated Group:			
Am Lead	10.81	11.56	+ .18
Exch Fd	30.35	N.L.	+ .45
Hi Incm	12.21	13.06	+ .03
Tax Free	9.13	9.56	...

Source: The Wall Street Journal, 25 February 1983, p. 33. Reprinted by permission of *The Wall Street Journal,*

Mutual Fund Cost Considerations

Unlike the cost of closed-end investment company share purchases and sales, which are treated in the same fashion as any common stock transaction, the cost of mutual fund (open-end investment company) transactions varies. Mutual fund shares are, therefore, classified as *load* or *no-load,* depending on whether or not transaction charges, or "loads," are assessed. In addition to such charges, management and operating costs and taxes may mean reduced returns for mutual fund investors.

Load Funds Load funds normally charge a purchase fee equal to from 7 to 8.5 percent of the purchase amount. The 8.5 percent maximum sales commission was established in 1975 as a result of actions taken by the National Association or Securities Dealers (NASD), which is a self-regulatory organization of brokers and dealers. This commission charge, or load, is normally levied only on the purchase; a commission is not charged on the sale of shares back to the investment company. The amount of the load is deducted from the money put up for the purchase of shares.

For example, if on 24 February 1983, you purchased one share of Dreyfus Fund, you would have to pay $14.89 for the share, which has an NAV of only $13.62. The $1.27 difference between these values ($14.89 − $13.62) represents the load. Expressing the load as a percentage of the offering price indicates that the maximum sales commission of 8.5 percent ($1.27 ÷ $14.89) is being levied on this transaction. A more realistic expression of the sales commission would be 9.3 percent because you are effectively paying $1.27 to purchase a share worth $13.62 ($1.27 ÷ $13.62 = 9.3%). Since the load is expressed as a percentage of the offering price, the actual cost tends to be understated when expressed as a percentage of NAV. As a percent of NAV, the maximum load allowable—which is commonly charged—is 9.3 percent. Recalling that on stock transactions, purchase and selling commissions were about 2 percent each, it should be clear that the cost of load funds is very high, even though the load is charged only on the purchase, not on the sale, of the shares. Because in certain instances, the load could be excessive, the SEC has the power to oversee the level of the loads and has provided a mechanism whereby any prepaid load is refunded if the shares are sold within a specified period of time after purchase.

No-Load Funds Well-managed no-load funds have a great deal of appeal. They are mutual funds that do not use formal sales channels requiring payment of sales commissions and, therefore, do not charge any load. Shares of no-load funds are sold through advertisements in newspapers and other financial media. For this reason, however, it is more difficult to become acquainted with no-load funds. Occasionally, a no-load fund will have a 1 to 2 percent *back-end load,* a fee for redeeming mutual fund shares.

Management and Operating Costs Mutual funds employ professional managers who are responsible for making all decisions about the purchase and sale of the securities owned by the fund. The fee the managers are paid for their services is normally set as a percentage of the total assets of the fund. The larger the fund, the lower the rate. These fees, as well as the operating costs of the fund, typically total between 0.50 and 1.50 percent of the dollar amount of the total assets of the fund. They are deducted from the value of the fund assets when calculating the net asset value per share.

Earnings and Taxes

Two important aspects of investment companies are the sources of their earnings and their tax consequences. The earnings of investment companies may be received in three basic forms: (1) interest income from corporate and government bonds, (2) dividends from stock, and (3) capital gains from selling securities for more than their initial purchase price. Each of these forms of earnings is taxable income. Of course, management fees and operating costs are deducted from all earnings prior to their taxation. To avoid double taxation, most investment companies choose to be taxed as *regulated investment companies.* This means that by meeting certain conditions and distributing at least 90 percent of all earnings to the shareholders, they can avoid having earnings taxed as company income. Of course, the earnings received by the investment company shareholders will be taxed according to the break-down provided them by the fund. Using the breakdown of earnings provided them, the shareholder for tax purposes will have to claim all interest and/or dividends (subject to the $100 dividend exclusion) and short-term capital gains as ordinary income, but only 40 percent of any long-term capital gains will have to be claimed as ordinary income (see Chapter 4 for a review of the various tax treatments).

Classification of Investment Companies

Investment objectives and types of securities purchased serve as means of classifying investment companies. Since objectives are usually clearly stated, the company managers are responsible for making purchase and sale decisions consistent with them. In fact, fund managers are typically hired on the basis of their expertise in the types of activities required by fund objectives.

Bond and Preferred Stock Funds Funds that purchase diversified portfolios of either *bonds* or *preferred stocks* attempt to provide safe, predictable returns to their investors. These types of funds are currently not especially popular investments.

Diversified Common Stock Funds The most popular types of funds, *diversified common stock funds,* account for more than 50 percent of all investment company assets (other than money market funds). Their investments in diversified portfolios of common stock provide a wide range of income-growth combinations. Some invest only in blue-chip stocks, while others are known to invest in more speculative types. Since there is a broad range of common stock funds, investors should identify the objectives and performance of any funds they are interested

Table 14.1 Industry and Issue Breakdown of the Securities Owned by the Dreyfus Fund (31 December 1981)

Industry	Number of Issues	Percent of Portfolio Value[a]
Common Stocks (90.7%)		
Air Transport	8	1.3
Automotive	1	.2
Banking	16	6.9
Building and Construction	5	1.0
Capital Goods	2	.3
Chemicals	13	5.1
Communications	4	2.1
Conglomerates	9	4.4
Drugs and Health Care	17	8.9
Electronic and Electrical Equipment	6	1.1
Finance	5	1.4
Food and Beverage	12	3.2
Insurance	3	.7
Machinery and Machine Tools	4	.8
Mining and Metals	6	.8
Motion Pictures	3	4.2
Natural Gas Pipelines	8	3.1
Oil Services	7	2.3
Paper and Forest Products	6	1.7
Petroleum Producers and Marketers	12	9.3
Pollution Control	3	1.0
Printing and Publishing	4	1.2
Public Utilities	34	8.3
Railroads and Equipment	5	2.2
Retail Trade	2	1.0
Savings and Loan	2	1.4
Security Services	1	.3
Tires and Rubber Goods	1	1.3
Tobacco	2	5.4
Miscellaneous	3	1.3
Foreign	42	8.2
Total Common Stocks	246	90.7
Convertible Preferred Stocks (0.2%)	2	.2
Notes and Bonds (4.2%)	10	4.2
Short-term Investments (5.3%)	2	5.3
Totals	260	100.4[b]

[a]Percentages based upon the 31 December 1981 market value of the portfolio; dollar value of that portfolio is $1,641,764,204.
[b]Percentages total to 100.4 percent because the fund had net liabilities equal to 0.4 percent of the portfolio's value on 31 December 1981.

Source: Dreyfus Fund, Inc., Prospectus, 3 May 1982, New York, N.Y., pp. 23–28.

in prior to investment. Table 14.1 provides an industry and issue breakdown of securities owned by the Dreyfus Fund, a diversified common stock fund with a primary objective of "long-term capital appreciation," or growth.

Balanced Funds Bonds, preferred stocks, and common stocks of a variety of industries or companies are combined in the portfolios of *balanced funds.* These funds are believed to account for as much as 15 percent of all mutual fund assets (other than money market funds). They attract investors who wish to receive a reasonably good—but safe—return on their investments. While the money invested in a balanced fund is usually fairly secure, capital growth is not as great as that expected from investment in a diversified common stock fund. The balanced fund generally appeals to persons who do not wish to build their own portfolios and would like to diversify across various security types.

Mutual-Fund Funds These funds invest in a portfolio of *mutual funds,* thereby spreading risk over a quite large group of securities. One disadvantage of this type of fund is that it must pay loading fees of 7 to 8.5 percent on the shares of load funds it acquires for its portfolio. The mutual fund itself, however, is permitted to charge only 1 to 3 percent loadings on the sale of its shares. Due to its probable overdiversification and the large amount of fees it must pay to set up a portfolio, this type of fund is not an especially attractive investment.

Specialty Funds *Specialty funds* often invest in relatively high-quality companies within a specific industry. Some specialty funds invest in firms in similar situations. For example, the Small Business Investment Company (SBIC) is a closed-end investment company that invests solely in small business firms. The objectives of specialty funds may be income, growth, or some combination of the two.

Money Market Funds As a result of the prevailing high interest rates being paid on money market instruments from 1973 to 1975, *money market funds* were established to invest in short-term debt instruments, such as certificates of deposit, commercial paper, and treasury bills. As noted in Chapter 5, money market funds became the most successful of the mutual funds. Prior to the introduction of the money market account offered by financial institutions in late 1982, assets held by money market funds totaled about $230 billion. Stockbrokerage firms offer a money market fund; Merrill Lynch's Ready Assets is the largest. Many other institutions also offer them, and you should review several before selecting one. They differ in yields and the kinds of securities they hold. *The Wall Street Journal* and *Barron's* report on them weekly, and for more details you should review magazines such as *Money* or *Forbes.*

A recent innovation in the money market fund is one that invests in very short-term municipal bonds. *Short-term municipal bond funds* are able to offer investors the instant liquidity of a money market fund, and

Table 14.2 Classification and Characteristics of Investment Companies

Classification of Investment Company	Types of Securities in Portfolio	Primary Objective Growth (G) or Income (I)
Balanced Funds	Bonds, Preferred Stock, and Common Stock	G-I Combination
Bond Funds	Bonds—Corporate or Government	I
Diversified Common Stock Funds	Common Stock	Variety of G-I Combinations
Index Funds	Common Stock	G-I Combination
Money Market Funds	Money Market Instruments	I[a]
Municipal Bond Funds	Bonds—State and Local Government	I (Tax Exempt)
Mutual Fund Funds	Mutual Funds	G
Performance (Go-Go) Funds	Speculative Common Stock	G
Preferred Stock Funds	Preferred Stock	I
Short-Term Municipal Bond Funds	Short-Term Municipal Bonds	I[a] (Tax Exempt)
Specialty Funds	Common Stock in a Specific Industry	G, I, or Combination

[a]These funds also provide liquidity.

the interest they pay is free of federal income taxes. While the yields on these funds are lower than those on the traditional funds, on an after-tax basis their yields may be considerably higher to someone in a high tax bracket. Even a person in a bracket as low as 30 percent should consider them.

Performance (Go-Go) Funds Performance as measured by total return earned on the shareholder's investment is the emphasis of *performance (go-go) funds.* The managers of these funds are aggressive in the way that they buy and sell securities, often holding them only for short periods of time. Their investment strategies are speculative in the sense that they attempt to trade securities in order to earn on small share-price movements. Investment in go-go funds should be made only by those willing to take the risks commensurate with the higher than average returns expected from them. It is probably best to let the professional fund manager make these investments for you rather than engage in such speculative ventures on your own.

Index Funds A recent development, the *index fund* is one that invests in a portfolio of common stock selected so that its performance echoes that of the market. These funds typically contain anywhere from 200 to 500 common stocks and are expected to provide levels of return similar to those of the market. The market is defined as all of the stocks included in one of the leading stock market averages/indexes such as Standard and Poor's 500 Composite Index (see Chapter 13). The specific common stocks chosen as well as their proportional holdings are set by the fund manager in order to provide risk-return behaviors similar to those of the market. Some fund managers will merely buy the same stocks in the same proportions to those in the given market average in order to assure that the fund behaves in the same way as the market. Although as of yet these funds have not achieved great popularity among small investors, their future popularity may increase since they do nearly ensure the investor of a return at least as good as the market—something many mutual funds have been unable to achieve consistently.

Although the most common types of investment companies are described in the preceding sections, numerous others have objectives with respect to income and growth that are different from those discussed. Table 14.2 classifies the investment companies according to types of securities held and primary objective. Many of the possible motives and considerations for making investments in these companies are discussed in the next part of the chapter.

Making Mutual Fund Investments

Since most investment company transactions are made in mutual fund shares, this part of the chapter is devoted to certain essential aspects of mutual fund transactions, in particular, motives for purchase, methods of purchase, special features, and considerations and techniques involved in buying mutual fund shares.

Motives for Purchasing Mutual Funds

The most common motives for purchasing mutual fund shares include diversification, professional management, financial return, and convenience.

Diversification The primary motive for investing in mutual funds is the *ability to diversify* and diminish risk by indirectly investing in a number of different types of securities and/or companies. A person with only $200 to invest might at most be able to diversify into only four securities, while the same $200 invested in mutual fund shares might provide a claim on a diversified portfolio of more than 100 securities. In order to better understand the degree of diversification achieved by mutual funds, refer to the historic portfolio diversification for mutual funds in Table 14.3.

Table 14.3 Portfolio Diversification of Mutual Funds (Percent of Total Common Stocks by Industry, 1971, 1976, 1981)

Industry	1971	1976	1981
Agricultural Equipment	0.12%	0.27%	1.02%
Aircraft Mfg. & Aerospace	0.97	2.16	1.71
Air Transport	3.15	1.61	1.63
Auto and Accessories (excl. Tires)	3.72	3.09	1.11
Building Materials and Equipment	3.93	2.67	1.39
Chemicals	4.79	6.88	5.82
Communications (TV, Radio, Motion Pictures)	1.40	3.02	2.48
Containers	0.54	0.45	0.62
Drugs and Cosmetics	4.85	6.65	8.54
Elec. Equip. and Electronics (excl. TV & Radio)	6.43	5.10	7.64
Foods and Beverages	2.86	3.68	3.03
Financial (incl. Banks & Insurance)	10.18	7.71	9.36
Machinery	1.30	2.45	1.56
Metals and Mining	2.05	2.69	1.55
Office Equipment	6.80	8.09	7.56
Oil	8.74	14.70	12.16
Paper	2.06	3.04	1.93
Public Utilities (incl. Telephone & Natural Gas)	7.46	6.72	11.18
Railroad	2.61	1.81	1.03
Railroad Equipment	0.22	0.30	0.49
Retail Trade	6.87	2.95	3.64
Rubber (incl. Tires)	1.37	0.94	0.61
Steel	1.03	2.04	1.44
Textiles	0.33	0.42	0.24
Tobacco	1.06	2.16	2.14
Miscellaneous[a]	15.16	8.40	10.12
Totals	100.00%	100.00%	100.00%

Note: Composite industry investments drawn from the portfolios of 40 of the largest investment companies as of the end of calendar year 1981 whose total net assets represented 39.1 percent of total net assets of all Investment Company Institute member companies excluding money market funds.

[a]Includes diversified industrial companies not readily assignable to specific industry categories.

Source: 1982 Mutual Fund Fact Book (Washington, D.C.: Investment Company Institute, 1982), p. 18.

Professional Management The second major appeal of the mutual fund is its professional management. Of course, management is paid a fee from the fund's earnings, but the contribution of a full-time expert manager should be well worth its cost. Purchase and sale decisions made by professionals may provide better results than those that the average investor could achieve.

Financial Return As indicated earlier, professional management can result in returns exceeding those that the small investor could generate. Still, the relatively high purchase fee coupled with the management and operating costs have a tendency to reduce the returns actually earned on mutual fund investments. Mutual fund investments must therefore earn higher returns than other investments. And while they are generally expected to earn a safer, more predictable return than self-made portfolios, there is no guarantee—only the expectation—that this will actually be the case.

Convenience Finally, the fact that mutual fund shares can be purchased through a variety of sources also adds to their appeal. Then, too, prospectuses of mutual funds, which clearly state their investment objectives, greatly simplify the selection. This convenience coupled with diversification, professional management, and expected financial returns makes the mutual fund appealing to the small investor.

Methods of Purchasing Mutual Funds

Mutual fund shares can be purchased using one of three possible methods: the regular account purchase, voluntary savings accumulation plans, and contractual savings accumulation plans.

Regular Account Purchase Persons who buy mutual fund shares on a transaction-by-transaction basis rather than under some type of prearranged purchase program make regular account purchases which are one-time purchase transactions. To make this kind of purchase, the investor expends a specified amount of money; the loading, or purchase, fee (on load funds) is then deducted from this amount. Although the percentage amount of this fee declines with the size of the transaction, it is usually in the range of 7 to 8.5 percent for most transactions made by the small investor. For example, if you wish to make a regular account purchase of $5,000 of mutual fund shares at their offering price and the loading fee is 8 percent, the cost of the transaction included in the offering price would be $400 (0.08 × $5,000). The purchase would, therefore, have an NAV of $4,600 ($5,000 − $400). Any interest, dividends, or capital gains earned on this investment are distributed to the shareholders at prespecified points in time or reinvested, depending on what arrangements have been made. Reinvestment plans are discussed in a later section.

Voluntary Savings Accumulation Plans In voluntary savings accumulation plans an investor opens an account by making an initial purchase of mutual fund shares, typically ranging from $25 to $500 depending on the fund's requirements. The investor is then expected to make regular minimum purchases of the fund's shares generally ranging from $25 to $100; larger purchases can, of course, be made at any time. This type of plan is similar to the monthly investment plans (MIPs) for security purchases described in Chapter 13. Since additional purchases of the fund's shares are made each period, the voluntary savings accumulation plan is a type of dollar cost averaging plan. The load on purchases of shares under this plan is calculated in the same fashion as is done on regular account purchases. Since these plans have no stated life, they may be liquidated at any time without penalty. Failure to make a planned purchase does not result in any penalty, but it may cause the company to put you on a regular account purchase arrangement. The advantage of the voluntary accumulation plan over the regular account purchase arrangement is that it may allow you to make smaller purchases than the minimums often required under the regular account arrangement. The forced savings aspect of these plans also has appeal for some investors.

Contractual Savings Accumulation Plans There is a built-in penalty for not abiding by a contractual savings accumulation plan. This type of plan differs from the voluntary plan in that the purchaser agrees to make regular contributions over a specified period of time. The period over which contributions are made is frequently 10 years. The total commissions on all purchases to be made over the life of the plan are paid in the first few years. This arrangement is referred to as a "front-end load," and because in effect it requires commissions to be paid in advance, it provides investors with an incentive to abide by the plan. Investors who drop out of this kind of plan sacrifice the prepaid loads on subsequent purchases and find that the number of shares they possess is less than what they could have obtained through a regular account purchase. The SEC requires contractual savings accumulation plans to give a full refund of prepaid loads to persons who cancel within 45 days of their enrollment and to give persons who cancel within 18 months of enrollment a refund of 85 percent of the total prepaid sales commissions.

Contractual savings accumulation plans are offered only by load funds, since no-load funds have no mechanism to provide an incentive to continue investing. Because of the high sales commissions in the early years of these plans, sales representatives have strongly promoted them. At the same time, the SEC as well as state regulatory agencies have imposed restrictions on them, since the high front-end loadings tend to severely penalize persons wishing to cancel. The SEC has attempted to force investment companies to spread the loadings over more years; and certain states, such as California, Illinois, Ohio, and Wisconsin, have gone so far as to prohibit entirely the sale of contractual savings accumulation plans. As a result of the growing governmental regulation of these plans, their popularity has declined dramatically during recent years.

Special Features of Mutual Funds

Mutual funds have a variety of features which can prove valuable to investors, including automatic reinvestment plans, systematic withdrawal plans, insurance against loss, and retirement plans.

Automatic Reinvestment Plans Plans are often available whereby the share owners can elect to have interest, dividends, and capital gains realized on their holdings automatically reinvested in additional shares. Fractional shares are issued, if needed, in order to permit the reinvestment of the total amount of earnings. The advantage of these plans, which are often required under the savings accumulation plans discussed earlier, is that no loading is charged on this purchase transaction. Note, however, that the net amount earned from interest, dividends, and realized capital gains is reduced by the management and operating costs prior to reinvestment. For tax purposes, of course, it makes no difference whether or not interest, dividends, and capital gains realized are automatically reinvested. For investors who wish to increase their investment in fund shares, these plans provide an excellent vehicle that can save loading fees.

Systematic Withdrawal Plan Often a mutual fund will provide some kind of *systematic withdrawal plan* which pays out specified amounts each period to the shareholders. To participate in these plans, the shareholders are usually required to have a minimum investment (that is, net asset value) in the fund of $5,000 to $10,000. The size of the withdrawal must normally be $50 or more per month. Depending on how well the fund has done and the specified amount of the withdrawals, the payout may or may not actually represent the return of part of the owner's initial investment. In other words, in some cases, the interest, dividends, and capital gains after management and operating costs may be greater than the withdrawal, resulting in an automatic accumulation of additional shares in the plan. On the other hand, if the fund has not performed well, the withdrawals could eventually completely deplete the original investment of funds.

Under systematic withdrawal plans, the most common arrangement is to specify the withdrawal as a *fixed dollar amount* per period as indicated earlier. Another type of arrangement specifies a *fixed number of shares* which are to be liquidated each period so that the shareholder may receive the proceeds. Since the net asset value of the shares is likely to fluctuate each period, this plan provides a varying amount of dollar income depending on the prevailing net asset value. In still another type of arrangement, only a *fixed percentage of the net asset growth* is paid to the shareholder. Under this plan, since the percentage is less than 100, some reinvestment is always provided for. When net asset values do not grow, no withdrawal takes place. Finally, one kind of plan provides for withdrawal of *all earnings* in the form of interest, dividends, and capital gains (less management and operating costs). Under this plan, the initial investment remains untouched since only earnings on it are paid out. None of these withdrawal plans is permanent and all may be altered or discontinued at any time at the option of the shareholder. They are most useful to those who desire periodic income from their investments. Investors interested in one of these plans should check to be sure that it is available from the mutual fund in which they intend to invest.

Insurance Against Loss A number of mutual funds currently make available insurance policies covering losses realized on the mutual fund investment. These insurance policies require that the investment be held for at least ten years and that all interest, dividends, and capital gains earned on the shares be reinvested in additional shares. The premiums on these policies are forfeited and the coverage canceled if the shares are sold prior to the minimum holding period specified in the policy. The insurance covers the loss experienced when mutual fund shares are sold for less than was originally paid for them. For example, assume you paid $12,000 for mutual fund shares which you purchased ten years ago, and today you sell those shares for $10,000. If you had a ten-year policy insuring against losses, the insurance company would pay you $2,000 ($12,000 − $10,000). The availability of mutual fund insurance is often used to stimulate the purchase of shares in a given fund. On an economic basis, the insurance is not worth its cost; the chance that you would experience a loss on shares held for ten or so years on which all earnings have been reinvested is small.

Retirement Plans As a result of certain government legislation, self-employed individuals are permitted to divert a portion of their pretax income into certain approved mutual fund investments. Moreover, the Economic Recovery Tax Act of 1981 simplified and expanded retirement plans by easing the limitations on Individual Retirement Accounts (IRAs) and making them available to all working Americans, even if covered by a company retirement plan. The eligibility of mutual funds as acceptable investments under these arrangements enhances their investment appeal to self-employed persons as well as wage earners. A more detailed discussion of the use of mutual funds as part of retirement planning is included in Chapter 15.

Buying Mutual Fund Shares

In order to buy mutual fund shares that are consistent with your investment objectives, you need to know not only how to make the transaction but also how to obtain and evaluate information with respect to the quality of specific funds. This section considers the various sources of mutual fund information, methods for measuring mutual fund performance, and the process of making the transaction.

Sources of Information Information on the objectives, characteristics, management, and past performance of a mutual fund can be obtained from the fund's prospectus, which is available from a sales representative. Both the SEC and the NASD require that mutual fund prospectuses and advertising be accurate representations of the facts.

Figure 14.3 Cover and Table of Contents of a Prospectus for a Mutual Fund

PROSPECTUS **May 3, 1982**

THE DREYFUS FUND INCORPORATED

767 FIFTH AVENUE, NEW YORK, N.Y. 10153
Outside New York State—Toll Free—1-800-645-6561
In the 212 Area—895-1206
Elsewhere in New York State Call Collect—516-794-5200

The Dreyfus Fund Incorporated (the "Fund") is a diversified, open-end investment company. Its primary objective is long-term capital appreciation; income is a secondary consideration. The Fund's management leans toward full investment in common stocks, although it may, of course, invest in fixed income securities such as preferred stocks, bonds and debentures.

Dreyfus Service Corporation (the "Underwriter") serves as the principal underwriter of the Fund's shares.

The investor is advised to read and retain this Prospectus for future reference.

THESE SECURITIES HAVE NOT BEEN APPROVED OR DISAPPROVED BY THE SECURITIES AND EXCHANGE COMMISSION, NOR HAS THE COMMISSION PASSED UPON THE ACCURACY OR ADEQUACY OF THIS PROSPECTUS. ANY REPRESENTATION TO THE CONTRARY IS A CRIMINAL OFFENSE.

TABLE OF CONTENTS

Source: Courtesy of Dreyfus Fund, Inc. Prospectus dated 3 May 1982, New York, New York, cover and back page.

Thus prospectuses and other sales brochures should provide reliable information. The cover, which contains a brief statement of the fund's objective, and the table of contents from the prospectus for the Dreyfus Fund is shown in Figure 14.3. (An industry and issue breakdown of the securities owned by that fund on 31 December 1981 is given in Table 14.1.)

Other sources of information are similar to those for stock and bond investments given in Chapter 13. Publications such as *The Wall Street Journal, Barron's,* and *Forbes* provide useful data and articles concerned with mutual funds. Probably one of the best general sources of information on mutual funds is *Investment Companies*—an annual publication (with quarterly updates) of Weisenberger Services, Inc.—which provides background information as well as performance data on the leading mutual funds. It is, of course, not advisable to rely solely on the information provided by a salesperson since, although it may be accurate, it may not include comparisons of the fund to other funds having similar objectives.

Measuring Fund Performance The performance of mutual funds is usually measured with reference to the investment of a certain amount at a specified time. Comparisons are made of the net asset values of shares that result after a period of years from $10,000 investments. Statistics based on the assumption that all interest, dividends, and capital gains were reinvested in additional shares are presented as either the dollar amount of net asset value achieved or the annual compound rate of growth in net asset value realized. For example, a $10,000 investment in the QRS Growth Fund ten years ago with all dividends and capital gains reinvested might have a net asset value of $21,650. This would represent an annual rate of return of approximately 8 percent. These types of performance statistics provide a useful basis for comparing the different funds.

Again, small investors should not rely solely on the statistics provided in a prospectus or by a mutual fund sales representative since the data from these two sources are intended to show only the positive aspects of the fund under consideration. One excellent source of comparative performance statistics is published annually each August in *Forbes.* An excerpt from the 1982 Forbes Fund Ratings is shown in Table 14.4. Other sources of comparative statistics which are sold on a subscription basis are *Johnson's Investment Company Charts* and Weisenberger's *Investment Companies.* These sources not only compare the performance of the funds' management, but they also relate fund performance generally to the behavior of the securities markets to permit the investor to assess the relative advantages of investing in mutual fund shares versus investing in individual securities. These sources can normally be obtained at your stockbrokerage firm.

Note that performance statistics report only what has happened in the past. Although past performance does act as a barometer for the

Table 14.4 Excerpt from 1982 Forbes Fund Ratings

Performance: In UP Markets	Performance: In DOWN Markets		Investment Results: Average Annual Total Return 1970–82	Investment Results: Latest 12 Months: Return from Capital Growth	Investment Results: Latest 12 Months: Return from Income Dividends	Total Assets: 30 June '82 (Millions)	Total Assets: % Change '82 vs. '81	Maximum Sales Charge	Annual Expenses per $100
		Standard & Poor's 500 stock average	8.4%	−16.5%	6.2%				
		Forbes stock fund composite	9.6%	−15.5%	4.6%				
		Forbes balanced fund composite	8.1%	− 9.1%	9.7%				
		Forbes bond and preferred stock fund composite	6.3%	− 5.1%	13.9%				
			Group Averages						
		Stock Funds (Load)	**9.6%**	**−13.7%**	**5.0%**				
D	C	Delaware Fund	10.5	− 8.9	7.2	219.6	−14.2	8.50	0.74
D	C	Delta Trend Fund	6.0	− 9.2	4.2	13.7	33.0	8.50	1.40
D	C	Diversified Fund of State Bond & Mtge Co	8.2	−17.5	7.1	6.5	−12.2	8.50	1.00
D	D	Dividend Shares	7.8	−10.7	6.5	217.8	−13.5	8.50	0.84
C	C	The Dreyfus Fund	9.8	−16.2	5.6	1,515.4	−13.5	8.50	0.75
B	C	The Dreyfus Leverage Fund	11.2	− 9.5	4.7	286.9	−11.0	8.50	1.00
B	C	Eagle Growth Shares	—	−10.1	5.9	4.5	−10.0	8.50	1.34
		Eaton & Howard Funds							
A	D	Growth	8.1	− 6.7	3.9	33.2	− 9.0	7.25	0.91
D	F	Stock	4.4	−14.2	6.0	57.5	−21.5	7.25	0.71
B	C	Eaton Vance Growth Fund	11.2	−17.1	4.1	48.4	−17.8	8.50	0.80
A	F	Fairfield Fund	8.5	−24.3	0.7	26.2	−20.1	8.50	1.15
D	D	Farm Bureau Growth Fund	—	−13.6	7.2	35.1	−10.2	8.50	0.84
B	A	Fidelity Destiny Fund	—	−12.9	5.0	245.8	5.5	—	0.80
A+	B	Fidelity Magellan Fund	19.0	− 5.1	1.7	146.8	40.6	2.00	1.34
C	D	First Investors Discovery Fund	4.6	−20.4	1.1	4.9	−18.3	8.50	1.47
B	F	First Investors Fund for Growth	7.5	−22.4	2.9	50.9	−27.2	8.50	0.99
D	F	First Investors Natural Resources Fund	3.1	−32.9	6.2	8.1	−27.0	8.50	1.28

Note: FORBES rates mutual funds on the basis of their performance in each of three rising markets and three declining markets beginning with the market low of May 26, 1970. To get a high score, a fund must perform consistently well in all three up or down periods.

Adjustments in the calculations prevent an exceptional performance (good or bad) in any one period from having an undue influence on a fund's average performance—calculated separately for up markets and down markets. For up markets, the 12.5% of all funds with the highest adjusted averages are initially awarded an A+ rating, the next 12.5% get an A, the next 25% B, the following 25% C and the lowest quartile D. For down markets, the ratings range from A to F, with an occasional A+ awarded for outstanding performance. In both up-market and down-market ratings, downward adjustments are made to the initial grades where performance in the most recent of the three periods has been substantially below the average of all three. Thus the breakdown of final grades is skewed somewhat from the distribution described.

Source: "Forbes Fund Ratings—1982," *Forbes,* 30 August 1982, p. 77 and p. 78. Excerpted by permission of *Forbes* Magazine from the 30 August 1982 issue.

future, you should make sure that major changes in fund management are not expected since management is of key importance to a fund's success. Also, if you consider investing in a new fund that has no past performance statistics, you must rely almost completely on knowledge of the expertise of the managers in order to develop expectations about future performance. The quality of fund managers is the key factor affecting the relative performance of mutual fund shares.

Making the Transaction Transactions in mutual fund shares can be made either through a broker who is authorized to sell shares or through a fund salesperson. If your broker is not authorized to sell fund shares, he or she might be able to put you in contact with a salesperson. If you respond to an advertisement for fund shares, you will probably be called on by an authorized salesperson. In the case of no-load mutual funds, the entire transaction can be carried out through the mail. In response to your request, you will be sent the relevant information for purchasing shares along with a prospectus describing key aspects of the fund. Investors should keep in mind that when salespersons are involved, they are compensated only if shares are purchased. Be sure if you make a mutual fund investment that it is consistent with your financial plans and is the best of the available alternatives. In other words, do not let the salesperson make your investment decisions; make them yourself.

Real Estate Investments

Although real estate purchased to provide housing is a key fundamental asset, many people hold additional real estate for investment purposes. In this part of the chapter the fundamental considerations that pertain to real estate investments and some of the more popular types of real estate investment are discussed.

Fundamental Considerations

Before property is purchased as an investment, an expert analysis of the costs, benefits, and risks that will result should be obtained and related to similar analyses for alternative investments. This section provides only a brief description of the basic factors that affect the value of an investment in real estate, including cash flow and taxes, appreciation in value, risk versus return, the use of leverage, and second mortgages.

Cash Flow and Taxes The *cash flow,* or annual after-tax earnings of the investor, depends on the project in which the investment is made. It is also affected by depreciation and taxes. Certain types of real estate investments make possible large depreciation write-offs that tend to lower taxable income. These tax deductions, which are intended to reflect the fact that certain real estate assets other than raw land deteriorate over time, provide the property owner with an allowance for this decline in value, or *depreciation.* Because of the importance of taxes to the cash flow, individual investors should employ a tax expert to evaluate proposed real estate investments in light of their income.

Appreciation in Value Certain types of real estate—especially raw land and residential lots—in many areas have experienced significant growth in value during certain periods such as 1975–1980. Other types, such as apartments and duplexes, have also appreciated in value in many areas of the country. The total assessment of a proposed real estate investment should include estimates of projected changes in value that may occur, as well as cash flow projections.

Risk versus Return If you can earn 6 percent on a savings deposit, any money you invest in a real estate project will have to provide a return higher than 6 percent in order to justify your investment. In addition, the 6 percent return you receive on your savings is certain—but what about the projected returns on a real estate investment? Clearly an element of risk must be taken into account. The anticipated level of total return on the investment, as well as the predicted level of periodic returns, is another important consideration in the evaluation of proposed real estate investments. The risk and return characteristics of proposed real estate investments should be viewed in light of the risks and returns associated with other fundamental and investment assets.

Use of Leverage One appeal of investment in real estate is the high degree of leverage it permits. *Leverage* is the use of borrowing to magnify returns. Because real estate is a tangible item, investors are able to borrow from 75 to 90 percent of the cost of investment property. If the total return on the investment is greater than the cost of borrowing, the net profit on the investment that takes advantage of leverage is proportionately greater than that on an investment that does not use leverage. For example, imagine that you have found a real estate investment costing $100,000. You can either purchase it for cash or put up $10,000 of your own money and borrow the remaining $90,000 at 12 percent annual interest. If the property earns $13,000 per year after all expenses, including real estate property taxes and depreciation, but before the deduction of interest and income taxes, the analysis of the return on your investment will be as shown in Table 14.5. In the no-leverage case, the investor's return on investment will be 8.45 percent; in the leverage case, it will be 14.30 percent. Note from this example,

Table 14.5 Using Leverage in Real Estate Investments

	No Leverage		Leverage
Owner Investment	$100,000		$ 10,000
Borrow	0		90,000
Total Investment	$100,000		$100,000
Earnings Before Interest and Income Taxes[a]	$ 13,000		$ 13,000
Less: Interest	0	(0.12)($90,000) =	10,800
Earnings Before Taxes	$ 13,000		$ 2,200
Less: Income Taxes (assumed 35% rate)	4,550		770
Earnings After Taxes	$ 8,450		$ 1,430
Return on Investment	$\frac{\$8,450}{\$100,000} = 8.45\%$		$\frac{\$1,430}{\$10,000} = 14.30\%$

[a]All expenses, including real estate property taxes and depreciation, are assumed to have been already deducted from earnings.

however, that when no borrowing is used, there is no risk of default; but in the leverage case, minimum earnings (before interest and taxes) of $10,800 are necessary to avoid default. The risk that comes with leverage must, therefore, be considered along with the potential benefits. Indeed, many people have been driven into bankruptcy as the result of using too much leverage.

Second Mortgages The use of mortgage financing to acquire a home is discussed in Chapter 6. It explains that a mortgage is simply a legal document conveying a legal interest in your property to a lender as security for the payment of a debt. If only one mortgage is outstanding on a property, it is called a *first mortgage.* Property may serve as collateral to support any number of additional loans, however; a second loan, for example, could be supported by a *second mortgage,* and so forth. In periods of high interest rates second mortgage financing is very popular, since it can be used by the seller to aid in selling his or her property when a prospective buyer lacks sufficient down payment to qualify for a first mortgage loan. Suppose you have found a buyer for your property who is willing to pay the asking price of $100,000 but has only $10,000 for a down payment, and who can borrow only $80,000 from a financial institution. If you thought the buyer was a good credit risk and could meet all the monthly payments, you could in effect loan the additional $10,000 to him or her by taking a second mortgage. Of course, you should use an attorney to set up the loan to make sure that, if secondary markets exist, you can eventually sell the mortgage.

As a potential buyer of investment property, second mortgage financing could increase your leverage. Thus it increases your risk and should therefore be used only with caution. When second mortgage financing is readily available—and it is not uncommon to find properties for which almost the entire purchase price can be financed—you should carefully evaluate potential cash flows and make sure the property has investment merit; easy financing is no substitute for careful economic analysis.

Speculating in Real Estate

The growth in the value of real estate in certain areas has been phenomenal over the past few decades. The increase in population, the rising affluence of Americans, and the fact that real estate is a scarce commodity have all contributed to this growth. Stories of people who bought land for $50 an acre ten years ago and have recently been offered $1,000 an acre are not unusual. The rapid growth of certain urban and recreational areas has also caused related real estate prices to skyrocket. Because many investors expect the value of selected real estate to continue to increase, real estate remains a quite popular investment. The key to speculation is to isolate certain areas of potential population growth and/or real estate demand and to purchase property in these areas in the hope that the expectations for their development are realized.

Raw Land Undeveloped acreage without any utilities or improvements is often purchased by land speculators either to hold for future development or merely to sell at a higher price at some later date. Speculation in raw land often occurs near an area where a new development of some type is anticipated. Both residential and commercial developments tend to increase the value of nearby property. Because of the high degree of uncertainty involved in raw land speculation, this activity should be reserved for the professional real estate investor.

Residential Lots Although builders typically predominate among purchasers of residential lots, the individual investor can often buy such lots as speculative ventures. The likelihood that these lots will appreciate is much greater than for raw acreage since the land would probably not have been subdivided had there been no positive indications of the demand for the lots. If lots are purchased when first offered for sale, there is a good chance that they will appreciate, because as homes are built on neighboring lots the value of available lots tends to increase. Of course, if you wish to invest in residential lots, you should carefully assess their quality and the demand for them in the subdivision you are considering. Opportunities to profit do exist, but risks are still high. The success of speculation in lots depends not only on location but also on the quality, size, and appeal of the houses built on them. These latter factors are obviously difficult to control.

Investing in Income Property

The purchase of *income property* is a relatively common type of real estate investment that provides a *tax shelter.* The real estate purchased is leased to tenants to generate income in the form of rent receipts. Because the buildings on income property can be depreciated to reduce an investor's taxable income, it is a popular type of investment among the wealthy. Although the primary purpose of investment in income property is to produce a cash flow, certain types of strategically located income properties also offer good opportunities for appreciation in value. The two basic types of income property are housing units and commercial property.

Housing Units Apartment houses, duplexes, and rental houses are all housing units that provide income. This type of income property is available in a variety of sizes, prices, and types ranging from multifamily apartment complexes to single-family rental homes. First-time investors in real estate usually choose investments of this type. Aside from purchase and financing cost considerations, the major factors influencing the profitability of these investments are the occupancy rate—the percentage of available space rented over the year—and maintenance and management costs.

Commercial Property Office buildings, stores, shopping centers, and mobile home parks are examples of the variety of investments included in the category commercial property. The risks and returns on commercial property are more dependent on business conditions and location than would be true for housing units. The value of commercial property—especially retail businesses—is usually enhanced by a location in a high-traffic area. Due to the need for professional management and the magnitude of the expense involved, investment in commercial types of income property is generally the domain of more sophisticated investors.

Real Estate Syndication: Limited Partnerships

Real estate syndicates are professionally managed *limited partnerships* which invest in various types of real estate. Managers assume the role of a general partner, which means that their liability is unlimited, while the other investors are limited partners, which means they are legally liable for only the amount of their initial investment. Most limited partnerships require a minimum investment of between $2,500 and $10,000. Their shares can be purchased directly through ads in financial newspapers, through a stockbroker, or with the assistance of a commercial real estate broker.

Types of Syndicates There are both single property and blind pool syndicates. The *single property syndicate* is established to raise money to purchase a specific piece of property. For example, 50 shares at $7,500 each could be sold to buy a piece of property for $1 million. A total of $375,000 (50 × $7,500) would come from the partners, and the remaining $625,000 would be borrowed.

Figure 14.4 Cover of a Prospectus for a Limited Partnership

PROSPECTUS

ANGELES PARTNERS XI

$30,000,000

30,000 Limited Partnership Units ($1,000 per Unit)
(With Selling Agent's option to increase to 40,000 Units)
Minimum Purchase — Five Units ($5,000)

Angeles Partners XI, a California limited partnership (the "Partnership") organized to invest in improved real properties, hereby offers limited partnership units (the "Units") up to a maximum of 30,000 Units (unless increased through exercise of the option to sell up to a maximum of 40,000 Units as described under "Underwriting"). The Partnership's general partners (referred to collectively as the "General Partners" and individually as a "General Partner") are Angeles Realty Corporation II, a California corporation (the "Managing General Partner"), the Elliott Family Partnership, Ltd., a California limited partnership and the Elliott Accommodation Trust (the "Non-Managing General Partners"). The Partnership's primary objective is to acquire properties which provide a potential for appreciation and to endeavor to preserve the purchasing power of capital, offset the impact of inflation and maximize investment results by making leveraged investments in apartment complexes and commercial, office and industrial buildings. The Partnership will also seek to provide tax sheltered cash flow and some additional tax shelter for income from other sources. In making investment decisions to implement these objectives, the Partnership intends to avoid investments which, after weighing the potential for appreciation, contain undue risks of loss of capital.

The Units are being offered by Mitchel, Schreiber, Watts & Co., Inc. (the "Selling Agent"), an affiliate of the General Partners, on a "best efforts" basis. The offering of Units will continue until the Partnership has received and accepted subscriptions for 30,000 Units (or up to 40,000 Units if the option described under "Underwriting" is exercised) or until such earlier time as the Managing General Partner has terminated the offering; provided, however, that the offering will be terminated in any event one year from the date of this Prospectus. If subscriptions for 1,150 Units have not been received and accepted prior to termination of the offering, all funds received will be refunded promptly to investors. Until subscriptions for 1,150 Units have been received and accepted, all subscription funds will be maintained in an escrow account at Bank of America National Trust and Savings Association, Los Angeles, California. Funds received from subscribers after the minimum number of subscriptions has been received will be deposited either in an escrow account at Bank of America National Trust and Savings Association or in a Partnership escrow account controlled by the Partnership but which is separate from all other Partnership assets. (See "Subscriptions to Partnership")

This offering involves certain risk factors. (See "Risk Factors")

THESE SECURITIES HAVE NOT BEEN APPROVED OR DISAPPROVED BY THE SECURITIES AND EXCHANGE COMMISSION NOR HAS THE COMMISSION PASSED UPON THE ACCURACY OR ADEQUACY OF THIS PROSPECTUS. ANY REPRESENTATION TO THE CONTRARY IS A CRIMINAL OFFENSE.

NEITHER THE ATTORNEY GENERAL OF THE STATE OF NEW JERSEY NOR THE BUREAU OF SECURITIES OF THE STATE OF NEW JERSEY HAS PASSED ON OR ENDORSED THE MERITS OF THIS OFFERING. ANY REPRESENTATION TO THE CONTRARY IS UNLAWFUL.

	Price to Public (1)	Selling Commissions(2)	Proceeds to the Partnership(3)(4)
Per Limited Partnership Unit	$ 1,000.00	$ 87.50	$ 912.50
Total Minimum	$ 1,150,000.00	$ 100,625.00	$ 1,049,375.00
Total Maximum excluding option(5)	$30,000,000.00	$2,625,000.00	$27,375,000.00

(Footnotes continued on next page)

ANY SUPPLEMENTS AND/OR STICKERS WHICH UPDATE THIS PROSPECTUS ARE CONTAINED INSIDE THE BACK COVER.

The date of this Prospectus is February 14, 1983.

(THE COVER PAGE IS CONTINUED ON THE FOLLOWING PAGE.)

Mitchel, Schreiber, Watts & Co., Inc.

Source: Courtesy of Angeles Realty Corporation II, Los Angeles, Calif.

The *blind pool syndicate,* on the other hand, is formed by a syndicator, often well known, in order to raise a given amount of money to be invested at the discretion of the syndicator. The cover of the prospectus for such a limited partnership is shown in Figure 14.4. The blind pool syndicator takes a specified percentage of all income generated as a management fee. Large real estate brokerage firms commonly arrange these types of syndications.

Returns and Risks The potential returns from real estate syndications lie in the tax shield provided by depreciation and in the gains due to appreciation in property values. In effect, the tax shield allows shareholders to receive tax-free cash flows from these investments. Appreciation in value yields a long-term capital gain, which is taxed at rates lower than those on ordinary personal income (see Chapter 4). The annual returns on these types of investments range between 10 and 25 percent of the amount invested; and because part of the income is used to repay the mortgage financing, the partner's equity in the property increases over time. The emphasis with respect to the type of return generated differs from syndicate to syndicate. Some emphasize tax shelters; others emphasize long-term capital gains. Uncertainty with respect to future price appreciation, occupancy rates, changes in tax laws, and the competence of the syndicate management introduces varying degrees of risk into these types of investments. The goals of the syndicate, the expected returns, and the perceived risks should all be carefully evaluated before limited partnership shares in a real estate syndicate are purchased.

Advantages and Disadvantages The key advantages of real estate syndicate investments are diversification, professional management, convenience, potentially high returns, and low operating costs. Because the professional manager is able to keep abreast of real estate conditions and pay close attention to the investment, the likelihood of success is much greater than for small real estate investors.

Syndicate investments do have some disadvantages, however. Shares generally cannot be sold easily; there are high risks in speculating on property appreciation and occupancy rates in housing units; and possible changes in the tax laws related to depreciation—the 1984 tax law lessened the favorable treatment given to depreciation by the 1981 law—heighten the general uncertainty as to the continued role of these investments as tax shelters.

Real Estate Investment Trusts

The *Real Estate Investment Trust (REIT)* is a type of closed-end investment company that invests money obtained through the sale of shares to investors and by borrowing in mortgages and various types of investment real estate. REITs must abide by the Real Estate Investment Trust Act of 1960, which established requirements for forming a REIT and rules and procedures for making investments and distributing income. These trusts channel money into various types of long-term real estate investments, such as mortgage loans, apartments, and office buildings. Since they are required to pay out nearly all of their earnings to the owners, they do quite a bit of borrowing to obtain funds for investments.

A number of insurance companies, mortgage banking houses, and commercial banks have formed REITs. The ownership of many is traded on the securities exchanges. Like mutual funds, the income of the REIT is not taxed, but the income distributed to owners is designated and taxed as either ordinary income or long-term capital gains. Although the poor performance of REITs during the 1973–1975 recession caused them to fall into disfavor among investors, subsequent restructuring of their portfolios has rekindled investor interest in them. While REITs may earn returns in the range of 5 to 15 percent and do provide a mechanism through which the small investor can make real estate investments, they are often risky. You should invest only in the shares of the better-known REITs such as General Growth Properties, ICM Realty, and Southmark Corporation, which are listed on major securities exchanges. Your stockbroker should be able to give you advice with respect to REITs and help you select REIT investments consistent with your investment objectives, if you wish.

Real Estate Investment Companies

The *real estate investment company* is nothing more than a corporation that sells its shares and uses the proceeds to make real estate investments. It differs from the REIT in that it must pay corporate income taxes and, therefore, is not regulated with respect to the distribution of its income. Such companies are able to retain earnings as well as borrow and thus can grow at a much faster rate than REITs. Although these companies specialize in real estate investments, they represent nothing more than another common stock investment. This perhaps explains the diversity of their performance; some have done well, while others have performed poorly. Your stockbroker should be able to provide detailed information with respect to these common stock investments.

Other Investment Vehicles

In addition to the more traditional forms of investment, such as stocks, bonds, mutual funds, and real estate, a variety of other investment vehicles are available. Although they are less commonly acquired by the small investor due to their relatively high risk and/or lack of liquidity, a very basic understanding of the more popular other investment vehicles should prove useful in developing your investment portfolio. In this part of the chapter specific attention is given to commodity futures, financial futures, options, precious minerals, and collectibles.

Table 14.6 Selected Commodity Contract Specifications

Commodity	Contract Size	Price Quotation
Cattle (Live)	40,000 pounds	cents/pound
Coffee	37,500 pounds	cents/pound
Pork Bellies	38,000 pounds	cents/pound
Silver	5,000 troy ounces	cents/troy ounce
Soybeans	5,000 bushels	cents/bushel
Wheat	5,000 bushels	cents/bushel

Commodity Futures

The commodities markets provide a mechanism through which producers of certain commodities can protect themselves against future price declines on their products. Suppliers of commodities, such as cattle, coffee, frozen pork bellies, silver, soybeans, and wheat, who believe that the price of their product is likely to drop prior to the time when they will have their commodity available for sale might sell a contract to deliver a specified quantity of the commodity at a specified price at some future date. The buyers of these contracts protect themselves against a price increase and guarantee themselves the future availability of a needed raw material at a known price. The various commodities are listed and traded on a number of exchanges, including the Chicago Board of Trade (the largest), the Chicago Mercantile Exchange, and the New York Mercantile Exchange.

The Contract *Futures contracts* are normally written to provide for delivery of a commodity three or more months in the future. The contract represents a guarantee by the seller that he or she will deliver the commodity at a certain price on a given date. The buyer must arrange to pay for and take delivery of the commodity on this date. Thus both the seller and the buyer of a futures contract accept certain contractual obligations as the result of their transaction.

Because a wide variety of commodities are available for trading, contracts vary depending on which commodity is being traded. Table 14.6 lists some of the more common commodities along with the number of units in a contract and the unit in which the prices are quoted. For example, if a silver futures contract for delivery six months from now is quoted at 1,350.0, this means that to buy a contract, it is necessary to pay 1,350.0 cents per troy ounce. Since a silver contract consists of 5,000 troy ounces, the price of the contract would be $67,500 (1,350.0 cents/troy ounce × 5,000 troy ounces). If you plan to trade in futures contracts, you must be familiar with the differing contract sizes and price quotations.

Logic of Futures Trading Because of the various changes in business, weather, and international conditions, the prices of commodities fluctuate on a day-to-day basis and affect the value of futures contracts. For example, a one-cent increase in the price of silver would cause the value of a futures contract in silver to increase by $50 (one cent troy ounce × 5,000 troy ounces/contract). Because of the sensitivity of the values of futures contracts to small movements in the prices of commodities, these contracts offer high potential returns (or losses). They are thus attractive to speculators, who make commodities transactions not with any intention of ever taking delivery but rather in the hope of obtaining high profits in a short period of time. Of course, high risks are associated with these high returns. The two basic approaches used to trade in commodities differ depending on whether the price of a commodity is expected to increase or decrease.

Expected Price Increase A person who expects the price of a given commodity to rise will purchase a contract for that commodity and hold it until the price increase occurs. For example, assume today is 1 January and you purchase a silver contract (5,000 troy ounces) for delivery in May at the current price of silver, which is 1,350 cents per troy ounce. If the price of silver increases to 1,650 cents per troy ounce over the next few months and you sell the contract, you will make (ignoring any commissions) 300 cents/troy ounce (1,650 cents − 1,350 cents), or a total of $15,000 (300 cents/troy ounce × 5,000 troy ounces/contract) on the transaction. The $15,000 profit resulted from a relatively small movement in the silver price. Of course, had the price of silver instead dropped by 300 cents per troy ounce to 1,050 cents, you would have experienced a $15,000 loss.

Expected Price Decrease An individual who expects the price of a commodity to decline can attempt to capitalize on this expectation by selling a contract to deliver the commodity and, when the price of the commodity drops, purchasing a contract to cover the obligation to deliver. This strategy is quite similar to short selling, which was described in Chapter 13. For example, assume that silver futures are currently selling at 1,350 cents per troy ounce, and you expect the price to decline. You could sell a silver contract for delivery in five months at this price. If, within the five-month period, the price declines to 1,240 cents and you then buy a contract to cover your promised delivery, you will have made 110 cents per troy ounce, or a total of $5,500 (110 cents/troy ounce × 5,000 troy ounces/contract). You have in effect sold something to be delivered in the future at a higher price than you had to pay in order to acquire it. Had the price of the commodity increased instead of decreased, you would have had to purchase the commodity to be delivered at a price higher than the price at which you sold it and thus would have suffered a loss.

Since there are numerous factors that can affect the price of a commodity at a certain future date, and since small movements in commodity prices can drastically affect the value of a contract, the high risks of trading in commodity futures should be evident. In addition, certain constraints placed on the commodities markets may make it difficult to sell a futures contract as the delivery date approaches. This means that a risk of having to take delivery of the commodity itself does exist.

Making Futures Transactions Futures transactions can be made through most stockbrokerage firms. The broker can execute both buy and sell orders in futures contracts, and the commission charged currently averages about $70 per contract. (This amount covers the commission cost at both ends of the transaction—to buy and sell a contract.) In order to make sure that their customers are financially able to take the risks associated with commodities trading, most brokerage firms establish a net worth minimum their clients must possess in the form of liquid assets before they can open a commodity trading account. Although these minimums vary from firm to firm, they are often in the neighborhood of $50,000. *The Wall Street Journal* provides daily commodity price quotations. Other information can be obtained from your stockbroker or directly from one of the commodity exchanges.

One significant aspect of commodity futures is the very low margin requirements placed on transactions. Persons with commodity trading accounts are required to put up between 5 and 20 percent of the value of the futures contract at the time of the transaction. Interest is normally not charged on the borrowed portion of the purchase price, since the money is not really paid out (or borrowed) until the actual delivery of the commodity takes place. If the price of the commodity declines over the holding period, the brokerage firm is likely to require the customer to put up additional money as collateral on the contract. The use of low margin on commodity transactions enhances returns received on investments but also notably increases the risks involved.

Refer back to the example from the silver market, in which an individual purchased one silver contract and sold it after the price of silver increased by 300 cents per troy ounce (from 1,350 cents to 1,650) to make a profit (ignoring any commissions) of $15,000 on the transaction. Had the margin been 10 percent, the trader would have had to invest $6,750 (10% × 1,350 cents/troy ounce × 5,000 troy ounces of silver/contract). If the contract had been held for three months (one-fourth of a year), the return on the investment would have been approximately 889 percent ([$15,000 ÷ $6,750] × 4)—a very high return! Of course, had the price of silver declined by the same amount, the trader would have lost approximately 889 percent of the investment in the transaction. (What this means is you would have lost everything invested about nine times during the year!) Although trading commodity futures can provide high potential returns, the risks of these transactions are so great that the small investor is advised to stay away from them.

Financial Futures

In addition to futures contracts on commodities, futures contracts are also available on financial instruments such as foreign currencies, treasury debt issues (bonds, notes, and bills), corporate commercial paper, negotiable certificates of deposit issued by commercial banks, and even stock indexes—Standard and Poor's 500 Stock Index, for example. Buyers and sellers of *financial futures* have the same reasons for trading as do their counterparts in the commodities markets. For instance, if you think that the stock market is going to significantly advance over the next several months, you may buy a six-month contract on the S & P 500 Index with the expectation that once this stock market index rises in response to heightened stock market activity you can sell it at its increased level, thereby profiting from the gain in the index. Not only are the risks of trading financial futures similar to those of commodity futures, but these contracts tend to be more complicated than commodity contracts. Because of their high risk and complexity, the small investor should avoid financial futures.

Options

Options are various types of contracts that permit an individual to either purchase or sell a specified security at a predetermined price within a certain period of time. The two most common types of options are calls and puts. A *call* is an option to purchase a specified number of shares (typically 100) of a stock at or before some future date for a specified price. Call options usually have initial lives of from one to nine months, and occasionally one year. The *striking price* is the price at which the holder of the option can buy the stock any time prior to the option's expiration date; it is generally set at or near the prevailing market price of the stock at the time the option is issued. For example, if the stock of ABC is currently selling for $50 per share, a call option on the stock initiated today would likely have a striking price set at $50 per share. In order to purchase a call option, a specified price of normally a few hundred dollars must be paid. A *put* is an option to sell a given number of shares of a stock at or before a specified future date for a stated striking price. Like the call option, the striking price of the put is close to the market price of the underlying stock at the time of issuance. The lives and costs of puts are also quite similar to those of the call option. Although other types of options made of some combination of calls and puts exist, because calls and puts are the most common types, the discussion here is devoted solely to them.

How the Options Markets Work There are two methods of making options transactions. The first involves making a transaction through 1 of 20 or so call and put options dealers with the help of a stockbroker. The other and more popular mechanism is the organized options exchanges. The dominant exchanges on which both call and put options are traded are the *Chicago Board Options Exchange (CBOE)* and the *American Stock Exchange (AMEX).* Although from their inception in April 1973 on the CBOE and January 1975 on AMEX until June 1977, each dealt only in call options. They now provide organized marketplaces in which purchases and sales of both call and put options can be made in an orderly fashion. The options traded on the options exchanges are standardized and are considered registered securities. Each option is for 100 shares of the underlying stock. The price at which options transactions can be made is determined by the forces of supply and demand. Options on over 100 listed securities are available on both the CBOE and AMEX.

A person can take one of two possible roles on the options exchanges and become either an option *buyer* or an option *writer.* The buyer of options purchases and sells options that were initially written by the writer. In other words, a three-month call option for 100 shares of ABC with a striking price of $50, if exercised, would allow the buyer to purchase 100 shares of ABC for $50 per share. The writer of the option would be responsible for providing the 100 shares of ABC. Therefore, when a person writes a call option, a contractual obligation is made to sell 100 shares of the stock to the buyer of the call at the exercise price. Writers of puts must be prepared to purchase from the buyer of the put 100 shares of the stock at the exercise price. Although far less than half of all options are ever exercised, the option writer must be prepared to fulfill his or her contractual obligations to the option buyer. Most small investors who speculate in options only buy and sell options; they normally do not write them.

Logic of Options Trading The most common motive for purchasing call options is the expectation that the market price of the underlying stock will rise by more than enough to cover the cost of the option and thereby allow the purchaser of the call to profit. For example, assume that you pay $250 for a three-month call option on ABC at a striking price of $50. This means that by paying $250 you are guaranteed that you can purchase 100 shares of ABC at $50 per share any time over the next three months. Ignoring any brokerage fees, the stock price must climb $2.50 per share ($250 ÷ 100 shares) to $52.50 per share in order to cover the cost of the option. If the stock price were to rise to $60 per share during the period, your net profit would be $750 ([100 shares][$60/share] − [100 shares][$50/share] − $250). Since this return would be earned on a $250 investment, it illustrates the high return on investment that options offer. Of course, had the stock price not risen above $50 per share, you would have lost the $250 since there would have been no reason to exercise the option. Had the stock price risen to anywhere between $50 per share and $52.50 per share, you probably would have exercised the option in order to reduce your loss to an amount less than $250.

Put options are purchased in the expectation that the share price of a given security will decline over the life of the option. Purchasers of puts normally own the shares and wish to protect a gain they have realized since their initial purchase. By buying a put, they insure their gain because it enables them to sell their shares at a known price over the life of the option. Persons gain from put options when the price of the stock declines by more than the per share cost of the option. The logic underlying the purchase of a put option is exactly the opposite of that underlying the use of call options.

Making Options Transactions Your broker can easily make transactions for you in any of the options listed on the CBOE, AMEX, or other options exchanges. Even when the desired options are not listed, most brokers can locate the appropriate option dealer and negotiate the transaction. The brokerage fees on the purchase or sale of options may differ slightly depending on the exchange on which they are traded or the options dealer through which the transaction is made. As a rule of thumb, the fees are normally similar to those charged on transactions in listed securities.

Information and price data on options can be obtained from your stockbroker. Price quotations on the more active listed options appear daily in *The Wall Street Journal.* Trading in options is not recommended for the beginning or small investor due to the high degree of risk involved. Although high potential returns exist, the probability of achieving high returns is quite low. In many situations the exercise of the option is not attractive and the option expires, which results in a 100 percent loss on the investment in the option. Before attempting to trade in options, consult your broker, talk to an experienced investor, and read a basic text on options markets and transactions. Be sure you are aware of the risk associated with options transactions. Avoid this type of speculative investment unless you can afford the losses.

Precious Minerals

Over the recent past, as a result of the relatively high rate of inflation, many investors have been able to earn favorable returns through investing in certain *precious minerals.* The most popular forms of precious mineral investments include gold, silver, and diamonds. Although ownership of such minerals can be obtained in a variety of ways, the basic return from these forms of investment comes in the form of growth in value. In other words, one attempts to "buy low and sell high." Because future prices tend to be impacted by inflation as well as the changing supply of these minerals, investment in precious minerals tends to be somewhat risky. A slowdown in inflation or a sizeable discovery of new sources of a given mineral can unfavorably affect its market price; on the other hand, increasing inflation and continued scarcity of a given mineral can favorably influence the return from such an investment. Another factor that tends to affect the market value—and therefore the return—of precious minerals is the international political environment; in favorable times these forms of investment are not especially popular, while in times of turmoil their popularity tends to rise due to their tangible nature. As a result of their somewhat speculative behavior, investment in precious minerals is not for everyone. Before making such an investment, you should be certain to assess its role and risk-return potential in view of your investment objectives.

Gold Beginning 1 January 1975, U.S. citizens were for the second time in history legally permitted to hold gold. Since then, gold has become a popular investment vehicle. Its price has risen from $35/ounce in 1968 to $200 per ounce in 1975 to over $800 an ounce in early 1980, from which it declined to around $300 in June 1982, rebounded to almost $600 in December 1982, and fell to around $390 in mid-1984. The most popular forms of gold investment include coins, bullion, and jewelry. *Gold coins,* whose value is determined by gold content rather than collection value, can be purchased through banks and gold dealers. The most popular one, the *Krugerrand,* contains varying amounts of gold, but the most popular size is one troy ounce. A 2 to 4 percent commission is generally levied on these transactions. *Gold bullion* is an ingot of gold containing anywhere from less than one ounce to 400 ounces. It can be purchased through banks and gold dealers at commissions ranging from 3 to 10 percent. *Gold jewelry* is somewhat more expensive than gold coins and bullion since it has been manufactured into a more refined form. Jewelry is commonly 14 or 18 carat gold while pure gold is 24 carat. Although jewelry is appealing to many, from a strict investment point of view coins and bullion are preferable. Before buying gold you should have it assayed in order to confirm its gold content weight. You must also arrange for its safekeeping. Because safekeeping is often a problem, some investors find *gold certificates,* which evidence the ownership of gold held in a bank vault, an attractive form of investment. They can be purchased through major banks; a commission of 1 to 3 percent plus an annual storage fee of around 1 percent is typically charged.

Silver Silver also experienced a phenomenal increase in value during the 1970s and continuing into 1980. Its price per ounce during the 1960s was around $2, but by early 1980 its price soared to over $40 per ounce; by mid-1982, its price had dropped to about $5, increased to about $12 by year-end 1982, and dropped to about $9 by mid-1984. The market price of silver tends to behave in a fashion similar to gold; silver is sometimes viewed as a substitute for gold as a precious metal investment. Silver can be purchased as bullion—10-ounce to 1,000-ounce bars, in pure silver coin form, or in bags of silver-clad coins. Silver exhibits similar risk-return behavior to gold and can be purchased in a fashion similar to that used to acquire gold.

Diamonds Diamonds are sometimes acquired as an investment—not solely for their beauty. Because one producer, DeBeers Consolidated Mines, Ltd., of South Africa, almost completely controls their production, they are often viewed as a risky investment. The price per carat of a top-quality diamond, on the other hand, exhibited a fairly stable increase in value from about $1,700 per carat for a flawless stone in 1972 to $60,000 per carat in early 1980, then dropped to about $20,000 per carat by late 1982, and remained at about this level through mid-1984. Because diamonds come in various sizes, shapes, and colors, an investor wishing to buy diamonds should get certified appraisals of the stones. Investment diamonds can be purchased through a diamond dealer, who may charge a commission of 10 percent or more. Diamonds tend to be more difficult to sell than gold and silver. Because of its specialized nature and high risk, diamond investments are generally not advisable for the small investor.

Collectibles

Collectibles include a broad range of items that are found desirable for any of a variety of reasons, such as beauty, scarcity, age, and so on. Probably most significant is their ability to provide a hedge against inflation—the major factor accounting for the rapid growth in popularity of collectibles as an investment during recent years. Some of the items commonly included in this market are stamps, coins, antiques, art, books, autographs, and so on. These forms of collecting often provide a great deal of pleasure and satisfaction as well as good potential returns. The investment returns from collectibles come in the form of appreciation in value. While certain psychic income may be realized from the pleasure provided the investor, the financial return, if any, is realized only when the item is sold. While the acquisition of collectibles commonly results from an individual's personal interests, on a strict financial basis, items that have a good market and are likely to appreciate in value are the ones to collect. If an item under consideration is expensive, its value and authenticity should be confirmed by an expert prior to purchase (there are many unscrupulous dealers in collectible items). After purchase, one should make certain to store collectibles in a safe place and adequately insure them against all relevant perils (see Chapter 11).

Summary

Investment companies, real estate, and other investment vehicles, such as commodity futures, financial futures, options, precious minerals, and collectibles, provide alternatives to stock and bond investments. Investment companies gather funds by selling shares to numerous investors and using the proceeds to purchase securities issued by a variety of corporations. These funds, therefore, provide small investors who do not have enough money to create their own diversified security portfolios with the benefits of diversification. The two basic types of investment companies are closed end and open end. The latter, often called a mutual fund, issues as many shares as are demanded and stands willing to buy or sell shares at a price equal to the net asset value (NAV) per share of the portfolio. While most mutual funds are load funds—commissions are charged on the purchase of their shares—some are no-load funds.

Since investment companies are required to state their objectives, investors can use this information to select companies that provide returns consistent with their financial goals. The various types of investment companies include bond and preferred stock funds, diversified common stock funds, balanced funds, mutual-fund funds, specialty funds, money market funds (including short-term municipal bond funds), performance (go-go) funds, and index funds. The most popular type of fund is the diversified common stock fund, which invests in diversified portfolios of common stock providing a broad range of risk-return opportunities. The basic advantages of mutual fund investments include diversification, professional management, financial return, and convenience. Mutual fund shares can be purchased on regular account or through either a voluntary or contractual savings accumulation plan. Features often available as part of mutual fund purchases are automatic reinvestment plans, systematic withdrawal plans, insurance against loss, and various retirement plans. Sources of mutual fund information and performance data are available over a wide range. Purchases of mutual fund shares are best transacted through stockbrokers or fund salespersons.

Real estate has appeal as an investment due to any of several factors: a favorable cash flow, tax effects provided by depreciation, and the general expectation of appreciation in property value that it offers. The use of leverage, sometimes enhanced with use of second mortgages, adds risk to a real estate investment but makes higher returns possible. Speculators in real estate often purchase raw land or residential lots in expectation of future price increases. Income property—both housing units and commercial property—may appreciate in value while buildings on it can be depreciated, thereby providing some tax shelter. Other types of real estate investment that offer a variety of risk-return opportunities include real estate syndications, or limited partnerships; Real Estate Investment Trusts (REITs); and real estate investment companies.

Other investment vehicles include commodity futures, financial futures, options, precious minerals, and collectibles. Commodity and financial futures are contracts to buy or sell a commodity or a financial instrument at a specified price on a given date. Because of the great deal of uncertainty associated with future price movements, this form of investment is risky. Options, which are contracts that permit either the purchase or sale of a specified security at a predetermined price within a specified period of time, are risky. The two most common options are the call, an option to buy, and the put, an option to sell. Precious minerals, such as gold, silver, and diamonds, can be purchased as an investment. They offer a return in the form of future price appreciation. These minerals can be purchased in a variety of forms and qualities and caution is required when acquiring them. Collectibles, such as stamps, coins, antiques, art, books, autographs, and so on also can be acquired as an investment in expectation of future price appreciation. Not only do they provide potentially attractive returns, they often provide pleasure and satisfaction to the investor. Collectibles typically act as excellent inflation hedges and obtain their value from such characteristics as beauty, scarcity, and age.

Retirement Planning: Social Security, Annuities, and Pensions 15

Although people die at all ages, most of us will live at least five to ten years in retirement. So, if you want to reduce the chance that your income in retirement will be inadequate, the time to start planning is now. You therefore need to answer questions such as: How do I develop retirement plans? What benefits does social security provide? What is an annuity, and how can I use it? How does a prospective or existing employer's pension plan stack up? Answering such questions will help you meet this likely distant—but possibly most important—financial goal.

Families must protect against loss of income resulting from death or disability during the working career of the breadwinner. However, they also must prepare for reduced earnings in retirement. Poor planning will often result in a lower standard of living and quality of life in retirement. Retirees have the time to travel, pursue hobbies, and indulge in postponed activities, but too often they are unable to afford their dreams. To avoid this dilemma, you should begin to implement plans that will provide for adequate retirement income. Even if you are wealthy, you still need to plan for retirement. In that circumstance, you need to plan for asset preservation and liquidity. This chapter focuses on the financial factors that should be considered in planning for retirement. Because of the unique and changing nature of individual retirement needs, detailed guidelines for developing retirement plans are not presented. The discussion begins with an overview of the retirement planning process and is followed by an examination of the leading sources of retirement income—social security, annuities, and pensions.

Overview of Retirement Planning

No one under the age of 40 can develop a final plan for retirement. Uncertainty about inflation, social security, family size, the type of pension to which one might be entitled, and the amount of assets one will have accumulated by the time one is ready to retire make accurate forecasting impossible. However, contrary to popular notion, it is this uncertainty that makes planning mandatory. In fact, if you knew what the future held, planning would decrease in importance. To cope with uncertainty, you must plan for a variety of outcomes, and you need to monitor and modify your plans as your hopes, your abilities, and your personal finances change.

Unfortunately, many of the elderly lack adequate finances. Income statistics clearly indicate that the median income of persons age 65 or over is below that of all other adult age groups (except for those age 20–24) in the U.S. population. After considering social security and other government benefits, government statistics show that nearly 25 percent of elderly families (single persons and couples with one person 65 and over) are classified as poor or near poor. The data indicate that self-sufficient families obtain much more of their income from earnings and unearned income, such as annuities, pensions, interest, dividends, and rental income, than do the poor families. This information tends to confirm the need for retirement income in excess of that available from social security and other government benefits.

The first step in retirement planning is to develop retirement goals. Once they have been established, you should develop specific plans aimed at attaining them. Plans must consider both retirement income needs and the sources of retirement income available for meeting those needs.

Retirement Goals

People have many different types of goals for retirement. Playing more golf, fishing, traveling, and camping are several of the popular activities people anticipate. To have the income to realize these goals, people should consider the age at which they will retire and what their financial position will be at retirement.

Age at Retirement Estimating when you are likely to retire is important because it affects the time that you have until retirement. Many workers were electing to retire at age 60, or even 55, several years ago. But over the last couple of years, a trend toward later retirement has occurred—some people now remain in the work force until age 70 or longer. While these divergent actions may seem to be inconsistent, they chiefly indicate that today fewer people fit their life into society's preconceived mold. If you think that a shorter working career is for you, you must plan, of course, to place larger amounts of money aside each year for retirement than others who plan to work as long as they are physically and mentally capable.

Financial Position and Goals Your financial position at retirement depends not only on your plans for retirement but perhaps even more so on your choice of career and lifestyle. Remember, as is discussed in Chapters 1 through 4, that your quality of life and lifestyle goals must be chosen on the basis of projected income and expenditures. Although retirement was not mentioned, devoting some income toward retirement goals is essential to economic security in old age. You must be careful not to satisfy low-priority, short-run desires with funds that are better used for high-priority, long-run objectives.

Estimating Retirement Income Needs

Retirement planning would be much simpler in a static economy. But both your personal budget and the general economy are subject to considerable change, and accurately forecasting retirement needs over a long period is difficult. A good strategy is to plan for retirement in a series of short runs. A good way to do this is to state your retirement income objectives as a percent of your present earnings. For example, if you desire a retirement income of 80 percent of your final take-home pay, you, along with your life insurance agent or financial planner, can determine the amount necessary to fund this need. Then, every three to five years you can revise your plan to keep it up to date. Deciding how much to save annually to help you achieve your goals for retirement requires an understanding of social security, life insurance, annuities, pensions, and other investment vehicles. In addition, awareness of the use of compound-interest functions is essential. (Tables showing various results are convenient, and most plans provide projections regularly; the mathematical functions governing the use of interest-related financial factors are beyond the scope of this text, so examples illustrating the retirement income estimates are not included.)

Sources of Retirement Income

The major sources of retirement income for wage earners are social security, annuities, employer pension and retirement plans, and individual retirement and savings plans. This chapter describes the key characteristics of each source. Another source of retirement funds is the sale of a family-sized house and a repurchase of a smaller and less expensive retirement home. For people who have large estates at retirement, income from life insurance cash values, stocks, bonds, mutual funds, real estate, and other investment vehicles may provide retirement income. Those sources are discussed in the chapters on life insurance and investment assets (see Chapters 5, 9, 12, 13, and 14).

Social Security

The Social Security Act established a number of social programs, other than the widely known *Old Age, Survivor's, Disability, and Health Insurance (OASDHI)* program. These include supplementary security income (SSI), unemployment insurance, public assistance, welfare services, and provision for black lung benefits. This chapter gives primary attention to the old age and survivor's portion of the act, since it has a direct bearing on retirement planning. The disability and health benefits of social security are discussed in Chapter 10, which is devoted to health care plans and insurance.

Table 15.1 Percent of Population Age 65 and Over for Selected Past, Present, and Future Years

Year	Percent of Population 65 and Over	Year	Percent of Population 65 and Over
1930	5.4	1990	12.1
1940	6.8	2000	12.1
1950	8.2	2010	12.6
1960	9.1	2020	15.5
1970	9.7	2030	18.4
1975	10.3	2040	18.1
1980	11.3	2050	17.1

Note: The projected values (that is, 1990 and beyond) are based upon the population projections for the central assumptions in the 1977 long-range cost estimates from the *1977 Annual Report of the Board of Trustees of the Federal Old-Age and Survivors Insurance and Disability Trust Funds.*

Source: Adapted from Robert M. Ball, *Social Security* (New York: Columbia University Press, 1978), p. 66, and *Information Please Almanac* (New York: A & W Publishers, Inc., 1983), p. 766.

Basic Concepts

Conceptual misunderstandings about social security are pervasive in three basic areas: financing, solvency, and investment attributes.

Financing The cash benefits paid under the social security program are derived from the payroll taxes (FICA) paid by covered employees and their employers. As pointed out in Chapter 4, a tax rate of 6.7 percent (1984) is paid by the employee and approximately the same amount is paid by the employer (Table 4.1 gives past, present, and future rates). Self-employed persons are also covered by social security. They must contribute 11.30 percent (1984) of their earnings up to the amount of the wage base. The maximum wage base on which taxes were computed in 1984 was $37,800. This amount increases each year at the same rate that the average annual wage increases.

Social security operates on a current funding basis. This means that the taxes collected today are soon thereafter paid out to social security beneficiaries. Although there is a social security trust fund, its purpose is only to act as a short-term financial cushion in periods when current revenues are insufficient to meet current obligations. This trust fund is not intended to be large enough to pay all benefits that have been earned under the program. Many covered workers incorrectly believe that their tax contributions are being held specifically for them by the Social Security Administration. Social security operates on the principle of an *intergenerational compact.* This means that today's working generation is paying for yesterday's workers, who are now retired, and tomorrow's workers will pay for today's workers when they retire.

Solvency People often remark that all of the social security benefit money will be gone by the time that they are ready to collect benefits.

Figure 15.1 Proportion of Retired Persons to Work Force for Selected Years

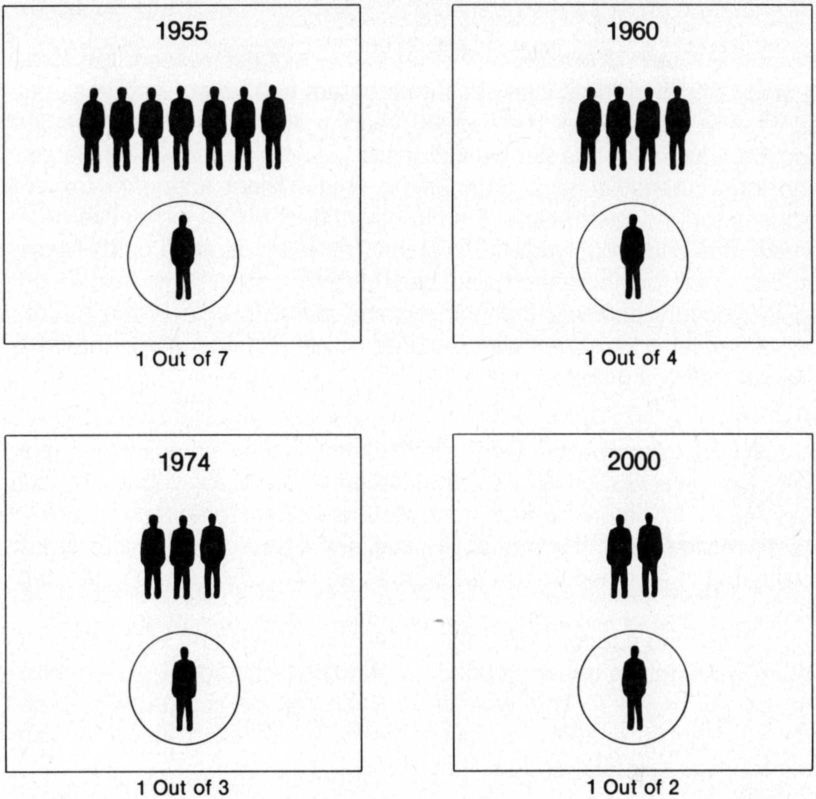

On the contrary, since revenues to pay benefits are derived from taxes, funds will be available as long as there is a work force to keep the system going. A basic financing problem to be overcome by the social security system stems from the fact that a larger percentage of our population will be elderly in future years than has been in the past. For example, as shown in Table 15.1, the percentage of persons age 65 or over is expected to increase to 18.4 percent by the year 2030, up from just 5.4 percent in 1930, and 11.3 percent in 1980. This trend indicates that proportionately fewer persons will be available in the work force to support the population of people over age 65 (see Figure 15.1).

Later Retirement People are now living much longer than when age 65 was selected as the "normal" retirement age. In 1935, life expectancy at age 65 was approximately 10 years. By 1983, at age 65 life expectancy exceeded 15 years. Furthermore, older people today generally experience better health than their counterparts of 50 years ago when social security was first enacted, and improvements in health and life expectancy are predicted to continue. As a result, increasing the normal retirement age to 68 would still leave tomorrow's retirees a longer period of retirement than that of their parents, and it would go a long way toward solving the social security financing problem.

Congressional Generosity Perhaps the biggest reason for forecasted deficits in the social security program has been Congressional generosity. Throughout the past 30 years a sure way to lose popular support was to oppose benefit increases in social security. Thus larger and larger benefits were forthcoming—but without adequate tax increases to fund them. Now, the financial effect of this legislative generosity has caught up with the system. The piper must be paid. Taxes probably will be increased and benefits reduced. Yet no expert on social security believes that the system will go broke. In the future, benefits will be legislated with a closer scrutiny of how much they will cost and who is going to pay for them.

Investment Attributes If you are like many people you might wonder what the "financial crisis" of social security means for you. First, you might ask, "Will there be any money left when I get to retirement age?" As discussed here, the probability that social security will have funds to pay out is as close to 100 percent as any future economic plan can be.

As a second concern you might question, "What kind of investment return will I get on my contributions? Wouldn't I be better off to invest the money myself?" This type of question can be answered in three parts: (1) social security vs. investment, (2) expected rates of return under social security, and (3) insolvency.

Social Security vs. Investment Social security should not be viewed as an investment. It is properly viewed as a social insurance system: an insurance system that insures covered workers and their families against poverty resulting from retirement, death, disability, or health problems. If you die or become disabled at age 30 and have a dependent spouse and two small children, your family could be eligible for monthly social security payments that would total more than $150,000—even though you may have paid in less than $10,000 in taxes.

Similarly, you might retire and live for 15, 20, or even 30 years. It makes no difference to social security. You will continue to draw benefits even though these benefits greatly exceed the amounts you paid into the system. On the other hand, you might contribute social security taxes for 40 years and then die (without dependents) the day you retire—and not collect a penny. An insurance system only works when some participants collect less than they pay in—otherwise no one could collect more. This principle holds regardless of whether we are talking about private life insurance, homeowner's insurance, or automobile insurance—or the retirement, life insurance, and disability coverages offered by social security.

Expected Rates of Return Many critics have complained that investment yields on social security could easily be exceeded through comparable investments in stocks, bonds, or real estate. Even if this claim were true, it would be irrelevant. But it is not true—even for workers entering the social security system during the 1980s. After allowing for all of the cash and noncash (e.g., medicare) benefits of social security, for the relatively safe nature of the benefits, and for a moderate premium for the risk reduction features of the program, the expected value of most workers' benefits exceeds the expected value of their tax payments into the system.

Insolvency What if the worst happens, though? What if taxes have to be raised much higher than expected, benefits have to be cut, and the retirement age is increased? Assume you do not get back a fair amount for what you paid in. Where has your money gone? The money has been paid to your aunts, uncles, grandparents, and parents. Perhaps as a dependent of a disabled or deceased worker, you have already received benefits yourself. (Many young people today have been paid thousands of dollars from social security before they even begin to work and pay social security taxes.)

Social security is not a perfect system. It is a blend of compromises and political trade-offs. It allocates too much money to some people, not enough to others. Its benefit and cost structure has emanated from emotion as much as it has from rational analysis. Improvements to maintain the system's financial integrity and basic insurance functions are long overdue. Yet, even if these problems are not worked out, even if today's workers do not personally receive as much as they paid in, those monies for the most part will have been paid to the older members of their families.

Who Is Covered?

Because of the broad coverage of social security, identifying who is not covered is simpler than listing all who do participate. Basically, the following classifications were excluded in 1983 from mandatory participation in social security: (1) employees of state and local governments, (2) employees of tax-exempt charitable or service institutions, (3) civilian employees of the federal government, (4) railroad workers who are covered under the Railroad Retirement Act, and (5) certain marginal employment positions such as newspaper delivery persons under age 18 and full-time college students working in fraternity and sorority houses. By far the largest number of workers in these excluded classifications are employees of state and local governments and charitable organizations. These groups are not forced to participate because the federal government is not empowered to impose a tax on their employers. However, any of these groups may voluntarily participate in social security if a majority of the employees in it elect coverage. Unlike private employees, public and charitable employees who voluntarily enroll in the social security program also have the option of withdrawing after five years of participation. Employees of the federal government do not participate in social security because they are covered by another retirement system that they believe is superior to social security and do not feel the need for additional coverage. Over the opposition of federal employees, however, legislation has been proposed that would include these workers in the social security system.

Benefits Important to Retirees

The basic social security disability and health care benefits are discussed in Chapter 10. Attention is given here only to the types of payments that can be important to retirees and their dependents throughout retirement: old-age and survivor's benefits.

Old-Age Benefits Workers who have become fully insured (the meaning of this term is discussed later) may receive old-age benefits for life once they reach the age of 65. In addition, workers may retire as early as age 62 with reduced benefits. If the retiree has a spouse age 65 or older, the spouse may be entitled to a benefit equal to one-half of the amount received by the retired worker. A spouse of a retired worker may also elect early receipt of reduced benefits at age 62. If the retired worker has a dependent child (or children), the spouse is entitled to a benefit, regardless of age, until the child (or children) reaches age 16. In addition, unmarried children under age 18 (or 19 if still in high school) of retired, deceased, or disabled workers are entitled to monthly social security benefits.

Survivor's Benefits If a covered worker dies, the spouse can receive survivor's benefits from social security. These benefits include a small lump sum payment of several hundred dollars followed by monthly benefit checks. The lump sum amount is paid automatically upon application. In order to be eligible for monthly payments, the widowed spouse generally must be at least age 60 or have a dependent and unmarried child of the deceased worker in his or her care. When the children of the deceased worker reach age 16 before the spouse reaches age 60, the monthly benefits cease and do not resume until the spouse does turn 60. This period of time during which survivor's benefits are not paid to the spouse is called the "black-out period."

Benefit Amounts

The amount of social security benefits that an eligible person is entitled to receive is scheduled under the law. The last enacted benefit sched-

Table 15.2 Monthly Retirement Benefits for Workers Who Reach 62 in 1979–1983

Average Yearly Earnings	For Workers: Retirement at 65	at 64	at 63	at 62	For Dependents[a]: Spouse at 65 or child	at 64	at 63	at 62	Family Benefits[b]
$ 1,200	$156.70	$146.30	$135.90	$125.40	$ 78.40	$ 71.90	$ 65.40	$ 58.50	$235.10
2,600	230.10	214.80	199.50	184.10	115.10	105.50	95.90	86.40	345.20
3,000	251.80	235.10	218.30	201.50	125.90	115.40	104.90	94.50	384.90
3,400	270.00	252.00	234.00	216.00	135.00	123.80	112.50	101.30	434.90
4,000	296.20	276.50	256.80	237.00	148.10	135.70	123.40	111.10	506.20
4,400	317.30	296.20	275.00	253.90	158.70	145.40	132.20	119.10	562.50
4,800	336.00	313.60	291.20	268.80	168.00	153.90	140.00	126.00	612.70
5,200	353.20	329.70	306.20	282.60	176.60	161.80	147.20	132.50	662.70
5,600	370.60	345.90	321.20	296.50	185.30	169.80	154.40	139.00	687.10
6,000	388.20	362.40	336.50	310.60	194.10	177.80	161.70	145.60	712.10
6,400	405.60	378.60	351.60	324.50	202.80	185.80	169.00	152.10	737.10
6,800	424.10	395.90	367.60	339.30	212.10	194.30	176.70	159.10	762.30
7,200	446.00	416.30	386.60	356.80	223.00	204.30	185.80	167.30	788.90
7,600	465.60	434.60	403.60	372.50	232.80	213.30	194.00	174.60	814.70
8,000	482.60	450.50	418.30	386.10	241.30	221.10	201.10	181.00	844.50
8,400	492.90	460.10	427.20	394.40	246.50	225.80	205.40	184.90	862.60
8,800	505.10	471.50	437.80	404.10	252.60	231.40	210.50	189.50	883.80
9,200	516.00	481.60	447.20	412.80	258.00	236.40	215.00	193.50	903.00
9,400	520.40	485.80	451.10	416.40	260.20	238.40	216.80	195.20	910.40
9,600	524.60	489.70	454.70	419.70	262.30	240.30	218.50	196.80	918.00
9,800	530.40	495.10	459.70	424.40	265.20	243.00	221.00	198.90	928.00
10,000	534.70	499.10	463.50	427.80	267.40	245.00	222.80	200.60	935.70

[a]If a person is eligible for both a worker's benefit and a spouse's benefit, the check actually payable is limited to the larger of the two.
[b]The maximum amount payable to a family is generally reached when a worker and two family members are eligible.
Source: Social Security Administration, U.S. Department of Health and Human Services.

ule as of 1983 is shown in Table 15.2. This schedule indicates the inception benefit amounts that beneficiaries will receive. However, although the schedule sets the first-year benefit amounts for a given beneficiary, that individual will then have his or her subsequent benefits increase with the cost of living.

Note that scheduled benefits do not increase proportionately as much as the corresponding average yearly earnings. This tendency results because one of the basic social objectives of social security is to help lower-income families more than the middle- and upper-income groups. A portion of social security benefits is taxable for recipients with adjusted gross income above a specified level. However, other features of social security favor the middle- and upper-income families. Social security benefits are paid to people without their proving a need. Consequently, a millionaire is entitled to benefits just the same as an impoverished family. Also, retired social security beneficiaries sixty-five or older may have their benefit payments reduced if they have annual income (for 1984) in excess of $6,960 per year. (*Note:* The annual exempt amount increases automatically to keep pace with increases in average wages.) Generally, the applicable rule states that for each $2 earned in excess of $6,600, the beneficiary loses $1 in benefits. In contrast, unearned income such as interest, dividends, and rent may be of an unlimited amount without a corresponding benefit reduction.

The fact that benefits are reduced because of earned income is one of the most frequently criticized features of social security. Consequently, this so-called *earnings test* may be eliminated in the future. The principle that underlies this rule in its present form is that social security benefits are intended to be wage replacement payments. Thus, if wages are still being earned (until age 70), the offset described is imposed. And since the program is supposed to encourage thrift and retirement financial planning by covered workers, those who have accumulated savings and investments are not penalized.

Receiving Social Security Benefits

Social security payments are not paid to eligible individuals (or their dependents) automatically. An application for benefits must be filed with the Social Security Administration. It then determines the applicant's eligibility for benefits based upon whether the covered worker had enough quarters (three-month periods) of participation in the social security system.

Retirement Benefit Eligibility In order to qualify for retirement benefits, nearly all workers today must be employed in a job covered by social security for at least 40 quarters. These quarters do not need to be consecutive. Once this 40 quarter requirement is met, the worker becomes fully insured and remains eligible for retirement payments even if he or she never again works in covered employment. Note, however, that in computing the average yearly earnings of covered wages, zeros are inserted for years in which no social security taxes were paid. This substantially reduces the size of monthly payments for which the retiree is eligible.

Survivor's Benefit Eligibility A spouse and/or dependent children of a deceased worker are eligible for monthly benefits if the worker was fully insured at the time of death or, in some special cases, if certain other requirements are met. The lump sum benefit mentioned earlier is payable if the worker was fully or currently insured. Workers are considered currently insured if they had 6 quarters of coverage during the full 13 quarter period preceding the date of death.

Student Benefit Eligibility In 1965, Congress extended social security benefit eligibility to full-time students aged 18–21. The basic requirements are that the student must be attending an approved educational institution and must be the child of a retired, deceased, or disabled parent who meets the criteria for benefit eligibility. These benefits, though, have been criticized as an inefficient use of social security funds. As a result they are being phased out, with the program scheduled to end in 1985.

Social Security and Retirement Planning

No one can accurately predict the amount of social security benefits that will be paid 30 or 40 years from now. For retirement planning purposes, however, it seems reasonable to expect social security to provide the retired average wage earner who is married with about 40 to 60 percent of the wages that he or she was earning in the year before retirement. This, of course, assumes that the retiree has had a full career working in covered employment. Social security should, therefore, be viewed as a foundation for your retirement income. By itself, it is insufficient to allow a worker and spouse to maintain their preretirement standard of living. For people who earn in excess of the wage base, a lower percentage of total preretirement wages will be replaced by social security. Consequently, both average and upper-middle-income families must plan to supplement their social security retirement benefits with income from other sources. Two of these other sources that are popular are annuities and pensions. These topics are discussed in the next two parts of this chapter.

Annuities

Since 1965, the number of annuity contracts in force with U.S. life insurance companies has increased from just over 1 million to more than 6 million. This growth has resulted primarily from the greater public awareness of annuities brought about by increased marketing efforts of life insurance companies. Furthermore, legislation allows widespread use of annuities in tax-sheltered retirement programs. The following sections discuss the annuity principle, the classification of annuities, their sources and costs, and an evaluation of their role in retirement planning.

The Annuity Principle

An annuity is actually the opposite of life insurance. As pointed out in Chapter 9, life insurance is the systematic accumulation of an estate for protection against financial loss resulting from premature death. In contrast, an *annuity* is the systematic liquidation of an estate to protect against the economic difficulties that could result from outliving personal financial resources. The period during which premiums are paid for the purchase of an annuity is called the *accumulation period,* and, correspondingly, the period during which annuity payments are made is called the *distribution period.*

Under a pure life annuity contract, a life insurance company will guarantee regular monthly payments to an individual for as long as that person lives. These benefits are composed of three parts: principal, interest, and survivorship benefits. The *principal* consists of the premium amounts paid in by the *annuitant* (person buying the annuity) during the accumulation period. *Interest* is the amount earned on these funds between the time they are paid and distributed. The portion of the principal and interest that has not been returned to the annuitant prior to death is the *survivorship benefit.* These funds are available to those members of the annuity group who survive in each subsequent period.

By using mortality tables (see Table 9.3) and estimated investment returns, life insurance companies can calculate for a group of annuitants of a given age the amount of monthly payment that can be guaranteed to each individual without prematurely depleting the total amounts that have accumulated. Consequently, the risk of outliving one's income is eliminated.

Classification of Annuities

Annuities may be classified by the following nonexclusive classifications: method of paying premiums, disposition of proceeds, inception date of benefits, number of lives covered, and method of calculating benefits. Figure 15.2 is a chart showing this classification system.

Method of Paying Premiums The two methods used to purchase an annuity are the single premium and the installment method. As the name implies, a *single-premium annuity contract* is one that is bought with a lump sum payment. Most single-premium annuities are purchased just before retirement. However, if a given single-premium amount is paid earlier, a larger monthly benefit will be paid at retirement. Frequently the cash values of death proceeds from a life insurance policy provide the funds used to acquire an annuity under the single premium method. Also, the majority of group annuities are funded with a single premium. As might be expected, many individuals buy annuities by paying *installments* (often annually) throughout their working career. During the period of accumulation, the contract serves as a medium for savings. If the annuitant dies before the distribution period, the premiums paid with interest earned are given to the beneficiaries or the estate. In addition, the annuitant may either terminate the contract at any time and withdraw the cash value or simply stop paying the periodic installments and take a paid-up annuity for a reduced amount. One potential advantage of purchasing an installment-type annuity early is that the scheduled benefits are based on mortality rates in effect when the contract is purchased. Even if the mortality rate improves, as is expected, you will not be required to pay the higher premium stipulated in contracts issued later on.

Figure 15.2 Major Classifications of Annuities

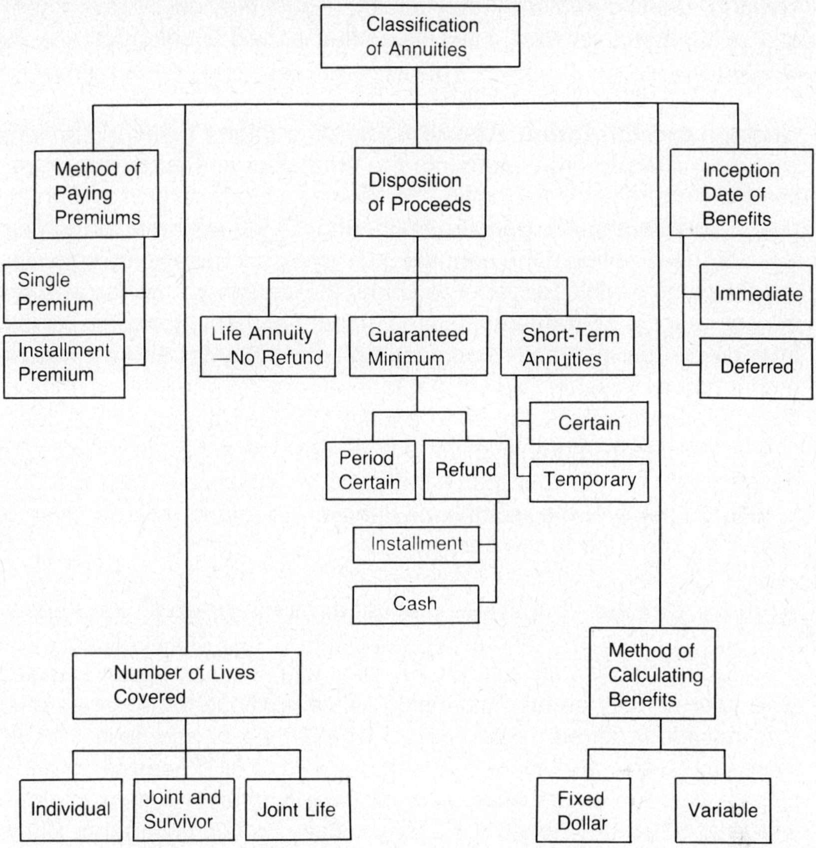

Source: Robert I. Mehr, *Life Insurance: Theory and Practice,* revised edition (Dallas, Texas: Business Publications, Inc., 1977), © 1977 by Business Publications, Inc. Reproduced with the permission of the publisher.

Disposition of Proceeds The four options that are most widely used in the distribution of annuity proceeds are the life annuity with no refund, the guaranteed minimum annuity, the annuity certain, and the temporary life annuity.

Life Annuity with No Refund (Straight Life) Under the *life annuity with no refund (straight life)* option, the annuitant receives a specified amount of income for life, regardless of whether the period over which income is distributed turns out to be 1 year or 50 years. No refunds or payments are made to the estate or family when the annuitant dies. This disposition procedure entitles the annuitant to the largest monthly payments of any of the distribution methods. These larger payments result since, when the annuitant dies, the issuer (a life insurance company) does not have to distribute the principal, if any, to the annuitant's heirs. Only a minority of individuals select the life annuity with no refund. Most people who purchase annuities are opposed to sacrificing the large unused portion of their capital should they die relatively soon after retirement. However, this option often is used under group annuity contracts.

Guaranteed Minimum Annuity The *guaranteed minimum annuity* was developed to help overcome the emotional and economic objections to the straight life annuity. The two basic types of such an annuity are (1) the life annuity, period certain, and (2) the refund annuity. With each of these options, the annuitant designates a beneficiary who also may become eligible for benefits. Under the *life annuity, period certain,* the annuitant is guaranteed a stated amount of monthly income for life. In addition, the insurance company agrees to pay for at least a minimum number of years (five or ten, for example), regardless of whether the annuitant survives. A *refund annuity* provides that upon the death of the annuitant, monthly payments will be made to the designated beneficiary until the total purchase price of the annuity has been refunded. In place of the monthly payments, the refund may be taken in cash if so provided in the contract.

Annuity Certain A specified amount of monthly income for a specified period of years without consideration of any life contingency is provided by the *annuity certain.* For example, if an annuitant selected a 10-year annuity certain, payments would continue for 10 years after that individual retired, regardless of whether he or she lived 2 or 20 more years. The annuity certain can be used to fill a need for monthly income that will expire after a certain length of time. For example, a widow at 52 could choose a 10-year annuity certain contract to fill the need for income until she reaches age 62, when she plans to apply for social security benefits.

Temporary Life Annuity Although similar to the annuity certain, the *temporary life annuity* differs from it in that benefits continue for the specified period only if the annuitant survives. If the widow had chosen a 10-year temporary life annuity but had died at age 60, no further payments would be made under the contract. Since a survivorship benefit is not provided by the temporary life annuity, it provides a larger monthly income than the annuity certain. The insurer that sells the temporary life annuity may not have to pay the benefits over the stated period, while the insurer that sells the annuity certain must. Therefore, unless the widow had a beneficiary who needed extra income, she would be wise to select the temporary life annuity instead of the annuity certain. In actuality, annuitants purchase a temporary life annuity contract only infrequently for the same basic reason that they avoid straight life annuities—they do not want a major portion of the purchase price of their annuity to be wasted if they should die shortly after payments begin.

Inception Date of Benefits An annuitant often has the choice of receiving monthly benefits immediately upon buying an annuity or of deferring receipt for a number of years. Logically, the first type is called an immediate annuity and the latter a deferred annuity. An *immediate annuity,* purchased with a single premium, is most often used in conjunction with the cash value or death proceeds of a life insurance policy to create a stream of cash receipts needed for retirement or to support a widow and/or dependent children. A *deferred annuity* can be bought with either a lump sum payment or through an installment plan. This contract is quite flexible and can be issued with numerous options to the annuitant for both paying the premiums and receiving the proceeds. Most annuities purchased under group contracts are immediate annuities, whereas those purchased by individuals are generally installment-type deferred annuities.

Number of Lives Covered Most annuities are written on the life of one individual. However, in some cases, a spouse or other dependent of the annuitant can be included. Such contracts are called joint annuities, and the most common of them is the joint and last survivorship annuity. Under the *joint and last survivorship annuity,* the monthly payments continue until the last survivor named in the contract dies. For example, assume that a husband and wife are covered under a joint and last survivorship annuity contract. If the husband dies first, payments will continue to be made to the wife for as long as she lives; while, if the wife dies before her husband, he still receives benefits for the remainder of his life.

These contracts can be written so that the same amount is paid monthly regardless of whether one or both parties are alive, or the benefits can be scheduled to decrease upon the death of the first mate. Most common, probably, is the annuity that reduces benefits by one third after the death of the spouse. The reasoning behind this plan is that, regardless of the popular expression, one *can* live more cheaply than two.

Method of Calculating Benefits Most annuity contracts are written on a *fixed dollar* basis. This means that once a payment schedule is selected, the amount of monthly income provided does not change. In contrast, a growing number of annuity plans are available that adjust the monthly income provided according to the actual investment (and sometimes mortality) experience of the insurer. These latter contracts are called *variable annuities.* The advantage of a fixed dollar annuity is that the dollar amount of monthly income is guaranteed to the annuitant regardless of how poorly or how well the investments of the insurer perform. A major disadvantage, however, is that in periods of inflation, the purchasing power of the dollar erodes. For example, with an 8 percent annual inflation rate, $1 is reduced in purchasing power to 68¢ in just five years.

Table 15.3 Comparison of CREF Variable Annuity Unit with the Consumer Price Index, 1970–1980

Year	Percent Increase in Consumer Price Index (CPI)	Percent Increase or Decrease in CREF Variable Annuity Unit
1970	5.9%	−11.0%
1971	4.3	6.0
1972	3.3	16.6
1973	6.2	−11.6
1974	11.0	−17.0
1975	9.1	−16.7
1976	5.8	20.1
1977	6.5	− 5.5
1978	7.7	− 6.1
1979	11.3	17.2
1980	13.5	− 3.7
1970–1980	**112.2%**	**− 9.1%**

Source: George E. Rejda, *Principles of Insurance* (Glenview, Ill.: Scott, Foresman and Company, 1982), p. 348.

To overcome the disadvantage of the fixed dollar contract, the variable annuity was developed. With this plan, annuitants face a different risk. They cannot be certain how well the insurer's investments, which consist primarily of common stocks, will do. Annuitants take a chance that they will receive even a lower monthly income in absolute dollars than a fixed dollar contract would provide. Most people who participate in variable annuity plans, of course, anticipate that they will at least be able to keep up with the cost of living. Unfortunately, though, variable annuity values and the CPI do not necessarily perform similarly. Table 15.3 shows that even though the CPI rose approximately 112 percent between 1970 and 1980, the College Retirement Equity Fund (CREF) variable annuity actually declined by 9.1 percent during this same period. This example shows that a real risk of a reduction in benefits from variable annuities does exist. Indeed, as a result of the dip in common stock values, the payments made under many variable annuity plans during the 1970s fell below the amounts paid by corresponding fixed dollar plans. Although most premiums paid into variable annuities are invested in common stocks, annuitants are sometimes given a choice as to whether they wish to have their monies placed in common stocks throughout the accumulation period as well as during the distribution period. In some cases, annuitants may prefer premium build-up in a variable plan and then switch to a fixed dollar plan at retirement. In this manner they participate in the growth of the economy over their working career but guard against short-term recessions that may occur during retirement years.

Table 15.4 Lump Sum Cost Necessary to Fund Payments of $100 per Month for Two Types of Annuities by Sex and Age at Issue

	Life Annuity with No Refund				Life—10 Years Certain			
	Male		Female		Male		Female	
Company	65	75	65	75	65	75	65	75
One	$10,430	$7,420	$11,560	$8,640	$11,220	$ 9,370	$12,090	$10,020
Two	11,300	8,350	12,444	9,230	11,980	9,930	12,820	10,350
Three	12,410	8,680	13,870	9,840	13,320	10,850	14,390	11,410

Source: Compiled from *Best's Flitcraft Compend,* 95th edition (Oldwick, N.J.: A.M. Best Company, 1982).

Sources and Costs of Annuities

Life insurance companies are the leading source of annuities. Since the marketing of annuities is similar to life insurance, this development has been quite logical. The cost of annuities varies considerably with the age of the annuitant at issue, the age of the annuitant when payments begin, the method of proceeds distribution, the number of lives covered, and the sex of the annuitant. Table 15.4 presents the lump sum costs of several leading companies for two types of immediate annuities. Note that substantial differences exist among the amount of companies' premiums. These differences confirm the need to shop around before making an annuity purchase. Note, too, that in every category the cost to females is more than the cost to males. This is due to the lower mortality rates among women. The differences in mortality rates for males and females can be seen in Table 15.5. Mortality differences not withstanding, legislation is now pending that would exclude sex as a criterion for annuity rate making.

An Evaluation of Annuities

The major value of annuities, for the most part, is that they are a source of income a person cannot outlive. While individuals might create a similar arrangement by simply living off the benefit of interest or dividends from investments, they would find it difficult to engage in the systematic liquidation of their principal in a manner that would be timed to exactly coincide with their death. Often viewed as a disadvantage, however, are the returns on funds used to purchase a deferred annuity. They typically range from 6 to 8 percent, a relatively low rate that can often be matched or exceeded through alternative investment media. Because of this, some persons may prefer to accumulate retirement funds in another investment medium and then use these funds at retirement to purchase an immediate annuity. Note, however, that when a deferred annuity is purchased, the monthly benefit is guaranteed at the time of purchase, even though benefits may not be payable for 30 or 40 years; thus, even if mortality rates for the elderly improve materially during the accumulation period, the annuity payments will not be reduced. On the other hand, if an immediate annuity is purchased, the

Table 15.5 Male vs. Female Mortality Rates and Life Expectancies

1980 Commissioners Standard Ordinary Mortality Table[a]

Age	Male Mortality Rate Per 1,000	Male Expectancy, Years	Female Mortality Rate Per 1,000	Female Expectancy, Years	Age	Male Mortality Rate Per 1,000	Male Expectancy, Years	Female Mortality Rate Per 1,000	Female Expectancy, Years
0	4.18	70.83	2.89	75.83	**50**	6.71	25.36	4.96	29.53
1	1.07	70.13	.87	75.04	**51**	7.30	24.52	5.31	28.67
2	.99	69.20	.81	74.11	**52**	7.96	23.70	5.70	27.82
3	.98	68.27	.79	73.17	**53**	8.71	22.89	6.15	26.96
4	.95	67.34	.77	72.23	**54**	9.56	22.08	6.61	26.14
5	.90	66.40	.76	71.28	**55**	10.47	21.29	7.09	25.31
6	.85	65.46	.73	70.34	**56**	11.46	20.51	7.57	24.49
7	.80	64.52	.72	69.39	**57**	12.49	19.74	8.03	23.67
8	.76	63.57	.70	68.44	**58**	13.59	18.99	8.47	22.86
9	.74	62.62	.69	67.48	**59**	14.77	18.24	8.94	22.05
10	.73	61.66	.68	66.53	**60**	16.00	17.51	9.47	21.25
11	.77	60.71	.69	65.58	**61**	17.54	16.79	10.13	20.44
12	.85	59.75	.72	64.62	**62**	19.19	16.08	10.96	19.65
13	.99	58.80	.75	63.67	**63**	21.06	15.38	12.02	18.86
14	1.15	57.86	.80	62.71	**64**	23.14	14.70	13.25	18.08
15	1.33	56.93	.85	61.76	**65**	25.42	14.04	14.59	17.32
16	1.51	56.00	.90	60.82	**66**	27.85	13.39	16.00	16.57
17	1.67	55.09	.95	59.87	**67**	30.44	12.76	17.43	15.83
18	1.78	54.18	.98	58.93	**68**	33.19	12.14	18.84	15.10
19	1.86	53.27	1.02	57.98	**69**	36.17	11.54	20.36	14.38
20	1.90	52.37	1.05	57.04	**70**	39.51	10.96	22.11	13.67
21	1.91	51.47	1.07	56.10	**71**	43.30	10.39	24.23	12.97
22	1.89	50.57	1.09	55.16	**72**	47.65	9.84	26.87	12.28
23	1.86	49.66	1.11	54.22	**73**	52.64	9.30	30.11	11.60
24	1.82	48.75	1.14	53.28	**74**	58.19	8.79	33.93	10.95
25	1.77	47.84	1.16	52.34	**75**	64.19	8.31	38.24	10.32
26	1.73	46.93	1.19	51.40	**76**	70.53	7.84	42.97	9.71
27	1.71	46.01	1.22	50.46	**77**	77.12	7.40	48.04	9.12
28	1.70	45.09	1.26	49.52	**78**	83.90	6.97	53.45	8.55
29	1.71	44.16	1.30	48.59	**79**	91.05	6.57	59.35	8.01
30	1.73	43.24	1.35	47.65	**80**	98.84	6.18	65.99	7.48
31	1.78	42.31	1.40	46.71	**81**	107.48	5.80	73.60	6.98
32	1.83	41.38	1.45	45.78	**82**	117.25	5.44	82.40	6.49
33	1.91	40.46	1.50	44.84	**83**	128.26	5.09	92.53	6.03
34	2.00	39.54	1.58	43.91	**84**	140.25	4.77	103.81	5.59
35	2.11	38.61	1.65	42.98	**85**	152.95	4.46	116.10	5.18
36	2.24	37.69	1.76	42.05	**86**	166.09	4.18	129.29	4.80
37	2.40	36.78	1.89	41.12	**87**	179.55	3.91	143.32	4.43
38	2.58	35.87	2.04	40.20	**88**	193.27	3.66	158.18	4.09
39	2.79	34.96	2.22	39.28	**89**	207.29	3.41	173.94	3.77
40	3.02	34.05	2.42	38.36	**90**	221.77	3.18	190.75	3.45
41	3.29	33.16	2.64	37.40	**91**	236.98	2.94	208.87	3.15
42	3.56	32.26	2.87	36.55	**92**	253.45	2.70	226.81	2.85
43	3.87	31.38	3.09	35.66	**93**	272.11	2.44	251.51	2.55
44	4.19	30.50	3.32	34.77	**94**	295.90	2.17	279.31	2.24
45	4.55	29.62	3.56	33.88	**95**	329.96	1.87	317.32	1.91
46	4.92	28.76	3.80	33.00	**96**	384.55	1.54	375.74	1.50
47	5.32	27.90	4.05	32.12	**97**	480.20	1.20	474.97	1.21
48	5.74	27.04	4.33	31.25	**98**	657.98	.84	655.85	.84
49	6.21	26.20	4.63	30.39	**99**	1000.00	.50	1000.00	.50

[a]Based on experience of years 1970–1975.

Source: Best's Flitcraft Compend, 95th edition (Oldwick, N.J.: A.M. Best Company, 1982), p. 572.

monthly benefit payable is that which is in effect at the time of retirement. Thus the deferred annuity approach could very well produce a higher benefit even though the cash values during the accumulation period earn only a nominal rate of interest. This trade-off of low returns for the level of guaranteed future income should be considered when the use of annuities in fulfilling specified retirement income needs is being evaluated. Expected investment returns also influence the relationship of premiums and benefits. Therefore, if interest rates are rising and mortality rates are decreasing, the premiums may decrease or increase depending upon the magnitude of change in each.

Pension and Retirement Plans

Accompanying the expansion of the social security program and the increase in annuity sales has been the growth of employer-sponsored pension and retirement plans. Presently, approximately 50 percent of all wage and salaried workers in the United States are covered by some employer-sponsored retirement or profit-sharing plan. In contrast, in 1940, when the social security program was in its infancy, less than 25 percent of the work force had the benefit of an employer-sponsored plan. This section examines the reasons for the dramatic increase in both the number and scope of pension and retirement plans, the effects of this growth, the basic features of the various plans, the classification of plans, types of employer plans, other types of plans, and government influence on pension plans.

Reasons for Growth

Although there are many reasons for the widespread development of pension and retirement plans, three are probably most important. Basically, pension plans have been developed by employers (1) to attract and retain quality employees, (2) to meet the demands of collective bargaining, and (3) to provide benefits to owners and key managers of firms. Many employers have stressed and will continue to stress the advantages of their retirement plan in attracting and keeping valuable employees. In fact, numerous firms have more or less been forced to implement retirement plans simply as a defensive measure to counteract the effects of plans of other employers who compete for the same workers. Of course, few representatives of these firms would go so far as to say that a good retirement plan encourages workers to put forth more effort. Nevertheless, evidence indicates that the lack of a good plan can serve as a job deterrent to prospective employees and may increase labor turnover, especially for employees age 40 and older.

In 1948, the National Labor Relations Board (NLRB) ruled that pensions and other types of insurance are a legitimate subject for collective bargaining. Since that time, many employers have established new pension plans or liberalized the provisions of existing ones to meet or anticipate union demands.

Qualified pension plans, which are discussed later, allow firms to deduct for tax purposes their contributions to employee retirement programs. These contributions are not included in the taxable income of the employee. As a result, many firms, especially smaller ones, have established pension or retirement plans to help owners and key managers accrue funds for retirement that are not subject to federal income taxes. Of course, eventually, when the funds are paid out as benefits, employees do have to pay taxes on them.

As a result of the rules and regulations it established for protecting employees participating in private employer retirement plans, the Employee Retirement Income Security Act (sometimes referred to as ERISA or the Pension Reform Act of 1974) now contributes to a reduction in the number of new retirement plans started among smaller firms. (This law is discussed in greater detail in a subsequent section of this chapter.) In addition, more liberal rules with respect to Individual Retirement Accounts (IRAs) also diminish the advantages of small employer-sponsored pension plans.

Effects of Growth in Plans

Still, the overall growth of employer-sponsored retirement plans is important in two major areas. First, payments made under these plans represent a needed source of income to millions of retired workers and their dependents. For example, more than 8 million persons received in excess of $20 billion from private employer retirement plans in 1980. In addition, retirement programs sponsored by federal, state, and local government employers will provide another $22 billion to more than 4.5 million benefit recipients. As more employer plans mature, both the number of persons and dollar payments involved can be expected to increase substantially. The total payments made to retired workers under employer-sponsored pension plans are still much less than those made by social security. But because a smaller number of persons are eligible for employer retirement benefits, some individuals receive a much larger monthly benefit from their pension.

The second major effect of growth in these pension funds is the related growth of their influence on the behavior of capital (security) markets in the United States. Assets of all pension and retirement programs (excluding social security) in the United States now total approximately $700 billion. The largest portion of this amount is invested in corporate and government bonds as well as corporate stocks. In fact, pension and retirement funds as a group are now the largest institutional owners of the corporate bonds and stocks traded on the

New York Stock Exchange. In addition, pension fund money is also becoming more widely available to buy commercial and investment real estate, as well as to provide mortgages to other investors.

Basic Features of Pension Plans

Apart from financing, which is discussed later, the basic features of pension plans that you should be familiar with pertain to participation requirements, contributory versus noncontributory plans, benefit rights, retirement age, and methods of computing benefits.

Participation Requirements In many pension plans, employees must meet certain criteria before they become eligible for participation. Most common are requirements that relate to years of service, minimum age, level of earnings, and employment classification. Years of service and/or minimum age requirements are often incorporated into retirement plans in the belief that a much greater labor turnover rate applies to newly hired employees and younger employees. Therefore, to reduce the administrative costs of these plans, employees in these categories are excluded from participation. Pension plans which limit enrollment to employees who earn in excess of a given salary amount do so generally when the private plan is designed to integrate with social security. Recall that social security replaces a much higher percentage of lost earnings for workers who receive relatively low pay, but employees who earn higher salaries need a supplemental plan to prevent a material reduction in income at retirement.

Contributory versus Noncontributory Plans A retirement plan is considered *noncontributory* if the employer pays the total cost of the benefits. Under a plan with a *contributory* feature, the employee also bears a portion of this cost. Most pensions established by corporations are noncontributory. In contrast, nearly all plans for employees of federal, state, and local government require a contribution from the employee. In contributory plans, the employee's share of the costs is frequently between 3 and 10 percent of annual wages and is typically paid through a payroll deduction. When employees who have participated in a contributory retirement plan terminate employment prior to retirement, they are legally entitled to some benefit based upon the amount of their own contributions. Usually this benefit is a cash lump sum, but in some cases it can be taken as a monthly payment at retirement. Whether departing employees receive any benefit from the employer's contributions to the pension plan depends on the benefit rights of the plan.

Benefit Rights Not everyone who participates in a pension plan will earn the right to receive retirement benefits. Pension plans impose criteria that must be met before the employee can obtain a nonforfeitable right to a pension. When nonforfeitable rights are secured by employees, those rights are said to be *vested.* Prior to 1974, employers often required employees to be employed for 25 years or more before vesting would occur. If the employee changed jobs before this specified period of employment was completed, the employee would lose all of the employer-sponsored pension benefits previously earned. Because there is high mobility of labor and capital, many workers at retirement faced the prospect of no pension. As a result, this practice contributed to the social problem of low incomes among the aged.

One of the principal purposes of the Pension Reform Act of 1974 (ERISA) was to reduce the number of employees who worked for most of their adult lives, but who still did not qualify for a pension. This legislation aimed to accomplish that goal by requiring covered employers to grant employees vested rights according to certain standards. Generally speaking, these standards are that full vesting of employer-provided benefits must require no more than 10 years of employment when there is no partial vesting prior to 10 years of service. As an alternative, employers can begin to vest an employee after 5 years, and then take up to 15 years to phase in fully vested benefits. Note, though, that these are minimum standards. Many employers grant vesting on more favorable terms.

Vesting can take different forms; in other words, the benefits employees receive when the employer contributions become vested vary in kind. In a growing minority of cases, the employee may choose a cash lump sum based upon these contributions. More frequently the employee becomes eligible for a monthly check at retirement based upon contributions to date. Under a contributory plan, if an employee dies before retirement, generally his or her contributions are refunded without any death benefits being paid.

To illustrate the vesting process, assume that a medium-size firm offers a plan in which vesting of benefits becomes complete for eligible employees after 10 years. The plan is contributory, with employees paying 3 percent of their salaries and the employer paying an amount equal to 6 percent of the employees' salaries. Under this plan, employees cannot withdraw as a cash payment the contributions made by their employer. The plan provides annual benefits in the amount of $11 per year of service for each $100 of an employee's final monthly earnings—the amount earned during the final month in the employ of the firm. Therefore, an employee who worked a minimum of 10 years for the firm would be eligible for a retirement benefit from that firm even if he or she transferred jobs at, say, age 35. However, because of inflation the value of the benefit for a worker who left the firm substantially before retirement age could be very small.

Two cases, one for a career employee and one for the minimum-years-of-service employee, might help to clarify this concept. A career employee with 40 years of service and final monthly earnings of $1,800 would be entitled to an annual pension of $7,920 (40 years × $11 ×

[$1,800 ÷ $100]). The employee with final monthly earnings of $1,800 who worked 10 years and left the firm at age 35 would receive $1,980 annually at retirement age (10 years × $11 × [$1,800 ÷ $100]). However, inflation over the 30-year period elapsing before achieving retirement age would seriously diminish the purchasing power of the $1,980. Consequently, the employee might be better off simply withdrawing his or her own contributions (which always vest immediately) and terminating participation in the plan at the same time he or she leaves the employer. Any worker who left the firm prior to accumulating 10 years of service would be entitled only to a return of his or her own contributions (plus investment earnings) to the plan.

Retirement Age Nearly all retirement plans specify when an eligible employee is entitled to benefits. In most plans, age 65 is specified. Often pension plans also provide an early retirement age. In these cases, employees may begin receiving benefits prior to the normal retirement age, but the amount of the benefit is less than that they would have received if retirement had been deferred. Many retirement plans for public employees also give employees the option of retiring after a stated number of years of service (30 or 35) at full benefit, regardless of their age at that time. In the past, the trend in pension plans has been toward earlier permissible retirement ages. But since many have now begun to argue in favor of increasing the age for mandatory retirement, it is expected that fewer plans will further reduce the normal retirement age.

Benefit Computations The method used to compute benefits at retirement is spelled out in every retirement plan. The two most common methods are the defined contribution plan and the defined benefit plan. A *defined contribution plan* is one that specifies the amount of contribution that the employer and employee must make to the pension plan. At retirement, the worker is then awarded whatever level of monthly benefits those contributions will purchase. Factors most often considered to determine this level are age, sex, amount of contributions, and the amount of income that has been earned on the investment of the contributions.

Under a *defined benefit plan,* the formula for computing benefits is stipulated in the plan provisions. This type of plan allows employees to determine before retirement how much their monthly retirement income will be. Often the number of years of service and amount of earnings are prime factors in the formula. For example, a worker might be paid annually 1 percent of his or her final three-year average annual salary for each year of service. Thus, the benefit to an employee whose final three-year average annual salary was $24,000 with 20 years of employment would equal $4,800 per year (1% × $24,000 × 20 years). Other types of defined benefit plans may simply pay benefits based upon (1) a consideration of earnings but not years of service, (2) a consideration of years of service but not earnings, or (3) a flat amount with no consideration given to either earnings or years of service. Regardless of the method used to calculate benefit amounts, the employee's basic concern should be with the percent of final take-home pay that the plan is likely to produce at retirement. A pension is usually thought to be good if, when combined with social security, it will result in a monthly income for the retiree of 70 to 80 percent of preretirement net earnings. Many pension plans also increase retirement benefits periodically to help retirees try to keep up with the cost of living. In periods of high inflation these increases are essential. Otherwise, retiree standards of living decline quickly.

Classification of Plans

Pension plans are often classified according to whether they are funded and whether they are qualified under the requirements of the Internal Revenue Code.

Funding Pension plans must in some way provide for the financing of benefits that will be paid to retired workers. If the plan merely allows the employer to make payments to retirees from current income, the plan is said to be *unfunded.* One pension expert has called unfunded pensions "owe as you go" plans. This name is appropriate since employers accumulate liabilities throughout the working careers of their employees but do not necessarily put any assets aside to offset them. In the past, only a small minority of employees have been covered under unfunded pension plans. Unfunded plans have received a large amount of unfavorable publicity as being too risky for employees. And consequently, the Employee Retirement Income Security Act (discussed in a subsequent section) sets forth minimum funding standards for pension plans.

Funded pension plans are those that formally establish charges against current income to allow for the pension liabilities as they accrue. The amount of liability that arises under the plan each year is determined by actuarial computations. (An *actuary* is an expert in calculating risks and premiums for insurance.) These computations take into account such factors as mortality rates among workers and retirees, actual and potential investment earnings, labor turnover, normal and early retirement ages, and salary levels. In order for a funded plan to be "actuarially sound," the assumptions concerning these foregoing factors must be realistic. In addition, the method of funding must be sound. Few persons advocate placing pension fund assets in speculative investments such as land development projects or commodity futures. On the other hand, many persons support the now common practice of investing a large percentage of the fund assets in common stocks and income-producing real estate.

Funding of pension plans represents an attempt to minimize the risk that benefits will not be available to an eligible employee upon retirement. Nonetheless, the unfunded plan of a large solvent governmental unit or a corporate employer sometimes can offer a better guarantee of payment than the funded plan of a financially weak firm. This may be particularly true when the primary objective of the actuarial assumptions of a funded system shifts from certainty of future payment to minimization of the employer's annual contributions to the plan. Requirements under the Employee Retirement Income Security Act attempt to control the lack of adequate funding in funded plans by requiring that reasonable actuarial estimates be used when calculating employer contributions.

Qualified Pension Plans The Internal Revenue Code permits a corporate employer making contributions to a retirement plan that is *qualified*—that meets a number of specified criteria—to deduct from taxable income its contributions to the plan. The employees on whose behalf the contributions are made do not include the employer's contributions in their taxable income until the benefits are actually received. Another tax advantage of these plans is that their investment income is allowed to accumulate untaxed. Many firms believe that the costs of regulation exceed any benefits that might result and, therefore, choose to forgo the procedures required to have a qualified plan.

Types of Employer Plans

The two most popular types of qualified pension plans are trust fund plans and insured plans. When an employer places its contributions with a trustee in a *trust fund plan,* this trustee becomes responsible for the investment of contributions and the payment of benefits. Under an *insured plan,* a life insurance company serves as the funding agency. In some cases, both a trust fund and an insurance contract are used. These plans are said to be *split funded.* Trust fund plans account for more than two-thirds of the employees covered under private pensions and nearly three-fourths of the assets held by private pension plans. Primarily smaller companies tend to use insured plans.

Other Types of Plans

In addition to the foregoing pension plans, numerous other mechanisms also exist for the organized accumulation of funds for retirement. Most frequently used are Keogh plans, individual retirement accounts (IRAs), SEP/IRAs, nonqualified deferred compensation plans, tax-deferred annuities for special types of employees, profit-sharing plans, thrift and savings plans, professional corporation plans, salary-reduction plans, and sale of residence. When structured properly, each of these plans will also result in certain tax deferral advantages for the individual.

Keogh Plans The *Self-Employment Individuals Tax Retirement Act of 1962*—HR-10, frequently called the Keogh Act—gave self-employed persons and partnerships the right to establish retirement plans for themselves and their employees that would give them the same tax advantages available to corporate employees covered by qualified pension plans. The primary groups that have benefited from *Keogh plans* are professionals, such as doctors, lawyers, and accountants, as well as owners of businesses that are not incorporated.

In 1984, people eligible for Keogh could contribute up to 20 percent of yearly income from self-employment or $30,000, whichever was less. Government approved investments under Keogh plans include bank savings plans, mutual funds, and life insurance annuity programs. Taxes are not levied against the investment earnings of these plans during the accumulation period. Funds may be removed from a Keogh plan prior to retirement, but a withdrawal penalty tax and income taxes are assessed.

Individual Retirement Accounts (IRAs) Under liberalized legislation provided by the Economic Recovery Tax Act of 1981, any working American can contribute up to $2,000 per year to a self-selected retirement fund known as an *Individual Retirement Account (IRA)*. The great advantage of this type of account is that for income tax purposes, the $2,000 contribution can be deducted from an individual's gross income. In addition, the investment earnings build each year tax-free. (Of course, the proceeds of an IRA are taxed as they are withdrawn at retirement.) The current IRA is viewed favorably by many financial planners and writers; *Money* magazine entitled a recent article on IRAs, "One Terrific Tax Shelter." As Figure 15.3 shows, depending on the interest rate earned, $2,000 per year can build over a 40-year period to very substantial sums—e.g., at 12 percent, $1,534,000.

If you are married and your spouse works, each of you can contribute up to $2,000 to your own IRA. If your spouse is not employed, then your annual tax deductible contribution can be increased to $2,250.

As might be expected, though, some qualifying government rules and regulations apply to IRA accounts. First of all, after establishing an IRA plan, you must leave all the money invested until at least age 59½, but no later than age 70½. Otherwise, you must pay taxes on the money during the year you withdraw it, plus a 10 percent penalty. So the cost of terminating an IRA before you are ready to start drawing retirement benefits from it is steep. However, even though early termination is costly, you can roll your funds over as often as once a year from the various plans that are available. If you choose the wrong bank, savings and loan, or life insurance company to administer your IRA, you are not stuck with that institution until you retire. In fact, as long as you do not exceed the maximum allowed annual contribution, you can open as many IRA plans as you want to. And this leads to a second rule. Although a wide variety of institutions and investments are per-

Figure 15.3 Future Value of $2,000 per Year for Various Years at Selected Rates of Interest

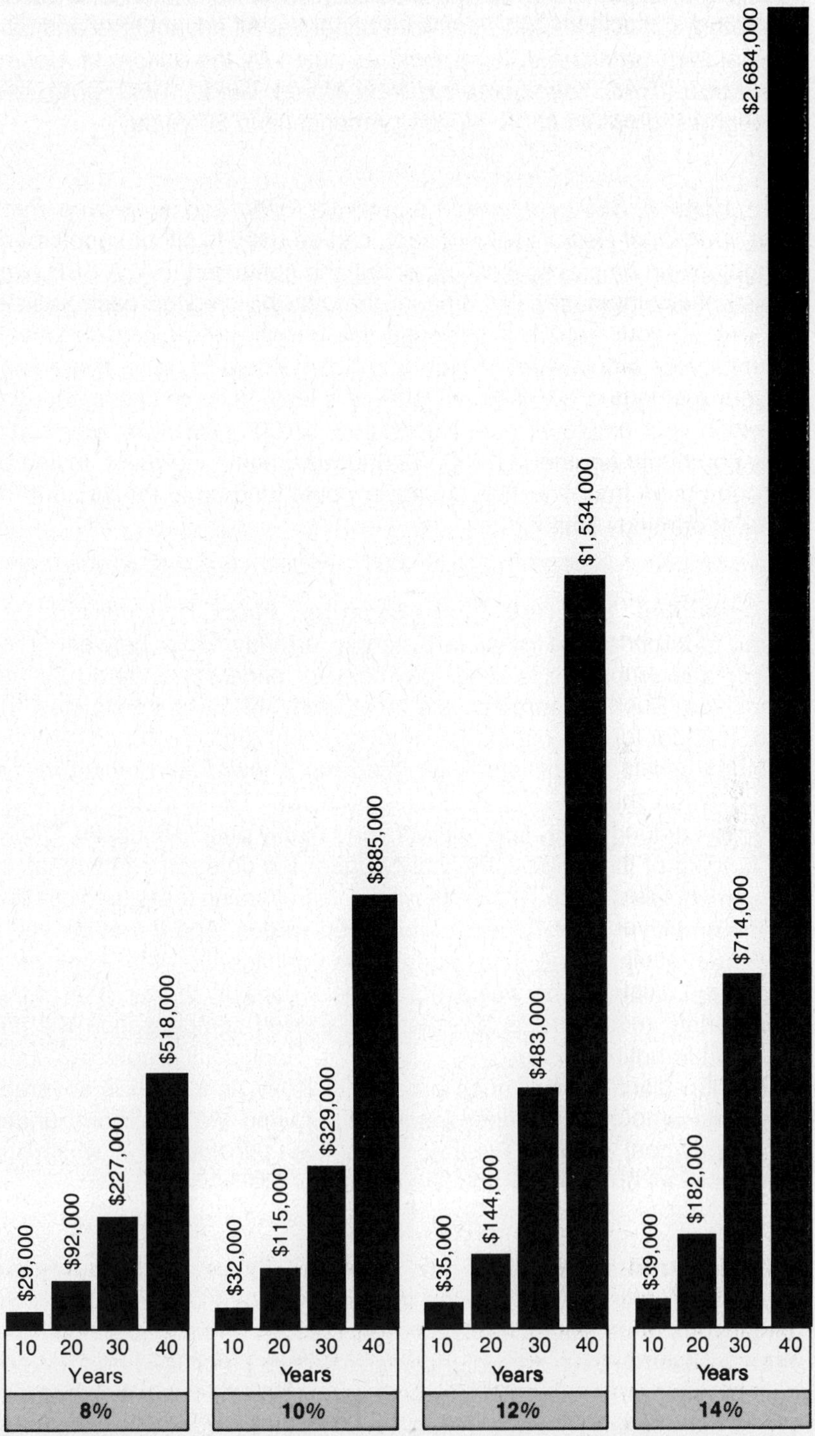

missible—e.g., bank certificates, money market funds, bonds, life insurer annuities, real estate limited partnerships—other types of investments are not permitted. They include cash value life insurance, antiques and other collectibles, and precious minerals. All advantages and disadvantages considered, IRAs look, as noted by the editors of *Money* magazine (*IRAs: Your Complete New Money Guide,* 1983, p. 6), like "Congress' greatest gift to working Americans in 50 years."

SEP/IRAs A *SEP/IRA,* which stands for *Simplified Employee Pension/Individual Retirement Account,* can be used to either supplement or replace an employee's self-selected and controlled IRA. A SEP plan substantially increases the amount that can be credited each year to an IRA on your behalf. It achieves this benefit because each year it permits your employer to invest an amount equal to up to 15 percent of your earnings or $15,000, whichever is less. In those cases, though, in which your employer contributes, say, $1,000 each year, you could only contribute another $1,000 ($2,000 maximum). However, in lieu of a contribution from you, the employer could fund up to the $15,000 or 15% of earnings limit.

Nonqualified Deferred Compensation Plans *Nonqualified deferred compensation plans* are simply arrangements between employer and employee to defer payment for services rendered by the employee. Such agreements are most useful when an employee's future need for funds exceeds his or her present requirements. Often the potential exists for the employee to be in a lower-tax bracket in the future when the funds are actually received. These plans are most common among highly paid athletes and highly paid executives. Often, no funding of the employer's liability under the deferred compensation agreement takes place. The employee is, therefore, an unsecured creditor of the employer with respect to the owed wages. And the employee's eventual receipt of the deferred funds is contingent on the employer's continued existence as well as its financial capacity to pay. If all of the appropriate requirements are met, the earned compensation will not be taxable until the employee receives it. Nonqualified deferred compensation plans permit much greater flexibility as to who is covered, what the amount of compensation will be, and the conditions under which payment will be made than do qualified pension plans, which are subject to all of the rules and regulations of ERISA.

Tax-Deferred Annuities for Special Types of Employees Presently Section 403(B) of the Internal Revenue Code (IRC) allows employees of qualified charitable organizations and public school systems to exempt from current income annuities purchased on their behalf by their employers. This benefit can supplement other retirement plans that the employer sponsors for its employees. However, it is not without limit. The IRS requires the complicated computation of an *exclusion allowance* for each participating employee. This exclusion allowance is used to determine the maximum amount of annuity premium provided by the employer for the employee upon which taxes can be deferred. Generally, contributions up to approximately 20 percent of the employee's annual compensation are allowed. When the employer is also making payments to an employer retirement plan for its employees, the amount available for the purchase of *tax-deferred annuities* is reduced accordingly. If an eligible employer does not contribute the maximum permissible amount to tax-sheltered plans for its employees, its employees may, on an individual basis, enter into a voluntary salary reduction agreement with the employer. The amount by which the salary is reduced (subject to the exclusion allowance) is then available for the purchase of the tax-deferred annuities. In essence, then, this IRC provision serves as an added benefit to eligible employees who wish to defer paying taxes on a relatively large percentage of their income.

Profit-Sharing Plans Profit-sharing plans permit employees to participate in the earnings of their employer. A *profit-sharing plan* may be qualified under the IRC and become eligible for essentially the same tax treatment as other types of pension plans. An argument in support of the use of profit-sharing plans is that they encourage employees to work harder because the employees benefit when the firm prospers. Whether these types of plans accomplish this goal is debatable. One advantage of profit-sharing plans from the viewpoint of the firm is that they do not impose any specific levels of contribution or benefits upon the employer. When profits are low, the employer is liable for a proportionately smaller contribution to the plan. And when profits are high, the firm pays proportionately more, and the employees benefit. In order to provide reasonable returns, many employers establish minimum and maximum amounts that will be paid as contributions to a profit-sharing plan, regardless of how low or high earnings are. Contributions from profit-sharing plans can be invested in life insurance annuity contracts, stocks and bonds, or (in many cases) securities issued by the employing firm. Employees who opt to purchase the firm's securities may benefit twice. When profits are good, larger contributions are made to the profit-sharing plan, and the price of the shares already purchased is also likely to increase. For many years, Sears Roebuck and Company has had one of the most widely known and best performing profit-sharing plans. Many low-level Sears career employees who have taken advantage of it have accumulated stocks worth hundreds of thousands of dollars.

Thrift and Savings Plans *Thrift and savings plans* have been established by many employers to supplement pension and other insurance fringe benefits. Most plans provide that the employer will make contributions to the savings plan in an amount equal to a set proportion of the amount contributed by the employee. For example, in some programs employers will match employee contributions at 50¢ on the dollar up to, say, 6 percent of salary. An employee making $20,000 a year could pay $1,200 into the plan annually, and the employer would add another $600. These contributions are then deposited with a trustee who invests the money in various types of securities, including (or sometimes exclusively) stocks and bonds of the employing firm. With IRS qualified thrift and savings plans, the employer's contributions and earnings on the savings are not included in the employee's taxable income until he or she withdraws these sums. However, the employee's contributions are *not* tax deductible when they are paid into the plan and accordingly are not counted as income when returned to them.

Usually thrift and savings plans have more liberal vesting and withdrawal privileges than pension and retirement programs. Often the employee's right to the contributions of the employer becomes nonforfeitable immediately upon payment, and the total savings in the plan can be withdrawn by giving proper notice. Those employees who terminate participation in such a plan, however, are frequently prohibited from rejoining it for a specified period such as one year. An employee who has the option should consider participation in a thrift plan since the returns are favorable.

Professional Corporation Plans In recent years, the trend has been for groups of lawyers, medical doctors, architects, dentists, and other professionals to establish *professional corporations.* While the reasons for forming these corporations extend far beyond pension and retirement planning, often this is an integral part of the total program. As will be recalled, self-employed persons and members of partnerships can set up a tax-sheltered retirement program under a Keogh plan. But while it is appealing, a Keogh plan does not generally permit the development of nearly as attractive a tax-sheltered retirement fund as can be organized by a corporation. In addition, the tax rules related to providing other insurance fringe benefits are more favorable to corporations than those that apply to persons who are self-employed or members of a partnership. Consequently, if you become a professional, you should explore with appropriate counsel the pros and cons of organizing a professional corporation.

Salary-Reduction Plans Another type of tax-sheltered plan offered by some employers is called the *salary-reduction plan,* which is sometimes called a 401(K) plan. Whereas the previously mentioned type of salary-reduction plan applies only to employees of certain nonprofit employers, other forms of salary-reduction agreements are available to employees of private companies. Like the nonprofit employer plans, these salary reduction plans provide that a portion of a covered employee's pay be withheld tax-free, and then invested in an annuity, the employer's common stock, or other eligible form of investment. A number of large companies such as J.C. Penney, Kodak, Mobil, and Quaker Oats now give their employees the right to elect a salary-reduction plan, and many other companies are beginning to.

This type of plan has one strong advantage over IRAs: you can withdraw cash from it to meet emergency needs, and you can withdraw all that you have put in if you leave your employer. Although you will have to pay taxes on the withdrawals, you suffer no additional penalties. In contrast to this potential advantage, salary-reduction plans generally offer you a limited number of investment options in which you can place your money.

Sale of a Residence Although not formally a retirement plan, many homeowners see their home as a potential source of retirement funds. With inflation pushing the prices of houses upward, many older people now have accumulated $50,000, $100,000, or even greater amounts of equity in their homes, and the high equity creates an incentive to sell.

The equity incentive is also bolstered by two other reasons. Often, an older couple has reduced their need for housing. Whereas a four-bedroom, three-bath house may have served them well in the past, a lower-priced, two-bedroom, one-and-a-half bath condominium might better fit their retirement lifestyle. In addition, the Internal Revenue Service gives homeowners age 55 or over a tax break when they sell their home. If married they can receive up to $125,000 in tax-free capital gains from a sale of their house. And a single homeowner 55 or older qualifies for a $62,500 exclusion. As a result of these three reasons, many people view their home as a potential nest egg for retirement.

Government Influence on Pension Plans

The two major areas of government influence on pension plans are the Internal Revenue Code requirements for plan qualification and the rules and regulations established by the *Employee Retirement Income Security Act of 1974 (ERISA)*. The major stipulations of the IRC are discussed earlier in the chapter. At this point, attention is devoted to the most important features of ERISA. As the name of the act implies, the primary objective is to increase the probability that employees who are covered by a retirement plan throughout their working career will in fact receive benefits upon retirement. ERISA covers nearly all pension and retirement plans created by private employers engaged in interstate commerce. It does not cover plans sponsored by government, charitable organizations, or firms exclusively involved in intrastate commerce. The law only regulates plans that are in existence. It does not require firms to begin a retirement plan for their employees; nor does it prohibit them from discontinuing an existing plan (as many have done to avoid the myriad ERISA rules and regulations). Similarly, ERISA does not force companies to pay any minimum amounts to employees other than those specified in the plan.

Basically, ERISA prescribes minimum standards with which covered plans must comply. These standards apply to plan provisions, funding, and administration. Among the major items treated are vesting, eligibility for participation, definition of service, minimum funding requirements, disclosure to participants, and employer fiduciary responsibility. Another important provision establishes the *Pension Benefit Guarantee Corporation (PBGC)*. The purpose of this organization is to guarantee to eligible workers that certain benefits will be payable to them even if their employer's plan has insufficient assets to fulfill its commitments. The funding for the PBGC comes from charges that are levied against all employers regulated by ERISA. In essence, the PBGC is providing plan termination insurance to covered employees. Although the implementation of ERISA has not been problem free, most observers agree that this law is a good start in insuring that employees who have earned pensions will receive them.

Summary

The first step in retirement planning involves setting retirement goals which specify desired retirement age and financial position. Once these goals are established, the retirement income needs required to fulfill them must be estimated. Finally, it is necessary to evaluate and plan for sources of retirement income in order to achieve retirement goals. The basic foundation of a retirement program for most families is social security. The social security system is designed to accomplish social objectives more than to provide a savings plan for each individual who participates in it. Social security is financed on a current funding basis. Consequently, the fact that the system does not have a trust fund established that is sufficient to pay all accumulating liabilities does not mean that it is insolvent. While considerable publicity has focused on the insufficiency of individual social security benefits, such publicity has been somewhat misleading. Nearly all present beneficiaries of social security are receiving larger monthly checks than their tax payments could have purchased from private insurers. Important benefits paid by social security include those for retirement, survivors, disability, health care, and eligible students.

Another major source of income useful in planning for retirement is the annuity. During the past 20 years, the sale of annuities has increased substantially. Basically, an annuity provides for the systematic liquidation of an estate. One of its primary advantages is that it can be arranged to provide payments for the life of an individual, no matter how long that might be. Annuities can be purchased either by paying a single premium or on an installment basis. The most important types of annuities are life annuities, guaranteed minimum annuities, annuities certain, and temporary life annuities. Annuity benefits can be scheduled to begin immediately or on a deferred basis. They can be written on the life of one individual or jointly on the lives of two (or more) persons, as for a husband and wife. They can be either fixed dollar or variable during both the accumulation and distribution periods.

Private and government employer pension and retirement plans provide a third source of retirement income. These plans have experienced considerable growth throughout the last 30 years and now cover more than 50 percent of all wage and salaried workers. Their basic features include participation requirements, a specified amount of employee contribution (if any), a period required for vesting of the employer contributions, the stipulation of normal and early retirement ages, and specification of the method used to compute benefits at retirement. The essentials of plan funding and qualification need to be understood.

In addition to basic employer-sponsored pension programs, several other types of retirement plans are also available to certain employees and self-employed persons. Keogh plans permit the self-employed as well as members of partnerships to deduct for tax purposes a portion of their earned income to be used for retirement investment. Individual retirement accounts (IRAs) serve to accomplish objectives similar to Keogh plans except that now any working American can establish an IRA plan. SEP/IRAs can be used to either supplement or replace an employee's self-selected and controlled IRA. Nonqualified deferred compensation plans are used to postpone earnings in an effort to defer and reduce the payment of income taxes. Under a special tax-deferred annuity provision of the Internal Revenue Code, employees of charitable organizations and public school systems are permitted to have their employer purchase annuities for them on a favorable tax basis. Profit-sharing plans operate such that employer contributions are related to the annual earnings of the employing firm. Thrift plans are supplemental savings plans offered by some employers as a special benefit to encourage and stimulate employee savings. Professional corporations are a form of organization that creates a favorable tax climate for providing retirement and other insurance fringe benefits. Salary-reduction plans offered by some employers provide for the withholding and tax-free investment of a portion of an employee's pay. And finally, although not formally a retirement plan, many homeowners view their homes as a potential source of retirement income. In 1974, a significant piece of pension legislation, ERISA, was passed in order to improve the chances that workers who have become eligible for a pension actually receive those benefits.

Estate Planning: Wills, Trusts, and Taxes

16

Someday you are going to die. Although this thought probably depresses you, its reality warrants attention. For if you do not give some consideration to the ultimate disposition of your accumulated wealth, chances are that little of your estate will be left for your heirs and beneficiaries to enjoy. Clearly, the importance of developing plans and taking action during your lifetime to assure that your wealth, or estate, is accumulated, preserved, and, upon your death, distributed in the desired fashion cannot be underestimated. This process, which is called estate planning, requires knowledge of wills, trusts, and taxes. An understanding of these components of estate planning and their interrelationships should make it possible for you to minimize the estate shrinkage that will occur after your death, while still achieving your lifetime personal financial goals.

The goal of estate planning is a continuous process of accumulating, preserving, and distributing an estate in the manner which most effectively accomplishes the estate owner's objectives. The emphasis of estate planning should be on personal objectives, the needs and desires of the individuals involved. In other words, estate planning should be "people planning"—placing primary emphasis on the satisfaction of human needs described here. Not only wealthy people need to plan their estates; it also makes good sense for individuals of modest or moderate means. *Estate planning* can be defined as a goal satisfaction-oriented activity that uses tax minimization tools and techniques to provide the greatest financial security possible for an individual and his or her heirs or beneficiaries. The goals that generally motivate people to engage in estate planning commonly include providing for a comfortable retirement, taking care of self and family during a long-term disability, assuring financial security for family members in the event of the death of the head of household, and securing enough capital to meet college education costs and other special needs.

Planning occurs in every estate. Some planning is controlled by the estate owner and/or his or her professional counselors. Other uncontrolled planning is done by the federal government and the government of the state in which the estate owner resides. Uncontrolled planning occurs when the estate owner forfeits the right to arrange for the disposition of assets and the minimization of tax and other estate settlement costs. This chapter discusses key factors in the estate planning process, particularly wills, trusts, and taxes. Special attention is given to types of planning and to the various means available for implementing estate plans.

Principles of Estate Planning

Individuals who wish to plan their estates must systematically uncover problems in a number of important areas and provide solutions for them. Table 16.1 itemizes the major types of problems along with their associated causes. These problems can be minimized or eliminated by maximizing the after-tax return on personal and business investments while minimizing the forces of estate impairment. Generally, the focus of estate planning is on reducing causes of estate impairment, such as taxes and administrative costs. Techniques for accomplishing this objective are discussed in later sections of the chapter.

Who Needs Estate Planning?

Some form of estate planning is required by almost all adults who have dependents. A more technical breakdown of persons who should plan their estates can be made on the basis of either "people planning" or wealth.

People Planning *People planning* means anticipating the psychological and financial needs of those people and organizations that you love—not only providing security but assuring your beneficiaries that they have enough income or capital or both to insure a continuance of their way of life. People planning also means keeping mother's cameo broach in the family and out of the pawnshop or preserving the business that granddad started in the early 1900s. People planning is especially important to those individuals with (1) children who are minors, (2) children who are exceptionally artistic or intellectually gifted, (3) children or other dependents who are retarded, emotionally and mentally disturbed, or physically handicapped, and (4) spouses who cannot or do not want to handle money, securities, or a business.

Minor children cannot legally handle large sums of money or deal with real estate or securities directly. Custodial accounts, guardianships, or trusts are necessary receptacles to provide administration, security, financial advice, and the legal capacity to act on behalf of minors. Few children are exceptionally artistic or intellectually gifted. But those few often need—or should have—special (and often expensive) schooling, travel opportunities, or equipment. Retarded, emotionally and mentally disturbed, or physically handicapped children (and other relatives) may need nursing, medical, or psychiatric care. Clearly, outright gifts of money or property to those who cannot care for themselves are foolishly inappropriate. These individuals may need more (or less) than other children. An individual who gives all of his or her children equal shares may not be giving them equitable shares.

How many of us have handled \$100,000 or \$200,000 or \$300,000? Think of the burden we place on others when we expect a spouse who

Table 16.1 Potential Estate Planning Problems: Their Major Causes or Indicators

Problem	Major Cause or Indicator
Excessive Transfer Costs	Taxes and estate administrative expenses higher than necessary.
Lack of Liquidity	Insufficient cash. Not enough assets that are quickly and inexpensively convertible to cash within a short period of time to meet tax demands and other costs.
Improper Disposition of Assets	Beneficiaries receive the wrong asset or the proper asset in the wrong manner or at the wrong time.
Inadequate Income at Retirement	Capital insufficient or not readily convertible to income-producing status.
Inadequate Income, If Disabled	High medical costs, capital insufficient or not readily convertible to income-producing status, difficulty in reducing living standards.
Inadequate Income for Family at Estate Owner's Death	Any one of the above causes can trigger this problem.
Insufficient Capital	Excessive taxes, inflation, improper investment planning.
Special Problems	A family member with a serious illness or physical or emotional problem, children of a prior marriage, beneficiaries who have extraordinary medical or financial needs, business problems, and opportunities.

cannot—or does not want to—handle such large sums of money or securities to do so with what may be his or her only assets. Is it fair or does it make sense to thrust the responsibilities of business upon those who are unequipped to handle them? The bottom line of "people planning" is that we engage in the process for only one reason: because we care. Even if there is no one else or no organization that is important, planning is important for us. Yes, sometimes, "spend it" is the best planning under the circumstances.

Wealth From a standpoint of wealth alone, estate planning is essential for anyone—single, widowed, married, or divorced—with estates exceeding $300,000 or $400,000. When a closely held business is involved, estate planning is essential to stabilize and maximize the asset and income-producing value at the owner's death or disability. Likewise, when an estate owner holds title to property in more than one state, estate planning is essential to avoid a multiplicity of problems—such as attorney's fees in each state or taxation by more than one state of the same assets.

Why Does an Estate Break Up?

Quite often, when people die, their estate dies with them. Sadly, the loss of the estate results not because they have done anything wrong but rather because they have not done anything. There are numerous forces which, if unchecked, tend to shrink an estate, reduce the usefulness of its assets, and frustrate the objectives of the person who built it. These include death-related costs, inflation, improper management, lack of liquidity, incorrect use of vehicles of transfer, and disabilities.

Death-Related Costs Last illness and funeral expenses are good examples of *first-level death-related costs.* Most people also die with some current bills unpaid and long-term obligations, such as mortgages, business loans, and installment contracts outstanding. Unpaid income taxes as well as property taxes also constitute debts often payable by the deceased's estate. *Second-level death-related costs* consist of the fees of attorneys, appraisers, and accountants and probate expenses—so-called administrative costs, federal estate taxes, and state death taxes (some states have both inheritance and estate taxes).

Inflation Death-related costs are only the tip of the estate impairment iceberg. Less obvious but often more damaging is the profound effect of inflation. Failure to continuously reappraise and rearrange an estate plan to provide a mechanism which will counter the effects of inflation can impair the ability of both fundamental and investment assets to provide steady and adequate levels of financial security.

Improper Management Business assets as well as some commercial real estate properties require continuous attention; often the estate beneficiaries are unable or unwilling to provide this needed care. The failure to note a change in consumer preferences or product or equipment obsolescence may result in a rapid decline in the value of a decedent's business or of various types of assets included within the estate.

Lack of Liquidity Insufficient cash to pay death costs and other estate obligations has always been a major factor impairing the value of estates. Forced sacrifice sales of assets with substantial income-producing power usually result in a disproportionately large loss of assets and family income. Furthermore, such sales—of the choicest parcel of farmland or a business which has been in the family for generations, for instance—often have undesirable psychological effects on the heirs. The outcome can be a devastating financial and emotional blow.

Incorrect Use of Vehicles of Transfer It would be criminally negligent to put a high-powered car in the hands of a child. Yet, assets are often put into the hands of beneficiaries who are unwilling or unable to handle them. Because of improper usage of vehicles of transfer, property often passes to unintended beneficiaries or to the proper beneficiaries in an improper manner or at an incorrect time. For example, spendthrift spouses or minors may be left large sums of money outright in the form of life insurance, through joint ownership of a savings account, or as the beneficiaries of an employee fringe benefit plan.

Disabilities A prolonged and expensive disability of a family wage earner is often called a *living death.* Loss of income due to disability is frequently coupled with a massive financial drain caused by the illness itself. The financial situation is further complicated by a lack of attention given to the management of currently owned assets. This not only causes the growth of the family's financial security to cease but also diminishes the value of the estate with incredible rapidity.

The Estate—What Is It?

Your *estate* is your property, whatever you own. The *probate estate* consists of the real and personal property that a person owns in his or her own name that can be transferred according to the terms of a will at death. A distinction must be made between the probate estate (a property law concept essentially encompassing assets passing by will) and the gross estate (a tax law term which may encompass a considerably larger amount of property). The *gross estate* includes all the property subject to federal estate tax at a person's death, both probate and nonprobate. Life insurance, jointly held property with rights of survivorship, and property passing under certain employee benefit plans are common examples of nonprobate assets that might be subject to federal (and perhaps state) estate taxes.

In addition, an individual may have property which is not probate property and will not be part of a decedent's gross estate for federal estate tax purposes, yet passes to his or her family and forms part of its financial security program. There are two types of such assets. One is the death benefit from qualified retirement plans, such as pension, Keogh, and profit-sharing plans. Individual Retirement Account (IRA) death benefits might also fall into this category. Arranged properly, the proceeds from such plans can pass outside the probate estate because of their contractual nature. For individuals dying prior to 1985, up to $100,000 could be excluded from the decedent's gross estate for federal estate tax purposes; the Tax Reform Act of 1984 repealed this exclusion for individuals dying after 1984. In many states qualified plan and IRA benefits will be wholly or partially inheritance tax exempt and pass directly to the specified beneficiaries of the deceased. The other type of financial asset that falls into this category is social security. Payments to a surviving spouse and minor children are generally neither probate assets nor subject to any federal (or state) estate taxes. Because of the freedom from administrative costs and taxes, this cat-

Table 16.2 Types of Factual Data Required by Professionals for Preparation of Detailed Estate Plans

Personal Data
Names, addresses, phone numbers, family consultants
Family birthdates, occupations, health problems, support needs
Citizenship, marital status, marital agreements, wills, trusts, custodianships, trust beneficiary, gifts or inheritances, social security numbers, education, and military service

Property (except Life Insurance or Business)
Classification, title, indebtedness, basis, date and manner of acquisition, value of marketable securities, and location

Life Insurance

Health Insurance
Disability income
Medical expense insurance

Business Interest
Name, address, ownership
Valuation factors; desired survivorship control; name, address, and phone number of business attorney and accountant

Employee Census Data

Employee Benefits

Family Income
Income of client, spouse, dependent children, income tax information

Family Finances
Budget information, investment preferences
Ranking of economic objectives, capital needs, other objectives

Income and Capital Needs
Retirement: Age, required amount, potential sources
Disability: Required amount, sources
Death: Expected sources of income

Liabilities
Classification of liabilities, creditors, amounts, whether insured or secured

Factors Affecting Plan
Gift propensity, charitable inclinations, emotional maturity of children, basic desires for estate distribution

Authorization for Information
Life insurance

Receipt for Documents
Personal and business

Observations from Interview

Source: Reprinted with permission from *Advanced Estate Planning Course.*

egory of assets provides unique and substantial estate planning opportunities.

The Estate Planning Process

The estate planning process consists of a number of important steps. (1) Comprehensive and accurate data on all aspects of the family must be gathered. Table 16.2 summarizes the types of factual data required by professionals in order to prepare detailed estate plans. (2) The data gathered must be categorized into general problem areas, and estate transfer costs must be estimated. (3) With this information, the estate plan is formulated and preparations are made for its implementation. The objective of estate plans, of course, is to maximize the usefulness of people's assets during their lives and to achieve their personal objectives after their death. (4) The final steps in the estate planning process involve testing and implementing the proposed plan.

Once the plan has been implemented, it is important to keep in mind that it is good only as long as it fits the needs, desires, and circumstances of the parties involved. As these elements change, the estate plan must also be modified. Marriage or remarriage, divorce, the birth of a child, a change of job or location, or substantial changes in income, health, or living standards are the types of events that indicate a need for a review. Even if none of these occur, a review of life insurance needs should automatically be scheduled at least once every two years, and a full estate audit should be made at least once every five to seven years (or whenever there has been a major change in the federal or state death tax laws). Because of the general complexity of the laws relating to estate transfer, the assistance of estate planners, life insurance professionals (CLUs), Certified Financial Planners (CFPs), Chartered Financial Consultants (ChFCs), accountants, and attorneys is often necessary in the planning and evaluation process. Due to the complexity and individual nature of estate planning, more specific guidelines are not included in this chapter.

The Will

A *will* is a written legal expression or declaration of a person's wishes as to the disposition of his or her property to be performed or to take effect upon his or her death. The importance of a valid will can be illustrated in light of what happens when a person dies without one.

Absence of a Valid Will: Intestacy

Intestacy describes the situation that exists when a person dies without a valid will. Some intestacy laws "draw the will the decedent failed to make" to determine the disposition of the probate property of persons who have died intestate. These statutes enumerate certain preferred classes of survivors. Generally, the decedent's spouse is favored, followed by the children and then other descendants. If the spouse and children or other descendants such as grandchildren or great-grandchildren survive, they will divide the estate, and other relatives or char-

Table 16.3 Distribution of a Typical Intestate Estate

Decedent Dies Leaving	Distribution	
Spouse and children or their descendants	Spouse receives one third	Children receive two thirds divided equally
Spouse and one child or child's descendants	Spouse receives one half	Child receives one half
Spouse but no children or their descendants, and decedent's mother or father survives	Spouse receives $10,000 plus one half of balance	Father and mother or surviving parent (if one is already deceased) receive one half of balance
Spouse but no children or their descendants, and no parent survives	Spouse receives $10,000 plus one half of balance	Brothers and sisters receive other half of balance divided equally
Spouse but no children or their descendants, and no parent, brother, sister, niece, nephew, grandparent, uncle, or aunt survives	Spouse receives all	
Child or children but no spouse		Child or children receive all divided equally
No spouse and no children or their descendants, and decedent's mother or father survives		Mother and father receive all
No spouse and no children or their descendants, and no parent of the decedent survives		Brothers and sisters receive all divided equally

Source: Courtesy of Stephan R. Leimberg, Esq., Bryn Mawr, Pa.

itable organizations will receive nothing. If no spouse, children, or other descendants survive, the deceased's parents, brothers, and sisters receive a share of the estate.

The disposition of a typical intestate estate can be illustrated by a simple example. Assume an individual dies with no valid will. That individual's separately owned property would be distributed as shown in Table 16.3 after deduction of debts, taxes, and state family exemptions. If the deceased leaves no wife or husband, child or descendant, parent, brother or sister or descendant, grandparent, or uncle or aunt or their children, the state normally takes all of the property. Had the deceased even in this situation had a will, the property could have been directed to some nonrelated individual or to a charity. Aside from having lost control of the disposition of property to individuals or charities, the person who dies intestate has also forfeited the privileges of naming a personal representative to guide the disposition of the estate, naming a guardian for persons and property, and specifying which beneficiaries are to bear certain tax burdens. In addition, with a valid will the amount of estate shrinkage can be minimized through the use of certain deductions and exclusions which may not be available when a person dies intestate. The importance of a valid will—regardless of the size of an estate—must not be overlooked in the personal financial planning process.

Preparation of the Will

A will can be defined as a written document that allows a person, called a *testator,* to determine the disposition of property at his or her death. A key characteristic of a will is that it can be changed or revoked at any time prior to the testator's (the will owner's) death. Upon the death of the testator, it becomes operative and applies to the situation which exists at that time. Will preparation, or drafting, varies with respect to difficulty and cost depending on individual circumstances. In some cases a two-page will costing $50 may be adequate, while in others it may be necessary to pay $500 to have a ten-page will prepared. A will must not only effectively accomplish the specified objectives for distribution of assets, but it must also take into consideration the income, gift, and estate tax laws. Often a knowledge of the corporate, trust, real estate, and securities laws is required as well. Note that a will, important as it is, is useless and perhaps even dangerous if it does not consider assets passing outside its limits.

Information Requirements A properly prepared will should (1) provide a plan for distributing the testator's assets in accordance with his or her wishes, the beneficiaries' needs, and due regard to federal and state dispositive and tax laws; (2) consider the changes in family circumstances which might occur after the execution of the will; and (3) be unambiguous and complete in describing the testator's desires. By following these general guidelines, the testator can generally develop a satisfactory will.

Use of an Attorney Will drafting, no matter how modest the size of the estate, should not be attempted by a lay person. The complexity and interrelationships of tax, property, domestic relations, and other laws make the homemade will a frivolous if not dangerous act. Nowhere is the old adage "He who has self for attorney has fool for client" more true, and nothing is more expensive in the long run than the do-it-yourself will—except, perhaps, the do-it-yourself heart transplant!

Common Features of the Will

Although there is no absolute format that must be followed in will preparation, most wills contain eight distinct parts: (1) introductory clause,

(2) direction of payments, (3) dispositive provisions, (4) appointment clause, (5) tax clause, (6) common disaster clause, (7) execution and attestation clause, and (8) witness clause. Generalized examples of each of these clauses are briefly illustrated and described as follows. These must be tailored to individual needs and circumstances by an attorney familiar with your own state's statutory requirements.

Introductory Clause An introductory clause, or preamble, would normally take the form shown:

I, ______, of the city of ______, state of ______, do hereby make my last will and revoke all wills and codicils made prior to this will.

The declaration of residence that is included here helps to determine the county which will have legal jurisdiction and be considered the testator's domicile for tax purposes. The portion of the clause related to revocation nullifies old and forgotten wills and codicils—legally binding modifications of an existing will.

Direction of Payments The clause related to directing the estate with respect to certain payments of expenses is typically formulated along the lines of the following example.

I direct payment out of my estate of all just debts and the expenses of my last illness and funeral.

In many states, the rights of creditors are protected by law and such a clause is largely useless. However, the will of a married woman should contain a direction to pay debts and expenses. Otherwise, in a number of states the burden of funeral and medical expenses lies primarily on her husband.

Dispositive Provisions Three examples of dispositive clauses follow:

I give and bequeath to my wife, Allene Murphy, all my jewelry, automobiles, books, and photography equipment, as well as all other articles of personal and household use.

I give to the Chicago Historical Society the sum of $100,000.

All the rest, residue, and remainder of my estate, real and personal, wherever located, I give in equal one-half shares to my children, Charlee and Lara, their heirs and assigns forever.

The first type of clause disposes of personal effects. A testator should make a detailed and specific list of intimate personal property and carefully identify each item. The second type of clause, called a *pecuniary legacy,* passes money to a specified party. The correct title of a charity should be ascertained by direct and discreet inquiry. Note that the popular name is seldom the correct or full legal name. The third clause describes the distribution of residual assets after specific gifts have been made. The share of a person who dies before the testator will normally pass to the other residual heirs unless provision is made to the contrary. Of course, this result varies from state to state.

Appointment Clause Examples of appointment clauses, which are typically included to appoint executors (the decedent's personal representatives), guardians, and trustees, as well as their successors, follow:

I hereby nominate, constitute, and appoint as Executor of this last Will and Testament my beloved husband Elrod Wilmeyer and my brother, Charles S. Warren III. In the event any persons named herein predecease me, or for any cause shall cease or fail to act, then I nominate, constitute, and appoint as Executor of my said will in the place and stead of any or one of said persons named herein, the Farmers and Merchants Bank of Omaha, Nebraska.

I appoint my brother, Eugene Smith, guardian of the person and property of my son, Farnsworth, during his minority.

The first clause is used to appoint executors and alternates, whose responsibility it is to administer the estate of the deceased. The importance of naming an executor and alternate is highlighted in a subsequent section of this chapter concerned with the administration of an estate. The second clause shown is used to appoint a guardian. In many states, the surviving parent of an unmarried minor child can appoint a guardian of the person and property of the child. Often, the surviving parent is not allowed to become sole guardian of the property of a minor child.

Tax Clause An example of the tax clause follows:

I direct that there shall be paid out of my residuary estate (from that portion which does not qualify for the marital deduction) all estate, inheritance, and similar taxes imposed by a government in respect to property includable in my estate for tax purposes, whether the property passes under this will or otherwise.

In the absence of a specified provision in the will, so-called *apportionment statutes* of the testator's state will allocate the burden of taxes among the beneficiaries. The result may be an inappropriate and unintended reduction of certain beneficiaries' shares or adverse income tax effects.

Common Disaster Clause A sample of the type of clause often included within the will to protect against a common disaster or simultaneous death follows:

If my wife and I shall die under such circumstances that there is not sufficient evidence to determine the order of our deaths, then it shall be presumed that she survived me. My estate shall be administered and distributed in all respects in accordance with such assumption.

The assumption that the spouse survives is used mainly to permit the marital deduction, which offers a tax advantage. Other types of clauses are similarly designed to avoid double probate of the same assets—duplication of administrative and probate costs. One such clause provides that the survivor must live for, say, 30 days in order to be a beneficiary under the will.

Execution and Attestation Clause An example of the execution and attestation clause follows:

In witness whereof, I have affixed my signature to this, my last will and testament, which consists of ______ pages, to each of which I have initialed, this ______ day of ______, One Thousand Nine Hundred and Eighty-four (1984).

____________(Seal)

Every will should be in writing and signed by the testator at its end as a precaution against fraud; many attorneys suggest initialing each page after the last line and including a signature on the left-hand margin of each page. Each page should, of course, be numbered.

Witness Clause The final clause, which helps to affirm that the will in question is really that of the deceased, is illustrated as follows:

Signed, sealed, and published by Terrell J. Michaels, the testator, as his last will, in the presence of us, who, at his request, and in the presence of each other, all being present at the same time, have written our names as witnesses.

It is wise to use at least three witnesses who sign in the presence of one another. Their addresses should be noted on the will. If the testator is unable to sign his or her name for any reason, most states allow the testator to make a mark and to have another person (properly witnessed) sign for him or her.

Requirements of a Valid Will

To be valid, a will must be the product of a person with a sound mind; there must have been no undue influence (influence that would remove the testator's freedom of choice); the will itself must have been properly executed; and its execution must be free from fraud.

Mental Capacity In order to be judged mentally competent, testators must have (1) a full and intelligent knowledge of the act they are involved in, (2) an understanding of the property they possess, (3) a knowledge of the dispositions they want to make of it, and (4) an appreciation of the objects they desire to be the recipients of their bounty. Generally, such capacity is presumed; clear and convincing proof of mental incapacity is required to set aside a will, and the burden of proof is on the contestant.

Freedom of Choice A will is considered invalid if it can be shown that the testator was subject to the undue influence of another person at the time the will was made and executed. Threats, misrepresentations, inordinate flattery, or some physical or mental coercion employed to destroy the testator's freedom of choice are all types of *undue influence.*

Proper Execution To be considered properly executed, a will must meet the requirements of the state's wills act or its equivalent. It must also be demonstrable that it is in fact the will of the testator. Most states have statutes which spell out (1) who may make a will—generally any person of sound mind, age 18 or older (age 21 in some states); (2) the form and execution a will must have—most states require a will to be in writing and signed by the testator at the logical end, preferably in black ink; and (3) requirements for witnesses. (Since no state requires more than three witnesses, this number should sign as witnesses in the presence of the testator and one another. If at all possible, a beneficiary should *not* sign as a witness since in a few states this could result in the disinheritance of that beneficiary. Many states have now provided for a "self-proving" will. For example, in Pennsylvania if a testator's signing of the will is witnessed by two individuals who sign in the presence of each other and in the presence of a notary, at the probate of the will, those witnesses do not have to appear. This saves time, money, and often a great deal of aggravation on the executor's part.)

Changing or Revoking the Will: Codicils

A will is inoperative until the testator's death and therefore can be changed at any time until then. Wills should be revised periodically for many reasons. Modification is generally in order if there is a significant change in the testator's (or the beneficiaries') health or financial circumstances; if births, deaths, marriages, or divorces have altered the operative circumstances; or if substantial changes in the tax law have occurred. An existing will can be either changed or revoked, although in certain states a so-called "right of election" (explained later) exists.

Changing the Will In order to change an existing will, a *codicil,* which is a simple and convenient legal means of modifying an existing will, is drawn up. It is used when the will needs only minor modifications and is often a single page document which reaffirms all the existing provisions in the will except the one to be changed. The codicil should be executed in accordance with the same formalities as a will and should be typed, signed, and witnessed in the same manner. Where substantial changes are required, usually a new will is preferable to a codicil. In addition, if a gift in the original will is removed, even though substantial changes are not required, sometimes it is best to draw a new will and destroy the old. This may avoid offending the omitted beneficiary. Sometimes the prior will should not be destroyed, even after the new will is made and signed. This is especially true when the testator is older or in poor health and if the will might be contested. One reason for retaining the prior will is that if the new will fails for some reason (because of the testator's mental incapacity, for example), the prior will may qualify. Another is that a prior will could help to prove a "continuity of testamentary purpose"—in other words, that the latest will (which may have provided a substantial gift to charity) was not an afterthought or the result of an unduly influenced mind.

Revoking the Will The revocation of a will may occur in two ways: A testator may revoke his or her will; or in some cases, the law will revoke or modify it automatically. A testator can revoke a will by (1) making a later will which expressly revokes prior wills; (2) making a codicil which expressly revokes any wills; (3) making a later will which is inconsistent with a former will; and (4) physically mutilating, burning, tearing, or defacing the will with the intention of revoking it. The law automatically revokes or modifies a will under certain circumstances, which vary from state to state. The more common ones are (1) divorce, (2) marriage, (3) birth or adoption, and (4) murder. If, after making a will, a testator is divorced, in many states all provisions in the will relating to the spouse become ineffective. If a testator marries after making a will, the spouse receives that portion of the estate which would have been received had the testator died without a valid will—unless the will gives the spouse a larger share. If a testator did not provide for a child born or adopted after the will was made (unless it appears that such lack of provision was intentional), the child receives that share of the estate not passing to the testator's spouse that would have been given to the child had the deceased not had a will. And almost all states have "slayer's statutes" of some type forbidding a person who participates in a willful and unlawful murder from acquiring property as the result of the murder.

Right of Election Many states provide one further way a will can be changed: through the "right of election." Most states give this right only to surviving spouses, while at least one state extends a similar right to the testator's children. The survivor with a *right of election* has the right to "take against the will"—to take a specified portion of the probate estate regardless of what the will provides. One state, for example, allows a surviving spouse to take at least that share that would have been allowed had the deceased died without a valid will. This right is generally forfeited by a spouse who deserted the testator or participated in the testator's willful and unlawful murder.

Safeguarding the Will

In most cases, the original of the will should be kept in a safe deposit box together with deeds, contracts, and other valuable papers. (Although some authorities and many attorneys recommend leaving the original of a will with the attorney who drafted it, this may make it awkward for the executor to choose his or her own attorney, a right which most states give the executor regardless of who drew the will or what the will states about who should be the estate's counsel. Furthermore, it discourages the estate owner from changing the will or engaging a new attorney even if he or she moves out of the state in which the will was drawn.) Table 16.4 contains an executor's checklist of documents and information that should be kept in a safe deposit box. If each spouse has a separate safe deposit box, the couple may want to keep their wills in each other's boxes. Some states provide for "lodging" of the will, a mechanism for filing and safekeeping the will in the office of the probate court (also called orphan's or surrogate's court). In those states, this procedure satisfies the need to safeguard the will.

The Letter of Last Instructions

Frequently, people will have thoughts they want to convey and instructions they wish to have carried out that cannot properly be included in their wills. These suggestions or recommendations should be included in a *letter of last instructions* in the form of an informal memorandum separate from the will (*Note:* Make no bequests in this letter of last instructions since such documents have no legal standing). Usually, it is best to make several copies of the letter and keep one at home and the others in the hands of the estate's executor or an attorney or accountant to be mailed or delivered to beneficiaries at the appropriate time.

A letter of last instructions might provide directions with respect to: (1) location of the will and other documents; (2) funeral and burial instructions—often a will is not opened until after the funeral; (3) suggestions or recommendations as to the continuance, sale, or liquidation of a business (it is easier to freely suggest a course of action in such a letter than it is in a will); (4) personal matters that the testator might prefer not to be made public in the will, such as statements which might sound unkind or inconsiderate but which would prove of great value to the executor (for example, comments about a spendthrift spouse or a reckless son); (5) legal and accounting services (executors are free, however, to choose their own counsel—not even testators can bind them in that selection); and (6) an explanation of the actions taken in the will, which may help avoid litigation (for instance, "I left only $1,000 to my son, John, because . . ." or "I made no provisions for my oldest daughter, Melissa, because . . .").

Table 16.4 An Executor's Checklist of Items That Should Be Kept in a Safe Deposit Box

________ 1. Birth Certificates	________ 7. Bonds, Stocks, and Securities
________ 2. Marriage Certificates (Including Any Prior Marriages)	________ 8. Real Estate Deeds
________ 3. Your Will (and Spouse's Will) and Trust Agreements	________ 9. Business (Buy-Sell) Agreements
________ 4. Listing of Life Insurance Policies or Certificates	________ 10. Automobile Titles and Insurance Policies
________ 5. Your Social Security Numbers	________ 11. Property Insurance Policies
________ 6. Military Discharge Papers	________ 12. Letter of Last Instructions
	________ 13. Additional Documents

List numbers of all checking and savings accounts including bank addresses and location of safe deposit boxes:

________________ ________________ ________________

________________ ________________ ________________

List name, address, and phone number of property and life insurance agent:

________________ ________________ ________________

________________ ________________ ________________

List name, address, and phone number of accountant:

________________ ________________ ________________

List name, address, and phone number of (current or past) employer. State date when you retired if applicable. Include employee benefits booklets:

________________ ________________ ________________

________________ ________________ ________________

List all debts owed to *and* owed by you:

________________ ________________ ________________

________________ ________________ ________________

List the names, addresses, telephone numbers, and birth dates of your children and other beneficiaries (including charitable beneficiaries):

________________ ________________ ________________

________________ ________________ ________________

________________ ________________ ________________

________________ ________________ ________________

Source: Stephan R. Leimberg, Herbert Levy, Stephen N. Kandell, Morey S. Rosenbloom, and Ralph Gano Miller, *Tools and Techniques of Estate Planning,* 4th ed. (Cincinnati, Ohio: National Underwriter Company, 1982). Reprinted by permission of the publisher.

Administration of an Estate

When people die, they usually own property and owe debts. Often, they will have claims (accounts receivable) against other persons. A process of liquidation similar to that which occurs when a corporation is dissolved must take place. In this process, money owed is collected, creditors (including the tax authorities) are satisfied, and what remains is distributed to the appropriate individuals or organizations. A local court generally supervises this *probate process* through a person designated as an *executor* in the decedent's will, or, if the decedent died intestate (without a valid will), through a court-appointed administrator.

An executor or administrator, who is sometimes also referred to as the decedent's personal representative, must collect the assets of the decedent, pay debts or provide for the payment of debts which are not currently due, and distribute any remaining assets to the persons entitled to them by will or by the intestate law of the appropriate state. Estate administration is important for many reasons. One of these reasons is that bank accounts and other contracts could not be collected without such a formal process because there would be no one who legally could bring suit or be entitled to give a release of liability. Another is that title to real estate could not be made marketable because there would be no assurance against the existence of a creditor with claims against the land. Due to the importance of the estate administration process, executors should be selected who are not only familiar with your affairs but who also exhibit good administrative skills.

What About Joint Ownership?

Many people take title to property jointly either through a "joint tenancy" or as "tenants by the entirety." (There is a third common form called *tenancy in common.* This means that each tenant owns an interest that can be left to whomever he or she desires rather than to the other joint tenant. Likewise, a tenancy in common can be sold or given away without the consent of the other joint tenant.) These two forms of joint ownership have the following characteristics. (1) The interest of a decedent passes directly to the surviving joint tenant (that is, to the other joint owner) by operation of the law and is free from the claims of the decedent's creditors, heirs, or personal representatives. (2) A *joint tenancy with right of survivorship* may consist of any number of persons—regardless if they are related by blood or marriage. A *tenancy by the entirety,* on the other hand, can exist only between husband and wife. (3) In the case of *joint tenancy,* each joint tenant can unilaterally sever the tenancy. This is not the case with a tenancy by the entirety, which can be severed only by mutual agreement or terminated by divorce or conveyance by both spouses to a third party. In some states a tenancy by the entirety can exist only with respect to real property, while others do not recognize such tenancies at all.

The advantages of joint tenancy, the more common form of joint ownership, are a sense of family security, quick and easy transfer to spouse at death, exemption of jointly owned property from the claims of the deceased's creditors, and avoidance of delays and publicity in the estate settlement process. The key disadvantage of joint tenancy is that the jointly owned property cannot be controlled by a will and, therefore, does not permit the first joint owner to die to control the property's disposition and management upon his or her death. Another disadvantage is that higher potential tax costs are often incurred in both the creation and the severance of a joint tenancy. A father, for example, who purchases and pays for property and places it in his name and his daughter's name is making a gift to her. Upon the termination of the tenancy, if the daughter receives the entire proceeds (for example, upon a sale of a jointly owned home) the father is making a second gift to her. In both situations he gratuitously transferred an interest to her which she did not have before. Fortunately, federal gift tax law does not tax most interspousal transfers and so the problem will not arise on a federal level between a married couple (but many states do tax such unintentional gifts). Because most persons believe the advantages of joint ownership of major assets, such as a home or automobile, far outweigh the potential disadvantages, it is commonly utilized by married couples.

Trusts

A *trust* is a relationship created when one party (called a *grantor,* settler, or creator) transfers property to a second party (the *trustee*) for the benefit of third parties (*beneficiaries*), which may or may not include the grantor. The property placed in the trust is called *trust principal* or *res* (pronounced race). The trustee holds the legal title to the property in the trust and must use the property and any income it produces solely for the benefit of trust beneficiaries. Generally, the trust is created by a written document. The grantor spells out the substantive provisions (such as how the property in the trust is to be allocated and how income is to be distributed) as well as certain administrative provisions. A trust may be *living* (created during the grantor's life) or *testamentary* (created in a will). A trust may be revocable or irrevocable. Property placed into a revocable trust can be regained, and the terms of the trust can be altered or amended. Property placed into an irrevocable trust cannot be recovered by the grantor during the term of the trust. Although the establishment of trusts is generally for those with substantial means, the features of trusts as they relate to estate planning are briefly described in this part of the chapter.

Purposes of Trusts

Trusts are designed for any of a number of reasons. The most common motives are (1) to attain income and estate tax savings and (2) to manage and conserve property.

Income and Estate Tax Savings The burden of paying taxes on the income produced by securities, real estate, and other investments can be shifted from a high-bracket taxpayer to a trust itself or to its beneficiary, both of whom are typically subject to lower income tax rates than the grantor. The savings due to this rate differential coupled with the addition of the beneficiary's $1,000 personal exemption can be significant. Furthermore, dramatic estate tax savings are possible because the appreciation in property placed into such a trust can be entirely removed from the grantor's estate and can possibly benefit several generations of family members without adverse federal estate tax consequences.

Management and Conservation of Trust Property Minors, spendthrifts, and mental incompetents need asset management for obvious reasons. But busy executives and others who cannot or do not want to take the countless hours necessary to learn to handle large sums of money and other property often utilize trusts to relieve themselves of those burdens. The trustee assumes the responsibility for managing and conserving the property on behalf of the beneficiaries. The use of independent trustees has recently been employed by members of Congress and presidents to avoid potential conflicts of interest regarding investments. In some cases, the management ability of the trustee is held in reserve in case a healthy and vigorous individual is unexpectedly incapacitated and becomes unable or unwilling to manage his or her assets.

Selecting a Trustee

Five qualities are essential in a trustee. A trustee must (1) possess sound business knowledge and judgment, (2) have an intimate knowledge of the beneficiary's needs and financial situation, (3) be skilled in investment and trust management, (4) be available to beneficiaries (specifically, this means the trustee should be young enough to survive through the trust term), and (5) be able to make decisions impartially. A corporate trustee, such as a trust company or bank that has been authorized to perform trust duties, may seem best able to meet these requirements. A corporate trustee is likely to have investment experience and will not be incapacitated by death, disability, or absence. Unlike a family member, a corporate trustee can be relied on to be impartial and obedient to the directions of the trust instrument. Such objectivity has added value if there are several beneficiaries. On the other hand, a corporate trustee may charge high fees or be overly conservative in investments, impersonal, or lacking in the familiarity with and understanding of family problems and needs that a family member would possess. Often a compromise is suggested: the appointment of one (or more) individual(s) and a corporate trustee as co-trustees.

Common Types and Characteristics of Trusts

Although there are various types of trusts, the most common are the living trust, the testamentary trust, and the life insurance trust and pour-over will.

Living Trust A *living* or *inter vivos trust* is one created during the grantor's lifetime. It can be either revocable or irrevocable and can last for a limited period or can continue long after the grantor's death.

Revocable Living Trust The grantor reserves the right to revoke the trust and regain the trust property in a *revocable living trust.* For federal income tax purposes, grantors of these trusts are treated as owners of the property in the trust—in other words, just as if they held the property in their own name. Therefore, they are taxed on any income produced by the trust. Three basic advantages of revocable living trusts are often cited. The first is that management continuity and income flow are assured even after the death of the grantor. No probate is necessary since the trust continues to operate after the death of the grantor just as it did while he or she was alive. A second advantage is that the burdens of investment decisions and management responsibility are assumed by the trustee. A good example of this can be found in the case of individuals who want to control investment decisions and management policy as long as they are alive and healthy but who set up a trust to provide backup help in case they become unable or unwilling to continue managing the assets. This type of living trust is appropriately called a *step-up trust* because the trustee steps up to take the grantor's place in decision making and day-to-day management. A final advantage of the revocable living trust is that the terms of the trust and the amount of assets placed into it do not become public knowledge. Unlike the probate process, the public has no right to know the terms or conditions of a revocable living trust. Disadvantages of such trusts include the fees charged by the trustee for management of the property placed into the trust as well as the legal fees charged for drafting the trust instruments.

Irrevocable Living Trust Grantors who establish an *irrevocable living trust* relinquish title to the property they place in trust as well as the right to revoke or terminate it. Such trusts have all the advantages of revocable trusts as well as the potential for reducing taxes. Income produced by property held in an irrevocable living trust is taxed to either the trust or, if distributed, to its beneficiaries rather than to the grantor, who is usually in a higher tax bracket than either the trust or its beneficiaries. Disadvantages of such a trust relate to the fees charged by trustees for management of assets placed in the trust, the gift taxes on assets put into the trust, the grantor's complete loss of the trust property and any income it may produce, and the grantor's forfeiture of the right to change the terms of the trust as circumstances change.

Testamentary Trust A trust created by a deceased's will is called a *testamentary trust.* Such a trust comes into existence only after the will is probated. No tax savings are realized by the grantor with this type of trust since there is no divestiture of property until the grantor's death.

Life Insurance Trust and Pour-Over Will A will can be written so that it "pours over" certain assets into a previously established *life insurance trust.* This type of trust can be revocable or irrevocable and is created during the grantor's lifetime. The trust is named beneficiary of the grantor's insurance policies and may be "funded" (contain income-producing assets) or "unfunded." Generally, a *pour-over will* contains a provision passing the estate—after debts, expenses, taxes, and specific bequests—to the specified trust. The trust contains provisions as to how those assets (together with insurance proceeds payable to the trust) will be administered and distributed. Such an arrangement provides for easily coordinated and well-administered management of estate assets.

Gift Taxes

Federal tax law provides for a tax on certain gifts made during one's lifetime (the *gift tax*) as well as on "death-time" gifts (the *estate tax*). Both lifetime gifts and death-time gifts are considered cumulatively and are subjected to the integrated progressive tax rate schedule given in Table 16.5. The tax on gifts is imposed on the right to transfer property and is measured by the value of the property transferred. The donor is primarily liable for the tax. The graduated table of rates is used for both gift and estate tax purposes and is known as the *unified rate schedule.* These rates are applied to all taxable gifts after a number of adjustments and computations are made. Due to the complex nature of the gift tax computation, an illustration is excluded from this discussion. This section describes the fundamental aspects of gift taxes that should be considered in the estate planning process.

Table 16.5 Unified Rate Schedule for Federal Gift and Estate Taxes in the Case of Gifts Made and Decedents Dying in 1981[a]

Amount with Respect to Which the Tentative Tax Is to Be Computed	Tentative Tax
Not Over $10,000	18% of such amount
Over $10,000 but Not Over $20,000	$1,800 plus 20% of the excess of such amount over $10,000
Over $20,000 but Not Over $40,000	$3,800 plus 22% of the excess of such amount over $20,000
Over $40,000 but Not Over $60,000	$8,200 plus 24% of the excess of such amount over $40,000
Over $60,000 but Not Over $80,000	$13,000 plus 26% of the excess of such amount over $60,000
Over $80,000 but Not Over $100,000	$18,200 plus 28% of the excess of such amount over $80,000
Over $100,000 but Not Over $150,000	$23,800 plus 30% of the excess of such amount over $100,000
Over $150,000 but Not Over $250,000	$38,800 plus 32% of the excess of such amount over $150,000
Over $250,000 but Not Over $500,000	$70,800 plus 34% of the excess of such amount over $250,000
Over $500,000 but Not Over $750,000	$155,800 plus 37% of the excess of such amount over $500,000
Over $750,000 but Not Over $1,000,000	$248,300 plus 39% of the excess of such amount over $750,000
Over $1,000,000 but Not Over $1,250,000	$345,800 plus 41% of the excess of such amount over $1,000,000
Over $1,250,000 but Not Over $1,500,000	$448,300 plus 43% of the excess of such amount over $1,250,000
Over $1,500,000 but Not Over $2,000,000	$555,800 plus 45% of the excess of such amount over $1,500,000
Over $2,000,000 but Not Over $2,500,000	$780,800 plus 49% of the excess of such amount over $2,000,000
Over $2,500,000 but Not Over $3,000,000	$1,025,800 plus 53% of the excess of such amount over $2,500,000
Over $3,000,000 but Not Over $3,500,000	$1,290,800 plus 57% of the excess of such amount over $3,000,000
Over $3,500,000 but Not Over $4,000,000	$1,575,800 plus 61% of the excess of such amount over $3,500,000
Over $4,000,000 but Not Over $4,500,000	$1,880,800 plus 65% of the excess of such amount over $4,000,000

Transfers Subject to the Tax

Almost all property can be the subject of a transfer on which the gift tax must be paid. There is no tax on services one person performs for another; nor is the rent-free use of property a taxable transfer. A tax may be payable on cash gifts, gifts of personal or real property, and both direct and indirect gifts. For example, if a father makes the mortgage payments on his adult son's home, the payment is an indirect gift from father to son. In fact, almost any shifting of financial advantage in which the recipient does not provide consideration in money or money's worth may be considered a gift. Gifts are generally defined with reference to the *consideration* received. In other words, a transfer for less than adequate and full consideration in money or money's worth is

Table 16.5 **(*Continued*)**

Over $4,500,000 but Not Over $5,000,000	$2,205,800 plus 69% of the excess of such amount over $4,500,000
Over $5,000,000	$2,550,800 plus 70% of the excess over $5,000,000

[a]The following modifications are required for gifts made and decedents dying after 1981.

For 1982
In the case of decedents dying and gifts made in 1982, the following substitution should be made to the 1981 schedule:

Over $2,500,000 but Not Over $3,000,000	$1,025,800 plus 53% of the excess of such amount over $2,500,000
Over $3,000,000 but Not Over $3,500,000	$1,290,800 plus 57% of the excess of such amount over $3,000,000
Over $3,500,000 but Not Over $4,000,000	$1,575,800 plus 61% of the excess of such amount over $3,500,000
Over $4,000,000	$1,880,800 plus $65% of the excess of such amount over $4,000,000

For 1983
In the case of decedents dying and gifts made in 1983, the following substitution should be made to the 1982 schedule:

Over $2,500,000 but Not Over $3,000,000	$1,025,800 plus 53% of the excess of such amount over $2,500,000
Over $3,000,000 but Not Over $3,500,000	$1,290,800 plus 57% of the excess of such amount over $3,000,000
Over $3,500,000	$1,575,800 plus 60% of the excess of such amount over $3,500,000

For 1984
In the case of decedents dying and gifts made in 1984, the following substitution should be made to the 1983 schedule:

Over $2,500,000 but Not Over $3,000,000	$1,025,800 plus 53% of the excess of such amount over $2,500,000
Over $3,000,000	$1,290,800 plus 55% of the excess of such amount over $3,000,000

For 1988
In the case of decedents dying and gifts made in 1988, the following substitution should be made to the 1984 schedule:

Over $2,500,000 but Not Over $3,000,000	$1,025,800 plus 50% of the excess of such amount over $2,500,000

Source: Copyright © 1984 by The American College. Reprinted from *Advanced Estate Planning Course.*

viewed as a partial gift. Where some consideration is received by the transferor, the measure of the gift is found by subtracting the consideration received from the value of the property transferred. For example, suppose your father gave you a summer home having a market value of $75,000 in exchange for $10,000. The $65,000 excess of the value received over the consideration paid would be treated as a gift. Of course, if you gave no consideration for the property, its market value ($75,000) would represent the amount of the gift.

When Is a Gift Made?

The question of when a gift is made is important because it determines (1) when the gift must be reported and the gift tax, if any, paid and (2) the date at which the value of the gift is measured. Usually, a gift is made when the donor relinquishes dominion and control over the property or property interest transferred. For example, if a husband places cash in a bank account held jointly with his wife, no gift is made until the wife makes a withdrawal. Until that time, the husband could completely recover the entire amount placed in the account. Similarly, when parents place property into a revocable trust for their children, no gift occurs since they have not relinquished control over the assets placed in the trust. But if they later make the trust irrevocable and thereby relinquish their right to revoke the gift, the transfer is considered a completed gift. For gift tax purposes, therefore, a transfer is not subject to gift taxes until the donor gives up (1) the power to take or reclaim the property and (2) the right to alter the time or manner of enjoyment of the gift by the recipient.

Determining the Amount of a Taxable Gift

All that is transferred by an individual is not necessarily subject to a gift tax. Annual exclusions, gift splitting, charitable deductions, and marital deductions are all means of reducing the total amount for tax purposes.

Annual Exclusions Almost all gifts are subject to the gift tax, but for reasons of administrative convenience, certain transfers, or gift equivalents, are not counted. The gift tax law eliminates from the computation of taxable gifts transfers by a donor of amounts up to $10,000 to each of any number of donees. For example, a person could give gifts of $10,000 each to 30 donees for a total of $300,000 without paying any gift tax. Furthermore, the ability to give tax-free gifts of $10,000 per donee regenerates *annually.* This *annual exclusion* is available only for gifts of a present interest in property—gifts which the donee has the immediate and unrestricted right to use, possess, or enjoy upon receipt. If the donee has to wait to use, possess, or enjoy a gift or if his or her use, possession, or legal right to enjoyment is conditioned in any substantive way, it is then a gift of a future interest in property, and, therefore, the donor will not be allowed the $10,000 annual exclusion.

Gift Splitting *Gift splitting* is permitted in order to equate the tax treatment of married taxpayers domiciled in common law states with the tax treatment of married taxpayers domiciled in community property states. When a spouse earns a dollar in a community property state, such as California or Texas, half of that dollar is deemed to be owned by the other spouse immediately and automatically. If a gift is made of that dollar, each spouse is considered to have given 50¢. Similarly, in common law states, such as Colorado, New York, and Pennsylvania, federal law provides that a married donor, with the consent of his or her spouse, can elect to treat gifts as if they were made one-half by each spouse. Because of this gift-splitting option, if a wife transfers $20,000 to her son and the required consent is given by her husband, for tax computation purposes her gift is viewed as $10,000, and her husband is considered to have given the other $10,000. The total amount, because of the split, is entirely gift tax free since a $10,000 annual exclusion is allowed to each spouse. The wife could give $20,000 to any number of donees and by splitting the gift with her husband avoid the tax on the entire gift. This tax reduction technique is available even if one spouse makes all the gifts and the other spouse gives nothing. Gift splitting is allowed, however, only for gifts from married couples to third parties.

Charitable Deductions There is no limit on the amount that can be given gift tax free to a qualified charity—one to which deductible gifts can be made for income tax purposes. Therefore, people could give their entire estate to charity and receive a gift tax deduction for the total amount. There would be no federal gift taxes, regardless of the type or amount of assets transferred.

Marital Deductions Federal law permits an unlimited deduction for gift-tax purposes for property given by one spouse to another. An individual could conceivably give the entire estate to his or her spouse during their lifetimes without gift tax cost.

Payment of the Gift Tax

An annual gift tax return must be filed and is due when the donor's income tax return is due (including extensions).

Reasons for Making Lifetime Gifts

There are several tax-oriented reasons why estate planners recommend gift giving.

Gift Exclusion A single individual can give any number of donees up to $10,000 each year entirely gift tax free. There are no tax costs to either the donee or the donor for making the transfer. If the donor is married and the donor's spouse consents, the gift tax free limit is increased to $20,000 even if the entire gift was made from the donor's assets.

Gift Tax Exclusion Regardless of the size of the gift, and even if it is made less than three years before the donor's death, typically the gift will not be treated as part of the donor's gross estate. But the taxable portion of a gift does have an effect on the estate tax return. The taxable portion of lifetime gifts (technically called an adjusted taxable gift) pushes up the rate at which the donor's estate will be taxed. Fortunately, to the extent to which cash or other property qualifies for the annual exclusion, it is not taxable and therefore is both gift and estate tax free in all respects. The estate tax savings from this exclusion can be significant.

Appreciation in Value One of the most important reasons for making a lifetime gift is that the appreciation on the gift from the time the gift is made will not be included in the donor's estate (unless the gift is, for some reason, includable in the estate—as, for instance, it would be if the donor retained the right to receive all the dividends for life). If Larry gives his son Steve a taxable gift of $10,000, and it grows to $60,000 by the date of Larry's death five years later, only the $10,000 taxable value of the stock at the time of the gift enters into the tax computation of Larry's estate (as an adjusted taxable gift).

Payment Limit Because of the credit that can be used to offset otherwise taxable gifts, gift taxes currently (1984) do not have to be paid on gifts totaling $325,000 or less. Of course, once this credit is taken, it cannot be used to offset the taxes generated by future lifetime (or death-time) gifts.

Impact of Marital Deduction Because of the gift tax marital deduction, it is possible to give a spouse an unlimited amount of money or other property entirely gift tax free.

Estate Taxes and Planning

The federal estate tax is levied on the transfer of property at death. The tax is measured by the value of the property which the deceased transfers (or is deemed to transfer) to others. The parenthetical phrase "deemed to transfer" is important because the estate tax reaches not only transfers that a deceased actually makes at death but also certain transfers made during the person's lifetime. In other words, to thwart tax avoidance schemes, the estate tax is imposed on certain lifetime gifts made to "beat the estate tax" or which are in essence the same as dispositions of property made at death. For example, if Max gives his son Eric a $1,000,000 policy on Max's life the day before Max's death, the tax law treats the gift as if it were actually made at Max's death. The $1,000,000 is therefore subject to the federal estate tax. This part discusses key facts related to estate taxes and the estate planning process.

Computation of the Federal Estate Tax

There are five stages involved in the process of computing federal estate taxes. The first involves determining the *gross estate,* the total of all property in which the decedent had an interest and which is required to be included in the estate. Second, the *adjusted gross estate* is determined. This is done by subtracting from the gross estate any allowable funeral and administrative expenses, debts, certain taxes, and losses incurred during administration. The calculation of the *taxable estate,* the third stage, is accomplished by subtracting any allowable marital deduction or charitable deduction from the adjusted gross estate.

The computation of the *estate tax payable before credits* is the fourth stage. After determining the value of the taxable estate, any "adjusted taxable gifts"—which include certain taxable lifetime transfers not included in the deceased's gross estate—are added to the taxable estate. The unified rate schedule—the same one applicable to gift taxes, shown in Table 16.5—is then applied to determine a tentative estate tax. After this tentative tax is found, gift taxes the decedent paid on certain gifts are subtracted. The result is the estate tax payable before reduction by any available credits.

The final stage involves the determination of the *net federal estate tax payable.* Certain credits are allowed against the estate tax payable. These result in a dollar for dollar reduction of the tax. They are (1) unified credit, (2) state death tax credit, (3) credit for tax on prior transfers, and (4) credit for foreign death taxes. After reducing the estate tax payable for any eligible credits, the net federal estate tax is payable by the decedent's executor, generally within nine months of the decedent's death. The form included in Table 16.6 depicts for a hypothetical situation, assuming death in 1984, the computations required to determine the net federal estate tax payable. The form is useful in following the flow of dollars from the gross estate to the net federal estate tax payable. Because of the technical nature involved in these computations, no further discussion of them is included here.

State Death Taxes

More individuals are subject to state *death taxes* than are liable for federal estate taxes. This is because (1) federal laws permit certain deductions such as the marital deduction that many state laws do not; (2) federal law exempts certain transfers that are not exempted under

Table 16.6 A Form for Computing the Net Federal Estate Tax Payable

Line	Computation	Item	Amount	Total Amount
1		*Gross Estate*		$700,000
	Subtract Sum of:	(a) Funeral Expenses	$ 5,000	
		(b) Administrative Expenses	30,000	
		(c) Debts	20,000	
		(d) Taxes	5,000	
		(e) Losses	—	
2	Result:	*Adjusted Gross Estate*		$640,000
	Subtract Sum of:	(a) Marital Deduction	$350,000	
		(b) Charitable Deduction	—	
3	Result:	*Taxable Estate*		$290,000
4	Add:	*Adjusted Taxable Gifts*		$100,000
5	Result:	*Tentative Tax Base*		$390,000
6	Compute:	*Tentative Estate Tax*	$118,400[a]	
7	Subtract:	Gift Taxes Payable on Post-1976 Gifts	—	
8	Result:	*Estate Tax Payable before Credits*		$118,400
9	Subtract Sum of:	(a) Unified Credit	$ 96,300	
		(b) State Death Tax Credit	1,040	
		(c) Credit for Tax on Prior Transfers	—	
		(d) Credit for Foreign Death Taxes	—	
10	Result:	*Net Federal Estate Tax Payable*		$ 21,060

[a]This value was calculated using the Unified Rate Schedule presented in Table 16.5. The calculation was made as follows: $70,800 + .34($390,000 − $250,000) = $118,400.

Source: Form from Stephan R. Leimberg, Herbert Levy, Stephen N. Kandell, Morey S. Rosenbloom, and Ralph Gano Miller, *Tools and Techniques of Estate Planning,* 4th ed. (Cincinnati, Ohio: National Underwriter Company, 1982). Reprinted by permission of the publisher.

many state laws—for instance, death benefits under qualified noncontributory corporate retirement plans; and (3) the amount of property exempted from tax under federal law is larger than that exempted by the laws of most states. The three basic types of state death tax are a state inheritance tax, a state estate tax, and a credit estate tax.

Inheritance Tax An *inheritance tax,* which is the most common type of state death tax, is a tax on the right to receive a decedent's property. The amount of the tax depends on the value of the property each beneficiary receives and the relationship of the beneficiary to the deceased. In most states, beneficiaries are divided into categories. The lowest rates and largest exemptions are allocated to lineal descendants or to those beneficiaries most closely related to the deceased. For example, in Pennsylvania, property left to a child of the deceased is taxed at 6 percent, while the same property left to a cousin is subject to a 15 percent rate. Real property held jointly with rights of survivorship by spouses is exempt from state death taxes, while the same property held jointly by brothers is subject to a 15 percent tax.

Estate Tax A state estate tax is imposed on the deceased's right to transfer property and is measured by the value of the property transferred. It is, therefore, similar to the federal estate tax. Some states impose both an inheritance and an estate tax.

Table 16.7 Federal Estate Tax Credit for State Death Taxes

Taxable Estate	Maximum Tax Credit
Not Over $150,000	8/10ths of 1% of the amount by which the taxable estate exceeds $100,000
Over $150,000 but Not Over $200,000	$400 plus 1.6% of the excess over $150,000
Over $200,000 but Not Over $300,000	$1,200 plus 2.4% of the excess over $200,000
Over $300,000 but Not Over $500,000	$3,600 plus 3.2% of the excess over $300,000
Over $500,000 but Not Over $700,000	$10,000 plus 4% of the excess over $500,000
Over $700,000 but Not Over $900,000	$18,000 plus 4.8% of the excess over $700,000
Over $900,000 but Not Over $1,100,000	$27,600 plus 5.6% of the excess over $900,000
Over $1,100,000 but Not Over $1,600,000	$38,800 plus 6.4% of the excess over $1,100,000
Over $1,600,000 but Not Over $2,100,000	$70,800 plus 7.2% of the excess over $1,600,000
Over $2,100,000 but Not Over $2,600,000	$106,800 plus 8% of the excess over $2,100,000
Over $2,600,000 but Not Over $3,100,000	$146,800 plus 8.8% of the excess over $2,600,000
Over $3,100,000 but Not Over $3,600,000	$190,800 plus 9.6% of the excess over $3,100,000
Over $3,600,000 but Not Over $4,100,000	$238,800 plus 10.4% of the excess over $3,600,000
Over $4,100,000 but Not Over $5,100,000	$290,800 plus 11.2% of the excess over $4,100,000
Over $5,100,000 but Not Over $6,100,000	$402,800 plus 12% of the excess over $5,100,000
Over $6,100,000 but Not Over $7,100,000	$522,800 plus 12.8% of the excess over $6,100,000
Over $7,100,000 but Not Over $8,100,000	$650,800 plus 13.6% of the excess over $7,100,000
Over $8,100,000 but Not Over $9,100,000	$786,800 plus 14.4% of the excess over $8,100,000
Over $9,100,000 but Not Over $10,100,000	$930,800 plus 15.2% of the excess over $9,100,000
Over $10,100,000	$1,082,800 plus 16% of the excess over $10,100,000

Source: Reprinted with permission from *Advanced Estate Planning Course*.

Credit Estate Tax The *credit,* or *gap, estate tax* is designed to bridge the gap between the state's inheritance and estate taxes and the maximum state death tax credit allowed against the federal estate tax. (See line 9b of the form for computing the net federal estate tax payable in Table 16.6.) The credit tax is best illustrated by a simple example. If a deceased's taxable estate for federal estate tax purposes is $500,000, a credit of up to $10,000 against the federal tax is allowed for taxes paid to the state as death taxes. (See Table 16.7, which gives federal estate tax credits for state death taxes, for determination of this credit.)

The amount of any state death taxes paid may be subtracted from the tax, provided, however, that the maximum to be subtracted not exceed the maximum shown in the table. If the state's inheritance tax amounts to only $8,000, an additional tax—a $2,000 credit estate tax—is imposed so that the total state death tax is increased to $10,000, the amount of credit given by the federal government for state death taxes.

Other Factors Affecting the Amount of State Death Tax Due These include (1) state exemptions and deductions, (2) multiple state taxation, and (3) tax rates.

Exemptions and Deductions Not all property is subject to taxation. Generally, states exempt property transferred to the United States, to the state itself, and to certain charitable organizations. A few states exempt property passing to a surviving spouse. Other states either totally or partially exempt life insurance proceeds unless payable to or for the benefit of the estate or its creditors. Most states allow deductions for administrative costs, debts, funeral and last illness expenses, and certain property taxes that are unpaid at the deceased's death.

Multiple Taxation Many individuals have summer and winter homes or land and other property in states other than where they live. Although most estates are taxed only by one state, in certain situations an estate or its beneficiaries may be liable for the taxes of more than one state. The right of a state to impose a death tax depends on the type of property involved. The general treatment of the major types of property is as follows.

Real Estate Land and permanent buildings can be taxed only by the state in which the property is located.

Tangible Personal Property Cars, boats, and household goods can be taxed only in the state where they are situated. A boat, for example, is taxed where it is permanently docked. Its registry and location for insurance purposes are examined in order to determine its legal location.

Intangible Personal Property Securities such as stocks, bonds, notes, and mortgages may, in the absence of interstate agreements, be taxed by several states. Generally, intangible personal property is taxed only by the state of the deceased's domicile. Unfortunately, if a deceased has residences in more than one state or does not clearly establish his or her state of domicile, two or more states can impose death taxes on the same intangible personal property.

Tax Rates The rates at which transfers or receipts of property are taxed vary widely from state to state. Some states have graduated rates similar to the federal tax, while others, such as Pennsylvania, have flat rates that do not grow progressively as the size of the estate increases.

In fact, because the impact of state death taxes can be so significant, many individuals go "domicile shopping" at retirement to find a state with favorable rates, exemptions, and deductions.

Tools and Techniques of Estate Planning

The federal and state tax laws described in the preceding paragraphs provide both problems and opportunities to the estate planner. Estate shrinkage can be minimized and financial security maximized by judicious use of certain tax-oriented arrangements and maneuvers. Techniques of estate planning can be summarized by the four Ds: divide, deduct, defer, and discount.

Dividing the Estate Each time a new taxpaying entity can be created, income taxes are saved and estate accumulation is stimulated. Some of the more popular techniques are:

1. Giving income producing property to minor children, either outright or in trust. Since each child has an exemption and can receive up to $1,000 of unearned income a year and pay no tax, a substantial income tax savings can be realized each year by persons in high-tax brackets.
2. Creating multiple trusts for short-term periods. The income on the trust property is taxed to the low-bracket beneficiary rather than the high-bracket grantor during the term of the trust, but the income-producing property is eventually returned to the grantor of the trust. A short-term trust usually lasts for the lifetime of the beneficiary or for at least ten years plus one day or more. These short-term trusts are also called *Clifford,* or *reversionary, trusts.*
3. Establishing a corporation. Incorporation permits individuals in high-tax brackets, such as doctors or other professionals, to save substantial sums by accumulating income in a manner subject to relatively lower income tax rates.
4. Fully qualifying for the federal estate tax marital deduction. This marital deduction allows an individual to pass—estate tax free—unlimited amounts to a spouse. It also helps obtain the full advantage from the surviving spouse's unified credit. (Properly qualifying—in some estates—may mean something less than fully qualifying. In other words, there are circumstances in which an advisor may properly recommend passing a lower amount of property than the maximum marital deduction amount, i.e., an individual's entire estate.)

Deducting Any dollar which is deductible from taxable income (or from a deceased's gross estate) is more useful to the taxpayer than a nondeductible dollar. The higher the income (or estate tax bracket), the more value that results from the privilege of deductibility. Some of the retirement plans discussed in Chapter 15 that enable an individual to obtain deductions for money set aside for retirement include (1) qualified pension plans, (2) Keogh plans, (3) Individual Retirement Accounts (IRAs), (4) SEP/IRAs, (5) qualified profit-sharing plans, and (6) salary-reduction plans.

Deferring Progressive tax rates (rates that increase as the income or size of the estate increases) penalize taxpayers whose maximum earnings (or estates) reach high peaks. This makes it extremely difficult to gain and retain financial security. Among the devices that help minimize the total tax burden by spreading income over more than one tax year or deferring the tax to a later period so that the taxpayer can invest the tax money for a longer period of time are:

1. Nonqualified deferred compensation plans for selected individuals in corporate businesses as well as private contractors.
2. The making of installment sales instead of cash sales so that the taxable gain can be spread over several years.
3. Private annuities, which are arrangements whereby one person transfers property to another, usually younger, family member. This recipient promises in return to pay an annuity to the original owner for as long as he or she lives. The income tax attributable to such an annuity can thereby be spread over a number of years.
4. Qualified pension and profit-sharing plans that allow tax deferral on the income and gains from investments.
5. Government Series EE Bonds, since their earnings can be treated as taxable income at maturity rather than each year as earned.
6. Stocks that yield low dividends but provide high price appreciation because management is retaining earnings for company development.
7. Life insurance policies in which lifetime growth is not taxed and death values are income tax free. If the insured survives, earnings inherent in policy values become taxable only as received, so the tax on any gain can be deferred over a lifetime.
8. Depreciable real estate that yields high write-offs in years when the estate owner is earning large amounts of taxable income.
9. Installment payment of federal estate taxes applicable to a business interest. Payments can be spread over as many as 15 years with only the interest being paid on the unpaid tax during the first 5 years.

Discounting After everything is done to accumulate an estate and reduce the income and estate tax burdens on it, there may still be a tax payable. There are two instruments which make it possible to, in effect, pay estate taxes at a discount: Flower Bonds and a special type of life insurance policy.

Flower Bonds, although no longer issued by the federal government, are now available through trust departments of banks, even to the terminally ill. They can be bought at less than par and are redeemed by the government at par in payment of the federal estate tax. Savings are reduced, however, by inclusion of the bond at par in the gross estate of the deceased.

Life insurance, one of the primary tools of estate planners, can be purchased by a person other than the insured or the insured's spouse, or by a trust, for an annual premium that is from 3 to 6 percent of the face (death) value of the policy. If proper arrangements are made, the proceeds of such insurance will pass to the decedent's beneficiaries free of income tax, estate tax, inheritance tax, and probate costs. Such proceeds may be used to pay death taxes, debts, and other probate and administrative costs. Life insurance can also be used to provide an income for family expenses, funds for special needs, such as the payment of college expenses, mortgage balances, or other large capital needs, and acts as an attractive form of loan collateral in the case of whole life and endowment policies. As pointed out in Chapters 8 and 9, some lending institutions and other creditors require borrowers to obtain life insurance in an amount sufficient to repay them in the event the borrower dies prior to fully repaying the loan.

Summary

Estate planning involves accumulating, preserving, and distributing an estate in a manner that will most effectively achieve an estate owner's personal goals. The forces that often thwart the accomplishment of financial security for the estate owner and his or her family include death-related costs, inflation, improper management, lack of liquidity, incorrect use of vehicles of transfer, and the prolonged disability of the estate owner. The estate planning process ideally consists of four elements or steps: (1) gathering of data, (2) identification of possible problems, (3) formulation of a plan and delegation of responsibilities for executing that arrangement, and (4) testing and implementing the plan. Once implemented, the estate plan should be subjected to periodic and regularly scheduled reviews.

Important privileges are forfeited when a person dies without a valid will. These include the right to decide how property will be transferred at death and who will receive it and the right to select someone to administer the estate, nominate a guardian, and decide who will bear the burden of taxes and administration expenses. The will should provide a clear and unambiguous expression of the testator's wishes, be flexible enough to encompass possible events or changes in family circumstances occurring after it is drawn, and give proper regard to minimization of federal and state taxes. A will is valid only if properly executed by a testator of sound mind. Wills can be changed by codicil or revoked by a later will. Estate administration can be described as a three-part process in which the decedent's personal representative, or executor, must (1) collect the decedent's assets, (2) pay his or her debts and taxes, and (3) distribute any remaining assets to the appropriate beneficiaries.

The trust relationship arises when one party, the grantor, transfers property to a second party, the trustee, for the benefit of third parties, the beneficiaries. Trusts are designed primarily to accomplish one or more of three purposes: (1) to save income and estate taxes, (2) to provide asset management, and (3) to conserve trust property. Trusts may be living (inter vivos)—revocable or irrevocable—or testamentary. The tax consequences of placing property in trust depend on which types of trusts are used.

The gift tax law imposes a graduated tax on the right to transfer property during one's lifetime. The federal estate tax is essentially a levy on the right to make gifts at death. It is unified (coordinated with) the gift tax so that the rates and credits are the same for both. Once the federal estate tax is computed, certain credits are allowed and the resulting amount is generally payable within nine months of the decedent's death. State death taxes are also payable by a decedent's executor. The three types of state death taxes are (1) an inheritance tax, (2) an estate tax, and (3) a credit, or gap, estate tax. The four Ds of estate planning—divide, deduct, defer, and discount—define four categories in which every major tool or tax saving technique of the estate planner can be classified. Dividing involves the creation of new tax entities; deducting includes any type of retirement or employee benefit plan that provides financial security with before-tax dollars; deferring gives an individual the use of money that otherwise would have been paid in taxes; and discounting involves paying all expenses with "discounted" dollars.

Index